The X Window System Series

The books in the X Window System Series are based in part on the original MIT X Window System documentation, but are far more comprehensive, easy to use, and are loaded with examples, tutorials and helpful hints. Over 20 major computer vendors recommend or license volumes in the series. In short, these are the definitive guides to the X Window System.

Volume 0:
X Protocol Reference Manual

A complete programmer's reference to the X Network Protocol, the language of communication between the X server and the X clients. 418 pages, $30.00.

Volumes 1 and 2:
Xlib Programming Manual
Xlib Reference Manual

Complete guide and reference to programming with the X library (Xlib), the lowest level of programming interface to X. 659 and 723 pages. $60.00 for the set, or $34.95 each.

Volume 3:
X Window System User's Guide

Describes window system concepts and the most common client applications available for X, Release 4. Includes complete explanation of the new window manager, *twm*, and a chapter on Motif. For experienced users, later chapters explain customizing the X environment. Useful with either Release 3 or Release 4. 586 pages. $30.00.

Volumes 4 and 5:
X Toolkit Intrinsics Programming Manual
X Toolkit Intrinsics Reference Manual

Complete guides to programming with the X Toolkit. The *Programming Manual* provides concepts and examples for using widgets and for the more complex task of writing new widgets. The *Reference Manual* provides reference pages for Xt functions, and Xt and Athena widgets. 582 and 545 pages. $55.00 for the set, or $30.00 each.

Volume 7:
XView Programming Manual

XView is an easy-to-use toolkit that is not just for Sun developers. It is available on MIT's R4 tape and System V Release 4, as well as being a part of Sun's Open Windows package. This manual provides complete information on XView, from concepts to creating applications to reference pages. 566 pages. $30.00.

For orders or a free catalog of all our books, please contact us.

O'Reilly & Associates, Inc.

Creators and Publishers of Nutshell Handbooks
632 Petaluma Avenue, Sebastapol, CA 95472
email: uunet!ora!nuts · 1-800-338-6887 · in CA 1-800-533-6887 · or 1-707-829-0515

Volume One

Xlib Programming Manual

for Version 11 of the
X Window System

by Adrian Nye

O'Reilly & Associates, Inc.

Revision and Printing History

August 1988:	First Printing.
November 1988:	Second Printing. Minor revisions.
May 1989:	Third Printing. Release 3 updates added. Minor revisions.
April 1990:	Second Edition covers Release 3 and Release 4. Major revisions.

Small Print

Table of Contents

4 Window Attributes

5 The Graphics Context

7 Color 181

8 Events 229

10 Interclient Communication

Figures

Examples

Tables

Preface

By convention, a preface describes the book itself, while the introduction describes the subject matter. You should read through the preface to get an idea of how the book is organized, the conventions it follows, and so on.

In This Chapter:

Preface

About This Manual

This manual describes the X library, the C Language programming interface to Version 11 of the X Window System. The X library, known as Xlib, is the lowest level of programming interface to X. This library enables a programmer to write applications with an advanced user interface based on windows on the screen, with complete network transparency, that will run without changes on many types of workstations and personal computers.

Xlib is powerful enough to write effective applications without additional programming tools and is necessary for certain tasks even in applications written with higher-level "toolkits."

There are a number of these toolkits for X programming, the most notable being the DEC/MIT toolkit Xt, the Andrew toolkit developed by IBM and Carnegie-Mellon University, and the InterViews toolkit from Stanford. These toolkits are still evolving, and only Xt is currently part of the X standard. Toolkits simplify the process of application writing considerably, providing a number of *widgets* that implement menus, command buttons, and other common features of the user interface.

This manual does not describe Xt or any other toolkit. That is done in Volumes Four, Five, and Six of our X Window System series.* Nonetheless, much of the material described in this book is helpful for understanding and using the toolkits, since the toolkits themselves are written using Xlib and allow Xlib code to be intermingled with toolkit code.

Summary of Contents

This manual is divided into two volumes. This is the first volume, the *Xlib Programming Manual*. It provides a conceptual introduction to Xlib, including tutorial material and numerous programming examples. Arranged by task or topic, each chapter brings together a group of Xlib functions, describes the conceptual foundation they are based on, and illustrates how they are most often used in writing applications (or, in the case of the last chapter, in writing window managers). Volume One is structured so as to be useful as a tutorial and also as a task-oriented reference.

Volume Six, *X Toolkit Widget Reference Manual*, is not available as of this printing.

The second volume, the *Xlib Reference Manual*, includes reference pages for each of the Xlib functions, organized alphabetically for ease of reference; a permuted index; and numerous appendices and quick reference aids.

Volume One and Volume Two are designed to be used together. To get the most out of the examples in Volume One, you will need the exact calling sequences of each function from Volume Two. To understand fully how to use each of the functions described in Volume Two, all but the most experienced X "hacker" will need the explanation and examples in Volume One.

Both volumes include material from the original Xlib and X11 protocol documentation provided by MIT, as well as from other documents provided on the MIT release tape. We have done our best to incorporate all of the useful information from the MIT documentation, to correct code references we found to be in error, to reorganize and present it in a more useful form, and to supplement it with conceptual material, tutorials, reference aids, and examples. In other words, this manual is not only a replacement but is a superset of the MIT documentation.

Those of you familiar with the MIT documentation will recognize that each reference page in Volume Two includes the detailed description of the routine found in Gettys, Newman, and Scheifler's *Xlib–C Language X Interface*, plus, in many cases, additional text that clarifies ambiguities and describes the context in which the routine would be used. We have also added cross references to related reference pages and to where additional information can be found in Volume One.

How to Use This Manual

Volume One is intended as an introduction to all the basic concepts of X programming and also as a useful reference for many of the most common programming techniques. It is divided into 14 chapters, which describe and demonstrate the use of the X programming library, and numerous appendices.

You will find it necessary to read at least Chapters 1, 2, and 3 before attempting to program with the X library. Chapter 1, *Introduction*, provides a discussion of the context in which X programs operate. Chapter 2, *X Concepts*, describes the conceptual foundations underlying X programming. Chapter 3, *Basic Window Program*, presents a simple program.

Chapters 4 through 9 (*Window Attributes*, *The Graphics Context*, *Drawing Graphics and Text*, *Color*, *Events*, and *The Keyboard and Pointer*) discuss various programming techniques that are used in all X programs. These chapters can be read as a tutorial and consulted for reference later.

Chapter 10, *Interclient Communication*, is a description of communication between applications and between applications and the window manager, including properties and selections. The proposed conventions for interclient communication are presented in Appendix L, *Interclient Communication Conventions*, of Volume Zero, *X Protocol Reference Manual* (as of the second printing).

Chapter 11, *Managing User Preferences*, describes the facilities provided for database management, parsing the command line, and managing user preferences. Xlib calls this the resource manager.

Chapter 12, *A Complete Application*, provides an example of a complete application. This chapter is especially useful in demonstrating managing user preferences with the resource manager.

Chapter 13, *Other Programming Techniques*, describes programming techniques that will be useful to some but not all programs. It should be scanned for applicable techniques and read in detail when needed for a particular project.

Chapter 14, *Window Management*, describes what window managers do and how they work. This information should provide a more complete knowledge of the variety of contexts in which X applications may function. It also describes the Xlib functions that are intended primarily for window management. A simple window manager program is described.

Appendix A, *Specifying Fonts*, describes how the programmer should specify default font names.

Appendix B, *X10 Compatibility*, describes the routines supported in X11 for compatibility with X Version 10.

Appendix C, *Writing Extensions to X*, is a guide to writing extensions to X. This is for experienced X programmers only. It is provided so that this manual can serve as a complete replacement for the MIT Xlib documentation.

Appendix D, *The basecalc Application*, presents the complete code for *basecalc*, the complete application described in Chapter 12, *A Complete Application*.

Appendix E, *Event Reference*, describes each event type in a reference page format. Included is how to select the events, when they are generated, the contents of the event structures, and notes on how to use them. This information is vital in using the numerous events.

Appendix F, *The Xmu Library*, describes the routines in this miscellaneous utilities library that are useful in Xlib programming. This library is not an X Consortium standard but is widely available.

Appendix G, *Sources of Additional Information*, lists where to get the X software, companies that offer training in X programming, and descriptions of additional published books on the subject.

Appendix H, *Release Notes*, describes the changes between Releases 1, 2, 3, and 4. This manual describes Release 3 and Release 4.

The *Glossary* gives you somewhere to turn should you run across a term with which you are unfamiliar. Some care has been taken to see that all terms are defined where they are first used in the text, but this assumes a sequential reading of the manual.

Volume Two consists of a permuted index, reference pages to each library function, and appendices that cover macros, structures, function groups, events, fonts, colors, cursors, keysyms, and errors. Finally, Volume Two concludes with at-a-glance charts that help in setting the graphics context (GC) and the window attributes. This volume should be consulted to obtain the specifics of calling each Xlib function.

Example Programs

The example programs in this book are on the X11 Release 4 distribution in the contributed section. There are many ways of getting this distribution; most are described in Appendix H.

The example programs are also available free from UUNET (that is, free except for UUNET's usual connect-time charges). If you have access to UUNET, you can retrieve the source code using *uucp* or *ftp*. For *uucp*, find a machine with direct access to UUNET and type the following command:

```
uucp uunet\!~uucp/nutshell/Xlib/xlibprgs.tar.Z yourhost\!~/yourname/
```

The backslashes can be omitted if you use the Bourne shell (*sh*) instead of *csh*. The file should appear some time later (up to a day or more) in the directory */usr/spool/uucp-public/yourname*.

To use *ftp*, *ftp* to *uunet.uu.net* and use *anonymous* as your user name and *guest* as your password. Then type the following:

```
cd /nutshell/Xlib
binary (you must specify binary transfer for compressed files)
get xlibprgs.tar.Z
bye
```

The file is a compressed shell archive. To restore the files once you have retrieved the archive, type:

```
uncompress xlibprgs.tar
sh xlibprgs.tar
```

The example programs are also available free by *ftp* from *expo.lcs.mit.edu*. The directory containing the examples is *contrib/examples/OReilly/Xlib*.

The examples will be installed in subdirectories under the current directory, one for each chapter in the book. Imakefiles are included. (Imakefiles are used with *imake*, a program supplied with the X11 distribution that generates proper Makefiles on a wide variety of systems.)

Assumptions

Readers should be proficient in the C programming language, although examples are provided for infrequently used features of the language that are necessary or useful when programming with X. In addition, general familiarity with the principles of raster graphics will be helpful.

Font Conventions Used in This Manual

Italic is used for:

- UNIX pathnames, filenames, program names, user command names, and options for user commands.

- New terms where they are defined.

`Typewriter Font` is used for:

- Anything that would be typed verbatim into code, such as examples of source code and text on the screen.

- The contents of include files, such as structure types, structure members, symbols (defined constants and bit flags), and macros.

- Xlib functions.

- Names of subroutines of the example programs.

`Italic Typewriter Font` is used for:

- Arguments to Xlib functions, since they could be typed in code as shown but are arbitrary.

Helvetica Italics are used for:

- Titles of examples, figures, and tables.

Boldface is used for:

- Chapter and section headings.

Related Documents

The C Programming Language by B. W. Kernighan and D. M. Ritchie.

The following documents are included on the X11 source tape:

> *Xt Toolkit Intrinsics* by Joel McCormack, Paul Asente, and Ralph Swick
> *Xt Toolkit Widgets* by Ralph Swick and Terry Weissman
> *Xlib–C Language X Interface* by Jim Gettys, Ron Newman, and Robert Scheifler
> *X Window System Protocol, Version 11* by Robert Scheifler

The following other books on the X Window System are available from O'Reilly and Associates, Inc.:

Volume Zero — *X Protocol Reference Manual*
Volume Three — *X Window System User's Guide*
Volume Four — *X Toolkit Intrinsics Programming Manual*
Volume Five — *X Toolkit Intrinsics Reference Manual*
Volume Six — *X Toolkit Widgets Reference Manual* (available summer 1990)
Volume Seven — *XView Programmer's Guide*

Requests for Comments

Please write to tell us about any flaws you find in this manual or how you think it could be improved, to help us provide you with the best documentation possible.

Our U.S. mail address, e-mail address, and telephone number are as follows:

O'Reilly and Associates, Inc.
632 Petaluma Avenue
Sebastopol, CA 95472
(800) 338-6887

UUCP: uunet!ora!adrian   ARPA: adrian@ora.UU.NET

Bulk Sales Information

This manual is being resold as the official X Window System documentation by many workstation manufacturers. For information on volume discounts for bulk purchase, call Linda Walsh at O'Reilly and Associates, Inc. at 617-354-5800, or send e-mail to linda@ora.com.

For companies requiring extensive customization of the book, source licensing terms are also available.

Acknowledgements

The information contained in this manual is based in part on *Xlib–C Language X Interface*, written by Jim Gettys, Ron Newman, and Robert Scheifler, and the *X Window System Protocol, Version 11*, by Robert Scheifler (with many contributors). The X Window System software and these documents were written under the auspices of Project Athena at MIT. In addition, this manual includes material from Oliver Jones' Xlib tutorial presentation, which was given at the MIT X Conference in January 1988, and from David Rosenthal's *Inter-Client Communication Conventions Manual*.

I would like to thank the people who helped this book come into being. It was Tim O'Reilly who originally sent me out on a contract to write a manual for X Version 10 for a workstation manufacturer and later to another company to write a manual for X Version 11, from which this book began. I have learned most of what I know about computers and technical writing while working for Tim. For this book, he acted as an editor, he helped me reorganize several chapters, he worked on the *Color* and *Managing User Preferences* chapters when time was too short for me to do it, and he kept my spirits up through this long project. While I was concentrating on the details, his eye was on the overall presentation, and his efforts improved the book enormously.

This book would not be as good (and we might still be working on it) had it not been for Daniel Gilly. Daniel was my production assistant for critical periods in the project. He dealt with formatting issues, checked for consistent usage of terms and noticed irregularities in content, and edited files from written corrections by me and by others. His job was to take as much of the work off me as possible, and with his technical skill and knowledge of UNIX, he did that very well.

This manual has benefitted from the work and assistance of the entire staff of O'Reilly and Associates, Inc. Susan Willing was responsible for graphics and design, and she proofed many drafts of the book; Linda Mui tailored the troff macros to the design by Sue Willing and myself and was invaluable in the final production process; John Strang figured out the resource manager and wrote the original section on that topic; Karen Cakebread edited a draft of the manual and established some conventions for terms and format. Peter Mui executed the "at-a-glance" tables for the inside back cover; Tom Scanlon entered written edits and performed copy fitting; Donna Woonteiler wrote the index of the book; Valerie Quercia, Tom Van Raalte, and Linda Walsh all contributed in some small ways; and Cathy Brennan, Suzanne Van Hove, and Jill Berlin fielded many calls from people interested in the X manual and saved me all the time that would have taken. Ruth Terry, Lenny Muellner, and Donna Woonteiler produced the Second Edition, with graphics done by Chris Reilly. A special thanks to everyone at O'Reilly and Associates for putting up with my habits of printer and terminal hogging, lugging X books around, recycling paper, and for generally being good at what they do and good-natured to boot.

Many people sent in corrections for this Second Edition of the manual. Those whose efforts were most noteworthy were Jane-Na Chang of NEC, Jonathan Saunders of Identification and Security Systems Inc., Saundra Miller, and Russell Ferriday.

I would also like to thank the people from other companies that reviewed the book or otherwise made this project possible: John Posner, Barry Kingsbury, Jeff MacMann and Jeffrey Vroom of Stellar Computer; Oliver Jones of Apollo Computer; Sam Black, Jeff Graber, and Janet Egan of Masscomp; Al Tabayoyon, Paul Shearer, and many others from Tektronix; Robert Scheifler and Jim Fulton of the X Consortium (who helped with the *Color* and *Managing User Preferences* chapters), and Peter Winston II and Aub Harden of Integrated Computer Solutions. Despite the efforts of the reviewers and everyone else, any errors that remain are my own.

— *Adrian Nye*

1

Introduction

This chapter gives the big picture: what X is all about and some fundamentals of how it works. Everyone should look at this chapter, though readers who are already familiar with X may only want to skim it.

In This Chapter:

1
Introduction

In September 1987, the Massachusetts Institute of Technology released the first snapshot of what may well become one of the most significant software technologies of the 1990s: Version 11 of the X Window System, commonly referred to as X11. X11 may not change the world, but it is likely to change the world of workstations.

The X Window System is being adopted as a standard by nearly every workstation manufacturer and should eventually replace or be supported under their proprietary windowing systems. Versions will also be available for personal computers and supercomputers.

For the first time, portable applications can be written for an entire class of machines rather than for a single manufacturer's equipment. Programmers can write in a single graphics language and expect their applications to work without significant modifications on dozens of different computers.

What's more, since X is a network-based windowing system, applications can run in a network of systems from different vendors. Programs can be run on a remote computer, and the results displayed on a local workstation. Proprietary networks have been around for a while. However, network cooperation of *different* computers has been held up by the lack of a common applications language. Now there is one.

Vendors hope that X will lead to a software explosion similar to the one that occurred in response to the PC standard on microcomputers.

1.1 Versions of X

X was developed jointly by MIT's Project Athena and Digital Equipment Corporation, with contributions from many other companies. It was masterminded by Robert Scheifler and colleagues at MIT, though it owes some debt to the "W" windowing package developed by Paul Asente at Stanford.

There have been numerous research versions of X. Version 10, Release 4 (popularly known as X10.4), which was released in 1986, became the basis for several commercial products. Development of most X10.4 products was curtailed, however, when it became apparent that

Version 11 would not be compatible with it. Version 11, Release 1 became available in September 1987, Release 2 in March 1988, Release 3 in February 1989, and Release 4 in January 1990.

Version 11 is a complete window programming package. It offers much more flexibility in the areas of supported display features, window manager styles, and support for multiple screens and provides better performance than X Version 10. It is fully extensible. But just as important, the X11 subroutine library (Xlib) is expected to be stable for several years and to be at least a de facto industry standard. That means that programs written with this library will not need major revisions because of software updates. While there may be additions to this library, there will not be incompatible changes to it.

With X11 Release 2, control of X has passed from MIT to the X Consortium, an association of major computer manufacturers who plan to support the X standard. The Consortium was formed in January 1988 and includes virtually all large computer manufacturers. Many software houses and universities are associate members, who also have a voice in controlling the standard and receive advance access to newly released software.

1.2 X Window System Concepts

The X Window System is complex, but it is based on a few premises that can be quickly understood. This section describes these major concepts.

1.2.1 Displays and Screens

The first and most obvious thing to note about X is that it is a windowing system for bit-mapped graphics displays.* It supports color as well as monochrome and gray-scale displays.

A slightly unusual feature is that a *display* is defined as a workstation consisting of a keyboard, a pointing device such as a mouse, and *one or more* screens. Multiple screens can work together, with mouse movement allowed to cross physical screen boundaries. As long as multiple screens are controlled by a single user with a single keyboard and pointing device, they comprise only a single display, as shown in Figure 1-1.

---

*In bitmapped graphics, each dot on the screen (called a *pixel*, or picture element) corresponds to one or more bits in memory. Programs modify the display simply by writing to display memory. Bitmapped graphics are also referred to as raster graphics, since most bitmapped displays use television-type scan line technology: the entire screen is continually refreshed by an electron beam scanning across the face of the display tube one scan line, or raster, at a time. The term bitmapped graphics (or memory-mapped graphics) is more general, since it also applies to other dot-oriented displays, such as LCD screens. We assume that you are familiar with the basic principles of bitmapped graphics.

Figure 1-1. A display consisting of more than one screen

1.2.2 The Server–Client Model

The next thing to note is that X is a network-oriented windowing system. An application need not be running on the same system that actually supports the display. While many applications will execute locally, other applications may execute on other machines, sending requests across the network to a particular display and receiving keyboard and pointer events from the system controlling the display.

At this point, only TCP/IP and DECnet networks are supported, though that may change before long.

The program that controls each display is known as a *server*. At first, this usage of the term server may seem a little odd—when you sit at a workstation, you tend to think of a server as something across the network (such as a file or print server) rather than the local program that controls your own display. The thing to remember is that your display is accessible to other systems across the network, and for those systems, the code executing in your system does act as a true display server.

The server acts as an intermediary between user programs (called *clients* or *applications*) running on either the local or remote systems and the resources of the local system. The server performs the following tasks:

- Allows access to the display by multiple clients.

- Interprets network messages from clients.

- Passes user input to the clients by sending network messages.

- Does two-dimensional drawing—graphics are performed by the display server rather than by the client.

- Maintains complex data structures, including windows, cursors, fonts, and "graphics contexts," as *resources* that can be shared between clients and referred to simply by resource IDs. Server-maintained resources reduce the amount of data that has to be maintained by each client and the amount of data that has to be transferred over the network.

Since the X Window System makes the network transparent to clients, these programs may connect to any display in the network if the host they are running on has permission from the server that controls that display. In a network environment, it is common for a user to have programs running on several different hosts in the network, all invoked from and displaying their windows on a single screen, as shown in Figure 1-2.

Figure 1-2. Applications can run on any system across the network

In practice, each user is sitting at a server and can start applications locally to display on the local server or can start applications on remote hosts for display on the local server, if the remote hosts have permission to connect to the local server. All other users in the network are in a similar situation—they can run applications on their own system or on yours, but they will, for the most part, be displaying on their own server. This use of the network is known as *distributed processing*. Distributed processing helps solve the problem of unbalanced system loads. When one host machine is overloaded, the users of that machine can arrange for some of their programs to run on other hosts.

One extreme of this arrangement is the PC server or X terminal. Because these single-task systems can run only the X server, a user sitting at one of these servers must run all clients on systems across the network, with their results displayed on the PC or X terminal screen. This makes the single-tasking PC or X terminal look and work just like X on a multitasking workstation.

1.2.3 Window Management

Another important concept in X programming is that clients do not actually control such things as where a window appears or what size it is. Given multiprocessor, multiclient access to the same workstation display, clients must not be dependent on a particular window configuration. Instead, a client gives *hints* about how long and where it would like to be displayed. The screen layout or appearance and the style of user interaction with the system are left up to a separate program, called the *window manager*.

The window manager is just another program written with the X library, except that it is given special authority to control the layout of windows on the screen. The window manager typically allows the user to move or resize windows, start new applications, and control the stacking of windows on the screen, but only according to the window manager's window layout policy. A *window layout policy* is a set of rules that specify allowable sizes and positions of windows and icons.

Unlike citizens, the window manager has rights but not responsibilities. Programs must be prepared to cooperate with any type of window manager or with none at all (there are fairly simple ways to prepare programs for these contingencies). The standard window managers *uwm* and *twm* do not enforce any window layout policy, but clients should still assume that there could be one. For example, the window manager must be informed of the desired size of a new window before the window is displayed on the screen. If the window manager does not accept the desired window size and position, the program must be prepared to accept a different size or position or be able to display a message such as "Too small!"

If you are having trouble visualizing this situation, imagine a window manager where no windows are allowed to overlap. This is known as a *tiled* window manager. The Siemens RTL tiled window manager lets only transient windows (such as pop-up menus) overlap. The window managers *uwm* and *twm*, on the other hand, are referred to as *real-estate-driven* because keyboard input is automatically assigned to whatever window the pointer currently happens to be in.

There is at least one other window manager variety that you might encounter, called a *listener* or *click-to-type*. Its distinguishing feature is that it assigns all keyboard input to a single window when that window is selected by clicking on it with the pointer. A listener may or may not allow windows to overlap. Apple Macintosh™ users will recognize this type of interface.

X is somewhat unusual in that it does not mandate a particular type of window manager. Its developers have tried to make X itself as free of window management or user interface policy as possible. And, while the X11 distribution includes *twm* as a sample window manager (*uwm* prior to Release 4), individual manufacturers are expected to write their own window managers and user interface guidelines. In fact, two commercial window managers with user interface guidelines are already becoming established. They are *olwm*, the OPEN LOOK™ window manager from AT&T and Sun, and *mwm*, the Motif™ window manager from Open Software Foundation.

In the long run, the developers of X may well have made the right choice, in that the lack of clear user interface guidelines will allow a period of experimentation in which the market-place could come up with better designs than are presently available. Some industry observers, however, decry this move, pointing out that it undercuts X's appeal as a standard user platform—X *programs* may be portable across systems from multiple vendors, but if users have to deal with a different user interface on each system, half the benefit of that portability will be lost. Until a clear user interface standard emerges from the marketplace, developers must be careful to write their programs in such a way that they can run under different window managers and user interface conventions.

1.2.4 Events

As in any mouse-driven window system, an X client must be prepared to respond to any of many different *events*. Events include user input (keypress, mouse click, or mouse movement) as well as interaction with other programs. (For example, if an obscured portion of a window is exposed when another overlapping window is moved, closed, or resized, the client must redraw it.) Events of many different types can occur at any time and in any order. They are placed on a queue in the order they occur and usually are processed by clients in that order. Event-driven programming makes it natural to let the user tell the program what to do instead of vice versa.

The need to handle events is a major difference between programming under a window system and traditional UNIX or PC programming. X programs do not use the standard C functions for getting characters, and they do not poll for input. Instead there are functions for receiving events, and then the program must branch according to the type of event and perform the appropriate response.

1.2.5 Extensions to X

The final thing to know about X is that it is *extensible*. The code includes a defined mechanism for incorporating extensions, so that vendors are not forced to hack up the existing system in incompatible ways when adding features. These extensions are used just like the core Xlib routines and perform at the same level.

Among the extensions currently being developed are support for 2-D spline curves, for 3-D graphics, and for display PostScript.

1.3 X Window System Software Architecture

By now, we have described enough to draw a simple picture of the X Window System architecture (see Figure 1-3).

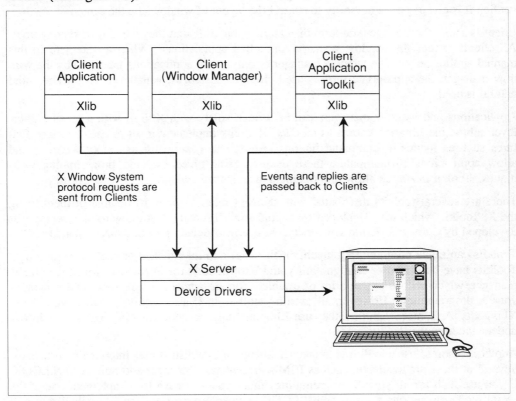

Figure 1-3. Clients communicate with the server via Xlib calls

A display server is a program that runs on each system that supports a graphics display, keyboard, and mouse. The X release from MIT includes sample monochrome and color servers for Sun 2, 3, and 4 systems; DEC systems under ULTRIX; Apollo systems under DOMAIN/IX; HP Topcat, Catseye, or Renaissance systems; IBM APA and megapel RT systems; Apple monochrome Macintosh II; and the Parallax color and video graphics controller. Commercially developed servers are or will be available from most major workstation vendors. In addition, companies such as Graphics Software Systems, Interactive Systems, and Locus Computing offer server implementations for PCs. Finally, there are X terminals, which are screens controlled by an X server running in ROM. X terminals are available from companies such as Visual, NCD, and GraphOn.

Applications communicate with the server by means of calls to a low-level library of C language routines known as *Xlib*. Xlib provides functions for connecting to a particular display server, creating windows, drawing graphics, responding to events, and so on. Xlib calls are translated to protocol requests that are passed either to the local server or to another server across the network. Some of the many sample applications available on the X release include *xterm* (a terminal emulator), *xcalc* (a calculator), *xmh* (a mail handler), *xclock* (a clock), and troff and teX previewers.

The window manager is just another program written with the X library, except that by convention it is given special authority to control the layout of windows on the screen.

Client is a slightly more general term than application, although they are almost synonymous. All clients except the window manager are called applications. When a statement in this manual applies only to the window manager or only to the applications managed by the window manager, the appropriate term is used. In other instances, whichever term seems more natural is used.

Applications and window managers can be written solely with Xlib or with a set of higher-level subroutine libraries known as *toolkits*. Toolkits implement a set of user interface features such as menus or command buttons (referred to generically as toolkit *widgets*) and allow applications to manipulate these features using object-oriented programming techniques. Toolkit *intrinsics* allow programmers to create new widgets.

There are several toolkits distributed with the X11 release, the most notable of them being the Xt Toolkit, which was developed by Digital and MIT, and the Andrew toolkit, which was developed by Carnegie-Mellon University. Xt is now officially part of the X11 standard.

Toolkits can make programming much, much easier and the finished project more thorough. Toolkits have built-in user configurability and built-in code for interaction with the window manager, which will save you a lot of trouble. You are advised to use a toolkit for most of your X programming. However, all existing toolkits in C also require or allow you to use Xlib code. And, more than that, they use Xlib internally; so understanding Xlib will help you understand how the toolkits work.

Another reason to use a toolkit is to take advantage of established user interface conventions. Several of these are available, such as IBM's Presentation Manager and Sun's OPEN LOOK. If you use Xlib for all your X programming, either you will have to reimplement one of the established conventions such as OPEN LOOK or your program will be an oddball that will not look or respond as people expect.

There are tradeoffs in using toolkits, however. One is that the executable for a given program using a toolkit is considerably larger than the equivalent program written using Xlib. Another is that the toolkits utilize highly abstract concepts and require strict programming conventions because of their object-oriented design in a nonobject-oriented language. These take time to learn.

This manual describes how to write programs with Xlib. Future volumes in our X Window System series will cover the toolkits.

1.4 Overview of Xlib

Just what does the X library contain? Table 1-1 groups the Xlib routines according to their major function and lists the chapter in which the group is discussed.

Table 1-1. Xlib Routines by Function

Function Group	Description	Chapter
Color	Routines to change the way colors drawn by an application are interpreted on the screen.	Chapter 7
Cursors	Routines to change the shape and colors of the image that tracks the pointer around the screen.	Chapter 6
Data Management	Several mechanisms to associate data with windows or numbers.	Chapter 13
Display Connection	Routines to connect and disconnect an application with a display, possibly across the network.	Chapter 3
Display and Server Specifications	Macros and equivalent functions are provided that provide information about a particular server implementation and the connected display hardware.	Volume One, throughout; Volume Two, Appendix C
Drawing	Routines to draw dots, lines, rectangles, polygons, and arcs, and an analogous set to fill the last three.	Chapter 6
Errors	Routines to set the functions called when errors occur.	Chapter 2
Events	Routines to get input from the user, from other applications, and from the server. In X, these are collectively called events.	Chapter 8
Extensions	Routines to find out what extensions are available on a particular server and get information about how to use one.	Chapter 13
Fonts	Routines to list available fonts, load fonts, and find out their characteristics.	Chapter 6
Geometry	Routines to manipulate and translate geometry specifications.	Chapter 11
Graphics Context	Routines to set the way drawing requests are interpreted.	Chapter 5
Host Access	Routines to control access to a server from other machines connected in a network.	Chapter 13

Table 1-1. Xlib Routines by Function (continued)

Function Group	Description	Chapter
Images	Routines to get, display, or manipulate screen images.	Chapter 6
Interclient Communication	Routines enabling any client to make available information for any other client to read.	Chapter 10
Keyboard	Functions to modify the way keyboard input is handled, including the keyboard mapping.	Chapter 9
Pointer	Functions to modify the way pointer input is handled.	Chapter 9
Regions	Routines to perform mathematical operations on polygonal regions.	Chapter 6
Resource Management	Routines to make managing user preferences and command line arguments easier.	Chapter 11, Chapter 12
Screen Saver	Routines to set the operating characteristics of the daemon that blanks the screen when the keyboard and pointer have been idle for a time.	Chapter 13
Text	Routines for drawing text and for determining the size of a string to be drawn.	Chapter 6
User Preferences	Routines for setting and getting the keyboard click and auto-repeat settings.	Chapter 9
Window Attributes	Routines for setting and getting the current characteristics of a window.	Chapter 4
Window Life	Routines to create or destroy a window.	Chapter 3
Window Management	Routines to allow the manipulation of windows around the screen, changing their size, their visibility on the screen, and their apparent position above or below other windows.	Chapter 14

As you can see, Xlib provides a lot of functionality. X was designed to allow any style of user interface, and that requires a very flexible set of routines. But not all the routines are necessary or intended for writing normal applications. Many are intended for window management or for other specialized purposes.

A more detailed listing that provides the name and a brief description of the routines in each group can be found in Appendix A, *Function Group Summary*, of Volume Two, *Xlib Reference Manual*.

2

X Concepts

This chapter introduces the concepts that underlie X programming. You should read this chapter even if you are the type of person who likes to jump right into the code. (If you are desperate, you can skip ahead to Chapter 3 and return to this chapter when you get confused.) "An hour or so spent reading about the system in general can save many hours of programming that leads to a dead end when the approach turns out to be wrong."

In This Chapter:

2
X Concepts

When learning a new programming language, many programmers prefer to look at a few code samples and then begin programming right away, looking up more information as they need it. This manual is organized so that most of it is useful both as a tutorial and as a reference. There are lots of code samples and fragments in this manual to help the person who likes to read code more than words. Around the code they will find many of the concepts described that are necessary for understanding that particular example.

The "just-look-at-the-examples" approach works up to a point. It allows a sharp individual to get "something" running in a very short time. Eventually, however, programmers find that in order to get the most out of a system—and sometimes even to get it do anything useful—a lot of underlying issues must be understood. In X, there are a lot of interrelated concepts and assumptions that are so basic that the programmer should know them cold. An hour or so spent reading about the system in general can save many hours of programming that leads to a dead end when the approach turns out to be wrong.

This chapter describes those underlying issues and assumptions that are so important to programming with Xlib. It goes into considerably more detail than the brief conceptual overview provided in Chapter 1, *Introduction*. After reading this chapter, you will be well prepared to understand the rest of this manual and will have a sound idea of what is required to write an X application. This chapter describes how Xlib works, including a description of window concepts and characteristics, graphics, and events, and reviews the issues that you will need to think about in order to program.

2.1 How Xlib Works

Let's start by describing the problem that X was designed to solve and then describe how it goes about solving it.

First of all, X was designed to provide windows on bitmapped terminals. This has been done before but not in a way designed to be easily portable to many different brands of hardware, from PCs to supercomputers. The code was designed to stress easy portability, even between different operating systems, but still to allow high performance.

Second, X was designed to allow many different types of machines to cooperate within a network. This was one of the major innovations in the X design. There are several standard networking protocols, but there was lacking a widely adopted standard for a higher-level protocol specifying what should be sent over the network to drive a window system. The first thing that was determined about X was the protocol used to communicate across the network.

Third, the developers of X decided that it should not require (or even imply) a particular style of user interface. Practically speaking, X would not have been adopted as a standard by many companies if it had implied a user interface incompatible with their proprietary window systems. In addition, the developers of X felt that the issues surrounding the design of a window-based user interface for X were not sufficiently worked out at present. An important design goal was thus to make X "policy free."

To accomplish these goals, the X Window System had to be designed from the bottom up. To work over a network, there had to be programs running at both ends of the connection to send and receive the information and to interpret it. The end that controls the display and input devices was named the server. At the other end are clients—programs written using Xlib to interface with the X protocol. This is shown in Figure 2-1.

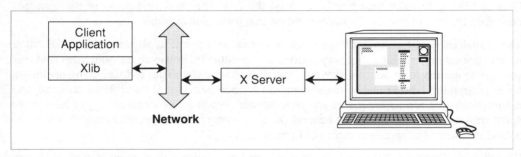

Figure 2-1. Clients and servers

Actually, although this manual describes Xlib, the C language interface to the X protocol, there is also a Lisp interface, and there are likely to be others. Any language binding that can generate and receive X protocol requests can communicate with a server and be used with the X Window System. But, at present, Xlib is the most popular programming interface used with X, because C is so widely available.

2.1.1 The X Protocol

The X protocol specifies what makes up each packet of information that gets transferred between the server and Xlib in both directions. Even when the server and Xlib are running on the same machine, the protocol is used for communication, through some internal channel instead of the external network. There are four types of packets that get transferred via the protocol: requests, replies, events, and errors.

A protocol *request* is generated by Xlib and sent to the server. A protocol request can carry a wide variety of information, such as a specification for drawing a line or changing the color value in a cell in a colormap or an inquiry about the current size of a window. Most Xlib routines generate protocol requests. The exceptions are routines that only affect data structures local to Xlib and do not affect the server (regions and the resource manager are the primary examples of these exceptions).

A protocol *reply* is sent from the server to Xlib in response to certain requests. Not all requests are answered by replies—only the ones that request information. Requests that specify drawing, for example, do not generate replies. When Xlib receives a reply, it places the requested data into the arguments or returned value of the Xlib routine that generated the request. An Xlib routine that requires a reply is called a *round-trip request*. Round-trip requests have to be minimized in clients because they lower performance when there are network delays.

An *event* is sent from the server to Xlib and contains information about a device action or about a side effect of a previous request. The data contained in events is quite varied, because it is the principal method by which clients get information. Events are kept in a queue in Xlib and can be read one at a time by the client. The range of types of events that the server sends to a client is specified by the client.

An *error* tells the client that a previous request was invalid. An error is like an event, but it is handled slightly differently within Xlib. Errors cannot be read by the Xlib calls that read events. Instead, errors are sent to an error-handling routine in Xlib. The default error handler simply prints a message and exits; it can be replaced by a client-specific error-handling routine.

2.1.2 Buffering

Xlib saves up requests instead of sending them to the server immediately, so that the client program can continue running instead of waiting to gain access to the network after every Xlib call. This is possible because most Xlib calls do not require immediate action by the server. This grouping of requests by the client before sending them over the network also increases the performance of some networks, because it makes the network transactions longer and less numerous, reducing the total overhead involved.

Xlib sends the buffer full of requests to the server under three conditions. The most common is when an application calls an Xlib routine to wait for an event but no matching event is currently available on Xlib's queue. Since, in this case, the application must wait for an appropriate event anyway, it makes sense to flush the request buffer. Second, Xlib calls that get information from the server require an immediate reply, and therefore, the request buffer is sent while the information is being returned. Third, the client would like to be able to flush the request buffer manually in situations where no user events and no calls to query the server are expected.

Let's look at how this works in practice. While an application is running, Xlib queues up requests for the server. The server, meanwhile, sends events to Xlib as soon after the user causes them as the network allows—it does not queue them or group them (except under rare conditions involving grabs discussed in Section 9.4). When the client application asks the user for input, it could, for example, draw a string that asks a question. This request sits on the request queue within Xlib. Then the application calls the event reading routine to get the answer. But, normally, the answer will not be there yet because the user hasn't seen the question! So, Xlib flushes the request buffer, and the question will appear on the user's screen. Then the user will type the answer, the event will be sent to Xlib, and the program can continue.

It is, of course, possible that a user familiar with the program will have typed the answer before the question even appears. This means that the request buffer may have been flushed once before the question is requested and will need to be flushed again to display the question. It is important to make sure that the event-reading code is able to handle this case, as it is quite possible to deadlock searching for an event that has already happened or that is a response to a question that has not been asked because the request buffer has not been flushed.

Using Xlib calls, the client can flush the connection in three ways: by calling a routine that requires an immediate reply (a routine with Query, Fetch, or Get in its name); by calling certain event-reading routines when no matching event exists on Xlib's queue; or by calling the routines XFlush or XSync.* The first of these actions says to the server, "I need some information; please act on these requests right away and then give me the information." The second says, "I'm waiting for a certain kind of event, so I'll check if you already sent the event over to Xlib. If not, please act on these requests immediately, and then I'll be waiting for the event." The last one says, "I don't need any information from you now, but I need you to act on these requests immediately." Normally, the last method is not used because there are enough of the first two types of Xlib calls in the client to make the transactions frequent enough.

You should already know that Xlib maintains a queue of the events for each server to which an application is connected, as shown in Figure 2-2. Whenever events arrive from the server, they are queued until the client reads them.

The fact that Xlib queues both input and output is very important in application programming and especially in debugging. It means that drawing requests will not appear in a window until the request buffer is flushed. It means that errors are not discovered by the server until the queue of requests arrive and are processed, which happens only after Xlib flushes the request buffer. Once discovered, the error is reported immediately to the client. In other words, several Xlib routines may be called before an error caused by an earlier routine is reported. These are two of the most visible examples of the effects of buffering. See Section 2.6.3 for more details on how buffering affects programming and debugging.

---

*In this manual, whenever you see typewriter font (such as that used for the routine XSync), it means this word would be typed verbatim into C code as a symbol, structure name, structure member, or Xlib routine. Italic typewriter font is used for dummy arguments to Xlib routines, since they could be typed into code as shown but are arbitrary. The argument names used in this volume are the same as the names used on the reference pages in Volume Two, *Xlib Reference Manual.*

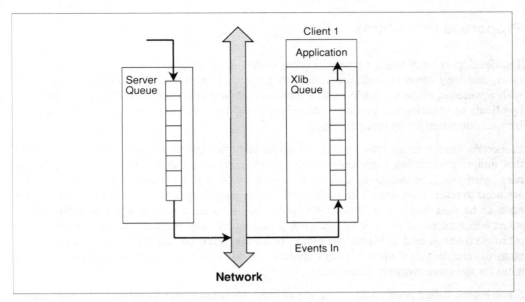

Figure 2-2. The server's event queue and a client's event queue

2.1.3 Resources

X uses several techniques to reduce network traffic. One major technique is to have the server maintain complex abstractions such as windows or fonts and have the client allocate an integer ID number for each one as a nickname. Each of these abstractions is called a *resource*. A resource can be a window, pixmap, colormap, cursor, font, or graphics context (these will be described in a moment).

Whenever an operation is to be performed on a window (or any other resource), the ID of the window is used in one argument to the Xlib routine. This means that instead of an entire structure full of data being sent over the network with an Xlib routine call, only a single integer that refers to that structure need be sent. Remember that since the client and the server may be running on different machines, pointers cannot be used to refer to structures. The caveat of the resource approach is that the client must query the server when it needs information about resources, which, as mentioned above, leads to network delays. As it turns out, clients normally do not need to query the server very often, and the resource abstraction greatly simplifies programs.

Be warned that there is another use of the term resource in X that pertains to the resource manager. A resource in the context of the resource manager is a user-preference specification that controls user-customizable elements of an application. Fortunately, these two uses of the term resource apply to completely different parts of X and therefore are not too difficult to keep separate. One use applies to server-maintained data structure, and the other to user customization of an application.

2.1.4 Properties and Atoms

The developers of X needed a way to allow clients to communicate arbitrary data with each other, and they came up with properties. A *property* is a packet of information associated with a window, made available to all the clients running under a server. Properties are used by clients to store information that other clients might need or want to know and to read that information when set by other clients.

Properties have a string name and a numerical identifier called an atom. An *atom* is an ID that uniquely identifies a particular property. Property name strings are typically all upper case, with words separated by underscores, such as "WM_COLORMAP_WINDOWS". Atoms are used to refer to properties in routine calls so arbitrary-length property name strings do not need to be sent over the network. An application gets the atom for a property by calling `XInternAtom`. You specify the string name for the property as an argument to `XInternAtom`, and it returns the atom. From this point on, the application uses only the atom to refer to that property. Every application that uses this procedure will get the same atom for the same property name string.

Some atoms, called *predefined atoms*, are defined when the server initializes. An application does not need to use `XInternAtom` to get these atoms. Instead, these atoms are available as symbolic constants beginning with `XA_`. These atoms identify properties whose contents have a certain meaning known by convention to all clients. The properties themselves do not have any contents until a client or the window manager sets them. Some of the properties described in this manual have predefined atoms and others do not, for historical reasons. Where predefined atoms are available, such as `XA_WM_HINTS`, we will use them in the text to refer to the property. For properties with no predefined atoms, we will use the string property name such as WM_COLORMAP_WINDOWS, which does not begin with XA_ and is not in Courier typeface. This tells you whether you will need to call `XInternAtom` before using the property.

A group of related clients or an extension may define other properties and atoms that will have a meaning known to all the clients in the group or using the extension.

Atoms for properties are analogous to the IDs used to refer to server resources, except that both an atom and a window are needed to uniquely identify a property. The same atom would be used to identify a property on one window as on another—only the window is different in the calls to set or read this property on two windows. Only the type `Atom` is ever used in client code; properties are the underlying data managed by the server.

One of the most important uses of properties is to communicate information from applications to the window manager and vice versa. The application sets the *standard properties* on its top-level window to specify the range of sizes it prefers for its top-level window and other information. These properties are called "standard" because they are the minimum set that an application should specify. Properties also communicate the other way; for example, the window manager specifies what sizes of icon pixmaps it prefers.

The atoms for window manager communication and for a few other standard uses are defined when the server initializes, but the corresponding properties are not set on particular windows until a client sets them.

For more information on properties and atoms, see Section 10.1.

2.1.5 The Window Manager

The window manager is just another client written with Xlib, but by convention, it is given special responsibilities. It mediates competing demands for the physical resources of a display, including screen space and the colormap. Usually it has a user interface to allow the user to move windows about on the screen, resize them, and start new applications.

Most window managers decorate the main windows of all applications with a titlebar and various tools for iconifying and resizing the application. The window manager does this by creating a separate window that fits behind the main window of each application. It is this separate window that has the decorations on it. This is important mainly because your application code does not need to handle this drawing. Figure 2-3 shows the titlebar added to an application by *twm*, the standard window manager in the MIT distribution as of R4. Note that *uwm*, the standard window manager in R3, does not decorate windows.

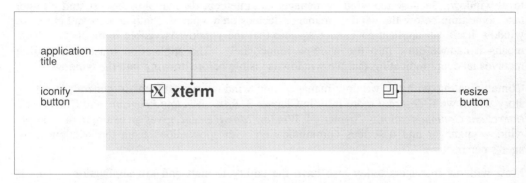

Figure 2-3. Titlebar added to applications by the twm window manager

Much of the communication between clients and the window manager and vice versa occurs through properties (the rest occurring through events). Many of the properties are known as *hints* because they may not necessarily be honored by the window manager, even if one is running. An application must be prepared for the window manager to ignore, modify, or honor the preferences it indicates through the window manager hints. The properties themselves do not have valid contents until applications or the window manager set them.

Quite a few of the features of Xlib exist only to give the window manager the mechanism to enforce its authority (and the protocol itself). These are described in Appendix L, *Interclient Communication Conventions*, of Volume Zero, *X Protocol Reference Manual* (as of the second printing). They will not be needed by normal applications.

One such feature is called *substructure redirection*. Substructure refers to the size, position, and overlapping order of the children of a window. Redirection refers to the requests by applications to change the configuration of these windows being sent to the window manager for approval instead of actually getting acted upon by the server. Substructure redirection allows a window manager to intercept any request by an application to change the size, position, border width, or stacking order (known collectively as the window configuration) of its top-level windows on the screen. Any application request to change the configuration of its top-level window will be canceled, and instead an event will be sent to the window manager indicating the arguments used in the reconfiguration request. The window manager can then decide what size, position, and stacking order to grant the application, and the window manager will reconfigure the window to those dimensions. For temporary windows such as pop-up menus and dialog boxes, the substructure redirect feature can be turned off using a window attribute.

Substructure redirection may seem obscure, but it has two significant implications for applications. The first is that the application cannot assume that the configuration it specifies for a window will actually be reflected in the window on the screen. This is true whether the configuration was set by creating the window or by reconfiguring the window. That means that the application must always determine the new configuration of the window before drawing into it. It can do this by selecting a certain event type which contains the window configuration.

The second important implication of substructure redirection concerns the mapping of a top-level window. Because the window manager can intercept the mapping request, and it might take some time before the window manager decides on a window configuration and maps the window itself, an application cannot assume that the window is visible immediately. That means it cannot draw into the window immediately. The application must wait until it receives an event indicating that the window is visible before drawing into the window.

Communicating with the window manager, and window management in general, is a long story which we'll describe more fully in Chapter 3, *Basic Window Program*, and Chapter 10, *Interclient Communication*. Chapter 14, *Window Management*, gives an example of a simple window manager and describes communication with applications from the window manager's perspective.

Most window managers today also have the ability to start and kill applications. This is known a session management. However, they can usually start only *xterm* and a few other basic clients. A true *session manager* can be a separate client. It would be able to start any client and control its command line arguments and save the state of a whole group of clients (before the user logs out) and later restore them to the same position on the screen (when the user logs back in). This level of capability is not yet available (but people are working on it). Each application supplies its command line as a hint so that the window or session manager has enough information to restart it in its current state.

Now you should have an idea of how Xlib works. Let's move on to a description of windows.

2.2 What are X Windows?

An X server controls a bitmapped screen. In order to make it easier to view and control many different tasks at the same time, this screen can be divided up into smaller areas called windows. A window is a rectangular area that works in several ways like a miniature screen. Windows on the screen can be arranged so they all are visible or so they cover each other completely or partially. A window may be any size.

Each window (on a screen running X) can be involved in a different activity, and the windows currently in use are placed so they are at least partially visible. The window manager lets you move a different window to the top when necessary or rearrange the size and position of the windows.

What you may not have realized is that some of these windows, such as the ones created by the mail handler *xmh*, are made up of many layered windows of various sizes. The scrollbars, titlebar, command buttons, and other features of the user interface are actually separate windows that provide information to the user or allow for input providing convenient control, as shown in Figure 2-4. There is more here than meets the eye.

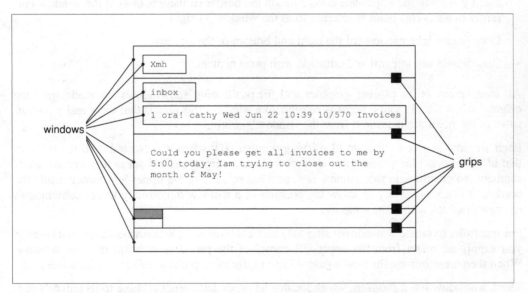

Figure 2-4. The windows used to create an instance of the xmh application

2.2.1 Window Characteristics*

What are the characteristics of a window? There are many.

First of all, a window always has a *parent* window, which is assigned as the window is created. Each window is contained within the limits of its parent. The window cannot display output in areas outside itself and cannot receive input from the keyboard or the pointer while the pointer is outside itself (unless a *grab* or *keyboard focus* is in effect, as described in Sections 8.3.2.1 and 8.3.2.2). Every window fits in a hierarchy set up by its children, its parent, its parent's parent, and so on. The very first window, the only one that has no parent, is called the root window and fills the entire screen. The root window is created by the X server as it starts up.

Second, each window has its own coordinate system. As shown in Figure 2-5, the origin of a window is the top-left corner of the window and the x and y coordinates increase to the right and bottom.

In the X Window System:

- The horizontal axis is *x*, and the vertical axis is *y*.

- *x* and *y* are 0 at the upper-left corner inside the border (if there is one) of the window currently in use. This point is referred to as the window's *origin*.

- Coordinates increase toward the right and bottom of the window.

- Coordinates are integral and coincide with pixel centers.

All measurements for placing graphics and for positioning subwindows are made from the origin. When we say that a point is *relative to* a window, this means that the x and y coordinates of the point are measured from the window's origin.

Each window is given a unique identifying number (ID) when it is created. All the routines that affect a particular window use a window ID as an argument and act in this window environment, so positions in the window are specified relative to the upper-left corner inside the border. It is not necessary to know the position of a window to correctly locate subwindows or draw graphics within the window.

For example, to create a window using XCreateWindow or XCreateSimpleWindow, you supply an offset from the upper-left corner of the parent to position the new window. When the parent moves, the new window stays in the same position relative to its parent.

Third, a window has a *position*, which locates its upper-left corner relative to its parent's corner, a certain *width* and *height* of usable pixels within the border, and a *border width*. These characteristics are shown in Figure 2-5. By convention, the window width and height do not include the border. Since several windows may have the same parent, a window must also have a *stacking order* among these windows to determine which will be visible if they overlap. These four characteristics are collectively known as the *window configuration* because they affect the layout of windows on the screen.

---

*Do read this section even if you are already familiar with windowing systems, to make sure you understand X's particular implementation of windowing.

Figure 2-5. Elements of the window configuration

To summarize, the window configuration includes:

- A window's width and height in pixels, not including the border.

- A window's border. It can vary in width; zero makes the border invisible.

- A window's particular position on the screen, specified by *x* and *y* in pixels, measured from the origin of the parent (the upper-left corner, inside the border) to the upper-left corner of the child, outside its border.

- A window's particular stacking order among the windows with the same parent.

The width, height, and position are collectively called the window *geometry*. Applications often allow users to specify the geometry and border width of the window as a command line argument or through the user defaults mechanism.

Fourth, a window has characteristics referred to as *depth* and *visual*, which together determine its color characteristics. The depth is the number of bits available for each pixel to represent color (or gray scales). The visual represents the way pixel values are translated to produce color or monochrome output on the monitor.

Fifth, a window has a *class* of either `InputOutput` or `InputOnly`. As the names imply, `InputOutput` windows may receive input and may be used to display output, and `InputOnly` windows are used for input only. There is no such thing as an output-only window because certain types of input, called events, are needed by all windows.

Sixth, a window has a set of *attributes*. The window attributes control many aspects of the appearance and response of the window:

- What color or pattern is used for the border and background of the window?

- How are partial window contents relocated during resizing?

- When are the contents of the window saved automatically as they become covered and then exposed?

- Which event types are received, and which types are thrown away (not passed on to ancestor windows)?

- Should this window be allowed to be displayed, moved, or resized without notifying the window manager?

- Which colormap is used to interpret pixel values drawn in this window?

- Which cursor should be displayed when the pointer is in this window?

This may seem like a dizzying array of variables, but in practice, many of them default to reasonable values and can be safely ignored. And the flexibility they provide makes the system much more powerful. All of these window characteristics will be explained in more detail later in this chapter, and most will be covered again later in the manual.

But first, a little more detail is necessary on the basic framework of X: the window hierarchy, the stacking order, and the concept of wrapping. These are the subjects of the next three sections.

2.2.2 Window Hierarchy

Windows are arranged in a hierarchy like a family tree, except that only one parent is required to create a child window. There is a separate hierarchy for each screen. At the top is the *root* window, which fills the entire screen and is created when the server initializes. The first windows to be created by each client are children of the root window. In the client's first call to `XCreateWindow` or `XCreateSimpleWindow` (either of which creates a new window), the root window is the parent.

The children of the root window are special, because they are the top-level windows of each application and they are managed by the window manager. Chapter 3, *Basic Window Program*, describes the special procedures required of a client before displaying, moving, or resizing this window.

Each child may also have its own child windows. These child windows of the top-level windows are used to create application features like command buttons and scrollbars.

Figure 2-6 shows a window hierarchy as it might appear on the screen, and Figure 2-7 shows the same hierarchy in schematic form. Note that the windows *A* through *G* represent subwindows of each application, which may not overlap like this in real applications. Normally the subwindows are used as command buttons or panes which are laid out in non-overlapping fashion, as was shown in Figure 2-4. However, this hypothetical hierarchy serves to demonstrate the effects of the stacking order and the window hierarchy.

Figure 2-6. A sample window hierarchy on the screen

A child may be positioned partially or completely outside its parent window, but output to the child is displayed and input received only in the area where the child overlaps with the parent. Figure 2-6 shows that the child windows do not extend beyond the borders of the parent even when they are positioned in such a way that they would otherwise overlap the parent's edge. (For example, in Figure 2-6, window *G* will not be drawn beyond the bottom of window *3* even if its height would suggest that it should.) If a window is moved in such a way that it would extend beyond the parent, it is clipped, so that only the part overlapping the parent is displayed.

These are the terms used to describe subsets of the window hierarchy:

Parent   The window used when creating a child window.

Child   A window created with another window as parent.

Subwindow   Synonymous with child. Not the same as descendant.

Figure 2-7. Sample window hierarchy in schematic form

Siblings   Windows created with the same parent (brothers and sisters).

Descendants   The children of a window, their children, and so on. Descendants could also be called *inferiors*. This term is more inclusive than *child* or *subwindow*, since it can include several generations in the window hierarchy.

Ancestors   The parent of a window, its parent, and so on, including the root window. Ancestors could also be called *superiors*.

2.2.3 Window Stacking Order

When one window overlaps one of its sibling windows, the one on top obscures part of the other. The stacking order determines which window appears on top. This order can be changed with various routines to raise, lower, or circulate windows relative to their siblings. These routines affect only a group of siblings and their descendants but not their ancestors.

Child windows always stay in front of their parent. When a window with children is moved in the stacking order, all its child windows move with it, just as they do (because of the window-based coordinate system) when the parent is moved around the screen.

Figures 2-6 and 2-7 showed a set of windows on the screen and their hierarchy, and if you look carefully, you can see how the stacking order affects each group of sibling windows. Notice that window *2* is above window *C* and all the other children of window *1*.

2.2.4 Mapping and Visibility

A newly created window does not immediately appear on the screen. It is an abstract entity that cannot be drawn to (unless a backing store feature—discussed later in this section—is implemented on that server and turned on with the appropriate window attribute). *Mapping* marks a window as eligible for display. If it is not obscured by siblings or siblings of ancestors, it may be visible, and only then can it be drawn to.

`XMapWindow` maps a window in its current position in the stacking order, while `XMapRaised` places the window at the top of the stacking order of its siblings before mapping it. For a new window never mapped before, these two calls are equivalent, since the initial stacking position of a new window is on top.

You must map a window before you have any chance of seeing it, but that alone is not enough. A number of factors can affect whether any window, newly created or already mapped, is visible:

1. The window must be mapped with `XMapWindow` or related routines.

2. All of the window's ancestors must be mapped.

3. The window must not be obscured by visible sibling windows or siblings of ancestors. If sibling windows are overlapping, whether or not a window is obscured depends on the stacking order. The stacking order can be manipulated with `XCirculateWindows`, `XConfigureWindow`, and `XRestackWindows`.

4. The request buffer must be flushed by a routine that gets events, with a call to `XFlush`, or by a function that requests information from the server. More information on this topic was provided in Section 2.1.2.

5. The initial mapping of a top-level window is a special case, since the window's visibility may be delayed by the window manager due to substructure redirection that was briefly described in Section 2.1.5. For complicated reasons, a client must wait for the first `Expose` event before assuming that its window is visible and drawing into it. It is not important to understand why this is true at this point.

An important consequence of these rules, and one of the reasons for them, is that unmapping a window (with `XUnmapWindow`) erases the window and all its descendants from the screen. X allows you (or, actually, the window manager) to control the placement and visibility of an entire client made up of a hierarchy of windows simply by manipulating the top-level window.

The window configuration and window attributes are maintained when a window is unmapped. But it is important to remember that the X server does not automatically preserve the visible contents of a window. Graphic operations on a window that is not visible or that is unmapped have no effect. Graphics visible in a window will be erased when that window is obscured and then exposed. For these reasons, it is important for the client to be prepared to redraw the contents of the window on demand, as described in Section 2.5.

On some high performance servers, a "backing store" feature is available that maintains the window contents when a window is unmapped or covered by other windows, so that the window is automatically refreshed with the current contents when it becomes visible again. This feature is expensive in terms of computing resources and should be invoked only for windows whose contents are difficult to recreate. On many types of equipment, this feature is not supported, so for the sake of portability, programs should be capable of recreating the contents of their windows in other ways. This portability is particularly important in X, because network environments often employ various brands of equipment.

Mapping is done with the `XMapWindow` or `XMapSubwindows` routines. Unmapping is done with the `XUnmapWindow` or `XUnmapSubwindows` routines.

2.3 Introduction to X Graphics

This section provides a brief introduction to the terms and concepts used in graphics under the X Window System. You will see these terms used in Chapters 3 and 4 before we get to a serious treatment of graphics in Chapters 5, 6, and 7.

2.3.1 Pixels and Colors

The X Window System is designed to control bitmapped graphics displays. In the simplest black-and-white display, there is a single bit per pixel: the state of that bit determines whether the pixel will be black or white. In color systems or on monochrome systems allowing gray-scale displays, there are multiple bits per pixel.

The state of the multiple bits assigned to each pixel does not directly control the color or gray-scale intensity of that pixel. Instead they are used as an index to a lookup table called a *colormap*, as shown in Figure 2-8. On a color display, a pixel consists of separate red, green, and blue phosphors, each sensitive to a separate electron beam; the relative intensity of these three colors fools the eye into thinking it sees a single color. Accordingly, the colormap contains an array of red, green, and blue (RGB) triples. In other words, if the value of the bits for a given pixel is 14, the RGB values of the fourteenth member of the colormap will be displayed at that location on the screen.

Each member of a colormap is called a *colorcell*, each of which translates a pixel value into a specified set of red, green, and blue values. All bitmapped displays have at least one hardware colormap, though in the case of a single-plane monochrome screen, it may consist of only two colorcells. In most cases, all clients share the single colormap by allocating only the number of colorcells they need and sharing as many as possible. When clients have special requirements, however, X allows them to have private colorcells or to create virtual colormaps which are then swapped into the hardware colormap (if it is writable) when necessary.

Figure 2-8. Mapping of pixel value into color through colormap

Note that each window can potentially specify a different colormap. This is the significance of the fact that the colormap is a window attribute.

2.3.2 Pixels and Planes

The number of bits per pixel is also referred to as the number of *planes* in the graphics display. Black-and-white systems have a single plane, color displays have from 4 to 28 planes, and gray-scale displays usually have from 2 to 4 planes. X11 supports up to 32 planes.

As can be inferred from the previous discussion of bits per pixel as an index to the colormap, the number of possible colors or shades of gray that can be *simultaneously* displayed on the screen is 2^n, where n is the number of planes in the display. (Of course, additional colors can be made available even on a system with only a few planes, at the cost of existing colors, simply by loading different RGB values into the hardware colormap if it is writable.)

All graphics calculations are performed on the pixel values before they are translated into RGB. The *source* pixel values specified in a drawing request and the *old destination* pixel values are combined according to a plane mask, clip mask, and logical function to arrive at the final *destination* pixel values. The plane mask, clip mask, and logical function are aspects of a structure called the graphics context (GC) and are described in Chapter 5, *The Graphics Context*.

The macros `BlackPixel` and `WhitePixel` return pixel values that map to black and white using the default colormap for that screen. These macros are intended for use in monochrome programs so that they will work on monochrome, gray-scale, or color displays. On color hardware, the colors of black and white may not actually be black and white, but they are guaranteed to be contrasting.

2.3.3 Pixmaps and Drawables

A window is not the only valid destination for drawing. Pixmaps are also valid destinations for most graphics requests. A *pixmap* is a block of off-screen memory in the server. Windows and pixmaps are collectively known as *drawables*.

A pixmap is an array of pixel values. It has a depth just like a window. It does not, however, have a position relative to any other window or pixmap, and it does not have window attributes such as a colormap. All of those things affect a pixmap only when it is copied into a window. And a pixmap becomes visible only when copied to a window.

Some routines operate only on pixmaps or only on windows. These routines specify either `Pixmap` or `Window` as the argument. If either is allowed, the argument to the Xlib routine will be specified as a `Drawable`. All the drawing routines specify the `Drawable` argument type.

A pixmap is not susceptible to being covered by other windows. Windows, on the other hand, may only be drawn to usefully when they are visible, since their contents are not maintained when they are obscured or unmapped (unless the backing store feature is available and in effect).

To be copied to a window with `XCopyArea`, a pixmap must have the same depth as the window it is to be copied to. Once copied, the colormap associated with the window is used to translate the pixel values from the pixmap to visible colors. After copying, additional drawing into the pixmap does *not* appear in the window. A single plane of a pixmap of any depth can be copied into any window with `XCopyPlane`.

In short, windows have the disadvantage that, when they are not visible, drawing to them will not do anything. A pixmap, which represents an area of the screen, resides in memory and can be drawn to at any time. Unfortunately, pixmaps must be copied into a visible window before the user can see them. This copying can have performance penalties. Perhaps more importantly, off-screen memory in the server used for pixmaps may be limited in quantity. Therefore, programs that use a lot of pixmaps may not work on PC servers and X terminals.

A pixmap of depth 1 is known as a *bitmap*, though there is no separate type or resource called Bitmap. A bitmap is a two-dimensional array of bits used for many purposes including cursor definitions, fonts, and templates for two-color pictures. Each bit represents a single pixel value that is either set (1) or unset (0). Depending on the visual type, these pixel values can be interpreted as two colors or simply as black and white.

2.3.4 Drawing and the Graphics Context

As in any graphics language, X provides routines for drawing points, lines, rectangles, polygons, arcs, text, and so on. Routines that draw graphics are generically called *graphics primitives*. But in X, a given graphics primitive does not contain all the information needed to draw a particular graphic. A server resource called the *graphics context* (GC) specifies the remaining variables, such as the line width, colors, and fill patterns. The ID of a GC is specified as an argument to the drawing routine and modifies the appearance of everything that is drawn into the drawable.

The GC must be created by the client before any drawing is done. The created GC is stored in the server, so that the information it contains does not have to be sent with every graphics primitive—only its ID is passed. This improves the performance of drawing significantly since it reduces the traffic over the connection between Xlib and the server. All GC settings apply to all graphics drawn using that GC.

More than one GC can be created, and each can be set with different values. This allows a program to switch between GCs and get different effects with the same graphics primitive.

2.3.5 Tiles and Stipples

When pixmaps are used for patterning an area, such as for the background of a window or in a GC, they are often referred to as tiles or stipples.

A *tile* is a pixmap with the same depth as the drawable it is used to pattern. The tile is typically 16 by 16 pixels but can be other sizes—certain sizes are drawn faster—depending on the hardware (see XQueryBestTile). It is typically composed of only two different pixel values since this is the easiest type to create, but multiple pixel values are permitted. Areas drawn by any of the drawing routines can be tiled by placing certain values in the GC. The background and border of windows can be tiled by specifying a pixmap in the window attributes.

A *stipple* is a pixmap of depth 1. A stipple is used in conjunction with a foreground pixel value and sometimes a background pixel value to pattern an area in a way similar to a tile. There are two styles of stippling that can be set in the graphics context. In one, set bits in the stipple are drawn in the foreground color and unset bits are drawn in the background color. In the other, only the set bits in the stipple are drawn in the foreground pixel value, and the pixels in the destination represented by unset bits in the stipple are not changed. Like tiling, stippling affects only those pixels that are selected by the graphics request, such as the pixels drawn for a line or a character. Stipples are only present in the GC and cannot be used for window backgrounds.

Figure 2-9 shows how a tile is used to pattern the background of a window.

Figure 2-9. Tiling of a window background

2.4 More on Window Characteristics

This section expands on the overview of window characteristics in Section 2.2.1 and describes in more detail the window attributes, window configuration, class, and depth and visual.

2.4.1 Window Attributes

The window attributes consist of information about how a window is to look and act. Each window has a separate set of attributes, which can be set with `XChangeWindow-Attributes` or, in some cases, with routines that change individual attributes. The attributes control the following window features:

Background   Can be a solid color, a tiled pixmap, or transparent.

Border   Can be a solid color or a tiled pixmap.

Bit Gravity   Determines how partial window contents are preserved when a window is resized.

Window Gravity   Determines how child windows are relocated when a window is resized.

Backing Store   Provides hints about when a window's contents should be automatically saved while the window is unmapped or obscured, which display planes should be saved, and what pixel value is to be used when restoring unsaved planes. Not all servers are capable of backing. Check the value returned from the `DoesBackingStore` macro to determine whether this feature is supported on a particular screen on your server.

Saving Under   Provides hints about whether or not the screen area beneath a window should be saved while a window, such as a pop-up menu, is in place to save obscured windows from having to redraw themselves when the pop up is removed. Not all servers can save under windows. You can find out whether this feature is supported on a particular screen with the `Does-SaveUnders` macro.

Events   Indicate which events should be received and which events should not be sent to ancestor windows.

Substructure Redirect Override
Determines whether this window should be allowed to be mapped on the screen without intervention by the window manager. This override is usually done for menus and other windows that are frequently mapped and then almost immediately unmapped again.

Colormap   Determines which virtual colormap should be used for this window.

Cursor   Determines which cursor should be displayed when the pointer is in this window.

It may clarify the picture to describe the features that window attributes *do not* affect. Setting the window attributes does not determine the size or position of a window, its parent, or its border width; these comprise the window configuration. Setting the window attributes does not affect the depth, class, or visual of a window; these are permanently set when the window is created. Attributes do not determine how graphics requests are interpreted; this is the job of the graphics context (GC).

2.4.2 Window Configuration

A window's configuration consists of its position, width and height, border width, and stacking position, as described in Section 2.2.1. These factors are handled differently from the window attributes (even though they are stored internally in the `XWindowAttributes` structure) for an important reason: changing the configuration of a top-level window (a child of the root window) must be done in cooperation with the window manager.

We will not go into detail here about how the application must interact with the window manager when attempting to map a window or change a window's configuration. For now, suffice it to say that there are certain rules the application must follow so that the window manager can be responsible for controlling what is on the screen and where. See Chapter 3, *Basic Window Program*, for an introduction to client-window manager interaction and Chapter 10, *Interclient Communication*, for a complete description.

2.4.3 Class: InputOutput and InputOnly Windows

The X Window System provides two classes of windows: `InputOutput` and `Input-Only`. The main difference between the two classes is that an `InputOnly` window cannot be used as a drawable (a destination for a graphics request). Consequently, `InputOnly` windows have a more limited set of window attributes, have no border and a transparent background, and cannot have `InputOutput` windows as children.

`InputOnly` windows make an invisible area of the screen in which input has a different purpose but the display is not changed. `InputOnly` windows usually are assigned a different cursor to distinguish them. `InputOnly` windows are rarely used.

The class of a window is assigned at creation and cannot be changed.

2.4.4 Depth and Visual

The depth and visual of a window are assigned at creation and cannot be changed. The depth is the number of planes that are to be used to represent gray scales or color within a window; depth is also the number of bits per pixel. The maximum depth allowable for an `Input-Output` window is the number of planes supported by the screen with which it is associated. If a screen has 12 planes, a window may have at most 12 bits per pixel, and therefore there are at most 2^{12} possible different shades of gray or color.

The depth of an `InputOnly` window is always 0. For `InputOutput` windows, the symbol `CopyFromParent`, when used as the *depth* argument in `XCreateWindow`, copies the depth of the parent window. Most windows use the default depth, inherited from the root window.

The visual accounts for the differences between various types of display hardware in determining the way pixel values are translated into visible colors within a particular window. A screen may support only one visual or several types of visuals. An `XVisualInfo` structure contains all the information about a particular visual. One member of `XVisualInfo` is the visual class, which has one of the values `DirectColor`, `GrayScale`, `PseudoColor`, `StaticColor`, `StaticGray`, or `TrueColor`. These values specify the characteristics of the colormaps that can be used with the window—whether the colormap is read-only or read/write, color or monochrome, split into three primary colors or composite. Other members of `XVisualInfo` specify the valid range of pixel values; how many bits of the pixel are allocated to red, green, and blue; and several other variables.

Both the depth and visual are inherited from the parent when a window is created with `XCreateSimpleWindow`. For more information on the visual class, see Chapter 7, *Color*.

2.4.5 Icons

An *icon* is a small marker window that indicates that a larger "main" window exists and is available but is not currently mapped on the screen.

Most window managers allow the user to *iconify* an application to get it out of the way without destroying it. Deiconifying an application is faster and more convenient than running the application from scratch. Also, the iconified application keeps running whatever processes it was at work on when iconified (unless the application is programmed to halt when it is iconified). When input is required, the program may either wait until the window is deiconified or accept input in the icon.

Figure 2-10 shows an *xterm* window before and after it is iconified. The *xterm* application does not create an icon pixmap, and therefore, the window manager *uwm* simply draws its icon name into the icon. The appearance and placement of icons varies between window managers.

Figure 2-10. An application and its icon

Icon windows are managed and, in many cases, created by the window manager. Through the window manager hints (which will be detailed in Section 3.2.8 and Chapter 10, *Inter-client Communication*), an application passes its icon's name and pixmap to be displayed in the icon window. If an application needs to perform operations on its own icon window (perhaps to be able to change the background at any time, as the mail handler *xmh* does to indicate that mail has arrived), it can create its own icon window and pass the window ID to the window manager. Otherwise, the window manager will create the icon window.

The window manager may specify in a property on the root window what sizes of icon pixmaps it prefers. If this property is set, the application should attempt to provide an icon pixmap of an acceptable size. The window manager may also specify where icons will be placed. These are optional features of the window manager that may not be present. In fact, most current window managers do not specify icon sizes or control icon location.

2.4.6 Special Characteristics of the Root Window

The root window is created when the X server program is initialized. The root window's characteristics differ slightly from those of other windows.

The root window is an InputOutput window. It is always mapped. Its size cannot be changed. Its upper-left corner is always at the upper-left corner of the screen, where the global coordinates are (0,0). The root window has a zero-width border. Its size is accessible through macros that will be described in Chapter 3, *Basic Window Program.*

The default window attributes of the root window include a background pixmap with diagonal cross-hatchings, the default colormap, and a default cursor that is a large X. Any of these can be changed. The event mask attribute can be changed, but by default, no events that occur in the root window are sent to any client. None of the other attributes are applicable to the root window. See Chapter 4, *Window Attributes*, for more information on setting window attributes.

The root window is never iconified by the window manager, because among other reasons, it cannot be unmapped.

2.5 Introduction to Events

This section provides a brief introduction to events. You will need this knowledge to fully understand Chapter 3, *Basic Window Program*, and some of the window attributes described in Chapter 4, *Window Attributes*. Events are covered completely in Chapter 8, *Events*, and Chapter 9, *The Keyboard and Pointer.*

2.5.1 What is an Event?

Moving the pointer or pressing a keyboard key causes an input event to occur. These are two of the simplest and most common event types, but there are many others. An event is a packet of information that is generated by the server when certain actions occur and is queued for later use by the client. The queued events can be read at any subsequent time in any order, but they are usually read and processed in the order in which they occurred.

Here are some other sorts of events:

- Mouse (or other pointer) button pressed or released. (ButtonPress, ButtonRelease)

- Window mapped or unmapped. (MapNotify, UnmapNotify)

- Mouse crossing a window boundary. (EnterNotify, LeaveNotify)

These event types are usually used for user input and to control a user interface.

A second group of events reports side effects of window operations. For example, when a window becomes visible after being obscured, it receives an `Expose` event. When window gravity (a window attribute that controls the position of a window when the parent is resized) takes effect, a `GravityNotify` event is generated.

A third purpose of events is to allow various clients to communicate with each other and with the window manager. The events that report the following actions are usually used for the second purpose.

- A client may request that all keyboard input be sent to a particular window regardless of the pointer position; this is called a *keyboard focus* window. Changing keyboard focus from one window to another causes `FocusIn` and `FocusOut` events, indicating to the client whether or not it can expect further keyboard events.

- Changing the mapping between keyboard keys and codes they generate causes a `KeymapNotify` event to be sent to all clients.

- Reparenting a window is sometimes done by the window manager to add a frame to windows on the screen. This action causes a `ReparentNotify` event.

- A `PropertyNotify` event is generated when a client changes a property on a window.

- `SelectionClear`, `SelectionNotify`, and `SelectionRequest` events are used to communicate back and forth between a client that is allowing a user to select a section of text (or other information) and a client that is allowing the user to place the information in its window. Some of these events are sent with `XSendEvent`.

At this point, it is only important to understand in general what events are, not precisely what each one is for or how to use them. Chapter 8, *Events*, and Chapter 9, *The Keyboard and Pointer*, will provide complete details.

2.5.2 Selection and Propagation of Events

A client must select the event types that it wants the server to send for each window. The selection is made by calling `XSelectInput`, which sets the `event_mask` window attribute, by setting that attribute with the more general `XChangeWindowAttributes` routine, or when calling `XCreateWindow`.

For example, a scrollbar may require mouse button events but not keyboard events, while the main window of an application may require keyboard but not mouse events. One would select different event types on each of these windows.

Keyboard and pointer events are generated in the smallest window enclosing the pointer (or grabbing the pointer, as discussed in Section 8.3.2.2). Then an event of one of these types (only) propagates upward through the window hierarchy until the event type is found in the `event_mask` or `do_not_propagate_mask` attributes of the window. If the event is found in an `event_mask` first (or in both on the same window), then the event is sent as if it occurred in that window, and if it is found in a `do_not_propagate_mask` first, then it is never sent. The ID of the window that finally received the event (if any) is put in the `window` member of the event structure.

The `do_not_propagate_mask` can only be set with `XChangeWindowAttributes` or `XCreateWindow`. Events other than keyboard and pointer events do not propagate. They occur in the window in which they were selected when the appropriate action occurs.

For most types of events, a copy of an event can be sent to more than one client if each client has selected that event type on that window. Each client has its own event mask for each window. The client that created the window need not do anything to cooperate. The second client that wants to get an event from a window that it did not create simply needs to find out the ID of the window and then select the desired event types with `XSelectInput` on that window. A duplicate event is sent to each window, and these events propagate independently up through the hierarchy in the two applications. This is rarely done, because there is usually no reason for any program other than the window manager to play with another application's windows.

2.5.3 The Event Queue

What do we mean when we say that an event is queued? Each client has its own event queue which receives the selected events in the order they are sent by the server, as was shown in Figure 2-2.

The client then can remove each event at any time and process it according to its type and the other information in each event structure. There are several functions that get input, and they differ in how many windows are monitored and what types of events are sought. The client can also read events on the queue without removing them, remove one and then put it back, or clear the queue by throwing away all the events. Events can also be created by a program and sent to the window manager or other programs.

2.5.4 An Event Structure

`Expose` is one of the most important event types, and its event structure is shown in Example 2-1. It is generated when an area of a window becomes visible on the screen and indicates that the client must redraw that area. This happens when a window is mapped, moved, resized, or deiconified or when an obscuring window is unmapped. Exposure events are common and can happen at any time, since they may be caused by the actions of other clients.

Example 2-1. An event structure

```
typedef struct {
    int type;
    unsigned long serial;    /* # of last request processed by
                              * server */
    Bool send_event;         /* True if this came from a SendEvent
                              * request */
    Display *display;        /* Display the event was read from */
    Window window;
    int x, y;
    int width, height;
    int count;               /* If nonzero, more expose events
                              * follow */
} XExposeEvent;
```

The type of event is reported in every event structure—in the XExposeEvent structure, the *type* field would be the symbolic constant Expose. The window to which the event propagated is reported in the *window* member, present in all but five event types (those dealing with selections and graphics exposure). All other information in the event structures is specific to certain event types and is described in detail in Appendix E, *Event Reference*.

2.5.5 The Event Loop

Because events can arrive in any order, the structure of code to handle them is predetermined. Every program contains an event loop in which each event is received and processed. Normally this loop is implemented as an infinite while loop, beginning with an event-getting routine and followed by a switch statement that branches according to the event type. Within each branch for an event type, there may be additional branches corresponding to the window in which the event occurred or other fields in the event structure.

The loop will almost always include exposure events. X does not normally keep track of the contents of the obscured regions of windows. It is the responsibility of the program to make sure that the window contents can be redrawn when exposure occurs. The program must be prepared to receive and act on an exposure event at any time, meaning at every invocation of the event-gathering routine. A program may work perfectly as long as there are no other programs running, but that is not good enough in a window environment!

When a window is first mapped, the first function of the program must be to read the exposure event that is generated by mapping the window. Then the program can draw the window's contents. As it turns out, this is also how the program should respond when an exposure event arrives at any later time. The first drawing and later redrawing are done in exactly the same way, using the same code.

Note, however, that another type of event, ConfigureNotify, must be handled in case the window manager modified the size of the application before mapping it and in case the user later resizes the window. More will be said about this in Chapter 3, *Basic Window Program*.

2.6 How to Program with Xlib

This section reviews what is important to know about X programming before you write any code. Describing what goes into the designing, writing, and debugging of X programs should give you a better start when you begin your own programming.

The basic program described in Chapter 3 illustrates many of the issues described here.

2.6.1 Designing an X Application

Let's begin by outlining the major tasks any X application must perform.

From the user's standpoint, almost any application under any window system will do the obvious things: create a window on the screen of an appropriate size, determine a position for some text and/or graphics within the window, draw into the window, and accept keyboard and/or pointer input, changing the screen accordingly. Essentially, the top-level window of the application is treated very much like the whole screen would be treated on a PC. These tasks are straightforward and most programmers should find them familiar.

There are, of course, a few complications resulting from the unique features of window systems in general and the X Window System in particular. These complications determine the design requirements for an application that is to run under X.

2.6.1.1 Design Requirements

The following four paragraphs describe the things X applications must do that are not obvious. These are things that must be done for the application to operate properly under X but that the average user might not notice or know about.

First, X allows workstations to be connected in a network in which any host or node may run X programs and display them on any other node, given permission. This means that the program must be able to accept the user's specification of which display to use. (Remember that each display has its own server, so choosing the display is equivalent to establishing the connection between the client and a particular server.) This requirement turns out to be built in and requires virtually no programming, as is described in Section 3.2.2.

Second, the application must be responsible in its use of the limited resources of the display, chiefly screen space and colormaps. This is because there may be many applications running concurrently on a single screen, sharing those limited resources. The client in charge of managing these limited resources is the window manager. There are certain requirements for communication between each application and the window manager to ensure that competing needs can be fairly arbitrated and to help make sure that the user sees a consistent user interface. These requirements are not difficult to meet for simple applications, but they get more complex for serious applications. This area is described in Chapter 10, *Interclient Communication*.

Third, other clients may be moved over your client and then moved away, requiring your client to redraw its window or windows. X cannot maintain the contents of an unlimited number of overlapping windows, and it is inefficient for it to try to maintain even a few. Your client will be told when redrawing is necessary and in what areas. This requirement is not hard to meet, but it encourages programming in a way that records the current "state" of each window so that it can be redrawn. The handling of exposure is described in Section 3.2.13.

Fourth, the user may resize your application, so it should be capable of recalculating the dimensions and placement of subwindows and graphics to fit within the given window.

In a nutshell, these four aspects are all that is required of an X program beyond its basic functionality. Fortunately, for most clients without unique needs such as a custom colormap, these requirements are straightforward to satisfy.

2.6.1.2 The User Interface

The first step in designing an application will be to determine what its features will be. Determining how the user will invoke those features is probably the next step. This means designing a user interface.

X was purposely designed to be "policy free," and therefore it does not come with a standard user interface like many other window systems do. You will have to write all parts of the user interface yourself, unless you choose to use one of the toolkits that are available. Using a toolkit makes building a user interface much easier and is strongly recommended. Otherwise, you must write menus, command buttons, dialog boxes, and so forth and determine how they are to be used. Although there are many ways to write these user interface features, there is a simple implementation of a menu in the *winman* program shown in Chapter 14, *Window Management*, and an example of a dialog box routine in Chapter 9, *The Keyboard and Pointer*. The writing of a command button routine should be straightforward.

The key elements that interact in the design of a user interface are the hierarchy of windows and the selection and processing of events, chiefly pointer and keyboard events. Since these device events propagate through the hierarchy depending on whether they are selected for each window, both the hierarchy and the selection together determine how events are received. For every user action, there must be a path (possibly unique, possibly common for several different user actions) through the event-handling code that yields some sort of response to the user, either by a visible change, a message, or a beep. Therefore, the job of the event loop is to distinguish all the possible user actions and invoke the proper code. In the main event loop, each case statement for an event type must then have another switch, depending on the window which received the event, before calling the function that performs the action the user requested. The event type and the window in which it occurred are only two of the most common event structure members—there may be additional switch statements based on other members, too, such as which keys or buttons were being held while a key or button press occurred.

Especially for complex programs, a careful design of the window hierarchy and selection of events can simplify the code and save hours of debugging. We recommend drawing out the hierarchy of windows and the types of events selected by each one and then drawing in the events that will be propagated to ancestor windows. This helps find problems before any code is written.

2.6.2 Writing an X Application

The best way to start writing an X application is probably to copy the existing application that is most similar to your intended purpose or to start from a skeleton program such as *basicwin*, described in Chapter 3, *Basic Window Program*. Select one from the core portion of the standard distribution from MIT, because these are the most likely to follow current conventions.

The following sections describe some basic facts about the actual process of coding and compiling an application.

2.6.2.1 Resources and User Customizability

An application should not hardcode all the options that are possible under X, such as colors and fonts. It should allow the user to specify the colors of all windows, the font to use, the display and screen to use, the initial size and position of the application, and a large number of other standard and application specific options.

An application should provide command line options, but there are too many variables to support all of them as command line options. The developers of X have designed a better way for the user to specify options, called resources. The user places the desired options in a file using a particular format and runs the X application *xrdb* specifying this file as a command line argument. *xrdb* places a property on the root window whose value is the contents of this file. Applications use a set of Xlib routines collectively called the resource manager to return a setting for each variable required. The routine XGetDefault makes this process quite easy for the application. If the user has not called *xrdb* to set the property on the root window, XGetDefault reads in a file called *Xdefaults* in the user's home directory. The application itself should contain a default value for each variable in case neither of these sources contains a value for one of them.

This use of the term resource is completely different from the term *server resource*, which refers to windows and GCs.

A resource specification is a key/value pair. A key/value pair may apply only to a particular window within a particular application, to an entire application, to a certain class of applications such as editors, or to all applications. The algorithm used to find the value for a particular variable operates quite differently from a normal database manager. Given an incomplete specification of a key, it uses an algorithm to determine which of the keys in the resource database is the best match and returns the indicated value. It always returns only one value. This is much different from a normal database manager which would return many values if the key were too general.

The resource manager and providing user customizability are described in detail in Chapter 11, *Managing User Preferences*.

2.6.2.2 Compiling and Linking X Programs

To use all the functions in the X library, you need to include *<X11/Xlib.h>*, *<X11/Xutil.h>*, *<X11/keysym.h>*, and *<X11/Xresource.h>*. These files define data structures, macros, and symbols and declare the types of functions. It is also a good idea to include *<X11/Xos.h>*, which includes certain header files commonly used in C programs that differ in name or location between various operating systems, notably System V and BSD. To compile and link your program with all the available Xlib libraries, including a symbol table for a symbolic debugger, use:

```
cc -g -o outputfile inputfile.c -lX11
```

The *-lX11* option specifies linking with the standard X library, Xlib.

A set of routines to make it easier to port programs from X Version 10 to Version 11 is provided in a separate library. To use the X Version 10 compatibility functions, include *<X11/X10.h>* in your source file and link with both the *-lX11* and *-loldX* options to your *cc* command. You may wish to include *<X11.Xos.b>* if you use system calls, file manipulation, or string manipulation utilities. This header file includes the right files for various operating systems.

Several other libraries are available in the X distribution from MIT: Xmu, the miscellaneous utilities library, and Xext, the extensions library (which requires additional server-side software in order to function). These are not yet adopted standards of the X Consortium but are widely available. If you use *-lXmu*, it must be placed before Xlib on the compiling command line. All toolkit libraries based on Xlib such as Xt must also appear before *-lX11* on the command line. *-lXext* can appear before or after *-lX11* because it does not use Xlib.

If, when compiling, you get errors about header files in *<X11/Xos.h>* not being found, you are probably on a System V system that does not define the symbol `SYSV`. To solve this problem, add *-DSYSV* to the command line.

You will probably want to use *make*(1) when compiling time could be saved by compiling smaller functions separately before linking. (For more information, see the Nutshell Handbook *Managing Projects with Make*.)

2.6.2.3 Naming Conventions

There are a number of conventions for the naming of Xlib functions and constants. You should be familiar with these conventions in order to name your own functions and constants properly. The major conventions are:

- The names of all Xlib functions begin with an X (capital x). Compound words are constructed by capitalizing the first letter of each word. For example, a typical function name is `XAllocColor`.

- The names of most user-visible data structures and structure types begin with an X. The only exceptions are `Depth`, `Display`, `GC`, `Screen`, `ScreenFormat`, and `Visual`. Pointers to these six structures are quite commonly used in programs, but their members should not be accessed except through pre-existing macros.

- The names of all members of data structures use lower case. Compound words, where needed, are constructed with underscores (_).

- The names of macros do not begin with an X. To distinguish macros from user symbols (which are all caps), the first letter of each word in the macro is capitalized. (The macros used for quarks are an exception to this rule, perhaps because they were once part of a separate library. Their names begin with Xrm.)

- The names of symbolic constants defined in X header files (#defined) use mixed case, with the first letter of each word capitalized, and do not begin with X. Lower-case symbols are reserved for variables and all upper-case for user symbols, according to existing convention. The only exception is that predefined atom names use all upper-case letters, with underscores separating the words. Atom names begin with XA_ to distinguish them from user symbols.

You should choose constants and routine names that will not be confused with standard Xlib functions, macros, or constants. User function names should not begin with X and perhaps should have the first letter of the first word lower case to avoid confusion with Xlib macros. User constants should be all upper case. Variable names can be lower case as usual, with underscores separating the words if desired, since X structure member references will always be accompanied by the variable declared as the structure.

2.6.2.4 Using Structures, Symbols, and Masks

Xlib programming takes advantage of many structure definitions and defined constants. This style of programming may be unfamiliar to some programmers. We will describe how structures and constants are typically used so that the idea will be familiar when you see the examples.

Pointers to structures are the major way of specifying data to and returning data from Xlib routines. If the routine returns data, the returned value will be a pointer to the data structure, unless the routine returns more than one structure, in which case one or all of the structures will be arguments. In some routines (primarily those concerning color), a pointer-to-structure argument specifies some information and returns some other information.

When setting the characteristics of an X resource, such as a set of window attributes, a graphics context, the cells in a colormap, or a hardware characteristic (such as key click), both a structure and a mask are specified as arguments. The *mask* specifies which values in the specified structure should be read when updating the resource values. One bit in the mask is assigned to each member in the structure, and a special constant is defined in the Xlib header files to represent that member when constructing the mask. Each of the mask constants has one bit set. The mask argument is made by combining any number of the mask constants with the bitwise OR operator (|). For example, the CWBackgroundPixmap constant is used to indicate that the background_pixmap member of the specified window attributes structure is to be read and the corresponding member in the resource changed.

The other major use of defined constants in Xlib (other than for masks) is as values for structure members themselves. They indicate which of a number of alternatives is true. For example, several of the structure members can have only the values True or False. As another example, the type member of each event structure can have one of 33 different values, each represented by a different defined constant such as `Expose`. Defined constants are also used as returned values.

Defined constants are also used for predefined atoms. As described in Section 2.1.4, an atom is an integer value identifying a property. Atoms are used to avoid passing arbitrary-length property name strings back and forth between the client and the server.

2.6.2.5 Performance Optimizing

While designing, writing, and debugging your application, you can look for ways to improve its performance.

Whenever possible, you should use Xlib functions that do not require protocol replies. That is, in functions that are called frequently, especially in the event loop, avoid Xlib routines with names containing `Fetch`, `Get`, or `Query`. Most of these functions return information from the server, and as such, they are subject to network delays and will slow down your application. Much of this information can be had from events.

In general, keep the feedback loop between the user's action and the program's response as short as possible.

2.6.3 Debugging an X Application

All programmers know that debugging is by far the most difficult and time consuming aspect of programming. This is where you catch all the problems caused during the writing stage and often also problems in the design stage. One can rarely foresee all the issues when designing a program.

There are some techniques that make debugging X applications easier. One, of course, is to have good tools. The C program checker *lint* helps find problems such as mismatches in the number of arguments to a function, variables declared but not used, or misused pointers. Although it often finds something to complain about that you do not consider an error, it also provides useful information.

Use of a good debugger such as *dbx* avoids the need to continually place `printf` statements in the code and recompile.

The standard application *xwininfo* is good for displaying information about a window, including its window ID and name, parent and children IDs and names, all the window attributes, and the window manager hints set for that window. Use the *-all* option or see the *xwininfo* reference page in Volume Three, *X Window System User's Guide*, for information on printing just the needed information.

The standard application *xprop*, which displays the name, type, and value of each property set on a window, is useful in debugging applications that set or read properties. It can also display font properties. This application is also described in Volume Three.

If your application generates protocol errors during debugging, it is easier to locate the error if you turn off Xlib's request buffering (described in Section 2.1.2). This is done with the XSynchronize call placed immediately after the call to connect with the sever (XOpen-Display).

One of the most common places to have difficulty debugging is in event handling. For this reason, we recommend that all programs under development contain printf statements at the beginning of each branch of their event handling, so that the programmer can watch the sequence of events in one window and the visible performance of the application in another. This print statement can be placed within a compile-time #ifdef DEBUG, #endif pair. Then define this symbol on the compiling command line. Later, all the print statements can be taken out of the compiled code by simply changing the command line when recompiling. Although the event types are coded as numbers and will normally be printed that way by the printf statements, they are easily translated back into strings that match their symbols using the technique described in Section 8.2.5.

X applications are difficult to test thoroughly. Here are some of the miscellaneous tests you should put your application through:

- Be sure to try all combinations of raising and and lowering different windows to test the application's response to exposure. Does it redraw unnecessarily?

- Try all combinations of pressing and releasing different pointer buttons to see if anything breaks.

- Try operating the program in a busy network environment.

- Try the application on a variety of different servers. Does it work on both color and monochrome systems?

- Try running the application on machines with different architectures and bit and byte orders.

- What happens when you type function keys or other unique keys on a particular keyboard?

- Is it possible to crash the application by specifying the wrong set of resources or command line arguments?

If your application can pass all these tests, you have done a good job.

2.6.3.1 Errors

There are really three levels of error handling in programs using Xlib. The first level you implement yourself by monitoring the return status of the routines that create server resources. This allows the client to modify the arguments of the request and try again. The second level, protocol errors, is usually caused by a programming error, and the third by a fatal system error such as a crash of the machine running the server or network failure. The second two types are handled by two separate error-handling functions that can be set by the client but, by default, simply print a message and exit the client.

As an example of the first level of error handling, a client should always check to see whether it was successfully connected to the display server with `XOpenDisplay` before proceeding. If this connection did not succeed, the client should print a message to *stderr* indicating what happened and which server it attempted to connect to. This process will be demonstrated in Chapter 3, *Basic Window Program*.

X protocol errors occur when routine arguments do not conform to accepted ranges or when IDs do not match existing resources, etc. These types of errors are sent to `XError-Handler`. Fatal errors, such as a broken connection with the server, are unrecoverable conditions and invoke the `XIOErrorHandler`. Both error handlers by default display an intelligible (if not intelligent) message and then exit.

The possible X protocol error messages and their general causes are listed in Appendix B, *Error Messages and Protocol Requests*, of Volume Two, *Xlib Reference Manual*. These error messages also specify which protocol request caused the error, which you can also look up in Volume Two, Appendix B to determine which Xlib routine may have caused the error. This mapping is not unique because several Xlib routines often generate the same protocol request.

User-defined error-handling routines will be called from the error handlers if you pass procedure names to `XSetIOErrorHandler` or `XSetErrorHandler`. If either is passed a `NULL` function pointer, the respective default handler will be reinstated.

If you write your own error-handling routines, it is recommended that you use `XGet-ErrorText` or `XGetErrorDatabaseText` to get the string describing an error code, so that the codes of extensions can be handled properly. `XGetErrorDatabaseText` uses the resource manager to provide error messages from the file *XErrorDB*, located by default in */usr/lib/X11*.

Only the error-handling routine `XErrorHandler` receives error events, and these events cannot be selected or received by windows.

2.6.3.2 The XErrorEvent Structure

Example 2-2 shows the `XErrorEvent` structure and its members. The value of each member of this structure is displayed by the default X protocol error handler.

Example 2-2. The XErrorEvent structure

```
typedef struct _XErrorEvent {
    int type;
    Display *display;            /* Display the event was read from */
    XID resourceid;              /* Resource ID */
    unsigned long serial;        /* Serial number of failed request */
    unsigned char error_code;    /* Error code of failed request */
    unsigned char request_code;  /* Major opcode of failed request */
    unsigned char minor_code;    /* Minor opcode of failed request */
} XErrorEvent;
```

The following list describes each member of the `XErrorEvent` structure in detail:

- The `serial` member is the number of requests sent over the network connection since it was opened, starting from 1. The difference between `serial` and the last request processed as reported in error messages tells you how many requests to count back in order to find the request that caused the error.

- The `request_code` is a protocol representation of the name of the protocol request that failed; these are decoded in Appendix B, *Error Messages and Protocol Requests*, of Volume Two, *Xlib Reference Manual*.

- The `error_code` is one of the items described in Volume Two, Appendix B, such as `BadWindow`.

- The `minor_code` is zero unless the request is part of an extension. If it is, the `minor_code` indicates which request in the extension caused the error.

- The `resource_id` indicates one of the server resources (window, colormap, etc.) that was associated with the request that caused the error.

2.6.3.3 Synchronizing Errors

Since error events are not displayed precisely when they occur, it is often informative to look up the protocol request as well as the error code to determine which function the error occurred in. You cannot rely on the debugger to indicate where the error occurred because of Xlib's request buffering and other delays.

It is useful to use `XSynchronize` to make sure that protocol errors are displayed as soon as they occur. When `XSynchronize` is invoked, the performance of graphics will be drastically reduced. The same result occurs by setting the global variable `_Xdebug` to any nonzero value when running a program under a debugger (UNIX only).

3

Basic Window Program

Every Xlib program has a similar structure. This chapter shows a simple program that puts up a window and handles events in that window. You can use this simple application as a template for your own more complex applications.

In This Chapter:

basicwin

3
Basic Window Program

This chapter presents a simple program that demonstrates the fundamentals of programming with the X library. All clients will use the techniques described and demonstrated here.

The basic program presented in this chapter fulfills all the requirements for a basic application outlined near the end of Chapter 2, *X Concepts*, and illustrates some of the most important X concepts and programming issues. You should have read Chapter 2 before proceeding.

The program will perform these operations:

- Connect the client to an X server with XOpenDisplay, and exit gracefully if the connection could not be made.

- Get information about the physical screen, and use it to calculate the desired size of the window.

- Create a window with XCreateSimpleWindow.

- Set standard properties for the window manager.

- Select the types of events it needs to receive.

- Load the font to be used for printing text.

- Create a graphics context to control the action of drawing requests.

- Display the window with XMapWindow.

- Loop for events.

- Respond to the Expose event resulting from mapping the window (and any other Expose event that might come along later) by calling routines to draw text and graphics. If the window is too small to perform its intended function, it will display an appropriate message.

- Receive ConfigureNotify events, indicating that the window has been resized by the window manager. The new window size is provided in the event structure.

- Keep handling events until a KeyPress or ButtonPress event arrives, then close the display connection and exits.

The program does not perform the following operations, which are required of a robust X client:

- Allow the user to specify command line options and read the resource database.

- Handle colors.

For more information on these topics, see Chapter 7, *Color*, and Chapter 12, *A Complete Application*.

3.1 Running the Program

If you have the sample programs (see the *Preface* for how to get them) and a workstation that runs X, you can try out this program by compiling *basic/basicwin.c*. See the description of how to compile X programs in Section 2.6.2.2.

The program just displays a window with some text and graphics drawn into it. Figure 3-1 shows the output of the program. The one useful thing it does is tell you the size and depth of the current screen.

Figure 3-1. Output of the basicwin program

Without further ado, let's begin to look at the code.

3.2 The Main of basicwin

As usual, the code is composed of a main program and several subroutines. The main does everything described at the start of this chapter except create the GC, load the font, and draw the text and graphics. These tasks are done in the `draw_graphics`, `draw_text`, `get_GC`, and `load_font`, routines, which are shown with the complete code in Section 3.2.20 but not described fully until Chapter 6, *Drawing Graphics and Text*. You can get the general idea of what they do just by looking at them, though.

In the following sections, the code is shown and described in small pieces. In some cases, the relevant declarations of variables are shown again in each segment of the code as well as at the top of the program (where they would normally appear). This has been done to increase clarity when showing the individual pieces of the program.

3.2.1 Include Files and Declarations

Example 3-1 shows the include files and declarations from *basicwin.c*.

Example 3-1. basicwin — include files and declarations

```
/* Xlib include files */
#include <X11/Xlib.h>
#include <X11/Xutil.h>
#include <X11/Xos.h>
#include <X11/Xatom.h>

/* Standard C include file */
#include <stdio.h>

/* Bitmap data for icon */
#include "bitmaps/icon_bitmap"

#define BITMAPDEPTH 1

/* Values for window_size in main -- is window big enough to be
 * useful? */
#define TOO_SMALL 0
#define BIG_ENOUGH 1

/* Display and screen_num are used as arguments to nearly every
 * Xlib routine, so it simplifies routine calls to declare them
 * global; if there were additional source files, these variables
 * would be declared ``extern'' in them */
Display *display;
int screen_num;

/* Name this program was invoked by; this is global because
 * it is used in several places in application routines, not
 * just in main */
static char *progname;

void main(argc, argv)
int argc;
char **argv;
{
```

Example 3-1. basicwin — include files and declarations (continued)

```
Window win;
unsigned int width, height;      /* Window size */
int x = 0, y = 0;                /* Window position */
unsigned int border_width = 4;   /* Border four pixels wide */
unsigned int display_width, display_height;
char *window_name = "Basic Window Program";
char *icon_name = "basicwin";
Pixmap icon_pixmap;
XSizeHints size_hints;           /* Preferred sizes for window man */
XEvent report;                   /* Structure for event information */
GC gc;                           /* ID of graphics context */
XFontStruct *font_info;          /* Structure containing
                                  * font information */
char *display_name = NULL;       /* Server to connect to */
```

Let's begin with the include files. The three include files *<X11/Xlib.h>*, *<X11/Xutil.h>*, and *<X11/Xos.h>* are needed in virtually all Xlib programs. The *<X11/Xlib.h>* file contains declarations of structure types used in Xlib functions. *<X11/Xlib.h>* in turn includes *<X11/X.h>*, which sets up many defined constants. *<X11/Xutil.h>* contains more structure definitions and defined constants for certain groups of Xlib functions. Many of the structures and constant definitions from these include files are described in this manual with the functions in which they are used. Structures and constants are also presented on many of the reference pages in Volume Two, *Xlib Reference Manual*, if the routine on that page uses a structure or defined constant as an argument or return value. Appendix F, *Structure Reference*, of Volume Two, *Xlib Reference Manual*, provides an alphabetical listing of structures; Appendix G, *Symbol Reference*, of Volume Two, *Xlib Reference Manual*, provides the definitions of constants.

The final include file referenced in the Example 3-1 is *<X11/Xos.h>*, which attempts to make programs as portable as possible by including certain files depending on the version of UNIX for which the program is being compiled. This include file is not absolutely necessary, but it is useful.

Now let's move on to all the strange new types that appear in Example 3-1. The Window, Display, Pixmap, XSizeHints, and XEvent types used in this program are all defined in *<X11/Xlib.h>*. A brief description of each is given here, but you will need to see the code that uses each variable to fully understand them.

Window
: A unique integer identifier (ID) that is returned by XCreateWindow or XCreateSimpleWindow and is thereafter used by the program to refer to the created window resource.

Display
: A large structure that contains information about the server and its screens. It is filled only after this program connects to a server by calling XOpenDisplay.

Pixmap
: An integer ID like Window but for a pixmap resource. The pixmap in this case is a picture to display in the icon for the window.

XSizeHints
: A structure that is used to provide the window manager with information about the preferred sizes and size increments for the top-level window of the application.

XEvent   A union that stores information about an event. It can be interpreted as
                one of many individual structure types depending on the type of event.

These declarations are repeated in the sections of code below in which they are used to avoid
the need to flip back and forth.

3.2.2 Connecting to a Server

XOpenDisplay connects an Xlib program to a server. The code shown in Example 3-2
that calls XOpenDisplay will appear in all Xlib programs.

Example 3-2. basicwin — connecting to the server

```
char *display_name = NULL;
Display *display;
int screen_num;
Screen *screen_ptr;
        .
        .
        .
progname = argv[0];
/* Connect to X server */
if ( (display=XOpenDisplay(display_name)) == NULL )
{
    (void) fprintf( stderr, "%s: cannot connect to \
            X server %s\n", progname, XDisplayName(display_name));
    exit( -1 );
}

screen_num = DefaultScreen(display);
screen_ptr = DefaultScreenOfDisplay(display);
```

The *display_name* argument to XOpenDisplay specifies which server to connect to.
This may be any server on the network and could be specified on the command line in a more
complete application than this one. (See Section 2.6.2.1 and Chapter 11, *Managing User
Preferences*, for a discussion of how to process command line arguments and user-specified
default values in an X program.) When *display_name* is not specified by the user, it
should be set to NULL, which causes XOpenDisplay to connect to the server specified in
the UNIX environment DISPLAY variable. You can view the current contents of the DISPLAY
environment variable by using the UNIX command:

```
echo $DISPLAY
```

It can be changed by typing:

```
setenv DISPLAY display_name                    (C Shell)
```

or:

```
DISPLAY=display_name; export DISPLAY           (Bourne Shell)
```

You must be careful to set the DISPLAY variable when you login to a remote machine to
make sure that when you execute X applications from that terminal, your output will be
displayed on the screen from which you typed the command.

basicwin

Both the DISPLAY environment variable and the *display_name* argument to XOpen-Display have the same format. The format is *host:server.screen*, in which *host* refers to the name of the machine running the server; *server*, the server number on that machine; and *screen*, the screen number on that server.*

The server number can be thought of as the number of the user on a particular host. The *server* number is always zero on a single-user workstation and may be nonzero only if a single host has a separate keyboard, pointer, and display for more than one user, all connected by wires (not networks) to the central host. Systems that run multiple X servers are rare.

The *.screen* part is optional and only specifies which screen is returned by the Default-Screen macro (more on macros in a minute). You can still use any or all of the screens controlled by the specified server. For example, Perseus:0.1 instructs the server you are running the program on to connect to server 0 on the host called Perseus and that the default screen on that server for this program will be screen 1.†

The XOpenDisplay routine returns a pointer to a structure of type Display. If the connection is successful, the structure will be filled with information about the server and each of its screens. If the attempt to create a connection fails, XOpenDisplay returns NULL. The code in Example 3-2 above checks to make sure this returned pointer is not NULL before proceeding. The message printed when the connection fails includes the text returned by the XDisplayName function. This function returns *display_name* or, if that is NULL, the UNIX environment DISPLAY variable. XDisplayName is necessary, since without it, there would be no way to tell the user to what server an attempt to connect was made.

The client might not succeed in connecting to a server for a number of reasons. Most likely, the *display_name* variable or DISPLAY environment variable does not specify a valid server that is connected via the network to the machine on which you are running the program. Or perhaps the network is out of order. Another possibility is that the server and client use different versions of the X protocol. X Version 11 programs are not compatible with X Version 10 and vice versa, so that if such a connection is attempted, an error message such as "protocol mismatch" should be printed, since the connection will partially succeed. All releases of X Version 11, however, *are* compatible since they use the same protocol.

The connection will also fail if the host you are running the client on is not on the *host access list* of the server you are trying to display on. The host access list is a simple permission mechanism. A server reads the list of hosts as it starts up and may be connected only to clients running on these hosts. There are commands to add and remove hosts from the access list, but these can be called only from clients running on the host whose list is being changed.

---

*MIT's manual describes this format as *host:display.screen*, using *display* instead of *server*. Since most people think of screens and displays as virtually the same thing, their description leads to confusion. The second member in the string really identifies which server on a particular host to connect to. Each of these servers would support a user.

†Note that most servers only control a single screen. However, an X server can support multiple screens. These may actually be separate physical devices, but they can also be logical devices. For example, the sample server for Sun workstations on the X11 distribution allows a single physical screen to be used as both a color screen and a monochrome screen. Both screens can be active at the same time: moving the pointer off the edge of one screen moves the pointer onto the other, showing the entire contents of the other screen in the process. This is a useful feature because color is by definition somewhat slower than monochrome, so programs can be edited and debugged on the monochrome screen but then tested on the color screen.

In all these cases, the code shown in Example 3-2 will simply print the name of the server to which the connection failed and no further information.

In R4, a simple authorization scheme has also been implemented. If the person operating the server has turned authorization on, Xlib must know a secret code in order to connect to that server. Xlib gets this code from a file, and the server puts it there to grant access.

If Example 3-2 executes successfully past opening the display, we can begin to set up variables for use in the rest of the program. The first of these is the global variable *screen_num*, set to the return value of the `DefaultScreen` macro. *screen_num* will be used throughout the program to indicate which screen on the server our operations are to affect. It is important to use the `DefaultScreen` macro rather than to hardcode 0 as the screen used by the client, because even without command line parsing in the client, this allows the user to set the default screen by setting the *.screen* element of the DISPLAY environment variable.

The variable *screen_num* can actually be any integral value between 0 and the value returned by (`ScreenCount(display)` − 1), inclusive. The `ScreenCount` macro returns the number of screens on the connected server. Since we only intend to use one of the screens, we can be satisfied with using the default screen.

3.2.3 Display Macros

We have just described all the macros used in the context of connecting with a display. They all get their information from the `Display` structure returned by `XOpenDisplay`. But this is not the only useful information we can get from the `Display` structure. There are numerous other macros that supply information about the characteristics of the server and its screens. We will describe these macros where they come in handy in this manual. The complete set of macros that access the members of the `Display` structure is listed and described in Appendix C, *Macros*, of Volume Two, *Xlib Reference Manual*. They tell you whether the server supports certain features like backing store and motion history buffers, the protocol version and release and the name of the server vendor, and much more. The `Display` structure also provides information about each screen, such as the root window dimensions and the number of planes.

The macros are provided both for convenience and because the `Display` structure is intended to be opaque; clients should not access its members directly. The reason for it being opaque is that Xlib's authors want to retain the option to change the members in the `Display` structure without making existing clients obsolete.

3.2.4 Getting Window Information

Most clients need to know the size of the screen so that the output can be tailored to look the same—or to look good—on any display. There are two ways to get this information: you can access members of the `Display` structure to get information about the root window or you can use `XGetGeometry` or `XGetWindowAttributes` to get the root window's dimensions. The first method, using the macros for accessing information from the

`Display` structure, works only for the root window but is more efficient. The second and third methods, reading the window geometry or attributes, work for any window.

To get the dimensions of a screen in pixels, you can use the macros `DisplayWidth` and `DisplayHeight`. The macros `DisplayWidthMM` and `DisplayHeightMM` return the screen dimensions in millimeters. These four macros get their information locally from the `Display` structure, so they are fast and efficient. The ratio of width in millimeters to width in pixels gives you a measurement of the spacing between pixels horizontally, and the same process can be used to determine the vertical pixel spacing. This can be important because when you draw a circle, it will look more like an ellipse on screens that do not have the same pixel spacing in both directions (usually inexpensive PC servers). You can tailor your drawing to compensate for this effect.

The second and third ways to get the geometry of a window are to use `XGetGeometry` or to get all the window attributes using `XGetWindowAttributes`. The difference between these two routines is that `XGetWindowAttributes` gets much more information and actually calls `XGetGeometry` itself. These methods have the disadvantage that they get information from the server, requiring a round-trip request that is subject to network delays. We show this method here because, for any window other than the root window, this is the only way to get window information.

The following code fragments demonstrate the three ways of getting root window information. *basicwin* uses the macros method because, in this case, we need information about the root window, and this is the most efficient way to get it.

Example 3-3 shows the macros method; Example 3-4, the `XGetGeometry` method; and Example 3-5, the `XGetWindowAttributes` method.

Example 3-3. Code fragment for getting display dimensions — using macros

```
Display *display;
int screen_num;
unsigned int display_width, display_height;
    .
    .
    .
/* Open display */
    .
    .
/* Display size is a member of display structure */
display_width = DisplayWidth(display, screen_num);
display_height = DisplayHeight(display, screen_num);
```

Example 3-4. Another way to get window size — using XGetGeometry

```
Display *display;
int screen_num;
Window root;
int x, y;
unsigned int width, height;
unsigned int border_width;
unsigned int depth;
    .
    .
```

Example 3-4. Another way to get window size — using XGetGeometry (continued)

```
/* Open display */
    .
    .
    .
/* Get geometry information about root window */
if (XGetGeometry(display, RootWindow(display, screen_num), &root,
        &x, &y, &width, &height, &border_width, &depth) == False)
    {
    fprintf(stderr, "%s: can't get root window geometry\n",
            progname);
    exit(-1);
    }
display_width = width;
display_height = height;
```

Note that the `root` argument of `XGetGeometry` returns the root window at the top of the hierarchy of the window being queried. This happens to be useless in this case, because it is the root window we are querying!

Example 3-5. A third way to get window size — using XGetWindowAttributes

```
Display *display;
int screen_num;
XWindowAttributes windowattr; /* (This declaration at top) */
    .
    .
    .
/* Open display */
    .
    .
    .
/* Fill attribute structure with information about root window */
if (XGetWindowAttributes(display, RootWindow(display, screen_num),
        &windowattr) == 0) {
    fprintf(stderr, "%s: failed to get window attributes.\n",
            progname);
    exit(-1);
}
display_width = windowattr.width;
display_height = windowattr.height;
```

3.2.5 Creating Windows

The next step is to create and place windows. Actually, a window's position relative to its parent is determined as the window is created, since these coordinates are specified as arguments to the routine that creates the window.

The *basicwin* application has only one window. Creating the first window of an application is a special case, because that window is a child of the root window and, therefore, is subject to management by the window manager. An application can suggest a position for this window, but it is very likely to be ignored. Most window managers allow the user to position the window as it appears on the screen. So most simple applications create the first window with its position set to (0,0). Example 3-6 shows the simplest call to create a window.

In Chapter 12, *A Complete Application*, we will show you a more complete approach that processes command line arguments to get the position of the top-level window. When the user specifies a position, there is a technique for making sure that the window manager will honor the position.

Example 3-6. basicwin — creating a window

```
Window win;
int border_width = 4;        /* Border four pixels wide */
unsigned int width, height; /* Window size */
int x,y;                /* Window position */
    .
    .

/* Open display, set screen, determine screen dimensions */
    .
    .

/* Note that in a real application, x and y would default to 0 but
 * would be settable from the command line or resource database */
x = y = 0;

/* Size window with enough room for text */
width = display_width/3, height = display_height/4;

/* Create opaque window */
win = XCreateSimpleWindow(display, RootWindow(display, screen_num),
        x, y, width, height, border_width, BlackPixel(display,
        screen_num), WhitePixel(display, screen_num));
```

The only new thing in Example 3-6 is the use of several new macros in the call to create a window.

Let's talk about the RootWindow macro. Each screen has its own root window. To create the first of your application's windows on a particular screen, you use the root window on that screen as the parent. That window can then only be used on that screen. The ID of the root window on a particular screen is returned by the RootWindow macro. The first generation of windows on a screen (known as the top-level windows) should always use this macro to specify the parent. XCreateSimpleWindow makes a new window given arguments for specifying it parent, size, position, border width, border pixel value, and background pixel value. All other attributes of the window are taken from the parent, in this case the root window. If we wanted to specify any or all the attributes instead of inheriting them from the parent, we would have to use XCreateWindow instead of XCreateSimpleWindow.

3.2.6 Color Strategy

Applications do not choose pixel values, they choose colors and are returned pixel values by a routine they call that allocates colors or they get pixel values from the display macros BlackPixel and WhitePixel.*

---

*BlackPixel and WhitePixel are no longer constants as they were in X Version 10. Pixel values must not be hardcoded.

This example is a monochrome application, but it will work on both monochrome and color screens. We use the `WhitePixel` macro to specify the background pixel value (in the call to create the window) and set the foreground in the GC to be the contrasting value returned by `BlackPixel`. The border pixel value is also set to `BlackPixel`. The background and border pixel values are set with the last two arguments of `XCreateSimpleWindow`. The foreground pixel value is set in the `get_GC` routine in the manner described in Section 5.1.1.

As you may recall from Chapter 2, *X Concepts*, pixel values represent colors, but they will be translated by a colormap before being displayed on the screen. `BlackPixel` and `White-Pixel` return the pixel values corresponding to two contrasting colors in the default colormap, which might not actually be black and white.

Every application should be made to work in monochrome, because many people have only monochrome screens.

How to add color handling to *basicwin* (or any application) is described in Chapter 7, *Color*.

3.2.7 Preparing an Icon Pixmap

An application should create an icon design for itself, so that if a window manager is running and the user iconifies the application, the icon will be recognizable as belonging to the particular application. Exactly how to tell the window manager about this pixmap will be described in the next section, but first let's talk about how to create the pixmap.

The program should take two steps in creating the pixmap: it should find out what sizes of icon are acceptable to the window manager and then create a pixmap of an appropriate size. Since most current window managers do not specify icon sizes, and it is difficult to know how to respond in a reasonable way, this issue can be ignored for the present. Eventually, when standard window managers specify standard icon sizes, applications would use `XGet-IconSizes` to determine which window manager was in operation and have a icon bitmap for each one.

Example 3-7 shows the simple process of creating a pixmap for the icon.

Example 3-7. basicwin — creating an icon pixmap

```
#include "bitmaps/icon_bitmap"

void main(argc, argv)
int argc;
char **argv;
{
    /* Other declarations */
      .
      .
      .
    Pixmap icon_pixmap;

    /* Open display, create window, etc. */

    /* Might someday want to use XGetIconSizes to get the icon
     * sizes specified by the window manager in order to determine
```

Example 3-7. basicwin — creating an icon pixmap (continued)

```
        * which of several icon bitmap files to use, but only when
        * some standard window managers set these */

     /* Create pixmap of depth 1 (bitmap) for icon */
     icon_pixmap = XCreateBitmapFromData(display, win,
             icon_bitmap_bits, icon_bitmap_width,
             icon_bitmap_height);
             .
             .
             .
```

An icon design can be created using the standard X application *bitmap*. You run *bitmap* with a filename and dimensions as command line arguments, like so:

```
     % bitmap icon_bitmap 40x40
```

Then you use the pointer to draw your bitmap. For more information on the *bitmap* editor, see Volume Three, *X Window System User's Guide*. Normally the icon carries some symbolic representation of the application, so use your imagination. *bitmap* creates an ASCII file that looks like Example 3-8. This particular bitmap is a bit small for an icon, being only 20 pixels on a side. A more typical size would be about 40 pixels on a side.

Example 3-8. Format of bitmap files

```
#define icon_bitmap_width 20
#define icon_bitmap_height 20
static char icon_bitmap_bits[] = {
   0x60, 0x00, 0x01, 0xb0, 0x00, 0x07, 0x0c, 0x03, 0x00, 0x04, 0x04, 0x00,
   0xc2, 0x18, 0x00, 0x03, 0x30, 0x00, 0x01, 0x60, 0x00, 0xf1, 0xdf, 0x00,
   0xc1, 0xf0, 0x01, 0x82, 0x01, 0x00, 0x02, 0x03, 0x00, 0x02, 0x0c, 0x00,
   0x02, 0x38, 0x00, 0x04, 0x60, 0x00, 0x04, 0xe0, 0x00, 0x04, 0x38, 0x00,
   0x84, 0x06, 0x00, 0x14, 0x14, 0x00, 0x0c, 0x34, 0x00, 0x00, 0x00, 0x00};
```

The bitmap format shown in Example 3-8 is not used only in `XCreateBitmapFrom-Data`. It is also used by the Xlib functions `XWriteBitmapFile` and `XReadBitmap-File`. An application can also read from a file the data used to create a pixmap, instead of including the data, but this is more complicated because it requires processing of filenames.

3.2.8 Communicating with the Window Manager

Before mapping the window (which displays it on the screen), an application must set the standard properties to tell the window manager at least a few essential things about the application.

You may remember from Chapter 2, *X Concepts*, that a property is a collection of information that is readable and writable by any client and is usually used to communicate between clients. The standard properties are part of the convention for communication between each application and the window manager.

You may also remember that a property is associated with a particular window. The standard properties are associated with the top-level window of the application. This is how the server keeps track of the standard properties of all the different applications and has them ready for the window manager to read them.

Several routines are provided that allow the application to easily set these properties; analogous routines allow the window manager to read them. The routines designed to set all the most important properties for a normal application are XSetStandardProperties and XSetWMHints under R3 and XSetWMProperties under R4.

The reason the function to use has changed in R4 is that a new standard for communication between the application and the window manager has been adopted by the X Consortium. The document describing this standard is called the *Inter-Client Communication Conventions Manual*; it is reprinted in Appendix L, *Interclient Communication Conventions*, of Volume Zero, *X Protocol Reference Manual* (as of the second printing). This chapter demonstrates how to satisfy either set of conventions. More information on the differences between conventions used in R3 (and earlier) and R4 (and later) can be found in Chapter 10, *Interclient Communication*, of this manual.

The minimum set of properties that an application must set are:

• Window name

• Icon name

• Icon pixmap

• Command name and arguments (the command line)

• Number of arguments

• Preferred window sizes

• Keyboard focus model

We'll say more about each of these after you have seen the code that sets them. Example 3-9 shows the code that sets the standard properties. Note that condition preprocessor symbols are used to allow this code to operate properly under either R3 or R4.

Example 3-9. basicwin — setting standard properties

```
void main(argc, argv)
int argc;
char **argv;
{
        .
        .
        .
    /* To be displayed in window manager's titlebar of window */
    char *window_name = "Basic Window Program";

    /* To be displayed in icon */
    char *icon_name = "basicwin";
    Pixmap icon_pixmap;

    XSizeHints size_hints; /* Structure containing preferred sizes */

    /* Open display, create window, create icon pixmap */
```

Example 3-9. basicwin — setting standard properties (continued)

```
                .
                .

        /* Before mapping, set size hints for window manager */
        /* Note that in a real application, if size or position were
         * set by the user, the flags would be USPosition and USSize
         * for both R3 and R4, and these would override the window
         * manager's preferences for this window; this is true even
         * in R4 when the x, y, width, and height fields are obsolete */
#ifdef X11R3 /* And earlier */
        size_hints.flags = PPosition | PSize | PMinSize;
        size_hints.x = x;
        size_hints.y = y;
        size_hints.width = width;
        size_hints.height = height;
        size_hints.min_width = 300;
        size_hints.min_height = 200;
#else /* X11R4 or later */
        /* x, y, width, and height hints are now taken from the
         * actual settings of the window when mapped; note that
         * PPosition and PSize must be specified anyway */

        size_hints.flags = PPosition | PSize | PMinSize;
        size_hints.min_width = 300;
        size_hints.min_height = 200;
#endif

#ifdef X11R3
        /* Set Properties for window manager (always before mapping) */
        XSetStandardProperties(display, win, window_name, icon_name,
                icon_pixmap, argv, argc, &size_hints);

#else /* X11R4 or later */
        {
        XWMHints wm_hints;
        XClassHint class_hints;

        /* Format of the window name and icon name arguments has
         * changed in R4 */
        XTextProperty windowName, iconName;

        /* These calls store window_name and icon_name into
         * XTextProperty structures and set their other fields
         * properly */
        if (XStringListToTextProperty(&window_name, 1, &windowName) == 0) {
            (void) fprintf( stderr, "%s: structure allocation for \
                    windowName failed.\n", progname);
            exit(-1);
        }

        if (XStringListToTextProperty(&icon_name, 1, &iconName) == 0) {
            (void) fprintf( stderr, "%s: structure allocation for \
                    iconName failed.\n", progname);
            exit(-1);
        }

        /* Whether application should be  normal or iconified
         * when first mapped */
        wm_hints.initial_state = NormalState;
```

Example 3-9. basicwin — setting standard properties (continued)

```
        /* Does application need keyboard input? */
        wm_hints.input = True;
        wm_hints.icon_pixmap = icon_pixmap;
        wm_hints.flags = StateHint | IconPixmapHint | InputHint;

        /* These are used by the window manager to get information
         * about this application from the resource database */
        class_hints.res_name = progname;
        class_hints.res_class = "Basicwin";

        XSetWMProperties(display, win, &windowName, &iconName,
                argv, argc, &size_hints, &wm_hints,
                &class_hints);
    }
#endif
```

It is important to realize that these properties are only hints. A hint is information that might or might not be used. There may be no window manager running, or the window manager may ignore some or all of the hints. Therefore, an application should not depend on anything having been done with the information provided in the standard properties. For example, take the window name hint. Some window managers will use this information to display a titlebar above or beside each top-level window, showing the application's name. The proper and obvious thing for the application to do would be to set the window name to be the application's name. But if the application were an editor, it could try to set its window name to the name of the current file. This plan would fall through if no window manager were running.

The icon name and icon pixmap should both set to allow the window manager to use either or both. Most current window managers often display just the icon pixmap, unless no pixmap is specified, in which case they use the icon name. If the icon name is not set, the convention within window managers is to use the window name as the icon name; if the window name is not specified either, then they will use the first element of the command line.

The UNIX shell command name and arguments are passed into *main* in the standard fashion from the command line, as `argv` and `argc`. These can be used directly as arguments in the call to set the standard properties. This information might be used by the session manager to restart or duplicate the application when so instructed by the user.

And last but not least (in R3), the window size hints property is a structure that specifies the sizes, positions, and aspect ratios preferred by the user or the program for this application. The XSizeHints structure is shown in Example 3-10.

Example 3-10. The XSizeHints structure

```
typedef struct {
        long flags;                       /* Marks defined fields
                                           * in this structure */
        int x, y;                         /* Obsolete in R4 */
        int width, height;                /* Obsolete in R4 */
        int min_width, min_height;
        int max_width, max_height;
        int width_inc, height_inc;
        struct {
```

basicwin

Example 3-10. The XSizeHints structure (continued)

```
                    int x;                      /* Numerator */
                    int y;                      /* Denominator */
        } min_aspect, max_aspect;
        int base_width, base_height;    /* New in R4 */
        int win_gravity;                /* New in R4 */
} XSizeHints;
```

You might ask, "How would the user be involved in specifying the size hints when they have to be set even before a window appears?" The answer: applications can be written to let the user specify the position and size of the top-level window through command line arguments or the resource database. A more complete application would get these values, use them to set the size of the window, and (in R3 only) use them to set the size hints. To tell the window manager that the user, not the application, supplied these values, the application would set the `flags` field to `USSize | USPosition` instead of `PSize | PPosition` (in both R3 and R4).

All this arranges a priority for the different settings of the position and size of a top-level window. The lowest priority is the application itself. Next higher is the window manager, and highest of all is the user. In Example 3-9, the symbols used to set `flags` are `PSize` and `PMinSize`. These indicate that the program is specifying its desired size and its minimum useful size. The symbols used for other members of `XSizeHints` are shown on the reference page for `XSetStandardProperties` in Volume Two, *Xlib Reference Manual*.

Let's describe the other members of `XSizeHints`. The `x`, `y`, `width`, and `height` members are simply the desired position and size for the window. In R3, these should be set to the same values used in creating the top-level window. In R4, these fields need not be set.

The rest of the size hints give the window manager information about how to resize the window. The `min_height` and `min_width` fields should be set to the minimum dimensions (in pixels) required so that the application can still function normally. Many window managers will not allow the user to resize the window smaller than `min_width` and `min_height`. `max_width` and `max_height` are analogous to `min_width` and `min_height` but are less critical for most applications.

In R4, the `base_width` and `base_height` fields have been added to the `XSizeHints` structure. They are used with the `width_inc` and `height_inc` fields to indicate to the window manager that it should resize the window in steps—in units of a certain number of pixels instead of single pixels. The window manager resizes the window to any multiple of `width_inc` in width and `height_inc` in height, but no smaller than `min_width` and `min_height` and no bigger than `max_width` and `max_height`. If you think about it, `min_width` and `min_height` and `base_width` and `base_height` have basically the same purpose. Therefore, in R4, `base_width` and `base_height` take priority over `min_width` and `min_height`, so only one of these pairs should be set.

The *xterm* application provides a good example of size increments. It wants its window to be resized in multiples of the font width and height, since it uses only constant-width fonts. This way, there are no partial characters along the edges of the window. What's more, the application can then interpret dimensions specified by the user in multiples of `width_inc` and `height_inc`, instead of pixels. The user specifies dimensions in characters (24 by 80 for a standard size terminal), which the application then translates into pixels by multiplying them by `width_inc` and `height_inc`. Most window managers display the dimensions of the window when the user is resizing it, and if `width_inc` and `height_inc` are set, they will use multiples instead of pixels as units.

In R4, the `win_gravity` field has also been added to the `XSizeHints` structure. This field suggests to the window manager how the window should be placed when mapped or, more accurately, how the position for the window specified by the user should be interpreted. Normally, when the user specifies a position, either by clicking a pointer button to position a window or through command line arguments, the window manager places the top-left corner of the application's top-level window at that point. The `win_gravity` field tells the window manager to place a different part of the window at that point. The values of this field are `Center`, `East`, `North`, `NorthEast`, `NorthWest`, `South`, `SouthEast`, `South-West`, and `West`. These refer to a corner or edge of the window that should be placed at the specified point. As mentioned, the default is `NorthWest`, which positions the top-left corner of the window at the specified point. Few applications need to use this feature.

3.2.9 Selecting Desired Event Types

The next step is to select the event types the application will require. Our simple program must receive events for three reasons: to redraw itself in case of exposure, to recalculate its contents when it is resized, and to receive a button or key press indicating that the user is finished with the application.

The program must select these types of events specifically since, by default, it will not receive the kinds of input it needs. Example 3-11 shows the line of code that selects events.

Example 3-11. basicwin — selecting desired event types

```
/* Select event types wanted */
XSelectInput(display, win, ExposureMask | KeyPressMask |
    ButtonPressMask | StructureNotifyMask);
```

The crucial argument of `XSelectInput` is the event mask. Each symbol used here selects one of more event types. The event mask constants are combined with a bitwise OR since they are really setting bits in a single argument.

`ExposureMask` selects `Expose` events, which occur when the window is first displayed and whenever it becomes visible after being obscured. `Expose` events signal that the application should redraw itself.

X provides separate events for depressing and releasing both keyboard keys and pointer buttons and separate symbols for selecting each of these types of events. `KeyPressMask` selects only `KeyPress` events, and `ButtonPressMask` selects only `ButtonPress` events. `ButtonRelease` and `KeyRelease` events can also be selected with `Button-ReleaseMask` and `KeyReleaseMask`, but they are not needed in this application.

`StructureNotifyMask` selects a number of event types, specifically `Circulate-Notify`, `ConfigureNotify`, `DestroyNotify`, `GravityNotify`, `MapNotify`, `ReparentNotify`, and `UnmapNotify`. The only one of these we need for our application is `ConfigureNotify`, which informs the application of its window's new size when it has been resized. However, there is no way to select just this one event type. We could get away without selecting this event type, but any real application would use it because it allows an increase in performance. Without this event type, on every `Expose` event the application would have to use `XGetGeometry` to find out its current size. This is a request that requires a reply from the server and therefore is subject to network delays.

The rest of the event types selected by `StructureNotifyMask` are described in Chapter 8, *Events*.

`XSelectInput` actually sets the `event_mask` attribute of the window. If you create the window with `XCreateWindow` (as opposed to `XCreateSimpleWindow`), you can select events at the same time by setting the `event_mask` attribute in the last two arguments of the call. This is slightly more efficient than calling `XSelectInput` separately. You can also set this attribute through `XChangeWindowAttributes` if, for some other reason, you need to call this function anyway.

3.2.10 Creating Server Resources

The next step in the application is to create any other server resources that are needed. Server resources are collections of information managed by the server and referred to in the application by an ID number. Items with the types `Colormap`, `Cursor`, `Font`, `GC`, `Pixmap`, and `Window` are server resources. They should be created once and the ID kept rather than creating and deleting them in frequently called subroutines. That is why they are normally created in `main` or in a subroutine called only once from `main`.

In this program, we have already created two resources: a window and the icon pixmap. We still need to load a font for the text and to create a graphics context to draw both text and graphics into the window. These operations are done in the routines `load_font` and `get_GC`, called just before mapping the window. We are going to delay describing these routines until Chapters 5 and 6, in order to keep this chapter to manageable proportions. However, the complete code for *basicwin*, including these functions, is listed at the end of this chapter, in case you want a sneak preview.

3.2.11 Window Mapping

Finally we are ready to display the window. Note that we have done all that preparation before mapping the window for good reason. The window manager hints must be set so that the window manager can handle the mapping properly, and events must be selected so that the first `Expose` will arrive and tell the application to draw into its window.

Example 3-12 shows the code that maps the window.

Example 3-12. basicwin — mapping the window

```
/* Display window */
XMapWindow(display, win);
```

You may remember from Chapter 2, *X Concepts*, that in order for a window to be visible, it must meet five conditions. These are so important that they bear repeating:

1. The window must be mapped with XMapWindow or related routines.

2. All its ancestors must be mapped. This condition is always satisfied for the children of the root window, the top-level windows of each application.

3. The window must not be obscured by visible sibling windows or their ancestors—this depends on the stacking order. When first mapped, a window appears on top of its siblings, which will be on top of all windows if its parent is the root window.

4. The request buffer must be flushed. This topic will be described in the next section.

5. The initial mapping of a top-level window is a special case, since the window's visibility may be delayed by the window manager. For complicated reasons, an application must wait for the first Expose event before assuming that its window is visible and drawing into it.

3.2.12 Flushing the Output Buffer

XMapWindow causes an X protocol request that instructs the server to display the window on the screen. Like all other X protocol requests, this one is queued until an event-reading routine such as XNextEvent, a routine that queries the server (most routines whose names contain Fetch, Get, or Query), or a routine such as XFlush or XSync is called. The server operates more efficiently over the network when X protocol requests are sent in groups.

The XNextEvent call performs the flushing frequently enough in applications that take user input. The routines that query the server should be called as infrequently as possible because they reduce performance over the network. The XFlush command instructs the server to process all queued output requests right away. XFlush is generally necessary only when an application needs to draw periodically even without user input.

3.2.13 Setting Up an Event-gathering Loop

X programs are event-driven, which means that after setting up all the server resources and window manager hints as described up to this point, the program performs all further actions only in response to events. The event-gathering loop is the standard way to respond to events, performing the appropriate action depending on the type of event and the information contained in the event structure.

The event loop is normally a closed loop, in which one of the event types with certain contents defined by the application indicates that the user wants to exit. In some existing applications such as *xclock*, the loop is completely closed, and therefore the only way to terminate the program is to find the process ID from the shell and kill it or use the window or session manager, but this can be inconvenient.

The choice of which events are received by the application was made earlier when the application selected input or set the `event_mask` attribute. The event loop must make sure to properly handle every event type selected. One of the most common debugging problems is for there to be a difference between the events handled and those selected.

Have a look at the code in Example 3-13, before we describe it in more specific terms.

Example 3-13. basicwin — processing events

```
        .
        .
        .
/* Get events, use first Expose to display text and graphics
 * ConfigureNotify to indicate a resize (maybe even before
 * first Expose); ButtonPress or KeyPress to exit */
while (1)   {
    XNextEvent(display, &report);
    switch  (report.type) {
    case Expose:
        /* Unless this is the last contiguous expose,
         * don't draw the window */
        if (report.xexpose.count != 0)
            break;

        /* If window too small to use */
        if (window_size == TOO_SMALL)
            TooSmall(win, gc, font_info);
        else {
            /* Place text in window */
            place_text(win, gc, font_info, width, height);

            /* Place graphics in window */
            place_graphics(win, gc, width, height);
        }
        break;
    case ConfigureNotify:
        /* Window has been resized; change width and height
         * to send to place_text and place_graphics in
         * next Expose */
        width = report.xconfigure.width;
        height = report.xconfigure.height;
        if ((width < size_hints.min_width) ||
                (height < size_hints.min_height))
            window_size = TOO_SMALL;
            else
            window_size = BIG_ENOUGH;
        break;
    case ButtonPress:
        /* Trickle down into KeyPress (no break) */
    case KeyPress:
        XUnloadFont(display, font_info->fid);
```

Example 3-13. basicwin — processing events (continued)

```
            XFreeGC(display, gc);
            XCloseDisplay(display);
            exit(1);
    default:
            /* All events selected by StructureNotifyMask
             * except ConfigureNotify are thrown away here,
             * since nothing is done with them */
            break;
    } /* End switch */
} /* End while */
```

Example 3-13 is framed by an infinite while loop. Just inside the top of the loop is the XNextEvent statement, which gets an event structure from the queue Xlib maintains for the application and puts the pointer to it in the variable report. You might assume that the event loop could have been written:

```
while (XNextEvent(display, &event)) {
    .
    .
    .
}
```

but this is not the case. XNextEvent returns void; it only returns when there is an event to return. Errors are handled through a separate error-handling mechanism, not through the returned value. So it is necessary to write the event loop:

```
while (1) {
    XNextEvent(display, &event);
    .
    .
    .
}
```

Right after XNextEvent is a switch statement that branches depending on the event type. There is one case for each of the four types of events: ButtonPress, Configure-Notify, Expose, and KeyPress.

The ConfigureNotify branch, in all applications, will calculate the values of variables based on the new window size. These variable values will then be used to calculate where to draw things in the Expose branch the next time an Expose event occurs. A ConfigureNotify event is always followed by one or more Expose events.

3.2.13.1 Repainting the Window

Expose events occur when a window becomes visible on the screen, after being obscured or unmapped. They occur because the X Window System does not normally save the contents of regions of windows obscured by other windows or not mapped. The contents of windows need to be redrawn when they are exposed.

The code for Expose events draws or redraws the contents of the application's window. This code will be reached when the window is first mapped, and whenever a portion of the window becomes visible.

An application can respond to Expose events by refreshing only the parts of the window exposed, or by refreshing the entire window. The former is possible because the event structure for each Expose event carries the position and dimensions of a single rectangular exposed area, as shown in Example 3-14.

Example 3-14. The XExposeEvent structure

```
typedef struct {
    int type;
    unsigned long serial;/* # of last request processed by server */
    Bool send_event;      /* True if this came from SendEvent
                           * request */
    Display *display;     /* Display the event was read from */
    Window window;
    int x, y;
    int width, height;
    int count;            /* If nonzero, at least this many more */
} XExposeEvent;
```

Several Expose events can occur because of a single window manager operation, as shown in Figure 3-2. If window *E* were raised, four Expose events would be sent to it. The height and width members in each event structure would correspond to the dimensions of the area where each of the windows overlapped window *E*, and the x and y members would specify the upper-left corner of each area relative to the origin of window *E*. All the Expose events generated by a single action are guaranteed to be contiguous in the event queue.

Whether an application should draw the whole window or just the exposed parts depends on the complexity of the drawing in the window. If all of the window contents are simple for both the application and the server to draw, the entire window contents can be redrawn without a performance problem. This approach works well as long as the window is only redrawn once, even if multiple Expose events occur because of a single user action. One trick is to monitor the count member of the Expose event structure and ignore the Expose events (do not redraw the window) until this member is 0. It might seem an even better method to search the entire queue, removing all Expose events that occurred on the window, before redrawing. But this is illegal because there may be intervening ConfigureNotify events in the queue, and responding to an Expose event that follows a Configure-Notify event too early will result in redrawing the wrong area or not redrawing at the right time. Only *contiguous* Expose events can be skipped.

On the other hand, if a window has any elements that can be time consuming for either the application or the server to redraw, then the application should only redraw the time-consuming elements if they are actually within the exposed areas.

The issue here is redrawing time, which has two components under the application's control: the time the application takes to process the redrawing instructions, and the time it takes for the server to actually do the redrawing. On most servers, a user must wait for the server to complete drawing before he or she can move the pointer or go on to other actions. Therefore, the time taken by the server is critical, since it translates directly into waiting by the user. Since the system running X clients is normally multitasking, the time taken by the application to minimize redrawing is not as important, since the user can still do work.

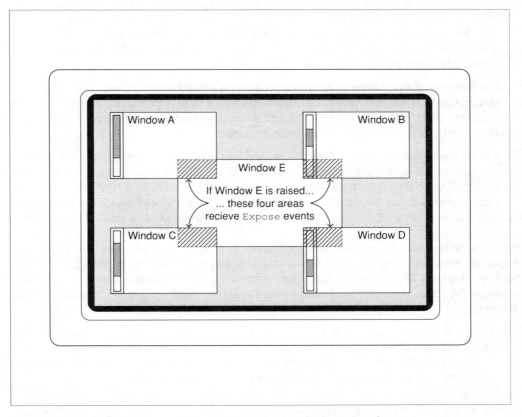

Figure 3-2. Multiple Expose events generated from a single user action

There are two approaches to assisting the server in redrawing exposed regions quickly. One is to avoid redrawing items in regions that have not been exposed. Doing this in an application requires identifying any items to be drawn that do not extend into any of the exposed areas and eliminating these drawing requests. There are a set of routines that perform intersecting calculations on regions that may help you implement this.

The second approach is to set the clip mask in the GC to draw only in the exposed areas. This second approach is much simpler in code, but it delegates the job of eliminating unnecessary drawing to the server. Many servers may not do this elimination, because there is again a tradeoff between the time saved in eliminating requests and the time spent in calculating which requests to eliminate.

If you are now confused and wondering which redrawing approach to take in your application, the general rules should be as follows:

- If the window is fast to draw, the whole window can be drawn in response to the last `Expose` event in a contiguous series; this means drawing only when `count` is zero. The definition of *fast* will vary from server to server, but anything that uses the more complex features of the GC, such as wide lines or join styles, or that may have lots of drawing requests should probably be considered slow.

- For windows that are slow to draw, the application should avoid drawing areas that were not exposed. If the application can figure out which slow drawing requests would draw only into areas that were not exposed and these calculations are not time consuming in themselves, then it should eliminate these requests.

- For windows that are slow to draw, the second best approach is to set a clip mask to allow the server to eliminate unnecessary requests. (This will work only if the server has been designed to do so.) The application can combine all the areas in a contiguous series of expose events into a single clip mask and set this clip mask into the GC. The code for this is only slightly more complex than the approach for the window that is fast to draw.

Since the image used by the *basicwin* application is simple, the application can redraw the entire window upon receiving the last contiguous `Expose` event with little performance penalty. But we will also show you the other approach, as if the window were more complex. Example 3-13 shows the first method from the list above, and Example 3-15 shows the third method.

The second method in the list above is not shown here because it is hard to demonstrate in a way that is transferable to other applications. We will just describe it in a little more detail instead. Let's say that we are writing a spreadsheet application and designing the exposure event handling. In the spreadsheet, it would be easy to determine which cells were affected by the exposure, because the cells are arranged along horizontal rows and in columns. Upon getting an `Expose` event, the application could easily determine which cells overlapped the exposed area and then redraw only those. The same could not be said of a painting program, in which some drawing primitives could be diagonal or drawn with wierd line styles. It would be very hard to determine whether a particular primitive drawn in the painting program intersects with an exposed region. In general, any application that draws most or all of its graphics horizontally or vertically can benefit from this technique. One example of an application written this way is *xterm*, and you can look at the code for that if you can get it. *xterm* redraws only the characters that are in exposed areas.

Example 3-15 shows a technique that could be used for more complicated windows. It creates a single `Region` composed of the union of the rectangles in all the `Expose` events. Regions are described fully in Chapter 6, *Drawing Graphics and Text*, but you should be able to understand this example anyway.

Example 3-15. Handling Expose events for complex window contents

```
int window_size = BIG_ENOUGH;    /* Or TOO_SMALL to display contents */
Region region;                   /* Coalesce rectangles from all Expose
                                  * events */
XRectangle rectangle;            /* Place Expose rectangles in here */
```

```
          .
          .
/* Create region for exposure event processing */
region = XCreateRegion();
while (1)  {
    XNextEvent(display, &report);
    switch  (report.type) {
    case Expose:
        if (window_size == TOO_SMALL) {
            TooSmall(win, gc, font_info);
            break;
        }
        /* Set rectangle to be exposed area */
        rectangle.x = (short) report.xexpose.x;
        rectangle.y = (short) report.xexpose.y;
        rectangle.width = (unsigned short) report.xexpose.width;
        rectangle.height = (unsigned short) report.xexpose.height;

        /* Union this rect into a region */
        XUnionRectWithRegion(&rectangle, region, region);

        /* If this is the last contiguous expose in a group,
         * set the clip region, clear region for next time
         * and draw */
        if (report.xexpose.count == 0) {
            /* Set clip region */
            XSetRegion(display, gc, region);
            /* Clear region for next time */
            XDestroyRegion(region);
            region = XCreateRegion();
            /* Place text in window */
            place_text(win, gc, font_info, width, height);

            /* Place graphics in window */
            place_graphics(win, gc, width, height);
        }
        break;
```

Being able to redraw the contents of its windows is important for most applications, but for a few applications, it might be very difficult or impossible. There is another method that might be used in such a situation. The application could draw into a pixmap and then copy the pixmap to the window each time the window needs redrawing. That way the complete window contents would always be available for redrawing the window on Expose events. The disadvantage of this approach is that the server might not have sufficient memory to store many pixmaps in memory (especially on color displays) or it might be slow about copying the pixmap into the window. But this would be a logical way to handle exposure in an application that performs double-buffering.* On high performance graphics workstations, a

---

*Double-buffering is an animation technique that hides the drawing process from the viewer. In this process, a pixmap is drawn into and then copied to a window when the image is complete.

On some hardware, it is possible to directly view a pixmap in a window without having to copy it, though this is an extension to X and not a standard feature. In this case, there would be an additional pixmap that swaps roles with the first whenever a new image is complete. The use of two pixmaps is the origin of the term *double-buffering*.

basicwin

feature known as a backing store might also be available to assist in redrawing windows. When available, this feature can be turned on for any window that really requires it. With the backing store on, the server can maintain the contents of the window when it is obscured and even when it is unmapped and capture drawing to the window while it is in one of these states. The one situation that the backing store cannot fully take care of is resizing the window. This is because it is assumed that most applications need to recalculate the dimensions of their contents to fit a new window size. The application can set an attribute called bit gravity to retain part of the window during a resize, but part of the window is still going to need redrawing if the window is resized larger.

In case you might be wondering, we have intentionally not described the `draw_text` and `draw_graphics` routines here. They are described in Sections 6.2.6 and 6.1.3. But if you are still curious, they are included in the listing of *basicwin* at the end of this chapter.

3.2.14 When Can I Draw?

There is often confusion about when an application is permitted to draw into its windows. You might think it would work to draw immediately after the `XMapWindow` request that displays a window on the screen. But that will not always work with all styles of window manager. The rule is that no drawing is allowed until the first `Expose` event arrives.

The reason involves a feature of X called substructure redirection, introduced in Section 2.1.5 and described more fully in Section 14.2.

3.2.15 When Will My Drawing Appear?

Another characteristic of X that often confuses newcomers is the fact that graphics drawn may not appear on the screen immediately. It is easy to write a program that properly performs a number of drawing calls but that never makes anything appear on the screen. This is a side effect of the fact that X is designed to buffer communications over a network, as was described in theoretical terms in Section 2.1.2. We will describe it in more practical terms here.

What happens is that the requests (to create windows, to map windows, or to draw into them) are queued up in Xlib, waiting for something to happen that requires an immediate communication with the server. Xlib will not send requests of any kind to the server until such an occurrence. The requests are saved up as a packet so they can be sent over the network more efficiently.

The queue of requests waiting to be sent to the server is called the *request buffer*. The requests are accumulated in the request buffer until a call to:

1. Any routine which requests information from the X server (for example, `XGetWindow-Attributes`, `XLoadQueryFont`, `XQueryPointer`)

2. Certain requests for getting events (`XMaskEvent`, `XNextEvent`, `XPending`, `XWindowEvent`)

3. `XFlush`

4. `XSync`

Actually, a routine in number 2 above that gets events triggers a communication with the server only if there is no event on Xlib's event queue that matches what the routine is looking for. Only if the routines are waiting for an event do they trigger the exchange. Any of these actions is said to *flush* the request buffer, which means that all requests up to this point will be acted on by the server. Novice programmers who neglect to call one of these routines will notice that their drawing requests have not been honored. They do not realize that perhaps *none* of their X requests that require communication with the server have been honored.

But does it really take a lot of care to make sure that the request buffer gets flushed? Not usually. Since X programs are event-driven, they often call routines that get events. If an application handles event types that occur frequently, such as pointer or keyboard events, there is nothing to worry about. If the application needs to get information from the server by making a call containing the word `Fetch`, `Get`, or `Query`, no problem is likely. On the other hand, an output-only application that handles only `Expose` events would certainly need to call `XFlush` once in a while to make sure that its drawing was honored in a timely fashion.

3.2.16 Handling Resizing of the Window

The `ConfigureNotify` event tells the application that the window was resized. In this program, we pass this information to the routines that draw, so that they can position things properly. We also see if the new size is less than the minimum useful size that we set as a size hint for the window manager. If it is smaller in either dimension, then we set the flag `window_size` so that the next time an `Expose` event arrives, we display the message "Too Small" instead of the usual text.

Example 3-16 shows the code that handles the `ConfigureNotify` event.

Example 3-16. basicwin — the ConfigureNotify event

```
        .
        .
        .
case ConfigureNotify:
    /* Window has been resized; change width and height to
     * send to place_text and place_graphics in next Expose */
    width = report.xconfigure.width;
    height = report.xconfigure.height;
    if ((width < size_hints.min_width) ||
            (height < size_hints.min_height))
        window_size = TOO_SMALL;
```

Example 3-16. basicwin — the ConfigureNotify event (continued)

```
          else
              window_size = BIG_ENOUGH;
          break;
      .
      .
      .
```

Note that when the window is first mapped, the `ConfigureNotify` event appears on the queue *before* the first `Expose` event. This means that the code works even if the window manager modifies the window's size before allowing it to be displayed. The initial `ConfigureNotify` updates the application's knowledge of the window size, and the following `Expose` event allows the application to draw the window's contents.

If we had not selected `ConfigureNotify` events, the code for `Expose` would have to be modified to check the dimensions in the first `Expose` event, so that it knew the correct window size. It would also have to query the server for the window size in response to subsequent `Expose` events, because these events describe only the exposed area, not the entire window.

3.2.17 Exiting the Program

This program uses a key or button press to exit. This is not a very demanding use of `Key-Press` and `ButtonPress` events. For a description of how to use keyboard and pointer events for more advanced purposes, see Chapter 9, *The Keyboard and Pointer*.

To cleanly exit, a client should free all the memory it has allocated, particularly X resources, and then close the display connection with `XCloseDisplay`. Example 3-17 shows the code that performs these functions in *basicwin*.

Example 3-17. Closing the display connection and freeing resources

```
case ButtonPress:
        /* Trickle down into KeyPress (no break) */
case KeyPress:
        XUnloadFont(display, font_info->fid);
        XFreeGC(display, gc);
        XCloseDisplay(display);
        exit(1);
```

It is good practice to use `XCloseDisplay` even though the connection to the server is closed automatically when a process exits. Otherwise, pending errors might not be reported.

3.2.18 Error Handling

Although there does not appear to be much in the way of error-handling code in this example, the question of error handling has been fully considered:

*   On the `XOpenDisplay` call, we check for the error return, tell the user what server the attempt was made to connect to, and exit gracefully.

- For all other errors, we depend on the default error-handling mechanisms. These errors might be a protocol errors caused by a programming error (all of which we hope to eliminate), a protocol error caused by the server running out of memory (the chance of which we cannot eliminate), or an IO error such as losing the connection with the server due to network failure. For protocol errors, the client gets an error event from the server, and Xlib invokes an error handler function. The client is free to provide its own error handler to replace the default handler, which prints an informative message and exits. For IO errors, there is a separate error handler function, which can be separately replaced by the application. But for this example, we have simply relied on the default handlers.

It is important to note that not all protocol errors cause the error handler to be invoked, though this fact does not show itself in *basicwin*. Some errors, such as failure to open a font, are indicated by returned values of type `Status` on the appropriate routine (in this case, `XLoadFont`). The returned values are zero on failure and nonzero on success. In general, any routine that returns `Status` will need its return value tested, because it will have bypassed the error-handling mechanism.

3.2.19 Summary

The basic steps that were taken in this program are as follows:

- Open connection to server.
- Make sure connection succeeded, print error and exit if not.
- Get display dimensions.
- Calculate desired size of window and create window.
- Create pixmap for icon.
- Initialize `XSizeHint` structure.
- Set standard properties for window manager.
- Select desired event types.
- Map window.
- Set up event gathering loop.
- If event is of type `Expose`, draw contents of window.
- If event is of type `ConfigureNotify`, recalculate dimensions of window.
- If event is `ButtonPress` or `KeyPress`, close the display and exit.

The order of these steps is important up to the point where the window is mapped. Within the event loop, the order of events cannot be completely predicted.

basicwin

3.2.20 Complete Code for basicwin

Now look at the complete code for *basicwin* and make sure you understand everything. Note that the `draw_graphics`, `draw_text`, `get_GC`, and `load_font` routines have not yet been described but will be covered in later chapters.

Example 3-18. basicwin — in its entirety

```
#include <X11/Xlib.h>
#include <X11/Xutil.h>
#include <X11/Xos.h>
#include <X11/Xatom.h>

#include <stdio.h>

#include "bitmaps/icon_bitmap"

#define BITMAPDEPTH 1
#define TOO_SMALL 0
#define BIG_ENOUGH 1

/* These are used as arguments to nearly every Xlib routine, so it
 * saves routine arguments to declare them global; if there were
 * additional source files, they would be declared extern there */
Display *display;
int screen_num;

/* progname is the string by which this program was invoked; this
 * is global because it is needed in most application functions */
static char *progname;

void main(argc, argv)
int argc;
char **argv;
{
    Window win;
    unsigned int width, height;     /* Window size */
    int x, y;                       /* Window position */
    unsigned int border_width = 4;  /* Four pixels */
    unsigned int display_width, display_height;
    unsigned int icon_width, icon_height;
    char *window_name = "Basic Window Program";
    char *icon_name = "basicwin";
    Pixmap icon_pixmap;
    XSizeHints size_hints;
    XIconSize *size_list;
    int count;
    XEvent report;
    GC gc;
    XFontStruct *font_info;
    char *display_name = NULL;
    int window_size = 0;                /* BIG_ENOUGH or TOO_SMALL to
                                         * display contents */

    progname = argv[0];

    /* Connect to X server */
    if ( (display=XOpenDisplay(display_name)) == NULL )
    {
        (void) fprintf( stderr, "%s: cannot connect to X server %s\n",
```

Example 3-18. basicwin — in its entirety (continued)

```
                    progname, XDisplayName(display_name));
        exit( -1 );
    }

    /* Get screen size from display structure macro */
    screen_num = DefaultScreen(display);
    display_width = DisplayWidth(display, screen_num);
    display_height = DisplayHeight(display, screen_num);

    /* Note that in a real application, x and y would default
     * to 0 but would be settable from the command line or
     * resource database */
    x = y = 0;

    /* Size window with enough room for text */
    width = display_width/3, height = display_height/4;

    /* Create opaque window */
    win = XCreateSimpleWindow(display, RootWindow(display,screen_num),
                x, y, width, height, border_width, BlackPixel(display,
                screen_num), WhitePixel(display,screen_num));

    /* Get available icon sizes from window manager */

    if (XGetIconSizes(display, RootWindow(display,screen_num),
            &size_list, &count) == 0)
        (void) fprintf( stderr, "%s: Window manager didn't set \
                icon sizes - using default.\n", progname);
    else {
        ;
        /* A real application would search through size_list
         * here to find an acceptable icon size and then
         * create a pixmap of that size; this requires that
         * the application have data for several sizes of icons */
    }

    /* Create pixmap of depth 1 (bitmap) for icon */
    icon_pixmap = XCreateBitmapFromData(display, win,
            icon_bitmap_bits, icon_bitmap_width,
            icon_bitmap_height);

    /* Set size hints for window manager; the window manager
     * may override these settings */
    /* Note that in a real application, if size or position
     * were set by the user, the flags would be USPosition
     * and USSize and these would override the window manager's
     * preferences for this window */
#ifdef X11R3
    size_hints.flags = PPosition | PSize | PMinSize;
    size_hints.x = x;
    size_hints.y = y;
    size_hints.width = width;
    size_hints.height = height;
    size_hints.min_width = 300;
    size_hints.min_height = 200;
#else /* X11R4 or later */
    /* x, y, width, and height hints are now taken from
     * the actual settings of the window when mapped; note
     * that PPosition and PSize must be specified anyway */
```

Example 3-18. basicwin — in its entirety (continued)

```
        size_hints.flags = PPosition | PSize | PMinSize;
        size_hints.min_width = 300;
        size_hints.min_height = 200;
#endif

#ifdef X11R3
        /* Set Properties for window manager (always before mapping) */
        XSetStandardProperties(display, win, window_name, icon_name,
                icon_pixmap, argv, argc, &size_hints);

#else /* X11R4 or later */
        {
        XWMHints wm_hints;
        XClassHint class_hints;

        /* Format of the window name and icon name arguments
         * has changed in R4 */
        XTextProperty windowName, iconName;

        /* These calls store window_name and icon_name into
         * XTextProperty structures and set their other fields
         * properly */
        if (XStringListToTextProperty(&window_name, 1, &windowName) == 0) {
            (void) fprintf( stderr, "%s: structure allocation for \
                    windowName failed.\n", progname);
            exit(-1);
        }

        if (XStringListToTextProperty(&icon_name, 1, &iconName) == 0) {
            (void) fprintf( stderr, "%s: structure allocation for \
                    iconName failed.\n", progname);
            exit(-1);
        }

        wm_hints.initial_state = NormalState;
        wm_hints.input = True;
        wm_hints.icon_pixmap = icon_pixmap;
        wm_hints.flags = StateHint | IconPixmapHint | InputHint;

        class_hints.res_name = progname;
        class_hints.res_class = "Basicwin";

        XSetWMProperties(display, win, &windowName, &iconName,
                argv, argc, &size_hints, &wm_hints,
                &class_hints);
        }
#endif
        /* Select event types wanted */
        XSelectInput(display, win, ExposureMask | KeyPressMask |
                ButtonPressMask | StructureNotifyMask);

        load_font(&font_info);

        /* Create GC for text and drawing */
        getGC(win, &gc, font_info);

        /* Display window */
        XMapWindow(display, win);
```

Example 3-18. basicwin — in its entirety (continued)

```
    /* Get events, use first to display text and graphics */
    while (1)  {
        XNextEvent(display, &report);
        switch  (report.type) {
        case Expose:
            /* Unless this is the last contiguous expose,
             * don't draw the window */
            if (report.xexpose.count != 0)
                break;

            /* If window too small to use */
            if (window_size == TOO_SMALL)
                TooSmall(win, gc, font_info);
            else {
                /* Place text in window */
                place_text(win, gc, font_info, width, height);

                /* Place graphics in window */
                place_graphics(win, gc, width, height);
            }
            break;
        case ConfigureNotify:
            /* Window has been resized; change width
             * and height to send to place_text and
             * place_graphics in next Expose */
            width = report.xconfigure.width;
            height = report.xconfigure.height;
            if ((width < size_hints.min_width) ||
                    (height < size_hints.min_height))
                window_size = TOO_SMALL;
            else
                window_size = BIG_ENOUGH;
            break;
        case ButtonPress:
            /* Trickle down into KeyPress (no break) */
        case KeyPress:
            XUnloadFont(display, font_info->fid);
            XFreeGC(display, gc);
            XCloseDisplay(display);
            exit(1);
        default:
            /* All events selected by StructureNotifyMask
             * except ConfigureNotify are thrown away here,
             * since nothing is done with them */
            break;
        } /* End switch */
    } /* End while */
}

getGC(win, gc, font_info)
Window win;
GC *gc;
XFontStruct *font_info;
{
    unsigned long valuemask = 0; /* Ignore XGCvalues and
                                  * use defaults */
    XGCValues values;
```

Example 3-18. basicwin — in its entirety (continued)

```
        unsigned int line_width = 6;
        int line_style = LineOnOffDash;
        int cap_style = CapRound;
        int join_style = JoinRound;
        int dash_offset = 0;
        static char dash_list[] = {12, 24};
        int list_length = 2;

        /* Create default Graphics Context */
        *gc = XCreateGC(display, win, valuemask, &values);

        /* Specify font */
        XSetFont(display, *gc, font_info->fid);

        /* Specify black foreground since default window background
         * is white and default foreground is undefined */
        XSetForeground(display, *gc, BlackPixel(display,screen_num));

        /* Set line attributes */
        XSetLineAttributes(display, *gc, line_width, line_style,
                cap_style, join_style);

        /* Set dashes */
        XSetDashes(display, *gc, dash_offset, dash_list, list_length);
}

load_font(font_info)
XFontStruct **font_info;
{
        char *fontname = "9x15";

        /* Load font and get font information structure */
        if ((*font_info = XLoadQueryFont(display,fontname)) == NULL)
        {
                (void) fprintf( stderr, "%s: Cannot open 9x15 font\n",
                        progname);
                exit( -1 );
        }
}

place_text(win, gc, font_info, win_width, win_height)
Window win;
GC gc;
XFontStruct *font_info;
unsigned int win_width, win_height;
{
        char *string1 = "Hi! I'm a window, who are you?";
        char *string2 = "To terminate program; Press any key";
        char *string3 = "or button while in this window.";
        char *string4 = "Screen Dimensions:";
        int len1, len2, len3, len4;
        int width1, width2, width3;
        char cd_height[50], cd_width[50], cd_depth[50];
        int font_height;
        int initial_y_offset, x_offset;

        /* Need length for both XTextWidth and XDrawString */
        len1 = strlen(string1);
        len2 = strlen(string2);
```

Example 3-18. basicwin — in its entirety (continued)

```
      len3 = strlen(string3);

      /* Get string widths for centering */
      width1 = XTextWidth(font_info, string1, len1);
      width2 = XTextWidth(font_info, string2, len2);
      width3 = XTextWidth(font_info, string3, len3);

      font_height = font_info->ascent + font_info->descent;

      /* Output text, centered on each line */
      XDrawString(display, win, gc, (win_width - width1)/2,
              font_height,
              string1, len1);
      XDrawString(display, win, gc, (win_width - width2)/2,
              (int)(win_height - (2 * font_height)),
              string2, len2);
      XDrawString(display, win, gc, (win_width - width3)/2,
              (int)(win_height - font_height),
              string3, len3);

      /* Copy numbers into string variables */
      (void) sprintf(cd_height, " Height - %d pixels",
              DisplayHeight(display,screen_num));
      (void) sprintf(cd_width, " Width  - %d pixels",
              DisplayWidth(display,screen_num));
      (void) sprintf(cd_depth, " Depth  - %d plane(s)",
              DefaultDepth(display, screen_num));

      /* Reuse these for same purpose */
      len4 = strlen(string4);
      len1 = strlen(cd_height);
      len2 = strlen(cd_width);
      len3 = strlen(cd_depth);

      /* To center strings vertically, we place the first string
       * so that the top of it is two font_heights above the center
       * of the window; since the baseline of the string is what
       * we need to locate for XDrawString and the baseline is
       * one font_info -> ascent below the top of the character,
       * the final offset of the origin up from the center of
       * the window is one font_height + one descent */

      initial_y_offset = win_height/2 - font_height -
              font_info->descent;
      x_offset = (int) win_width/4;
      XDrawString(display, win, gc, x_offset, (int) initial_y_offset,
              string4,len4);

      XDrawString(display, win, gc, x_offset, (int) initial_y_offset +
              font_height,cd_height,len1);
      XDrawString(display, win, gc, x_offset, (int) initial_y_offset +
              2 * font_height,cd_width,len2);
      XDrawString(display, win, gc, x_offset, (int) initial_y_offset +
              3 * font_height,cd_depth,len3);
}

place_graphics(win, gc, window_width, window_height)
Window win;
GC gc;
unsigned int window_width, window_height;
```

Example 3-18. basicwin — in its entirety (continued)

```
{
     int x, y;
     int width, height;

     height = window_height/2;
     width = 3 * window_width/4;
     x = window_width/2 - width/2;   /* Center */
     y = window_height/2 - height/2;
     XDrawRectangle(display, win, gc, x, y, width, height);
}

TooSmall(win, gc, font_info)
Window win;
GC gc;
XFontStruct *font_info;
{
     char *string1 = "Too Small";
     int y_offset, x_offset;

     y_offset = font_info->ascent + 2;
     x_offset = 2;

     /* Output text, centered on each line */
     XDrawString(display, win, gc, x_offset, y_offset, string1,
             strlen(string1));
}
```

4

Window Attributes

*The window attributes control a window's background and border pattern or
color, the events that should be queued for it, and so on. This chapter
describes how to set and get window attributes and provides a detailed
description of each attribute. Everyone should read this chapter.*

In This Chapter:

4

Window Attributes

Now that you know the basic X concepts and you have seen the code for an X application, we can go back and describe the window attributes thoroughly. The window attributes were introduced in Section 2.2.1 and described in more detail in Section 2.4.1. You should read those sections before proceeding. You will continue to find this chapter useful as a reference even when you are an experienced X programmer. A useful quick reference to the window attributes is also provided inside the back cover of Volume Two, *Xlib Reference Manual*.

4.1 Setting Window Attributes

Window attributes can be set while creating a window with `XCreateWindow` or afterward with a call to `XChangeWindowAttributes`. When creating a window with `XCreateSimpleWindow`, the attributes are inherited from the parent. There are also several routines for changing individual window attributes, including the `event_mask`, background and border.

The procedure for setting the attributes is the same with `XCreateWindow` or `XChange-WindowAttributes`. You set the members of an `XSetWindowAttributes` structure to the desired values, create a mask indicating which members you have set, and call the routine to create the window or change the attributes.

4.2 The Window Attribute Structures

There are actually two structures associated with window attributes. `XWindow-Attributes` is an internal, read-only structure that contains all the attributes, while `XSetWindowAttributes` is a structure that contains only those attributes that a program is allowed to set. We will not show you `XWindowAttributes` until Section 4.4, since it is used in programming only for getting the values of the window attributes.

Example 4-1 shows the structure that is used to set the window attributes.

Example 4-1. The XSetWindowAttributes structure
```
typedef struct _XSetWindowAttributes {
    Pixmap background_pixmap;   /* Pixmap, None, or ParentRelative */
    long background_pixel;      /* Background pixel value */
    Pixmap border_pixmap;       /* Pixmap, None, or CopyFromParent */
    long border_pixel;          /* Border pixel value */
    int bit_gravity;            /* One of the bit gravity symbols */
    int win_gravity;            /* One of the window gravity symbols */
    int backing_store;          /* NotUseful, WhenMapped, or Always */
    long backing_bitplanes;     /* Planes to be preserved, if
                                 * possible */
    long backing_pixel;         /* Value to use in restoring planes */
    Bool save_under;            /* Should bits under window be saved */
    long event_mask;            /* Events that should be queued */
    long do_not_propagate_mask; /* Events that shouldn't propagate */
    Bool override_redirect;     /* Override redirected configuration
                                 * requests */
    Colormap colormap;          /* Colormap associated with window */
    Cursor cursor;              /* Cursor to be displayed or None */
} XSetWindowAttributes;
```

To set the window attributes, you need to set the elements of the XSetWindow-Attributes structure to the desired values and then set a valuemask argument that represents which members are to be changed in the server's internal structure. A symbol specifying each member to be changed is combined with the bitwise OR operator (|). These symbols are shown in Table 4-1. They begin with the letters CW ("Create Window" or "Change Window") because the routines they are used in have those capital letters in their names.

Table 4-1. Window Attribute Mask Symbols

Member	Flag	Bit
background_pixmap	CWBackPixmap	0
background_pixel	CWBackPixel	1
border_pixmap	CWBorderPixmap	2
border_pixel	CWBorderPixel	3
bit_gravity	CWBitGravity	4
win_gravity	CWWinGravity	5
backing_store	CWBackingStore	6
backing_planes	CWBackingPlanes	7
backing_pixel	CWBackingPixel	8
override_redirect	CWOverrideRedirect	9
save_under	CWSaveUnder	10
event_mask	CWEventMask	11
do_not_propagate_mask	CWDontPropagate	12
colormap	CWColormap	13
cursor	CWCursor	14

For example, if you want to set the initial values of the background and border pixel values, you would follow the procedure shown in Example 4-2.

Example 4-2. Setting window attributes while creating a window

```
Display *display;
Window parent, window;
int x, y;
unsigned int width, height, border_width;
int depth;
Visual *visual;
unsigned int class;
XSetWindowAttributes setwinattr;
unsigned long valuemask;

/* (Must open display) */

valuemask = CWBackPixel | CWBorderPixel;
setwinattr.background_pixel = WhitePixel(display, screen_num);
setwinattr.border_pixel = BlackPixel(display, screen_num);
window = XCreateWindow(display, parent, x, y, width, height,
     border_width, depth, class, visual, valuemask, &setwinattr);
```

If the window already exists, you can change those same attributes with the procedure shown in Example 4-3.

Example 4-3. Changing window attributes of existing window

```
Display *display;
Window window;
XSetWindowAttributes setwinattr;
unsigned long valuemask;

/* (Must open display, create window) */

valuemask = CWBackPixel | CWBorderPixel;
setwinattr.background_pixel = WhitePixel(display, screen_num);
setwinattr.border_pixel = BlackPixel(display, screen_num);
XChangeWindowAttributes(display, window, valuemask, &setwinattr);
```

You can also use separate calls to `XSetWindowBackground` and `XSetWindow-Border` to set these particular attributes. These and a few other attributes have routines for setting them individually. (These routines are referred to as *convenience routines*. They are provided for the attributes that most often need to be set without modifying any other attributes.) Table 4-2 lists the attributes that can be set individually and the routines that set them. But it is important to realize that each of these routines would generate a separate protocol request to the server, so if more than one attribute is to be set, it is more efficient to use the procedures shown above in Examples 4-2 and 4-3.

Table 4-2. Attributes that can be Set Individually

Attribute	Routine for Setting It
`background_pixmap`	`XSetWindowBackgroundPixmap`
`background_pixel`	`XSetWindowBackground`
`border_pixmap`	`XSetWindowBorderPixmap`
`border_pixel`	`XSetWindowBorder`
`event_mask`	`XSelectInput`
`colormap`	`XSetWindowColormap`
`cursor`	`XDefineCursor` or `XUndefineCursor`

Section 4.3 describes all of the attributes and the routines for setting them.

4.3 Settable Attributes

The sections that follow describe the options and default values for each member of the `XSetWindowAttributes` structure. The attributes control a wide variety of ways for a window to act. They can be grouped loosely to help you understand when you might want to set each attribute.

One group of attributes controls the appearance of a window. These are `background_pixel`, `background_pixmap`, `border_pixel`, `border_pixmap`, `colormap`, and `cursor`. Most clients will set the border, background, and cursor but use the default colormap.

A second group is provided to allow clients to improve their redrawing performance under certain conditions. These are `backing_pixel`, `backing_planes`, `backing_store`, `bit_gravity`, and `save_under`. These attributes do not affect the appearance or operation of a client. It is advisable to consider `bit_gravity` when designing a client, but the code for using these attributes can be added after a client's functionality is complete.

The `event_mask` and `do_not_propagate_mask` attributes control the selection and propagation of events. These attributes are described briefly in this chapter but also in much more detail in Chapter 8, *Events*.

The `win_gravity` attribute provides a means for relocating a window automatically when its parent is resized. Applications can take advantage of this feature to simplify the code that positions their subwindows when they are resized.

The `override_redirect` attribute controls whether requests to map or reconfigure the window can be intercepted by the window manager. `override_redirect` is meant to be set for the most temporary types of windows such as pop-up menus. In practice, this attribute only affects the top-level windows of an application (all children of the root window).

InputOutput windows have all of the attributes described in the sections below. InputOnly windows have only the following subset of attributes:

- win_gravity
- event_mask
- do_not_propagate_mask
- override_redirect
- cursor

Any attempt to set attributes other than these five on an InputOnly window will cause an X protocol error.

4.3.1 The Window Background

The background of a window is the drawing surface on which other graphics are drawn. It may be a solid color, or it may be patterned with a pixmap. This choice is mostly an aesthetic decision for the programmer. However, users expect to be able to specify the background color on the command line or in the resource database. Also, if a pixmap is used, the code for creating the pixmap should use two colors specified by the user.

The two attributes that control the background are background_pixmap and background_pixel, and XSetWindowBackgroundPixmap and XSetWindow-Background set them.

These two attributes are not independent since they affect the same pixels. Either attribute can take precedence over the other, the winner being the one that is set last. If both are set in the same call to XCreateWindow or XChangeWindowAttributes, the background_pixel value is used.

The background of exposed areas of windows is automatically repainted by the server, regardless of whether the application selects Expose events.

However, changes in background attributes will not take effect until the server generates the next Expose event on that window. If you want the new background to be visible immediately, call XClearWindow and flush the request buffer with XFlush.

Applications must set one or the other for all windows. Otherwise, the results are undefined. Most applications set backgrounds to a solid color by setting the background_pixel attribute. The easiest way to do this is by setting the last argument of XCreateSimple-Window to BlackPixel or WhitePixel.

Window
Attributes

4.3.1.1 background_pixmap

If the background is set to a pixmap, the background is tiled with the pixmap. *Tiling* is the laying out of a pixmap to cover an area. The first pixmap is applied at the origin of the window (or its parent's origin if using the parent's background pixmap by specifying `Parent-Relative`, as described below). Another copy of the same pixmap is applied next to that one and another below it and so on until the window is filled.

The pixmap may be any size, though some sizes may be tiled faster than others. To find the most efficient tile size for a particular screen, call `XQueryBestTile`.

A pixmap must be created with `XCreatePixmap` or `XCreatePixmapFromBitmap-Data` before being set as the `background_pixmap` attribute. The pixmap must have the same depth as the window and be created on the same screen. These attributes are assigned to a pixmap as it is created. (For more information on creating pixmaps for tiles, see Section 6.1.5.)

The `background_pixmap` attribute has the following possible values:

`None` (default)
  : Specifies that the window has no defined background pixmap. The window initially will be invisible and will share the bits of its parent but only if the `background_pixel` attribute is not set. When anything is drawn by any client into the area enclosed by the window, the contents will remain until the area is explicitly cleared with `XClearWindow`. The background is not automatically refreshed after exposure.

a pixmap ID
  : The background will be tiled with the specified pixmap. The background tile origin is the window origin. If the pixmap is not explicitly referenced again, it can be freed, since a copy is maintained in the server.

`ParentRelative`
  : Specifies that the parent's background is to be used and that the origin for tiling is the parent's origin (or the parent's parent if the parent's `background_pixmap` attribute is also `Parent-Relative` and so on). The difference between setting `Parent-Relative` and explicitly setting the same pixmap as the parent is the origin of the tiling. The difference between `Parent-Relative` and `None` is that for `ParentRelative`, the background is automatically repainted on exposure.

    The window must have the same depth as the parent, or a `Bad-Match` error will occur. If the parent has background `None`, then the window will also have background `None`. The parent's background is re-examined each time the window background is required (when it needs to be redrawn due to exposure). The window's contents will be lost when the window is moved relative to its parent, and the contents will have to be redrawn.

Changing the `background_pixmap` attribute of the root window to `None` or `Parent-Relative` restores the default background, which is server-dependent.

By the way, the symbol `CopyFromParent` is not used for setting the background, but it will not cause an error, since its value is the same as `None`.

4.3.1.2 background_pixel

If the background pixel value is specified, the entire background will take on the color (or shade of gray) indicated for that pixel value in the current colormap.*

The `background_pixel` attribute has the following possible values:

undefined (default)   Indicates that the background is as specified in the `background_pixmap` attribute. This value is possible only by creating a window with `XCreateWindow` and not setting the `background_pixel` attribute.

a pixel value   The background is filled with the specified pixel value. This is set with the last argument of `XCreateSimpleWindow`.

4.3.2 The Window Border

Like the window background, the window border may have a solid color or may be tiled with a pixmap. This choice is again up to the programmer, though the user should be allowed to determine the color or colors.

Unlike changes to the window background, changes to a window's border attributes are reflected immediately. No call to `XClearWindow` or call to flush the request buffer is necessary. This feature makes it possible to use the window border for indicating a client's state. But you cannot use the border of the top-level window, since some window managers manipulate this border to indicate the keyboard focus window (see Section 8.3.2.1 for a description of the keyboard focus).

The design of a pattern for the border will be different from the background pixmap, because the border width is usually narrow (at most four pixels).

The two attributes that affect the border are `border_pixmap` and `border_pixel`. `XSetWindowBorder` and `XSetWindowBorderPixmap` can be used to set these attributes. Like the window background, whenever one of these routines is called, it overrides the previous setting of the border. If they are both set simultaneously with `XCreate-Window` or `XChangeWindowAttributes`, the `border_pixel` attribute takes precedence.

Most applications simply set the `border_pixel` to `BlackPixel` or `WhitePixel` in the next-to-last argument of `XCreateSimpleWindow`.

---

*We should inform you here that a pixel value is not something you choose yourself; you choose a color name, and the pixel value is returned to you from `BlackPixel` or `WhitePixel` or one of the routines that allocate colors. We go into this subject in detail in Chapter 7, *Color*.

Window Attributes

4.3.2.1 border_pixmap

If the `border_pixmap` is set to a pixmap, the border is tiled with the pixmap. Tiling is performed as described previously for the background pixmap; the border tile origin is the same as the background tile origin.

The `border_pixmap` attribute has the following possible values:

CopyFromParent (default)
> Specifies that the border pixmap is to be copied from the parent. Subsequent changes to the parent's border attributes do not affect the child, but changes to the pixmap used by the parent may be reflected in the child border (server-dependent).

None
> Specifies that the window has no border pixmap. If the window has no border pixel value either, then it uses the same border pixel value as the parent.

a pixmap ID
> Specifies a pixmap to be tiled in the border. The border tile origin is always the window origin; it is not taken from the background tile origin. If the pixmap is not explicitly referenced again, it can be freed since a copy is maintained in the server.

For the root window, CopyFromParent indicates that the default border will be inherited by subsequently created children of the root window, instead of any other border that was set for the root window. Setting the border_pixmap of the root window to CopyFromParent restores the default border pixmap for later inheritance.

4.3.2.2 border_pixel

If a border pixel value is specified, the entire border will take on the color (or shade of gray) indicated for that pixel value in the current colormap.

The `border_pixel` attribute has the following possible values:

undefined (default)
> Indicates that the border is as specified in the `border_pixmap` attribute. This value is possible only by creating a window with XCreateWindow and not setting the `border_pixel` attribute.

a pixel value
> Overrides the default and any `border_pixmap` given, and fills the border with the specified pixel value. This is set by the next-to-last argument of XCreateSimpleWindow.

4.3.3 Bit Gravity

When an unobscured window is moved, its contents are moved with it, since none of the pixel values needs to be changed. But when a window is enlarged or shrunk, the server has no idea where in the resulting window the old contents should be placed, so it normally throws them out. The `bit_gravity` attribute tells the server where to put the existing bits in the larger or smaller window. By instructing the server where to place the old contents, bit gravity allows some clients (not all can take advantage of it) to avoid redrawing parts of their windows.

Bit gravity is never *necessary* in programs. It does not affect the appearance or functionality of the client. It is used to improve performance in certain cases. Some X servers may not implement bit gravity and may throw out the window contents on resizing regardless of the setting of this attribute. This response is the default for all servers. That is, the default bit gravity is `ForgetGravity`, which means that the contents of a window are always lost when the window is resized, even if they are maintained in backing store or because of a `save_under` (to be described in Sections 4.3.5 and 4.3.6).

The window is tiled with its background in the areas that are not preserved by the bit gravity, unless no background is defined, in which case the existing screen is not altered.

There is no routine to set the `bit_gravity` individually; it can be set only with `XChangeWindowAttributes` or `XCreateWindow`.

The `bit_gravity` attribute has 11 possible values:

ForgetGravity (default) Specifies that window contents should always be discarded after a size change. Note that some X servers may not implement bit gravity and may use `ForgetGravity` in all cases.

StaticGravity Specifies that window contents should not move relative to the origin of the root window. This means that the area of intersection between the original extent of the window and the final extent of the window will not be disturbed.

Each constant below specifies where the old window contents should be placed in the resized window.

NorthWestGravity Upper-left corner of the resized window.
NorthGravity Top center of the resized window.
NorthEastGravity Upper-right corner of the resized window.
WestGravity Left center of the resized window.
CenterGravity Center of the resized window.
EastGravity Right center of the resized window.
SouthWestGravity Lower-left corner of the resized window.
SouthGravity Bottom center of the resized window.
SouthEastGravity Lower-right corner of the resized window.

Here are two examples of applications that could take advantage of bit gravity. Figure 4-1 shows a fictional application that draws a two-axis graph in a window, with the origin at the lower-left corner. If that window were resized, the application would want the old contents to be placed against the new lower-left corner, no matter which sides of the window were moved in or out. That application would set the `bit_gravity` attribute of this window to `SouthWestGravity`. Figure 4-1 shows the response of this window to resizing with this bit gravity setting.

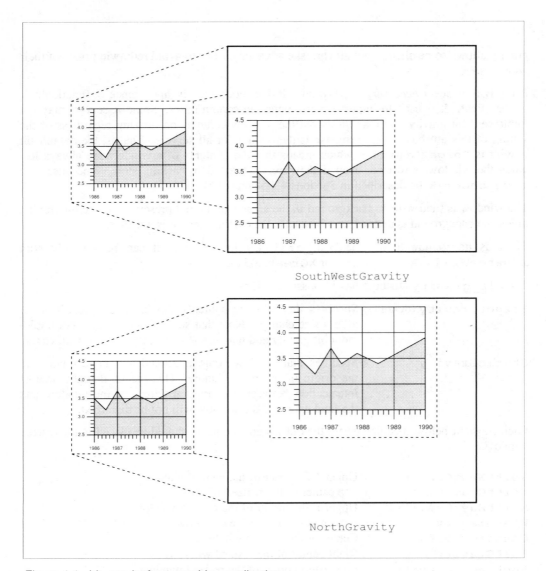

Figure 4-1. bit_gravity for a graphing application

Each compass constant, such as SouthWestGravity, indicates the placement of the retained region in the window after resizing. In this case, the lower-left corner of the existing pixels is placed against the lower-left corner of the resulting window. When an Expose event arrives, the application need only redraw the two new strips of the window at the top and right side. No Expose event will be generated on the area that was saved because of bit_gravity.

For another example, think of a window containing centered text. If that window were resized either larger or smaller, we would still like the text to be centered. In this case, the bit_gravity should be set to CenterGravity. Then only if the window is resized smaller than the length of the text would we have to redraw the area and only then to break the line or use a shorter message. We could see whether changing the message would be necessary by looking at the `ConfigureNotify` event that occurs as a result of the resize (see *basicwin* in Chapter 3, *Basic Window Program*). The window would still have to be redrawn if it were obscured and then exposed, of course—bit gravity only saves *some* of the redrawing that would otherwise have to be done.

If the constant were `NorthGravity`, the top center of the pixels in the window before the resize would be placed against the top center of the resulting window. This would be appropriate if we had a line of text centered at the top of the window that we wished to preserve when possible.

4.3.4 Window Gravity

The `win_gravity` attribute controls the repositioning of subwindows when a parent window is resized. The attribute is set on the children. Normally, each child has a fixed position measured from the origin of the parent window. Window gravity can be used to tell the server to unmap the child or to move the child an amount depending on the change in size of the parent. The constants used to set `win_gravity` are similar to those for bit gravity, but their effect is quite different.

`NorthGravity` specifies that the child window should be moved horizontally by an amount one-half as great as the amount the window was resized in the horizontal direction. The child is not moved vertically. That means that if the window was originally centered along the top edge of the window, it will also be centered along the top edge of the window after resizing. If it was not originally centered, its relative distance from the center may be accentuated or reduced depending on whether the parent is resized larger or smaller.

Window gravity is only useful for children placed against or very near the outside edges of the parent or directly in its center. Furthermore, the child must be centered along one of the outside edges or in a corner. Figure 4-2 shows the nine child positions where window gravity can be useful and the setting to be used for each position.

If any other setting is used for any of these positions, the window gravity may move the child outside the resized parent, since there are no checks to prevent this. The application can try to prevent it by getting the new position of the child from a `ConfigureNotify` event (see Section 3.2.16) and moving the child inside if necessary. But this will cause a flash when the child window is automatically placed incorrectly and then moved to the correct position by the application. And if an application has to go to the trouble to check the position and move the child, it might as well just forget about window gravity and place the child itself.

`NorthWestGravity` (the default) indicates that the child (for which this attribute is set) is not moved relative to its parent.

`UnmapGravity` specifies that the subwindow should be unmapped when the parent is resized. This might be used when a client wishes to recalculate the positions of its children. Normally, the children would appear in their old positions before the client could move them into their recalculated positions. This can be confusing to the user. By setting the `win_gravity` attribute to `UnmapGravity`, the server will unmap the windows. They can be repositioned at the client's leisure, and then the client can remap them (with `XMap-Subwindows`) in their new locations.

Figure 4-2. Child positions where window gravity is useful

There is no routine to set the `win_gravity` attribute individually; it can be set only with `XChangeWindowAttributes` or `XCreateWindow`.

The `win_gravity` attribute has the following possible values:

UnmapGravity   Specifies that the child is unmapped (removed from the screen) when the parent is resized, and an `UnmapNotify` event is generated.

StaticGravity   Specifies that the window contents should not move relative to the origin of the root window.

One of the compass constants below

     The list below shows the distance the child window will be moved; *W* is the amount the parent was resized in width, and *H* is the amount the parent was resized in height:

NorthWestGravity (default)	(0, 0)
NorthGravity	(W/2, 0)
NorthEastGravity	(W, 0)
WestGravity	(0, H/2)
CenterGravity	(W/2, H/2)
EastGravity	(W, H/2)
SouthWestGravity	(0, H)
SouthGravity	(W/2, H)
SouthEastGravity	(W, H)

4.3.5 Backing Store

A *backing store* automatically maintains the contents of a window while it is obscured or even while it is unmapped. Backing is like having a copy of the window saved in a pixmap, automatically copied to the screen whenever necessary to keep the visible contents up to date. Backing store is only available on some servers, usually on high performance work-stations.

These servers can be instructed when to back up a window and which planes to save, through the backing store attributes. Even when it is available, the backing store should be avoided since it may carry a heavy performance penalty on the server. You can find out whether backing is supported on a particular screen with the `DoesBackingStore` macro.

A client might use this feature to back up a window it is incapable of redrawing for some reason or to be able to draw into a window that is obscured or unmapped.

Three separate attributes control backing: `backing_store`, `backing_planes`, and `backing_pixel`. There are no routines for setting these attributes individually (use `XChangeWindowAttributes` or `XCreateWindow`). The `backing_store` attribute determines when and if a window's contents are preserved by the server. The `backing_planes` attribute specifies which planes must be preserved, and `backing_pixel` specifies the pixel value used to fill planes not specified in `backing_planes`. The X server is free to save only the bit planes specified in `backing_planes` and to regenerate the remaining planes with the specified pixel value.

When the backing store feature is active and the window is larger than its parent, the server maintains complete contents, not just the region within the parent's boundaries. If the server is maintaining the contents of a window, `Expose` events will not be generated when that window is exposed.

Use of the backing store does not make a window immune to the other window attributes. If the `bit_gravity` is `ForgetGravity`, the contents will still be lost whenever the window is resized.

The `backing_store` attribute has the following possible values:

`NotUseful` (default) Advises the server that maintaining contents is unnecessary. A server may still choose to maintain contents.

`WhenMapped` Advises the server that it would be beneficial to maintain contents of obscured regions when the window is mapped.

`Always` Advises the server that it would be beneficial to maintain contents even when the window is unmapped.

The `backing_planes` attribute specifies a mask (default all 1's) that indicates which planes of the window hold dynamic data that must be preserved in the backing store.

The `backing_pixel` attribute specifies a pixel value (default 0) to be used in planes not specified in the `backing_plane` attribute.

4.3.6 Saving Under

The `save_under` attribute controls whether the contents of the screen beneath a window should be preserved just before the window is mapped and replaced just after it is unmapped. This attribute is most useful for pop-up windows, which need to be on the screen only briefly. No `Expose` events will be sent to the windows that are exposed when the pop-up window is unmapped, saving the time necessary to redraw their contents.

Pop-up windows are usually children of the root window and, therefore, are not constrained to appear within the application's top-level window. Therefore, both your application and other applications on the screen would otherwise need to redraw areas when the pop-up window is unmapped.

Setting `save_under` is never necessary, but it can improve the performance of the server running clients that frequently map and unmap temporary windows. The user would otherwise have to wait for the area under the menu to be redrawn when the menu was unmapped.

There is no routine for setting the `save_under` attribute individually; it can only be set with `XChangeWindowAttributes` or `XCreateWindow`.

The `save_under` attribute is different from the backing store; `save_under` may save portions of several windows beneath a window for the duration of the appearance of the window on the screen, while the backing store saves the contents of a single window while it is mapped or even when unmapped, depending on the attributes.

Not all servers are capable of saving under windows. You can find out whether this feature is supported on a particular screen with the `DoesSaveUnders` macro.

The `save_under` attribute has the following possible values:

`False` (default) Specifies that covered clients should be sent `Expose` events when the window is unmapped, unless they are preserved in the backing store.

`True` Specifies that the server should save areas under the window and replace them when the window is unmapped.

Setting the `save_under` attribute to `True` does not prevent all `Expose` events on the area underneath. For example, assume there is a window whose `bit_gravity` is `ForgetGravity`, and this window lies under a window that has the `save_under` attribute set to `True`. The contents of the obscured window will be lost if the underlying window is resized while partially obscured, and `Expose` events will be generated even on the saved area.

4.3.7 Event Handling

The `event_mask` and `do_not_propagate_mask` attributes control the propagation of events through the window hierarchy. The `event_mask` attribute is normally set with `XSelectInput`, but it can also be set directly with `XChangeWindowAttributes` or `XCreateWindow`.

The `event_mask` attribute specifies which event types are queued for the window when they occur. The `do_not_propagate_mask` attribute defines which events should not be propagated to ancestor windows when the event type is not selected in this window. Both masks are made by combining the constants listed below using the bitwise OR operator (|).

`Button1MotionMask`	`KeyPressMask`
`Button2MotionMask`	`KeyReleaseMask`
`Button3MotionMask`	`LeaveWindowMask`
`Button4MotionMask`	`NoEventMask`
`Button5MotionMask`	`OwnerGrabButtonMask`
`ButtonMotionMask`	`PointerMotionHintMask`
`ButtonPressMask`	`PointerMotionMask`
`ButtonReleaseMask`	`PropertyChangeMask`
`ColormapChangeMask`	`ResizeRedirectMask`
`EnterWindowMask`	`StructureNotifyMask`
`ExposureMask`	`SubstructureNotifyMask`
`FocusChangeMask`	`SubstructureRedirectMask`
`KeymapStateMask`	`VisibilityChangeMask`

Much more information on setting the event masks, including examples, is presented in Chapter 8, *Events*. This is a very important topic.

4.3.8 Substructure Redirect Override

A feature called *substructure redirect* allows a window manager to intercept any requests to map, move, resize, or change the border width of windows. This allows the window manager to modify these requests, if necessary, to ensure that they meet its window layout policy.

Setting the `override_redirect` attribute `True` for a window allows a window to be mapped, moved, resized, or its border width changed without the intervention of the window manager. This override is usually done for menus that are frequently mapped and almost immediately unmapped again.

Under properly designed window managers, there is a property you can set to tell the window manager to allow a window to pop up with minimal intervention (`XA_WM_TRANSIENT_FOR`). This is used for dialog boxes, as described in Section 10.2.1.4.6.

There is no routine for setting the `override_redirect` attribute individually; it must be set with `XChangeWindowAttributes` or `XCreateWindow`.

The `override_redirect` attribute has the following possible values:

`False` (default)   Specifies that map, move, and resize requests may be processed by the window manager.

`True`   Specifies that map, move, and resize requests are to be done verbatim, bypassing any window manager involvement.

4.3.9 Colormap

The `colormap` attribute specifies which colormap should be used to interpret the pixel values in a window.

For the large majority of clients without special color needs, this attribute can be left in its default state. By default, the `colormap` attribute from the parent is taken, which, if all ancestors of the window have used the default, will be the default colormap. This means that the default colormap for the screen will be used to translate into colors the pixel values drawn into this window.

If the client requires its own colormap for some reason, the client can create a colormap and set the `colormap` attribute to the ID of the new colormap. A colormap ID is of type `Colormap`.

The window manager will read this attribute and install the specified colormap into the hardware colormap when the user indicates that the application should be active. If the system only has one hardware colormap, all other applications will appear in false colors. This is one good reason that applications are encouraged not to create their own colormaps but to use the default colormap instead.

To understand this process, you need to know more about colormaps in X, and for that, see Chapter 7, *Color*.

`XSetWindowColormap` sets the `colormap` attribute, which can be set to the following values:

CopyFromParent (default)
> Specifies that the colormap attribute is to be copied from the parent (subsequent changes to the parent's attribute do not affect the child), but the window must have the same visual type as the parent and the parent must not have a colormap of `None` (otherwise a `BadMatch` error occurs).

a colormap ID
> The specified colormap will be used for displaying this window, at least while the window manager considers the application active.

4.3.10 Cursor

The cursor is the object that tracks the pointer on the screen. In X, a *cursor* is an X resource which defines a cursor pattern, its colors, and the point within the pattern that will be reported in events (called the *hotspot*). The ID of a cursor is of type `Cursor`.

Most clients will define a suitable cursor for their top-level window and other cursors for each subwindow if needed. For example, *xterm* specifies the thin text cursor for the main window and a vertical bidirectional arrow for the scrollbar.

A cursor can be associated with any InputOutput or InputOnly window using the cursor attribute. Then the specified cursor will track the pointer while the pointer is within the window's borders.

A primary purpose for having a different cursor in a window is to indicate visually to the user that something different will happen to keyboard or button input while in the window. Another reason might be to change a cursor's color to increase its visibility over the background of certain windows (although there are other ways to obtain contrast, with the cursor mask). There are probably other uses for a separate cursor.

A call to XDefineCursor sets this attribute to a Cursor, and a call to XUndefine-Cursor sets it back to None, which means that the cursor of the parent is used. The resource Cursor must be created before calling XDefineCursor. This can be done with XCreateFontCursor, as described in Section 6.5.1. XCreateGlyphCursor, or XCreatePixmapCursor; The cursor resource can be freed with XFreeCursor when no further explicit references to it are to be made. See Section 6.5.1.

The cursor attribute has the following possible values:

None (default)   Specifies that the parent's cursor will be used when the pointer is in the window.

a cursor ID   Specifies a cursor that will be used whenever the pointer is in the window.

The cursor of the root window is initially a large X, but this may be changed like the cursor in any other window if desired. However, this should only be done by the window manager or by the user using the *xsetroot* application. See Volume Three, *X Window System User's Guide*, for a description of *xsetroot*.

4.3.11 Default Attributes

Table 4-3 summarizes the default attributes for an InputOutput window. Only five of the attributes are relevant for InputOnly windows: cursor, do_not_propagate_mask, event_mask, override_redirect, and win_gravity. These attributes have the same defaults as for InputOutput windows.

The background, border, and event_mask attributes need to be set for virtually all windows.

Table 4-3. Default Window Attributes

Member	Default Value
background_pixmap	None
background_pixel	Undefined
border_pixmap	CopyFromParent
border_pixel	Undefined
bit_gravity	ForgetGravity
win_gravity	NorthWestGravity
backing_store	NotUseful
backing_planes	All 1's (ones)
backing_pixel	0 (zero)
override_redirect	False
save_under	False
event_mask	0
do_not_propagate_mask	0
colormap	CopyFromParent
cursor	None

4.4 Information from the XWindowAttributes Structure

We have been describing the programmable window attributes stored in the XSetWindow-Attributes structure. Many of the other window characteristics described in Chapter 2, *X Concepts*, including the window configuration, are also stored with the window attributes by the server but are not programmable using XChangeWindowAttributes. For example, depth, class, and visual are assigned at window creation and cannot be changed. The window size, position, and border width are changed with a separate mechanism, because there must be cooperation of the window manager.

The current state of most of the programmable attributes, the read-only attributes, and the window configuration can be read with XGetWindowAttributes. All this information is returned in an XWindowAttributes structure (not an XSetWindowAttributes structure).

Example 4-4 shows the fields of the XWindowAttributes structure that are not present in XSetWindowAttributes.

Example 4-4. Read-only XWindowAttributes members

```
typedef struct {
    /* Members writable with XChangeWindowAttributes omitted */
    .
    .
    .
    /* Window geometry -- set by window configuration functions
```

Example 4-4. Read-only XWindowAttributes members (continued)

```
       * in cooperation with window manager */
    int x, y;              /* Location of window */
    int width, height;     /* Width and height of window */
    int border_width;      /* Border width of window */

    /* This is the event_mask attribute set by XSelectInput */
    long your_event_mask; /* My event mask */

    /* Set when the window is created, not changeable */
    Visual *visual;        /* The associated visual structure */
    int class;             /* InputOutput, InputOnly */
    int depth;             /* Depth of window */
    Screen *screen_num;    /* Pointer to screen the window is on */

    /* Server sets these members */
    Window root;           /* Root of screen containing window */
    Bool map_installed;    /* Is colormap currently installed */
    int map_state;         /* IsUnmapped, IsUnviewable, or
                            * IsViewable */
    long all_event_masks; /* Events all clients have interest in */
} XWindowAttributes;
```

As you can see, the members of XWindowAttributes that cannot be directly written with XChangeWindowAttributes are separated into four groups.

The first group provides a way to get the window geometry. This information is also returned by XGetGeometry, but it might be useful to use XGetWindowAttributes instead if you need both the geometry and a few attributes.

The your_event_mask member can be useful if you want to add event mask symbols to those already selected. In a call to XSelectInput, you must always specify all the desired event masks. If you do not know which event masks are already selected or do not want to bother passing an event_mask argument into one of your routines, you could read the existing event mask here. Then you could OR in any additional event mask symbols before calling XSelectInput or XChangeWindowAttributes. See Chapter 8, *Events*, for more information on the use of event masks.

The depth, class, visual, and screen_num members are set when the window is created. If the window was created with XCreateSimpleWindow, they were inherited from the parent. If the window was created with XCreateWindow, these members were specified as arguments, except screen_num, which is indirectly specified by the *parent* argument. The screen_num member points to a structure that tells you about the screen on which this window was created. This is one of the Screen structures from the list in the Display structure, and therefore, the information it contains can also be gotten from the macros as described in Section 3.2.3 and Appendix C, *Macros*, of Volume Two, *Xlib Reference Manual*. Again, these should only be needed for convenience to avoid having to pass around these values as arguments or global variables.

The root member tells you the ID of the root window on the screen on which your window was created. It is usually more convenient to use the RootWindow macro.

The map_installed member can be monitored to tell your application whether the colormap it has set in its colormap attribute is currently installed. If not, the application will be displayed in false colors. See Chapter 7, *Color*, for more details.

The `map_state` member can be monitored by a program and used to turn off processing while a window is unviewable. Some applications that continuously poll for input can stop doing so and save processor cycles when there is no chance of getting input.

The `all_event_masks` member tells you all the event types that are selected by all clients on the window requested. This is the OR of all the `event_mask` attributes for that window for all clients. By contrast, `your_event_mask` specifies only the events selected by *your* client.

Also note that `XWindowAttributes` is missing a few fields that are present in `XSetWindowAttributes`. This means that there are some fields that can be set but not queried. These fields are the background and border pixel value or pixmap and the cursor. The designers of X decided to make these fields nonreadable to reduce restrictions on the implementation of backgrounds, borders, and cursors in the server.

5

The Graphics Context

The graphics primitives supplied with X are quite simple. Most of the details about the graphics to be generated are stored in a resource called a graphics context (GC). GCs are stored in the server, thus reducing the amount of information that needs to be transmitted for each graphics request. This chapter describes how to use GCs and provides details on each member of the XGCValues structure. Everyone should read this chapter.

In This Chapter:

5
The Graphics Context

The routines that draw graphics are called graphics primitives. They draw dots, lines, text, images, and tile or fill areas. But a given graphics primitive does not contain all the information needed to draw a particular graphic. A resource called the graphics context (GC) specifies many variables that apply to each graphic primitive. The appearance of everything that is drawn within a window (except the border and background of a window, which are window attributes) is controlled by the GC that is specified with each graphics request. What is drawn into a pixmap is also controlled by the GC used in the drawing to the pixmap and, again, possibly with a different GC, if the pixmap is copied into a window.

There are two performance-related reasons for having GCs. First, they reduce the traffic between Xlib and the server because the GC information is held in the server and only needs to be sent once before the first graphics request. Each subsequent primitive that specifies the same GC will use the same values. When a few settings of the GC need to be changed, only the selected few need to be sent, not the entire GC. Second, you can create several GCs and then simply specify which GC you want applied to each graphic request. This has important performance benefits on servers that are capable of caching multiple GCs in their display hardware.

The GC also allows for more convenient programming, since to provide the same flexibility without the GC, you would need to specify an absurd number of arguments every time you called a graphics primitive.

Before we can go on to describe what the GC does in particular, you must understand what a primitive does in general.

You should think of a graphics primitive as specifying which pixels in a *source rectangle* are to be drawn and where this rectangle should be placed in the *destination drawable*. Note that the source rectangle does not correspond to any area of the screen (except in XCopyArea and XCopyPlane, which are not really primitives). The source is an internal entity that is drawn as an intermediate stage in the drawing process. Primitives select pixels in the source rectangle by generating a bitmap with bits set for the pixels to be drawn. In the case of XFillPolygon, this bitmap might look like Figure 5-1.

Information in the GC is then applied to this bitmap to give it pixel values (which represent colors and are returned by BlackPixel or WhitePixel or a routine that allocates colors).

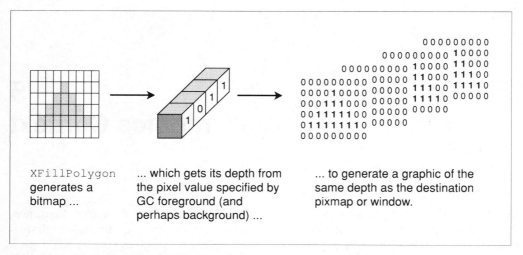

XFillPolygon generates a bitmap ...

... which gets its depth from the pixel value specified by GC foreground (and perhaps background) ...

... to generate a graphic of the same depth as the destination pixmap or window.

Figure 5-1. A "source" for a filled polygon

This modified source may then go through a number of other transformations before it appears on the screen. A graphics primitive does not draw on the screen as if it were simply a blank sheet of paper. Remember that there are multiple bits per pixel (multiple planes); a plane mask can be used to define which planes can be affected by the graphics request. Furthermore, bits on the screen have existing pixel values; while it is possible simply to overwrite them with new values, a wide range of other logical functions can be applied to combine the pixel values generated by the graphics request with what is already on the screen. It is also possible to define a clip mask that limits the effect of a graphics request to a particular area or particular pixels in a window. This is just the beginning of the possibilities controlled by the GC.

The following list gives an overview of the characteristics controlled by the GC, which are described in detail in the following sections. Some of these characteristics are specified by more than one member of the GC.

- The source* and old destination pixel values can be combined to compute the new destination pixel values, according to a *logical function*.

- In all primitives, the foreground determines the pixel value of set bits in the source. In a few primitives, the background of the GC specifies the pixel value for unset bits in the source. For example, the characters in a font would be drawn with the foreground pixel value by both XDrawString and XDrawImageString. However, the latter also fills the bounding rectangle of the string with the background pixel value.

- Line characteristics determine the width, dot pattern, and line-end type for lines.

---

*Later in this chapter, when we discuss logical functions, we will use the term *source* to refer to the actual pixels selected by a graphics request plus the pixel values specified by the GC's foreground and background members.

- Fill characteristics determine the tile and fill style for filled areas and lines.

- `GraphicsExpose` and `NoExpose` events can be selected to indicate when visibility affects `XCopyArea` and `XCopyPlane` requests.

- The font used for text-drawing requests may be specified.

- Subwindows may or may not obscure graphics drawn on the parent.

Now we will discuss how to create and set the GC, before moving on to details of individual members of the GC.

5.1 Creating and Setting a Graphics Context

Before a GC can be used, you must create it by calling `XCreateGC`. `XCreateGC` requires only four arguments: *display*, *drawable*, *values*, and *valuemask*.

- The *display* argument (pointer to a `Display` structure) should be familiar by now; it specifies the connection to the X server. The *display* argument is used in virtually every Xlib routine.

- The *drawable* argument is a window or pixmap ID. You might think that the *drawable* argument specifies which window or pixmap the GC is to be used in, but this is not necessarily the case. It really indicates which screen the GC resource is associated with and the depth of windows it can be used with. A GC can be used on any window or pixmap of the same depth and on the same screen as the drawable specified. Drawables were introduced in Section 2.3.3.

- The *values* argument is an `XGCValues` structure (shown in Example 5-1) filled with the desired settings for the GC.

- The *valuemask* argument specifies which members of the `XGCValues` structure are actually read. The members not represented by a bit set to 1 in the *valuemask* are given the default values listed in Section 5.13. The symbols used to make this bitmask correspond to the members of `XGCValues` and are shown in Table 5-1.

The GC is set very much like the window attributes, as described in Section 4.2. Of course, there is a different structure and there are different masks for specifying which members are to be set. One other difference in practice is that every member of the GC can be set with an individual "convenience routine." Therefore, it can be preferable to create a default GC and then modify it with the individual routines rather than to set all the members in both the structure and the mask before calling `XCreateGC` or `XChangeGC`. Both of these approaches are demonstrated below.

Example 5-1 and Table 5-1 present the `XGCValues` structure and the masks used when calling `XCreateGC` or `XChangeGC`.

Example 5-1. The GCValues structure

```
/* Data structure for setting graphics context  */

typedef struct {
    int function;              /* Logical function */
    unsigned long plane_mask;  /* Plane mask */
    unsigned long foreground;  /* Foreground pixel */
    unsigned long background;  /* Background pixel */
    int line_width;            /* Line width */
    int line_style;            /* LineSolid, LineOnOffDash,
                                * LineDoubleDash */
    int cap_style;             /* CapNotLast, CapButt, CapRound,
                                * CapProjecting */
    int join_style;            /* JoinMiter, JoinRound, JoinBevel */
    int fill_style;            /* FillSolid, FillTiled, FillStippled,
                                * FillOpaqueStippled */
    int fill_rule;             /* EvenOddRule, WindingRule */
    int arc_mode;              /* ArcChord, ArcPieSlice */
    Pixmap tile;               /* Tile pixmap for tiling operations */
    Pixmap stipple;            /* Pixmap of depth 1 */
    int ts_x_origin;           /* Offset for tile or stipple operations */
    int ts_y_origin;
    Font font;                 /* Font for text operations (except
                                * XDrawText) */
    int subwindow_mode;        /* ClipByChildren, IncludeInferiors */
    Bool graphics_exposures;   /* Should events be generated on
                                * XCopyArea, XCopyPlane   */
    int clip_x_origin;         /* Origin for clipping */
    int clip_y_origin;
    Pixmap clip_mask;          /* Bitmap for clipping */
    int dash_offset;           /* Patterned/dashed line information */
    char dashes;
} XGCValues;
```

The meaning and possible values for each member are described in Sections 5.3 through 5.9.

Table 5-1 shows the symbols used to specify which members of the XGCvalues structure actually contain meaningful values. The *valuemask* is made up of these symbols combined by means of a bitwise OR (|).

Table 5-1. Symbols for Setting the XGCValues Structure

Member	Mask	Set Bit	Default
function	GCFunction	0	GXcopy
plane_mask	GCPlaneMask	1	all 1's
foreground	GCForeground	2	0
background	GCBackground	3	1
line_width	GCLineWidth	4	0
line_style	GCLineStyle	5	LineSolid
cap_style	GCCapStyle	6	CapButt
join_style	GCJoinStyle	7	JoinMiter
fill_style	GCFillStyle	8	FillSolid
fill_rule	GCFillRule	9	EvenOddRule
arc_mode	GCArcMode	22	ArcPieSlice

Table 5-1. Symbols for Setting the XGCValues Structure (continued)

Member	Mask	Set Bit	Default
tile	GCTile	10	pixmap filled with foreground pixel
stipple	GCStipple	11	pixmap filled with 1's
ts_x_origin	GCTileStipXOrigin	12	0
ts_y_origin	GCTileStipYOrigin	13	0
font	GCFont	14	(implementation dependent)
subwindow_mode	GCSubwindowMode	15	ClipByChildren
graphics_exposures	GCGraphicsExposures	16	True
clip_x_origin	GCClipXOrigin	17	0
clip_y_origin	GCClipYOrigin	18	0
clip_mask	GCClipMask	19	None
dash_offset	GCDashOffset	20	0
dashes	GCDashList	21	4 (i.e., the list [4, 4])

A *valuemask* composed of the symbols shown in Table 5-1 is used in XChangeGC, XCopyGC, and XCreateGC. In XCopyGC, though, the *valuemask* indicates which members are copied from the source GC to the destination GC, and the rest of the members in the destination are left unchanged. In XChangeGC, the specified members are changed and the rest are left unchanged.

5.1.1 Example of Creating and Setting a GC

Example 5-2 shows a simple way of setting some of the values for a GC before creating it. This example uses the default values except for the foreground and background pixel values.

Example 5-2. Example of setting a GC while creating it

```
GC gc;
XGCValues values;
unsigned long valuemask;
     .
     .
/* Open display, create window, etc. */
     .
     .
values.foreground = BlackPixel(display,screen_num);
values.background = WhitePixel(display,screen_num);

gc = XCreateGC(display, RootWindow(display, screen_num),
        (GCForeground | GCBackground), &values);

/* Now you can use gc in drawing routines */
```

In Example 5-2, the foreground pixel value is set to the value returned by the `BlackPixel` macro. This will result in a color of black if the default colormap is installed (more on this in Chapter 7, *Color*). To obtain a pixel value that represents any color other than black or white, you will need to allocate the color as described in Chapter 7.

Convenience functions are also available to change most elements of a GC after it is created. These functions are listed in Sections 5.3 through 5.9, which describe each GC element in detail. Example 5-3 performs the same functions as Example 5-2 but by creating a default GC and then modifying the contents with convenience functions.

Example 5-3. Example of setting default GC then changing it

```
GC gc;
    .
    .
    .
/* Open display, create window, etc. */
    .
    .
    .
gc = XCreateGC(display, RootWindow(display, screen_num), 0, NULL);
XSetForeground(display, gc, BlackPixel(display,screen_num));
XSetBackground(display, gc, WhitePixel(display,screen_num));

/* Now you can use gc in drawing routines */
```

You may wonder which of these two ways is more efficient, setting the `XGCValues` and `valuemask` or calling the convenience functions. Actually, there is not much difference, since in both cases, the individual requests to change the same GC are packaged into a single protocol request before being sent to the server. The method chosen is mainly a matter of personal preference.

5.2 Switching Between Graphics Contexts

One purpose of the GC is to store information about how to interpret graphics requests so that the same information does not have to be sent with every request. Another useful feature of this approach is that you can create several GCs with the different characteristics you need and then switch between them. Example 5-4 demonstrates how this is done. It creates two slightly different GCs with swapped foreground and background pixel values.

Example 5-4. Example of switching graphics contexts

```
GC gc1, gc2;
XGCValues values;
unsigned long valuemask;
    .
    .
    .
/* Open display, create window, etc. */

values.foreground = BlackPixel(display,screen_num);
values.background = WhitePixel(display,screen_num);
```

Example 5-4. Example of switching graphics contexts (continued)

```
gc1 = XCreateGC(display, RootWindow(display, screen_num),
    (GCForeground | GCBackground), &values);

values.foreground = WhitePixel(display,screen_num);
values.background = BlackPixel(display,screen_num);

gc2 = XCreateGC(display, RootWindow(display, screen_num),
    (GCForeground | GCBackground), &values);

/* Now you can use either gc in drawing routines, thereby
 * quickly swapping the foreground and background colors */
```

Whether it is faster to switch between GCs or to modify a few values of a single GC depends on the particular server implementation. On some types of display hardware, several or many GCs can be cached. On these servers, it is faster to change between GCs than to change members of them. On servers that do not cache or that cache only one GC, it is faster to change one or two elements of the GC than to switch between two slightly different GCs. There is no way for the application to tell which of these two server types are in use. Therefore, accepted practice is to compromise by creating a small number of GCs.

Now that you know how to create, set, and modify the GC and how to set up multiple GCs, we can go into more detail about each element of the GC. The following sections describe each member of the graphics context. A useful quick reference to the graphics context is provided inside the back cover of Volume Two, *Xlib Reference Manual*.

5.3 Controlling the Effect of a Graphics Primitive

The GC provides a flexible way to control exactly which pixels and which planes are affected by graphics requests and how the source and old destination pixel values are used to compute the new destination pixel values. As mentioned earlier, the bitmap generated by a graphics request (the source) has pixel values applied to it by the `foreground` and `background` members of the GC and is then transformed by a logical operation between it and the existing value of the pixels (the destination), as well as by a plane mask and a clip mask.

As shown in Example 5-5, the logical operation, the plane mask, the clip mask, and the origin of the clip mask are all components of the GC.

Example 5-5. Members of XGCValues that control combining of source and destination pixels

```
int function;            /* Logical function */
unsigned long plane_mask;  /* Plane mask */
int clip_x_origin;       /* Origin for clipping */
int clip_y_origin;
Pixmap clip_mask;        /* Bitmap clipping; other calls
                          * for rects */
```

The source and existing destination pixels are combined by performing a logical function on the corresponding bits for each pixel. The `plane_mask` restricts the operation to a subset of planes, so that some bits in the source may be excluded from the computation. The `clip_mask` restricts the operation to a subset of the pixels, likewise eliminating some from the result.

The source, destination, `clip_mask`, and `plane_mask` are combined using the algorithm shown below to yield the new destination pixel values. For each bit in each pixel of the destination drawable, if the corresponding bit in `clip_mask` is set, the following expression defines whether that bit is set:

```
((src FUNC dst) AND plane_mask) OR (dst AND (NOT plane_mask))
```

That is, if the `plane_mask` bit is set, the source and existing destination pixels are combined using the logical function represented by `FUNC`. If the `plane_mask` bit is not set, the existing bit in the destination is not changed. Note that the `clip_mask` is placed relative to the drawable with the `clip_x_origin` and `clip_y_origin` members of the GC, which are described in Section 5.3.3.

In the next three sections, we'll look at the actual values that can be specified for each of these members.

5.3.1 Logical Function

The `function` member of the GC selects a logical function. *Logical functions* control how the *source* pixel values generated by a graphics request are combined with the *old destination* pixel values already present on the screen or drawable to result in the *final destination* pixel values. Logical functions are also sometimes called *raster operations*, *raster ops*, or *display functions*. The logical function can be changed by a call to `XSetFunction`.

The source is the output of a graphics primitive or an area of the screen or drawable (for an `XCopyArea`); the destination is the area of the drawable or window that is to receive the output. The 16 logical functions defined in *<X11/X.h>* are shown in Table 5-2.

Table 5-2. Logical Functions in the GC

Logical Function	Hex Code	Definition
GXclear	0x0	0
GXand	0x1	src AND dst
GXandReverse	0x2	src AND (NOT dst)
GXcopy	0x3	src
GXandInverted	0x4	(NOT src) AND dst
GXnoop	0x5	dst
GXxor	0x6	src XOR dst
GXor	0x7	src OR dst
GXnor	0x8	(NOT src) AND (NOT dst)

Table 5-2. Logical Functions in the GC (continued)

Logical Function	Hex Code	Definition
GXequiv	0x9	(NOT src) XOR dst
GXinvert	0xa	(NOT dst)
GXorReverse	0xb	src OR (NOT dst)
GXcopyInverted	0xc	(NOT src)
GXorInverted	0xd	(NOT src) OR dst
GXnand	0xe	(NOT src) OR (NOT dst)
GXset	0xf	1

Figures 5-2a, 5-2b, and 5-2c illustrate the effect of three logical functions on a single pixel of an eight-plane screen given a particular set of source and destination bit values.

Figure 5-2a. The effect of logical function GXcopy

GXcopy, the default logical function, is the most frequently used because it copies without reference to the existing destination pixels, with predictable effects on both monochrome and color displays. GXxor and GXinvert are also used quite frequently. Rarely, programs may use other functions in concert with particular planes of a color display. Here is some more detail on the most frequently used logical functions:

GXcopy   Ignores the bits already in the destination drawable. It is used for both monochrome and color.

GXinvert   Ignores the source and inverts the old destination. This logical function is used to change black to white and vice versa when modifying only one plane. This can be used for highlighting on monochrome or color screens.

Figure 5-2b. The effect of logical function GXxor

Figure 5-2c. The effect of logical function GXand

GXxor   Combines the source and existing bits in such a way that, if the operation is repeated, the drawable is returned to its initial condition. It is important that these two operations occur without intervening manipulation of the selected bits (for windows, the server should be grabbed but for a very short time).* Otherwise, the second XOR operation will not leave the drawable unchanged. GXxor has these properties on both monochrome and color screens.

5.3.2 Plane Mask

The plane_mask member of XGCValues determines which planes of the destination drawable are modified. By default, all planes are modified. The plane_mask can be changed by a call to XSetPlaneMask.

Destination planes represented by a bit set to 1 in the plane_mask can be changed by the graphics command, and the others cannot. The defined constant AllPlanes provides a plane_mask with all bits set, which should be used when every plane is to be affected. A plane_mask of 0 cancels the effect of the graphics primitive. A plane_mask with only 1 bit set is useful for highlighting on both color and monochrome displays. The macro DisplayPlanes returns the number of planes available on the screen. However, the depth of the window is the upper limit on the number of meaningful bits in the plane_mask. Figure 5-3 illustrates the use of the plane_mask.

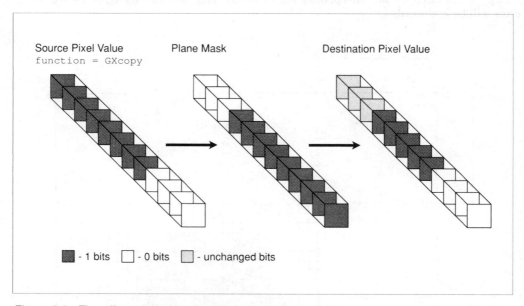

Source Pixel Value
function = GXcopy

Plane Mask

Destination Pixel Value

■ - 1 bits   □ - 0 bits   ▨ - unchanged bits

Figure 5-3. The effect of the plane_mask on a 12-plane display

---

*When the server is grabbed, the client that grabbed it has sole control over the server and the screen. All other clients are put on hold; the server saves up events queued for them and does not change the screen on their behalf until the server grab is released. The server is grabbed and released with XGrabServer and XUngrabServer, but this should be done only when really necessary.

5.3.3 Clip Mask

Clipping allows you to limit the effect of graphics requests to a particular area of the display. The `clip_mask` member of `XGCValues` is a bitmap that indicates which pixels of the destination drawable are to be affected by graphics requests. By default, all pixels in the destination drawable are affected.

Pixels not represented by a set bit in the clip mask will not be drawn. The `clip_mask` can be set with `XSetClipMask`, `XSetClipRectangles`, or `XSetRegion`. `XSetClipMask` sets a clip mask composed of an arbitrary set of bits, as shown in Figure 5-4. `XSetClipRectangles` specifies an array of rectangles that will collectively be used as a clip mask. `XSetRegion` is another way to set the clip mask to a set of rectangles, sometimes more convenient than `XSetClipRectangles`. `XUnionRectWithRegion` can be used to add the rectangle from an `Expose` event into a region. Then `XSetRegion` sets the GC to clip output to those areas. This is useful for redrawing only the areas that have been exposed. See Example 3-15, which uses this technique.

If the `clip_mask` is set manually with `XSetClipMask` or while creating the GC, a pixmap of depth 1 must be created. Then the only pixels drawn are those for which the `clip_mask` has a set bit. This pixmap must have the same root as the GC, or a `BadMatch` error will be generated.

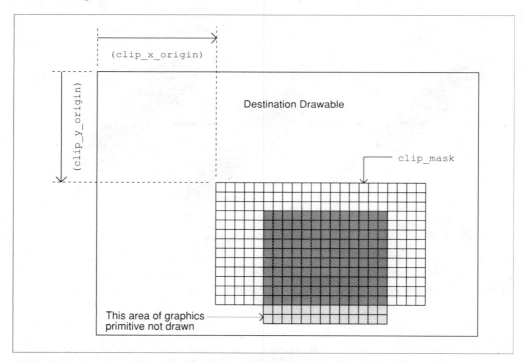

Figure 5-4. Use of clip origin to locate the clip_mask relative to drawable

The clip origin, which places the `clip_mask` relative to the destination drawable, is specified by two other members of the GC structure: `clip_x_origin` and `clip_y_origin`. Figure 5-4 shows how these coordinates specify the upper-left corner of the clip mask relative to the upper-left corner of the destination drawable specified in the graphics request. The origin of the `clip_mask` can be set with `XSetClipOrigin`. The gray area in the figure represents the data to be drawn. The rectangle filled with unshaded squares represents the clip mask, which has all bits set to one. The lighter gray at the bottom shows the area outside the clip mask; this data will not be drawn.

5.4 Foreground and Background

The `foreground` and `background` elements of the GC specify the pixel values to be applied to the source. These are the "colors" used when drawing graphics.* They can be set by `XSetForeground` and `XSetBackground`.

The `foreground` member in the GC is used as the pixel value for set bits in the source in all primitives. The `background` is used for unset bits in the source in just four situations: using `XDrawImageString` (see Section 6.2.4), using `XCopyPlane` (see Section 6.1.7), drawing with `line_style` of `LineDoubleDash` (see Section 5.5.2), and filling with `fill_style` of `FillOpaqueStippled` (see Section 5.6.4).

Figure 5-5 shows the use of the `foreground` and `background` values when drawing a character with `XDrawImageString`. This primitive draws both the character and its bounding box. The character itself is drawn in the foreground pixel value; the remainder of the pixels in the bounding box are drawn with the background pixel value.

5.5 Line Characteristics

There are six line characteristics that are part of the graphics context and members of `XGCValues`:

`line_width`	Specifies the width of the line in pixels. Zero means to draw using the server's fastest algorithm with a line width of one pixel.
`line_style`	Specifies whether the line is solid in foreground, dashed in foreground, or alternating foreground and background. Possible values are `Line-Solid`, `LineOnOffDash`, or `LineDoubleDash`.

---

*For practical purposes, you can loosely think of a pixel value as the "color" in which an object will be drawn, though it applies to both color and monochrome systems. Even on a color system, the actual color resulting from the specified foreground or background pixel value will depend on the plane mask and logical function in effect, as well as the red, green, and blue values stored in the colormap entry to which the resulting value points! Later references in this chapter to drawing in the "foreground color" should be interpreted in this light.

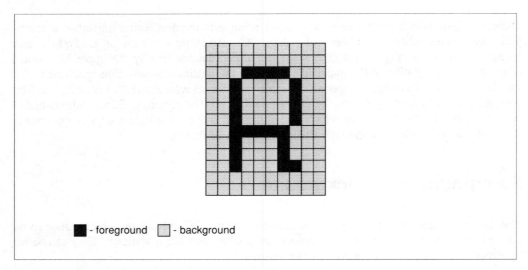

Figure 5-5. Use of foreground and background in XDrawImageString character

cap_style   Controls the appearance of the ends of a line and the ends of dashes in a line in some cases. Possible values are CapButt, CapNotLast, CapProjecting, and CapRound.

join_style   Controls the appearance of joints between consecutive lines drawn within a single graphics primitive. Possible values are JoinBevel, JoinMiter, and JoinRound.

dashes   Specifies a pattern of dash lengths for custom-designed dashed lines.

dash_offset   Specifies the starting point of the dash pattern for custom-designed dashed lines.

All these line characteristics play a part in selecting which pixels will be drawn. Therefore, the "source" as used by the logical function is what results *after* these have been applied.

The line_width, line_style, cap_style, and join_style can be set using XSetLineAttributes, while the dashes and dash_offset can be set with XSetDashes. Now we'll describe each of these line characteristics in more detail, followed by an example that sets them.

5.5.1 Line Width

The line_width member of XGCValues is measured in pixels. The line width can be set with XSetLineAttributes.

A line_width greater than or equal to 1 is considered a *wide* line, and the value 0 is a special case, considered a *thin* line. Wide and thin lines often use different drawing algorithms. The thin line is intended to be a fast algorithm for drawing a line of width 1 but may not be as uniform between different servers.

Wide lines are drawn centered on the path described by the graphics request. A wide line drawn from [x1,y1] to [x2,y2] always draws the same pixels as a wide line drawn from [x2,y2] to [x1,y1], not counting cap and join styles. This is not necessarily the case for thin lines.

Unless otherwise specified by the join or cap style, the bounding box of a wide line with endpoints [x1,y1], [x2,y2] and width w is a rectangle with vertices at the following real coordinates:

Lower Left:	[x1-(w*sin(θ)/2), y1+(w*cos(θ)/2)]
Upper Right:	[x1+(w*sin(θ)/2), y1-(w*cos(θ)/2)]
Lower Left:	[x2-(w*sin(θ)/2), y2+(w*cos(θ)/2)]
Lower Right:	[x2+(w*sin(θ)/2), y2-(w*cos(θ)/2)]

where θ is the angle of the line measured from horizontal.

A pixel is drawn if the center of the pixel is fully inside the bounding box (which is viewed as having infinitely thin edges). If the center of the pixel is exactly on the bounding box, it is part of the line only if the interior of the box is immediately to the pixel's right. Pixels with centers on a horizontal edge are part of the line only if the interior of the box is immediately below the pixel.

Thin lines (line_width == 0) are one-pixel-wide lines drawn using an unspecified, device-dependent fast algorithm. The set of points comprising this type of a line will not be affected by clipping.

A wide line of width 1 and a thin line with line_width 0 drawn between the same two points may not be exactly alike. Because of their different drawing algorithms, thin lines may not mix well with wide lines, aesthetically speaking. For precise and uniform results across all displays, use a line_width of 1 rather than 0. If speed is the goal, use a line_width of 0.

5.5.2 Line Style

The line_style member of XGCValues defines which sections of a line are drawn and in which pixel value, as shown in Figure 5-6. The line style can be set with XSetLine-Attributes. The actual length of each dash and gap is set by the dashes member of XGCValues, described in Section 5.5.5. The constants used to set line_style are as follows:

LineSolid	Specifies that the full path of the line is drawn using the foreground pixel value.
LineOnOffDash	Specifies that only the dashes are drawn with the foreground pixel value and cap_style applies to the ends of each dash (except that CapNotLast is treated as CapButt for dash ends).
LineDoubleDash	Specifies that the full path of the line is drawn, dashes with the foreground pixel value, gaps with the background pixel values, with CapButt style always used where dashes and gaps meet.

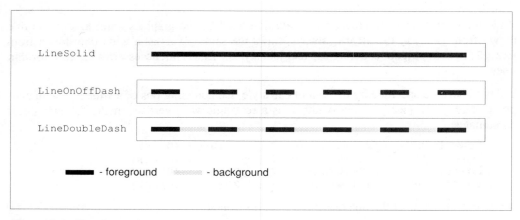

Figure 5-6. The line styles

5.5.3 Cap Style

The `cap_style` member of `XGCValues` defines how the endpoints of lines are drawn, as shown in Figure 5-7. The cap style can be set with `XSetLineAttributes`. The constants used to set `cap_style` are as follows:

CapNotLast   Is equivalent to `CapButt`, except that for a `line_width` of 0 or 1, the final endpoint is not drawn. If specified with `line_style` `LineOnOffDash` or `LineDoubleDash`, the ends of the dashes or where even and odd dashes meet are treated as `CapButt`.

CapButt   Specifies that lines will be square at the endpoint with no projection beyond. The end is perpendicular to the slope of the line.

CapRound   Specifies that lines will be terminated by a circular arc with the diameter equal to the `line_width`, centered on the endpoint (equivalent to `CapButt` for `line_width` of 0 or 1).

CapProjecting   Specifies that lines will be square at the end but with the path continuing beyond the endpoint for a distance equal to half the `line_width` (equivalent to `CapButt` for `line_width` of 0 or 1).

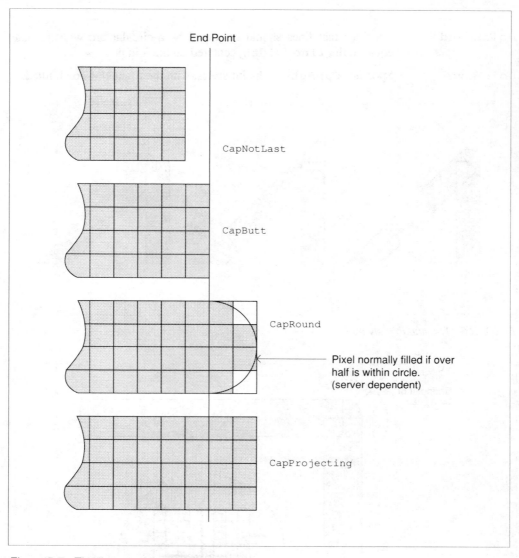

Figure 5-7. The line cap (end) styles

5.5.4 Join Style

The `join_style` member of `XGCValues` defines how corners are drawn for wide lines drawn within a single graphics primitive, as shown in Figures 5-8 and 5-9. The join style can be set with `XSetLineAttributes`. The constants used to set `join_style` are as follows:

JoinMiter   Specifies that the outer edges of the two lines should extend to meet at an angle. If the angle between the two lines is less than 11 degrees, `JoinBevel` is used.

`JoinRound`   Specifies that lines should be joined by a circular arc with diameter equal to the `line_width`, centered on the join point.

`JoinBevel`   Specifies `CapButt` endpoint styles, with the triangular notch filled.

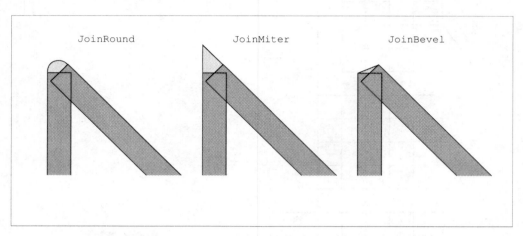

Figure 5-8. The line join styles

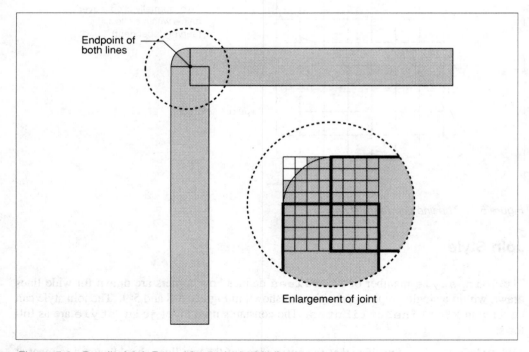

Figure 5-9. Detail of JoinRound for 8-pixel-wide lines

5.5.5 Dash List and Offset

The `dashes` member of `XGCValues` must be a single, nonzero value specifying the length in pixels of both the dashes and the gaps. More complicated patterns can be set with `XSet-Dashes`.

In `XSetDashes`, the *dash_list* argument is a real list, with each value representing the length of a single dash or gap in the line. The initial and alternating members of *dash_list* are the length of the *even* dashes; the others are the *odd* dashes (gaps). All members must be nonzero. The length of the *dash_list* is also an argument to `XSet-Dashes`. The `dashes` element of `XGCValues` is equivalent to specifying a two-member *dash_list* [N, N] in `XSetDashes`, where *N* is the single value specified in `XGCValues.dashes`.

The `dash_offset` for `XSetDashes` defines the phase of the pattern, specifying how many pixels into the pattern the line should actually begin.

Example 5-6 shows a code segment that creates and sets the line dashes of five GCs. Figure 5-10 shows the lines that result from drawing with these GCs.

Example 5-6. Code segment specifying five styles of dashed line in five GCs

```
#define NUMLINES 5
#define DOTTED_LIST_LENGTH 2
#define DOT_DASHED_LIST_LENGTH 4
#define SHORT_DASHED_LIST_LENGTH 2
#define LONG_DASHED_LIST_LENGTH 2
#define ODD_DASHED_LIST_LENGTH 3

void main(argc, argv)
int argc;
char **argv;
{
    GC gca[NUMLINES];
        .
        .
        .
    /* Open display, create windows, etc. */

    set_dashes(gca);

        while (1)  {
                XNextEvent(display, &report);
                switch  (report.type) {
                case Expose:
                        if (report.xexpose.count == 0)
                                draw_lines(win, gca, width, height);
                        break;
            .
            .
            .
}

set_dashes(gca)
GC gca[];
{
```

```
    XGCValues gcv;
    int i;
    static int dash_list_length[] = {
        DOTTED_LIST_LENGTH,
        DOT_DASHED_LIST_LENGTH,
        SHORT_DASHED_LIST_LENGTH,
        LONG_DASHED_LIST_LENGTH,
        ODD_DASHED_LIST_LENGTH
    };

    /* Must be at least one element in each list */
    static unsigned char dotted[DOTTED_LIST_LENGTH] =
            {3, 1};
    static unsigned char dot_dashed[DOT_DASHED_LIST_LENGTH] =
            {3, 4, 3, 1};
    static unsigned char short_dashed[SHORT_DASHED_LIST_LENGTH] =
            {4, 4};
    static unsigned char long_dashed[LONG_DASHED_LIST_LENGTH] =
            {4, 7};
    static unsigned char odd_dashed[ODD_DASHED_LIST_LENGTH] =
            {1, 2, 3};

    static unsigned char *dash_list[] = {
        dotted,
        dot_dashed,
        short_dashed,
        long_dashed,
        odd_dashed,
    };

    int dash_offset = 0;

    /* Open display, create window, etc. */

    gcv.line_style = LineOnOffDash;
    for (i = 0 ; i < NUMLINES; i++) {
        gca[i] = XCreateGC(display, RootWindow(display, screen_num),
                GCLineStyle, &gcv);
        XSetDashes(display, gca[i], dash_offset, dash_list[i],
                dash_list_length[i]);
    }
}

draw_lines(win, gca, window_width, window_height)
Window win;
GC gca[];
unsigned int window_width, window_height;
{
        int i;
        for (i=0;i < NUMLINES; i++) {
                XDrawLine(display, win, gca[i],
                        window_width/4, 40 + (10 * i),
                        3 * (window_width/4), 40 + (10 * i));
        }

}
```

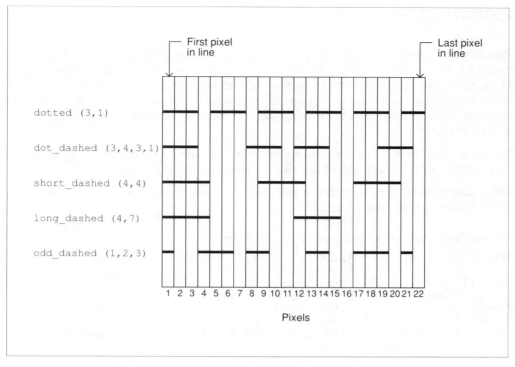

Figure 5-10. Lines drawn with GCs set in Example 5-6

5.5.6 Example of Setting Line Characteristics

Example 5-7 demonstrates how to set the line characteristics with XSetLine-
Attributes. This routine and XSetDashes (which sets dashes, demonstrated in
Example 5-6) are the only ways to set line characteristics, other than with XCreateGC or
XChangeGC.

Example 5-7. Setting line characteristics in a GC

```
set_line_attributes(gc)
GC gc;
{
    unsigned int line_width = 3; /* 0 would be fast line of width 1 */
    int line_style = LineSolid;  /* If LineOnOffDash or LineDoubleDash,
                                  * must set dashes */
    int cap_style = CapRound;    /* else CapNotLast, CapButt, or
                                  * CapProjecting */
    int join_style = JoinRound;  /* else JoinMiter or JoinBevel */

    XSetLineAttributes(display, gc, line_width, line_style,
            cap_style, join_style);
}
```

5.6 Patterning

Typically, any image drawn by a graphics primitive is drawn using the pixel value specified by the `foreground` member of the GC as the source. However, particularly when drawing filled figures, you may not want to draw using that value as a "solid color"—instead, you might want it to be patterned. In other words, all the set bits in the source can be filled with a repeating pattern. You can tile anything you can draw, including text. However, lines of width 0 are not affected.

Two separate types of patterning can be used: tiling and stippling. Tiling and stippling were introduced in Section 2.3.5 and are described in more detail in this section.

The members of `XGCValues` shown in Example 5-8 affect patterning. They are described in the Sections 5.6.4 through 5.6.6.

Example 5-8. Members of XGCValues affecting filling

```
int fill_style;      /* FillSolid, FillTiled, FillStippled,
                      * FillOpaqueStippled */
int fill_rule;       /* EvenOddRule, WindingRule */
int arc_mode;        /* ArcChord, ArcPieSlice */
Pixmap tile;         /* tile pixmap for tiling operations */
Pixmap stipple;      /* single-plane pixmap for stippling */
int ts_x_origin;     /* offset for tile or stipple operations */
int ts_y_origin;
```

5.6.1 Tiles

A tile is a pixmap used to pattern the pixels specified by set bits in the source bitmap. The `tile` member of the GC can be set with `XSetTile`.

Tiles are so named because they are laid out next to each other in an array like bathroom tile. The origin of the first tile is specified with `ts_x_origin` and `ts_y_origin`, which are relative to the origin of the destination drawable. These members of the GC are set with `XSetTSOrigin`. Only pixels specified by set bits in the source bitmap are tiled. Figure 5-11 shows how tiles are used to pattern an area. Instead of being filled with a solid color (or shade of gray), the area is filled with the tile pattern.

Creating a tile is described in Section 6.1.5. The tile pixmap must be created on the same root window and have the same depth as the destination drawable. If these conditions are not satisfied, a `BadMatch` error is generated. If a pixmap is used simultaneously in a graphics request both as a destination and as a tile, the results are not defined.

If the depth of the drawable and tile is 1, tiling is identical to stippling with `fill_style` `FillOpaqueStippled`, which we'll describe next.

tile

Figure 5-11. Tiling an area

5.6.2 Stipples

Stippling is similar to tiling, except that a stipple is a pixmap of depth 1, not of the depth of the drawable. The pixel values used to draw the pattern are the foreground and background in the GC.

There are two styles of stippling, selected by the fill_style of the GC (to be described in the next section): FillOpaqueStippled and FillStippled. For a fill_style of FillOpaqueStippled, the foreground pixel value in the GC is used for bits set in the stipple and the source, and the background pixel value is used for bits unset in the stipple but set in the source. For a fill_style of FillStippled, only the foreground pixel value is drawn for set bits in the stipple, and other pixels are not affected.

When the depth of the drawable is one, there is no difference between tiling with fill_style of FillTiled and stippling with fill_style of FillOpaque-Stippled.

The stipple member of the GC may be changed with XSetStipple. If both the stipple and tile members of the GC are set, the fill_style determines which is used. Both cannot be used in a single graphics request.

5.6.3 Tile and Stipple Sizes

A pixmap of any size can be used for tiling or stippling, but on some types of hardware, particular tile or stipple sizes run much faster than arbitrary sizes. `XQueryBestSize` returns the closest tile or stipple size to the one you specify and also the largest allowable cursor. `XQueryBestTile` and `XQueryBestStipple` perform the same functions, but only for tiles and stipples, respectively.

For how to create a tile or stipple, see Section 6.1.5.

5.6.4 Fill Style

The `fill_style` member of `XGCValues` controls whether the source graphics are drawn with a solid color, a tile, or one of the two stipple styles. The `fill_style` member of the GC may be changed with `XSetFillStyle`.

The `fill_style` affects all line, text, and fill requests except lines drawn with `line-width` 0. It affects only set bits in the source; that is, those areas selected by the graphics request. Possible values are:

`FillSolid`   Specifies that graphics should be drawn using the `foreground` pixel value.

`FillTiled`   Specifies that graphics should be drawn using the `tile` pixmap.

`FillStippled`   Specifies that graphics should be drawn using the `foreground` pixel value masked by `stipple`. In other words, bits set in the source and `stipple` are drawn in the `foreground` pixel value.

`FillOpaqueStippled`
        Specifies that graphics should be drawn using `stipple`, using the `foreground` pixel value for set bits in stipple and the `background` pixel value for unset bits in stipple.

Figure 5-12 demonstrates the four fill styles.

Odd dashes in dotted lines are a special case. For the gaps (odd dashes) in lines with `line_style` of `LineDoubleDash`, `FillSolid` means to draw the gaps in the `background` pixel value, and `FillStippled` means to draw in the `background` pixel value masked by `stipple`. With a `line_style` of `LineDoubleDash`, `Fill-Tiled` and `FillStippled` have the effect of wiping out the odd dashes, so that the line looks like `LineOnOffDash` with the specified fill style.

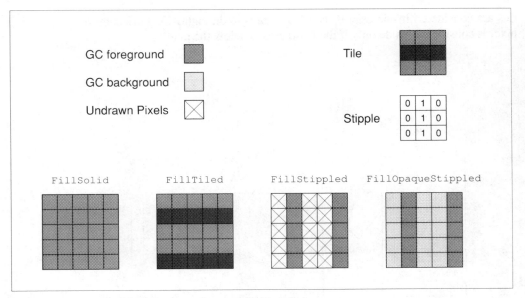

Figure 5-12. fill_style demonstrated on small pixmaps

5.6.5 Fill Rule

The `fill_rule` member of `XGCValues` defines what pixels are drawn for paths given in `XFillPolygon` requests. The *fill_rule* is also an argument to `XPolygonRegion`, which is described in Section 6.3. The `fill_rule` in the GC is set with `XSetFillRule`. The `fill_rule` may be `EvenOddRule` (the default in the GC) or `WindingRule`.

As shown in Figure 5-13, `EvenOddRule` means that if areas overlap an odd number of times, they are not drawn. Technically, it specifies that a point is drawn if an infinite ray with the point as origin crosses the path an odd number of times.

`WindingRule`, also shown in Figure 5-13, means that overlapping areas are always filled, regardless of how many times they overlap. Technically, this rule specifies that a point is inside the filled area if an infinite ray with the point as origin crosses an unequal number of clockwise- and counterclockwise-directed path segments.

Since polygons are drawn as a series of points connected by lines, the order of the points determines the direction of each line. A clockwise-directed path segment is one which crosses the ray from left to right as observed from the point. A counterclockwise-directed segment is one which crosses the ray from right to left as observed from the point. The case where a directed line segment is coincident with the ray is uninteresting, because you can simply choose a different ray that is not coincident with a segment.

All calculations are performed on infinitely small points, so that if any point within a pixel is considered inside, the entire pixel is drawn. Pixels with centers exactly on vertical boundaries are considered inside only if the filled area is to the right. On horizontal boundaries, the pixel is considered inside only if the filled area is below the pixel.

Outline of polygon to fill   EvenOddRule   WindingRule

Figure 5-13. fill_rule constants for filling closed polygons

5.6.6 Arc Mode (for Filling)

The arc_mode member of XGCValues controls filling of arcs drawn with XFillArc and XFillArcs. The arc_mode is set with XSetArcMode.

An arc is specified for XFillArc or XFillArcs as follows:

- The arc is bounded by a rectangle whose center is the center of the arc.

- The position of the upper-left corner of the rectangle is relative to the origin of the destination drawable.

- Two angles indicate the starting and stopping position of the arc. These are measured in sixty-fourths of a degree starting from the three-o'clock position, with positive angles indicating counterclockwise measurement.

The arc_mode can be either ArcPieSlice or ArcChord. Figure 5-14 demonstrates the two modes. For ArcChord, the arc and the single line segment joining the endpoints of the arc create a closed figure to fill. For ArcPieSlice, the arc and the two line segments joining the endpoints of the arc with the center point are used.

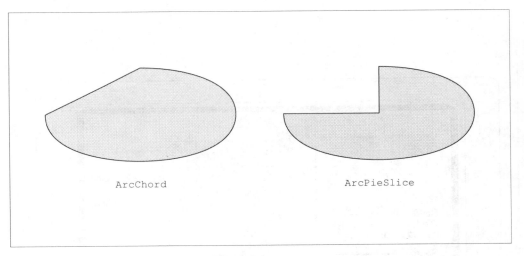

Figure 5-14. arc_mode constants for filling arcs

5.7 Graphics Exposure

When using XCopyArea and XCopyPlane to copy data from one drawable to another, it is possible that certain portions of the source region will be obscured, unmapped, or otherwise unavailable. If this is the case, it may be desirable to generate an event to signal the client that one or more areas in the destination window could not be copied to and should be redrawn some other way.

The graphics_exposures flag in the GC specifies whether or not events should be generated in such a case. There are actually two event types that can be generated if graphics_exposures is set to True:

• One or more GraphicsExpose events are sent when a destination region cannot be completely drawn because the source region was obscured, unmapped, or otherwise unavailable.

• A single NoExpose event occurs when the specified source region is completely available.

These event types are not selected by XSelectInput or in the event_mask attribute; setting graphics_exposures to True is the only way to select them. The graphics_exposures member of the GC can be set with XSetGraphics-Exposures.

Figure 5-15 shows a typical XCopyArea request where the source region is obscured. It shows the areas that would be specified in the GraphicsExpose events generated.

As shown in Figure 5-15, a single XCopyPlane or XCopyArea can result in more than one GraphicsExpose event, since the resulting area to be redrawn may be composed of several rectangles. A copy such as the one shown in Figure 5-15 would generate two GraphicsExpose events. One rectangle is specified by each event.

Figure 5-15. Copying a partially unavailable area

When `graphics_exposures` is `False`, neither of these events is sent under any circumstances. By default, `graphics_exposures` is `True`.

5.8 The Font

The `font` member of the GC specifies which font will be used in graphics requests that use this GC and can be set with `XSetFont`. If the specified font has not been loaded by this client, a graphics primitive that tries to draw text will not fail; it just will not draw. Therefore, you should make sure you load the font.

The X server actually loads a requested font into memory only when `XLoadFont` or `XLoadQueryFont` is called and if the specified font has not already been loaded by another client. A font is unloaded when the last program using the font exits or unloads it. Duplicate copies of a font are never stored in the server.

There are several ways to deal with fonts. Most programs will use `XLoadQueryFont` to load a font and get information about the dimensions of each character. `XLoadQuery-`

Font returns a pointer to an XFontStruct. The font in the GC can then be set to XFontStruct.fid. See Chapter 6, *Drawing Graphics and Text*, for details.

5.9 Subwindow Mode

The subwindow_mode member of XGCValues controls whether subwindows obscure their parent for purposes of drawing on the parent. This member is set with XSet-SubwindowMode.

The value ClipByChildren sets the default condition, in which drawing into the area of a window obscured by its visible children produces no effect.

If the subwindow_mode is set to IncludeInferiors, drawing appears through visible children even when they have opaque backgrounds. The use of IncludeInferiors on a window of depth 1 with mapped inferiors of differing depth is not illegal, but the results are not defined in standard Xlib.

One familiar use of IncludeInferiors is the window manager's "rubber banding" of window outlines while they are being moved or resized. The outline is drawn on the root window with the GC set to IncludeInferiors.

5.10 Sharing GCs Between Clients

Despite the fact that a GC is a resource, and theoretically shareable, separate clients should not attempt to share GCs, because of the way GCs are implemented.

5.11 GCs and Server Efficiency

Some servers can cache a limited number of GCs in their display hardware. These systems achieve highest performance when the number of GCs created by an application is less than the number that can be cached at one time. Furthermore, each GC takes up some amount of server memory. Therefore, it is a general principal that an application should create as few GCs as reasonably possible.

However, this should not be taken to extremes. For example, all applications could be written to use only one GC, changing it frequently every time different characteristics are needed. But this defeats two of the purposes of the GC, which are to reduce network traffic and simplify programming. There are also performance costs when GCs are changed too often.

Deciding how many GCs to create and when to change them is a tradeoff between the benefits of a more efficient server against the benefits of reduced network traffic and simpler programming. The designers of X still think that using a small number of GCs is, overall, the best approach.

5.12 Querying the Graphics Context

When you call a number of the GC convenience routines, such as XSetForeground and XSetLineAttributes, you might expect each to generate a separate protocol request to change the GC. But this is not what happens. Xlib saves up the changes in an internal structure and makes a single request to the server just before the GC is actually used by a drawing request.

The type of this internal structure is GC! All Xlib routines use a pointer to this internal structure, not a integer ID, as we have previously implied. However, this fact does not impact how you write Xlib code at all. In practice, a pointer to an opaque structure and an integer ID such as a window ID are treated exactly the same.

In R4, the XGetGCValues function has been added to allow clients to read Xlib's cache of the fields in each GC. This can save an application from having to maintain its own cache of GC values, when it needs to change the GC in several different places in ways that depend on the current contents.

Note that XGetGCValues is not the same as a true round-trip query to the server—there is no protocol request that actually asks the server for these values. This has good and bad consequences. The good part is that XGetGCValues is fast because it is not subject to network delays. The bad side is that the values in Xlib's cache do not include the default values for certain of the GC members. The tile, stipple, and font fields contain invalid IDs when XGetGCValues is called on a default GC. Therefore, even though there is actually a default font that is always loaded on a server, you cannot use XGetGCValues to find out its ID. But it turns out that this is unnecessary anyway, because you can pass the default GC to XQueryFont and it will get information about the default font. Neither is there any obvious reason for needing the IDs of the tile and stipple in the default GC.

Also note that the clip mask and dash list cannot be queried.

5.13 The Default Graphics Context

Table 5-3 shows the default values for all members of a graphics context.

Table 5-3. The Default Graphics Context

Component	Value
function	GXcopy
plane_mask	all 1's
foreground	0
background	1
line_width	0
line_style	LineSolid
cap_style	CapButt
join_style	JoinMiter

Table 5-3. The Default Graphics Context (continued)

Component	Value
`fill_style`	`FillSolid`
`fill_rule`	`EvenOddRule`
`arc_mode`	`ArcPieSlice`
`tile`	pixmap filled with foreground pixel
`stipple`	pixmap filled with 1's
`ts_x_origin`	0
`ts_y_origin`	0
`font`	(implementation dependent)
`subwindow_mode`	`ClipByChildren`
`graphics_exposures`	`True`
`clip_x_origin`	0
`clip_y_origin`	0
`clip_mask`	`None`
`dash_offset`	0
`dashes`	4 (i.e., the list [4, 4])

A useful quick reference to the graphics context is provided inside the back cover of Volume Two, *Xlib Reference Manual*.

6

Drawing Graphics and Text

This chapter describes the routines used to draw lines, geometrical figures, and text. It also discusses the use of pixmaps, images, and regions. You should be familiar with the use of the graphics context before attempting to use these routines.

In This Chapter:

6

Drawing Graphics and Text

Drawing with computers is a little like drawing by hand. Holding the pencil is not hard, but getting anything recognizable to appear on the page is a different matter. Similarly, drawing with X is quite easy, but designing what to draw and where can be a challenge. We can do little more in this chapter than tell you how to hold the pencil; the rest is up to you.

This chapter describes various techniques that have to do with drawing: drawing lines, rectangles, and arcs; using bitmaps; placing and drawing text; using regions; creating and using cursors; and using images.

The draw_text and draw_graphics routines called in the *basicwin* program in Chapter 3, *Basic Window Program*, are used as examples in this chapter. Also described here are various versions of the draw_box routine, which is called in the simple window manager *winman* described in Chapter 14, *Window Management*.

Note that, before you draw anything, you must set up a graphics context to specify, at minimum, the foreground and background pixel values for drawing and the font if you are drawing text. For monochrome applications, you should set these values using the BlackPixel and WhitePixel macros described in Chapter 3, *Basic Window Program*. For color applications, you should use one of the color allocation routines described in Chapter 7, *Color*. While the foreground and background values in the default GC *may* work on some servers, they are hardcoded (0 and 1) and should *not* be relied upon by any client, since they will give inconsistent results on color displays.

6.1 Drawing

The X drawing primitives are easy-to-use routines capable of drawing points, connected lines (polylines), disconnected lines (disjoint polylines), rectangles, and circles, ellipses, or arcs.

These primitives select the source pixels that will be operated on according to the graphics context. The GC is described in Chapter 5, *The Graphics Context*.

XDrawPoint requires only the coordinates of the point to be drawn. XDrawPoints requires a pointer to an array of coordinates for the points, the number of points, and a mode flag which controls whether the coordinates are interpreted relative to the origin of the drawable or relative to the previous point drawn.

XDrawLine is similar to XDrawPoint but requires two points, a beginning and an end. XDrawLines works just like XDrawPoints but draws lines between consecutive points in the list. If the first and last points coincide, the lines will be joined properly according to the join_style in the GC.

XDrawSegments draws lines that are not necessarily connected end to end. It requires an array of pairs of endpoints. There is no mode flag for XDrawSegments, so the coordinates are always relative to the origin of the drawable. If the end point of one segment and the beginning of the next coincide, the lines will be joined according to the join_style in the GC. The remaining end points will be drawn according to the cap_style in the GC.

XDrawRectangle draws the outline of a rectangle when given the upper-left corner and the height and width. XDrawRectangles draws multiple rectangles from an array of corner coordinates and dimensions. The actual width and height of a rectangle is one pixel larger than the dimensions specified, according to the X protocol, as shown in Figure 6-2. These actual dimensions maintain consistency with the definition of a filled rectangle or a clipping region, which are exactly the size specified. The corners of rectangles are drawn according to the join_style in the GC.

XDrawArc is similar to XDrawRectangle, except that it draws an arc that fits inside the rectangle. This function can draw circles and ellipses (or parts thereof) whose axes are parallel to the window coordinates. An elliptical arc occurs if the rectangle is not a square. The extent of the arc is specified by two angles: the first is the starting angle relative to the three-o'clock position, and the second is the angle relative to the starting position. The angles are signed integers in sixty-fourths of a degree (0 to 360 * 64 is a complete circle), with positive values drawing the arc counterclockwise. This scale factor is required so that angles can be specified more accurately than allowed by integral values between 0 and 360 degrees. Figure 6-1 demonstrates the arguments needed for XDrawArc.

X Version 11 also supports the XDraw and XDrawFilled routines that were available in X Version 10, though the performance of these is low. These routines are described in Appendix B, *X10 Compatibility*.

Xlib does not provide routines for drawing Bezier or cubic spline curves, but extensions for drawing these are publicly available.

6.1.1 The Request Size Limit

One caveat of all the Xlib routines that draw multiple objects is that there is a maximum number of objects that can be drawn with a single call, and this number varies according to the server your application is connected to. This affects the calls XDrawArcs, XDraw-Lines, XDrawPoints, XDrawRectangles, XDrawSegments, XDrawText, XDrawText16, XFillArcs, and XFillRectangles.

Figure 6-1. Angle measurement for XDrawArc or XDrawArcs

To determine how many objects you can draw in a single call, you find out your server's maximum request size using `XMaxRequestSize`. Subtract 3, and this is the maximum number of points you can draw in a single `XDrawPoints` request. You can draw one-half this many lines, segments, or rectangles, and one-third this many arcs.*

For `XDrawText` and `XDrawText16`, which draw a series of strings as will be described later, the maximum number is based on the number and length of these strings.

---

*Solutions to this problem are being investigated. The obvious answer is to have Xlib chop these requests into smaller pieces automatically. However, this would not work for `XDrawLines`, because this would disturb the server's joining of the lines.

6.1.2 Scaling Graphics

All drawing measurements in X are made in pixels. The positions you specify are relative to the origin (upper-left corner inside border) of the window specified in the drawing request. The width and height of a rectangle or bounding box for an arc are also specified in pixels.

Basing scaling on pixels has a weakness caused by the fact that pixels are not always the same size on the screen. Imagine a desktop publishing application. Its goal is to make everything drawn on the screen as close as possible to what will appear on the printed page. People may run the application from a PC which has a 9.5" by 7.25" screen with an 640 by 480 array of pixels or from a workstation which has a 13.5" by 10.5" screen with an array of, perhaps, 1152 by 900 pixels. The ruler lines drawn by the application would look much different on the two screens if their sizes were not adjusted accordingly. The application should calculate the ratio of the size in millimeters of the screen to its size in pixels, in both directions. The required information is returned by the `DisplayHeight`, `DisplayHeight-MM`, `DisplayWidth`, and `DisplayWidthMM` macros.

This correction of size distortion also solves a second, smaller problem. The relative density of pixels in the x and y directions on the screen may vary. For example, a square drawn with equal width and height may appear rectangular on the screen, since some (but, fortunately, not many) screens have more space between rows of pixels than between columns. By correcting for size variation, this problem goes away. It is also possible to allow size variations but correct for the aspect ratio distortion by multiplying the height measurements in pixels by the ratio:

$$\frac{DisplayHeight \ + \ DisplayHeight \ MM}{DisplayWidth \ + \ DisplayWidth \ MM}$$

or by multiplying the width measurements in pixels by the inverse of this ratio. Do not multiply both the width and height measurements.

6.1.3 Example of Drawing Graphics

All drawing routines are used in essentially the same way:

- First, create and set the graphics context.
- Then calculate the dimensions and placement of what you want to draw.
- Finally, do the actual drawing.

Example 6-1 shows a routine named `draw_graphics` that places and draws a rectangle. As you can tell from the brevity of the routine, most of the trouble goes into setting the GC properly and positioning the item to be drawn. The actual drawing is very simple.

This routine is called from the *basicwin* program described in Chapter 3, *Basic Window Program*. By the time it is called, we have already done many things. The display is opened, windows and resources created (including the GC), and window manager hints set. Most importantly, `draw_graphics` is called only in response to `Expose` events. It is used to draw the window for the first time and to redraw the contents of areas exposed later.

Example 6-1. The draw_graphics routine

```
draw_graphics(win, gc, window_width, window_height)
Window win;
GC gc;
unsigned int window_width, window_height;
{
        int x, y;
        unsigned int width, height;

        height = window_height/2;
        width = 3 * window_width/4;
        x = window_width/2 - width/2;   /* Center */
        y = window_height/2 - height/2;
        XDrawRectangle(display, win, gc, x, y, width, height);
}
```

The calling routine gets the `window_width` and `window_height` arguments from `ConfigureNotify` events because the window being drawn into is a top-level window which might get resized by the window manager. Routines to draw into descendents of the top-level window may also require size arguments if the sizes of the windows will be adjusted in response to a resized top-level window.

6.1.4 Filling

The `XFillArc`, `XFillArcs`, `XFillPolygon`, `XFillRectangle`, and `XFill-Rectangles` commands act much like the drawing routines described at the start of Section 6.1 instead of drawing the outline.

Surprisingly, the filling and drawing versions of the rectangle routines do not draw the same outline if given the same arguments. The routine that fills a rectangle draws an outline one pixel shorter in width and height than the routine that just draws the outline, as shown in Figure 6-2. It is easy to adjust the arguments for the rectangle calls so that one draws the outline and another fills a completely different set of interior pixels. Simply add 1 to *x* and *y* and subtract 1 from *width* and *height*.

The `XFillPolygon` routine is somewhat different from the other filling routines, since there is no directly analogous routine that draws a polygon with lines (though `XDrawLines` can be used to draw a polygon). Like the other routines, `XFillPolygon` uses an array of points to specify the nodes to be connected, but it connects the first and last points to form a closed figure and then fills the resulting shape. The `shape` flag (which can be one of the symbols `Complex`, `Convex`, or `Nonconvex`) is a hint that may enable the server to improve the performance of the filling operation. The *mode* argument indicates whether the coordinates of the vertices are interpreted relative to the origin of the drawable or relative to the previous point.

The `fill_rule` member of the GC controls how complex, self-intersecting polygons are filled. The `WindingRule` setting of the `fill_rule` specifies that overlapping areas of a

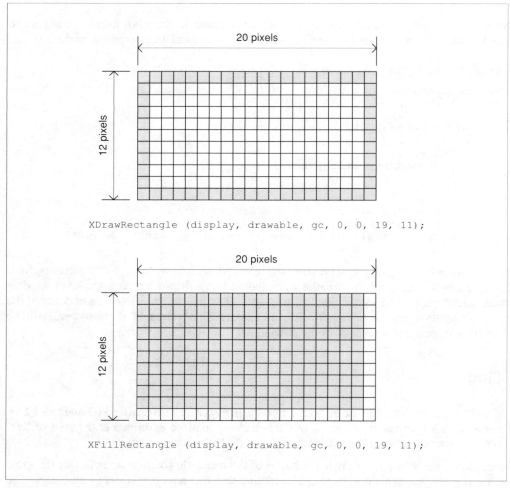

```
XDrawRectangle (display, drawable, gc, 0, 0, 19, 11);
```

```
XFillRectangle (display, drawable, gc, 0, 0, 19, 11);
```

Figure 6-2. The pixels affected by XFillRectangle vs. XDrawRectangle with the same
arguments.

polygon drawn in a single call are filled. With `EvenOddRule`, areas overlapping an odd number of times are not filled. See Section 5.6.5 for more information.

6.1.5 Creating Bitmaps, Pixmaps, Tiles, and Stipples

Bitmaps, tiles, and stipples are all forms of pixmaps, all of type `Pixmap`. Applications often need to create pixmaps for icon patterns, cursors, and tiles.

The data used to create a pixmap for any purpose can be included in a program at compile time or read in at run time. In both methods, you must have a bitmap file created with `XWriteBitmapFile` or the *bitmap* application.

In the first method, you use an #include statement to read the bitmap file at run time and then call XCreateBitmapFromData or XCreatePixmapFromBitmapData if you want a pixmap with depth for a window background or a tile.

In the second method, you create a single-plane Pixmap with XCreatePixmap and call XReadBitmapFile to fill the Pixmap with the data from the file. Then if you want a pixmap with depth for the background of a window or for a tile, you can create another pixmap of the desired depth and call XCopyPlane to copy the bitmap into the pixmap. Normally, an application would choose reading the data from a file if the user needs to be able to change the bitmap between invocations of the client.

XWriteBitmapFile can be used to write the contents of a bitmap into a file conforming to X Version 11 bitmap file format.

Example 6-2 shows some bitmap data in standard X11 bitmap file format and two subroutines, one that creates a stipple from included data and the other that reads the bitmap data from a file.

Example 6-2. Creating a stipple from included data and from data read from a file

```
#define icon_bitmap_width 40
#define icon_bitmap_height 40
static char icon_bitmap_bits[] = {
   0xc3, 0xc3, 0x7f, 0x00, 0x78, 0x00, 0x00, 0x00, 0x00, 0xc0, 0x00, 0x00,
   0x00, 0x00, 0x80, 0x38, 0x00, 0x40, 0x00, 0x80, 0x24, 0x00, 0x00, 0x00,
      .
      .
      .
   0x0c, 0x30, 0x18, 0x00, 0x84, 0x04, 0x60, 0x0e, 0x00, 0xdc, 0x02, 0x80,
   0x03, 0x00, 0x70, 0x00, 0x00, 0x00, 0x00, 0x00};

void main(argc, argv)
int argc;
char **argv;
{
      .
      .
      .

     Pixmap stipple;
     unsigned int stip_width, stip_height;
     char *filename = "bitmaps/icon_bitmap";

     if (create_included_stipple(&stipple, &stip_width,
             &stip_height) == False)
     fprintf(stderr, "basic: couldn't create included bitmap\n");
     printf("stipple is %dx%d\n", stip_width, stip_height);
     if (create_read_stipple(&stipple, filename, &stip_width,
             &stip_height) ! = BitmapSuccess)
     fprintf(stderr, "basic: can't read bitmap\n");
     printf("stipple is %dx%d\n", stip_width, stip_height);
      .
      .
      .
}

create_included_stipple(stip, width, height)
```

```
Pixmap *stip;                       /* Returned created stipple */
unsigned int *width, *height;  /* Returned */
{
    if ((*stip = XCreateBitmapFromData(display,
            RootWindow(display, screen_num), icon_bitmap_bits,
            icon_bitmap_width, icon_bitmap_height))
            == False)
        return(False);
    *width = name_width;
    *height = name_height;
    return(True);
}

create_read_stipple(stip, filename, width, height)
Pixmap *stip;                       /* Returned created stipple */
char *filename;
unsigned int *width, *height;  /* Returned */
{
    int value;
    int x_hot, y_hot;               /* Don't care about these unless for
                                     * cursor */

    value = XReadBitmapFile(display, RootWindow(display, screen_num),
            filename, width, height, stip, &x_hot, &y_hot);
    if (value == BitmapFileInvalid)
        fprintf(stderr, "Filename %s contains invalid bitmap data\n",
                filename);
    else if (value == BitmapOpenFailed)
        fprintf(stderr, "Filename %s could not be opened\n",
                filename);
    else if (value == BitmapNoMemory)
        fprintf(stderr, "Not enough memory to allocate pixmap\n");
    return(value);
    /* Returns BitmapSuccess if everything worked */
}
```

6.1.6 Copying and Clearing Areas

XClearWindow clears an entire window. If the window has a background_pixmap attribute, then the window is redrawn with this tile. If the window has background_pixmap or background_pixel attribute None, then the contents of the window are not changed. No exposure events are generated by XClearWindow, since the usual intent of this command is to clear the window, not to refresh the old contents (which would be the normal response to an exposure event). Conversely, XClearWindow is not needed to clear a window before redrawing it due to an Expose event, because the server automatically draws the exposed area with the background pixel value or pixmap.

XClearArea is like XClearWindow but acts on a particular area within a window defined by the call's *x, y, height,* and *width* arguments. If the *height* or *width* argument is 0, then some special rules take effect that clear an area to the right and/or the bottom of the window, as shown in Figure 6-3.

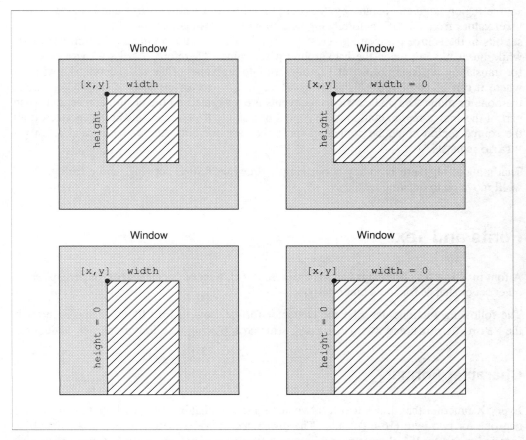

Figure 6-3. XClearArea - area cleared with various width and height arguments

If the *width* argument is 0, the left edge of the cleared area is *x* and the right edge is the right border of the window. If the *height* is 0, the top is *y* and the bottom is the bottom of the window. If both *height* and *width* are 0, then the area between *x* and *y* and the bottom and right sides of the window are cleared. The *exposures* argument indicates whether an Expose event is generated on the cleared area.

XCopyArea is used for many purposes, including copying off-screen pixmaps to the screen and copying one screen area to another. You need to specify the source and destination drawables, the upper-left corner of the source and destination locations, and the width and height of the area. Note that the source and destination drawables must have the same depth, or an error occurs.

Areas of the source that are not visible, not preserved in the backing store, or outside the boundaries of the source drawable are not copied. If the destination has a background tile attribute other than None, the destination areas corresponding to the uncopyable areas of the source are filled or tiled according to the background attributes.

The operation of XCopyPlane is quite different from XCopyArea. A single plane of the source region is given "depth" by "coloring" it with the foreground and background pixel values from the GC, before being written into the destination drawable. In other words, set bits in the source plane are given the foreground pixel value in the destination drawable, while unset bits are given the background pixel value. Therefore, XCopyPlane is useful for translating a pixmap of depth 1 (a bitmap) into a pixmap of the same depth as a window where it can be displayed. If the graphics_exposures member of the GC is True, then one or more GraphicsExpose events are generated on the destination region when part of the source region could not be copied or a single NoExpose event is generated if all the source region could be copied. This is the case for both XCopyArea and XCopy-Plane requests.

That's about all there is to say about simple drawing, filling, copying, and clearing. Now we'll move on to drawing text.

6.2 Fonts and Text

A font in X is a set of bitmaps and may represent text, a set of cursor shapes, or perhaps some other set of shapes for some other purpose.

The following sections describe the character format, how to load fonts, character metrics, the XFontStruct and XCharStruct structures, placing text, font properties, and more.

6.2.1 Character Format

Every X function that draws text has two versions: one that handles single-byte (8-bit) fonts and one for two-byte (16-bit) fonts. The difference between these two is that a single-byte font is limited to 256 characters, while a two-byte font may have up to 256 rows each with 256 characters, a total of 65,536 characters. Large numbers of characters are necessary for Oriental languages.

On many servers, only single-byte fonts can be used with the routines whose names do not end in 16 and only two-byte fonts may be used with the routines that do end in 16. However, some servers may handle either type in either routine. At the moment, there is only one two-byte font on the standard X distribution, the Kanji font used by the *kterm* program, a terminal emulator for Japanese.

6.2.2 Loading Fonts

A font must be loaded before being used. If one or more clients are using the same font, they share the same copy in the server, but each must request that the font be loaded, if only to get the font ID.

The available fonts are stored in a database that is accessible with the XListFonts and XListFontsWithInfo commands.

XListFonts lists the fonts that match the specified pattern (with wildcards) that are available on the current server. The list of font names generated by XListFonts can be freed when no longer needed using XFreeFontNames.

Once the desired font name is found, it can be used as a string in XLoadFont. Some fonts, such as "fixed" and "9x15," are almost always available and should not require a search through the list of fonts. The XLoadFont command loads a font and returns the font ID, which is used in all subsequent references to that font. The font ID is used in XSetFont to associate the font with a GC to be used in drawing text. XLoadFont returns a value that must be checked to make sure the loading succeeded.

If the font is constant width, then it is ready for use as soon as it is loaded. If the font is proportionally spaced and your program needs to calculate the extent of many strings in the same font, then you may want to get the table of the extents of the font characters and perform this calculation locally in order to save repeated round-trip requests to the server. This information is stored in an XFontStruct, which is filled by calling the XQueryFont routine (that structure is described in Section 6.2.3.2). Both the XLoadFont and XQueryFont operations may be done together with XLoadQueryFont.

If the font ID passed to the XQueryFont routines is of type GContext, the information about the font associated with the specified GC is returned. This is how you get information about the default font, which is always loaded. Pass the value returned by:

```
XGContextFromGC(DefaultGC(display, screen_num))
```

to XQueryFont.

The load_font routine shown in Example 6-3 is called in the *basicwin* program described in Chapter 3, *Basic Window Program*. It loads a font and gets the font information structure for later use in the routines that actually draw the text.

Example 6-3. The load_font routine

```
load_font(font_info)
XFontStruct **font_info;
{
    char *fontname = "9x15";

    /* Access font */
    if ((*font_info = XLoadQueryFont(display,fontname)) == NULL)
    {
        (void) fprintf( stderr, "Basic: Cannot open 9x15 font\n");
        exit( -1 );
    }
}
```

In a more general client, the font name should be an argument to load_font, and provision should be made to read it from the command line or resource database.

XListFontsWithInfo returns a list of the loaded fonts matching a font name (with wildcards) and returns the information structure associated with each loaded font. The information returned is identical to that returned by XQueryFont except that per-character metrics are not returned. Only the maximum metrics over the entire font are returned. If `XFontStruct.min_byte1` and `XFontStruct.max_byte1` are 0, the font is a single-byte font.

`XFreeFontInfo` should be used to free the font information structure when the font is no longer needed but before the font is unloaded using `XUnloadFont`. `XFreeFont` combines `XFreeFontInfo` and `XUnloadFont`.

6.2.3 Character Metrics

Before going on to the structures that specify characters and fonts, we should go over some terminology. The measurements shown in Figure 6-4 are some of the *font metrics* that are the measurements in pixels that describe both a font as a whole and each character in the font. The names shown for the metrics are members of the font information structures.

Figure 6-4. The metrics of two characters

Notice that the origin is not at the upper-left corner of each character, as in most of the rest of X. The origin of each character is on the *baseline*, which is a row of pixels somewhere near the lower middle of a line of text. This part of X has been written to conform closely to the existing standards for fonts provided by companies like Adobe.

Notice that two structures are mentioned in Figure 6-4, XFontStruct and XCharStruct. XFontStruct holds information about the entire font, while XCharStruct (itself the type of several members of XFontStruct) holds information about a single character. These two structures have some common member names, but their meanings are different.

There is a difference between the font ascent and descent members in XFontStruct and the ascent and descent members in each individual XCharStruct. The former specifies the largest of each measurement in any character in the font, and the latter specifies the measurements of single characters.

6.2.3.1 The XCharStruct Structure

One XCharStruct structure contains the metrics of a single character in a font. XCharStruct is shown in Example 6-4. Refer back to Figure 6-4 for the meaning of each of its members.

Example 6-4. The XCharStruct structure

```
/* Per character font metric information */
typedef struct {
    short lbearing;              /* Origin to left edge of character */
    short rbearing;              /* Origin to right edge of character */
    short width;                 /* Advance to next char's origin */
    short ascent;                /* Baseline to top edge of character */
    short descent;               /* Baseline to bottom edge of
                                  * character */
    unsigned short attributes;   /* Per char flags (not predefined) */
} XCharStruct;
```

The attributes member is for font-specific information. It does not have any standard use or meaning.

6.2.3.2 The XFontStruct Structure

Example 6-5 shows the XFontStruct structure. This structure contains information about the font as a whole.

Example 6-5. The XFontStruct structure

```
typedef struct {
    XExtData *ext_data;          /* Hook for extension to hang data */
    Font fid;                    /* Font ID for this font */
    unsigned direction;          /* Direction the font is painted */
    unsigned min_char_or_byte2;  /* First character */
    unsigned max_char_or_byte2;  /* Last character */
    unsigned min_byte1;          /* First row that exists (for two-byte
```

Example 6-5. The XFontStruct structure (continued)

```
                                    *  fonts) */
    unsigned max_byte1;             /* Last row that exists (for two-byte
                                    *  fonts) */
    Bool all_chars_exist;           /* Flag if all characters have nonzero
                                    *  size */
    unsigned default_char;          /* Char to print for undefined character */
    int n_properties;               /* How many properties there are */
    XFontProp *properties;          /* Pointer to array of additional
                                    *  properties*/
    XCharStruct min_bounds;         /* Minimum bounds over all existing char*/
    XCharStruct max_bounds;         /* Maximum bounds over all existing char*/
    XCharStruct *per_char;          /* first_char to last_char information */
    int ascent;                     /* Max extent above baseline for spacing */
    int descent;                    /* Max descent below baseline for spacing */
} XFontStruct;
```

XFontStruct includes three members of type XCharStruct: one describes the smallest measurement for each character metric among all the characters in the font; one describes the largest; and one points to a list of structures, one for every character in the font. Note that the minimum character metrics (min_bounds) do not describe the smallest character in the font, but the smallest of every measurement found anywhere in the font. The same goes for max_bounds.

The following list describes in detail each member of the XFontStruct structure. Only font developers need to learn all these members. In general, an application programmer will use only the ascent and descent members and occasionally the min_bounds, max_bounds, min_byte1, and max_byte1 members. These members are placed first so you can just scan the rest if you are interested. Refer back to Figure 6-4 for a visual representation of ascent and descent.

- The min_bounds and max_bounds are structures containing the minimum and maximum extents of the characters in the font, ignoring nonexistent characters. The bounding box of the font (the smallest rectangle that could contain any character bitmap in the font), by superimposing all of the characters at the same origin (specified by x, y), has its upper-left coordinate at:

      [x + min_bounds.lbearing, y - max_bounds.ascent]

  The bounding box's width is:

      max_bounds.rbearing - min_bounds.lbearing

  Its height is:

      max_bounds.ascent + max_bounds.descent

- ascent is the logical extent of the font above the baseline and is used for determining line spacing. Specific character bitmaps may extend beyond this ascent.

- descent is the logical extent of the font below the baseline and is used for determining line spacing. Specific character bitmaps may extend beyond this descent. If the baseline is at absolute y coordinate y, then the logical extent of the font is between the y coordinates (y-XFontStruct.ascent) and (y+XFontStruct.descent-1), inclusive.

- **direction** can be either **FontLeftToRight** or **FontRightToLeft**. This member is a hint about whether most **XCharStruct** members have a positive (**Font-LeftToRight**) or a negative (**FontRightToLeft**) character-width metric, indicating the preferred direction of drawing the font.

- **min_byte1** and **max_byte1** are both 0 for single-byte fonts, since the second byte is not used. These members can be tested to see if a font is single- or two-byte. If single-byte, **min_char_or_byte2** specifies the index of the first member of the **per_char** array and **max_char_or_byte2** specifies the index of the last member.

  min_byte1 and **max_byte1** represent the first and last rows that exist in the font. There may be up to 256 rows in a font, but no normal font is likely to need all 256 rows (256 * 256 characters). For two-byte fonts, both **min_char_or_byte2** and **max_char_or_byte2** will be less than 256, and the two-byte character index values corresponding to **per_char** array member N (counting from 0) are:

  $byte1 = N/D$ min_byte1   /* Row offset */

  $byte2 = N\%D$ min_char_or_byte2   /* Column offset */

  where:

D	=	number of characters per row (max_char_or_byte2 - min_char_or_byte2 + 1)
$/$	=	integer division
$\%$	=	integer modulus

- If the **per_char** pointer is **NULL**, then all glyphs (characters in the font) between the first and last character, inclusive, have the same extent and other information, as given by both **min_bounds** and **max_bounds**.

- If **all_chars_exist** is **True**, then all characters in the **per_char** array have nonzero bounding boxes.

- **default_char** specifies the index that will be used when an undefined or nonexistent index is used. **default_char** is a single-byte character. For a font using two-byte matrix format, **default_char** has **byte1** in the most significant byte and **byte2** in the least significant byte. If **default_char** itself specifies an undefined or nonexistent character, then no printing is performed for undefined or nonexistent index values.

The **XFontProp** member of **XFontStruct** is provided to allow additional properties (over and above the predefined properties) to be associated with a font. See Section 6.2.8 for a description of predefined and additional font properties.

6.2.4 Positioning of Text

All the routines that draw text require the same basic techniques for positioning text on the screen.

Let's consider a string drawn with XDrawImageString. XDrawImageString draws the entire rectangle described by the max_bounds of the font, with the character drawn in the foreground pixel value and the rest drawn in the background pixel value (both from the GC). Figure 6-5 demonstrates the drawing of three strings. The origin of the base-line of each text line is specified in the XDrawImageString call. The offset of the first line of text in Figure 6-5 is (20 + ascent). Subsequent lines are placed (ascent + descent) below the origin of the first line. For routines other than XDraw-ImageString*,† these coordinates still position the background rectangle even though that rectangle is not filled.

- If you want the upper-left corner of the background rectangle to be at pixel coordinate (x,y), then pass (x, y+ascent) as the baseline origin coordinates to the text drawing routines, where ascent is the font ascent as given in XFontStruct.

- If you want the lower-left corner of the background rectangle to be at pixel coordinate (x,y), then pass (x, y−descent+1) as the baseline origin coordinates to the text routines, where descent is the font descent as given in XFontStruct.

It is important to find out how wide a given string is going to be in the chosen font. This width must be smaller than the width of the drawable if you want to be able to read the end of the text!

Listed below are several routines that return either a string width or its extent (both width and height). Both types of routines return the width of the specified string in pixels. The routines that return an extent also provide vertical size information in the form of ascent and descent measurements for the particular string in question and for the font as a whole.

XTextWidth and XTextWidth16
    Return the width in pixels of a string in a particular font.

XTextExtents and XTextExtents16
    Return string and font metrics, which include the width and height of the bound-ing box containing the string in the specified font. Use these routines if making repeated calls with the same XFontStruct.

XQueryTextExtents and XQueryTextExtents16
    Perform the same function as XTextExtents and XTextExtents16, but they query the server instead of requiring a filled XFontStruct and perform-ing the computation locally. Use these routines if you only need to calculate metrics once (or so) for a given font.

To position text vertically using the returned extents, normally you should use the font ascent and descent (rather than the string ascent and descent) if you will be drawing other strings that you want lined up. If you are seriously pressed for space, it is pos-

---

†The * (wildcard) notation is used occasionally in this manual to indicate a number of events or routines with similar names. In this case, there are two functions, XDrawImageString and XDrawImageString16, which differ only slightly in name, features, and arguments, as described in Section 6.2.1. Instead of always listing them both, we may use the wildcard notation.

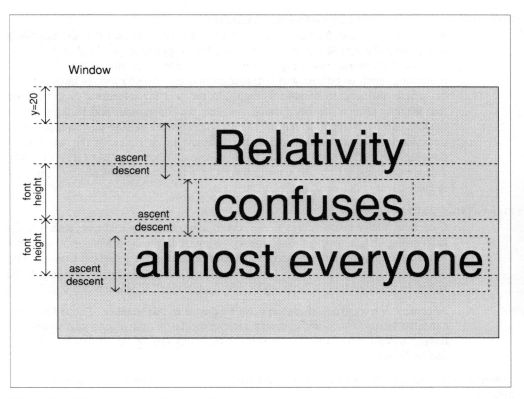

Figure 6-5. The vertical positioning of strings.

sible to save a few pixel rows with certain strings by using the string `ascent` and `descent` measurements.

Whether you center, left justify, or right justify text is completely up to you. The only crucial test is to see that there is enough room for the height and width of the string at the chosen position.

6.2.5 Text-drawing Routines

The following routines draw text into a drawable:

`XDrawString` and `XDrawString16`
> Draw a string into a drawable. They require only the string, its length, and the position of the baseline origin. The font in the GC is used both as a source for the graphics operation and as a clip mask, so that pixels in the destination drawable that are not in each font character are not drawn.

`XDrawImageString` and `XDrawImageString16`

Act just like `XDrawString` and `XDrawString16` except that the bounding box around the text string is filled with the `background` pixel value defined in the GC. This avoids annoying flicker on many screens in clients that do a lot of redrawing, such as editors and terminal emulators. These routines are very useful when you need to be able to highlight the text for selections or to indicate that a menu choice has been made, because the foreground and background of the GC can be swapped to redraw the text highlighted. Using the other text routines to do this requires changing the background attribute of the window or copying the entire area to itself with a logical function of `GXinvert`. The `function` and `fill_style` in the GC are ignored for this request, but they are effectively `GXcopy` and `FillSolid`.

`XDrawText` and `XDrawText16`

Can draw one or more strings to the screen using one `XTextItem` structure for each string. Each structure contains the string of text to be drawn, specifies what font to use, and provides a horizontal offset (the `delta` member) from the end of the last item of text. A font member other than `None` causes the font to be stored in the specified GC; otherwise, the font in that GC is used.

Accented or overstruck characters can be drawn in this manner. These functions can also be used to draw complex arrangements of text in one call instead of having to call `XDrawString` several times, changing the position, text, and font in between each call.

Example 6-6 displays the `XTextItem` structures used by `XDrawText` and `XDrawText16`.

Example 6-6. The XTextItem and XChar2b structures

```
typedef struct {
    char *chars;            /* Pointer to string */
    int nchars;             /* Number of characters */
    int delta;              /* Delta between strings */
    Font font;              /* Font to print it in, None don't change */
} XTextItem;

typedef struct {
    XChar2b *chars;         /* Two-byte characters */
    int nchars;             /* Number of characters */
    int delta;              /* Delta between strings */
    Font font;              /* Font to print it in, None don't change */
} XTextItem16;

typedef struct {           /* Normal 16-bit characters are two bytes */
    unsigned char byte1;
    unsigned char byte2;
} XChar2b;
```

The `font` member of `XTextItem` specifies the font to be used to draw the string in the `chars` member and is stored in the GC for use in subsequent text requests.

The `delta` member specifies a change in horizontal position before the string is drawn. The delta is always added to the character origin and is not dependent on the draw direction of the font. For example, if x = 40, y = 20, and items[0].delta = 8, then the string specified by items[0].chars would be drawn starting at x = 48, y = 20. If items[0].chars pointed to two characters with a combined width of 16 pixels, the next delta, items[1].delta, would begin at x = 64. The next text item would begin at the end of this delta. The `delta` member can also be used to backspace for overstriking characters.

6.2.6 The draw_text Routine

Example 6-7 shows the `draw_text` routine, called from the *basicwin* program described in Chapter 3, *Basic Window Program*. `draw_text` draws three strings in different locations in the window. It demonstrates how to calculate the vertical position of a string using the font ascent.

Example 6-7. The draw_text routine

```
draw_text(win, gc, font_info, win_width, win_height)
Window win;
GC gc;
XFontStruct *font_info;
unsigned int win_width, win_height;
{
    char *string1 = "Hi! I'm a window, who are you?";
    char *string2 = "To terminate program, press any key";
    char *string3 = "or button while in this window.";
    char *string4 = "Screen Dimensions:";
    int len1, len2, len3, len4;
    int width1, width2, width3;
    char cd_height[50], cd_width[50], cd_depth[50];
    int font_height;
    int initial_y_offset, x_offset;

    /* Need length for both XTextWidth and XDrawString */
    len1 = strlen(string1);
    len2 = strlen(string2);
    len3 = strlen(string3);

    /* Get string widths for centering */
    width1 = XTextWidth(font_info, string1, len1);
    width2 = XTextWidth(font_info, string2, len2);
    width3 = XTextWidth(font_info, string3, len3);

    /* Output text, centered on each line */
    font_height = font_info->ascent + font_info->descent;

    /* Output text, centered on each line */
    XDrawString(display, win, gc, (win_width - width1)/2,
            font_height, string1, len1);
    XDrawString(display, win, gc, (win_width - width2)/2,
            (int)(win_height - (2 * font_height)),
            string2, len2);
    XDrawString(display, win, gc, (win_width - width3)/2,
            (int)(win_height - font_height),
```

Example 6-7. The draw_text routine (continued)

```
                            string3, len3);
        /* Copy numbers into string variables */
        (void) sprintf(cd_height, " Height - %d pixels",
                DisplayHeight(display,screen_num));
        (void) sprintf(cd_width, " Width  - %d pixels",
                DisplayWidth(display,screen_num));
        (void) sprintf(cd_depth, " Depth  - %d plane(s)",
                DefaultDepth(display, screen_num));

        /* Reuse these for same purpose */
        len4 = strlen(string4);
        len1 = strlen(cd_height);
        len2 = strlen(cd_width);
        len3 = strlen(cd_depth);

        /* To center strings vertically, we place the first string
         * so that the top of it is two font_heights above the center
         * of the window; since the baseline of the string is what
         * we need to locate for XDrawString and the baseline is
         * one font_info->ascent below the top of the character,
         * the final offset of the origin up from the center of
         * the window is one font_height + one descent */

        initial_y_offset = win_height/2 - font_height -
                font_info->descent;

        x_offset = (int) win_width/4;

        XDrawString(display, win, gc, x_offset, (int) initial_y_offset,
                string4,len4);

        XDrawString(display, win, gc, x_offset, (int) initial_y_offset +
                font_height,cd_height,len1);
        XDrawString(display, win, gc, x_offset, (int) initial_y_offset +
                2 * font_height,cd_width,len2);
        XDrawString(display, win, gc, x_offset, (int) initial_y_offset +
                3 * font_height,cd_depth,len3);
}
```

Note that this routine may be called repeatedly in response to Expose events. That is why the font is loaded, a GC is created, and its font member is set to the loaded font in separate routines before the event loop. The font information structure (containing the font ID) and GC resource ID are passed to draw_text as arguments.

6.2.7 Vertical Text

Xlib provides routines that draw horizontal strings, but not vertical ones. If you want to draw strings vertically that read normally, you need to use a separate text drawing call for each character. You use a baseline with the same x coordinate but a different y coordinate for each character.

Drawing strings vertically that read sideways is even more of a problem. The core X protocol provides no way to rotate text.* Therefore, you are limited to using fonts that have their characters sideways. There is only one of these in the distribution from MIT, called *rot-s16*.

6.2.8 Font Properties

Font properties give detailed information about a font, usually for use only in desktop publishing applications. A font is not guaranteed to have any properties. When possible, fonts should have at least the properties represented by the atoms listed in Table 6-1. These atoms are defined in *<X11/Xatom.h>*. XGetFontProperty returns the value of a property given the atom for that property. In the descriptions in Table 6-1, the data associated with a property is referred to with the same name as the property, but in mixed case. For example, the property atom XA_SUPERSCRIPT_X contains a value that is referred to as SuperscriptX in the description.

Applications that make heavy use of proportionally spaced text may use these properties to space various characters properly.

For a further description of font properties and associated conventions, see Appendix M, *Logical Font Description Conventions*, of Volume Zero, *X Protocol Reference Manual* (as of the second printing).

Table 6-1. Font Properties

Property Name	Type	Description
XA_MIN_SPACE	unsigned int	The minimum interword spacing.
XA_NORM_SPACE	unsigned int	The normal interword spacing.
XA_MAX_SPACE	unsigned int	The maximum interword spacing.
XA_END_SPACE	unsigned int	The additional spacing at the end of sentences.
XA_SUPERSCRIPT_X	int	Offset (in pixels) from the character origin where superscripts should begin. If the origin is at [x,y], then superscripts should begin at: [x + SuperscriptX, y - SuperscriptY]
XA_SUPERSCRIPT_Y	int	Offset (in pixels) from the character origin where superscripts should begin. If the origin is at [x,y], then superscripts should begin at: [x + SuperscriptX, y - SuperscriptY]

---

*Extensions to scale and rotate text are under development, as is an extension for Display PostScript that allows this.

Table 6-1. Font Properties (continued)

Property Name	Type	Description
XA_SUBSCRIPT_X	int	Offset (in pixels) from the character where subscripts should begin. If the origin is at [x,y], then subscripts should begin at: [x + SubscriptX, y + SubscriptY]
XA_SUBSCRIPT_Y	int	Offset (in pixels) from the character where subscripts should begin. If the origin is at [x,y], then subscripts should begin at: [x + SubscriptX, y + SubscriptY]
XA_UNDERLINE_ POSITION	int	Y offset (in pixels) from the baseline to the top of an underline. If the baseline is y-coordinate y, then the top of the underline is at: [y + UnderlinePosition]
XA_UNDERLINE_ THICKNESS	unsigned int	Thickness in pixels of an underline.
XA_STRIKEOUT_ ASCENT	int	Vertical extents (in pixels) for boxing or voiding characters. If the baseline is at y-coordinate y, then the top of the strikeout box is at: [y − StrikeoutAscent] and the height of the box is: [StrikeoutAscent + StrikeoutDescent]
XA_STRIKEOUT_ DESCENT	int	Vertical extents (in pixels) for boxing or voiding characters. If the baseline is at y-coordinate y, then the top of the strikeout box is at: [y − StrikeoutAscent] and the height of the box is: [StrikeoutAscent + StrikeoutDescent]
XA_ITALIC_ANGLE	int	The angle of the dominant staffs of characters in the font, in degrees scaled by 64, relative to the three-o'clock position from the character origin, with positive indicating counterclockwise motion (as in XDrawArc).
XA_X_HEIGHT	int	"1 ex" as in TeX, but expressed in units of pixels. Often the height of lower-case *x*.

Table 6-1. Font Properties (continued)

Property Name	Type	Description
XA_QUAD_WIDTH	int	"1 em" as in TeX, but expressed in units of pixels. The width of an *m* in the current font and point size.
XA_CAP_HEIGHT	int	Y offset from the baseline to the top of the capital letters, ignoring accents, in pixels. If the baseline is at y-coordinate y, then the top of the capitals is at: (y - CAP_HEIGHT)
XA_WEIGHT	unsigned	The weight or boldness of the font, expressed as a value between 0 and 1000.
XA_POINT_SIZE	unsigned	The point size, expressed in tenths of a point, of this font at the ideal resolution. There are 72.27 points to the inch.
XA_RESOLUTION	unsigned	The number of pixels per point, expressed in hundredths, at which this font was created.

It is also possible for fonts to have properties not in this predefined list. If there are such properties, they will be stored in a list of XFontProp structures in the XFontStruct for the font. Example 6-8 shows the XFontProp structure. The documentation for each font must describe these additional properties if they are defined.

Example 6-8. The additional font property structure

```
/* Additional properties to allow arbitrary information with fonts */
typedef struct {
    Atom name;
    unsigned long card32;
} XFontProp;
```

6.2.9 Setting the Font Path

XFreeFontPath, XGetFontPath, and XSetFontPath are available to get or set the current search path for fonts. These functions are very rarely needed, but you should know that they exist. Their purpose is to allow for additional directories of fonts besides the default, which is */usr/lib/X11/fonts* on UNIX-based systems. The font path is common to all clients of the server, so it should be modified with care. If the directory that contains the standard fonts is removed from the path, neither any client nor the server can access fonts.

6.3 Regions

An X *region* is an arbitrary set of pixels on the screen. But usually a region is either a rectangular area, several overlapping or adjacent rectangular areas, or a general polygon. Regions are chiefly used to set the `clip_mask` member of the GC. `XSetRegion` sets the `clip_mask` to a region so that output will occur only within the region. Using `XSet-Region` is a lot easier than defining a single-plane pixmap with the desired size and shape and then using that bitmap to set the `clip_mask` with `XSetClipMask`, and it is more flexible than the `clip_mask` you can set with `XSetClipRectangles`.

The most common use of setting the `clip_mask` to a region is to combine the rectangle from each of multiple contiguous `Expose` events on a single window into a single region and clip the redrawing to that region. This provides a performance improvement in some situations. See Section 3.2.13.1 for more information and an example.

A region has an x and y offset, which is used internally when making calculations with regions (offsets for all regions have a common origin). The offset has an effect if the region is used as a `clip_mask`. When making a graphics request with the `clip_mask` of the GC set with `XSetRegion`, the offset of the region is added to `clip_x_origin` and `clip_y_origin` to determine the placement of the region relative to the destination drawable.

Regions can be created with `XCreateRegion` or `XPolygonRegion`. `XCreate-Region` creates an empty region to which rectangles can be added with `XUnionRect-WithRegion` and various other functions that perform mathematical operations on regions. `XCreateRegion` and `XPolygonRegion` return a pointer to the opaque type `Region`, whose definition a program does not need to know. Just the pointer is used to refer to the region. `XPolygonRegion` creates a region of the same shape as `XDrawLines` would draw given the same arguments (except that `XPolygonRegion` does not require a drawable or a GC and therefore interprets the lines as thin lines). It specifies a list of points and has a flag that indicates whether areas overlapping an odd number of times should be included or not included in the region (just like the `fill_rule` in the GC).

Each region is implemented as a group of nonoverlapping rectangles. Therefore, performance will be best if the regions you use have sides parallel to the coordinate axes. Nonetheless, nonrectangular regions can be created with `XPolygonRegion`.

A region is destroyed with `XDestroyRegion`. The best way to clear a region is to destroy it and create a new one.

`XClipBox` returns the size and position of the smallest rectangle that completely encloses the given region. This function returns an `XRectangle` structure that contains the coordinates of the upper-left corner and the width and height of the rectangle enclosing a region.

6.3.1 Moving and Resizing Regions

`XOffsetRegion` changes the offset of the specified region by the number of pixels specified by its arguments *dx* and *dy*. `XShrinkRegion` reduces the size of the given region by the number of pixels specified by *dx* and *dy*, with positive values indicating that the region is to be increased in size. `XShrinkRegion` also modifies the offset of the region to keep the center of the region near its original position.

6.3.2 Computations with Regions

Several functions are available to combine two regions in various ways. Each function takes three regions as arguments: two operands and a region in which to place the result.

`XIntersectRegion`	Computes the intersection (overlapping area) of two regions.
`XUnionRegion`	Computes the union (total of both areas) of two regions.
`XSubtractRegion`	Subtracts two regions. The result is the region listed first minus the intersection of the two regions.
`XXorRegion`	Computes the difference between the union and the intersection of two regions.
`XUnionRectWithRegion`	Computes the union of a rectangle and region and sets the region to the result.

6.3.3 Returning Region Information

This group of region functions makes logical determinations about regions. All of these routines return nonzero if their conditions are satisfied.

`XEmptyRegion`	Determines whether there is any area in the specified region.
`XEqualRegion`	Determines whether two regions have the same offset, size, and shape.
`XPointInRegion`	Determines whether a specified point resides in a region.
`XRectInRegion`	Determines whether a rectangle specified by *x*, *y*, *width*, and *height* occurs completely inside, completely outside, or overlapping a given region. It returns `RectangleIn` if the rectangle is completely inside the region, `RectanglePart` if the rectangle overlaps the edge of a region, and `RectangleOut` if the rectangle and the region are nonintersecting.

Drawing

6.4 Images

Xlib provides an image structure that is capable of storing all the data corresponding to a screen area or pixmap. The major difference between an image and a pixmap is that an image is a structure on the client side, so its contents can be manipulated directly by the client, instead of solely through X protocol requests. Xlib provides the routines XGetImage and XPutImage that use the X protocol to transfer the contents of a window or pixmap into an image structure and to write the contents of an image structure back into a window or pixmap.

Xlib provides a few minimal routines for manipulating image structures, including routines to create and initialize an empty image structure, destroy an image structure, get a pixel, set a pixel, extract a subimage of an image, and add a constant value to all pixels in an image. These routines can be relatively slow, because they change the byte- and bit-order of the image before performing the operation and then change it back before placing it back in the image. However, in some implementations of Xlib, optimized versions of these routines will automatically be used when the byte- and bit-order used by the server happens to be the same as that used by the machine running the client. This should be quite fast but is not always available.

The image-processing routines provided by Xlib are minimal—they do not provide a complete image manipulation package. However, the image structure does contain all the information necessary to implement a complete package. An application can implement its own routines to manipulate the image data directly. However, this code is difficult to write in a portable and efficient fashion because of the large number of data formats that are possible.* XGetImage returns data that uses the byte- and bit-order of the server. The application will need to swap this into the native byte- and bit-order before doing image processing. XPutImage takes care of swapping it back before sending it to the server, so that the application need not convert the data back to the server-native byte- and bit-order. However, XPutImage does not convert images of different depths.

The XImage data structure is shown in Example 6-9.

Example 6-9. The XImage structure

```
struct _XImage {
int width, height;          /* Size of image */
int xoffset;                /* Number of pixels offset in
                             * x direction */
int format;                 /* XYBitmap, XYPixmap, ZPixmap */
char *data;                 /* Pointer to image data */
int byte_order;             /* Data byte order, LSBFirst,
                             * MSBFirst */
int bitmap_unit;            /* Quantity of scan line 8, 16, 32 */
int bitmap_bit_order;       /* LSBFirst, MSBFirst */
int bitmap_pad;             /* 8, 16, 32 either XY or Z format */
int depth;                  /* Depth of image */
int bytes_per_line;         /* Accelerator to next line */
```

---

*Anyone thinking of trying to write their own routines to manipulate images should get access to the Xlib code that manipulates images. This code will make you think again.

Example 6-9. The XImage structure (continued)

```
    int bits_per_pixel;        /* Bits per pixel (ZPixmap format) */
    unsigned long red_mask;    /* Bits in z arrangement */
    unsigned long green_mask;
    unsigned long blue_mask;
    char *obdata;              /* Hook for the object routines to
                                * hang on */
    struct funcs {             /* Image manipulation routines */
        struct _XImage *(*create_image)();
        int (*destroy_image)();
        unsigned long (*get_pixel)();
        int (*put_pixel)();
        struct _XImage *(*sub_image)();
        int (*add_pixel)();
        } f;
} XImage;
```

The function pointers in the image object allow Xlib implementors to replace MIT's generic functions with functions optimized for the byte- and bit-order used in the machine that is running Xlib.

- The `height`, `width`, and `xoffset` are set when an image is created. The offset is used to align an image to even-addressable boundaries.

- The `format` member may be `XYBitmap`, `XYPixmap`, or `ZPixmap`.

  In `XYBitmap`, the bitmap is represented in scan line order, with each scan line made up of multiples of the `bitmap_unit` and padded with meaningless bits. Within each `bitmap_unit`, the bit order depends on `bitmap_bit_order`.

  In `XYPixmap`, each plane is represented as a bitmap, and the planes appear in most significant to least significant bit order, with no padding between planes.

  In `ZPixmap`, the pixels (instead of bits) are listed in scan line order. Each pixel has `bits_per_pixel` bits, and the bits in the pixel that are allocated to red, green, and blue for `DirectColor` and `TrueColor` are specified by `red_mask`, `blue_mask`, and `green_mask`. See Chapter 7, *Color*, for more information. At the end of each scan line, a pad is used as for `XYBitmap`.

- The `byte_order` is the data byte order, either `LSBFirst` or `MSBFirst`. The `bitmap_bit_order` is the bit order within each byte, again either `LSBFirst` or `MSBFirst`. The `bitmap_unit` specifies how many bits make up a unit of image data (usually the same as the word size), and it can be 8, 16, or 32. Together, these members determine the exact arrangement of bits in memory. Figure 6-6 shows the effect of the various `byte_order` and `bit_order` combinations assuming a `bitmap_unit` of 16. VAXes and 80*86 systems use `byte_order` of `LSBFirst`, while 68000-family systems use `MSBFirst`. Note that with these three variables alone there are 12 different data formats. The `ImageByteOrder` and `BitmapBitOrder` macros return which byte order and bit order is used by the server.

- The `bitmap_pad` member can be 8, 16, or 32, and it specifies the quantum of the scan line. In other words, the start of one scan line and the start of the next are separated by an integer multiple of this number.

- The depth of an image is assigned as the image is created. The depth of a window from which image data is read must match this depth.

- The bytes_per_line member specifies how many bytes make up a scan line.

- The bits_per_pixel member is for ZPixmap images only. This member of the XImage structure must match the member of the same name in the ScreenFormat structure (itself a member of Display).

- The red_mask, green_mask, and blue_mask members are for ZPixmap only and specify the number of bits in the pixel that are allocated to red, green, and blue. This implies that the visual is DirectColor or TrueColor. See Chapter 7, *Color*, for more information.

```
Pixel#    0    1    2    3    4    5    6    7    8    9   10   11   12   13   14   15
-------------------------------------------------------------------------------------
byte_order = LSBFirst, bitmap_bit_order = LSBFirst
byte      0                                      1
bit       0    1    2    3    4    5    6    7    8    9   10   11   12   13   14   15

byte_order = LSBFirst, bitmap_bit_order = MSBFirst
byte      0                                      1
bit       7    6    5    4    3    2    1    0   15   14   13   12   11   10    9    8

byte_order = MSBFirst, bitmap_bit_order = LSBFirst
byte      0                                      1
bit       8    9   10   11   12   13   14   15    0    1    2    3    4    5    6    7

byte_order = MSBFirst, bitmap_bit_order = MSBFirst
byte      0                                      1
bit      15   14   13   12   11   10    9    8    7    6    5    4    3    2    1    0
```

Figure 6-6. Bit and byte order possibilities for images when bitmap_unit = 16

6.4.1 Manipulating Images

These are the available functions that operate on images:

XCreateImage   Allocates memory for an XImage structure and sets various members. Note that it uses the server's data format, which is often not appropriate. The byte- and bit-order fields should usually be changed directly to the client-native format. However, then the call _XInitImageFuncPtrs(image) should be issued to reset the mapping to the appropriate versions of the functions for manipulating the image. This call is supposed to be private to Xlib and, therefore, should be watched for changes in later releases, but this is currently the accepted method.

XGetImage	Fills an XImage structure with data corresponding to a visible area of the screen or a pixmap.
XPutImage	Dumps an XImage structure with data into an area of a window or a pixmap.
XDestroyImage	Frees the data field in an image structure if the image structure was allocated in the application. If the image was created using XCreateImage, XGetImage, or XGetSubImage, XDestroyImage frees both the data and the image structure. Note that if the image data is stored in static memory in the application, it cannot be freed—to free an image created with XCreate-Image that has statically allocated data, you must set NULL into the data field before calling XDestroyImage.
XGetPixel	Gets a single pixel value specified by an x,y location from an image.
XPutPixel	Puts a single pixel value into an image in a specified location.
XAddPixel	Increments each pixel in a pixmap by a constant value.
XSubImage	Creates a new image that is a subset of an existing image. It executes XCreateImage and then performs multiple executions of XGetPixel and XPutPixel, so it may be slow.
XGetSubImage	Creates an image from a subsection of a drawable.

Functions to read and write images to and from disk files have not yet been defined by the X Consortium.

Example 6-10 demonstrates the use of images. See Volume Two, *Xlib Reference Manual*, for more information on the image-handling functions.

6.4.2 Examples Using Images

Images are one of the areas of X that has not yet been extensively used. Therefore, there are few examples available that use images to their potential.

The unique feature of images is that all the data is stored and is directly accessible in Xlib, rather than in the server like Pixmap and Window resources. Since images completely represent a screen area, you can do anything you want to any of the pixel values in the image. Applications like image processing and machine vision would probably use images.

Example 6-10 shows a routine using images. This routine reads an image from the screen, manipulates it, and puts a reflected version of the contents in a new window of the same size. It uses XGetImage, XPutImage, and XPutPixel.

Example 6-10. Example using images — reflect_window

```
/* Window and newwindow must have the same size and depth,
 * and window must be visible */
reflect_window (window, newwindow, gc, width, height)
Window window, newwindow;
```

Example 6-10. Example using images — reflect_window (continued)

```
GC gc;
unsigned int width, height;
{
XImage *xi;
unsigned long pixelvalue1, pixelvalue2;
int y;
int left_x, right_x;

xi = XGetImage(display, window, 0,0, width, height, AllPlanes,
        XYPixmap);
printf("calculating reflection -- this may take awhile...\n");

for (left_x=0 ; left_x<width/2 ; left_x++)
        {
        for (y=0 ; y<height ; y++)
                {
                pixelvalue1 = XGetPixel(xi, left_x, y);
                right_x = width - left_x;
                if (left_x != right_x)
                        {
                        pixelvalue2 = XGetPixel(xi, right_x, y);
                        XPutPixel(xi, left_x, y, pixelvalue2);
                        }
                XPutPixel(xi, right_x, y, pixelvalue1);
                }
        }
printf("putting image\n");
XPutImage(display, newwindow, gc, xi, 0, 0, 0, 0, width, height);
}
```

With sufficient understanding of the format of image data, this routine could be rewritten without XGetPixel and XPutPixel, which would speed it up substantially. However, there would have to be separate code for the many different image formats to make the code as portable as the version shown.

6.5 Cursors

The cursor is different from other types of output to the screen since it is transient, passing over the screen without permanently changing it. The cursor is drawn where the pointer is pointing and removed as soon as the pointer moves.

Each window can have a different cursor defined in its window attributes (using XDefine-Cursor). Whenever the pointer is in a visible window, the cursor is set to the cursor defined for that window. If no cursor was defined for that window, the cursor will be the one that was defined for the parent window unless otherwise specified in the attributes.

From X's perspective, a cursor consists of a cursor shape, mask, foreground and background colors, and hotspot (defined in a moment):

• The cursor bitmap determines the shape of the cursor.

• The mask bitmap determines the pixels on the screen that will be modified by the cursor.

- The pixel values determine the foreground color (the 1 bits in the cursor bitmap) and the background color (the 0 bits in the cursor bitmap).

- The *hotspot* defines the point on the cursor that will be reported when a pointer event occurs. The hotspot is the actual tracking position—for example, the center for a crosshair cursor or the point of an arrow.

There usually are limitations imposed by the hardware on cursors as to size, shape, and whether a mask is implemented. `XQueryBestCursor` is used to find out what sizes are possible.

You need to create a `Cursor` resource to call `XDefineCursor`. Read on for a description of the various ways to create cursors.

6.5.1 The Standard Cursor Font

Many popular cursor shapes are provided in the standard cursor font, *<X11/cursorfont.h>*. Each of these cursor shapes can be turned into a `Cursor` resource using `XCreateFont-Cursor`. Example 6-11 demonstrates this process.

The cursor font is shown in Appendix I, *The Cursor Font*, of Volume Two, *Xlib Reference Manual*, and on the reference page for `XCreateFontCursor` in Volume Two. Each of these cursors uses two characters in the cursor font, only one of which is shown. One determines the shape of the cursor, and the other is a mask which selects which pixels on the screen are disturbed by the cursor. The mask for each standard cursor is very similar to the shape for that cursor but one pixel wider in all directions. This means that when the cursor is black and over a black background, this one pixel outline of the cursor will appear in white around the cursor, making the cursor visible over any background.

Example 6-11. Creating a Cursor from the standard cursor font

```
#include <X11/cursorfont.h>
int cursor_shape = XC_arrow;
Window window;
Cursor cursor;
cursor = XCreateFontCursor(display, cursor_shape);
XDefineCursor(display, window, cursor);
/* Now cursor will appear when pointer is in window */
```

If your client is operating on a color screen and it allows the user to specify window background colors, it may also allow the user to specify cursor colors, since this could improve contrast between the window background and cursor. These pixel values may be specified in the calls to `XCreateGlyphCursor` and `XCreatePixmapCursor`, or `XRecolorCursor` may be called for an existing cursor.

`XCreateGlyphCursor` allows you to do the same thing as is done with the standard cursors but using font characters you specify from any font. The hotspot of these cursors and those created by `XCreateFontCursor` is the origin of each font character (just as if it were text). Usually the hotspot is placed in a logical location, but it is not possible to determine where the hotspot is from within the program or to change its location.

XCreatePixmapCursor allows you to create a cursor from shape and mask pixmaps and foreground and background pixel values, with an explicit hotspot. XQueryBestCursor should be called to determine the allowed cursor sizes before preparing the pixmaps.

You can free the cursor with XFreeCursor right after the XDefineCursor call if no further explicit references to it are made.

6.5.2 Loading and Changing Cursors

The following routines are used to manipulate cursors:

XCreateFontCursor	Creates a cursor from the font of standard cursors. This is the easiest way to create a cursor.
XCreateGlyphCursor	Creates a cursor from a font character (glyph) and a mask.
XCreatePixmapCursor	Creates a cursor from pixmap data.
XDefineCursor	Associates a cursor with a window, so that the specified cursor is displayed in the window whenever the pointer is in the window.
XUndefineCursor	Reverses XDefineCursor, so that the window uses the cursor assigned to its parent.
XFreeCursor	Frees memory associated with a cursor.
XQueryBestCursor	Returns the supported cursor sizes on the given display.
XRecolorCursor	Changes the foreground and background color of a cursor.

See Volume Two, *Xlib Reference Manual*, for more information on these routines.

7

Color

This chapter describes how to use color in your programs. Color handling in X can be more complex than in other graphics systems because of the need for portability to many different types of displays. Certain advanced topics in color handling are still poorly defined in the X standard. This chapter starts with the basics, which everyone working with color should read, and gradually moves to more advanced topics. Pick and choose from the later sections as appropriate.

In This Chapter:

Color

A typical X application allows the user to specify colors for the background and border of each of its windows, colors for the cursor, and foreground and background colors to be set in GCs for drawing text and graphics. More complex applications (such as Computer Aided Design (CAD) applications) might use color to distinguish physical or logical layers. Still more complex applications, such as in imaging, might use fine gradations of color to represent real-world data. Yet in discussing the background and border window attributes and how to set the foreground and background members of the GC, we have spoken only of pixel values.

How are these pixel values translated to colors? And how must an X client manage color if it is to run successfully on the wide variety of screen hardware available in the X environment?

Because X must support a wide variety of systems with differing screen hardware, the Xlib color-handling mechanisms are fairly complex. Even programmers who have previously written color graphics applications will find there are some new concepts to learn.

This chapter starts out by describing the different types of screens that an X application may run on and the mechanisms Xlib provides for determining the screen type. It then describes the simplest color-allocation mechanisms, which could be used by applications whose principal use of color is for decoration. It proceeds to discuss more complex color applications and concludes with a section on writing applications that will be portable across different types of color and monochrome screens.

7.1 Basic Color Terms and Concepts

Most color screens on the market today are based on the RGB color model. Each pixel on the screen is actually made up of three phosphors: one red, one green, and one blue. Each of these three phosphors is sensitive to a separate electron beam. When all three phosphors are fully illuminated, the pixel appears white to the human eye. When all three are dark, the pixel appears black. When the illumination of each primary color varies, the three phosphors generate an additive color that might seem surprising. For example, equal portions of red and green, with no admixture of blue, make yellow. Most people are more familiar with subtractive color mixing, used in paints, where red, yellow, and blue are the three primary colors from which all other colors (except white and shades of gray) can be made.

You, no doubt, know that a color screen uses multiple bits per pixel (also referred to as multiple planes) to specify colors. A *colormap* is used to translate each pixel's value into the visible colors you see on the screen.

A colormap is no more than a lookup table stored in the server. Any given pixel value is used as an index into this table—for example, a pixel value of 16 will select the sixteenth element, or *colorcell*.

On the most common type of color system, each colorcell contains separate 16-bit intensity values for each of the three primary colors.

As shown in Figure 7-1, a pixel value uniquely identifies a particular colorcell. Each pixel value in the visible portions of a window is continuously read out of screen memory and looked up in the colormap. The RGB values in the specified colorcell control the intensity of the three primary colors and thus determine the color that is displayed at that point on the screen.

Figure 7-1. Pixel value to RGB mapping with the colormap on a color screen

The range of colors possible on the screen is a function of the number of bits available in the colormap for RGB specification. If eight bits is available for each primary, then the range of possible colors is 256^3 (about 16 million colors).

However, the number of different colors that can be displayed on the screen at any one time is a function of the number of planes. A 4-plane system could index 2^4 colorcells (16 distinct colors); an 8-plane system could index 2^8 colorcells (256 distinct colors); and a 24-plane system could index 2^{24} colorcells (over 16 million distinct colors).

A client attempting to use color does not *specify* a pixel value and the color to be put in that cell in order to draw in a given color. Instead, it requests access to a colorcell in a colormap (managed by the server) and is *returned* a pixel value. This is called *allocating* a color.

When a client allocates a color, it asks the server, "Which colorcell can I use?" and the server responds by saying, "You can use the colorcell specified by this pixel value." There are three functions that allocate colors, which are described in detail and demonstrated in later sections in this chapter.

7.1.1 The Color Name Database

In order to simplify color specification and to promote sharing of colors, X provides a color database that translates string color names into RGB values. As described above, sharing of colorcells can happen only if two clients allocate a read-only cell with the exact same RGB values. If both clients allocate a color specified by one of the 300-odd string names, there is a much better chance of them selecting the exact same RGB values and thereby sharing a cell than if they use one of the 2^{48} possible combinations of RGB values.

Because of differences in screen hardware, the same RGB values may generate quite different colors on different hardware. Therefore, server implementors will change the RGB values corresponding to each color name to make sure that the appropriate color appears on their screen. This is called *gamma correction*. By using names from this database, you are more sure of getting a color close to the one you request. If the server implementor has not provided a gamma-corrected color database, there is no way a program can tell exactly what color is being displayed even when it knows the RGB values.

It is also important to note that the color names are not specified by the X11 protocol or Xlib. Therefore, server implementors may change them, but more often, they will simply add to the list. (Note that some servers allow users to customize this file. For more information, see Volume Three, *X Window System User's Guide*.)

Table 7-1 shows the color names and corresponding RGB values in the default color database for R3. The R4 database is much more extensive and is shown in Appendix D, *The Color Database*, of Volume Two, *Xlib Reference Manual*. The text version of this database in the standard distribution on a UNIX-based system is in the file */usr/lib/X11/rgb.txt*. The location of this file may vary.

The color names in the color database are strings in which each character uses the ISO Latin-1 encoding. The ISO (International Standards Organization) encoding is used by virtually all workstations manufacturers. What this means is that the first 127 character codes correspond to 7-bit ASCII and are the normal English characters that appear on U.S. keyboards. But ISO characters are 8-bit, and the characters from 128 to 255 are used for characters with accents and other variations, necessary for other Western languages.

Server vendors should be able to supply a color database file for each foreign language. The RGB values would be the same, but the names would be different. In the English file, the entry for green is encoded with the ISO character codes 103 (g), 114 (r), 101 (e), 101 (e), 110 (n). In German, the same entry would be for *grün*, encoded with the ISO codes 103 (g), 114 (r), 252 (ü), 110 (n). In a workstation configured for German, there will be an easy way to type *ü*.

Note that keysyms also use the ISO Latin standard, as shown in Chapter 8, *Events*.

*Table 7-1. The R3 Color Database**

English Words	Red	Green	Blue	English Words	Red	Green	Blue
aquamarine	112	219	147	medium blue	50	50	204
black	0	0	0	medium forest green	107	142	35
blue	0	0	255	medium goldenrod	234	234	173
blue violet	159	95	159	medium orchid	147	112	219
brown	165	42	42	medium sea green	66	111	66
cadet blue	95	159	159	medium slate blue	127	0	255
coral	255	127	0	medium spring green	127	255	0
cornflower blue	66	66	111	medium turquoise	112	219	219
cyan	0	255	255	medium violet red	219	112	147
dark green	47	79	47	midnight blue	47	47	79
dark olive green	79	79	47	navy	35	35	142
dark orchid	153	50	204	navy blue	35	35	142
dark slate blue	107	35	142	orange	204	50	50
dark slate gray	47	79	79	orange red	255	0	127
dark slate grey	47	79	79	orchid	219	112	219
dark turquoise	112	147	219	pale green	143	188	143
dim gray	84	84	84	pink	188	143	143
dim grey	84	84	84	plum	234	173	234
firebrick	142	35	35	purple	176	0	255
forest green	35	142	35	red	255	0	0
gold	204	127	50	salmon	111	66	66
goldenrod	219	219	112	sea green	35	142	107
gray	192	192	192	sienna	142	107	35
green	0	255	0	sky blue	50	153	204
green yellow	147	219	112	slate blue	0	127	255
grey	192	192	192	spring green	0	255	127
indian red	79	47	47	steel blue	35	107	142
khaki	159	159	95	tan	219	147	112
light blue	191	216	216	thistle	216	191	216
light gray	168	168	168	turquoise	173	234	234
light grey	168	168	168	violet	79	47	79
light steel blue	143	143	188	violet red	204	50	153
lime green	50	204	50	wheat	216	216	191
magenta	255	0	255	white	252	252	252
maroon	142	35	107	yellow	255	255	0
medium aquamarine	50	204	153	yellow green	153	204	50

*Also defined are the color names "gray0" through "gray100", spelled with an "e" or an "a". "gray0" is black and "gray100" is white. See Appendix D, *The Color Database*, of Volume Two, *Xlib Reference Manual*, for a listing of the R4 database.

7.1.2 Hexadecimal Color Specification

It is also possible to specify colors using a hexadecimal string.

The hexadecimal form of color specification is necessary, since you may want the user to be able to specify an exact color, not just the rough approximation allowed by an string name. The hexadecimal specification must be in one of the following formats:

```
#RGB            (4 bits each of red, green, and blue)
#RRGGBB         (8 bits each of red, green, and blue)
#RRRGGGBBB      (12 bits each of red, green, and blue)
#RRRRGGGGBBBB   (16 bits each of red, green, and blue)
```

Each of the letters represents a hexadecimal digit. In the shorter formats, the specified values are interpreted as the most significant bits of a 16-bit value. For example, #3a7 and #3000a0007000 are equivalent.

Use of hexadecimal color specifications does not preclude colorcell sharing, since the user could specify the same hexadecimal value for the color for two or more clients. However, it probably tends to make sharing less likely, since a window manager might allocate all the colors in the color database as read-only cells, and then any client that uses hexadecimal specifications will probably be allocating a separate cell instead of sharing.

7.2 Differences in Display Hardware

The description of color mapping given in the previous section was actually somewhat over-simplified. There are significant differences in how the colormap is used on mid-range color screens, monochrome and gray-scale screens, and high performance color screens. Color handling in X was designed to work with any of these hardware types.

7.2.1 Mid-range Color Displays

The most common type of color screen has between four and eight planes and uses the color-map indexing technique described above. This type of screen is so widespread because it provides a flexible color system while being moderately priced. The mapping of pixel values to colorcells, with arbitrary RGB values stored in each colorcell, allows a very large range of possible colors, even though a more limited number can be shown on the screen at any one time.

Mid-range color screens usually have only one hardware colormap. In other words, the pixel values in all the windows on the screen are mapped to colors using the same colormap. On most of these systems, however, the color in any colorcell in the hardware colormap can be individually changed, and therefore, the entire colormap can be replaced with a new set of values. X provides the concept of the *virtual colormap*, so that more than one set of color-cells can be maintained, even though only one of them can be in use at a time. Virtual color-maps are swapped in and out of the hardware colormap by the window manager. This makes it possible for an application that has special color needs to create its own virtual colormap, which the window manager will load into the hardware colormap when that application is in use. However, since only one hardware colormap is available and all applications share it, when any one application creates a new virtual colormap and the window manager installs it, all other applications will screen in false colors, since the pixel values they use now point to cells in the other client's colormap. This is acceptable, since the window manager always installs the correct colormap for the application in use, but it is obviously not ideal. On high performance systems, described below, this problem is solved by having multiple hardware colormaps.

7.2.2 Monochrome and Gray Scale

Monochrome (black and white) screens have only a single plane of screen memory. Each pixel is made up of a single phosphor, which can be either on or off.

Gray-scale screens are sometimes used for publishing applications, since pixels made up of a single phosphor are smaller than those made up of three phosphors and the resolution is, therefore, better. As shown in Figure 7-2, a gray-scale screen works by looking up the intensity of the pixel in the colormap, which, for this screen type, contains only a single value. This controls the intensity of a single electron beam. Gray scale can be simulated on a color screen by making the red, green, and blue values equal in a given colorcell to determine the brightness of gray pixels on the screen.

Figure 7-2. Pixel value to RGB mapping: gray scale and monochrome displays

A gray-scale screen might have a read-only colormap, so that the gray levels in each cell could not be changed. A monochrome screen is an example of this type; it is a single-plane screen with a two-element read-only colormap.

7.2.3 High Performance Color Displays

As memory has become cheaper and applications more advanced, workstations with 24 planes and more have become more common. With 24 bits per pixel, it is possible to screen every discernable color at the same time. This makes it possible to do smooth shading and other applications that use a large number of closely spaced colors.

The problem with having so many planes is that a colormap of the style used in mid-range color screens would be impossibly large: it would contain over 16 million entries. Instead, the available bits per pixel are broken down into three separate colormap indices, one for each primary color, as shown in Figure 7-3. This approach still allows the full range of colors to be generated but makes the job of loading the colormap much more manageable. This scheme requires three primary colormaps of only 256 entries each to specify all 16 million colors on a 24-plane system.

Figure 7-3. Pixel value to RGB mapping: high-performance color displays

In high performance screens, having a read-only colormap makes just as much sense as having it read/write, because nearly every color imaginable can be simultaneously available. With a read-only colormap, there is a fixed relationship between the pixel values used to select a color and the actual RGB values generated. This makes possible applications that want to calculate pixel values directly instead of having to calculate colors and then determine which pixel value represents that color, as is necessary when the colormap is read/write.

In reality, most screens in this class let you use the color resources in either fashion, using virtual colormaps. There can be one read-only virtual colormap and one read/write virtual colormap. However, unlike on mid-range color screen hardware, most high performance color systems have multiple hardware colormaps, so that both virtual colormaps can be installed and used at the same time. In fact, on many of these systems, each window can have its own virtual colormap installed in the hardware at the same time.

7.2.4 How X Describes Color Support with Visuals

A *visual* describes the characteristics of a virtual colormap that has been or can be created for use on a particular screen. As used by Xlib, a visual is actually a pointer to a structure (of type `Visual`) containing information about one way of using a particular screen. A visual must be specified when creating a colormap or a window, and the same visual must be used in creating a window as is used to create the colormap to be used in that window.

Most windows inherit their parent's visual, and windows will often share the root window's visual, which is known as the default visual. The default visual describes, naturally, the default colormap. If you create all your windows with `XCreateSimpleWindow`, you will be using the default visual and colormap.

The `Visual` structure is intended to be opaque; programs are not supposed to access its contents. This is so that Xlib implementors can change the structure without breaking existing clients. The procedure used to avoid accessing its members is not all that cumbersome but is just beginning to come into use by application writers. Up to this point, most programmers have broken this rule. We will show you only the correct method here, since it adds only a few lines to the application.

Even more existing applications have avoided visuals altogether and used only the `DefaultDepth` or `DisplayPlanes` macros to attempt to determine whether the screen is monochrome or color. However, this does not work in general, because it does not distinguish between gray-scale screens and color screens (both have more than one plane). The only way to make this distinction is to get information about visuals.

Remember that a visual is only one way to use color on a particular screen. There may be a list of supported visuals on a screen, with each visual describing a different depth and writeability of the colormap. On a color system, there may be both monochrome and color visuals available.

The correct method to get information about the visuals supported on a particular screen is to use `XMatchVisualInfo` or `XGetVisualInfo`. These functions return `XVisual-Info` structures that contain information about the available visuals and are public so their fields can be safely accessed.

The `class` member of `XVisualInfo` contains a constant specifying one of six different visual classes,* corresponding to the basic ways of using a screen: `DirectColor`, `GrayScale`, `PseudoColor`, `StaticColor`, `StaticGray`, or `TrueColor`.

As summarized in Table 7-2, the visual classes distinguish between color or monochrome, whether the colormap is read/write or read-only, and whether a pixel value provides a single index to the colormap or is decomposed into separate indices for red, green, and blue values.

Table 7-2. Comparison of Visual Classes

Colormap Type	Read/Write	Read-only
Monochrome/Gray	`GrayScale`	`StaticGray`
Single Index for RG&B	`PseudoColor`	`StaticColor`
Decomposed Index for RG&B	`DirectColor`	`TrueColor`

There may be more than one way of using color on a particular screen, and therefore, there may be more than one supported visual. This is usually true of high-end workstations. There are ways to search through the available visuals to select the one that most closely meets the needs of your application, as will be described later. Several visuals of the same class may be provided but at different depths. On high performance screens, it is possible to create the colormap as read/write or as read-only. Both methods have certain advantages and would be used for different applications. There would be a separate visual for each of these ways of using the screen hardware. One of these visuals would be `TrueColor` class and the other `DirectColor` class. Some 24-plane screens allow the screen to be treated as two separate 12-plane `PseudoColor` visuals. (This allows for "double-buffering," a technique useful for animation, or for storing distance data to simplify hidden line and plane calculations in 3-D applications.) In fact, on some advanced workstations, you can use a different visual in each window.

Figure 7-4 schematically represents the visual classes that can theoretically be supported by each type of screen hardware. A screen that supports the `DirectColor` class can theoretically support any of the six visual classes. A screen that supports the `PseudoColor` visual class can support `GrayScale`, `PseudoColor`, `StaticColor`, or `StaticGray` visual classes. A screen that supports the `GrayScale` visual class can also support `StaticGray` visual classes. The three types of screen with read-only colormaps can only support visuals of their own class. But remember that just because a certain visual class can theoretically be supported by a certain screen hardware does not mean that the server implementors will decide to support that class.

---

*Do not confuse *visual* class with *window* class. While both are represented in certain structures as the `class` member and both are set when a window is created and cannot be changed, they are quite different. The window class is `InputOutput` or `InputOnly`. The visual class is only part of the overall visual, which is the way color is represented for a window.

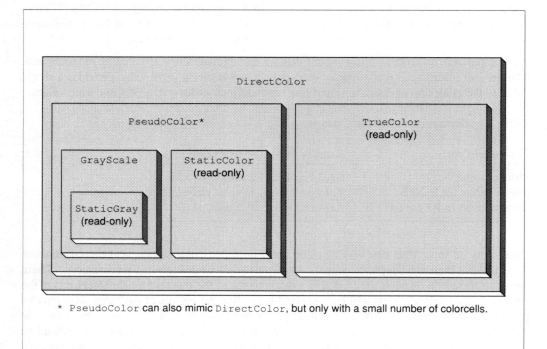

Figure 7-4. Hierarchy of visual classes

7.2.5 Shareability vs. Changeability

Notice that DirectColor, GrayScale, and PseudoColor visuals have changeable colormaps, but StaticColor, StaticGray, and TrueColor have immutable colormaps. Within the changeable colormaps, it is possible to have two types of colorcells: read-only and read/write. The color in a read-only cell is set once by one client and from then on can be shared by any client but not changed. A read/write cell can have its color changed at any time by the client that allocated it but cannot be shared by other clients. In immutable colormaps, you are limited to only read-only cells.

One advantage of immutable colormaps is that all the cells are read-only and can be shared between clients, so all the cells are available to every client. Immutable colormaps also make it possible to calculate pixel values from the colors desired without querying the server, since the mapping between pixel values and colors is predictable. This technique is necessary for smooth shading and 3-D rendering algorithms. As you will see, this is usually not possible with changeable colormaps. The disadvantages of immutable colormaps are that there may not be the exact color you desire (if there are a small number of planes) and you cannot allocate read/write cells, so you cannot change a colorcell to change the color of existing pixels on the screen. To change a color, you have to redraw the graphics with a new pixel value.

In general, the advantage of changeable colormaps is that you can have both private read/write cells and shareable read-only cells. That is why PseudoColor and Direct-Color are the most useful visuals, when a screen supports them. PseudoColor and DirectColor allow you to decide whether your client really needs read/write cells or whether it can use read-only cells. Read-only usage is preferred, since these cells can be shared by all clients, which means that the colormap is less likely to run out of free cells.

Try not to confuse the writeability of colormaps with the writeability of colorcells. A colorcell in a read/write colormap can be allocated read/write or read-only. A colorcell in a read-only colormap can only be allocated read-only. A changeable colormap could be made entirely read-only if the window manager or any other client allocates all available colorcells read-only.

The advantages of read/write colorcells, available only in changeable colormaps, are that your program can select exactly the color you want (as long as it is physically possible on the screen) and you can change the color at will, which instantly changes the visible color of everything drawn with that pixel value if the colormap is currently installed. Although any other client can also change the values in a read/write cell, it is a convention that only the client that allocated the cell should change its contents. You *own* that pixel value. Since most clients cannot be satisfied with having no control over their displayed colors, this pixel value is not shareable. That means that if several clients that use read/write colorcells are running, all the colorcells might be used. Then some client will be forced to create its own colormap, with the negative consequences described in Section 7.7.

7.3 Allocating Shared Colors

Since free colorcells can quickly become a scarce resource when clients store private color values, simple clients that mainly use color for decoration are encouraged always to allocate read-only colors, so that these colorcells can be shared by other clients that allocate the same colors read-only.

The returned pixel value can be used to set the background_pixel or border_pixel attribute of a window or to set the foreground or background member of a GC, which are used by drawing requests. (See Chapter 4, *Window Attributes*, and Chapter 5, *The Graphics Context*, for more information.)

Read-only colorcells can be allocated with the following routines:

XAllocColor   Returns the index of the colorcell (a pixel value) that contains the RGB values requested or that contains the closest RGB values physically possible on the screen.

XAllocNamedColor   Returns the index of the colorcell that contains the RGB values associated with a specified color name from the string color name database or the closest RGB values physically possible on the screen.

By convention, clients allow the user to specify colors on the command line or in the resource database using a color name. When the RGB values are chosen from the color database by specifying color name strings, sharing of read-only colorcells is much more likely than if colors are specified as raw RGB values or using hexadecimal specifications.

XParseColor parses a color name string or a hexadecimal color specification string and returns RGB values. It can be used with XAllocColor or the routines that allocate read/write cells, which will be described later. For color names, it gets the RGB values from the server's color database just like XAllocNamedColor. You may have noticed that XAllocNamedColor is very similar to the combination of XParseColor and XAllocColor. The difference is slight: XAllocNamedColor can interpret color names but not hexadecimal specifications—but hexadecimal specifications are rarely made by users anyway. The two-routine combination is more often used because it allows you to separately report errors in parsing the color specified and allocating the colorcell.

Using XQueryColor and XQueryColors you can find out what RGB values are in each colorcell. But there is no way to determine whether a given cell is read-only or read/write or how many cells are currently unallocated.

A request to allocate a color may fail because there are no free colormap cells and, for read-only colorcells, because no existing colorcell contains the closest color possible on the hardware to the exact color requested. Applications must allocate colors by trial and error. The routines that allocate colorcells all have Status return values. If the call to allocate colorcells returns False, the client may modify the arguments and try again. If repeated attempts fail, the client can settle with BlackPixel and WhitePixel or, if these colors are inadequate, create a new virtual colormap. An application with picky color needs that cannot be satisfied can simply report to the user that its color needs cannot be met and exit.

7.3.1 The XColor Structure

Both XAllocColor and XAllocNamedColor (as well as other functions that manipulate colorcells) take as an argument an XColor structure. This structure is used to specify the desired RGB values, as well as to return the pixel value.

The XColor structure is shown in Example 7-1. The information it contains closely matches the information in each cell of the colormap.

Example 7-1. The XColor structure

```
typedef struct {
    unsigned long pixel;                /* Pixel value */
    unsigned short red, green, blue;    /* RGB values */
    char flags;                         /* DoRed,  DoGreen, and/or
                                         * DoBlue */
    char pad;                           /* Unused; pads structure
                                         * to even word boundary */
} XColor;
```

In XAllocColor and XAllocNamedColor, the pixel member returns the pixel value that will be used to set the foreground or background pixel value in the GC or window attributes. In XStoreColor and XQueryColor, which you will see later, the pixel member indicates which cell in the colormap is having its color set (read/write cells only) or is having its RGB values queried.

The red, green, and blue members are 16-bit values. Full brightness in a color is a value of 65535, half brightness is 32767, and off is 0. (The server automatically scales these values if the hardware colormap includes fewer bits for RGB values.)

The flags member of the XColor structure is a bitwise OR of the symbols DoRed, DoGreen, and DoBlue. These flags are used to specify which of the red, green, and blue values should be read while changing the RGB values in a read/write colorcell. How these are used is demonstrated in Section 7.4.1.

7.3.2 Code to Allocate Read-only Colors

As we have said, applications that have basic color needs should allocate read-only, shareable color cells. Example 7-2 shows code to allocate a color specified using a name from the color name database. In this case, we have simply hardcoded the color name strings. In a real application, you would hardcode the default color but allow user specification of the string, as is done in *basecalc*, described in Chapter 12, *A Complete Application*.

This routine uses XMatchVisualInfo to determine whether color is supported on the screen. If any of the four color visual classes are supported, it proceeds to attempt to allocate read-only colors. Whenever anything fails or if color is not supported, the routine uses black and white. For some applications, this could be modified to allocate levels of gray on GrayScale visual class screens.

The code for all the examples in this chapter is in the example source in the directory */basicwin/color/*. This example is called *basic.ro*.

Example 7-2. Allocating read-only colorcells

```
#include <X11/Xlib.h>
#include <X11/Xutil.h>
#include <X11/Xos.h>
#include <stdio.h>

extern Display *display;
extern int screen_num;
extern Screen *screen_ptr;
extern unsigned long foreground_pixel, background_pixel,
        border_pixel;
extern char *progname;

#define MAX_COLORS 3

/* This is just so we can print the visual class intelligibly */
static char *visual_class[] = {
    "StaticGray",
    "GrayScale",
    "StaticColor",
    "PseudoColor",
    "TrueColor",
    "DirectColor"
```

Example 7-2. Allocating read-only colorcells (continued)

```
};

get_colors()
{
    int default_depth;
    Visual *default_visual;
    static char *name[] = {"Red", "Yellow", "Green"};
    XColor exact_def;
    Colormap default_cmap;
    int ncolors = 0;
    int colors[MAX_COLORS];
    int i = 5;
    XVisualInfo visual_info;

    /* Try to allocate colors for PseudoColor, TrueColor,
     * DirectColor, and StaticColor; use black and white
     * for StaticGray and GrayScale */

    default_depth = DefaultDepth(display, screen_num);
    default_visual = DefaultVisual(display, screen_num);
    default_cmap   = DefaultColormap(display, screen_num);
    if (default_depth == 1) {
        /* Must be StaticGray, use black and white */
        border_pixel = BlackPixel(display, screen_num);
        background_pixel = WhitePixel(display, screen_num);
        foreground_pixel = BlackPixel(display, screen_num);
        return(0);
    }

    while (!XMatchVisualInfo(display, screen_num, default_depth,
            /* visual class */i--, &visual_info))
        ;
    printf("%s: found a %s class visual at default depth.\n",
            progname, visual_class[++i]);

    if (i < StaticColor) { /* Color visual classes are 2 to 5 */
        /* No color visual available at default depth;
         * some applications might call XMatchVisualInfo
         * here to try for a GrayScale visual if they
         * can use gray to advantage, before giving up
         * and using black and white */
        border_pixel = BlackPixel(display, screen_num);
        background_pixel = WhitePixel(display, screen_num);
        foreground_pixel = BlackPixel(display, screen_num);
        return(0);
    }

    /* Otherwise, got a color visual at default depth */

    /* The visual we found is not necessarily the default
     * visual, and therefore it is not necessarily the one
     * we used to create our window; however, we now know
     * for sure that color is supported, so the following
     * code will work (or fail in a controlled way) */
    /* Let's check just out of curiosity: */
    if (visual_info.visual != default_visual)
    {
        printf("%s: %s class visual at default depth\n",
```

Example 7-2. Allocating read-only colorcells (continued)

```
                    progname, visual_class[i]);
            printf("is not default visual! Continuing anyway...\n");
    }

    for (i = 0; i < MAX_COLORS; i++) {
        printf("allocating %s\n", name[i]);
        if (!XParseColor (display, default_cmap, name[i],
                &exact_def)) {
            fprintf(stderr, "%s: color name %s not in database",
                    progname, name[i]);
            exit(0);
        }
        printf("The RGB values from the database are %d, %d, %d\n",
                exact_def.red, exact_def.green, exact_def.blue);
        if (!XAllocColor(display, default_cmap, &exact_def)) {
            fprintf(stderr, "%s: can't allocate color:\n",
                    progname);
            fprintf(stderr, "All colorcells allocated and\n");
            fprintf(stderr, "no matching cell found.\n");
            exit(0);
        }
        printf("The RGB values actually allocated are %d, %d, %d\n",
                exact_def.red, exact_def.green,
                exact_def.blue);
        colors[i] = exact_def.pixel;
        ncolors++;
    }

    printf("%s: allocated %d read-only color cells\n",
            progname, ncolors);

    border_pixel = colors[0];
    background_pixel = colors[1];
    foreground_pixel = colors[2];
    return(1);
}
```

This code begins by setting variables to the default depth, visual, and colormap for later use. If the default depth is one, then the application is displaying on a monochrome screen, and black and white are returned. Then the code calls XMatchVisualInfo in a loop to look for a color visual at the default depth—it is called up to four times, until a color visual is found. If none is found, it again returns black and white, since this screen must support only a GrayScale visual (at this depth, anyway). Some applications may wish to allocate grays in this branch. The rest of the code loops through the list of color names to be allocated, looks them up in the color database, and then allocates them. If either the lookup stage or the allocation stage fails for any color, the routine prints an error and exits. It could instead simply fall back on black and white again; your choice.

As noted in the code, the visual found might not necessarily be the default visual. This does not always matter, because if any color visual is available, it is a good bet that the default visual is also color, and so colors can be allocated without doing any further research. With XMatchVisualInfo, it is difficult to develop an algorithm that is guaranteed to find the default visual. This is much easier with XGetVisualInfo, which returns a list of available visual structures that match a set of criteria you specify. If you pass no criteria, it simply returns the entire list of available visuals. You can then search through the list matching the `visual` member of the `XVisualInfo` structures to the default visual. This will be demonstrated in Section 7.5.

The `XParseColor` call specifies a color name, and the RGB values corresponding to that name are returned from the color database in the passed `XColor` structure. This structure is then passed to `XAllocColor`, and the pixel value allocated is returned in the `pixel` field of the structure.

The same calls would be used to parse a hexadecimal color string. Pink could be specified in the call to `XParseColor` as "#bc8f8f" instead of "pink". But, as we have said before, color names are preferred, because there is a better chance that they will specify a color already allocated or later to be allocated by another client.

It is also possible to specify the desired RGB values explicitly. This is good for default colors because it saves a call to `XParseColor`, but on the other hand, you might not get a consistent color on all systems because you are bypassing the gamma correction implemented through the color database. Simply declare an `XColor` structure and set its `red`, `green`, and `blue` members to the desired RGB values. Of course, these values can be specified as integers, hexadecimal values, or any other way that the C language allows. Then pass this structure to `XAllocColor`. But remember, as we have said, it is better to use color names when allocating read-only colorcells than to use any of these explicit RGB values.

7.3.3 Highlighting in Two Colors

It is easy to highlight graphics on a monochrome system. The simplest way is to set the GC to the `GXxor` logical function and draw your graphics once to draw them and again to undraw them. You must grab the server between the drawing and undrawing so that no other client changes the same pixels in between (by, for example, covering part of the area with another window). On a monochrome system, this always changes white to black and black to white if you set the foreground in the GC to 1 (setting it to `BlackPixel` or `WhitePixel` is not guaranteed to work on all systems, because either may be 0).

When drawing in `BlackPixel` and `WhitePixel` on a color system, the color drawn by the `GXxor` operation is random if `BlackPixel` or `WhitePixel` are used for the foreground pixel value in the GC. This is because there is no restriction on which pixel value `BlackPixel` and `WhitePixel` can be on a server—they are not necessarily 1 and 0 and not necessarily different by just one bit. For example, the pixel value drawn if the foreground pixel value in the GC is `BlackPixel` and the pixel value on the screen is `WhitePixel` is `BlackPixel` XOR `WhitePixel`, which, unless `BlackPixel` and `WhitePixel` are different by only one bit, is a third pixel value not allocated by this client. The colorcell identified by this pixel value might contain black, in which case the operation would not change the screen.

The solution to this problem, which works on monochrome and color systems, is to set the foreground pixel value in the GC used in drawing with `GXxor` to the exclusive OR of `BlackPixel` and `WhitePixel` or by setting the logical function to `GXinvert` and using a plane mask which is the exclusive OR of `WhitePixel` and `BlackPixel`. All applications that highlight graphics drawn in `BlackPixel` and `WhitePixel` on a color system should use one of these two methods. The following example illustrates how this works using two arbitrarily chosen pixel values (which could be `BlackPixel` and `WhitePixel` or could be any two colors).

Let's assume that we draw in two pixel values, which we will call `color1` and `color2`. The pixel values for these could be:

```
color1 = 11111111111111110000000000000000
color2 = 00000000111111111111111100000000
```

The pixel value we will use to draw is generated by taking the exclusive OR of `color1` and `color2`:

```
color1 XOR color2 = 11111111000000001111111100000000
```

Now we set the `foreground` in the GC to this pixel value and the `function` in the GC to `GXxor` and draw. This changes existing pixels that contained `color1` to `color2` and existing pixels that were `color2` to `color1`.

```
foreground =              11111111000000001111111100000000
existing pixel (color1) = 11111111111111110000000000000000
resulting pixel (color2) = 00000000111111111111111100000000
```

The other way to do this is to set the `plane_mask` in the GC to (`color1 ^ color2`) and then use a logical function of `GXinvert`. This is equally effective.

7.3.4 Choosing Default Colors

A client that uses color should allow the user to specify the colors either on the command line or in the resource database, or both. The resource manager (described in Chapter 11, *Managing User Preferences*) can be used to merge these preferences with the defaults of the program. However, the client needs to have reasonable default colors in case the user does not specify any preferences.

Follow these guidelines for your application's default colors:*

- Use string color names for read-only colorcells if possible, since this maximizes the chance of sharing cells.

- Use colors with large contributions from two or all three primary colors—they light the screen more brightly.

- Avoid shades of pure blue—the human eye is relatively insensitive to and unable to focus on images made of pure blue light. Mix blue shades with white (white contains equal parts of all three primary colors).

- Remember that some users are color blind. Do not use the same intensity of green and red for "safe" and "danger"—use colors with differing intensity.

---

*Courtesy Oliver Jones, Apollo Computer.

7.4 Allocating Private Colors

In colormaps of the `PseudoColor` or `TrueColor` visual classes, a client can allocate read/write cells. Read/write colorcells should be allocated when:

- The application draws something whose color must be changed dynamically without redrawing it. For example, in a color mixing program, the palette must be drawn in colors that change frequently. If this were done with read-only colors, cells would have to be allocated and freed frequently and the palette area redrawn with each new color. However, with read/write colorcells, the steps of allocation and color setting are separate, so that the color of an already allocated cell can be changed at will. Anything drawn using the pixel value of this colorcell will change color immediately when the RGB values in the colorcell are changed.

- The application needs to overlay graphics on top of other graphics in such a way that the overlayed graphics can be erased without disturbing the underlying graphics. For example, in a Computer Aided Design (CAD) package for chip design, it is often useful to overlay the various layers of a chip in different colors on the screen. When one of the layers is removed, you want to avoid having to redraw all the underlying layers. How to do this by allocating read/write cells will be described.

- The system has a huge colormap, and the application needs to set a large number of colorcells. The calls for manipulating read/write colorcells allow you to manipulate multiple cells per call, whereas with read-only cells, you are limited to one cell per call.

Note that read/write colorcell allocation never works on `TrueColor` or `StaticColor` visuals. Therefore, on systems that only support these visuals, an application that uses read/write colorcells cannot work. Read/write colorcells should only be used when really needed.

`XAllocColorCells` allocates read/write colorcells. At its simplest, it allows you to allocate read/write cells so you can change the RGB values dynamically.

But to simply allocate just a few cells, you set the `ncolors` argument to the number of colorcells desired and `nplanes` to 0, and all the pixel values you need will be returned in the `pixels` array. The real reason for the `nplanes` and `plane_masks` arguments will become clear in Section 7.4.2. The RGB values of the allocated cells are set with `XStoreColor`, `XStoreColors`, or `XStoreNamedColor`.

`XAllocColorPlanes`, on the other hand, is only used when you want to be able to vary a primary color component of graphics already drawn without redrawing them. It allocates read/write cells, so that a preset number of bits are reserved for each primary color. Primarily for `DirectColor`, it also allows you to simulate a small `DirectColor` colormap on a `PseudoColor` visual but uses up colorcells quickly. It treats the colormap as three separate lookup tables, allocating $ncolors * 2^{nreds}$ entries in the red lookup table, $ncolors * 2^{ngreens}$ entries in the green lookup table, and $ncolors * 2^{nblues}$ entries in the blue lookup table.

The following routines are used to actually store colors into read/write colorcells once they are allocated:

XStoreColor   Changes the read/write colormap cell corresponding to the speci-
                       fied pixel value to the hardware color that most closely matches
                       the RGB values specified.* The flags DoRed, DoGreen, and
                       DoBlue in the XColor structure indicate which primary colors
                       in the cell are to be changed.

XStoreColors   Like XStoreColor, except it does multiple cells per call.
                       Changes the read/write colormap cell corresponding to the speci-
                       fied pixel value to the hardware color that most closely matches
                       the RGB values specified. The flags DoRed, DoGreen, and
                       DoBlue in each XColor structure indicate which primary
                       colors in each cell are to be changed.

XStoreNamedColor   Performs the same function as StoreColor, except that it
                       stores the RGB values associated with a string color name in the
                       RGB database. This call would be useful for loading a private
                       colormap with each of the default named colors.

7.4.1 Allocating Read/Write Colorcells for Dynamic Colors

As described above, the simplest use of read/write colors is to allocate colorcells whose colors can by changed at any time. Example 7-3 is analogous to the code just shown to allo-cate read-only colors, except that it allocates read/write colors instead. Note that it calls XAllocColorCells with the *ncolors* argument set to the number of colorcells desired and *nplanes* set to zero.

Example 7-3. Allocating read/write colorcells for dynamic colors

```
#include <X11/Xlib.h>
#include <X11/Xutil.h>
#include <X11/Xos.h>
#include <stdio.h>

extern Display *display;
extern int screen_num;
extern unsigned long foreground_pixel, background_pixel,
        border_pixel;

#define MAX_COLORS 3

get_colors()
{
        int default_depth;
        Visual *default_visual;
    static char *name[] = {"Red", "Yellow", "Green"};
```

---

*Even when storing explicit RGB values, you may not get the precise color you specify. For example, if the hard-ware colormap supports only four bits of intensity in each primary and you specify eight-bit values, the server will scale the values you provide to the closest possible equivalent on the hardware.

```
    XColor exact_defs[MAX_COLORS];
    Colormap default_cmap;
    int ncolors = MAX_COLORS;
    int plane_masks[1];
    int colors[MAX_COLORS];
    int i;
    XVisualInfo visual_info;
    int class;

    class = PseudoColor;
    default_depth = DefaultDepth(display, screen_num);
    default_visual = DefaultVisual(display, screen_num);
    default_cmap   = DefaultColormap(display, screen_num);
    if (default_depth == 1) {
        /* Must be StaticGray, use black and white */
        border_pixel = BlackPixel(display, screen_num);
        background_pixel = WhitePixel(display, screen_num);
        foreground_pixel = BlackPixel(display, screen_num);
        return(0);
    }

    if (!XMatchVisualInfo(display, screen_num, default_depth,
            PseudoColor, &visual_info)) {
        if (!XMatchVisualInfo(display, screen_num, default_depth,
                DirectColor, &visual_info)) {
            /* No PseudoColor visual available at default_depth;
             * some applications might try for a GrayScale
             * visual here if they can use gray to advantage,
             * before giving up and using black and white */
            border_pixel = BlackPixel(display, screen_num);
            background_pixel = WhitePixel(display, screen_num);
            foreground_pixel = BlackPixel(display, screen_num);
            return(0);
        }
    }

    /* Got PseudoColor or DirectColor visual at default_depth */

    /* The visual we found is not necessarily the default
     * visual, and therefore it is not necessarily the one
     * we used to create our window; however, we now know
     * for sure that color is supported, so the following
     * code will work (or fail in a controlled way) */

    /* Allocate as many cells as we can */
    ncolors = MAX_COLORS;
    while (1) {
        if (XAllocColorCells (display, default_cmap, False,
                plane_masks, /* nplanes */0, colors, ncolors))
            break;
        ncolors--;
        if (ncolors = 0)
            fprintf(stderr, "basic: couldn't allocate read/write \
                    colors\n");
        exit(0);
    }

    printf("basic: allocated %d read/write color cells\n", ncolors);
```

Example 7-3. Allocating read/write colorcells for dynamic colors (continued)

```
        for (i = 0; i < ncolors; i++) {
            if (!XParseColor (display, default_cmap, name[i],
                    &exact_defs[i])) {
                fprintf(stderr, "basic: color name %s not in database",
                        name[i]);
                exit(0);
            }

            /* Set pixel value in struct to the allocated one */
            exact_defs[i].pixel = colors[i];
            exact_defs[i].flags = DoRed | DoGreen | DoBlue;
        }
    /* This sets the color of read/write cell */
    XStoreColors (display, default_cmap, exact_defs, ncolors);
    border_pixel = colors[0];
    background_pixel = colors[1];
    foreground_pixel = colors[2];
}
```

The `main` that calls this `get_colors` function, shown in Example 7-4 contains an `XQueryColor` call that gets the current RGB values in the colorcell (necessary because `main` and `get_colors` are in separate source files and the RGB values used in `get_colors` are not global variables) and an `XStoreColor` call that changes the color of what is drawn in the foreground pixel value every time you press a button in the window. In the example source, this application is in the directory *basicwin/color/* and is called *basic.rw*.

Example 7-4. Main of basic.rw — changing colors of dynamic colorcells

```
        .
        .
        .
void main(argc, argv)
int argc;
char **argv;
{
        .
        .
        .

    XColor color;
    unsigned short red, green, blue;
        .
        .
        .
    /* Open display, etc. */

    color.pixel = foreground_pixel;
    XQueryColor(display, DefaultColormap(display, screen_num),
            &color);
    printf("red is %d, green is %d, blue is %d\n", color.red,
            color.green, color.blue);

    while (1)  {
        XNextEvent(display, &report);
```

```
        switch  (report.type) {
            .
            .
            .
        case ButtonPress:
            color.red += 5000;
            color.green -= 5000;
            color.blue += 3000;
            printf("red is %d, green is %d, blue is %d\n",
                    color.red,
            color.green, color.blue);
            XStoreColor(display, DefaultColormap(display,
                    screen_num), &color);
            break;
            .
            .
            .
        }
    }
```

7.4.2 Allocating Read/Write Colorcells for Overlays

XAllocColorCells has another use: it allows you to nondestructively overlay one set of graphics over another. The underlying graphics will not be visible where the overlay is drawn, but they can be refreshed by simply setting or clearing one or more complete planes in the drawable. This technique can improve the performance of a client by reducing the amount of complicated graphics that have to be redrawn. It can be useful for highlighting graphics for selection. However, as noted earlier, read/write colorcells can only be allocated in PseudoColor and DirectColor visuals, so any application that attempts to use this technique should also provide a fallback technique for use on other visuals or in case of failure.

The trick that allows drawing without destroying what is already drawn relies on the fact that we can draw in one plane of the drawable, changing the pixel values and therefore the color, without changing any other plane. This is possible using the plane_mask component of the GC. It is these other planes that contain the information about the drawing that was already there. The disadvantage of this approach is that we have to allocate more colorcells than we would normally need. Some of the colorcells will need to be loaded with duplicate RGB values. Because of this waste of colorcells, this technique should be used only when the graphics being preserved are slow for the client or the server to redraw.

To illustrate this trick, we are going to draw in one color (the foreground in the GC), set the `background_pixel` attribute of the window to a second color, and then draw something temporary over the top with a third color.* To do this, we need to allocate four colorcells with `XAllocColorCells`. The pixel values allocated will look something like this:

Color	Important Bits	Remaining bits
foreground:	----0--0------------------------	*all other bits don't matter*
background:	----0--1------------------------	*all other bits don't matter*
highlight1:	----1--0------------------------	*all other bits don't matter*
highlight2:	----1--1------------------------	*all other bits don't matter*

The bits indicated could have been any bits, but it is significant that only two bits distinguish the four pixel values. The first pixel value is used for the foreground, and the second for the background. We draw overlays in the third or fourth pixel value. Since we do not want to erase what was drawn in the foreground and background pixel values, we use a plane mask to restrict the drawing of the highlighting pixel value to a single plane, the one where bits in the highlighting pixel values are set to 1. When this entire plane (indicated by the 1 in pixel values `highlight1` and `highlight2`) is cleared, anything drawn in `highlight1` or `highlight2` disappears, and anything that was drawn in the foreground or background will reappear. The color in the colorcell indicated by `highlight2` must be the same as the color of colorcell `highlight1` so that the same highlighting color appears regardless of the bit already in the drawable that distinguishes the foreground and background pixel values.

`XAllocColorCells` does not return these four pixel values directly. Instead it returns the arrays *colors* and *plane_masks* that are more convenient for actually using the overlays than a single array of pixel values. (Each of these arrays has the number of members that was specified in the *ncolors* and *nplanes* arguments.) Both arrays consist of unsigned long values like pixel values. One array contains the plane masks of the overlay planes, and the other contains the pixel values that can be used for drawing independent of the overlay planes. Here are the values returned in each array after we call `XAlloc-ColorCells` with *ncolors* = 2 and *nplanes* = 1. These values are then used to generate the pixel values shown above.

Array Members		Important Bits	Remaining Bits
colors[0]	=	----0--0------------------------	*other bits don't matter*
colors[1]	=	----0--1------------------------	
plane_masks[0]	=	----1------------------------	*all other bits 0*

The two members of the *colors* array are used for the foreground and background. Pixel values `highlight1` and `highlight2` are composed by combining with a bitwise OR

---

*Note that the background of a window is redrawn by the server when Expose events occur, but this does not effect the process of drawing and removing overlays, because no Expose event will be triggered in this process. In other words, even though the background color is set as a window attribute and drawn by the server, the response to other graphics drawn on top is the same as if the background were drawn by the application. The background counts as a color that must be preserved.

each item in the *colors* array with each item in the *plane_masks* array. In this case, `highlight1` is (*colors*[0] | *plane_masks*[0]). The `plane_mask` in the GC used when highlighting should be set to the OR of the members of *plane_masks* used to make the highlighting pixel value. In this simplest case, highlighting should be done with the `plane_mask` in the GC set to *plane_masks*[0].

Note that `highlight2`, generated with (*colors*[1] | *plane_masks*[0]), can be useful. As mentioned earlier, `highlight2` can be used interchangeably with `highlight1`, as long as the `plane_mask` in the GC is set to *plane_masks*[0]. But `highlight2` has another use. With a GC that does not have its `plane_mask` set to *plane_masks*[0] (the GC used for drawing with the foreground or background), this fourth pixel value can be used for drawing in the highlighting color while wiping out the underlying graphics, so that when the highlight is removed, the background color appears regardless of the contents of the drawable before the highlighting.

We have been hinting at the fact that this overlay technique can be used with more than two colors and more than one plane. *ncolors* specifies the number of colors than can be drawn and preserved while drawing in the overlays. *nplanes* specifies how many separate one-color overlays you may have or how many bits of color are available in a single overlay. The pixel values in the *colors* array are the ones that will be preserved through overlays. By ORing together each *colors* with any combination of *plane_masks*, you get the pixel values that are used for drawing the overlays. Note, however, that the plane mask of the GC used for the overlaying must be the OR of the same combination of members of the *plane_masks* array as were used to generate the pixel value.

The total number of pixel values (colorcells) allocated by `XAllocColorCells` is $ncolors * 2^{nplanes}$. Note that the more planes you try to allocate, the less likely this request is to succeed, particularly on `PseudoColor` visuals. Therefore, if you are trying for multiple overlays or one multicolor overlay, this will probably work reliably only on `DirectColor` visuals, so make sure you have a backup plan for more common systems. In most cases, the underlying graphics can be redrawn if the overlays that would preserve them cannot be allocated. It is also possible to use backing store (which can save selective planes) or to manage your own off-screen pixmaps for use in fast redrawing of complicated graphics.

`XAllocColorCells` takes a *contig* argument that specifies whether the planes returned in *plane_masks* must be contiguous. The *contig* argument is normally set to `False`, specifying that the allocated planes need not be contiguous, because then the chances of success of the `XAllocColorCells` call are greater. There are more likely to be a number of noncontiguous planes available than the same number of contiguous planes. The *contig* argument may have to be set to `True` for imaging applications that want to be able to perform mathematical operations on the pixel values. It is easier to perform operations by shifting bits with contiguous planes than to achieve the same effect with random planes.

Each plane mask has one bit for `GrayScale` and `PseudoColor` or three bits for `DirectColor` or `TrueColor`, and none of the masks have bits in common.

Example 7-5 demonstrates allocating the read/write cells for a single overlay plane. It implements the overlay scheme described above. If this overlay plan fails, it allocates three colors so that a highlight can still be implemented even though the underlying graphics will have to be redrawn. If the color allocation fails completely, it uses black and white, which can be highlighted using the GXxor logical function to invert the color, as described in Section 7.3.3.

Example 7-5. Using XAllocColorCells to allocate read/write colorcells for overlay plane

```
#include <X11/Xlib.h>
#include <X11/Xutil.h>
#include <X11/Xos.h>
#include <stdio.h>

extern Display *display;
extern int screen_num;
extern unsigned long foreground, background_pixel, overlay_pixel_1,
        overlay_pixel_2;
extern unsigned long overlay_plane_mask;

#define MAX_COLORS 2
#define MAX_PLANES 1
#define MAX_CELLS 4             /* MAX_COLORS * 2 ^ MAX_PLANES */
#define CANNOT_OVERLAY 0
#define CAN_OVERLAY 1

int
get_colors()
{
    int default_depth;
    static char *name[] = {"Red", "Yellow", "Green", "Green"};
    XColor exact_defs[MAX_CELLS];
    Colormap default_cmap;
    int ncolors = 4;
    int plane_masks[MAX_PLANES];
    int colors[MAX_COLORS];
    int i;
    XVisualInfo visual_info;
    int class;

    default_depth = DefaultDepth(display, screen_num);
    default_cmap  = DefaultColormap(display, screen_num);
    if (default_depth == 1) {
        /* Must be StaticGray, use black and white */
        background_pixel = WhitePixel(display, screen_num);
        foreground = BlackPixel(display, screen_num);
        printf("using black and white\n");
        return(CANNOT_OVERLAY);
    }

    if (!XMatchVisualInfo(display, screen_num, default_depth,
            PseudoColor, &visual_info)) {
        if (!XMatchVisualInfo(display, screen_num, default_depth,
                DirectColor, &visual_info)) {
            /* No PseudoColor or TrueColor visual available
             * at default_depth; some applications might try
             * for a GrayScale visual here if they can use
             * gray to advantage, before giving up and using
             * black and white */
            background_pixel = WhitePixel(display, screen_num);
            foreground = BlackPixel(display, screen_num);
            printf("using black and white\n");
```

```
                    return(CANNOT_OVERLAY);
            }
    }

    /* Got PseudoColor or TrueColor visual at default depth */

    /* The visual we found is not necessarily the default
     * visual, and therefore it is not necessarily the one
     * we used to create our window; however, we now know
     * for sure that color is supported, so the following
     * code will work (or fail in a controlled way) */

    if (XAllocColorCells (display, default_cmap, False, plane_masks,
            1, colors, 2) == 0) {
        /* Can't get enough read/write cells to overlay;
         * try at least to get three colors */
        if (XAllocColorCells (display, default_cmap, False,
                plane_masks, 0, colors, 3) == 0) {
            /* Can't even get that; give up and use
             * black and white */
                    background_pixel = WhitePixel(display,
                            screen_num);
                    foreground = BlackPixel(display, screen_num);
            printf("using black and white\n");
            return(CANNOT_OVERLAY);
        }
        else
            ncolors = 3;
    }

    /* Allocated three or four colorcells succesfully,
     * now set their colors -- three and four are set
     * to the same RGB values */
    for (i = 0; i < ncolors; i++)
    {
        if (!XParseColor (display, default_cmap, name[i],
                &exact_defs[i])) {
            fprintf(stderr, "basic: color name %s not in database",
                    name[i]);
            exit(0);
        }
        /* This needed before calling XStoreColors */
        exact_defs[i].flags = DoRed | DoGreen | DoBlue;
    }
    printf("got RGB values\n");

    /* Set pixel value in struct to the allocated ones */
    exact_defs[0].pixel = colors[0];
    exact_defs[1].pixel = colors[1];
    exact_defs[2].pixel = colors[0] | plane_masks[0];
    exact_defs[3].pixel = colors[1] | plane_masks[0];

    /* This sets the color of the read/write cells */
    XStoreColors (display, default_cmap, exact_defs, ncolors);
    printf("stored colors\n");

    background_pixel = exact_defs[0].pixel;
```

```
        foreground = exact_defs[1].pixel;
        if (ncolors == 4) {
            overlay_pixel_1 = exact_defs[2].pixel;
            overlay_pixel_2 = exact_defs[3].pixel;
            overlay_plane_mask = plane_masks[0];
            printf("set can\n");
            return(CAN_OVERLAY);
        }
        else {
            /* This must be used as a normal color, not overlay */
            overlay_pixel_1 = exact_defs[2].pixel;
            printf("set can't\n");
            return(CANNOT_OVERLAY);
        }
}
```

7.4.3 Using XAllocColorPlanes

XAllocColorPlanes also allocates read/write colorcells but in a different way than XAllocColorCells. XAllocColorPlanes is used when you want to be able to change the amount of a primary color in graphics without having to redraw them. In other words, perhaps you are looking at an image and would like to increase the redness of it. The best way to do this is to increase the amount of red in every pixel value. XAllocColorPlanes would be the way to allocate colors to allow this. It is rarely used except in imaging applications and 3-D graphics and will rarely work except on 24-plane workstations with a DirectColor visual.

Note that for applications like a paint mixing program, in which you have three bars for the three primary colors and a palette that shows the mixed color, you would not use XAllocColorPlanes. The correct way to implement this is to allocate a single read/write color for the palette and to change it dynamically. (If the primary colors are displayed, they should be allocated using read-only colors.)

The piece of code shown in Example 7-6 is similar to Example 7-5 but it uses XAllocColorPlanes. It is somewhat sketchy, because real applications that use XAllocColorPlanes are complicated.

After allocating colors with XAllocColorPlanes, you can then use XStoreColors to set the colors. When *nred*, *ngreen*, and *nblue* are each 8, only one call to XAllocColorPlanes and one call to XStoreColors are necessary to allocate and set all 16 million colors of an entire 24-plane colormap.

Example 7-6. Using XAllocColorPlanes to allocate colorcells for DirectColor

```
#define PIXELS 256

Display *display;
int screen_num;
int contig = False;              /* Noncontiguous planes */
unsigned long pixels[PIXELS];    /* Return of pixel values */

/* Number of independent pixel values allocate */
unsigned int ncolors = PIXELS;

/* Need PIXELS * 2 ^ maxplanes defs, where maxplanes
 * is the largest of nred, ngreen, and nblue */
XColor defs[2048];

/* Number of planes to allocate for each primary */
unsigned int nreds = 3, ngreens = 3, nblues = 2;

/* Returned masks, which bits of pixel value for each primary */
unsigned long red_mask, green_mask, blue_mask;

Colormap colormap;
Status status;

/* Open display, etc. */
/* Get or create large DirectColor colormap */

while (status = XAllocColorPlanes(display, colormap,
        contig, pixels, ncolors, nreds, ngreens, nblues,
        &red_mask, &green_mask, &blue_mask) == 0) {
    /* Make contig False if it was True; reduce value of
     * ncolors; reduce value of nreds, ngreens, and/or
     * nblues; or try allocating new map; break when
     * you give up */
    break;
}
if (status == 0) {
    fprintf(stderr, "%s: couldn't allocate requested colorcells",
            argv[0]);
    exit(-1);
}

/* Define desired colors in defs */

while (status = XStoreColors(display, colormap, defs,
        ncolors) == 0) {
    fprintf(stderr, "%s: can't store colors", argv[0]);
    /* Try to fix problem here, exit or break */
    exit(-1);
}

/* Draw your shaded stuff! */
```

7.5 Getting Complete Visual Information

As mentioned earlier, some systems define more than one visual. The default visual might not be the most appropriate for your application. Moreover, the visual found using the technique described in Section 7.3.2 using XMatchVisualInfo is fine for applications with routine color needs but is not necessarily the best. As you may recall, XMatchVisualInfo returns a single visual arbitrarily selected from the list that matches the passed visual class and depth. The most thorough method is to get a complete list of visual information for every available visual using XGetVisualInfo and then choose from these.

XGetVisualInfo returns a list of visual structures that match the attributes specified by template and mask arguments. The template is an XVisualInfo structure with members set to the required values, and the mask indicates which members are matched with the list of available visuals. By passing an empty template structure, you can get a complete list of XVisualInfo structures.

7.5.1 The XVisualInfo Structure

The XVisualInfo structure returns information about the available visuals. It is used both to select a visual type from those available and as a source of information while using a particular visual.

The XVisualInfo structure is shown in Example 7-7.

Example 7-7. The XVisualInfo structure

```
typedef struct {
    Visual *visual;
    VisualID visualid;
    int screen_num;
    unsigned int depth;
    int class;
    unsigned long red_mask;
    unsigned long green_mask;
    unsigned long blue_mask;
    int colormap_size;   /* Same as map_entries member of Visual */
    int bits_per_rgb;
} XVisualInfo;
```

The visual member is a pointer to the internal Visual structure. This pointer is used as the *visual* argument of XCreateWindow and XCreateColormap.

The visualid member is not normally needed by applications.

As discussed earlier, the class member specifies whether the screen is to be considered color or monochrome and changeable or immutable. The class member can be one of the constants DirectColor, GrayScale, PseudoColor, StaticColor, Static-Gray, or TrueColor.

The red_mask, green_mask, and blue_mask members are used only for the DirectColor and TrueColor visual classes, where there is a separate map for each primary color. They define which bits of the pixel value index into the colormap for each primary color. Each mask has one contiguous set of bits, with no bits in common with the other masks. These values are zero for monochrome and most four- to eight-plane color systems.

The colormap_size member of the structure tells you how many different pixel values are valid with this visual. For a monochrome screen, this value is two. For the default visual of an eight-plane color system, this value is typically 254 or 256 (two colors are often reserved for the cursor). For DirectColor and TrueColor, colormap_size will be the number of cells for the biggest individual pixel subfield. The colormap_size member is the same as the map_entries member of the visual structure.

The bits_per_rgb member specifies how many bits in each of the red, green, and blue values in a colorcell are used to drive the RGB gun in the screen. For a monochrome screen, this value is one. For the default visual of an eight-plane color system, this value is typically eight. The pixel subfields (the red, green, and blue values in each colorcell) are 16-bit unsigned short values, but only the highest bits_per_rgb bits are used to drive the RGB gun in the screen. This number corresponds the number of bits of resolution in the Digital to Analog Converter (DAC) in the screen hardware.

7.5.2 Example of Choosing a Visual

Example 7-8 shows a routine that uses XGetVisualInfo to get all the visuals of depth 8 on the current screen, as defined by the X server, and then creates a colormap and window.

Example 7-8. Code to match visuals

```
#include <X11/Xlib.h>
#include <X11/Xutil.h>

visual()
{
Display *display;
Colormap colormap;
Window window;
XSetWindowAttributes attributes;
unsigned long valuemask;
int screen_num;

    .
    .
    .
XVisualInfo vTemplate;      /* Template of the visual we want */
XVisualInfo *visualList;    /* List of XVisualInfo structs that
                             * match */
int visualsMatched;         /* Number of visuals that match */
    .
    .
    .
/* Set up the XVisualInfo template so that it returns a list
 * of all the visuals of depth 8 defined on the current screen
```

Example 7-8. Code to match visuals (continued)

```
 * by the X server */
vTemplate.screen = screen_num;
vTemplate.depth = 8;
visualList = XGetVisualInfo (display, VisualScreenMask |
        VisualDepthMask, &vTemplate, &visualsMatched);
if ( visualsMatched == 0 )
    fatalError ("No matching visuals\n");

/* Create a colormap for a window using the first of the
 * visuals in the list ov XVisualInfo structs returned by
 * XGetVisualInfo */
colormap = XCreateColormap (display, RootWindow(display, screen_num),
    visualList[0].visual, AllocNone);

/* Must specify colormap attribute if using nondefault visual */
attributes.colormap = colormap;
valuemask |= CWColormap;
    .
    .
    .
window = XCreateWindow (display, RootWindow(display, screen_num),
    x, y, width, height, border_width, vTemplate.depth,
    InputOutput, visualList[0].visual, valuemask, &attributes);
XSetWindowColormap(display, window, colormap);

/* All done with visual information; free it */

XFree(visualList);
    .
    .
    .
} /* End routine */
```

Notice that the list of XVisualInfo structures is freed with XFree after use.

7.6 The GrayScale Visual

On a gray-scale workstation or a GrayScale visual on a color workstation, a color application should still work correctly. The only problem might be that when colors are allocated, the closest physically possible colors (returned by XAllocColor) will result in shades of gray that provide insufficient contrast. The best way to avoid this is to explicitly check for the StaticGray visual. For true bulletproof operation, it is a good idea to check any user-specified colors to make sure they contrast.

The color names "gray0" through "gray100", spelled with an "e" or an "a", can be used with XParseColor to get RGB values for various grays.

You must set the red, green, and blue values to be equal. Some servers only use one of the values, and others combine all three according to the NTSC standard that makes color television signals work on black-and-white televisions:

```
intensity = (.30 * red) + (.59 * green) + (.11 * blue)
```

MIT's implementations use a least-squares algorithm that determines the closest RGB values in the (gray) colormap to the RGB values specified. Exactly what algorithm is used is up to the server implementor.

7.7 Creating and Installing Colormaps

In discussing colormaps earlier in this chapter, we mentioned that there are hardware colormaps and virtual colormaps, but we did not discuss the ramifications of this fact.

A hardware colormap is a physical register from which the screen hardware reads the RGB intensity values that generate the colors on the screen. Most workstations have only one hardware colormap, in which case all windows on the screen are interpreted using the same colormap. Some high performance workstations have multiple hardware colormaps, in which case separate windows may have their own independent colormaps.

If the hardware colormap cannot be changed, it is termed *immutable*. Monochrome systems normally have an immutable colormap, since it does little good to swap the two entries or make them both black or white. Some low-cost color systems and X terminals have immutable hardware colormaps. The StaticColor, StaticGray, and TrueColor visuals are the only visuals that can possibly work on systems that have immutable hardware colormaps. In immutable colormaps, no client can allocate private colorcells and all RGB values are preset. On these systems, XCreateColormap succeeds, but it just gives you another copy of the default colormap (or one of the default colormaps if there are multiple immutable colormaps). The application should check for this when creating colormaps.

On most color workstations, you can write new values into the hardware colormap or colormaps to change that mapping. These hardware colormaps are termed *changeable*. The DirectColor, GrayScale, and PseudoColor visuals are available only on systems that have changeable colormaps.

X manages multiple colormaps by keeping *virtual colormaps* in memory and installing them as instructed by the window manager. *Installing* a colormap is the process of moving a virtual colormap into the hardware colormap. Only installed colormaps are used to determine the colors appearing on the screen. When there is only one hardware colormap and a new virtual colormap is installed, the virtual colormap that was previously installed becomes *uninstalled*.

Up to this point in this chapter, we have been allocating colors out of the default colormap, which is created and installed when the server starts up. On the most common color workstations, with four to eight planes, it is quite easy for clients that require precise colors to allocate all the available colorcells. Virtual colormaps are a response to this problem. When a client cannot get the colorcells it needs from the installed colormap, it can create a new virtual one. The window manager will then install this virtual colormap when this application is in use.

When a virtual colormap is installed and there is only one hardware colormap, all the clients that used the old colormap will be displayed in false colors, since the pixel values in their windows will be interpreted according to the new colormap.

When an application creates a virtual colormap, it must set the colormap window attribute of its top-level window so that the window manager can find out what colormap to install. By default, this attribute indicates the default colormap. If its subwindows use different colormaps from the main window, there is a property that can be set to tell this to the window manager, as described in Chapter 10, *Interclient Communication*.

Several of the older window managers do not install colormaps properly. Under these, an application that creates its own colormap also has to install it. However, as these window managers are revised or go out of use, it becomes a hard rule that application should never install their own colormaps. This is required by the current conventions described in Chapter 10.

By now you should be getting the idea that it is much better to arrange to share the default colormap with the other applications than to try to create one of your own. The only time when you should really need to create a special colormap is when you are doing smooth shading or similar applications that need many strangely distributed colors. On the other hand, creating a virtual colormap might be the only way to make your application that has demanding color needs work on a system that provides only a PseudoColor visual. On systems with multiple hardware colormaps, you can create your own colormap and have it installed without affecting other applications. You can use XListInstalled-Colormaps to get information about how many colormaps are installed into the hardware.

7.7.1 Functions for Manipulating Colormaps

The following functions should be used by applications only if they need a special purpose colormap:

XCreateColormap
: Creates a virtual colormap resource, either with no allocated entries or with all allocated read/write, that matches the passed visual. If no entries are allocated, they can be allocated either as read/write or as read-only cells. If all entries are allocated read/write, the colormap is completely private and just needs its colors set with XStoreColors.

XFreeColormap
: Uninstalls the specified virtual colormap and frees the resources associated with the colormap. Applications are allowed to use this. Sends a ColormapNotify event to any windows that were using the colormap.

XListInstalledColormaps
: Lists the installed colormaps.

XCopyColormapAndFree
: Moves all the client's existing colormap entries to a new colormap and frees those entries of the old colormap. This is used when colorcell allocation fails and some cells have already been allocated. It saves needing to create a colormap and start from the beginning allocating colors. For applications with special color needs that can't make do, they can

call `XCopyColormapAndFree`, set their colormap window attribute, and continue allocating colors in the new colormap where they left off.

`XSetWindowColormap`   Sets the colormap window attribute of a window.

The following functions are use by the window manager to install and uninstall colormaps:

`XInstallColormap`   A function only to be used by window managers to install a colormap. Any window using that colormap ID as its colormap attribute receives a `ColormapNotify` event.

`XUninstallColormap`   A function only to be used by window managers to uninstall a colormap. Removes a virtual colormap from the set of installed hardware colormaps. On systems with only one hardware colormap, the default colormap is reinstalled. Sends `ColormapNotify` event to windows that are using the specified map.

7.7.2 The ColormapNotify Event

`ColormapNotify` events notify an application when the colormap specified in the colormap attribute for a particular window has been installed, uninstalled, or freed or when the attribute itself has been changed. The former is used by applications, and the latter by window managers.

If your application wants to know when your colormap is installed or uninstalled, it should watch for these events and act accordingly. To receive `ColormapNotify` events, pass `ColormapChangeMask` (ORed with the other masks you need) to `XSelectInput`. Example 7-9 shows the `XColormapEvent` structure.

Example 7-9. The ColormapEvent structure

```
typedef struct {
    int type;
    unsigned long serial;    /* # of last request processed by server */
    Bool send_event;         /* True if this came from SendEvent
                              * request */
    Display *display;        /* Display the event was read from */
    Window window;
    Colormap colormap;       /* Colormap or None */
    Bool new;
    int state;               /* ColormapInstalled, ColormapUninstalled */
} XColormapEvent;
```

Here is a brief explanation of each member of the `XColormapEvent` structure:

window
: The window for which this event was selected, whose colormap attribute was changed or whose colormap specified in that attribute was installed, uninstalled, or freed.

colormap
: The colormap associated with the window, either a colormap ID or the constant `None`. It will be `None` only if this event was in response to an `XFreeColormap` call.

new
: `True` when the colormap attribute has been changed, or `False` when the colormap is installed or uninstalled.

state
: Either `ColormapInstalled` or `ColormapUninstalled`; it indicates whether the colormap is installed or uninstalled.

`XFreeColormap`, `XInstallColormap`, and `XUninstallColormap` generate this event for windows that have their colormap attribute set to the colormap that was affected. `XSetWindowColormap` and `XChangeWindowAttributes` can also generate this event. From the information in the structure, you can tell which of these calls generated the event and what the current status of the colormap is. See Chapter 10, *Interclient Communication*, in this manual and Appendix L, *Interclient Communication Conventions*, of Volume Zero, *X Protocol Reference Manual*, (as of the second printing) for an additional description of the conventions regarding colormaps.

7.7.3 The Required Colormap List

The X protocol specifies that each server can specify a required list of colormaps, which affects what happens when other colormaps are installed or uninstalled. Here is what the protocol specification says about the required list (translated into Xlib terms):

> At any time, there is a subset of the installed maps, viewed as an ordered list, called the required list. The length of the required list is at most `min_maps`, where `min_maps` is a member of the `Display` structure. The required list is maintained as follows. When a colormap is an explicit argument to `XInstallColormap`, it is added to the head of the list, and the list is truncated at the tail if necessary to keep the length of the list to at most `min_maps`. When a colormap is an explicit argument to `XUninstallColormap` and it is in the required list, it is removed from the list. A colormap is not added to the required list when it is installed implicitly by the server, and the server cannot implicitly uninstall a colormap that is in the required list.

In less precise words, the `min_maps` most recently installed maps are guaranteed to be installed. This number will often be one; clients needing multiple colormaps should beware.

7.8 Standard Colormaps

A *standard colormap* is one in which the mapping between pixel values and colors is predictable. The purpose of standard colormaps is to encourage sharing of entire colormaps (not just individual cells) between applications that have too demanding color needs to be able to allocate read-only colors out of the default colormaps.

X defines a set of properties that contain information describing commonly used colormaps. An application reads these properties by calling XGetRGBColormaps (XGetStandardColormap prior to R4). This call returns an XStandardColormap structure that contains enough information so that the application can calculate the colors in every colormap cell (or a certain range within the colormap). This structure may also include the ID of a colormap matching this description that was created by the window manager or another client. Otherwise, the application then creates a new colormap and uses this information to allocate and set the colors according to the information in the property.

But how does the sharing work? After creating this colormap, the application sets the ID of the created colormap into the colormap field of the XStandardColormap structure and then calls XSetRGBColormaps (XSetStandardColormap prior to R4). This resets the property, so that the next time another client calls XGetRGBColormaps, the colormap field of the returned structure will actually contain the ID of the appropriate colormap.

Therefore, although an application must have the code to create, allocate, and set colors in a standard colormap, in some cases this code will not be executed because some other client will have already done the work. After calling XGetRGBColormaps, if the colormap field is zero, the application must create the colormap. Otherwise, the colormap field holds the ID of an appropriate colormap.

When an application uses standard colormaps, two (or more) instances of the application can run at the same time without increasing the load on the system caused by creating multiple copies of the same colormap. Applications that do not use standard colormaps will end up creating separate but identical colormaps. The window manager will switch these in and out of the hardware colormap whenever a different instance is in use. Although nothing on the screen will change color because both the colormaps are identical, the server will be performing unnecessary installing and uninstalling, and the extra colormaps will waste server memory.

In some cases, the window manager or even the server will create one or more standard colormaps. This does not change how applications work at all. Applications do not care whether it was the window manager, the server, or some other client that created a standard colormap.

If your application does not create or use a custom colormap, you can skip this section if pressed for time.

Applications can also use the knowledge about a standard colormap to optimize the process of figuring out which existing pixel values correspond to required colors and which colors must be allocated and set from scratch.

7.8.1 The Standard Colormap Properties

The standard colormap properties contain information about a few commonly used colormaps. However, note that even if an application creates a custom colormap unlike any of these, it should still use the standard property mechanism by creating its own standard colormap structure.

Properties were introduced in Section 2.1.4. For a more complete description of properties, see Section 10.1.

In the call to XGetRGBColormaps (or XGetStandardColormap), you specify one of these atoms like XA_RGB_BEST_MAP (or, if necessary, one unique to your application).

The following list names the atoms and describes the colormap associated with each one:

XA_RGB_DEFAULT_MAP
>This property defines part of the system default colormap. This colormap may be initially completely unallocated, or it may contain a selection of read-only colorcells with the RGB values from the color database and a few unallocated cells for use by applications that need read/write cells. A typical allocation of the XA_RGB_DEFAULT_MAP on eight-plane screens is all the colors produced from any combination of six reds, six greens, and six blues. This gives 216 uniformly distributed colors and leaves 40 for other programs or for special purpose colors for text, borders, and so on. A typical allocation for the XA_RGB_DEFAULT_MAP on 24-plane screens is 64 reds, 64 greens, and 64 blues. This gives about one million uniformly distributed colors (64 intensities of 4096 different hues) and leaves lots of colorcells available for other purposes.

XA_RGB_BEST_MAP
>This property defines the "best" RGB colormap available on the screen. Of course, this is a subjective evaluation. Many image-processing and 3-D programs need to use all available colormap cells and to distribute as many perceptually distinct colors as possible over those cells. In this case, there may be more green values available than red and more green or red than blue.

>On an eight-plane DirectColor visual, XA_RGB_BEST_MAP is usually a 3/3/2 allocation. On a 24-plane DirectColor visual, XA_RGB_BEST_MAP is usually an 8/8/8 allocation. On other screens, XA_RGB_BEST_MAP is purely up to the implementor of the server.

XA_RGB_RED_MAP, XA_RGB_GREEN_MAP, XA_RGB_BLUE_MAP
>These properties define all-red, all-green, and all-blue colormaps, respectively. These maps are used by programs that make color-separated images. For example, a user might generate a full color image on an eight-plane screen by rendering an image once with high color resolution in red, once with green, and once with blue and exposing a single frame in a camera with three images.

XA_RGB_GRAY_MAP
>This property describes the "best" gray-scale colormap available on the screen.

7.8.2 The XStandardColormap Structure

As described above, an application that wants to use a standard colormap must get the structure that contains the specification for the colormap using XGetRGBColormaps (XGet-StandardColormap prior to R4). Some servers and window managers, particularly on high performance workstations, create some or all of the standard colormaps when they initialize. If the desired colormap has already been created, it is returned in the colormap member of the XStandardColormap structure shown in Example 7-10. If the colormap does not yet exist, the colormap member will be zero. In that case, the application can create a colormap and allocate entries to match the specification in the members of XStandardColormap, then call XSetRGBColormaps (XSetStandard-Colormap prior to R4) to allow other clients to share this colormap.

Example 7-10. The XStandardColormap structure

```
typedef struct _XStandardColormap {
    Colormap colormap;
    unsigned long red_max, green_max, blue_max;
    unsigned long red_mult, green_mult, blue_mult;
    unsigned long base_pixel;
    VisualID visualid;              /* Added in R4:  ICCCM version 1 */
    XID killid;                     /* Added in R4:  ICCCM version 1 */
} XStandardColormap;
```

The members of the XStandardColormap structure are as follows:

- The colormap member is the ID of a colormap created by the XCreateColormap function or the default colormap. This ID can be used to install a virtual colormap into the hardware colormap.

- The red_max, green_max, and blue_max fields give the maximum red, green, and blue values, respectively. A typical allocation that provides = 216 read-only, shareable colors in a PseudoColor colormap on a standard eight-plane workstation is red_max = 5, green_max = 5, and blue_max = 5. This leaves 40 cells available for special colors and private, nonshareable purposes. On a 24-plane workstation, there would be eight bits available for each color in a TrueColor visual, which would allow 256 shades of each primary color. In this case, red_max = 255, green_max = 255, and blue_max = 255. This map would include = 16.38 million total colors.

- The red_mult, green_mult, and blue_mult fields scale each pixel subfield into the proper range in the 16-bit RGB value in the colorcell with the range 0 to 65535. The red pixel subfield is moved red_mult bits toward the most significant bit of the pixel value.

For a 3/3/2 DirectColor allocation (eight reds, eight greens, four blues), red_mult might be 32, green_mult might be 4, and blue_mult might be 1 (as shown in Figure 7-5). These effectively move the red value into the most significant bits of the RGB value in the colorcell, the green into the middle, and the blue into the least significant bits. This arrangement is arbitrary but useful. For a six-colors-each allocation, which must be PseudoColor since the planes cannot be evenly allocated to separate primaries, red_mult might be 36, green_mult might be 6, and blue_mult might be 1.

- The `base_pixel` field gives the base value that is added to the pixel value calculated from the RGB values and scale factors. Usually the `base_pixel` is obtained from a call to the `XAllocColorPlanes` function.

- The `visualid` field is the ID of a server resource associated with each visual, of type `VisualID`. You will need this ID only if you intend to use standard colormaps. This field was added in R4 because only with this information can standard colormaps be used with other than the default visual. Prior to R4, standard colormaps were not in wide use, partly because they could only be used with the default visual.

- The `killid` field returns a number that is used if the application needs to free the colormap for some reason. If `killid` is greater than one, then the resources should be freed by calling `XKillClient` with the `killid` field as the argument. If `killid` is one, then the resources should be freed by calling `XFreeColormap` with the `colormap` field as the argument. If `killid` is zero, then no attempt should be made to free the resources.

Only the `colormap`, `red_max`, `red_mult`, and `base_pixel` fields of the `XStandardColormap` structure are use for `GrayScale` colormaps.

7.8.3 The 3/3/2 Standard Colormap

Now let's look at a typical standard colormap. The following example describes the 3/3/2 `DirectColor` standard colormap used on eight-plane screens. Three planes are used for red, three planes for green, and two planes for blue. This 3/3/2 allocation allows values in the range of:

```
red     0-7     thus    red_max     =   7
green   0-7             green_max   =   7
blue    0-3             blue_max    =   3
```

To obtain the pixel value, these RGB values must be shifted to their corresponding planes. If the red value is contained in the three most significant planes or bits, the green values in the three next most significant planes or bits, and the blue value in the two least significant planes or bits, then the pixel can be constructed as shown in Figure 7-5.

In a `DirectColor` system like this, the multiples are equal to 2^n, where n is their lowest plane or bit position. If the red, green, and blue were stored in a different order, the multiples would not be 32, 4, 1 but would still be calculated from the above description and formula. The 3/3/2 standard colormap allocation is fairly standard.

7.8.4 Creating and Using a Standard Colormap

Two members were added to the `XStandardColormap` structure in Release 4 to comply with the ICCCM (interclient communication conventions, described in Chapter 10). Because of this, there are two different sets of routines that manage standard colormaps, one for use with R3 (and earlier) and the other for use with R4 (and later). The R3 routines will also work under R4, but an application using them will not comply with current conventions. The

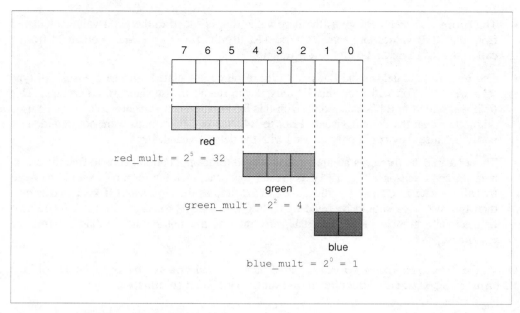

Figure 7-5. Shifting pixel subfields into pixel value

R3 routines are XGetStandardColormap and XSetStandardColormap, and the R4 routines are XGetRGBColormaps and XSetRGBColormaps. The reason for the plural form of the R4 routine XGetRGBColormaps is that it returns a list of colormaps; it also has a *count* argument not present in the R3 routine. According to the ICCCM, only queries of the XA_RGB_DEFAULT_MAP standard colormap can return more than one structure.

Example 7-11 gets information about the XA_RGB_BEST_MAP standard colormap, creates it if no other client already has, calculates pixel values from it, and sets the colormap window attribute of the window. Note that under R3, the created colormap can be used only with windows created using the default visual, because the standard colormap information under R3 does not include a visual. This example gives up and falls back on read-only colorcell allocation if the standard colormap property is not defined by the server or if creating a colormap returns the default colormap (which happens on systems with an immutable hardware colormap).

Example 7-11. Code to create and use XA_RGB_BEST_MAP

```
        .
        .
        .
#define USE_DEFAULT_COLORMAP 1
#define USE_STANDARD_COLORMAP 0

void main(argc, argv)
int argc;
char **argv;
{
    XStandardColormap best_map_info;
    XColor *exact_defs;
```

Example 7-11. Code to create and use XA_RGB_BEST_MAP (continued)

```
      XSetWindowAttributes attrib;
      unsigned long attribmask;
      int i, j, k, l;
      int ncells;
      XVisualInfo *vlist, vinfo_template, *v;
      int num_vis;
      int count;
      Visual *visual;
      int strategy = USE_STANDARD_COLORMAP;
         .
         .
         .
      /* Open display */

      visual = DefaultVisual(display, screen_num);
#ifdef X11R3
        if (XGetStandardColormap(display, RootWindow(display,
                       screen_num), &best_map_info,
             XA_RGB_BEST_MAP) == 0) {
#else /* R4 or later */
        if (XGetRGBColormaps(display, RootWindow(display,
                       screen_num), &best_map_info, &count,
             XA_RGB_BEST_MAP) == 0) {
#endif /* X11R3 */
                printf("%s: RGB_BEST_MAP colormap property not set.\n",
                    argv[0]);
          /* Give up standard colormaps; use one of the
           * basic color strategies */
          get_colors();
          strategy = USE_DEFAULT_COLORMAP;
    }
        else if (best_map_info.colormap) {
        /* Someone else created the map we need; make sure
         * it's valid, then we'll use it below */
        if (best_map_info.red_max == 0) {
            printf("%s: RGB_BEST_MAP colormap property is set\n",
                    argv[0]);
            printf("but is missing data.\n");
            strategy = USE_DEFAULT_COLORMAP;
        }
                attrib.colormap = best_map_info.colormap;
        }
    else if (best_map_info.visualid == 0) {
        printf("%s: Standard colormap property is set\n", argv[0]);
        printf("but is missing data.");
        /* Some systems define the properties but don't
         * place any data in them; this is a server bug,
         * but we'll check for it anyway */
        /* Fall back on a basic color strategy */
        strategy = USE_DEFAULT_COLORMAP;
    }
    else {
        /* Got information, but the described colormap
         * has not been created yet; create it and
         * allocate all cells read/write */
```

Example 7-11. Code to create and use XA_RGB_BEST_MAP (continued)

```
                /* XCreateColormap requires a visual argument
                 * (pointer to a Visual structure); however, the
                 * XStandardColormap structure returns a VisualID,
                 * which might not be the default visual;
                 * Converting between these two is painful */
                vlist = XGetVisualInfo(display, VisualNoMask,
                        &vinfo_template, &num_vis);
                for (v = vlist; v < vlist + num_vis; v++) {
                    if (v->visualid == best_map_info.visualid) {
                        visual = v->visual;
                        break;
                    }
                }

                best_map_info.colormap = XCreateColormap(display,
                        RootWindow(display, screen_num),
                        visual, AllocAll);

                if (best_map_info.colormap ==
                        DefaultColormap(display, screen_num)) {
                    printf("%s: hardware colormap is immutable:\n",
                            argv[0]);
                    printf("cannot create new colormap.\n");
                }

                attrib.colormap = best_map_info.colormap;

                ncells = best_map_info.base_pixel +
                        ((best_map_info.red_max + 1) *
                        (best_map_info.green_max + 1) *
                        (best_map_info.blue_max + 1));

                exact_defs = (XColor *) calloc(sizeof(XColor), ncells);

                /* Permute the levels of red, green, and blue */
                l = best_map_info.base_pixel;
                for (i = 0; i < best_map_info.blue_max; i++) {
                    exact_defs[l].blue = 65536 * i / best_map_info.blue_max;
                    for (j = 0; j < best_map_info.green_max; j++) {
                        exact_defs[l].green = 65536 * j /
                                best_map_info.green_max;
                        for (k = 0; k < best_map_info.red_max; k++) {
                            exact_defs[l].red = 65536 * k /
                                    best_map_info.red_max;
                            l++;
                        }
                    }
                }

                XStoreColors (display, best_map_info.colormap, exact_defs,
                        ncells);

                /* If to be used in a window not created with the
                 * default visual, must create the window first and
                 * use instead of RootWindow in this call; here we
                 * assume the default visual */
#ifdef X11R3
                XSetStandardColormap(display, RootWindow(display,
                        screen_num), &best_map_info, XA_RGB_BEST_MAP);
```

Example 7-11. Code to create and use XA_RGB_BEST_MAP (continued)

```
#else /* R4 or later */
        XSetRGBColormaps(display, RootWindow(display, screen_num),
                count, &best_map_info, XA_RGB_BEST_MAP);
#endif /* X11R3 */
    }

    if (strategy == USE_STANDARD_COLORMAP) {
        /* We must not have called get_colors above,
         * must be using standard colormaps strategy */

        /* Note that we act like we have already allocated pixel
         * pixel values, even though actually another client did */
        background_pixel = best_map_info.base_pixel  +
                (best_map_info.red_max * best_map_info.red_mult) +
                (best_map_info.green_max * best_map_info.green_mult) +
                (best_map_info.blue_max * best_map_info.blue_mult);

        attribmask = CWBackPixel | CWColormap;

        foreground_pixel = (best_map_info.green_max *
                best_map_info.green_mult / 2) +
                best_map_info.base_pixel;

        border_pixel = (best_map_info.blue_max *
                best_map_info.blue_mult / 2) +
                best_map_info.base_pixel;
    }

    /* Create opaque window */
    win = XCreateWindow(display, RootWindow(display,screen_num), x,
            y, width, height, borderwidth,
            DefaultDepth(display, screen_num),
            InputOutput, visual, attribmask, &attrib);
        .
        .
        .

}
```

This code begins by reading the XA_RGB_BEST_MAP property using the XGet-RGBColormaps or XGetStandardColormap call. (The name XGet-RGBColormaps suggests that the function returns a description of multiple colormaps—but this is true only for XA_RGB_DEFAULT_MAP. Therefore, the R3 and R4 functions are truly equivalent as used here.) If one of these calls succeeds, the property is defined and its contents have been placed in the best_map_info structure. Since any other, perhaps buggy, client might have set this property (like your own application while you are debugging it), it is a good idea not to trust its contents any more than necessary. (Properties set on the root window remain defined even after the client that set them has exited.) The code checks to make sure that the fields contain reasonable values before using them.

If the colormap field of best_map_info is nonzero, it should be the ID of a standard colormap that another client has created. Your application can immediately proceed to use the pixel values in this colormap as though your application had already allocated them read-only, even though in reality some other client allocated them read/write.

On the other hand, if the `colormap` field is zero, your application needs to create, allocate, and set the values of the standard colormap itself. You allocate the cells read/write, because this allows you to explicitly set the RGB values of each pixel value. Even though you allocate the cells read/write, you should use them as if they were read-only, so that other applications can share them after you reset the `XA_RGB_BEST_MAP` property to include the new colormap ID. As this suggests, a read/write cell, even though described earlier as being private and changeable by that one client, can be public if all the applications agree not to change its RGB values.

The algorithm used to store RGB values into the cells in the colormap is somewhat arbitrary. Conventions for it will probably be adopted by the X Consortium when there is more interest in standard colormaps. Any algorithm is good enough to allow two instances of the same application to share a colormap. But for two different applications to share the colormap, each must know exactly what RGB values the other would place in the colormap if the other were run before the colormap was created.

The `XGetVisualInfo` call is described in Section 7.5.

If you pass `AllocAll` to `XCreateColormap`, you do not need to make an `XAlloc-ColorCells` call to allocate all the cells read/write. However, you can use `AllocAll` only if you intend the entire colormap to be read-only to all clients. Some clients want a few cells preserved to be rewriteable for dynamically changing colors. If yours is that way, you must use `AllocNone` and then call `XAllocColorCells` once to create the standard portion of the colormap and again to allocate the cells your application will treat as private.

Once the colormap window attribute of a window is set, the window manager will take care of installing the colormap. When there is only one hardware colormap, the window manager usually installs an application's colormap when that application contains the pointer (for real-estate type window managers) or is given the keyboard focus (for click-to-type style window managers).

When a window manager creates a standard colormap, it can use a slightly different technique to make sure that the standard colormap remains defined even after the window manager exits. Assuming that it has already checked to see whether some other client has created a standard colormap and none has, it performs the following sequence of steps:

- Create a new connection to the same server.

- Determine the color capabilities of the screen. Choose a visual.

- Create a colormap (not required for `XA_RGB_DEFAULT_MAP`).

- Call `XAllocColorPlanes` or `XAllocColorCells` to allocate cells in the colormap (if did not use `AllocAll` flag when creating the colormap).

- Call `XStoreColors` to store appropriate color values in the colormap.

- Fill in the descriptive fields in the `XStandardColormap` structure, including the ID of the created colormap.

- Call `XSetRGBColormaps` or `XSetStandardColormap` to set the property on the root window. Under R4, the `killid` field should be set to the colormap ID.

- Use `XSetCloseDownMode` to make the resource permanent.

- Close the new connection to the server.

7.8.5 RGB-to-Pixel Conversion

The standard colormaps such as `XA_RGB_BEST_MAP` are useful when you want to calculate pixel values from RGB values.

Consider a 3-D display program that draws a smoothly shaded sphere. At each pixel in the image of the sphere, the program computes the intensity and color of light reflected to the viewer. The result of each computation is a triple of red, green, and blue coefficients in the range 0.0 to 1.0. To draw the sphere, the program needs a colormap that provides a large range of uniformly distributed colors. The colormap must be arranged so that the program can convert its RGB triples into pixel values very quickly, because drawing the entire sphere will require many such conversions. An example of one such calculation is shown in Example 7-12. Example 7-11 demonstrated how to do this for integral RGB values.

Example 7-12. Calculating pixel values from floating point RGB values

```
XStandardColormap best_map_info;
float red, green, blue;
unsigned long pixelvalue;

pixelvalue = best_map_info.base_pixel +
    ((unsigned long)(0.5 + (red * best_map_info.red_max)) *
        best_map_info.red_mult) +
    ((unsigned long)(0.5 + (green * best_map_info.green_max)) *
        best_map_info.green_mult) +
    ((unsigned long)(0.5 + (blue * best_map_info.blue_max)) *
        best_map_info.blue_mult);
```

For gray scale colormaps, only the `colormap`, `red_max`, `red_mult`, and `base_pixel` fields of the `XStandardColormap` structure are defined. The other fields are ignored. Pixel values for a `StaticGray` or `GrayScale` visual must be in the range:

```
base_pixel <= pixel_value < (red_max * red_mult) + base_pixel
```

To compute a gray pixel value, use the following expression:

```
pixel_value = gray * red_mult + base_pixel;
```

where:

`gray`	=	the gray value you desire (0 to `red_max`)
`red_mult`	=	value from `XStandardColormap` structure
`base_pixel`	=	value from `XStandardColormap` structure

7.9 Miscellaneous Color-handling Functions

The following miscellaneous functions provide additional ways to use the color database, to find out the RGB values in a colormap cell, and to free cells that are no longer needed:

XLookupColor   Looks up a string color name in the color database and returns separate color structures containing the exact RGB values specified in the database for that name and the closest RGB values available on the hardware. This function does not look at any cells in the colormap, even though it has a *colormap* argument! This argument specifies which screen the color should be looked up on. The difference between XLookupColor and XParseColor is that XParseColor accepts the hexadecimal color specification (which XLookupColor does not), while XLookupColor returns the closest colors available on the hardware (which XParseColor does not). XLookup-Color might be useful for making sure that user-specified colors are contrasting.

XQueryColor   Fills an XColor structure with the RGB values corresponding to the colormap cell indicated by a pixel value. Also sets the flags member of the structure to (DoRed | DoGreen | DoBlue).

XQueryColors   Fills multiple XColor structures with the RGB values and flags corresponding to the colormap cells indicated by a pixel values. Also sets each flags member to (DoRed | DoGreen | DoBlue).

XFreeColors   Frees the colormap cells associated with the given pixel values and/or frees the given planes. Since all the colorcells an application allocates are freed when the application exits, this routine is needed only when an application is finished with cells before it exits. Freeing a read/write colorcell makes that cell available to other applications. Freeing a read-only cell may make the cell unallocated, but only if no other application is sharing that cell.

8

Events

This chapter is another must-read. Events are central to X. The fundamental framework for handling events was given in Chapter 3, but this chapter gives much more detail, both on selecting events for a window and on handling them when they arrive. It discusses each of the masks used to select events; for a description of the event structures themselves, see Appendix E.

In This Chapter:

8
Events

An event, to quote the Oxford English Dictionary, is an "incident of importance" or a "consequence, result, or outcome." This definition holds for X. An event reports some device activity or is generated as a side effect of an Xlib routine.

From a programmer's point of view, an event reports:

- Something that your program needs to know about, such as user input or information available from other clients.

- Something your program is doing that other clients need to know about, such as making text available for pasting to another client.

- Something the window manager needs to know, such as a request by your program for a change to the layout of the screen by mapping a window.

Programming with events is quite different from traditional methods of programming for input. You cannot simply wait for a user to type something and expect nothing else to happen in the meantime. Other programs are running concurrently and sharing the same system resources including the screen. They can affect your program. What happens if another window is placed over yours in the middle of the instruction your user is typing? The program must be able to listen to several types of events at once and jump back and forth when acting on them. Events imply a philosophy that the program should respond to the user's actions, not the other way around. Events make this type of programming straightforward.

Events occur asynchronously and get queued for each client that requested them. It is possible for more than one client to get copies of the same event. Usually a program handles each one in turn and performs the appropriate action before reading the next one. But there is usually no way for a program to predict in what order it will find the events on the queue.

This chapter covers events in detail, going further than the introduction to events in Chapter 2, *X Concepts*. Here we discuss the event union and structure types, the selection and propagation of events, how each event type is usually used, how events are received and handled in a program, and how they are sent by one client to another.

After you have read and understood this chapter, see Chapter 9, *The Keyboard and Pointer*, which demonstrates how to use events to handle the user's input, and Appendix E, *Event Reference*, which describes all the event types in a reference format.

8.1 Overview of Event Handling

There are three important steps in a program's handling of events. First, the program selects the events it wants for each window. Then it maps the windows. Finally, it provides an event loop which reads events from the event queue as they occur.

This process is quite simple, the only complication being the variety of events that may occur, each perhaps having a different meaning when it occurs in a different window. You have to know every circumstance in which a particular event is generated and make sure that your program does the right thing with it. But you will not need to understand the details of every event in order to begin using the most important ones.

The easiest way to select events is to call `XSelectInput` for each window that you want to receive events. You can also set the `event_mask` attribute directly with `XChange-WindowAttributes` or `XCreateWindow`. You specify a mask which specifies which event types you want, combining any number of the event mask symbols with the bitwise OR operator (|).

You must make sure that every window that is to receive events appears on the screen after the events are selected for that window but before the event loop begins. Otherwise, the client will miss the first `Expose` event that triggers the drawing of the window's contents. For top-level windows, the client might also miss the `ConfigureNotify` event that reports the size of the window granted by the window manager. For a window to appear on the screen, it must be mapped and all its ancestors must be mapped. It is permissible to map all the windows except the top-level ones at any time, but the mapping of children of the root window must be done between the `XSelectInput` call and the routine that gets events for the event loop.

A simple event loop was shown in Chapter 3, *Basic Window Program*. The only difference between this loop and the loops in real clients is in the number of different event types handled and the complexity of each branch.

Even though selection of events must be done first, we are going to start by describing how to handle events once you have them, because there are fewer details involved. We will return to the exact procedure for selecting events and the meaning of each event mask symbol in Section 8.3.

8.2 Event Processing

This section describes what an event type is and what an event structure contains, reviews how the event queue stores events and how a program reads events from it, and summarizes all the routines that can be used to get events.

8.2.1 The Event Structures

An event is implemented as a packet of information stored in a structure. The simplest event structure is shown in Example 8-1.

Example 8-1. The XAnyEvent structure

```
typedef struct {
    int type;                /* The type of event */
    unsigned long serial;    /* # of last request processed by server */
    Bool send_event;         /* True if sent from a SendEvent request */
    Display *display;        /* Display the event was read from */
    Window window;           /* Window that receives event */
} XAnyEvent;
```

There are 30 different event structures. Virtually all of them have the members shown in the XAnyEvent structure. Most of the event structures also contain various additional members that provide useful information for clients. The first member of every event structure, type, indicates the type of event. We will come back to the type in Section 8.2.2. The serial member identifies the last protocol request processed by the server, for use in debugging. The send_event flag indicates whether this event was sent from the server (False) or from another client (True). Other clients can send events with XSendEvent, as described in Section 8.4.

Many of the event structures also have a display member or a root member or both. The display member identifies the connection to the server that this event came from. (Some applications connect with more than one server.) The root member indicates the screen on which the event occurred (a server may control more than one screen). Most programs only use a single screen and therefore do not need to worry about the root member. The display member can be useful for passing the display variable into routines by simply passing a pointer to the event structure.

Most event structures also have a window member, which indicates the window that selected and received the event. This is the window where the event arrives if it is a keyboard or pointer event and has propagated through the hierarchy, as described in Section 8.3.2. One event type may have two different meanings to a client, depending on which window the event appears in.

8.2.2 Event Types and XEvent Union

All the event structures are padded when necessary to be the same size. The XEvent union contains all the event structures, as shown in Example 8-2.* The first member of the XEvent union is the type of event. Each event structure within the XEvent union also begins with the type of event. A client determines the type of event by looking at the type member of XEvent. Then the client branches to specific code for that event type. After the initial determination of the event type, only the event structure containing the specific information for each event type should be used in each branch. For example, assuming you have

---

*See a C language tutorial or reference manual if you are unfamiliar with unions.

Events

declared an XEvent variable called report, the report.xexpose structure should be used within the branch for Expose events. This lets you use the fields unique to the Expose event structure.

The value of type is any one of the constants listed in the center column of Table 8-3, presented later in this chapter. After determining the event type, you know which event structure from the XEvent union contains specific information about the event. You can then use the appropriate event structure name, such as xkey, to access the specific information unique to that event structure. The event structure name is also shown on each event reference page in Appendix E, *Event Reference*.

Example 8-2. The XEvent union

```
typedef union _XEvent {
        int type;               /* Must not be changed; first member */
        XAnyEvent xany;
        XKeyEvent xkey;
        XButtonEvent xbutton;
        XMotionEvent xmotion;
        XCrossingEvent xcrossing;
        XFocusChangeEvent xfocus;
        XKeymapEvent xkeymap;
        XExposeEvent xexpose;
        XNoExposeEvent xnoexpose;
        XGraphicsExposeEvent xgraphicsexpose;
        XVisibilityEvent xvisibility;
        XCreateWindowEvent xcreatewindow;
        XDestroyWindowEvent xdestroywindow;
        XUnmapEvent xunmap;
        XMapEvent xmap;
        XMappingEvent xmapping;
        XMapRequestEvent xmaprequest;
        XReparentEvent xreparent;
        XConfigureEvent xconfigure;
        XGravityEvent xgravity;
        XResizeRequestEvent xresizerequest;
        XConfigureRequestEvent xconfigurerequest;
        XCirculateEvent xcirculate;
        XCirculateRequestEvent xcirculaterequest;
        XPropertyEvent xproperty;
        XSelectionClearEvent xselectionclear;
        XSelectionRequestEvent xselectionrequest;
        XSelectionEvent xselection;
        XColormapEvent xcolormap;
        XClientMessageEvent xclient;
} XEvent;
```

8.2.3 Xlib's Event Queue

The event structures are placed on an event queue in the order they occur, so that the program can read them and act accordingly. As shown in Figure 8-1, the server maintains one event queue, on which all events are placed, and distributes events to the Xlib in each client. The events in the server's queue are periodically transferred over the network to the Xlib queues. Two clients can receive copies of the same events if they each select them.

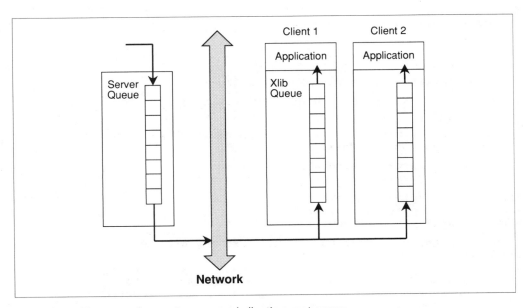

Figure 8-1. The server's event queue and client's event queue

The client sets up an event-receiving loop to handle the events that arrive on its event queue. There are several routines a client can use to get events. They differ in how many windows they monitor, how many types of events they look for, and whether they wait for events to appear before returning. For a description of the event-getting routines, see Section 8.2.6.

8.2.4 Writing the Event Loop

In *basicwin* (the example program in Chapter 3, *Basic Window Program*), you have already seen the structure of the code you should write to handle events. In a more complex application, the code for each event type will simply be divided according to the values in the members in each event structure. Usually, the next branch after the event type will test the window in which the event occurred.

The branch for `Expose` events in Example 8-3 demonstrates how an event might be handled when there are several windows involved. The example also notes when each of the selected events—and the events that may be delivered without your selecting them—should be handled within your event loop. Depending on your application, other events might need to be handled as well.

Notice how the specific event structure names such as `xexpose` are used to access information in the event structures.

Example 8-3. An event-handling loop

```
XEvent report;
Window window1, window2, window3;
    .
    .
    .

/* Open display, create windows, etc. */

/* Window 1 is a top-level window, window 2 is a child
 * of window 1 */
XSelectInput(display, window1, StructureNotifyMask | ExposureMask
        | ButtonPressMask);

XSelectInput(display, window2, ExposureMask);
XSelectInput(display, window3, ExposureMask);

XMapWindow(display, window1);
XMapWindow(display, window2);
XMapWindow(display, window3);

/* Get events, use first to display text and graphics */
while (1)
{
    /* Get any type of event on any window; this gets
     * events on every window for which we have selected
     * events (three in this case) */
    XNextEvent(display, &report);

    switch (report.type)  {
    case Expose:
        printf("got an Expose event\n");
        /* Redraw contents of windows; note that we can't
         * use switch because window IDs are not constant */
        if (report.xexpose.window == window1)
            /* Redraw window 1 */;
        else if (report.xexpose.window == window2)
            /* Redraw window 2 */;
        else (report.xexpose.window == window3)
            /* Redraw window 3 */;
        break;
    case ButtonPress:
        printf("got a ButtonPress event\n");
        /* Respond to buttonpress, probably depending on
         * which window is reported in report.xbutton.window */
        break;
    case ConfigureNotify:
        printf("got a ConfigureNotify event\n");
        /* Window was resized, moved, or restacked or border
```

Example 8-3. An event-handling loop (continued)

```
                         * width was changed; reset application variables
                         * so Expose branch will scale graphics properly */
                    break;
             case MappingNotify:
                    printf("got a MappingNotify event\n");
                    /* Keyboard or Pointer mapping was changed by another
                     * client; if keyboard, should call XRefreshKeyboardMapping,
                     * unless keyboard events are not used */
                    break;
             case ClientMessage:
                    printf("got a ClientMessage event\n");
                    /* Primarily used for transfering selection data,
                     * also might be used in a private interclient
                     * protocol; otherwise, not needed in event loop */
                    break;
             case SelectionClear:
                    printf("got a SelectionClear event\n");
                    /* If this application previously called
                     * XSetSelectionOwner, it may get this event;
                     * otherwise, you don't need it in your
                     * event loop */
                    break;
             case SelectionNotify:
                    printf("got a SelectionNotify event\n");
                    /* If this application calls XConvertSelection,
                     * it will get this event; otherwise, you don't
                     * need it in your event loop */
                    break;
             case SelectionRequest:
                    printf("got a SelectionRequest event\n");
                    /* If this application previously called
                     * XSetSelectionOwner, it may get this event;
                     * otherwise, you don't need it in your
                     * event loop */
                    break;
             case GraphicsExpose:
                    /* Fall through into NoExpose */
             case NoExpose:
                    printf("got a GraphicsExpose or NoExpose event\n");
                    /* If this application calls XCopyArea or XCopyPlane
                     * and the graphics_exposures member of the GC is
                     * True and the source is a window, these events may
                     * be generated; handle GraphicsExpose like Expose */
             default:
                    printf("Event being thrown away\n");
                    /* All *Notify events except ConfigureNotify will
                     * be thrown away; they are not needed by most
                     * applications but are sent because ConfigureNotify
                     * can't be selected independently */
                    break;
          }   /* End switch on event type */
      } /* End while (1) */
```

The XNextEvent routine gets the next event on the queue for our client or waits until one
appears before returning. There are many other routines that get events of particular types, in

particular windows, with or without waiting for the event to appear. These routines are described in Section 8.2.6.

The first member of the XEvent report contains the type of event. This information is used in a "switch" statement to branch according to the event type. Once the type is known, the specific event structure is known, and its contents can be accessed. For example, the width of the exposed area in the window is contained in the XExposeEvent structure as report.xexpose.width, where report is the XEvent variable, xexpose is the member of the XEvent union, and width is a member of the XExposeEvent structure type.

8.2.5 Printing the Event Type

We recommend that you print the event type and perhaps other event information in each branch of the event loop while you are in the application debugging stage. Be very careful that the loop handles all the events that can occur and that the Xlib routine you choose to get events is capable of getting all the events you need. If your program hangs and cannot be interrupted with Control-C, it is probably waiting for an event that you did not select. For example, you may have called XMaskEvent with a mask of ButtonReleaseMask but you did not select ButtonReleaseMask in the XSelectEvent call. The event-getting routines do not check to make sure you have selected the events you are requesting.

Instead of printing the event type as a number which you then have to interpret using the <X11/X.h> include file, you can have your program print the real name of the event. Example 8-4 creates an include file containing an array of strings spelling out the event type names. Example 8-5 then prints the correct event name.

Example 8-4. An include file for printing the event type — eventnames.h

```
static char *event_names[] = {
    "",
    "",
    "KeyPress",
    "KeyRelease",
    "ButtonPress",
    "ButtonRelease",
    "MotionNotify",
    "EnterNotify",
    "LeaveNotify",
    "FocusIn",
    "FocusOut",
    "KeymapNotify",
    "Expose",
    "GraphicsExpose",
    "NoExpose",
    "VisibilityNotify",
    "CreateNotify",
    "DestroyNotify",
    "UnmapNotify",
    "MapNotify",
    "MapRequest",
    "ReparentNotify",
```

```
        "ConfigureNotify",
        "ConfigureRequest",
        "GravityNotify",
        "ResizeRequest",
        "CirculateNotify",
        "CirculateRequest",
        "PropertyNotify",
        "SelectionClear",
        "SelectionRequest",
        "SelectionNotify",
        "ColormapNotify",
        "ClientMessage",
        "MappingNotify"
};
```

Note that *eventnames.h* is not a standard include file but one we have written for the purpose of printing the event type more legibly. You could use a similar method to identify windows, but since their IDs are not constants, you would need to load the array dynamically after you have created the windows.

Example 8-5 demonstrates printing an event using the include file shown in Example 8-4.

Example 8-5. Printing the event type

```
#ifdef DEBUG
#include "eventnames.h"
#endif

XEvent event;
XNextEvent(display, &event);

#ifdef DEBUG
fprintf(stderr, "winman: got a %s event\n", event_name[event.type]);
#endif
```

8.2.6 Routines that Get Events

There are several functions that get event structures from the queue. They differ in the following respects:

- The number of windows they monitor (whether they inspect the `window` member).

- Whether they look for particular event types.

- Whether the event is removed from the queue when it is read.

- Whether a routine you write is used to determine whether the event should be returned.

- Whether Xlib waits until an event meeting the criteria arrives or immediately returns a success or failure code.

- Whether the connection to the server is flushed to see if any more events become available.

The following is a list of the event-handling routines and their differences. In all of these routines, you pass a pointer to an XEvent structure to be filled.

XNextEvent	Gets the next event of any type on any window. This function flushes the request buffer if Xlib's queue does not contain an event and waits for an event to arrive from the server connection.
XMaskEvent	Gets the next event matching the specified mask on any window. This function flushes the request buffer if Xlib's queue does not contain a matching event and waits for a matching event to arrive from the server connection.
XCheckMaskEvent	Behaves like XMaskEvent but immediately returns False if there is no matching event in Xlib's queue and none could be read from the server connection after flushing the request buffer. Returns True if a matching event was found.
XWindowEvent	Gets the next event matching both the specified mask and the specified window. This function flushes the request buffer if Xlib's queue does not contain a matching event and waits for a matching event to arrive from the server connection.
XCheckWindowEvent	Behaves like XWindowEvent but immediately returns False if there is no matching event in Xlib's queue and none could be read from the server connection after flushing the request buffer. Returns True if a matching event was found.
XIfEvent	Looks for an event on the queue that matches the conditions set by a user-supplied predicate procedure. This function flushes the request buffer if Xlib's queue does not contain a matching event and waits for a matching event to arrive from the server connection.
XCheckIfEvent	Behaves like XIfEvent but immediately returns False if there is no matching event in Xlib's queue and none could be read from the server connection after flushing the request buffer. Returns True if a matching event was found.
XPeekEvent	Gets the next event of any type from any window without removing the event from the queue. This function flushes the request buffer if Xlib's queue is empty and waits for an event to arrive from the server connection.
XPeekIfEvent	Gets the next event that matches the specified predicate procedure, without removing the event from the queue. This function flushes the request buffer if Xlib's queue does not contain a matching event and waits for a matching event to arrive from the server connection.
XCheckTypedEvent	Searches the queue from the oldest event for the desired event type, without discarding all those searched that do not match. If no matching event is found in Xlib's queue, this function flushes the request buffer and returns False.

`XCheckTypedWindowEvent`
　　Searches the queue from the oldest event for the desired window and event type, without discarding those searched that do not match. If no matching event is found in Xlib's queue, this function flushes the request buffer and returns `False`.

`XEventsQueued`
　　Returns the number of events on the queue but has three modes that specify what else is done. All three modes count the events already in Xlib's queue and return if there are any. `Queued-Already` returns even if there are not any events in the queue. `QueuedAfterFlush` flushes the request buffer and attempts to read more events from the connection before returning. `QueuedAfterReading` attempts to read more events from the connection without flushing the buffer.

`XPending`
　　Returns the number of events on the queue. This is identical to `XEventsQueued` with mode `QueuedAfterFlush`.

`XPutBackEvent`
　　Puts an event you supply back on Xlib's queue, so that it will be the next to be received by `XNextEvent`.

`XGetMotionEvents`
　　Gets all the motion events that occurred on the specified window in a specified time period. This function will not work if there is no motion history buffer implemented on the server, which is true if `XDisplayMotionBufferSize(display) == 0`.

You may notice that there are two broad categories of routines that get input: those that wait for a matching event and those that do not wait. The latter may be used in porting applications that use the "polling" style of programming, which checks to see if input has arrived at regular intervals by continuously calling a "polling" function in a loop. Given the choice, however, it is much better to use the routines that wait for events as much as possible, since this technique does not waste processor cycles. This is true event-*driven* programming.

Table 8-1 organizes the event-receiving functions according to whether they wait for events if none are present on Xlib's queue.

Table 8-1. Event-getting Routines

Event Specifications	Desired Result		
	Wait if necessary	Return `False` immediately if none queued	Leave in queue (may wait)
Any event	`XNextEvent`	n/a	`XPeekEvent`
With predicate	`XIfEvent`	`XCheckIfEvent`	`XPeekIfEvent`
For window	`XWindowEvent`	`XCheckWindowEvent`	n/a
For event mask	`XMaskEvent`	`XCheckMaskEvent`	n/a
For type	n/a	`XCheckTypedEvent`	n/a
For window and type	n/a	`XCheckTypedWindowEvent`	n/a

Note that most of the routines apparently missing from Xlib according to Table 8-1 can be simulated with other routines and fairly simple code. The hole on the top row can be filled by calling `XCheckMaskEvent` with a mask set to all 1's. For the four routines missing in the last column, you can write a predicate procedure and call `XPeekIfEvent`. An example predicate procedure is shown in Example 8-6. The two routines missing in the first column can also be replaced with a predicate procedure and `XIfEvent`.

The event-getting routines with `Check` in their names are useful for programs that need to poll for input to handle interrupts. To illustrate the handling of interrupts, let's say you have a routine in a program that performs a complex, lengthy calculation like a Fourier transform. You want to be able to abort the calculation midway. Therefore, you need to be able to check the keyboard to see if a Control-C or other interrupt character has been typed. You also might want to provide for exposure events during the long wait, though you might be able to get away without this provision. This would be a good application for `XCheckTyped-Event` or `XCheckTypedWindowEvent`, since these routines poll without waiting if no events can be read. When an event does arrive, you can decide from the type or window whether to bother processing it.

8.2.7 Predicate Procedures

The routines `XCheckIfEvent`, `XIfEvent`, and `XPeekIfEvent` allow you to supply a procedure that returns `True` or `False` depending on some characteristic of the event. You would use one of these routines if you have a matching algorithm that is complicated or simply to enable you to clear up the code by putting some of the event processing in a separate routine.

Your predicate procedure is called with the same arguments as the event-getting routine (except for the predicate procedure pointer, of course). Example 8-6 shows a predicate procedure and the `XIfEvent` call that uses it. This code would normally use `XNextEvent`, but we have substituted `XIfEvent` so that we can filter out button events on buttons other than button 1. This predicate procedure returns `True` for all events except the undesirable button events.

Example 8-6. A predicate procedure and XIfEvent call

```
void main(argc, argv)
int argc;
char **argv;
{
        .
        .
        .
    Bool predproc();
    static char *stuff = "do this or that";
        .
        .
        .
    XSelectInput(display, wint, ExposureMask | ButtonPressMask
            | ButtonReleaseMask | ButtonMotionMask
            | PointerMotionHintMask);
        .
```

Example 8-6. A predicate procedure and XIfEvent call (continued)

```
        .
       .
      .
        while (1)   {
                XIfEvent(display, &report, predproc, stuff);
                switch   (report.type) {
        /* Note that no code here for eliminating button
         * events on other buttons, because only button
         * one events are returned by XIfEvent */
                case ButtonPress:
                        points[index].x = report.xbutton.x;
                        points[index].y = report.xbutton.y;
                        break;
                case ButtonRelease:
                        index++;
                        points[index].x = report.xbutton.x;
                        points[index].y = report.xbutton.y;
                        break;

                          .
                          .
                          .

        }
    }
}
Bool predproc(display, event, arg)
Display *display;
XEvent *event;
char *arg;
{
        printf("The arg is %s\n", arg);
        switch (event->type) {
                case Expose:
                case MotionNotify:
                case ConfigureNotify:
                case KeyPress:
                        return(True);
                        break;
                case ButtonPress:
                case ButtonRelease:
                        if (event->xbutton.button == Button1)
                                return(True);
                        else
                                return(False);
                        break;
                default:
        }
}
```

8.3 Selecting Events

For each window, a client must select which event types it wants placed in its queue when they occur in that window. This is normally done with XSelectInput, which sets the event_mask attribute of a window. The client need not select events on all of its windows, only those in which it wants to see the events that occur.

To select event types for a window, pass an event_mask as an argument to XSelect-Input or set the event_mask member of the XSetWindowAttributes structure and call XChangeWindowAttributes or XCreateWindow. (For more information on the XSetWindowAttributes structure, see Section 4.1.)

The event_mask is formed by combining the event mask symbols listed in the first column of Table 8-2 with the bitwise OR operator (|). Each mask symbol sets a bit in the event_mask.

Table 8-2 also describes briefly the circumstances under which you would want to specify each symbol. You will need to read about each mask in Section 8.3.3; see the examples using the events in Chapter 9, *The Keyboard and Pointer*, and throughout this manual; and look at the event structures in Appendix E, *Event Reference*, before you will really understand when to use each of these symbols.

Table 8-2. Event Mask Definitions

Event Mask Symbol	Circumstances
NoEventMask	No events
KeyPressMask	Keyboard down events
KeyReleaseMask	Keyboard up events
ButtonPressMask	Pointer button down events
ButtonReleaseMask	Pointer button up events
EnterWindowMask	Pointer window entry events
LeaveWindowMask	Pointer window leave events
PointerMotionMask	All pointer motion events
PointerMotionHintMask	Fewer pointer motion events
Button1MotionMask	Pointer motion while button 1 down
Button2MotionMask	Pointer motion while button 2 down
Button3MotionMask	Pointer motion while button 3 down
Button4MotionMask	Pointer motion while button 4 down
Button5MotionMask	Pointer motion while button 5 down
ButtonMotionMask	Pointer motion while any button down
KeymapStateMask	Any keyboard state change on EnterNotify, LeaveNotify, FocusIn or FocusOut
ExposureMask	Any exposure (except GraphicsExpose and NoExpose)
VisibilityChangeMask	Any change in visibility
StructureNotifyMask	Any change in window configuration.
ResizeRedirectMask	Redirect resize of this window
SubstructureNotifyMask	Notify about reconfiguration of children

Table 8-2. Event Mask Definitions (continued)

Event Mask Symbol	Circumstances
SubstructureRedirectMask	Redirect reconfiguration of children
FocusChangeMask	Any change in keyboard focus
PropertyChangeMask	Any change in property
ColormapChangeMask	Any change in colormap
OwnerGrabButtonMask	Modifies handling of pointer events

The `do_not_propagate_mask` window attribute is formed in the same way as `event_mask` but can only be set with `XChangeWindowAttributes` or `XCreate-Window`. Its function is described in Section 8.3.2.

Example 8-7 shows how to set the `event_mask` and call `XSelectInput`.

Example 8-7. An example of selecting input

```
Display display;
Window window;
unsigned long event_mask;
    .
    .
    .
/* Must open display, create window, etc. */

/* Select key events */
event_mask = ExposureMask | KeyPressMask | KeyReleaseMask;
XSelectInput(display, window, event_mask);

/* Map window after selecting */

/* Get events */
```

In Example 8-7, events are selected *before* the window is mapped. This sequence is important, since otherwise the window will not receive the first `Expose` event that occurs after a new window is mapped and it will not know when to redraw the window. You will remember from *basicwin* that an `Expose` event signifies that a window has become visible and needs to be redrawn. Every `Expose` event, including the first, should trigger the drawing of the window's contents.

Also, note that you cannot add to the selected events by calling `XSelectInput` with a single additional mask. You must specify all the desired event masks every time you call it.

8.3.1 Correspondence Between Event Masks and Events

Each event mask symbol indicates that a certain type of event or group of event types should be queued when they occur. For example, when used alone as an *event_mask* argument to `XSelectInput`, a `KeyPressMask` symbol indicates that only `KeyPress` events are desired. A `FocusChangeMask` symbol, on the other hand, indicates an interest in two types of events: `FocusIn` and `FocusOut`.

On the other hand, there is more than one event mask symbol for `MotionNotify` events; the different masks specify the conditions under which pointer motion events are desired. For example, if both `Button1MotionMask` and `Button3MotionMask` symbols are combined to form an `event_mask` argument to `XSelectInput`, only one event type is requested: `MotionNotify` events. However, this event type will be queued only if the pointer moves while the first or third button (or both) is held down.

Table 8-3 lists each event mask, its associated event types, and the associated structure definition. The structures for each event type are described in Appendix E, *Event Reference*.

Table 8-3. Event Masks, Event Types, and Event Structures

Event Mask	Event Type	Structure
KeyPressMask	KeyPress	XKeyPressedEvent
KeyReleaseMask	KeyRelease	XKeyReleasedEvent
ButtonPressMask	ButtonPress	XButtonPressedEvent
ButtonReleaseMask	ButtonRelease	XButtonReleasedEvent
OwnerGrabButtonMask	n/a	n/a
KeymapStateMask	KeymapNotify	XKeymapEvent
PointerMotionMask PointerMotionHintMask ButtonMotionMask Button1MotionMask Button2MotionMask Button3MotionMask Button4MotionMask Button5MotionMask	MotionNotify	XPointerMovedEvent
EnterWindowMask	EnterNotify	XEnterWindowEvent
LeaveWindowMask	LeaveNotify	XLeaveWindowEvent
FocusChangeMask	FocusIn FocusOut	XFocusInEvent XFocusOutEvent
ExposureMask	Expose	XExposeEvent
(Selected in GC by `graphics_expose` **member)**	GraphicsExpose NoExpose	XGraphicsExposeEvent XNoExposeEvent
ColormapChangeMask	ColormapNotify	XColormapEvent
PropertyChangeMask	PropertyNotify	XPropertyEvent
VisibilityChangeMask	VisibilityNotify	XVisibilityEvent
ResizeRedirectMask	ResizeRequest	XResizeRequestEvent
StructureNotifyMask	CirculateNotify ConfigureNotify DestroyNotify	XCirculateEvent XConfigureEvent XDestroyWindowEvent

Table 8-3. Event Masks, Event Types, and Event Structures (continued)

Event Mask	Event Type	Structure
	GravityNotify	XGravityEvent
	MapNotify	XMapEvent
	ReparentNotify	XReparentEvent
	UnmapNotify	XUnmapEvent
SubstructureNotifyMask	CirculateNotify	XCirculateEvent
	ConfigureNotify	XConfigureEvent
	CreateNotify	XCreateWindowEvent
	DestroyNotify	XDestroyWindowEvent
	GravityNotify	XGravityEvent
	MapNotify	XMapEvent
	ReparentNotify	XReparentEvent
	UnmapNotify	XUnmapEvent
SubstructureRedirectMask	CirculateRequest	XCirculateRequestEvent
	ConfigureRequest	XConfigureRequestEvent
	MapRequest	XMapRequestEvent
(Always selected)	MappingNotify	XMappingEvent
(Always selected)	ClientMessage	XClientMessageEvent
(Always selected)	SelectionClear	XSetSelectClearEvent
(Always selected)	SelectionNotify	XSelectionEvent
(Always selected)	SelectionRequest	XSelectionRequestEvent

There is no event mask for several of the event types listed at the end of this table, because the X server or another client can send them to any client without them being selected. For example, MappingNotify indicates that the keyboard mapping (see Section 9.1.2.3) or pointer mapping has changed. This event is reported to all clients by the server when any client changes those mappings. The selection events are a means of interclient communication, where one client announces with an event that it has a selection of text or graphics available for pasting, and another client responds with an event specifying in what format it would like the information. Similarly, ClientMessage events are always selected because they are sent from one client directly to another using the XSendEvent routine.

Also note that SubstructureNotifyMask and StructureNotifyMask select the same event types but on different windows. The former selects the events when they occur in any *child* of the window specified in the call to XSelectEvent, and the latter only when they occur in the window specified. (These are perhaps the two least often used masks.)

Events

8.3.2 Propagation of Device Events

The fifth member in almost every event structure, `window`, contains the ID of the window in which the event appears to have occurred. This is called the *event window*. For `Button-Press`, `ButtonRelease`, `KeyPress`, `KeyRelease`, and `MotionNotify` events, the event window is not necessarily the window in which the event originally happened, which is called the *source window*.

Which window is reported in the event on the queue depends on the results of propagation up through the window hierarchy and is controlled by the `event_mask` and `do_not_propagate_mask` window attributes.

The source window is the *lowest* visible window in the hierarchy that encloses the pointer when the device event occurs. It is also the *smallest* visible window enclosing the pointer. The `window` member of the event in the queue (the event window) will be the source window only if the `event_mask` attribute (set with `XSelectInput`) of the source window selected the event's type.

If the event was not selected for the source window, then the event is sent to the parent and so on until the event arrives at an ancestor window that has selected the right event type. The ID of this window is then placed in the `window` member of the event structure and that structure is placed on the queue for this client. Once a window that has selected the event is found, the event no longer propagates. If no window selected the event anywhere in the hierarchy up to and including the root window, the server never sends the event.

The `do_not_propagate_mask` window attribute also gets involved in this process. When an event arrives at a window but finds it has not been selected, the `do_not_propagate_mask` determines whether the event will be sent to ancestor windows. By default, all events that can propagate do. If the mask for the event type that occurred is included in the `do_not_propagate_mask`, the event is never sent.

Figures 8-2a, 8-2b, and 8-2c demonstrate the propagation of an event through the hierarchy, given three different `event_mask` and `do_not_propagate` attribute settings.

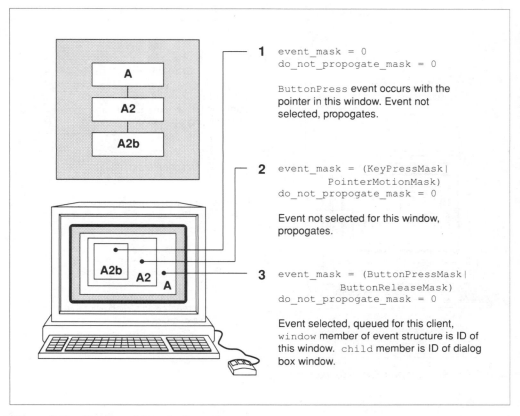

Figure 8-2a. One possible selection scheme

The `do_not_propagate_mask` is rarely used. However, here is one scenario in which setting the `do_not_propagate_mask` attribute would be useful. Consider an application with two windows, a parent and a child. The program lets the user draw in the child by moving the pointer while holding down a pointer button. However, like *basicwin*, the application exits on a `ButtonPress` event in the parent window. Since `ButtonPress` events are not selected in the child window, they will be propagated to the parent and will cause the application to exit. But a `ButtonPress` is necessary because we want the drawing in the child window to occur only when a button is held. By setting the `do_not_propagate_mask` attribute of the child window to `ButtonPressMask`, this problem is solved.

Figure 8-2b. Another possible selection scheme

Figure 8-2c. Yet another possible selection scheme

> For brevity, we need conventions for describing the distribution of events. We'll say that an event is *sent* to a window when it is generated in that window either because of device action or as a side effect to an Xlib routine. A window *receives* an event sent to it only if the window has selected that event type or if the event type is always selected. Only when a window *receives* an event is it placed on the queue for that client.
>
> Another convention is helpful in describing the selection of events. We will say that "the window has selected that event type" rather than the more cumbersome "the program has called XSelectInput, specifying the window and the mask that selects that event type."

We have described the way device events propagate normally. But two other actions can modify this operation: changing the keyboard focus window or grabbing the keyboard or pointer. Not only do these change the distribution of normal events, they create new events as side effects. We'll just introduce these here and return to them in Chapter 9, *The Keyboard and Pointer*.

8.3.2.1 The Keyboard Focus Window

The keyboard focus window affects the distribution of KeyPress and KeyRelease events. Normally, the window manager allows the user to specify which window, if any, should be the keyboard focus. Only the focus window and its descendants receive keyboard input, and within them, event propagation occurs normally. Events occurring outside the focus window are delivered to the focus window. By default, the focus window is the root and keyboard events are normally distributed to all windows on the screen, since all the windows on a screen are descendants of the root.

The keyboard focus is set to a window with XSetInputFocus. The focus window must be viewable.* If it is not viewable or later becomes not viewable, the focus reverts to another window specified in the XSetInputFocus call, the *revert_to* window.

The current focus window can be read with XGetInputFocus.

FocusOut events are delivered to the old focus window, and FocusIn events to the window which receives the focus. Windows in between these two windows in the hierarchy are said to be virtually crossed and receive focus change events depending on the relationship and direction of transfer between the origin and destination windows. Some or all of the windows between the window containing the pointer at the time of the focus change and that window's root can also receive focus change events. By checking the detail member of

---

*For a window to be viewable, it must be mapped and all its ancestors must be mapped, but it may be obscured.

`FocusIn` and `FocusOut` events, a client can tell which of its windows can receive input. See Chapter 9, *The Keyboard and Pointer*, for more information about tracking the keyboard focus.

Applications should set the keyboard focus to one of their own windows only when absolutely necessary, because this will prevent other clients from receiving keyboard events. It is permissible for clients to set the focus window when the mouse enters their top-level window, as long as they set it back to the root window when the pointer leaves again. A client might want to do this to send all keyboard input to one of its subwindows. See Chapter 10, *Interclient Communication*, for more information about what a client should do regarding the keyboard focus.

8.3.2.2 Keyboard and Pointer Grabbing

The keyboard and/or the pointer can be grabbed when their input should not be allowed to be interrupted by other clients. As the name implies, grabbing prevents other clients from receiving input and, therefore, can be antisocial. It should not be done unless absolutely necessary. Grabbing the pointer is particularly troublesome, because there is no event to announce to other clients that this has happened. See Appendix L, *Interclient Communication Conventions*, of Volume Zero, *X Protocol Reference Manual* (as of the second printing).

In general, grabbing is an advanced topic that you do not need to understand in detail until you find a reason to use it. But there are two exceptions to this rule. You do need to know what will happen when other clients grab, so that your client can prepare for it. Secondly, an automatic grab takes place between `ButtonPress` and `ButtonRelease` events if your client has selected both. You must understand grabbing to understand the implications of this automatic grab.

An *active grab* causes pointer and keyboard events to be sent to the grabbing window regardless of the current position of the pointer. Active grabs are invoked directly by calling `XGrabPointer` and `XGrabKeyboard`. A *passive grab* (invoked by calling `XGrabKey` or `XGrabButton`) causes an active grab to begin when a certain key or button combination is pressed. Passive grabs are useful in implementing menus.

When you grab a device, you have the option of confining the pointer to any window within the grabbing client and of controlling the further processing of both keyboard and pointer events.

Grabbing the keyboard effectively selects all keyboard events, whether you selected them previously or not. Grabbing the keyboard also causes `FocusIn` and `FocusOut` events to be sent to the old and new focus windows, but they must be selected by each window to be received. In the call to grab the pointer, however, you specify what types of pointer, button, and enter/leave events you want.

Grabs take precedence over the keyboard focus window. Grabs of the keyboard generated `FocusIn` and `FocusOut` events, so that if your client selects these, it can determine whether or not it can get keyboard events. Pointer grabbing is more problematic, since no event notifies other clients when one client has grabbed it. However, pointer grabs are almost always temporary.

For more on keyboard and pointer grabbing, see Section 9.4. For a description of server grabbing, which is a different topic though still related to events, see Chapter 14, *Window Management*.

8.3.3 Event Masks

This section describes the event masks and the events they select. After reading this section, you should have a good idea of what types of events exist, what they are for, how to select them, and when to use them. Chapter 9, *The Keyboard and Pointer*, and the sections listed in Table 8-5 provide practical examples and describe the use of some of the more commonly used events in more detail. Appendix E, *Event Reference*, provides a complete reference to each event type.

8.3.3.1 KeyPressMask and KeyReleaseMask

`KeyPress` and `KeyRelease` events report when a keyboard key has been pressed or released. Most, but not all, servers are capable of generating `KeyRelease` events. Shift, Control, and other modifier keys generate events just like the main keyboard.

The `KeyPress` and `KeyRelease` events provide a keycode that identifies the key, but the keycodes are server-dependent and should not be used to interpret the event. Instead you can use `XLookupString` to translate the keycode into a portable symbol called a keysym, which represents the symbol on the cap of the key, and into an ASCII character string. Both the mapping between keycodes and keysyms and the mapping between keysyms and ASCII strings can be modified.

In `XLookupString`, the main routine used for interpreting `KeyPress` and `KeyRelease` events, there is a provision for a special Compose key which is available on some keyboards, so that multikey sequences, usually used to type characters for languages other than English, can be entered and translated into the appropriate keysym. The Compose key feature, however, is not implemented in the versions of Xlib provided by MIT.

The events selected by `KeyPressMask` and `KeyReleaseMask` are used in the examples in Section 9.1.1.

Events

8.3.3.2 ButtonPressMask, ButtonReleaseMask, and OwnerGrabButtonMask

ButtonPress and ButtonRelease events occur when the pointer buttons are pressed. There are generally between three and five buttons on the pointer, and the event structure specifies not only the button that caused the event but also the current state of all the pointer buttons and the modifier keys on the keyboard. The mapping between the bits in the button mask and the physical buttons can be changed with XSetPointerMapping and read with XGetPointerMapping and is global to the server.

The pointer is automatically grabbed between the ButtonPress and ButtonRelease events on behalf of the client for whose window the ButtonPress was selected. This way, you always expect to receive button events in pairs since the release will be sent to your client regardless of the position of the pointer at that time. Only one client can select button events on any one window at one time, due to the grab that automatically takes place.

The OwnerGrabButtonMask does not select any event by itself, but it controls the distribution of button events to your client during the automatic grab between the ButtonPress and ButtonRelease (and during any grab your client might make). If it is selected, the automatic grab has the same effect as an XGrabButton call with the *owner_events* argument set to True, so that the ButtonRelease event is sent to whichever of the client's windows the pointer is in. If the ButtonRelease occurs outside the client's windows or if OwnerGrabButtonMask is not selected, all events will be sent only to the window where the ButtonPress occurred. Current wisdom suggests that you should always select OwnerGrabButtonMask with ButtonPressMask.

The events selected by ButtonPressMask and ButtonReleaseMask are discussed in Section 9.2.2 and demonstrated in Examples 9-9, 14-1, and 14-6.

8.3.3.3 The Pointer Motion Masks

There are eight pointer motion masks: PointerMotionMask, PointerMotion-HintMask, ButtonMotionMask, Button1MotionMask, Button2Motion-Mask, Button3MotionMask, Button4MotionMask, and Button5MotionMask. Up to five pointer buttons are supported, even though most mice have only three buttons and some have only one.

- PointerMotionMask selects motion events that occur when any or none of the pointer buttons are pressed. Each event includes the position of the pointer within the event window and the position relative to the origin of the root window. All motion events contain a mask that gives the current status of the modifier keys and pointer buttons and the current server time. MotionNotify events occur in large numbers while the pointer is moving steadily. Therefore, this mask is selected alone only by clients that require a complete record of pointer position, such as painting programs.

- PointerMotionHintMask is used in concert with other pointer motion masks to reduce the number of events generated. By itself, it does not select any events. PointerMotionHintMask specifies that the server should send only one Motion-Notify event when the pointer moves, until a key or button state changes, the pointer leaves the window, or the client calls XQueryPointer or XGetMotionEvents. The idea is that instead of processing hundreds of pointer motion events, the client gets only one event per movement and then queries the pointer position or examines the motion history buffer (the latter may not exist on some servers) for the current position. This approach is suitable for clients that need the pointer position at particular times but that do not need all the intermediate positions. Even though each query for the pointer position is a round-trip request, the performance of this approach is better than that of selecting all the events with `PointerMotionMask`, because of the reduced network traffic.

- `ButtonMotionMask` selects any pointer motion events that occur when at least one button is pressed.

- `Button1MotionMask`, `Button2MotionMask`, `Button3MotionMask`, `Button4MotionMask`, and `Button5MotionMask` select pointer motion events that occur when the specified button is pressed. If two or more of these masks are used, events with any combination of the specified buttons (except both released) will be selected.

Handling the events selected by these masks is described in Section 9.2.1 and demonstrated in three examples in that section.

8.3.3.4 FocusChangeMask

`FocusIn` and `FocusOut` events occur when the keyboard focus window is changed. A window that selects `FocusChangeMask` receives a `FocusOut` event if it was the old focus window or is in the same branch of the hierarchy as the old focus window. It receives a `FocusIn` event if it is the new focus window or is in the same branch of the hierarchy as the new focus window. The `detail` member in the event tells the relationship of the window to the new or old focus window. With this information, it is possible to tell whether the window can receive keyboard input. You can read the details of what events are delivered in Appendix E, *Event Reference*.

`EnterNotify`, `LeaveNotify`, `FocusIn`, and `FocusOut` events are often used together to track whether the pointer is in a window and whether the client has the keyboard focus. If the focus is the root, `EnterNotify` and `LeaveNotify` events are used. With any other focus, the `FocusIn` and `FocusOut` events take precedence.

`FocusIn` and `FocusOut` events are described and used in Section 9.3.

8.3.3.5 EnterWindowMask and LeaveWindowMask

`EnterNotify` and `LeaveNotify` events are typically used to inform a client that the pointer just entered or just left one of its windows. If the client receives a `LeaveNotify` event in its top-level window, the client will not be receiving any more key, button, or motion events until it gets an `EnterNotify` event, unless it is the keyboard focus window or has grabbed the keyboard or pointer.

Events

An `EnterNotify` event is also generated when a window is mapped over the current position of the pointer, and a `LeaveNotify` is generated when a window containing the pointer is unmapped.

`EnterNotify` and `LeaveNotify` events are described and used in Section 9.3.

8.3.3.6 KeymapStateMask

A `KeymapNotify` event notifies the client about the keyboard state when the pointer or keyboard focus enters a window. The keyboard state is represented (in the event structure) by 32 bytes of data called a *keyboard vector*, with one bit for each keyboard key. The number of a bit in the vector for a particular key is the same as the key's keycode. This vector is the same as the vector returned by `XQueryKeymap`.

This event type, if it is selected, always follows immediately after an `EnterNotify` or `FocusIn` event. It allows a client to find out which keys were pressed when the pointer or the keyboard focus entered the window. Since the state of the modifier keys is already reported in `EnterNotify` and `FocusIn` events, the `KeymapNotify` event is only useful for reporting the state of other keys.

`KeymapState` events are not used in the examples in this manual, because they are rarely needed. For more information about them, see Appendix E, *Event Reference*.

8.3.3.7 ExposureMask

An `Expose` event tells a client which window or area within a window has just become visible. The usual response is to redraw the contents of the area or of the entire window, if that is easier and comparably fast. Figure 8-3 shows a typical window hierarchy before and after window *C* is lowered. Two `Expose` events are sent to window *A* specifying areas *E1* and *E2*, and one `Expose` event is sent to window *B* specifying area *E3*.

The handling of `Expose` events is fully described and demonstrated in Section 3.2.13.1.

8.3.3.8 VisibilityChangeMask

A `VisibilityNotify` event is sent when a window makes any change in visibility, as shown in Table 8-4, except when the window becomes not viewable. (Becoming not viewable means that the window or one of its ancestors was unmapped, which generates an `UnmapNotify` event.) This event might be used by a client that must be completely visible in order to be useful.

Figure 8-3. Expose events generated by lowering of window C

The symbol returned in the `state` flag of the event is shown in the third column of the table.

Table 8-4. Visibility Transitions Causing VisibilityNotify Events

Beginning State	Final State	`state` Flag
unobscured	partially obscured	`VisibilityPartiallyObscured`
unobscured	fully obscured	`VisibilityFullyObscured`
partially obscured	unobscured	`VisibilityUnobscured`
partially obscured	fully obscured	`VisibilityFullyObscured`
fully obscured	unobscured	`VisibilityUnobscured`
fully obscured	partially obscured	`VisibilityPartiallyObscured`
not viewable	unobscured	`VisibilityUnobscured`
not viewable	partially obscured	`VisibilityPartiallyObscured`
not viewable	fully obscured	`VisibilityFullyObscured`

`VisibilityNotify` events are not demonstrated in this manual. For more information on them, see Appendix E, *Event Reference*.

8.3.3.9 ColormapChangeMask

A `ColormapNotify` event reports when the colormap attribute of the window (for which this mask was selected) changes and when the colormap specified by the attribute is installed, uninstalled, or freed. `XChangeWindowAttributes` can generate this event when the `colormap` window attribute is changed. `XFreeColormap`, `XInstallColormap`, and `XUninstallColormap` generate this event if called on the colormap specified in the attribute of the window. From the information in the structure, you can tell which of these calls generated the event and what the current status of the colormap is. The conventions for what the client should do in response to each of these contingencies has not yet been determined. See Chapter 10, *Interclient Communication*.

`ColormapNotify` events are dicussed in Section 7.7.2.

8.3.3.10 PropertyChangeMask

A `PropertyNotify` event indicates that a property of a certain window was changed or deleted. This event is generated when `XChangeProperty`, `XDeleteProperty`, or `XRotateWindowProperties` is called or when `XGetWindowProperty` is called with certain arguments. Beyond its normal purpose, this event can be used to get the current server time. This is done by appending zero-length data to a property using `XChange-Property`, which generates a `PropertyNotify` event containing the time.

The uses of `PropertyNotify` events are described in Chapter 10.

8.3.3.11 StructureNotifyMask and SubstructureNotifyMask

`StructureNotifyMask` selects a group of event types that report when the state of a window has changed. This includes the window's configuration (size, position, border width, stacking order), whether it was destroyed, whether it was moved due to its `win_gravity` window attribute, whether it was mapped or unmapped, and whether it was reparented.

`SubstructureNotifyMask` selects the same events plus one that indicates that a window has been created; it monitors all the *subwindows* of the window specified in the `XSelectInput` call that used this mask. Only `SubstructureNotifyMask` selects `CreateNotify` events, because the window does not exist beforehand, and therefore, no ID exists to use in a call to `XSelectInput` using `StructureNotifyMask`.

Applications often select `StructureNotifyMask` to be notified that they have been manipulated by the window manager or some other client, so that they can act accordingly.

The following list describes the events selected by `StructureNotifyMask` and `SubstructureNotifyMask`:

- A `CirculateNotify` event reports a call to change the stacking order and includes whether the final position is on top or on bottom. This event is generated by `XCirculateSubwindows`, `XCirculateSubwindowsDown`, or `XCirculateSubwindowsUp`.

- A `ConfigureNotify` event reports changes to a window's configuration, including its size, position, border width, and stacking order. This event is generated by `XConfigureWindow`, `XLowerWindow`, `XMapRaised`, `XMoveResizeWindow`, `XMoveWindow`, `XRaiseWindow`, `XResizeWindow`, `XRestackWindows`, and `XSetWindowBorderWidth`.

- A `CreateNotify` event reports that a new window has been created with either `XCreateSimpleWindow` or `XCreateWindow`.

- A `DestroyNotify` event reports that a window has been destroyed with `XDestroyWindow` or `XDestroySubwindows`. When a window is destroyed, this event is delivered to all subwindows of the window before it is delivered to the window itself, unless the subwindows are in another client's save-set (see Chapter 14, *Window Management*, for a description of save-sets).

- A `GravityNotify` event reports when a window is moved because its parent was resized and had its window gravity attribute set.

- A `MapNotify` event reports when a window is mapped. This event is generated by `XMapWindow`, `XMapRaised`, and `XMapSubwindows`.

- A `ReparentNotify` event reports when a client successfully reparents a window (see Chapter 14 for a description of window reparenting).

- An `UnmapNotify` event reports when a mapped window is unmapped. This event also indicates whether the unmapping of a child window was due to the fact that the parent window was resized and the child had a window gravity attribute of `UnmapGravity`.

The `ConfigureNotify` event is used in the *basicwin* application described in Chapter 3, *Basic Window Program*. The rest of these events are used in a similar fashion by applications that need detailed knowledge of their state.

8.3.3.12 SubstructureRedirectMask

The three event types selected by `SubstructureRedirectMask`—`CirculateRequest`, `ConfigureRequest`, and `MapRequest`—can be used by a client (virtually always the window manager) to intercept and cancel window-configuration-changing requests made by other clients to change the window configuration. Only one client at a time can select `SubstructureRedirectMask` on a particular window. Normally, `SubstructureRedirectMask` is selected on the root window to allow the window manager to intercept layout-changing requests for the top-level windows of each application. When these events are selected, the Xlib requests noted in the paragraphs below do not perform their usual function but instead simply generate these events. The window manager is then able to modify the requests according to its layout policy before repeating the requests itself with its modified arguments.

These events differ from `CirculateNotify`, `ConfigureNotify`, and `MapNotify` in that the `*Request` events† deliver the parameters of the request before the requests are carried out and indicate that the original request has been cancelled. The `*Notify` requests indicate the final outcome of such requests, unhindered.

Each of the event structures associated with the following event types includes an `override_redirect` member, which is either `True` or `False`. If it is `True`, the window manager should ignore the event, since this indicates that the client has set the `override_redirect` attribute to indicate that this is a temporary window. (For more information, see Section 14.2.)

- `CirculateRequest` events report when an Xlib function, such as `XCirculate-Subwindows`, `XCirculateSubwindowsDown`, `XCirculateSubwindowsUp`, or `XRestackWindows` is called to change the stacking order of a group of children.

- `ConfigureRequest` events report when an Xlib function, such as `XConfigure-Window`, `XLowerWindow`, `XMoveResizeWindow`, `XMoveWindow`, `XRaise-Window`, `XResizeWindow`, or `XSetWindowBorderWidth` is called to resize, move, restack, or change the border width of a window.

- `MapRequest` events report when `XMapWindow` or `XMapSubwindows` is called to map a window.

The uses of the event types selected by `SubstructureRedirectMask` are described in Chapter 14, *Window Management*.

8.3.3.13 ResizeRedirectMask

The `ResizeRequest` event is generated when some other client (usually the window manager) attempts to resize the window on which `ResizeRedirectMask` is selected. `XConfigureWindow`, `XMoveResizeWindow`, and `XResizeWindow` generate this event. Only one client can select `ResizeRedirectMask` at a time on a particular window.

This event includes the *requested* size. The final size may be adjusted by the window manager and can be found from the resulting `ConfigureNotify` event or, if the window is visible, from the `Expose` event.

A client might wish to select this mask if it has only one acceptable size. Then when any client attemped to resize the window, the request would be sent as an event and can be safely ignored. However, if some client (say, the window manager) has selected `SubstructureRedirectMask` for the parent of the window on which `Resize-RedirectMask` was selected, the substructure redirect takes precedence. Therefore, this usually will not work. `ResizeRedirectMask` is not very useful, given that most window managers select `SubstructureRedirectMask`.

---

†The * (wildcard) notation is used occasionally in this manual to indicate a number of events or routines with similar names. In this case, `*Request` means all event types whose symbols end in `Request`.

8.3.3.14 Automatically Selected Events

Seven types of events can be sent to your program even if you do not explicitly select them. Your client must handle or throw away `MappingNotify` events regardless of whether the client reads the keyboard. All the others are generated in response to your own actions (either by the server or by other clients), and therefore, you should know that you are going to get them. Example 8-3 described when each of these events should be present in your event loop.

- `MappingNotify` events are caused by `XChangeKeyboardMapping`, `XSet-ModifierMapping`, and `XSetPointerMapping` calls that set the pointer button, keyboard key, and keyboard modifier key mappings. Since these mappings are global to the server, each client must call the correct function to refresh its knowledge of the mappings.

  If the changed mapping is of the keyboard, a receiving client should call `XRefresh-KeyboardMapping`, which updates a client's knowledge of the server's mapping between keycodes and keysyms.

  If the changed mapping is of the pointer, the client can call `XGetPointerMapping` to update its knowledge. Most current clients do not do this, however, because it is assumed that the button mappings were intentionally changed by the user. That means that the client should not attempt to adjust its operation so that the buttons have their old meanings.

- `ClientMessage` events are sent as a result of a call to `XSendEvent` by a client to a particular window. They contain data described by an `Atom`. These events are normally used to transfer selection data. The `send_event` member of the event structure will always be set.

- `SelectionClear`, `SelectionNotify`, and `SelectionRequest` events are used to communicate back and forth between two applications that are transferring information. This process is described in Section 10.3.

- `GraphicsExpose` and `NoExpose` events are selected not by an event mask but by the `graphics_exposures` member of the GC. One or the other of them (or both) is generated by each `XCopyArea` or `XCopyPlane` request when the GC specified for the request has this member set to `True`. Otherwise, the events are not generated. The `GraphicsExpose` event indicates that a source area could not be completely copied into a destination because the source was partially or fully obscured. The `NoExpose` event indicates that the copy was not affected by an obscured source. More than one `GraphicsExpose` event can be generated by a single `XCopyArea` or `XCopyPlane` request, depending on the number and position of the obscuring windows, but only one `NoExpose` is possible as a result of a single copy. `GraphicsExpose` events are often handled just like `Expose` events.

8.4 Sending Events

The XSendEvent function may be used to send a ClientMessage event or any other event type to a particular window, to the current keyboard focus window, or to the window in which the pointer is located. Sending events is necessary in selection processing, as described in Section 10.3. It may also be useful for designing test procedures for your input handling or for making demonstration programs that simulate user input.

The send_event member of each event structure indicates the origin of the event. If True, it was sent from another client rather from the server. Note that, unless this flag is explicitly checked, events from the server and from other clients will appear the same to your application.

8.5 Where to Find More on Each Event

All event types are described in reference format in Appendix E, *Event Reference*. The information on each page includes the event structure definition, description of each event structure member, XEvent union name, how to select the event, when it is generated, and notes on its use. Table 8-5 shows other places in this manual where you can find information about using certain event types.

Table 8-5. Where Events are Described Further

Event Type	Section
KeyPress KeyRelease	Section 9.1.1.1
ButtonPress ButtonRelease	Section 9.2.2
KeymapNotify	Section 9.3.1
MotionNotify	Section 9.2.1
EnterNotify LeaveNotify	Section 9.3
FocusIn FocusOut	Section 9.3
Expose	Section 3.2.13.1
GraphicsExpose NoExpose	Section 5.7
ColormapNotify	Section 7.7.2
PropertyNotify	Section 10.1
ConfigureNotify	Section 3.2.16

Table 8-5. Where Events are Described Further (continued)

Event Type	Section
CirculateRequest ConfigureRequest MapRequest	Section 14.2
MappingNotify	Section 9.1.2.3
SelectionClear	Section 10.3*
SelectionNotify	Section 10.3*
SelectionRequest	Section 10.3*

---

*Also in Appendix L, *Interclient Communication Conventions*, of Volume Zero, *X Protocol Reference Manual* (as of the second printing).

9

The Keyboard and Pointer

This chapter not only describes how to handle keyboard and pointer events but also describes many other topics related to these two input devices. In particular, it discusses X's use of keysyms as portable symbols for character encoding, keyboard remapping, keyboard and pointer "grabs," and keyboard and pointer preferences.

In This Chapter:

The Keyboard and Pointer

In Chapter 3, *Basic Window Program*, we showed you quite thoroughly how to deal with Expose events. But all we did with pointer and keyboard events was to exit the program. As you can guess, there can be more to it than that. This chapter describes and demonstrates the handling of keyboard and pointer events, describes keyboard and pointer mapping, and describes how to set keyboard preferences.

9.1 The Keyboard

The keyboard is an area like color, where X clients have to be made portable across systems with different physical characteristics. In the case of the keyboard, these variations are in two areas: whether the keyboard provides KeyPress and KeyRelease events or just KeyPress events, and the symbols on the caps of the keys.

Almost all serious workstations provide both KeyPress and KeyRelease events. Some personal computers, however, may not. Therefore, avoid depending on KeyRelease events if you want your client to be portable to the lowest classes of machines.

The second problem is adjusting for variations in the keys available on each keyboard and the codes they generate. We'll start explaining how this problem is solved by describing the contents of a key event.

KeyPress and KeyRelease events are stored in XKeyEvent structures, shown in Example 9-1. Each key event contains the keycode of the key that was pressed and state, a mask which indicates which modifier keys and pointer buttons were being held down just before the event. A *modifier key* is a key like Shift or Control that can modify the meaning of a key event. In addition to their effect on the processing of other keys, the modifier keys also generate key events with unique keycodes.

Example 9-1. The XKeyEvent structure

```
typedef struct {
    int type;                    /* Of event */
    unsigned long serial;        /* Last request processed by server */
    Bool send_event;             /* True if from a SendEvent request */
    Display *display;            /* Server connection */
    Window window;               /* "event" window reported in */
```

Example 9-1. The XKeyEvent structure (continued)

```
    Window root;              /* Root window event occurred on */
    Window subwindow;         /* Child window */
    Time time;                /* Milliseconds */
    int x, y;                 /* Coordinates in event window */
    int x_root, y_root;       /* Coordinates relative to root */
    unsigned int state;       /* Key or button mask */
    unsigned int keycode;     /* Detail */
    Bool same_screen;         /* Same screen flag */
} XKeyEvent;
typedef XKeyEvent XKeyPressedEvent;
typedef XKeyEvent XKeyReleasedEvent;
```

The keycode member of XKeyEvent is a number between 8 and 255. The keycode is the same regardless of whether a key is pressed or released. The keycode for each physical key never changes on a particular server, but the key with the same symbol on it on different brands of equipment may generate different keycodes. For portability reasons and because the keycode by itself without the state of the modifier keys does not provide enough information to interpret an event, clients cannot use keycodes by themselves to determine the meaning of key events.

Instead of using the keycode alone, X clients call XLookupString to translate the key event into a keysym. A *keysym* is a defined constant that corresponds to the meaning of a key event. For example, the translation of the keycode generated by the "a" key on any system would be XK_a if no other keys were being held and XK_A if the Shift key were being held or if Shift Lock was in effect (all keysyms begin with XK_). The translation of the keycode for the Return key (which is labeled Enter or just with an arrow on some keyboards) would be XK_Return. The Enter key on the keypad, if any, would have the keysym XK_KP_Enter. Example 9-2 shows some keysym definitions. All keysyms are defined in *<X11/keysymdef.h>*.

Example 9-2. Some sample keysym definitions

```
#define XK_BackSpace     0xFF08    /* Back space, back char,... */
#define XK_Left          0xFF51    /* Move left, left arrow */
#define XK_Undo          0xFF65    /* Undo, oops */
#define XK_Num_Lock      0xFF7F
#define XK_KP_Multiply   0xFFAA
#define XK_Shift_L       0xFFE1    /* Left shift */
#define XK_space         0x020     /* Space */
#define XK_numbersign    0x023     /* # */
#define XK_3             0x033
#define XK_question      0x03f     /* "?" */
#define XK_A             0x041
#define XK_e             0x065
```

XLookupString also provides an ASCII string that corresponds to the keysym or NULL if there is no associated string. By default, all the keys that have ASCII values will have that value as their string. For example, XK_A would have the string "A", XK_ampersand would have the string "&", and XK_4 would have the string "4". XK_Return, XK_Escape, and XK_Delete have ASCII values, but they are not printable. XK_Shift_L (the Shift key on the left side of the keyboard) would not normally have an associated string.

The ASCII value for a particular keysym as returned by `XLookupString` can be changed by the client using XRebindKeysym, and it can be a string of any length, not just a single character. Even though keysyms like `XK_F1` (the F1 key) have no default ASCII mapping, they can be given strings. This mapping would apply only to the client that calls `XRebind-Keysym`.

With these introductory comments, we'll move right to the examples that handle keyboard input. Then we'll return to discuss keysyms in more detail and the various keyboard mappings and how they can be changed.

9.1.1 Simple Keyboard Input

Example 9-3 shows the framework of the code for translating a keyboard event into both a keysym and an ASCII string. You will need the keysym to determine what the keystroke means, and the ASCII string if the keystroke is a printable character. If the keystroke is printable, the program would append the ASCII interpretation of the key event to the end of the result string (and display it). If the keystroke is a modifier key being pressed, the event can normally be ignored, since the modifier status of events on other keys is already dealt with by `XLookupString`. But `XK_Delete` or `XK_Backspace` would indicate that a character should be removed from the string.

The function keys are not initially mapped to ASCII strings and can be ignored, but if the client allows the user to map them to an arbitrary string, it should treat them like any other printable character.

You may notice in Example 9-3 that `XLookupString` returns something called an `XComposeStatus`. Some keyboards provide a Compose key, which is used to type characters not found on the keyboard keys. Its purpose is to make it possible to type characters from other languages without disturbing the normal operation of the keyboard. As it usually works, you press the Compose key followed by some other key to generate characters like é. A table is usually provided which tells you which keys correspond to each foreign character. Processing of multikey sequences using the Compose key may one day be provided by `XLookupString`, but it is not supported in Release 2, even though the `XCompose-Status` argument is already present.*

Example 9-3. Translating a key event to keysym and ASCII

```
Display *display;
XEvent event;
char buffer[20];
int bufsize = 20;
KeySym key;
XComposeStatus compose;
int charcount;
        .
        .
        .
        /*  Open display, create window, select, map */
```

---

*If your *lint* program complains about the variable `compose` which is declared but not used, you may be able to trick it with a line such as `compose=compose;`.

Example 9-3. Translating a key event to keysym and ASCII (continued)

```
XNextEvent(display, &event);
switch( event.type ) {
    .

    .

    .
case KeyPress:
    charcount = XLookupString(&event, buffer, bufsize, &keysym,
            &compose);
    /* Branch according to keysym, then use buffer
     * if the key is printable */
    break;
case MappingNotify:
    XRefreshKeyboardMapping(&event);
    break;
}
```

Keysyms for accented vowels, tildes, and most combinations found in Western languages are provided in the LATIN1 set. If you want to display an accented *e*, for example, the keysym is XK_eacute. If the desired character is not present in the desired font, the client can prepare two or more text items for XDrawText for displaying the desired overstrike character and use the delta member to move the second character back over the first. XDrawText is capable of drawing in a different font for each text item, in case the desired accent is in a separate font from the desired character.

9.1.1.1 Getting a String — A Dialog Box

Let's say you are porting a nonevent-driven program to X, and you have a routine called get_string that gets an ASCII string from the user. It gets the entire string before returning. But under X, the user might stop typing midway through, pop some other window on top to check some bit of information, then pop the original application back on top. That means you need to handle exposure in the middle of the input string, which, in turn, means you need a function that remembers the string's state so that it can be redrawn in the get_string routine. You also have to be prepared in case the keyboard gets remapped by some other client. Suddenly your tiny subroutine to get a string now must be integrated into the event loop.

Example 9-4 is a modification to the *basicwin* program described in Chapter 3, *Basic Window Program*, that puts up a pop-up dialog box. If the user presses a button in the *basicwin* window, the application puts up a dialog box, which the user can type into until a carriage return is typed. All the printable characters except Tab are supported, and Delete or Backspace operate as would be expected. The code allows the user to type the string while also handling the other events that might occur. This is done by placing the code for popping up the dialog in the branch for ButtonPress events, placing the code to redraw the dialog string in the branch for Expose events, and placing the code to process key events in the branch for KeyPress events.

Example 9-4. Implementing a dialog box

```
/* Other include files */
#include <X11/keysym.h>

/* Other defined constants */
#define MAX_POPUP_STRING_LENGTH 40
#define MAX_MAPPED_STRING_LENGTH 10

/* Global variables display and screen */

void main(argc, argv)
int argc;
char **argv;
{
    /* Declarations from basicwin */

      .
      .
      .

    /* The following are for pop-up window */
    static Window pop_win;
    char buffer[MAX_MAPPED_STRING_LENGTH];
    int bufsize=MAX_MAPPED_STRING_LENGTH;
    int start_x, start_y;
    KeySym keysym;
    XComposeStatus compose;
    int count;
    unsigned int pop_width, pop_height;
    char string[MAX_POPUP_STRING_LENGTH];
    int popped = False;
    int length;

    /* Create main window (win) and select its events */

      .
      .
      .

    XMapWindow(display, win);

    /* Get events, use first to display text and graphics */
    while (1)   {
        XNextEvent(display, &report);
        switch  (report.type) {
        case Expose:
            if (report.xexpose.window == pop_win) {
                /* If pop_win is nonzero, it has been created,
                 * and window in Expose is never zero */
                if (popped)
                    XDrawString(display, pop_win, gc, start_x,
                        start_y, string, strlen(string));
            }
            else {  /* It's the main window */
                /* Refresh main window as in basicwin */
            }
            break;
        case ConfigureNotify:
            /* Same as in basicwin */

              .
              .
```

Keyboard/
Pointer

Example 9-4. Implementing a dialog box (continued)

```
                  .
            break;
    case ButtonPress:
        /* Put up pop-up window, create if necessary */
        if (!pop_win) {   /* Create it and pop it */
    /* Determine pop-up box size from font information */
    pop_width = MAX_POPUP_STRING_LENGTH *
            font_info->max_bounds.width + 4;
    pop_height = font_info->max_bounds.ascent +
            font_info->max_bounds.descent + 4;
    pop_win = XCreateSimpleWindow(display, win, x, y,
            pop_width, pop_height, border_width,
            BlackPixel(display, screen),
            WhitePixel(display, screen));
    /* Calculate starting position of string in window */
    start_x = 2;
    start_y = font_info->max_bounds.ascent + 2;
    XSelectInput(display, pop_win, ExposureMask | KeyPressMask);
        }
        /* If window is already mapped, no problem */
        XMapWindow(display, pop_win);
        popped = True;
        break;
    case KeyPress:
        if (report.xkey.window == win) {
            /* Key on main window indicates exit */
            XUnloadFont(display, font_info->fid);
            XFreeGC(display, gc);
            XCloseDisplay(display);
            exit(1);
        }
        else {
            /* Get characters until you encounter a
             * carriage return; deal with backspaces, etc. */
            count = XLookupString(&report, buffer, bufsize,
                &keysym, &compose);
            /* Now do the right thing with as many
             * keysyms as possible */
            if ((keysym == XK_Return) || (keysym == XK_KP_Enter)
                    || (keysym == XK_Linefeed)) {
                XUnmapWindow(display, pop_win);
                popped = False;
                printf("string is %s\n", string);
                break;
            }
            else if (((keysym >= XK_KP_Space)
                    && (keysym <= XK_KP_9))
                    || ((keysym >= XK_space)
                    && (keysym <= XK_asciitilde))) {
                if ((strlen(string) + strlen (buffer)) >=
                    MAX_POPUP_STRING_LENGTH)
                    XBell(display, 100);
                else
                    strcat(string, buffer);
            }
            else if ((keysym >= XK_Shift_L)
```

Example 9-4. Implementing a dialog box (continued)

```
                             && (keysym <= XK_Hyper_R))
                        ;/* Do nothing because it's a modifier key */
                else if ((keysym >= XK_F1)
                        && (keysym <= XK_F35))
                    if (buffer == NULL)
                        printf("Unmapped function key\n");
                    else if ((strlen(string) + strlen (buffer)) >=
                            MAX_POPUP_STRING_LENGTH)
                        XBell(display, 100);
                    else
                        strcat(string, buffer);
                else if ((keysym == XK_BackSpace) ||
                        (keysym == XK_Delete)) {
                    if ((length = strlen(string)) > 0) {
                        string[length - 1] = NULL;
                        XClearWindow(display, pop_win);
                    }
                    else
                        XBell(display, 100);
                }
                else {
                    printf("keysym %s is not handled\n",
                            XKeysymToString(keysym));
                    XBell(display, 100);
                }
                XDrawString(display, pop_win, gc, start_x,
                    start_y, string, strlen(string));
                break;
            }
        case MappingNotify:
            XRefreshKeyboardMapping(&report);
            break;
        default:
            /* All events selected by StructureNotifyMask
             * except ConfigureNotify are thrown away here,
             * since nothing is done with them */
            break;
        } /* End switch */
    } /* End while */
}
```

Example 9-4 takes advantage of the fact that the keysyms are constants arranged in groups with consecutive values. By looking for any keysym in a given range, you do not need to specify every keysym you intend to match.

Notice that the program uses keysyms to match all the keystrokes and then does different things depending on whether the keysym is a normal key, a modifier key, a function key, a delete key, or an enter key. If the key is printable, it copies the ASCII values returned by XLookupString into the result string.

Keyboard/
Pointer

This program does have some weaknesses.* One of them is that it redraws the entire string instead of just the character being changed. Secondly, using XTextItem structures for each character and calling XDrawText instead of XDrawString would support Tab characters and functions keys mapped to strings. Since a tab has to be expanded into a number of spaces before being drawn and function keys may be mapped to arbitrary strings, it is difficult to properly implement them with the approach we have used in Example 9-4.

9.1.2 The Keyboard Mappings

As we have said, there are several translations that take place between the pressing of a key and its interpretation within a program. The first, the mapping between physical keys and keycodes, is server-dependent and cannot be modified. A client cannot determine anything about this first mapping, and it is just a fact that certain physical keys generate certain keycodes. The second mapping, keycodes to keysyms, can be modified by clients but is server-wide, so it usually is not modified. The specification of which keycodes are considered modifiers is also part of the second level of mapping, because it affects the mapping of keycodes to keysyms. The third mapping, from keysyms to strings, is local to a client. This is the mapping with which a client can allow the user to map the function keys to strings for convenience of typing.

We are going to describe the mapping between keysyms and strings first, because this is the mapping that applications are most likely to change. Following that, we'll describe what you need to know about the keycode-to-keysym mapping and modifier mapping to write normal applications. These mappings are normally only changed by clients run from the user's startup script that do nothing else, because they change the keyboard mapping for all applications.

After that, Sections 9.1.3.1 and 9.1.3.2 are optional reading. They describe the background and development of keysyms and how to write special purpose programs to change the server-wide mapping of keycodes to keysyms and the modifier mapping. These techniques are not needed in normal applications.

9.1.2.1 Keysyms to Strings

The default mapping of keysyms to ASCII is defined by the server. The ASCII representation of the keys on the main keyboard are the ASCII codes for the single characters on the caps of the keys. Keysyms that do not have ASCII representations, such as the function keys, initially have mappings to NULL, but they can sometimes be mapped to strings, as we'll describe. However, the modifier keys on some machines cannot be mapped to strings at all.

---

*We could say we left it this way because it is simpler, and it is, but that is not why we wrote it this way. We did not realize the other way would be better until the program was already done. We will leave it as an exercise for you to modify it as described!

Any client in which the user is expected to type a large amount of text should support remapping of the function keys to strings. XRebindKeysym is the only function that can change this string, the one returned by XLookupString. The string can be any length. This change affects only the client that calls XRebindKeysym.

Example 9-5 is a short code sample that demonstrates how to remap function keys to strings. It binds the string "STOP" to Shift-F1 and "ABORT" to Control-Shift-F1. Since keyboards may have two Shift and two Control keys, one on each side, the process has to be done for both. Mapping the function keys combined with modifiers will not work on all servers. (On the Sun sample server, this code results in STOP being generated when F1 is pressed with any modifiers and ABORT never being generated.) However, mapping of unmodified function keys should work on all servers.

Example 9-5. Mapping keys to strings

```
#include <X11/keysym.h>
    .
    .
Display *display;

KeySym modlist[2];                    /* Array of modifier keysyms */
unsigned int string_length;
unsigned int list_length;
    .
    .
/* Open display */
    .
/* Map Shift-F1 to "STOP"  */
string_length = 4;
list_length = 1;
modlist[0] = XK_Shift_R;    /* Do right shift key */
XRebindKeysym(display, XK_F1, modlist, list_length, "STOP",
        string_length);
modlist[0] = XK_Shift_L;    /* Do left shift key */
XRebindKeysym(display, XK_F1, modlist, list_length, "STOP",
        string_length);

/* Map Control-Shift-F1 to "ABORT"  */
string_length = 5;
list_length = 2;

/* Both right pressed */
modlist[0] = XK_Shift_R; modlist[1] = XK_Control_R;
XRebindKeysym(display, XK_F1, modlist, list_length, "ABORT",
        string_length);

/* Left Shift, Right Control */
modlist[0] = XK_Shift_L; modlist[1] = XK_Control_R;
XRebindKeysym(display, XK_F1, modlist, list_length, "ABORT",
        string_length);

/* Right Shift, Left Control */
modlist[0] = XK_Shift_R; modlist[1] = XK_Control_L;
XRebindKeysym(display, XK_F1, modlist, list_length, "ABORT",
        string_length);

/* Both left pressed */
```

Example 9-5. Mapping keys to strings (continued)

```
modlist[0] = XK_Shift_L; modlist[1] = XK_Control_L;
XRebindKeysym(display, XK_F1, modlist, list_length, "ABORT",
        string_length);
```

XLookupString currently uses a linear search to find the keysym corresponding to each key event, and each call to XRebindKeysym causes XLookupString to run somewhat slower. This problem is exacerbated if you want a function key (or any other key) to generate the same string with any combination of modifier keys, since this requires 15 or more calls to XRebindKeysym.

9.1.2.2 The Modifier Keys

A keysym represents the meaning of a certain combination of a key and modifier keys such as Shift and Control. For example, XK_A represents the letter "a" pressed while the Shift key is held down or while Shift Lock is on. As in this example, the keysym depends on what modifier key is being held.

Although Shift is present on all keyboards and Control on most, the remaining modifier keys are not standardized. There may be Meta, Hyper, Super, Left, Right, or Alternate keys. X, however, has a fixed set of logical modifiers, listed in the first column of Table 9-1. Each of these logical modifier symbols corresponds to a bit in the state member of the XKey-Event structure. On each keyboard, there is a mapping between the physical modifier keys and these logical modifiers. Table 9-1 also shows the keysyms of the keys that are by default mapped to the logical modifiers on a Sun-3 system and the corresponding keycodes for that system. You can use the *xmodmap* command without arguments to find out the default modifier mapping on any system.

Table 9-1. Logical Modifiers and a Typical Modifier Key Mapping

Logical Modifier	Default Keycodes of Modifier Keys (Sun-3)	Modifier Keysym (Sun-3)
ShiftMask	(0x6a), (0x75)	XK_Shift_L, XK_Shift_R
ShiftLockMask	(0x7e)	XK_Caps_Lock
ControlMask	(0x53)	XK_Control_L
Mod1Mask	(0x7f), (0x81)	XK_Meta_L, XK_Meta_R
Mod2Mask	(unmapped)	
Mod3Mask	(unmapped)	
Mod4Mask	(unmapped)	
Mod5Mask	(unmapped)	

Each keycode may have a list of keysyms, one for every logical modifier. Each list, of varying length, conveys the set of meanings for the key with each of the modifier keys pressed. This array of keysyms for each keycode is initially defined by the server. In most cases, only two keysyms are defined for the keys that represent single printable characters and only one for the rest.

9.1.2.3 Keycodes to Keysyms

Clients can change the mapping of keycodes to keysyms (with `XChangeKeyboard-Mapping`), but they rarely do because this mapping is global to the server. This change would affect every client operating on the server. Every client would receive a `Mapping-Notify` event (regardless of whether they selected it or whether they actually use keyboard input) and must then get a new keysym table from the server with `XRefreshKeyboard-Mapping`. (This table is stored in the `Display` structure and is used by `XLookup-String` and the other routines that return keysyms.) `XRefreshKeyboardMapping` works by erasing the copy of the keyboard and/or modifier mappings that are present in the `Display` structure (the `keysyms` and `modifiermap` members). The next time that an Xlib call is made that requires either of these mappings, a request is made to the server, the new mappings are transferred to Xlib, and the pointers in the `Display` structure are reset to the new mapping data. Subsequent calls to access this data use the `Display` structure instead of querying the server.

One of few applications that might change the mapping between keycodes and keysyms would be an application that converted between QWERTY and DVORAK keyboard layout. These are the nicknames for two different layouts for the alphabetic characters on English language keyboards. The QWERTY keyboard in common use was originally designed to be slow enough so that mechanical typesetting machine operators would not be able to type fast enough to jam their machines. The DVORAK keyboard, on the other hand, was designed to place the most common letters in the English language under the home row of keys and is much faster.

Let's say a user wanted to use the DVORAK layout instead of the default, which is QWERTY. This application would not even need to create a window, but it would change the mapping of keycodes to keysyms with `XChangeKeyboardMapping`. The user could then move the keycaps around on the keyboard or label them somehow. Except for calling `XRefreshKeyboardMapping`, other applications would operate as usual. From then on, while the server was running, all applications would work properly with the DVORAK layout.

9.1.3 Background on Keysyms

Keysyms are a concept developed especially for X. It may help you to understand them better to read about how they were designed. But this is optional reading, and you can skip to Section 9.2 if you do not plan to write programs that change the mapping of keycodes to keysyms.

The keysyms are defined in two include files, *<X11/keysym.h>* and *<X11/keysymdef.h>*. Together these files define several sets of keysyms for different languages and purposes. There are sets for Latin, Greek, Cyrillic, Arabic, and so on, intended to allow for internationalization of programs. There are also sets for publishing and technical purposes, because these fields have their own "languages." *<X11/keysym.h>* defines which character sets are active, and *<X11/keysymdef.h>* defines the symbols in all the sets. Only *<X11/keysym.h>* needs to be included in an application because it includes *<X11/keysymdef.h>*.

By default, the enabled sets of defined keysyms include the ISO Latin character sets (1-4), a set of Greek characters, and a set of miscellaneous symbols common on keyboards (Return, Help, Tab, and so on). These are sufficient for making an application work in any Western language. Symbols for Katakana, Arabic, Cyrillic, Technical, Special, Publishing, APL, and Hebrew character sets are defined in *<X11/keysymdef.h>* but are not enabled in *<X11/keysym.h>* and may not be available on all servers. This is because some C compilers have a limit to the number of allowable defined symbols.

Many of the keysym sets share keysyms with sets earlier in the *<X11/keysymdef.h>* include file. For example, there is only one XK_space keysym because a space is common to all languages. XK_space is in LATIN1 so that it is always available. The LATIN2 and LATIN3 sets are quite short because they share most of their symbols with the previous sets.

9.1.3.1 The Design of Keysyms

English language keyboards tend to be quite standard in the alphanumeric keys, but they differ radically in the miscellaneous function keys. Many function keys are left over from early timesharing days or are designed for a specific application. Keyboard layouts from large manufacturers tend to have lots of keys for every conceivable purpose, whereas small workstation manufacturers often have keys that are solely for support of some unique function.

There are two ways of thinking about how to define keysyms given such a situation: the *Engraving* approach and the *Common* approach.

The Engraving approach is to create a keysym for every unique key engraving. This is effectively taking the union of all key engravings on all keyboards. For example, some keyboards label function keys across the top as F1 through Fn, others label them as PF1 through PFn. These would be different keys under the Engraving approach. Likewise, Lock would differ from Shift Lock, which is different from the up-arrow symbol that has the effect of changing lower case to upper case. There are lots of other aliases such as Del, DEL, Delete, Remove, and so forth. The Engraving approach makes it easy to decide if a new entry should be added to the keysym set: if it does not exactly match an existing one, then a new one is created. One estimate is that there would be on the order of 300 to 500 miscellaneous keysyms using this approach, not counting foreign translations and variations.

The Common approach tries to capture all of the keys present on a number of common keyboards, folding likely aliases into the same keysym. For example, Del, DEL, and Delete are all merged into a single keysym. Vendors would be expected to augment the keysym set (using the vendor-specific encoding space) to include all of their unique keys that were not included in the standard set. Each vendor decides which of its keys map into the standard keysyms. It is more difficult to implement this approach, since a judgement is required whether a sufficient set of keyboards implement an engraving to justify making it a keysym in the standard set and which engravings should be merged into a single keysym. Under this scheme, there are an estimated 100 to 150 keysyms for an English language keyboard.

While neither scheme is perfect, the Common approach has been selected because it makes it easier to write a portable application. Having the Delete functionality merged into a single keysym allows an application to implement a deletion function and expect reasonable bindings on a wide set of workstations. Under the Common approach, application writers are still free to look for and interpret vendor-specific keysyms, but because they are in an extended set, application developers should be more conscious that they are writing applications in a nonportable fashion.

9.1.3.2 Conventions for Keysym Meaning

For each keycode, the server defines a list of keysyms, corresponding to the key pressed while various modifier keys are being held. There are conventions for the meanings of the first two keysyms in the list. The first keysym in the list for a particular key should be construed as the symbol corresponding to a `KeyPress` when no modifier keys are down. The second keysym in the list, if present, usually should be construed as the symbol when the Shift or Shift Lock modifier keys are down. However, if there is only one keysym for a particular keycode, if it is alphabetic, and if case distinction is relevant for it, then the appropriate case should be based on the Shift and Lock modifiers. For example, if the single keysym is an upper-case *A*, you have to use the `state` member of `XKeyEvent` to determine if the Shift key is held. `XLookupString` should translate the event into the correct ASCII string anyway.

X does not suggest an interpretation of the keysyms beyond the first two and does not define any spatial geometry of the symbols on the key by their order in the keysym list. This is because the list of modifier keys varies widely between keyboards. However, when programming, it should be safe to assume that the third member in the keysym list would correspond to the key pressed with the next most common modifier available on the keyboard, which might be Control.

For keyboards with both left-side and right-side modifier keys (for example, Shift keys on each side that generate different keycodes), the bit in the `state` member in the event structure defines the OR of the keys. If electronically distinguishable, these keys can have separate keycodes and up/down events generated and your program can track their individual states manually.

9.1.4 Changing the Server-wide Keyboard Mappings

Both the keycode-to-keysym mapping and the modifier mapping affect all clients when they are changed by any client. That is why normal applications will not change them. Special purpose programs, however, can be written to change these mappings, usually to be run from a user's startup script. These sections describe how to write such programs. If you do not plan to write one, you can skip ahead to Section 9.1.5.

9.1.4.1 Changing the Keycode-to-Keysym Mapping

XChangeKeyboardMapping changes the current mapping of the specified range of key-codes to keysyms.

Example 9-6 shows a simple program called *mapkey* that changes the keyboard mapping for all the applications running on the server. This application takes pairs of arguments that are keysyms and maps the keycode associated with the first keysym to the second keysym. In other words, you could use it to map the F1 key to be Escape and Home to be a Control key on the right side of the keyboard by typing the following:

```
$ mapkey F1 Escape Home Control_R
```

Use mapkey with care, because it is easy to disable a server by remapping an alphanumeric key. Such a remapping cannot be reversed except by restarting the server.

Example 9-6. An application for server-wide keymapping

```c
#include <stdio.h>
#include <X11/Xlib.h>
#include <X11/Xutil.h>
#include <X11/Xatom.h>
#include <X11/keysym.h>

main(argc, argv)
int argc;
char **argv;
{
    KeySym old, new;
    int old_code;
    Display *display;

    if (!(display = XOpenDisplay(""))) {
        fprintf(stderr,"Cannot open display '%s'\n",
                    XDisplayName(""));
        exit(1);
    }
    argv++, argc--;

    if (argc & 0x1) {
        fprintf(stderr,"Usage:  Keysymfrom Keysymto Keysymfrom \
                    Keysymto ...\n");
        exit(1);
    }
    while (argc > 1) {
        old = XStringToKeysym(*argv++);
        new = XStringToKeysym(*argv++);
        argc--, argc--;
        old_code = XKeysymToKeycode(display, old);
        XChangeKeyboardMapping(display, old_code, 1, &new, 1);
    }
    XFlush(display);
    XCloseDisplay(display);
    exit(0);
}
```

The application in Example 9-6 could be rewritten on a larger scale to change a keyboard from QWERTY to DVORAK layout as described in Section 9.1.2.3. Since the keycodes are server-dependent, the QWERTY-to-DVORAK conversion program would not be portable between machines unless it used XGetKeyboardMapping to get the current mapping of keycodes to keysyms and then remapped them.

XGetKeyboardMapping returns an array of keysyms that represent the current mapping of the specified range of keycodes.

9.1.4.2 Changing Modifier Mapping

X allows you to control which physical keys are considered modifier keys. Normal applications will not do this. The modifier mapping might be changed for a left-handed user if, by default, there was only one Control key on the left side of the keyboard and the user preferred to have a Control key on the right side. In that case, a conveniently placed key on the right side could be mapped to a logical Control key. Like keycode-to-keysym remapping, this would typically be done by a special purpose application run from the user's startup script.

While modifier keys generate KeyPress and KeyRelease events like other keys, modifier keys are the only keys reported in the state member of every key, button, motion, or border crossing event structure. The state member is a mask that indicates which logical modifiers were pressed when the event occurred. Each bit in state is represented by a constant such as ControlMask. state is used by XLookupString to generate the correct keysym from a key event. Note that the state member of events other than key, button, motion, and border crossing events does not have the meaning described here.

XInsertModifiermapEntry and XDeleteModifiermapEntry provide the easiest ways by far to add or delete a few keycodes for a modifier.

Using XInsertModifiermapEntry and XDeleteModifiermapEntry is straightforward. You get the current modifier mapping stored in an XModifierKeymap structure with a call to XGetModifierMapping. You specify this structure, a keycode, and one of the eight modifier symbols as the three arguments to XInsertModifiermap-Entry or XDeleteModifiermapEntry. Both routines return a new XModifier-Keymap structure suitable for calling XSetModifierMapping. You should add or delete all the keycodes you intend to change before calling XSetModifierMapping.

You should not need to understand how the modifiers are stored to use the procedure described above for adding or deleting keycodes. To change the modifier map without the aid of XInsertModifiermapEntry or XDeleteModifiermapEntry, read Section 9.1.4.3.

XSetModifierMapping is the routine that actually changes the mapping. As such, it is when calling XSetModifierMapping that any errors appear, even though they are usually caused by an invalid XModifierKeymap structure that was set earlier.

Keyboard/
Pointer

These are the requirements for the XModifierKeymap structure specified to XSet-ModifierMapping:

- Zero keycodes are ignored.

- No keycode may appear twice anywhere in the map (otherwise, a BadValue error is generated).

- All nonzero keycodes must be in the range specified by min_keycode and max_keycode in the Display structure (else a BadValue error).

- A server can impose restrictions on how modifiers can be changed. For example, certain keys may not generate up transitions in hardware or multiple modifier keys may not be supported. If a restriction is violated, then the status reply is MappingFailed, and none of the modifiers are changed.

If the new keycodes specified for a modifier differ from those currently defined and any (current or new) keys for that modifier are in the down state, then the status reply is Mapping-Busy, and none of the modifiers are changed.

XSetModifierMapping generates a MappingNotify event on a Mapping-Success status.

When finished mapping the keyboard, you can free the XModifierKeymap structures by calling XFreeModifiermap.

9.1.5 Other Keyboard-handling Routines

Several routines in addition to XLookupString provide ways to translate key events. None of these routines are commonly needed in applications.

You might think that XKeysymToString and XStringToKeysym describe the mapping between keysyms and strings, but they don't. XKeysymToString does not return the same string as is placed in the *buffer* argument of XLookupString, when XKeysym-ToString is given the keysym that XLookupString returns. XKeysymToString changes the symbol form of a keysym (XK_Return), which is a number, into a string form of the symbol ("Return"), and XStringToKeysym does the reverse. XKeysym-ToString(XK_F1) would return "F1" regardless of what string is currently mapping to the F1 key. Only XLookupString returns the string mapped to a particular keysym with XRebindKeysym.

XKeycodeToKeysym and XKeysymToKeycode make the mapping between single keycodes and keysyms more accessible. (XLookupKeysym actually takes a key event, extracts the keycode, and calls XKeycodeToKeysym.) For XKeycodeToKeysym and XLookupKeysym, you must specify which keysym you want from the list for the keycode, with the *index* argument. Remember that the list of keysyms for each keycode represents the key with various combinations of modifier keys pressed. The meaning of the keysym list beyond the first two (unmodified, Shift or Shift Lock) is not defined. Therefore, the *index* values of 0 and 1 are the most commonly used.

9.2 The Pointer

The pointer generates events as it moves, as it crosses window borders, and as its buttons are pressed. It provides position information that can define a path in the two-dimensional space of the screen, tell you which window the pointer is in and allow the user to "point and click," generating input without using the keyboard. In fact, the pointer is the most unique feature of a window system.

This section describes how to track the pointer and how to handle the pointer buttons. Border crossing events are discussed in Section 9.3, because they must be handled in concert with keyboard focus change events.

9.2.1 Tracking Pointer Motion

There are three ways of handling pointer motion events:

- Getting all motion events. The program simply receives and processes every motion event. This option is suitable for applications that require all movements to be reported, no matter how small. Since many motion events are generated and reporting the processing of the events may lag behind the pointer, this approach is not suitable for applications that require the most current information about pointer position.

- Getting hints and querying pointer position. This method greatly reduces the number of motion events sent but requires that XQueryPointer be called to get the current pointer position. This option is suitable for applications that require only the final position of the mouse after each movement.

- Reading the motion history buffer. After checking that the buffer exists, call XGet-MotionEvents when you want the array of events occurring between two specified times. This option is not available on all servers, but it is suitable for detailed pointer position reporting. Its advantage over getting all motion events is that the list of pointer positions in the motion history buffer can be used for undoing or responding to exposure events in drawing applications.

Let's look at each of these methods in detail.

9.2.1.1 Getting All Motion Events

The most obvious way to handle motion events is to get all motion events. The only complication is that you must keep the processing of each event to a minimum so that the feedback loop to the user is reasonably fast.

Example 9-7 shows another modification to *basicwin*, the program described in Chapter 3, *Basic Window Program*. It creates a child window of the top-level window of the application and allows the user to draw into it by moving the pointer with any button held down.

Example 9-7. Getting all motion events

```
/* Global declarations of display and screen */

  .
  .
  .

#define BUF_SIZE 2000

void main(argc, argv)
int argc;
char **argv;
{
    /* Declarations from basicwin */

      .
      .
      .

    Window wint;
    int xpositions[BUF_SIZE], ypositions[BUF_SIZE];
    int i;
    int count = 0;
    Bool buffer_filled = False;

    /* Open display and create window win */

      .
      .
      .

    wint = XCreateSimpleWindow(display, win, 20, 20, 50, 50,
            border_width, BlackPixel(display, screen),
            WhitePixel(display,screen));

    XSelectInput(display, wint, ExposureMask | PointerMotionMask);

    XMapWindow(display, wint);

      .
      .
      .

    /* Select events for and map win */

    while (1)  {
        XNextEvent(display, &report);
        switch  (report.type) {
        case MotionNotify:
            printf("got a motion event\n");
            xpositions[count] = report.xmotion.x;
            ypositions[count] = report.xmotion.y;
            XDrawPoint(display, wint, gc,
                    report.xmotion.x, report.xmotion.y);
            /* The following implements a fast ring buffer
             * when count reaches buffer size */
            if (count <= BUF_SIZE)
                count++;
            else {
                count = 0;
                buffer_filled = True;
            }
            break;
        case Expose:
            printf("got expose event\n");
```

Example 9-7. Getting all motion events (continued)

```
                    if (report.xexpose.count != 0)
                        break;
                    if (report.xexpose.window == wint) {
                        /* This redraws the right number of points;
                         * if the ring buffer is not yet filled,
                         * it draws count points; otherwise, it
                         * draws all the points */
                        for (i=0 ; i < (buffer_filled ?
                                    BUF_SIZE : count) ; i++)
                            XDrawPoint(display, wint, gc, xpositions[i],
                                        ypositions[i]);
                    }
                    else {
                        if (window_size == SMALL)
                            TooSmall(win, gc, font_info);
                        else {
                            /* Place text in window */
                            draw_text(win, gc, font_info, width, height);

                            /* Place graphics in window */
                            draw_graphics(win, gc, width, height);
                        }
                    }
                break;
                /* Other event types handled same as basicwin */
                    .
                    .
                    .
            } /* End switch */
    } /* End while */
}
```

The program keeps a record of the points drawn so that they can be redrawn in case of an Expose event. The event record is a ring buffer so that the latest BUF_SIZE pointer positions are always maintained.

The program requires that one or more of the pointer buttons must be held down while drawing. (Most drawing applications require a button to be held, because otherwise it is impossible to move the pointer into a different application without drawing a trail of points to the edge of the window.) Therefore, drawing applications normally select ButtonMotion-Mask.

It would be quite easy to extend this program by giving each button a different meaning. Drawing with button 1 could mean drawing in black, button 2 could mean drawing in white, and button 3 could mean toggling the previous state of the drawn pixels. The only change necessary to implement this would be code that changes the foreground pixel value and logical operation in a GC or creates three GCs with these variations. The routine would determine which button was pressed from the state member of the event structure and determine what to do if more than one button was pressed.

9.2.1.2 Using Pointer Motion Hints

If you do not need a record of every point the pointer has passed through but only its current position, using motion hints is the most efficient method of handling pointer motion events. This method could be used for dragging in menus or scrollbars, in a window manager when it moves the outlines of windows, or in a drawing application in a line drawing mode. We'll demonstrate the technique in a line drawing application.

To use this method, select `PointerMotionHintMask` in addition to the specific event masks you desire. `PointerMotionHintMask` is a modifier; it does not select events by itself.

Example 9-8 demonstrates how to read pointer events with `PointerMotionHintMask` selected. The code shown in the example draws lines between the series of points the user specifies with button clicks. The `ButtonPress` event indicates the beginning of a line, `MotionNotify` events allow the application to draw a temporary line to the current pointer position, and `ButtonRelease` events indicate that the line should be drawn permanently between the points indicated by the `ButtonPress` and `ButtonRelease` events.

Example 9-8. Using pointer motion hints

```
/* Declare global variables display and screen */
    .
    .
    .
void main(argc, argv)
int argc;
char **argv;
{
    /* Declarations from basicwin */
        .
        .
        .
        int root_x, root_y;
        Window root, child;
        unsigned int keys_buttons;
    Window wint;
    XPoint points[BUF_SIZE];
    int index = 1;
    int pos_x, pos_y;
    int prev_x, prev_y;
    GC gcx;

    wint = XCreateSimpleWindow(display, win, 20, 20, 50, 50,
            border_width, BlackPixel(display, screen),
            WhitePixel(display,screen));

    XSelectInput(display, wint, ExposureMask | ButtonPressMask
            | ButtonReleaseMask | ButtonMotionMask
            | PointerMotionHintMask);

    gcx = XCreateGC(display, win, 0, NULL);
    XSetFunction(display, gcx, GXxor);
    XSetForeground(display, gcx, BlackPixel(display, screen));
```

Example 9-8. Using pointer motion hints (continued)

```
    XMapWindow(display, wint);
    while (1)   {
        XNextEvent(display, &report);
        switch  (report.type) {
        case ButtonPress:
            points[index].x = report.xbutton.x;
            points[index].y = report.xbutton.y;
            break;
        case ButtonRelease:
            index++;
            points[index].x = report.xbutton.x;
            points[index].y = report.xbutton.y;
            break;
        case MotionNotify:
            printf("got a motion event\n");
            while (XCheckMaskEvent(display,
                    ButtonMotionMask, &report));
            if (!XQueryPointer(display, report.xmotion.window,
                    &root, &child, &root_x, &root_y,
                    &pos_x, &pos_y, &keys_buttons))
                /* Pointer is on other screen */
                break;

            /* Undraw previous line, only if not first */
            if (index != 1)
                XDrawLine(display, wint, gcx, points[index].x,
                        points[index].y, prev_x, prev_y);

            /* Draw current line */
            XDrawLine(display, wint, gcx, points[index].x,
                    points[index].y, pos_x, pos_y);
            prev_x = pos_x;
            prev_y = pos_y;
            break;
        case Expose:
            printf("got expose event\n");

            if (report.xexpose.window == wint) {
                while (XCheckTypedWindowEvent(display,
                        wint, Expose, &report));
                XSetFunction(display, gcx, GXcopy);
                XDrawLines(display, wint, gcx, points,
                        index, CoordModeOrigin);
                XSetFunction(display, gcx, GXxor);
            }
            else {
                /* Same code as basicwin */
            }
            break;
        } /* End switch */
    } /* End while */
}
```

In some applications, you do not need to track pointer motion events to know where the pointer is at particular times. The pointer position is given in ButtonPress, Button-Release, KeyPress, KeyRelease, EnterNotify, and LeaveNotify events. You can use any of these events to locate objects in a window.

9.2.1.3 Motion History

If the motion history buffer exists on the server (XDisplayMotionBufferSize (display) > 0), all selected motion events are placed in a list of XTimeCoord structures. There is no macro for accessing this member of the display structure. You specify the desired range of times to XGetMotionEvents, and it returns a pointer to a list of XTimeCoord structures, representing all the pointer positions during the range of times.

The XTimeCoord structure is shown in Example 9-9.

Example 9-9. The XTimeCoord structure

```
typedef struct _XTimeCoord {
     short x,y;   /* Position relative to root window */
     Time time;
} XTimeCoord;
```

Example 9-10 shows another version of the program used to demonstrate getting all motion events. (This code has not been tested because few if any existing servers have the motion history buffer.) An application that uses motion history should also support the all-motion-events approach for use on servers that do not have the buffer.

Example 9-10. Reading the motion history buffer

```
/* Global declarations of display and screen */
    .
    .
    .
#define BUF_SIZE 2000

void main(argc, argv)
int argc;
char **argv;
{
    /* Declarations from basicwin */
        .
        .
        .
    Window wint;
    int xpositions[BUF_SIZE], ypositions[BUF_SIZE];
    int i;
    int count = 0;
    Bool buffer_filled = False;

    /* Open display and create window win */
        .
        .
        .
    if (display->motion_buffer <= 0)
```

Example 9-10. Reading the motion history buffer (continued)

```
        {
        printf("%s: motion history buffer not provided on server",
                argv(0));
        exit(-1);   /* Or use all events method instead */
        }
    wint = XCreateSimpleWindow(display, win, 20, 20, 50, 50,
            border_width, BlackPixel(display, screen),
            WhitePixel(display,screen));

    XSelectInput(display, wint, ExposureMask | ButtonMotionMask
            | PointerMotionHintMask);

    XMapWindow(display, wint);
        .
        .
        .

    /* Select events for and map win */

    while (1)  {
        XNextEvent(display, &report);
        switch  (report.type) {
        case MotionNotify:
                printf("got a motion event\n");
                while (XCheckTypedEvent(display, MotionNotify, &report));
                start = prevtime;
                stop = report.xmotion.time;
                xytimelist = XGetMotionEvents(display, window, start,
                        stop, &nevents);
                for (i=0;i<nevents;i++)
                    XDrawPoint(display, window, gc, xytimelist[i]->x,
                            xytimelist[i]->y);
                break;
            case Expose:
                printf("got expose event\n");
                if (report.xexpose.window == wint) {
                    while (XCheckTypedWindowEvent(display,
                            wint, Expose, &report));
                    xytimelist = XGetMotionEvents(display, window,
                            0, CurrentTime, &nevents);
                    for (i=0 ; i < nevents ; i++)
                        XDrawPoint(display, window, gc, xytimelist[i]->x,
                                xytimelist[i]->y);
                }
                else {
                    while (XCheckTypedWindowEvent(display,
                            win, Expose, &report));
                    if (window_size == SMALL)
                        TooSmall(win, gc, font_info);
                    else {
                        /* Place text in window */
                        draw_text(win, gc, font_info, width, height);

                        /* Place graphics in window */
                        draw_graphics(win, gc, width, height);
                    }
                }
```

Keyboard/
Pointer

Example 9-10. Reading the motion history buffer (continued)

```
            break;
        /* Other event types handled same as basicwin */
        .
        .
        .
        } /* End switch */
    } /* End while */
}
```

9.2.2 Handling Pointer Button Events

The examples of tracking pointer motion in Section 9.2.1 use the buttons to some extent, but they do not tell you the whole story. There is the subject of automatic button grabs, and there are issues involved in making each button perform a different function. Let's tackle grabs first.

When a pointer button is pressed, an active grab is triggered automatically (as described in Section 8.3.2.2, an active grab means that all button events before the matching `Button-Release` event on the same button always goes to the same application, or sometimes the same window, as the `ButtonPress`). The automatic grab does not take place if an active grab already exists or a passive grab on the present key and button combination exists for some higher level window in the hierarchy than the window in which the `ButtonPress` occurred.

The `OwnerGrabButtonMask` that you can specify in calls to `XSelectInput` controls the distribution of the `ButtonRelease` event (and any other pointer events that occur between the `ButtonPress` and `ButtonRelease`). If `OwnerGrabButtonMask` is selected, the `ButtonRelease` event will be sent to whichever window in the application the pointer is in when the event occurs. If the pointer is outside the application or if `OwnerGrabButtonMask` is not selected, the event is sent to the window in which the `ButtonPress` occurred.

`OwnerGrabButtonMask` should be selected when an application wants to know in which window `ButtonRelease` events occur. This information is useful when you require that both the `ButtonPress` and the matching `ButtonRelease` events occur in the same window in order for an operation to be executed. In practice, it does not hurt to select `OwnerGrabButtonMask` even if you do not need the response it provides. If you do not select `OwnerGrabButtonMask`, any changes you try to make to the event mask of the grabbing window before the `ButtonRelease` will not take effect, unless done with `XChangeActivePointerGrab`.

The automatic grabs affect only the window to which button events are sent. To be more precise, they affect the value of the `window` member in the button event structures in the application's event queue. And for the event to be placed on the queue in the first place, it must have been selected on the window specified in the `window` member.

Now let's talk about distinguishing which pointer button was pressed. Two members of the XButtonEvent structure contain information about the button state. The button member specifies the button that changed state to trigger the event. The state member gives the state of all the buttons and modifier keys just before the event. You will need the state member only if you require that certain key or button combinations be pressed to trigger an operation.

Especially if you require that the same button must be pressed and released in a certain window, be sure to account for the case where, for example, button 1 is pressed, then buttons 2 and 3 are pressed and released (perhaps repeatedly) or pressed and held, before button 1 is again released. You must be careful if you structure your code as shown in Example 9-11 to handle ButtonPress and ButtonRelease events in pairs.* There is no case for ButtonRelease in the example. Instead the code for ButtonPress looks for the matching ButtonRelease event. The matching ButtonRelease might not be the next button event, so intervening events must be dealt with. This problem appears only if you are trying to distinguish the button that was pressed.

Example 9-11. Accepting button events in pairs

```
case ButtonPress:
    /* Draw pane in white on black */
    paint_pane(event.xbutton.window, panes, gc, rgc,
            font_info, BLACK);

    /* Keep track of which button was pressed */
    button = event.xbutton.button;

    /* Keep track of which window press occurred in */
    inverted_pane = event.xbutton.window;

    /* Get the matching ButtonRelease on same button */
    while (1) {
        /* Get rid of presses on other buttons */
        while (XCheckTypedEvent(display, ButtonPress,
                &event));
        /* Wait for release; if on correct button, exit */
        XMaskEvent(display, ButtonReleaseMask, &event);
        if (event.xbutton.button == button)
            break;
    }

    /* All events are sent to the grabbing window
     * regardless of whether this is True or False,
     * because owner_events only affects the
     * distribution of events when the pointer is
     * within this application's windows; we don't
     * expect it to be for a window manager */
    owner_events = True;

    /* We don't want pointer or keyboard events
     * frozen in the server */
    pointer_mode = GrabModeAsync;
    keyboard_mode = GrabModeAsync;
```

---

*This code is an excerpt from *winman*, the simple window manager described in Chapter 14, *Window Management*.

Example 9-11. Accepting button events in pairs (continued)

```
    /* We don't want to confine the cursor */
    confine_to = None;

    GrabPointer(display, menuwin, owner_events,
            ButtonPressMask | ButtonReleaseMask,
            pointer_mode, keyboard_mode,
            confine_to, hand_cursor, CurrentTime);

    /* If press and release occurred in same window,
     * do command; if not, do nothing */
    if (inverted_pane == event.xbutton.window)
        {
        /* Convert window ID to window array index  */
        for (winindex = 0; inverted_pane !=
                panes[winindex]; winindex++)
            ;
        switch (winindex)
            {
        case 0:
            raise_lower(display, screen,
                    RAISE);
            break;
          .
          .
          .

        case 9: /* Exit */
            XSetInputFocus(display,
                RootWindow(display,screen),
                RevertToPointerRoot,
                CurrentTime);
            /* Turn all icons back into windows */
            /* Must clear focus highlights */
            XClearWindow(display, RootWindow(display, screen));
            /* Need to change focus border width back here */

            XFlush(display);
            XCloseDisplay(display);
            exit(1);
        default:
            (void) fprintf(stderr,
                    "Something went wrong\n");
            break;
            } /* End switch */
        } /* End if */

    /* Invert back here (logical function is GXcopy) */
    paint_pane(event.xexpose.window, panes, gc, rgc,
            font_info, WHITE);

    inverted_pane = NONE;
    draw_focus_frame();
    XUngrabPointer(display, CurrentTime);
    XFlush(display);
    break;
case DestroyNotify:
  .
  .
  .
```

9.2.3 Changing the Pointer Button Mapping

Some applications may allow the user to modify the mapping between the physical pointer buttons and the logical buttons that are reported when a button is pressed. In other words, if physical button 1 were mapped to logical button 3, then when either button 3 or button 1 were pressed, it would appear to all applications that only button 3 was pressed.

There are five logical buttons, but the number of physical buttons may range from one up to and perhaps greater than five. Mapping the pointer buttons might be done, for example, to simulate buttons 4 and 5 on a system with a three-button mouse. However, while physical buttons 1 and 2 were mapped to logical 4 and 5, no buttons would be mapped to logical 1 and 2. Therefore, there would have to be a way of toggling between the modes, perhaps using a function key.

The mapping of pointer buttons is analogous to the mapping between keycodes and keysyms in that it is global to the server and affects all clients. However, since the translation of a pointer event takes place in the server, unlike key event processing routines that use information stored in Xlib whenever possible, no routine is necessary to update the pointer mapping like XRefreshKeyboardMapping updates the keyboard mapping.

XGetPointerMapping returns the current mapping between physical and logical pointer buttons. XSetPointerMapping sets this mapping.

9.2.4 Moving the Pointer

The XWarpPointer routine moves the pointer to a relative or global position. Its use should be minimized and constrained to particular predictable circumstances, because it often confuses the user.

XWarpPointer has various features for moving only in certain situations. See the reference page in Volume Two, *Xlib Reference Manual*, for details.

Warping the pointer generates MotionNotify and border crossing events just as if the user moved the pointer.

9.3 Border Crossing and Keyboard Focus Change Events

LeaveNotify and EnterNotify events are generated when the pointer crosses a window border. If the window manager is of the real-estate-driven variety (as is *uwm*), you might be tempted to assume that a LeaveNotify event indicates that the window will not receive keyboard input until it receives a matching EnterNotify. However, this assumption is not true if the user has been allowed to set a keyboard focus window. It is also not true if the window manager is of the listener variety (see Chapters 1, 10, and 14). Ideally, you should be prepared to deal with either type of window manager.

Keyboard/ Pointer

Pointer input can only be delivered to a window when the pointer is inside the window (unless the window grabs the pointer). Therefore, an application that depends on pointer input can expect to be idle when the pointer leaves the window and to be active again when the pointer enters. Notice that keyboard input can be diverted with the keyboard focus or grabs, while pointer input can only be diverted by grabs.

`FocusIn` and `FocusOut` events occur when the keyboard focus window changes (when some client calls `XSetInputFocus`). By using focus events together with the border crossing events, an application should be able to determine whether or not it can get keyboard input. If it cannot get keyboard input, it may change its behavior somewhat. If it polls for keyboard input to allow for interrupts, it can stop polling. If it normally highlights a window when the pointer enters it, it should not do so if the keyboard focus is not the root window.

In general, to determine if it will get keyboard input, an application should first check `FocusIn` and `FocusOut` events. If the focus window is the root window, then the application should check `LeaveNotify` and `EnterNotify` to see if keyboard events are possible.

Additional focus change and border crossing events are generated when the origin and destination of the focus or pointer crossing do not have a parent-child relationship. These events are called *virtual crossing* events. See Appendix E, *Event Reference*, for a description of when these events are generated and how to distinguish them from normal crossing events.

Example 9-12 shows the code that would be used to monitor whether the application will receive keyboard input. When `keyboard_active` is `True` in this code, the application could highlight its main window.

Example 9-12. Monitoring whether keyboard input will be available

```
Bool keyboard_active;
Bool focus;

/* Open display, create window, select input */

/* Select input before setting keyboard focus, if application does */

while (1)  {
    XNextEvent(display, &report);
    switch  (report.type) {
        .
        .
        .
    case EnterNotify:
        printf("enter\n");
        /* Make sure focus is an ancestor */
        (report.xcrossing.focus) ?
                (keyboard_active = True)
                : (keyboard_active = False);
        break;
    case LeaveNotify:
        printf("leave\n");
        /* We get input only if we have the focus */
        (focus) ? (keyboard_active = True)
                : (keyboard_active = False);
        break;
```

```
    case FocusIn:
        /* We get keyboard input for sure */
        printf("focus in\n");
        focus = True;
        keyboard_active = True;
        break;
    case FocusOut:
        /* We lost focus, get no keyboard input */
        printf("focus out\n");
        focus = False;
        keyboard_active = False;
        break;

        .
        .
        .

    }
} /* End while */
```

Example 9-12 could be used as a basis for code that highlights a portion of an application when it can get keyboard input. It would be in *active* mode when the `keyboard_active` flag is `True`. When an `EnterNotify` event is received, the `focus` member of the event structure is checked to see that the focus window is an ancestor of the window in question. If so, `keyboard_active` is `True`. When a `LeaveNotify` event is received, `keyboard_active` is `True` only if the application has the focus. On `FocusIn` events, `keyboard_active` is `True`, and a flag (`focus`) is set to indicate whether the keyboard will be active after `LeaveNotify` events.

9.3.1 The KeymapNotify Event

The `KeymapNotify` event, when selected, always follows on the queue immediately after a `FocusIn` or `EnterNotify` event. Its purpose is to allow the application to easily determine which combination of keys were pressed when the focus was transferred to the window or the pointer entered it. The `KeymapNotify` event contains a keyboard *vector*, which is a 32-element array of type `char`, in which each bit represents a key. For a given key, its keycode is its position in the keyboard vector.

The `XQueryKeymap` function also returns this keyboard vector. Keyboard vectors are always independent of all the keyboard mapping and reading functions, since the bits in the vector correspond to keycodes that cannot be changed. This way of reading the keyboard is just like reading the pointer buttons. It can be useful for applications that treat the keyboard not as characters but, for example, as piano keys or drum pads.

Since `XQueryKeymap` makes a routine trip request, reading the keyboard this way could not achieve the same performance when operating over a network as the same program implemented using events.

Keyboard/
Pointer

9.4 Grabbing the Keyboard and Pointer

There are times when a program might want to bypass the normal keyboard or pointer event propagation path in order to get input independent of the position of the pointer. This is the purpose of grabbing the keyboard and pointer. There are routines to grab the keyboard (XGrabKeyboard) or the pointer (XGrabPointer), or to arrange that they become grabbed when a certain combination of keys and/or buttons is pressed (XGrabButton, XGrabKey). There are corresponding calls to ungrab (XUngrabButton, XUngrabKey, XUngrabKeyboard, XUngrabPointer), and there is one call to change the characteristics of a pointer grab (XChangeActivePointerGrab).

One of the most common situations where grabbing takes place is with button events. Most applications want both a ButtonPress and a ButtonRelease, so that they can compare the two positions. Since this is such a common desire, the server *automatically* grabs the pointer between the ButtonPress and ButtonRelease if both are selected, so that you do not have to make an explicit grab.

One reason for grabbing a device is so that you can handle a series of events contiguously without fear of intervening events. But when you grab a device, no other application can receive input from that device. Therefore, it is something to do only when absolutely necessary.

The routines that grab take several arguments that tailor the input response in these ways:

- When the pointer is grabbed, the cursor may be confined to any window (the *confine_to* argument).

- The distribution of events to windows within the application can be modified by the *owner_events* argument. If *owner_events* is True, then the grabbed events will be sent to the window within the application that the pointer indicates. If *owner_events* is False or the pointer is outside the applications, then the events are always sent only to window specified by *window*.

- A window called the *grab_window* is specified. All events that occur outside the calling application's windows are reported to the grab window. All events within the application's windows will be sent to the grab window if the *owner_events* argument is False, or they will be reported normally within the application (to the window indicated by the pointer or propagating from that window if it did not select the event) if *owner_events* is True.

- For events that occur outside the calling application's windows, and events that occur inside when *owner_events* is False, the *event_mask* argument specifies which types of events are selected for the grab window. This *event_mask* overrules the existing *event_mask* for the grab window unless *owner_events* is True.

- Event processing for either keyboard or pointer events or both may be halted altogether during the grab until a releasing XAllowEvents call is invoked by setting the *pointer_mode* or *keyboard_mode* arguments to GrabModeSync.

- The *cursor* argument specifies a particular Cursor to be displayed while the grab is active. This cursor indicates to the user that input is going to the grabbing window, since the cursor will not change when moved across the screen as it normally would.

- Grabbing calls may specify a time when the grab should take place (the *time* argument).

You can change several of the conditions of an active pointer grab, namely the *event_mask*, *cursor*, and *time*, using XChangeActivePointerGrab.

XGrabKey and XGrabButton arrange for a grab to take place when a certain combination of keys or buttons is pressed. After one of these routines is called, a passive grab is said to be in effect, until the specified keys and buttons are pressed. At that time, the grab is active and is indistinguishable from a grab generated by a call to XGrabKeyboard or XGrabPointer. After a passive grab, an active pointer grab will take effect when the following four conditions are met:

- The specified button is pressed when an optional set of modifier keyboard keys is pressed and no other keys or buttons are pressed.

- The pointer is contained in the grab window specified in the grabbing call.

- The cursor-confining window (specified in the *confine_to* argument of XGrab-Pointer or XGrabButton) must be visible, if one is specified.

- These conditions are not satisfied by any ancestor.

Grabbing the keyboard is similar to setting the keyboard focus window, but grabbing is more flexible, since there are more arguments to modify the effect. Focus changes and keyboard grabs and ungrabs all generate the same FocusIn and FocusOut events.

If pointer grabs and ungrabs cause the pointer to move in or out of a window, they generate EnterNotify and LeaveNotify events.

The XAllowEvents routine is used only when the *pointer_mode* or *keyboard_mode* in previous grabbing calls were set to GrabModeSync. Under these conditions, the server queues any events that occur (but does not send them to the Xlib event queues for each application), and the keyboard or pointer is considered "frozen." XAllow-Events releases the events that are queued in the server for the frozen device. After the call, the device is still frozen, and the server again queues any events that occur on that device until the next XAllowEvents or Ungrab* call. In effect, XAllowEvents allows events to come in a batch through the network to the event queues for each application in Xlib.

The pointer modes have no effect on the processing of keyboard events and vice versa.

Both a pointer grab and a keyboard grab may be active at the same time by the same or different clients. If a device is frozen on behalf of either grab, no event processing is performed for the device. It is possible for a single device to be frozen by both grabs. In this case, the freeze must be released on behalf of both grabs before events can again be processed.

9.5 Keyboard Preferences

Xlib provides routines to control beep pitch and volume, key click, Shift-Lock mode, mouse acceleration, keyboard lights and keyboard auto-repeat. Not all servers will actually be able to control all of these parameters.

There are five routines that deal with the keyboard and pointer preferences. XGet-KeyboardControl and XChangeKeyboardControl are the primary routines for getting or setting all these preferences at once. XAutoRepeatOff and XAutoRepeat-On set the global keyboard auto-repeat status but are not able to control the auto-repeat of individual keys as XChangeKeyboardControl can.

9.5.1 Setting Keyboard Preferences

XChangeKeyboardControl uses the standard X method of changing internal structure members. The *values* argument to XChangeKeyboardControl specifies the structure containing the desired values; the *value_mask* argument specifies which members in the structure specified in *values* should replace the current settings. See the reference page for XChangeKeyboardControl in Volume Two, *Xlib Reference Manual*, for a list of the mask symbols.

Example 9-13 shows the XKeyboardControl structure.

Example 9-13. The XKeyboardControl structure

```
typedef struct {
    int key_click_percent;
    int bell_percent;
    int bell_pitch;
    int bell_duration;
    int led;
    int led_mode;               /* LedModeOn or LedModeOff */
    int key;
    int auto_repeat_mode;       /* AutoRepeatModeOff, AutoRepeatModeOn,
                                 * AutoRepeatModeDefault */
} XKeyboardControl;
```

The following list describes each member of the XKeyboardControl structure:

- key_click_percent sets the volume for key clicks between 0 (off) and 100 (loud), inclusive.

- bell_percent sets the base volume for the bell (or beep) between 0 (off) and 100 (loud), inclusive.

- bell_pitch sets the pitch (specified in Hz) of the bell.

- bell_duration sets the duration (specified in milliseconds) of the bell.

- led_mode controls whether the keyboard LEDs are to be used. If led is not specified and led_mode is LedModeOn, the states of all the lights are changed. If led_mode is LedModeOff, then the states of the lights are not changed. If led is specified, the light specified in `led` is turned on if `led_mode` is `LedModeOn` or turned off if `led_mode` is `LedModeOff`.

- `led` is a number between 1 and 32, inclusive, which specifies which light is turned on or off, depending on `led_mode`.

- `auto_repeat_mode` specifies how to handle auto-repeat when a key is held down. If only `auto_repeat_mode` is specified, then the global auto-repeat mode for the entire keyboard is changed, without affecting the per-key settings. If the `auto_repeat_mode` is `AutoRepeatModeOn`, the keys that are set to auto-repeat will do so. If it is set to `AutoRepeatModeOff`, no keys will repeat. If it is set to `AutoRepeatModeDefault`, all the keys or the specified key will operate in the default mode for the server. Normally the default mode is for all nonmodal keys to repeat (everything except Shift Lock and similar keys). The `auto_repeat_mode` can also be set using the `XAutoRepeatOff` and `XAutoRepeatOn` routines. None of the other members of the `XKeyboardControl` structure have convenience routines for setting them.

- `key` specifies the keycode of a key whose auto-repeat status will be changed to the setting specified by `auto_repeat_mode`. If this value is specified, `auto_repeat_mode` affects only the key specified in `key`. This is the only way to change the mode of a single key.

Setting any of `bell_duration`, `bell_percent`, `bell_pitch`, or `key_click_percent` to −1 restores the default value for that member.

The initial state of many of these parameters may be determined by command line arguments to the X server. On systems that operate only under the X Window System, the server is executed automatically by *xdm* during the boot procedure, and the defaults may have been modified in one of the *xdm* configuration files.

Table 9-2 shows the ranges for each member when no command line arguments are specified for the server. The defaults when these values are not set are server-dependent.

Table 9-2. Keyboard Preference Settings — Ranges

Parameter	Range
`key_click_percent`	0 to 100
`bell_percent`	0 to 100
`bell_pitch`	hertz (20 to 20K)
`bell_duration`	milliseconds
`led`	1 to 32
`led_mode`	`LedModeOff`, `LedModeOn`
`key`	8 to 255
`auto_repeat_mode`	`AutoRepeatModeDefault`, `AutoRepeatModeOff`, `AutoRepeatModeOn`

9.5.2 Getting Keyboard Preferences

To obtain the current state of the user preferences, use `XGetKeyboardControl`. This routine returns an `XKeyboardState` structure, as shown in Example 9-14.

Example 9-14. The XKeyboardState structure

```
typedef struct {
    int key_click_percent;
    int bell_percent;
    unsigned int bell_pitch, bell_duration;
    unsigned long led_mask;
    int global_auto_repeat;
    char auto_repeats[32];
} XKeyboardState;
```

Except for `led_mask`, `global_auto_repeat`, and `auto_repeats`, these members have the same range of possible values listed in Table 9-2.

The `led_mask` member is not directly analogous to any member of `XKeyboard-Control`. Each bit set to 1 in `led_mask` indicates a lit LED. The least significant bit of `led_mask` corresponds to LED one.

The `global_auto_repeat` member is either `AutoRepeatModeOff` or `Auto-RepeatModeOn`. It reports the state of the parameter set by the `auto_repeat_mode` member of `XKeyboardControl`.

The `auto_repeats` member is a key vector like the one in `KeymapNotify` events and returned by `XQueryKeymap`. Each bit set to 1 in `auto_repeats` indicates that auto-repeat is enabled for the corresponding key. The vector is represented as 32 bytes. Byte *N* (from 0) contains the bits for keycodes *8N* to *8N+7*, with the least significant bit in the byte representing keycode *8N*. Every key on the keyboard is represented by a bit in the vector.

9.6 Pointer Preferences

`XChangePointerControl` sets the parameters that control pointer acceleration, and `XGetPointerControl` gets them. *Pointer acceleration* is a feature that allows the user to move the cursor more quickly across the screen. If pointer acceleration is active, when the pointer moves more than a certain *threshold* amount in a single movement, the cursor will move a *multiple* of the amount the physical pointer moved. The effect of acceleration is that you can have detailed control over the pointer for fine work and, by flicking the wrist, you can also move quickly to the far reaches of the screen.

`XChangePointerControl` takes three arguments (in addition to the ubiquitous *display*): `accel_numerator`, `accel_denominator`, and `threshold`.

The `accel_numerator` and `accel_denominator` arguments make up a fraction that determines the multiple used to determine how many pixels to move the cursor based on how much the physical pointer moved. The `threshold` argument specifies how many pixels the physical pointer must have moved for acceleration to take effect.

10

Interclient Communication

*As a multi-window environment, X must support a mechanism for communi-
cation between applications. There are three: properties, selections, and
cut buffers, all of which are described in this chapter. The special case of
communication between an application and the window manager is also
covered here. Standard conventions for additional aspects of interclient
communication are covered in Appendix L of Volume Zero, X Protocol Reference Manual.*

In This Chapter:

10
Interclient Communication

Communication is necessary to make sure that all applications running under X cooperate properly with the window manager and share the system resources politely. Communication also allows applications to interchange data. Most applications in an integrated computing environment should have the ability to transfer data to and accept data from other applications.

Communication between clients takes place through *properties*. Sometimes properties are set directly by one application and read by another. This is the case with most communication between the window manager and the clients.

There is also a simple but limited means of communication through properties called *cut buffers*. But the preferred and most powerful method of general communication between clients is called *selections*. Selections actually establish a dialog between the two applications, not just a one-way communication. Both cut buffers and selections are ways of using properties for communication.

Successful communication depends on conventions for the meanings of the data communicated through properties and selections. The conventions in this area have changed between Release 3 and Release 4, with the adoption as an X Consortium standard of the *Inter-Client Communication Conventions Manual*, which is reprinted in Appendix L, *Interclient Communication Conventions*, of Volume Zero, *X Protocol Reference Manual*.

Unfortunately, these old and new conventions are not completely compatible. To make sure that applications written under R3 and earlier still work under R4 and later, all R3 routines are still supported in R4. However, several R3 routines are made obsolete by routines added to Xlib in R4. Since this edition of the manual covers both R3 and R4, both interfaces will be described.

10.1 Properties and Atoms

Properties allow you to associate arbitrary information with windows, usually to make that data available to the window manager or other applications. Properties are stored in the server.

Each property has a unique integer ID, called an atom. An atom is just a nickname for a property, so that arbitrary length property name strings do not have to be transferred back and forth between Xlib and the server. The atom is assigned by the server and will remain defined in the server even after the client that defined it terminates. The atoms for the pre-defined properties are constants defined in *<X11/Xatom.h>*; all of them begin with the prefix XA_. This naming convention avoids name clashes with user-defined symbols.

A property is uniquely identified by an atom and a window. Therefore, there may be one property on each window identified by a given atom. In other words, there can be a XA_WM_NAME property on each and every window, even though by convention this property is only set or read on the top-level windows of each application. A property on a window takes up space only once it is set.

Each property also has a name, which is an ASCII string. For the predefined properties, the name is never used in code. That is why we have chosen for this manual to refer to all pre-defined properties by their atoms. But for properties defined by convention between related clients (not predefined), the property name string is used so that the applications can deter-mine the correct atom for the property. The first client to call XInternAtom with the prop-erty name string as an argument gets a new atom. Subsequent clients that call XIntern-Atom with the same string will get the same atom. After each client has called XIntern-Atom, they use the atom rather than the string to refer to the property. They use this process because for properties defined by clients, the actual number used for an atom may differ between invocations of the server.

Once created, an atom remains defined in the server even after the client that created it has exited. A server remembers all atoms that were ever defined since the server started up. This means that one client can refer to an atom first interned by another client even if that other client has already exited.

Each property has a type, which itself is a property. There are several predefined properties for use as some of the more often needed types.

The data associated with a property can be stored as an array of 8-bit quantities, 16-bit quan-tities, or 32-bit quantities only. Properties can contain structures or raw data, but if one is to contain a structure of complex type, it must be encoded into one of the three byte formats by the program before being sent to the server and decoded when read from the server. The pre-defined property types have been carefully designed to match one of the data formats so that encoding and decoding are not necessary.

Properties remain set until the window to which they are attached is destroyed, which hap-pens automatically when the client that created the window exits. However, properties set on the root window remain defined even after the client that set them has exited, since the root window is never destroyed.

There are 68 predefined properties for window manager communication, selections, standard colormaps, and font specifications. The properties used for window manager communication and selections are described in this chapter. The standard colormap properties are described in Chapter 7, *Color*, and the font properties are described in Chapter 6, *Drawing Graphics and Text*.

Properties are set with XChangeProperty and read with XGetWindowProperty. Whenever XChangeProperty is called, a PropertyNotify event is generated.

10.2 Communicating with the Window Manager

To permit window managers to perform their role of mediating the competing demands for screen space and colormaps, the clients being managed must adhere to certain conventions. These conventions specify things that clients must do, things they should or can do if desired, and things that they must not do. The most basic thing clients are expected to do is to set certain properties so that the window manager has information on which to base its decisions.

It is a fundamental principle of client-window manager communication that a general client should not care which window manager is running or, indeed, if one is running at all. The choice of window manager is up to the user or perhaps the system administrator, not the client.

The fact that window managers need information about the clients they are managing and yet that window managers vary and might not be running lead to the concept of the hint. A *hint* is a suggestion to the window manager about a preference of the application made by setting a property. Xlib makes this easy by providing routines that conveniently set the right properties. The window manager is encouraged to honor as many of the hints as possible, but it is not required to honor any of them. Therefore, the application must not depend on its hints being honored; it must be capable of operating when any of its hints are ignored or denied.*

In general, the object of the X11 design is that clients should, as far as possible, do exactly what they would do in the absence of a window manager, except for:

- Hinting to the window manager about the screen space and colormaps they would like to use.

- Cooperating with the window manager by accepting the resources they are allocated, even if not those requested.

- Being prepared for hardware-limited resource allocations to change at any time. The client can select events that will announce these changes.

---

*Under R4, applications that create their own colormap are the only ones that will not be able to run without a window manager if they honor the conventions, because the window manager is responsible for installing the colormap. However, under R3, few if any window managers installed colormaps, so the application had no choice but to install the colormap itself; this meant that it would successfully run without a window manager. But it also meant that there was no coordination between the various applications attempting to install their own colormaps.

Note that these procedures are not required for the virtually unlimited X resources such as windows or cursors.

Clients create one or more windows that are children of the root window. All these windows are known as top-level windows. It is these windows that the window manager controls, and it is also these windows on which the application sets window manager hint properties.

10.2.1 Standard Properties for Window Manager

Once the client has created one or more top-level windows but before it maps them, it must place properties on those windows to help the window manager manage them effectively. The following sections describe each property that must or should be set and how to set it.

As mentioned earlier, there are two sets of conventions—the "old" conventions which were used through Release 3 and the "version 1" conventions adopted as an X Consortium standard for Release 4 and later. We will refer to these as the "R3" and "R4" conventions for brevity, since although they were developed and released independently of the X releases, they actually became widely available along with the R3 and R4 releases. It is important to remember that the R4 conventions are the accepted X Consortium standard from July 1989 on and will continue to be valid in R5 and later; there will be additions but not incompatible changes.

The Xlib supplied in R4 continues to support both sets of conventions as much as possible, so that older applications will continue to compile and run without changes. To allow this, some new routines have been added that parallel older routines. We will describe both sets of routines.

Some of the properties that a client sets for the window manager are mandatory (the *standard properties*), and some are optional. XSetStandardProperties (R3) or XSet-WMProperties (R4), which were introduced and used in *basicwin* in Chapter 3, *Basic Window Program*, set all the required properties. The purpose of XSetStandard-Properties and XSetWMProperties is to provide a simple interface for the programmer who wants to code an application quickly. Other functions are provided to communicate the optional information to the window manager.

In order to work well with most window managers, every program should call XSet-StandardProperties and XSetWMHints (under R3) or XSetWMProperties (under R4) for each top-level window. These provide the window manager with the following information:

- Name of the application for titlebar.

- Name string for the icon.

- Command and arguments used to invoke the program.

- Icon pixmap and mask or window.

- Preferred initial icon position.

- Size hints for window in normal state.

- Startup state (normal or iconified).

- Keyboard focus model used by the application.

- Window group; for applications with multiple top-level windows, this describes which window is the main window for iconifying (added in R4).

The window manager, not Xlib, chooses its own default response when any of these properties are not set. Also, they are only hints. A window manager determines what to do with this information and is allowed to ignore it. They will, of course, be ignored if no window manager is running.

The following sections describe the properties set by the client that indicate its preferences to the window manager. Table 10-1 shows all the predefined properties that clients can set and the section in this chapter where they are described.

Table 10-1. The Window Manager Hints Property Atoms

Property	Property Type (R3 | R4)	C Type (R3 | R4)	Description	See
For window manager:				
XA_WM_CLASS	XA_STRING	XClassHint	Application class and name for resource database lookup.	Section 10.2.1.5
XA_WM_HINTS	XA_WM_HINTS	XWMHints	Additional hints set by client for use by window manager.	Section 10.2.1
XA_WM_ICON_NAME	XA_STRING | "TEXT"	char * | XText- Property	Name to be used in icon.	Section 10.2.1.2
XA_WM_NAME	XA_STRING | "TEXT"	char * | XText- Property	Application name.	Section 10.2.1.1
XA_WM_NORMAL_HINTS	XA_WM_SIZE_HINTS	XSizeHints	Size hints for window in normal state (not iconified or zoomed).	Section 10.2.1.3
XA_WM_TRANSIENT_ FOR_HINT	XA_STRING	char *	Tells window manager which window is the real main window with which a temporary window is associated.	Section 10.2.1.4.6
XA_WM_ZOOM_HINTS	XA_WM_SIZE_HINTS	XSizeHints	Size hints for zoomed window.	Section 10.2.1.3

Table 10-1. The Window Manager Hints Property Atoms (continued)

Property	Property Type (R3 | R4)	C Type (R3 | R4)	Description	See
For session manager:				
WM_CLIENT_MACHINE	"TEXT"	XText-Property	The name of machine running the client, as seen from the machine running the server. (*Added in R4.*)	Section 10.2.1
XA_WM_COMMAND	XA_STRING | "TEXT"	char * | XText-Property	Command and arguments, separated by ASCII 0's, used to invoke application.	Section 10.2.2.1

In addition to the functions mentioned above that set all of the standard properties, Xlib also provides separate functions for setting and getting each property. These are referenced in the sections below describing each property. See the relevant pages in Volume Two, *Xlib Reference Manual*, for full details on each function. Applications set these properties and never read them, and the window manager gets them but never sets them. Therefore, if you are writing an application, you will only use the routines that set these properties.

10.2.1.1 Application Name – XA_WM_NAME

The XA_WM_NAME property is a string that the client wishes displayed in association with the window (for example, in a window titlebar).

Window managers are expected to make an effort to display this information; simply ignoring XA_WM_NAME is not acceptable window manager behavior. Clients can assume that at least the first part of this string is visible to the user, unless the user has made an explicit decision to make it invisible by placing the headline off-screen or covering it by other windows. But XA_WM_NAME should not be used for application-critical information nor to announce changes of application state that require timely user response. The expected uses are:

- To permit the user to identify one of a number of instances of the same client.

- To provide the user with noncritical state information.

Even window managers that support headline bars will place some limit on the length of string that can be visible; brevity here is important.

In R3, the window name is stored by the client with XStoreName and read by the window manager with XFetchName. In R4, new functions that set the XA_WM_NAME property are provided, XSetWMName and XGetWMName. These were added because the earlier interfaces assumed an ASCII encoding, which precluded use with non-Western languages.

As mentioned above, the `XStoreName` and `XFetchName` interfaces are still supported in R4 for backwards compatibility, but they have become obsolete.

10.2.1.2   Icon Name – XA_WM_ICON_NAME

The `XA_WM_ICON_NAME` property is a string that the client wishes displayed in association with its icon window when the client is iconified (for example, an icon label). In other respects, it is similar to `XA_WM_NAME`. Fewer characters will normally be visible in `XA_WM_ICON_NAME` than `XA_WM_NAME`, for obvious geometric reasons.

If an icon pixmap has been specified in the standard properties or `XA_WM_HINTS`, it may be displayed in the icon in addition to or instead of the icon name. In R3, the icon name is set by the application with `XSetIconName` and read by the window manager with `XGet-IconName`. In R4, new functions that set the `XA_WM_NAME` property are provided, `XSetWMIconName` and `XGetWMIconName`. As mentioned above, the `XSetIconName` and `XGetIconName` interfaces are still supported in R4 for backwards compatibility, but they do not comply with the current ICCCM, for the reasons described in Section 10.2.1.1.

10.2.1.3   Window Size Hints – XA_WM_NORMAL_HINTS

An application must tell the window manager its geometry preferences for each of its top-level windows before mapping them.* These hints specify not only the preferred initial size (and sometimes position) of the window but also the preferred increments of sizes and aspect ratios the window manager should respect when allowing the user to resize the application. (The aspect ratio is the ratio of the width of the application to its height.)

In R3, there is a concept of a normal state and a zoomed state, and two properties may be set to indicate different size preferences in the two states. `XSetNormalHints` individually sets the `XA_WM_NORMAL_HINTS` property for a window in normal state, and `XSetZoom-Hints` sets the `XA_WM_ZOOM_HINTS` property for a window in zoomed state. In R4, the zoomed state has been declared obsolete.

Both the `XA_WM_NORMAL_HINTS` and `XA_WM_ZOOM_HINTS` properties are `XSizeHints` structures, shown in Example 10-1.

Example 10-1. The XSizeHints structure

```
typedef struct {
    long flags;                         /* Marks defined members in
                                         * structure */
    int x, y;                           /* Obsolete as of R4 */
    int width, height;                  /* Obsolete as of R4 */
    int min_width, min_height;
    int max_width, max_height;
    int width_inc, height_inc;
    struct {
        int x;                          /* Numerator */
```

---

*The pop-up menu is the only type of top-level window that does not need to have `XA_WM_NORMAL_HINTS` set for it. Instead, the `override_redirect` window attribute should be set to `True`.

Example 10-1. The XSizeHints structure (continued)

```
            int y;                      /* Denominator */
    } min_aspect, max_aspect;
    int base_width, base_height;        /* Added in R4 */
    int win_gravity;                    /* Added in R4 */
} XSizeHints;
```

- The `x`, `y`, `width`, and `height` members describe a desired position and size for the window. The coordinate system for `x` and `y` is the root window, irrespective of any reparenting that may have occurred. As of R4, these fields are obsolete, because the window manager will use the initial size and position of the window when mapped to get this information. (The window manager *redirects* the application's mapping request to itself, so that the window manager can inspect the position and size of the window set by the application, and perhaps change them, before mapping the window.)

- The `min_width` and `min_height` members specify the minimum size that the window can be for the application to be useful. Most window managers will not allow the user to resize the application smaller than this size. In R4, the `base_width` and `base_height` fields if set are used instead of `min_width` and `min_height`. If they are not set, `min_width` and `min_height` are used.

- The `max_width` and `max_height` members specify the maximum useful size.

- The `width_inc` and `height_inc` members define an arithmetic progression of sizes, from the minimum size to the maximum size, into which the window prefers to be resized. For example, *xterm* prefers size increments matching the dimensions of the font being used.

The following algorithm should be used by the window manager to calculate the displayed size of the top-level window. `i` and `j` are nonnegative integer loop variables within the window manager that would be incremented until a size that matches the window manager's window management policy is reached.

```
width = base_width + (i * width_inc)
height = base_height + (j * height_inc)
```

(In R3, and in R4 when `base_width` and `base_height` are not set, `min_width` and `min_height` are used instead of `base_width` and `base_height`.) Window managers will use `i` and `j` instead of `width` and `height` in reporting window sizes to users. Similarly, applications should interpret the command line or user default geometry using `width_inc` and `height_inc` pixels instead of single pixels as the unit. *xterm*, for example, interprets size specifications in terms of multiples of the font dimensions, not in pixels. A default *xterm* window has 80 columns and 24 rows of characters. To create an *xterm* window with more rows, you can use the command:

```
spike% xterm -geometry 80x40
```

- The `min_aspect` and `max_aspect` members specify the desired range of ratios of width to height for the window and are each expressed as a ratio of the `x` and `y` members of `min_aspect` and `max_aspect`. (The ratio `x` / `y` in `min_aspect` or `max_aspect` is the minimum or maximum value for `width` / `height`.)

- In R4, the `win_gravity` field was added to `XSizeHints`. This field controls how the window's initial position will be interpreted by the window manager. By default, this hint is `NorthWestGravity`, which means that the position of the window when mapped by the application is used by the window manager as the position of the north-west corner (top-left) of the window. The other values for this field are `Center-Gravity`, `EastGravity`, `NorthEastGravity`, `NorthGravity`, `South-EastGravity`, `SouthGravity`, `SouthWestGravity`, and `WestGravity`. If the hint is set to `CenterGravity`, the window manager will place the center of the window where the origin of the window was when the application mapped it.

- The `flags` member of `XSizeHints` indicates which members in the structure contain important information. The constants in Table 10-2 can be combined with bitwise OR to set `flags`. The `USPosition` and `USSize` flags indicate that the user specified the desired values, while `PPosition` and `PSize` indicate that the program determined the values. This distinction is important since it supports the power structure—the user overrides the window manager, and the window manager overrides the program in decisions about window layout. The window manager can override the program's choice of window location or geometry when `PPosition` or `PSize`, respectively, are set, but the user's choices should override the window manager's choice when `USPosition` or `USSize` are set.

Table 10-2. The XSizeHints Flags

Flag	Description
USPosition	User-specified x, y
USSize	User-specified width, height
PPosition	Program-specified position
PSize	Program-specified size
PMinSize	Program-specified minimum size
PMaxSize	Program-specified maximum size
PResizeInc	Program-specified resize increments
PAspect	Program-specified min and max aspect ratios
PBaseSize (R4)	Program-specified base size
PWinGravity (R4)	Program-specified window gravity
PAllHints	Program-specified all hints

There are actually several sets of calls that read and write properties containing the `XSize-Hints` structure—one each to send and receive the hints for the program in normal state, one for zoomed state, and one that uses the R4 conventions. All these functions use the `XSizeHints` structure described above. Table 10-3 lists these functions.*

---

*Actually, there are several more functions that set properties with `XSizeHint` structures, but they are very rarely used. `XSetSizeHints` and `XGetSizeHints` (for R3) and `XSetWMSizeHints` and `XGetWMSizeHints` (for R4) are only useful if an application and a window manager agree on a private protocol that defines a new type of size hint atom beyond the two for R3 and the one in R4 or if a new type of size hint is added in later conventions.

Table 10-3. Functions to Set and Get Size Hints

Window State	To Set	To Get
Normal (R3)	XSetNormalHints	XGetNormalHints
Normal (R4)	XSetWMNormalHints	XGetWMNormalHints
Zoomed (R3)	XSetZoomHints	XGetZoomHints

In R4, the XAllocSizeHints function was added. It allocates an XSizeHints structure and zeros all the fields. This function should be used so that new fields can be added in later releases while maintaining binary compatibility of applications written with earlier releases. In other words, using this function avoids compiling in the size of this structure, which may change. You declare only a pointer to this structure and then set it by calling XAllocSizeHints.

XGetNormalHints (and XGetWMNormalHints in R4) is normally used by the window manager to read the hints.

10.2.1.4 Additional Window Manager Hints – XA_WM_HINTS

The hints stored in the XA_WM_HINTS property provide an assortment of information to the window manager. Setting this property is required according to the R4 ICCCM and suggested in R3. The XA_WM_HINTS property includes:

- Whether the program sets the keyboard focus window independently or only when assigned by the window manager.

- Whether the program desires to begin life as a window or as an icon.

- A window to be used by the window manager as an icon, or a pixmap and mask to be used by the window manager to draw on an icon window it creates.

- The initial position of the icon.

In R3, this property is set by the client with XSetWMHints and read by the window manager with XGetWMHints. In R4, however, the property is normally set by the client with XSetWMProperties, and you should use the new XAllocWMHints function to allocate an XWMHints structure, then set its fields, and then call XSetWMHints. The XWMHints structure is shown in Example 10-2.

Example 10-2. The XWMHints structure

```
typedef struct {
    long flags;             /* Marks defined members in structure */
    Bool input;             /* Does application need window
                             * manager for keyboard input */
    int initial_state;      /* See below */
    Pixmap icon_pixmap;     /* Pixmap to be used as icon */
    Window icon_window;     /* Window to be used as icon */
    int icon_x, icon_y;     /* Initial position of icon */
    Pixmap icon_mask;       /* Pixmap to be used as mask
```

Example 10-2. The XWMHints structure (continued)

```
                              * for icon_pixmap */
    XID window_group;    /* ID of related window group */
    /* This structure may be extended in the future */
} XWMHints;
```

The following sections describe each member of XWMHints and how it should be set.

10.2.1.4.1 Flags Field. The client must set the flags field to indicate which members of the XWMHints structure are to be read by the window manager. This is done by combining the symbols shown in Table 10-4 using bitwise OR (|).

Table 10-4. Flags for Window Manager Hints

Member	Flag	Bit
input	InputHint	0
initial_state	StateHint	1
icon_pixmap	IconPixmapHint	2
icon_window	IconWindowHint	3
icon_x, icon_y	IconPositionHint	4
icon_mask	IconMaskHint	5
window_group	WindowGroupHint	6
All of the above	AllHints	0-6

10.2.1.4.2 Input Field and the Keyboard Focus. The input member of XWMHints is used to communicate to the window manager the keyboard focus model used by the application.* For the input hint to be read by the window manager, the InputHint constant must be specified in the flags field of XWMHints.

There are four input models:

- **No Input.** The client never expects keyboard input. An example would be *xload* or another output-only client.

- **Passive Input.** The client expects keyboard input but never explicitly sets the keyboard focus. An example would be a simple client with no subwindows, which will accept input in PointerRoot mode, or when the window manager sets the keyboard focus to its top-level window (in click-to-type mode).

---

*To remind you, the keyboard focus is the window to which keyboard events go, sometimes ignoring the pointer position. When the pointer is outside the keyboard focus window, all keyboard events are delivered to that window. When the pointer is inside the keyboard focus window or any of its descendants, keyboard events are delivered to the window containing the pointer.

- **Locally Active Input**. The client expects keyboard input and explicitly sets the keyboard focus but only does so when one of its windows already has the focus.

  An example of a Locally Active style client would be a client with subwindows defining various data entry members. Such an application might use Next and Prev keys to move the keyboard focus between the members, once its top-level window has acquired the focus in pointer-following mode or when the window manager sets the keyboard focus to its top-level window (in click-to-type mode).

- **Globally Active Input**. The client expects keyboard input and explicitly sets the keyboard focus even when the focus is set to a window the client does not own. An example would be a client with a scrollbar that wants to allow users to scroll the window without disturbing the keyboard focus even if it is in some other window. The client wants to acquire the keyboard focus when the user clicks in the scrolled region, but not when the user clicks in the scrollbar itself, and then set the focus back to its original window. Thus, the client wants to prevent the window manager setting the keyboard focus to any of its windows.

Clients using the Globally Active and No Input models should set the `input` flag to `False`. Clients using the Passive and Locally Active models should set the `input` flag to `True`.

Under R4 conventions, clients that use the Locally Active or Globally Active focus models must participate in one of the WM_PROTOCOLS called WM_TAKE_FOCUS, as described in Section 10.2.3.2.

10.2.1.4.3 Initial State Field. The `initial_state` member of `XWMHints` indicates to the window manager whether the application prefers to start off in iconified, zoomed, normal, or inactive state. In R4, the inactive and zoomed states have been made obsolete, and an application can only ask to be normal or iconified.

`initial_state` specifies the state the client prefers to be in at the time the top-level window is mapped.

NOTE

Under R3 conventions, clients could ask the window manager to switch between states by setting the `initial_state` flag. In R4, this no longer works because the window manager does not reread the property. See Section 10.2.6.1 for a description of the current procedure for doing this.

The `initial_state` flags are shown in Table 10-5.

Table 10-5. Initial State Hint Flags

Flag	Description
For use in R3 or R4:	
IconicState	Client wants to be iconified.
NormalState	Client wants top-level normal window visible.
For use in R3 only:	
DontCareState	Client doesn't care what state it is in.
InactiveState	Client wants to be inactive. (Inactive windows might be available from a pop-up menu.)
ZoomState	Client wants to be in zoomed state.

When setting the `initial_state` member of `XWMHints`, you must OR the `State-Hint` constant set into the `flags` member of `XWMHints` to indicate that the field is to be set.

Even under the R4 conventions, which have no flag for an inactive state, a window manager might implement a concept of inactive state in which an infrequently used client's window would be represented as a string in a menu. But this state is invisible to the client, which would see itself merely as being in `IconicState`.

10.2.1.4.4 Icon Hints Fields. Under X, icons are by convention managed by the window manager, except that the client is allowed to provide a variety of pixmap patterns, names, and an icon window among which the window manager may pick and choose. The four members of `XWMHints` shown in Example 10-3 provide this information to the window manager.

Example 10-3. The icon hints elements of the XWMHints structure

```
typedef struct {
    .
    .
    Pixmap icon_pixmap;     /* Pixmap for icon */
    Pixmap icon_mask;       /* Pixmap to be used as mask for
                             * icon_pixmap */
    Window icon_window;     /* Window to be used as icon */
    int icon_x, icon_y;     /* Initial position of icon */
    .
    .
} XWMHints;
```

`icon_pixmap` is the pattern to be used to distinguish the icon from other clients. This pixmap should be:

- One of the sizes specified in the `XA_WM_ICON_SIZE` property on the root, as described in Section 10.2.4.1.

- One bit deep. The window manager will select, through the resource database, suitable background (for the 0 bits) and foreground (for the 1 bits) colors. These resources can, of course, specify different colors for the icons of different clients.

The `icon_mask` is a one-bit-deep pixmap that determines which pixels in `icon_pixmap` are drawn on the icon window. This allows for icons that appear to be nonrectangular. Some window managers (including *uwm*) use the icon pixmap as a background tile for the icon window, a method which does not allow for the use of a mask.

`icon_window` is a window created but not mapped by the client. Clients that need to know their icon's ID or want to draw more than a simple two-color bitmap on the icon should set this hint. For example, *xbiff* and *xmh* change their icon pixmap when mail arrives, and they need to know their icon's ID to do this. Therefore, they must supply an icon window.

The `icon_window` hint should not be used unless needed. When it is not specified, the window manager creates the icon window itself.

You do not know which of the hints the window manager will honor. With current window managers, you can be confident that if `icon_window` is set, the window it names will be visible. If not, if `icon_pixmap` is set, the pixmap it names is visible. Otherwise, the window's `XA_WM_ICON_NAME` string is visible.

Under R3, it is dangerous to depend on `icon_window` actually being the icon window being used, since some window managers do not read `icon_window` hints and map a different icon window. Under R4, the conventions specify that the window manager must use the icon window.

An application that sets an `icon_window` is responsible for redrawing the window in case of `Expose` events. One way to set the icon design to be displayed is to set the background pixmap attribute of the icon window. The advantage of this approach is that there is no need to handle `Expose` events for the icon, because the background is automatically redrawn by the server. The disadvantage is that there is no way to apply a mask to generate a non-rectangular icon.

The icon window:

- Must be an `InputOutput` child of the root window.

- Should be one of the sizes specified in the `XA_WM_ICON_SIZE` property on the root (described in Section 10.2.4.1).

- Must use the default visual and default colormap for the screen in question.

- Should not be mapped, unmapped, or configured by the client.

- Should not have the `override_redirect` window attribute set to `True` (should be left as the default).

The client must not:

- Select `ResizeRedirectMask` on the icon.

- Depend on being able to receive input events via their icon windows, although most window managers will allow some subset of key and button events through.

- Manipulate the borders of their icon windows.

To summarize the client procedures regarding icons:

- Use XSetIconName or XSetWMIconName to set a string in XA_WM_ICON_NAME. All clients should do this, since it provides a fallback for window managers whose ideas about icons differ widely from those of the client.

- Set a pixmap into the icon_pixmap member of the XA_WM_HINTS property and possibly another into the icon_mask member. The window manager is expected to display the pixmap masked by the mask. The pixmap should be one of the sizes found in the XA_WM_ICON_SIZE property on the root. Window managers will normally clip or tile pixmaps which do not match XA_WM_ICON_SIZE.

Or:

- Set a window into the icon_window member of the XA_WM_HINTS property. The window manager is expected to use that window instead of creating its own and to map that window whenever the client is in IconicState. In general, the size of the icon window should be one of those specified in XA_WM_ICON_SIZE on the root, if that property exists. Window managers may resize icon windows. If the client supplies an icon window, it is responsible for redrawing it when necessary.

10.2.1.4.5 Window Group Field. The window_group member of XWMHints lets the client specify that it has multiple top-level windows which should be iconified together or managed by the window manager as a group. For example, group leaders may have the full set of decorations and other group members a restricted set.

Applications with only one top-level window need not set this hint.

One of the top-level windows is known as the group leader. The window_group member of the hints for each of the other top-level windows should be set to the window ID of the group leader.

The group leader may be a window which exists only for that purpose and may never be mapped. Its window_group member should contain its own ID. The properties of the window group leader are those for the group as a whole (for example, the icon to be shown when the entire group is iconified). Every other top-level window may also have its own hints applicable only to itself.

10.2.1.4.6 Transient Window Field. All temporary subwindows of the root, such as pop-up menus and dialog boxes, should use XSetTransientForHint to set the XA_WM_TRANSIENT_FOR property to the ID of the top-level window of the application that is creating the temporary window. This allows the window manager to process the temporary window accordingly (perhaps by decorating it differently than if it were a separate application). In particular, window managers will present newly mapped transient windows without requiring any user interaction, even if mapping top-level windows normally does require interaction.

The calling sequences and conventions are the same in both R3 and R4.

It is important not to confuse XA_WM_TRANSIENT_FOR with the override_redirect window attribute. The override_redirect attribute specifies that the window manager does not get the chance to intercept the mapping request and thus no chance at all to decorate the window. This should be done only on the most temporary of windows, such as menus, or on windows that the programmer wants to be mapped without window manager intervention, such as automated demonstration programs. XA_WM_TRANSIENT_FOR should be used when other windows are allowed to be active while the transient window is visible, such as when the pointer is not grabbed while the window is popped up. If other windows must be frozen, use override_redirect and grab the pointer while the window is mapped.

Temporary windows that are popped up frequently should also set the save_under window attribute so that windows beneath the window may not need to redraw themselves quite so often.

To summarize, clients wishing to pop up a window should do one of three things:

- They can create and map another normal top-level window, which will get decorated and managed as a separate client by the window manager. See the discussion of window groups in Section 10.2.1.4.5.

- If the window will be visible for a relatively short time and deserves a somewhat lighter treatment, they can set the XA_WM_TRANSIENT_FOR property. They can expect less decoration but should set all the normal window manager properties on the window. An example of an appropriate case would be a dialog box.

- If the window will be visible for a very short time and should not be decorated at all, the client can set the override_redirect window attribute. In general, this should be done only if the pointer is grabbed while the window is mapped. The window manager will never interfere with these windows, which should be used with caution. An example of an appropriate use is a pop-up menu.

10.2.1.5 Application Class Name and Instance Name – XA_WM_CLASS

The XA_WM_CLASS property is a string containing two null-separated elements, res_class and res_name, that are meant to be used by the window manager to look up resources applicable to this application in the resource database, or as identification information. They are in general the *class* and *instance* of the application, as the terms are used in object-oriented programming and the X Toolkit (see Chapter 2, *Introduction to the X Toolkit*, of Volume Four, *X Toolkit Intrinsics Programming Manual*, for a conceptual introduction to classes and instances).

The two strings are, respectively:

- A string naming the particular instance of the application to which the client owning this window belongs. Resources that are specified by instance name override any resources that are specified by class name. Instance names may be specified by the user in an operating-system-specific manner. Under UNIX, the following conventions are used:

- If "-name NAME" is given on the command line, NAME is used as the instance name.

- Otherwise, if the environment variable RESOURCE_NAME is set, its value will be used as the instance name.

- Otherwise, the trailing part of the name used to invoke the program (`argv[0]` stripped of any directory names) is used as the instance name.

- A string naming the general class of applications to which the client owning this window belongs. Resources that are specified by class apply to all applications that have the same class name. Class names are specified by the application writer. Examples of commonly used class names include "Emacs," "XTerm," "XClock," "XLoad," etc. Note that the class is not as general as "Editor."

Note that WM_CLASS strings, being null-terminated, differ from the general conventions that STRING properties are null-separated. This inconsistency is necessary for backwards compatibility.

An application should look up its own resources in the resource database using `XGet-Default` or with the resource manager routines described in Chapter 11, *Managing User Preferences*. If the user defaults are not found under `res_name`, the application should use `res_class`.

The `XA_WM_CLASS` property should only be written once and must be present when the window is mapped; window managers will ignore changes to it while the window is mapped.

The `XA_WM_CLASS` property contains a structure of type `XClassHint`. Example 10-4 shows the `XClassHint` structure.

Example 10-4. The XClassHint structure

```
typedef struct {
    char *res_name;
    char *res_class;
} XClassHint;
```

In R4, the `XAllocClassHint` function should be used to allocate and zero the `XClass-Hint` structure.

`XA_WM_CLASS` can be set by the client with `XSetClassHint` and read by the window manager with `XGetClassHint`.

10.2.2 Standard Properties for Session Manager

A session manager is in charge of starting and stopping applications in a controlled manner, so that a session made up of several running applications can be halted and restarted in its original state. This is useful, for example, when the user wants to log out without having to start from scratch when logging back in.

Note that session managers are rare or nonexistent at the present time. Nonetheless, these conventions should be honored because it is only a matter of time before session managers become available. And the session manager does not necessarily need to be a separate client from the window manager. A window manager may have session-management capabilities.

There are two properties that need setting for the benefit of session managers, WM_COMMAND and WM_CLIENT_MACHINE. These supply the command and arguments needed to invoke an application in its current state and the machine on which it should be run. Together they supply enough information to restart the application. These are described in the following sections.

10.2.2.1 Application Command and Arguments

The XA_WM_COMMAND property stores the shell command and arguments used to invoke the application, separated by NULL characters.

Applications use XSetCommand function to set the command property. In Release 3, there is no matching XGetCommand; window managers must use XGetWindowProperty to read this property. Release 4 provides XGetCommand.

Clients should ensure, by resetting this property as often as necessary, that it always reflects a command that will restart them in their current state.

10.2.2.2 Client Machine

To restart a client, the session manager needs to know not only the command and arguments but also the machine on which the client was running. The application sets the WM_CLIENT_MACHINE property to contain this information, using XSetWMClient-Machine. This function (and convention) is new in R4.

This property should be set to a string forming the name of the machine running the client as seen from the machine running the server.

10.2.3 Optional Properties for Window and Session Manager

The client will need to set one or more of the following properties if it uses multiple colormaps, if it takes the keyboard focus, if it has data that must be saved before the session manager kills it, or if it has multiple top-level windows and it would like to survive when the user deletes one of them.

10.2.3.1 Using Created Colormaps – WM_COLORMAP_WINDOWS

Under R4 conventions, an application never installs its own colormap. The window manager needs certain information from the application to be able to install colormaps at the appropriate times. An application that uses colormaps other than the default must do two things to make sure that the window manager knows which colormaps to install for each window:

- Set the `colormap` window attribute of each window that is to use a colormap other than the default.

- Set the WM_COLORMAP_WINDOWS property on the application's top-level window to tell the window manager which windows use colormaps different from the top-level window's colormap. In other words, you do not need to set WM_COLORMAP_WINDOWS unless your application uses more than one colormap.

The top-level window is always assumed to need its colormap installed. Applications set the WM_COLORMAP_WINDOWS property with `XSetWMColormapWindows`, and the window manager reads it with `XGetWMColormapWindows`. These routines are supplied beginning in R4.

Under R3, most window managers do not install colormaps. Therefore, applications that create their own colormaps will need to install them when they get the keyboard focus or when the pointer is moved inside. You should make this code easy to remove to ease conversion to R4.

10.2.3.2 Window Manager Protocols – WM_PROTOCOLS

Setting the WM_PROTOCOLS property is optional. It is for applications that can benefit from being notified by the window manager or session manager of certain conditions. It is a new part of the R4 conventions, not supported in R3.

The WM_PROTOCOLS property contains a list of atoms, each identifying a communication protocol between the application and the window manager in which the application wants to participate. Atoms can identify both standard protocols and private protocols specific to individual window managers. All the protocols in which a client can volunteer to take part involve the window manager sending the client a `ClientMessage` event marked with a certain flag to indicate with which protocol this event is associated. The client then takes appropriate action. Table 10-6 lists the protocols that have been defined to date.

Table 10-6. Current Standard WM_PROTOCOLS

Protocol	Purpose
WM_TAKE_FOCUS	Assignment of keyboard focus.
WM_SAVE_YOURSELF	Save client state warning.
WM_DELETE_WINDOW	Request to delete top-level window.
More to come ...	

Note that none of the above properties are represented by predefined atoms. Therefore, you will need to call `XInternAtom` once for each one that you intend to use.

An application sets the WM_PROTOCOLS property using `XSetWMProtocols`, and the window or session manager reads it with `XGetWMProtocols`.

10.2.3.2.1 **WM_TAKE_FOCUS.** Applications that use the Locally Active and Globally Active focus models should specify that they want to participate in this protocol. Under both these focus models, the application explicitly sets the keyboard focus to one of its windows. Any application that does not set the keyboard focus to any of its windows does not need to participate in this protocol.

To applications that specify WM_TAKE_FOCUS, the window manager may send a `Client-Message` event with the atom corresponding to WM_TAKE_FOCUS in their `data[0]` field. If the application wants the keyboard focus, it should respond by calling `XSetInput-Focus` with its *window* argument set to the window of theirs that last had the keyboard focus or to their default input window and with the *time* argument set to the timestamp in the message. The *revert_to* argument should be set to `RevertToParent`.

A client could receive WM_TAKE_FOCUS when opening from an icon or when the user has clicked outside the top-level window in an area that indicates to the window manager that it should assign the focus (for example, clicking in the headline bar can be used to assign the focus).

The goal of WM_TAKE_FOCUS is to support window managers that want to assign the keyboard focus to a top-level window in such a way that the top-level window can either assign it to one of its subwindows or decline the offer of the focus. A clock, for example, or a text editor with no currently open frames might not want to take focus even though the window manager generally believes that clients should take the keyboard focus after being deiconified or raised.

Clients that call `XSetInputFocus` must set the *time* argument to the timestamp of the event that caused them to make the attempt. Note that this cannot be a `FocusIn` event, since they do not have timestamps, and that clients may acquire the focus without a corresponding `EnterNotify`. Clients must not use `CurrentTime` in the *time* field.

Clients using the Globally Active model can only use `XSetInputFocus` to acquire the input focus when they do not already have it on receipt of one of the following events: `ButtonPress`, `ButtonRelease`, passive-grabbed `KeyPress`, and passive-grabbed `KeyRelease`.

In general, clients should avoid using passive-grabbed key events for this purpose except when they are unavoidable (as, for example, a selection tool that establishes a passive grab on the keys that cut, copy, or paste).

Clients that set the input focus should set the *revert_to* argument of the `XSetInput-Focus` request to the parent of the window that is to be the new focus window. This determines the behaviour of the input focus if the window the focus has been set to becomes not viewable. All other settings lead to problems, as described in Appendix L, *Interclient Communication Conventions*, of Volume Zero, *X Protocol Reference Manual* (as of the second printing).

Clients should not give up the input focus of their own volition. They should ignore input that they receive instead.

10.2.3.2.2 WM_SAVE_YOURSELF. This protocol is for applications that would like to be notified before the window or session manager terminates them, so that they can save their state and place themselves in a state from which they can be restarted. Such termination, from the application's perspective, would otherwise bypass all the application's internal safety measures (such as when an editor reminds you to save before exiting).

Applications that express interest in this protocol may receive a `ClientMessage` event the atom for WM_SAVE_YOURSELF in its `data[0]` field.

Clients receiving WM_SAVE_YOURSELF should place themselves in a state from which they can be restarted and should update XA_WM_COMMAND (by calling `XSetCommand`) to be a command that will restart them in this state. The session manager will be waiting for a `PropertyNotify` event on XA_WM_COMMAND as a confirmation that the client has saved its state, so that XA_WM_COMMAND should be updated (perhaps with a zero-length append) even if its contents are correct. No interactions with the user are permitted during this process.

After receiving the WM_SAVE_YOURSELF message through the event, saving its state, and updating XA_WM_COMMAND, the client should not change its state (in the sense of doing anything that would require a change to XA_WM_COMMAND) until it receives a mouse or keyboard event. Once it does so, it can assume that the danger is over. The session manager will ensure that these events do not reach clients until the danger is over or until the clients have been killed.

Clients with multiple top-level windows should ensure that only one of their top-level windows has a nonzero-length XA_WM_COMMAND property. They should also respond to a WM_SAVE_YOURSELF message by (in this order):

1. Updating the nonzero length XA_WM_COMMAND property if necessary.

2. Updating the XA_WM_COMMAND property on the window for which they received the WM_SAVE_YOURSELF message if it was not updated in step 1.

10.2.3.2.3 WM_DELETE_WINDOW. This protocol prevents the possibility of an application with multiple top-level windows being terminated unexpectedly by the session manager. It should be selected by applications whose server connection must survive the deletion of some of their top-level windows. Clients which choose not to include WM_DELETE_WINDOW in the WM_PROTOCOLS property will be disconnected from the server if the user asks for one of the client's top-level windows to be deleted.

Once an application has expressed interest in this protocol, if one of the top-level windows is deleted, the application will receive a `ClientMessage` event whose `data[0]` field is the atom for WM_DELETE_WINDOW.

Clients receiving a WM_DELETE_WINDOW message should behave as if the user selected "delete window" from a (hypothetical) menu. They should perform any confirmation dialogue with the user, and if they decide to complete the deletion, either:

- Change the window's state to Withdrawn (as described in Section 10.2.6.1) and release all associated state (backing store, for example) or

- Destroy the window.

If the user aborts the deletion during the confirmation dialogue, the client should continue as if it never received the ClientMessage event that began the dialogue.

If the client aborts a destroy and the user then attempts to delete the window again, the window manager should start the WM_DELETE_WINDOW protocol again. Window managers should not use XDestroyWindow on a window that has WM_DELETE_WINDOW in its WM_PROTOCOLS property.

Note that the WM_SAVE_YOURSELF and WM_DELETE_WINDOW protocols are orthogonal to each other and may be selected independently.

10.2.4 Properties Set by the Window Manager

The properties described above are those which the client is responsible for maintaining on its top-level windows. This section describes what the client can do with the properties that the window manager sets to give information to the client. There are currently two such properties. XA_WM_ICON_SIZE stores information about the sizes of icons that the window manager prefers. The application should use this information to create an icon pixmap or window of one of the right sizes.

The other property, WM_STATE, stores the current state (normal, iconic, or withdrawn) of the application. This is mostly for communication between the window manager and session manager but may also be used by some applications.

10.2.4.1 XA_WM_ICON_SIZE

The window manager may set the XA_WM_ICON_SIZE property on the root window to specify the icon sizes it allows. Clients should read this property using XGetIconSizes and provide an icon window or pixmap of an appropriate size as part of the XWMHints described in Section 10.2.1.4.4. This property is an XIconSize structure shown in Example 10-5.

Example 10-5. The XIconSize structure

```
typedef struct {
    int min_width, min_height;
    int max_width, max_height;
    int width_inc, height_inc;
} XIconSize;
```

The width_inc and height_inc members define an arithmetic progression of sizes, from the minimum size to the maximum size, representing the supported icon sizes.

`XGetIconSizes` actually returns a list of these structures, in case the window manager needs more than one to specify all of its accepted icon sizes.

Some commercial window managers set this property. Clients should be prepared to create an icon pixmap to fit the hint of each of the standard window managers and can even use the hint to determine which window manager is in operation.

Window managers use `XSetIconSize` to set this property for clients.

In R4, `XAllocIconSize` function should be used to allocate and zero the `XIconSize` structure.

10.2.4.2 WM_STATE

According to the ICCCM adopted as of Release 4, the window manager sets this property on top-level windows. The contents of this property is for communication between window managers and session managers. However, the existence of the property set on a window may be used to identify the top-level windows of other applications, for applications that need this information.

Xlib currently provides no routines for reading or writing this property, but of course, you can use `XChangeProperty` or `XGetWindowProperty`.

This property does not have a predefined atom—to read or write this property you will need to call `XInternAtom` to get the atom for this property.

10.2.5 Text Properties

As mentioned earlier, new versions of the routines that set and read text properties have been added in R4. The purpose of the new routines is to allow these properties to be set in an encoding suitable for non-Western languages. The R3 routines provided room for eight bits of data, which is sufficient for English and other Western languages, but not for a language with numerous characters such as Kanji.

The following routines were added in R4 to solve this problem: `XGetWMClient-Machine`, `XGetWMCommand`, `XGetWMIconName`, `XGetWMName`, `XSetWMClient-Machine`, `XSetWMCommand`, `XSetWMIconName`, and `XSetWMName`.

The R4 routines use the `XTextProperty` structure, which contains enough information to read and write the property in any format (8-bit, 16-bit, or 32-bit). The `XTextProperty` structure is shown in Example 10-6.

Example 10-6. The XTextProperty structure

```
typedef struct {
    unsigned char *value;       /* Property data */
    Atom encoding;              /* Type of property */
    int format;                 /* 8, 16, or 32 */
    unsigned long nitems;       /* Number of items in value */
} XTextProperty;
```

You also need to set the fields in two copies of this structure before calling XSet-WMProperties, in order to set the window name and icon name properties, as was done in *basicwin* in Chapter 3, *Basic Window Program*. There are two ways to do this: one is to set the fields directly one at a time, and the other is to use XStringListToText-Property. The latter is easier and better, because it does not require hardcoding the format or encoding. See Example 3-9 for a demonstration of how to do this.

Four more routines are provided in R4 to manipulate the XTextProperty structure:

XTextPropertyToStringList

> Creates a list of strings from an XTextProperty structure. This is used internally by XGetCommand—it is useful for reading properties composed of multiple strings. This is rarely used in normal application code.

XFreeStringList
> Frees memory allocated by XTextPropertyToString-List.

XSetTextProperty
> Convenience routine for XChangeProperty that sets a property according to the information in an XTextProperty structure.

XGetTextProperty
> Convenience routine for XGetWindowProperty that reads a property into an XTextProperty structure. This helps because XGetWindowProperty is complicated.

10.2.6 Constraints on Client Actions

The window manager is allowed to change the border width, color, or pattern of an application's top-level window's border (usually to indicate which window has the keyboard focus), so this window must be an InputOutput window. This also means that the application should not try to use the border to indicate any application state.

The client may receive notification that its window has been reparented, moved, resized, raised, or lowered or that its border width has been changed by selecting Structure-NotifyMask on its top-level window. It should not respond to these events by trying to change any of these characteristics, however.

10.2.6.1 Changing Application State

Some applications may need to tell the window manager that they wish to be iconified, deiconified, or taken completely off the screen. There are right and wrong ways to do this.

In R4, an application can call XIconifyWindow to have one of its top-level windows iconified. This function sends a ClientMessage event to the window manager, telling it to iconify this application. There is no equivalent routine to have the window manager return the application to normal state.

In R3, an application told the window manager to iconify it by resetting the `initial_state` field of `XWMHints`. However, few window managers honor this request.

Under R4, it is also possible to tell the window manager to unmap both the top-level window and its icon. This is done by calling `XWithdrawWindow`. This is useful because the window manager rereads all the standard properties when the window returns from withdrawn to normal state.* There is no defined way for the application to tell an R3 window manager to unmap an application.

R4 supplies no routine to tell the window manager to change a withdrawn application back into normal state. The technique under R4 conventions is for client to set the `initial_state` field of the `XWMHints` structure to `NormalState`, then call `XSetWMHints` to reset this property, and then map the top-level window.

Under R4, to change from withdrawn state to iconic state, the application should follow the same procedure but set the `initial_state` field to `IconicState`.

To change from iconic state to normal state, the client needs only to map the window—it need not reset the property.

If a client selects `StructureNotifyMask` on the top-level window, it will receive an `UnmapNotify` event when it moves to iconic state and a `MapNotify` when it moves to normal state.

Clients can also select `VisibilityChangeMask` on their top-level or icon windows. They will then receive a `VisibilityNotify` event (with the `state` field set to `VisibilityFullyObscured`) when the window concerned becomes completely obscured even though mapped (and thus perhaps a waste of time to update) and a `VisibilityNotify` event (with `state` field not set to `VisibilityFullyObscured`) when it becomes even partly viewable.

10.2.6.2 Reconfiguring the Top-level Window

Under R4 conventions, clients can resize, reposition, and restack their top-level windows using `XReconfigureWMWindow`. This routine is the same as `XConfigureWindow`, except that it takes care of an error condition possible when running under a reparenting window manager. `XReconfigureWindow` lets you specify a sibling window relative to which your top-level window should be stacked, and this will work even if the window manager has reparented your top-level window so that what once was a sibling is no longer a sibling.

Even when the client is not attempting to change the stacking order, the entire reconfigure request is sent by the server to the window manager for approval, and the window manager has the opportunity to honor, modify, or deny the request. The client finds out the window manager's decision through `ConfigureNotify` events.

---

*Remember that resetting a property with a complex structure such as `XA_WM_HINTS` or `XA_WM_NORMAL_HINTS` redefines all members in that property. You must reset all fields, even those which you are not changing since the last time you set the property.

Most applications do not need to specify or even suggest the position of their top-level windows. However, when doing so, the position the client specifies should be relative to the root window regardless of reparenting.

Client requests to reconfigure the top-level window are interpreted by the window manager in the same manner as the initial window geometry mapped from withdrawn state. There is no guarantee that the window manager will allocate the requested size or location, and clients must be prepared to deal with *any* size and location.

The window manager has several options in deciding how to respond to a request by the application to reconfigure a top-level window:

- Not changing the size or location of the window at all, a client will receive a synthetic `ConfigureNotify` event describing the (unchanged) state of the window. The (x,y) coordinates will be in the root coordinate system, adjusted for the border width the client requested, irrespective of any reparenting that has taken place. The `border_width` will be the border width the client requested. The client will not receive a real `ConfigureNotify`, since no change has actually taken place.

- Moving the window without resizing it, a client will receive a synthetic `Configure-Notify` event following the move describing the new state of the window, whose (x,y) coordinates will be in the root coordinate system adjusted for the border width the client requested. The `border_width` will be the border width the client requested. The client may not receive a real `ConfigureNotify` event describing this change, since the window manager may have reparented the top-level window. If it does receive a real event, the synthetic event will follow the real one.

- Resizing the window (whether or not it is moved), a client which has selected `StructureNotifyMask` will receive a `ConfigureNotify` event. Note that the coordinates in this event are relative to the parent, which may not be the root if the window has been reparented, and will reflect the actual border width of the window, which the window manager may have changed. `XTranslateCoordinates` can be used to convert the coordinates if required.

The general rule is that coordinates in real `ConfigureNotify` events are in the parent's space, whereas in synthetic events, they are in the root space.

Clients should be aware that their borders may not be visible. Most window managers use reparenting techniques to decorate client's top-level windows with titles, controls, and other details. Ones that do are likely to override the client's attempts to set the border width and set it to zero. Clients should, therefore, not depend on the top-level window's border being visible nor use it to display any critical information. Other window managers will allow the top-level windows' borders to be visible.

Clients should ignore the `above` field of all `ConfigureNotify` events that they receive on their top-level windows, since they cannot be guaranteed to contain useful information.

10.3 Selections

Selections are the primary mechanism X11 defines for clients that want to exchange information with other clients. A selection transfers arbitrary information between two clients. You can think of a selection as a piece of text or graphics that is highlighted in one application and can be pasted into another, though the information transferred can be almost anything. Clients are strongly encouraged to use this mechanism so that there is a uniform procedure in use by all applications.

The user may want to transfer information from an application and, at other times, to the application. Many applications need to be able to assume either role. In particular, clients should not display text in a permanent window without allowing the user to select it and convert it into a string, and any application that requires the user to type extensively should allow the user to paste in text from other applications.

Selections communicate between an *owner* client and a *requestor* client. The owner has the data representing the value of a selection, and the requestor wants it. The selection mechanism provides a way to notify other clients when useful data is placed in a property and to allow the owner of the data to convert it to a type asked for by the requestor.

Note that in the X11 environment, *all* data transferred between clients must go via the server (unless they are running on the same host, but that is a special case). An X11 client can neither assume that another client can open the same files nor communicate directly through IPC channels. The other client may be talking to the server via a completely different networking mechanism (for example, one client might be DECnet and the other TCP/IP). Thus, passing indirect references to data such as file names, hostnames, port numbers, and so on is permitted only if both clients specifically agree.

10.3.1 The Selection Mechanism

Let's look how a typical selection transaction occurs and then go into all the details of how to make it happen. From the user's point of view, it works like this:

1. The user highlights a selection of text or graphics in one application. For example, in *xterm*, selections are highlighted with the foreground and background colors reversed.

2. The user moves the pointer into another application and presses the key or button that indicates that the selection should be pasted. The keys or buttons used for this purpose in all applications probably should be the ones used by *xterm*, since most users use the cutting and pasting feature of *xterm* frequently.

The desired result is that the text or graphics should appear in the application in which it was pasted. Now how do two applications actually make this happen?

The application in which the text or graphics is being selected must first of all figure out what information is being selected and be able to convert it into a format that can be transferred to other applications. If the selection is text (usually the selection is a string) and the selected area is highlighted, by having the user drag the pointer over the area, then this application has to become the owner of a selection atom.

There are two built-in selection atoms: XA_PRIMARY and XA_SECONDARY. Unless the client foresees needing two simultaneous selections, it should use XA_PRIMARY. It calls XSet-SelectionOwner, specifying the selection atom, any window that it created (this window is used by other applications to identify the owner), and the time. The time used should be from the event that triggered the bid to own the selection (not CurrentTime) because of race conditions that can otherwise occur. If the client does not already own the selection atom, then this call will generate a SelectionClear event for the old owner, telling it to unhighlight the old selection.

Each client that wants to be able to have a selection pasted into it must set aside a key or button combination to indicate that the user wishes to paste in the current selection. In response to the event that occurs when that key or button combination is pressed, the client calls XConvertSelection. This call specifies which selection the application wants (XA_PRIMARY until other conventions are established), the property to place the data in, the window on which to set this property, and the time. These arguments are quite clear. But the XConvertSelection call also specifies a target type that the application wants the data in. You need to understand what happens after the XConvertSelection call to understand the purpose of the target type property.

The server places all the arguments of the XConvertSelection call into an XSelectionRequestEvent and sends the event to the selection owner. The owner then tries to convert the selection data into the format specified in the target type property. If the selection owner knows how to convert the data into the requested type, it puts the data in the property specified in the event and returns the atom of this property in the property member of a SelectionNotify event. If the selection owner cannot convert the selection into the requested type, it returns None as the property member in the SelectionNotify event. The owner sends this SelectionNotify event using XSendEvent.

When the requestor receives the SelectionNotify event, it either reads the property if it is set, repeats the request with a different target type if the owner returned None, or gives up on pasting data from that selection owner. It could be that the user is trying to do something like paste graphics into a text-only application.

Now you should understand the selection mechanism in general, so let's look at a more tangible example of how it takes place.

10.3.2 An Example of Selection

Let's say a text editor is the owner of the selection XA_PRIMARY. The user is editing a C program and debugging the same C program in another window. The user would like to select a line in the source code and instruct the debugger to stop at that same line without having to type in the line number. Perhaps the debugger would have a button labeled "stop at," which, when pressed, would tell the debugger to request a value for the primary selection. The text editor would allow the user to select text on a line and would be able to convert that selection into a string if it were pasted into another text editor or into a line number if it were pasted into the debugger. Which type the text editor would choose would depend on the target type of the selection request.

Assuming the text editor already uses the selection mechanism to transfer text to other applications, adding the line number capability should be easy. It would simply need to look for a new target type that indicated to it to figure out what line number the selected text is on. It might choose the first line, if more than one line were selected, or simply display an error message telling the user to select a single line.

The debugger application would then make the call shown in Example 10-7.

Example 10-7. Setting the primary selection to a line number

```
Display display;
Atom target;
Window debugger_window;
Time time;
Bool only_if_exists;
Atom data_prop;

/* We create atom for data to be put into */
data_prop = XInternAtom(display, "STOP_LINE_NUM",
        only_if_exists = False);

/* Target type atom must have been created by owner */
target_type = XInternAtom(display, "LINE_NUMBER",
        only_if_exists = True);

if (target_type == None) {
    fprintf(stderr, "%s: selection owner did not create \
            LINE_NUMBER atom", argv[0]);
    return(False);
}

XConvertSelection(display, XA_PRIMARY, target_type,
        data_prop, debugger_window, time = triggering_event_time)

/* Wait for a SelectionNotify event and, if the property
 * member is the same as data_prop, the conversion went fine;
 * if the property member is None, the conversion failed */
```

The server sends all of the above information in a `SelectionRequest` event to the text editor client (which had previously made itself the owner of the selection with `XSetSelectionOwner`).

The text editor stores the data in the property specified in the `SelectionRequest` event on `debugger_window`, then sends a `SelectionNotify` event (using `XSendEvent`) to the requesting application. Upon receiving this event, the debugger reads this property and uses its value to place a break point in the C program.

Now that you have seen a more practical application of selections, we'll move on to a more precise description of each step in the selection transfer process.

10.3.3 Acquiring Selection Ownership

When the user decides to select something in an application, the application needs to become the selection owner. Being the selection owner means that when any other application requests the value of the selection with XConvertSelection, the owner gets the resulting XSelectionRequest event. The transfer of selection ownership also makes sure that only one application at a time is attempting to set the properties. The previous application to call XSetSelectionOwner, if it was another application, receives a SelectionClear event, which indicates to it that it should clear any area it has highlighted.

Note that if the time in the XSetSelectionOwner request is in the future relative to the server's current time or if it is in the past relative to the last time the selection concerned changed hands, the XSetSelectionOwner request appears to the client to succeed, but ownership is *not* actually transferred. To ensure that ownership has been transferred, a client must perform the sequence shown in Example 10-8.

Example 10-8. Code to ensure transfer of selection ownership

```
XSetSelectionOwner(display, selection_atom, owner, time);
if (XGetSelectionOwner(display, selection_atom) != owner) {
    /* We didn't get the selection */
}
```

If XGetSelectionOwner returns a window ID rather than None, then the selection ownership was successfully transferred.

10.3.4 Responsibilities of the Selection Owner

When a requestor wants the value of a selection, the owner receives a Selection-Request event. Example 10-9 shows the XSelectionRequestEvent structure.

Example 10-9. The XSelectionRequestEvent structure

```
typedef struct {
    int type;
    unsigned long serial;   /* # of last request processed by
                             * server */
    Bool send_event;        /* True if this came from SendEvent
                             * request */
    Display *display;       /* Display the event was read from */
    Window owner;
    Window requestor;
    Atom selection;
    Atom target;
    Atom property;
    Time time;
} XSelectionRequestEvent;
```

The owner and the selection members will be the values specified in the XSet-SelectionOwner request, and therefore, the selection owner is interested in them only if it owns more than one selection.

The owner should convert the selection into the type specified by the target member and set the property specified by the property member of the SelectionRequest event. Current conventions hold that all properties used to reply to SelectionRequest events should be placed on the requestor window. If the data comprising the selection cannot be stored on the requestor window (for example, because the server cannot provide sufficient memory), the owner must refuse the selection request as above.

The owner should also send the requestor a SelectionNotify event using XSend-Event with an *event_mask* of 0. The members of the SelectionNotify event should be set to the same values received in the SelectionRequest event, except that if the selection could not be converted to the requested type, the property member should be set to None. Example 10-10 shows the XSelectionEvent structure which is used for SelectionNotify events.

Example 10-10. The XSelectionEvent structure

```
typedef struct {
    int type;
    unsigned long serial;    /* # of last request processed by
                              * server */
    Bool send_event;         /* True if this came from SendEvent
                              * request */
    Display *display;        /* Display the event was read from */
    Window requestor;
    Atom selection;
    Atom target;
    Atom property;           /* Atom or None */
    Time time;
} XSelectionEvent;
```

The selection, target, and property members should be set to the values received in the SelectionRequest event. Setting the property member to None indicates that the conversion requested could not be made.

The data stored in the property must eventually be deleted. According to the current conventions, selection requestors are responsible for deleting the converted properties whose names they receive in SelectionNotify events. Owners are responsible for deleting all other properties involved in communicating selections.

A selection owner may need confirmation that the data comprising the selection has actually been transferred. They should express interest in PropertyNotify events for the requestor window and wait until the property in the SelectionNotify event has been deleted before assuming that the selection data has been transferred.

10.3.5 Giving Up Selection Ownership

When some other client becomes the owner of a particular selection, the previous owner receives a `SelectionClear` event. The `XSelectionClearEvent` structure is shown in Example 10-11.

Example 10-11. The XSelectionClearEvent structure

```
typedef struct {
    int type;
    unsigned long serial;   /* # of last request processed by
                             * server */
    Bool send_event;        /* True if from a SendEvent request */
    Display *display;        /* Display the event was read from */
    Window window;
    Atom selection;
    Time time;
} XSelectionClearEvent;
```

The `time` member is the time at which the ownership changed hands, and the `owner` member is the window the new owner specified in its `XSetSelectionOwner` request.

If an owner loses ownership while it has a transfer in progress, that is to say before it receives notification that the requestor has received all the data, it must continue to service the ongoing transfer to completion.

To relinquish ownership of a selection voluntarily, a client should execute a `XSetSelectionOwner` call for that selection atom, with *owner* specified as `None` and *time* specified as `CurrentTime`. Alternatively, the client may destroy the window used as the *owner* argument of the `XSetSelectionOwner` call, or it may exit. In both cases, the ownership of the selection involved will revert to `None`.

10.3.6 Requesting a Selection

A client wishing to obtain the value of a selection in a particular form issues an `XConvertSelection` call. The arguments of the call are three atoms, a window, and the time. The first atom is the selection, usually `XA_PRIMARY`. The second atom is the target type, the type in which the requestor wants the data. The conventions will specify a standard list of target type atoms. The third atom specifies the property that the owner should set to the converted data. The window argument is the window on which the property containing the data is to be set. The `time` member should be set to the timestamp on the event triggering the request for the selection value. Note that the requestor of a selection does not need to know the owner of the selection or the window it specified in the `XSetSelectionOwner` call.

The client that calls `XConvertSelection` call will get a `SelectionNotify` event sent to it from the selection owner. The *requestor*, *selection*, *time*, and *target* arguments of this event will be the same as those on the `XConvertSelection` request.

If the `property` member is `None`, the conversion has been refused. This can mean that there is no owner for the selection, that the owner does not support the conversion implied by `target`, or that the server did not have sufficient space to accommodate the data.

If the `property` member is not `None`, then that property will exist on the requestor window. The value of the selection can be retrieved from this property using `XGet-WindowProperty`. When using `XGetWindowProperty` to retrieve the value of a selection, the *property* argument should be set to the `property` member in the `SelectionNotify` event. The `type` member should be set to `AnyPropertyType`, because the requestor has no way of knowing beforehand what type the selection owner will use.

The property in the `SelectionNotify` should be deleted by invoking `XGetWindow-Property` with the *delete* argument set to `True`. As discussed above, the owner has no way of knowing when the data has been transferred to the requestor unless the property is removed.

10.3.7 Large Data Transfers

Selections can get large, and this poses two problems:

- Transferring large amounts of data to the server is expensive, and it would be beneficial to be able to reuse the data once it has been sent to answer further `XConvert-Selection` requests.

- All servers will have limits on the amount of data that can be stored in a single property. Exceeding this limit will result in a `BadAlloc` error on the `XChangeProperty` call that the selection owner uses to store the data.

The proposed conventions for dealing with these problems are given in Appendix L, *Interclient Communication Conventions*, of Volume Zero, *X Protocol Reference Manual*.

10.3.8 More on Selection Properties and Types

A given selection has a *type* associated with it. Built-in property types that might apply to selections are `XA_BITMAP`, `XA_CARDINAL`, `XA_INTEGER`, `XA_PIXMAP`, `XA_POINT`, `XA_RECTANGLE`, and `XA_STRING`. Other types that clients could define might be `XA_FILE_NAME` or `XA_PICTURE` (a sequence of graphics primitives to reproduce a picture—the Macintosh uses this type of selection to cut and paste graphics into text applications and vice versa).

It is important to observe that defining a new atom consumes resources in the server, and they are not released until the server reinitializes. Thus, it must be a goal to reduce the need for newly minted atoms.

The selection named by `XA_PRIMARY` is used for all commands which take only a single argument. It is the principal means of communication between clients which use the selection mechanism.

It is suggested that the selection named by XA_SECONDARY be used:

- As the second argument to commands taking two arguments. For example, it might be used when exchanging the primary and secondary selections.

- As a means of obtaining data when there is a primary selection, and the user does not wish to disturb it.

A CLIPBOARD selection has been added in the R4 conventions to hold deleted data (it has no predefined atom). There is a client called *xclipboard* that will display the contents of the CLIPBOARD, even if the client where the data was selected has already been killed.

10.3.9 Target Atoms

The atom that a requestor supplies as the `target` argument of XConvertSelection determines the form of the data supplied. The set of such atoms is extensible, but a generally accepted base set of `target` atoms is needed. The set specified in the R4 conventions is shown in Appendix L, *Interclient Communication Conventions*, of Volume Zero, *X Protocol Reference Manual*. However, some types are already predefined properties, and these can safely be used.

Target properties describe types of data. They contain the C language types of the structures that are used for many of the Xlib functions. The predefined target atoms are shown in Table 10-7.

Table 10-7. Predefined Target Type Atoms

Type Atom	C Language Type
XA_ARC	XArc
XA_POINT	XPoint
XA_ATOM	Atom
XA_RGB_COLOR_MAP	Atom (standard colormap)
XA_BITMAP	Pixmap (of depth 1)
XA_RECTANGLE	XRectangle
XA_CARDINAL	int (dimensionless)
XA_STRING	char *
XA_COLORMAP	Colormap
XA_VISUALID	VisualID
XA_CURSOR	Cursor
XA_WINDOW	Window
XA_DRAWABLE	Drawable
XA_WM_HINTS	XWMHints
XA_FONT	Font
XA_INTEGER	int
XA_WM_SIZE_HINTS	XSizeHints
XA_PIXMAP	Pixmap

The owner should not translate the selection into some arbitrary fallback target type (such as XA_STRING) and return the fallback target to the requestor in the SelectionNotify event, because this might confuse the requestor. The conversion should simply fail. The requestor then has the option of requesting another type. The requestor can supply the target TARGETS to get a list of target types the owner supports.

10.4 Cut Buffers

Cut buffers are provided as a simple but limited method of communication between applications. Cut buffers are particularly good for editors, because they can act like a stack of buffers, recording the history of deletions.

The selection mechanism is superior for many applications, since it allows communication regarding the type of the data transferred. Selections are described in Section 10.3. It is also possible for an application to use both cut buffers and selections.

The cut buffers are eight properties on the root window of screen 0 of a server. The buffers are numbered 0 to 7. Cut buffers rely on a prior agreement between the two clients regarding the format of the data to be placed in the cut buffers. The data that can be placed in a single cut buffer is limited to the maximum size of a single property, which is server-dependent.

Because the cut buffers are properties, it is possible to be notified when they have been written into. PropertyNotify events can assist applications in timing their communication. These are selected with PropertyChangeMask.

The functions that are used to read and write to cut buffers are XFetchBuffer, XFetchBytes, XStoreBuffer, and XStoreBytes. The routines with Bytes in the name use cut buffer 0 only, while the others may use any of the eight. XRotateBuffers moves the contents of the eight buffers any number of positions.

The cut buffer properties are named by the predefined atoms XA_CUT_BUFFER0 to XA_CUT_BUFFER7.

The cut buffers can let applications implement a first-in, last-out stack of data. A client using this cut buffer mechanism must initially ensure that all eight buffer properties exist, using XChangeProperty to append zero-length data to each. A client storing data in the cut buffers (an owner) must first rotate the ring of buffers by +1, using XRotateProperties to rename XA_CUT_BUFFER0 to XA_CUT_BUFFER1 to .... to XA_CUT_BUFFER7 to XA_CUT_BUFFER0. It must then store the data into XA_CUT_BUFFER0, using XStoreBytes.

A client obtaining data from the cut buffers should use XFetchBytes to retrieve the contents of XA_CUT_BUFFER0.

A client may, in response to a specific user request, rotate the cut buffers by -1, using XRotateProperties to rename XA_CUT_BUFFER7 to XA_CUT_BUFFER6 .... and so on and XA_CUT_BUFFER0 to XA_CUT_BUFFER7.

Data should be stored to the cut buffers and the ring rotated only when requested by explicit user action. Users depend on their mental model of cut buffer operation and need to be able to identify operations that transfer data to and from the buffers.

Note that there is nothing magic about the properties used by Xlib's cut buffer routines or those routines themselves. If an application needs more buffers, it can intern additional atoms for CUT_BUFFER8 and so on and write its own equivalent of XStoreBuffer and XFetchBuffer that can write and read these properties.

11

Managing User Preferences

It is a fundamental part of the X philosophy that the user, not the application, should be in control of the way things work. For this reason, applications should allow the user to specify window geometry and many other characteristics both via command line options and in a file that specifies default preferences. This chapter discusses the use of the resource manager, which helps an application to evaluate and merge its own default with user preferences. While the information in this chapter is not essential for X programming, it is essential for writing programs that will work in ways that users will come to expect. For additional information on the resource manager at work, see Chapter 12.

In This Chapter:

11

Managing User Preferences

Applications can and should be made user customizable. Every application should provide command line options for the most important configurable elements of the application, such as colors or patterns for the window border and background, foreground colors for drawing, desired geometry of the application, fonts, and so on. Furthermore, an application should allow users to set all options through the resource database.

A *resource* is a configurable program option (completely different from a server resource, such as a window). There are a set of *resource files* and *resource properties* that may contain settings for program options. When all the resource files and properties are merged into a single database by Xlib, the result is called the *resource database*. Each setting for a resource in any of these files or properties or in the resource database is called a *resource specification*. The routines and database structures used for managing user preferences are collectively referred to as the *resource manager*.

Prior to X11 Release 2, users stored their resource specifications in a file in their home directory called *.Xdefaults*. Additional resource specifications could be stored in a file pointed to by the shell environment variable XENVIRONMENT or in a system-specific file called *.Xdefaults-system*.

However, experience showed that this approach caused problems for users running clients from multiple machines across the network. A separate *.Xdefaults* file had to be maintained on each machine. For this reason, the *xrdb* program was designed to install the user's preferences in the XA_RESOURCE_MANAGER property on the root window of the current server. In this way, all clients running on the same server share the same user preferences. The old mechanism is still supported for compatibility, but *.Xdefaults* is read only if the XA_RESOURCE_MANAGER property has not be set with *xrdb*. Another advantage of having the user's resource specifications set with *xrdb* is that they are stored in a property instead of a file, and therefore, they can be more easily managed by the session manager (although none of these exist yet), since changing a property from a program is much easier than editing a file from a program.

XGetDefault provides a simplified interface that applications can use to read options from the resource database. However, there is also a complete set of resource manager routines, which were originally developed for the Xt Toolkit, which can be used to process resources in a more thorough and expandable way. The Xt Toolkit resource manager was merged into Xlib because the task of managing user preferences is common to all X applications. By making the resource manager part of Xlib, the developers ensured that all toolkits layered on Xlib will use the same mechanism, providing users with a consistent interface. In the Xt Toolkit, all objects (called *widgets*) are configurable through the resource database. And as you will see, the object-oriented nature of the Xt Toolkit is also apparent in the resource manager. Even though most Xlib applications are not object-oriented and therefore cannot take full advantage of the capabilities of the resource manager, they can still benefit from using it.

All resource manager routines except `XGetDefault` have names beginning with *Xrm*, so they are conveniently grouped together in Volume Two, *Xlib Reference Manual*. You must include *<X11/Xresource.h>* to use `XGetDefault` or the other resource manager functions.

In the following sections, we'll talk about handling user preferences using `XGetDefault` and using the resource manager routines. We'll also talk about how to use `XParse-Geometry` and `XGeometry`, which parses the standard format for window size and placement preferences (whether specified on the command line or in a resource file or property).

After that, we'll discuss the format of the data in the resource manager database. The rules for specifying preferences are fairly complex, although for most Xlib applications, using them is quite simple.

Finally, we'll talk briefly about some more advanced resource manager routines.

11.1 Using XGetDefault

`XGetDefault` allows a program to determine a value for an option by searching the resource database. It reads the resource specifications from the `XA_RESOURCE_MANAGER` property in the server or, if that is not set, the user's *Xdefaults* file. Next, if there is an XENVIRONMENT environment variable, then the file specified in it is loaded as well. The value returned by `XGetDefault` for a particular program/option key will be the last match found in this list.

Actually, the `XA_RESOURCE_MANAGER` property is automatically copied from the server into the `Display` structure returned by `XOpenDisplay`. Therefore, each call to `XGet-Default` does not really read that property directly but, instead, a local copy of it. Therefore, `XGetDefault` does not require a round-trip request and is quite fast.

Unfortunately, `XGetDefault` does not do the whole job of handling program options. `XGetDefault` does not parse the command line options or read the application-specific resource file. You need to use the other resource manager routines to handle these.

Normally, the command line options are read one at a time, and if a command line argument is present for a particular option, it overrides any value that might be present in the resource database, and therefore `XGetDefault` does not need to be called. But if no value for a particular option is found, `XGetDefault` must be called. If `XGetDefault` returns a non-null string, that is the option value, which usually has to be converted into a useful type for the program. If `XGetDefault` returns NULL, your program needs a default value, which it can read from a database file in the *app-defaults* directory using `XrmGetFile-Database` and `XrmGetResource` or, less desirable but easier, it can hardcode the default values.

The sequence of operation for using XGetDefault is shown in Figure 11-1.

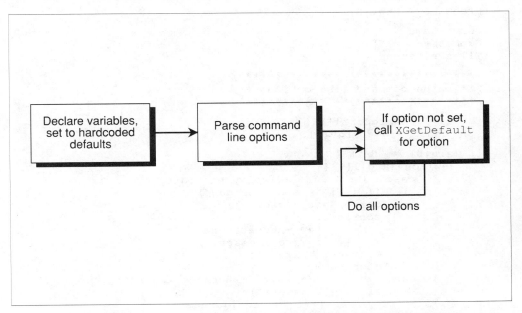

Figure 11-1. Procedure for processing user resource specifications with XGetDefault

Example 11-1 shows the code for one way to handle program options using XGetDefault. It is taken without modification from the X demo *puzzle*.*

Example 11-1. Handling program options with XGetDefault

```
#define DEFAULT_SPEED           2
int       PuzzleSize = 4;
int       PuzzleWidth=4, PuzzleHeight=4;
char      *ProgName;
int       UsePicture = 0;
int       CreateNewColormap = 0;
char      *PictureFileName;
int       TilesPerSecond;

/* Other global declarations */

main(argc,argv)    /* This is complete */
int argc;
char *argv[];
{
    int i, count;
    char *ServerName, *Geometry;
    char *puzzle_size = NULL;
    char *option;
```

---

*Be sure to try the puzzle program using the mandrill face picture (*puzzle -picture mandrill.cm*) on an eight-plane color screen. It is the most visually impressive X application we have seen, and the program is very well written, too.

Example 11-1. Handling program options with XGetDefault (continued)

```
        ProgName = argv[0];

        ServerName = "";
        Geometry   = "";
        TilesPerSecond = -1;

        /********************************/
        /** parse command line options **/
        /********************************/

        for (i=1; i<argc; i++) {
            char *arg = argv[i];

        if (arg[0] == '-') {
            switch (arg[1]) {
                case 'd':       /* -display host:display */
                    if (++i >= argc) usage ();
                    ServerName = argv[i];
                    continue;
                case 'g':       /* -geometry geom */
                    if (++i >= argc) usage ();
                    Geometry = argv[i];
                    continue;
                case 's':       /* -size WxH or -speed n */
                    if (arg[2] == 'i') {
                        if (++i >= argc) usage ();
                        puzzle_size = argv[i];
                        continue;
                    } else if (arg[2] == 'p') {
                        if (++i >= argc) usage ();
                        TilesPerSecond = atoi (argv[i]);
                        continue;
                    } else
                        usage ();
                    break;
                case 'p':       /* -picture filename */
                    if (++i >= argc) usage ();
                    UsePicture++;
                    PictureFileName = argv[i];
                    continue;
                case 'c':       /* -colormap */
                    CreateNewColormap++;
                    continue;
                default:
                    usage ();
            }   /* End switch */
        } else
            usage ();
        }   /* End for */

        /* Open display here */
        SetupDisplay (ServerName);

        if (!Geometry) {
            Geometry = XGetDefault (display, ProgName, "Geometry");
        }

        if (!puzzle_size) {
            option = XGetDefault (display, ProgName, "Size");
```

Example 11-1. Handling program options with XGetDefault (continued)

```
            puzzle_size = option ? option : "4x4";
    }

    if (TilesPerSecond <= 0) {
        option = XGetDefault (display, ProgName, "Speed");
        TilesPerSecond = option ? atoi (option) : DEFAULT_SPEED;
    }

    if (!UsePicture) {
        option = XGetDefault (display, ProgName, "Picture");
        if (option) {
        UsePicture++;
        PictureFileName = option;
        }
    }

    if (!CreateNewColormap) {
        option = XGetDefault (display, ProgName, "Colormap");
        if (option) {
        CreateNewColormap++;
        }
    }
    sscanf (puzzle_size, "%dx%d", &PuzzleWidth, &PuzzleHeight);
    if (PuzzleWidth < 4 || PuzzleHeight < 4) {
        fprintf (stderr, "%s:  Puzzle size must be at least 4x4\n",
                 ProgName);
    exit (1);
    }
    PuzzleSize = min((PuzzleWidth/2)*2,(PuzzleHeight/2)*2);

    Setup (Geometry,argc,argv);
    ProcessInput();
    exit (0);
}
static char *help_message[] = {
    "where options include:",
    "      -display host:display    X server to use",
    "      -geometry geom           geometry of puzzle window",
    "      -size WxH                number of squares in puzzle",
    "      -speed number            tiles to move per second",
    "      -picture filename        image to use for tiles",
    "      -colormap                create a new colormap",
    NULL
};

usage()
{
    char **cpp;

    fprintf (stderr, "usage:  %s [-options ...]\n\n", ProgName);
    for (cpp = help_message; *cpp; cpp++) {
        fprintf (stderr, "%s\n", *cpp);
    }
    fprintf (stderr, "\n");
    exit (1);
}
```

In Example 11-1, as in most existing applications, the program default values are hardcoded. Ideally, they should be taken from a file so that the code does not have to be recompiled to change them. Example 11-2 shows how this could be added to the code in Example 11-1. Only the processing of a single option is shown.

Example 11-2. Processing geometry option using program resource specifications file

```
}
    XrmDatabase applicationDB;
    char *classname = "puzzle";
    char name[255];            /* Would be 15 for System V */
    char Geometry[20];
    char Geostr[20];
    char *str_type[20];
    XrmValue value;
    unsigned int border_width;
    unsigned int font_width, font_height;
    int pad_x, pad_y;

    /* Width and height are *not* type unsigned when
     * returned from XGeometry -- don't ask us why... */
    int x, y, width, height;

    for (i=1; i<argc; i++) {
        char *arg = argv[i];
        if (arg[0] == '-') {
            switch (arg[1]) {
                .
                .
                .

                case 'g':/* -geometry geom */
                    if (++i >= argc) usage ();
                    Geometry = argv[i];
                    continue;
                .
                .
                .
            }
        }
        else
            usage();
    }

    if (!Geometry) {
        Geometry = XGetDefault (display, ProgName, "Geometry");
    }

    (void) strcpy(name, "/usr/lib/X11/app-defaults/");
    (void) strcat(name, classname);
    /* Get application resource specifications file, if any */
    if ((applicationDB = XrmGetFileDatabase(name)) == NULL)
        fprintf(stderr, "%s: program default file not found",
                ProgName);

    /* Get the program default geometry string regardless of
     * whether it has been specified on command line or in
     * resource database, because those specifications may be
     * partial; we're going to use XGeometry to fill in the gaps */
    if (XrmGetResource(applicationDB, "puzzle.geometry",
```

```
                "Puzzle.Geometry",
                str_type, &value) == True) {
(void) strncpy(Geostr, value.addr, (int) value.size);
} else {
        fprintf(stderr, "%s: default geometry option not found",
                ProgName);
Geostr[0] = NULL;
}

XGeometry(display, screen_num, Geometry, Geostr,
        (border_width = 0), (font_width = 1), (font_height = 1),
        (pad_x = 0), (pad_y = 0), &x, &y, &width, &height);
/* Now x, y, width, and height are the specs to use when
 * creating the window and nothing has been hardcoded */
```

11.2 Using the Low-level Resource Manager Routines

As you can see, handling program options properly with XGetDefault is not trivial, even though XGetDefault is supposed to be the simple interface to the resource manager. Whether it is any easier to use the resource manager calls is debatable, but the resource manager calls do have certain advantages.

For one, there is a single routine that takes care of parsing the command line and loading the values found there into the resource database. Secondly, there are several more resource files that XGetDefault does not read but that an application really should. You can mechanize the whole process of handling program options by turning every set of options into a database, merging them into a single database, and then extracting the correct values. The resulting code is easier to expand or modify than code that uses XGetDefault.

First, let's describe the additional resource files that we will handle with the low-level resource manager routines. All applications need fallback settings for all configurable options in case the user does not set these options. Instead of hardcoding these as defined constants, they can be placed in another resource file. Then if they need to be changed by the application writer, only the resource file needs editing, and the application does not need to be recompiled. Another advantage of this approach is that it allows all fixed text in the application to be specified in resource files instead of in the code, and this makes it easier to convert an application to a foreign language. The application-specific resource specifications can also be stored in a file in the directory */usr/lib/X11/app-defaults*. (Each file should have the same name as the application itself, except with the first letter capitalized, unless the application name begins with an X, in which case the first two letters should be capitalized.)

The other additional resource files add flexibility; each is intended to be set by either the user, the application writer, or the system administrator. More will probably be added for foreign language conversion. The user will only be expected to use the *.Xdefaults* file or the property set by the *xrdb* utility. The complete set of resource files and properties and the order in which they are merged is as follows:

- *Classname* file in the *app-defaults* directory.

- *Classname* file in the directory specified by the XUSERFILESEARCHPATH or XAPPLRESDIR environment variables.

- Property set using *xrdb*, accessible through the `XResourceManagerString` macro or, if that is empty, the *Xdefaults* file in the user's home directory.

- File specified by the XENVIRONMENT environment variable or, if not set, the *Xdefaults-hostname* file in the user's home directory.

- Command line arguments.

The order in which the various options are merged is important. A value for an option in the user's resource specifications should override the program's default for that option, but a value on the command line would override both the program's and the user's default value.

The basic routines that every application that processes resources this way will include:

`XrmInitialize`	Initializes the resource manager database. Must be called before any other routines.
`XrmParseCommand`	Parses command line options into a data structure compatible with other resource manager routines. Various styles of command line options (with or without arguments and with various styles of arguments) are supported.
`XrmGetFileDatabase`	Reads a resource file and stores the data in a resource manager database structure. This routine can be used to read the *Xdefaults* file, the *app-defaults/** file, and the file (if any) pointed to by the XENVIRONMENT environment variable.
`XrmGetStringDatabase`	Reads preferences from a string. This routine can be used to read resource specifications from the copy of the `XA_RESOURCE_MANAGER` property stored in the `Display` structure.
`XrmMergeDatabases`	Merges databases created with other routines into a single combined database. This routine is used to combine the separate resource databases created with the functions described immediately above. The order in which the various databases are merged determines which databases take precedence.
`XrmGetResource`	Extract a resource definition from the database so that it can be used to set program variables.

The sequence of operations for a typical application is shown in Figure 11-2.

Routines that use these functions are shown and described in Chapter 12, *A Complete Application*.

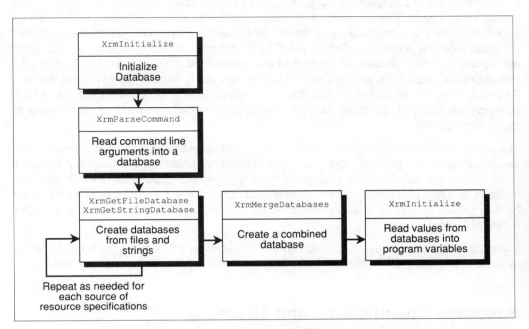

Figure 11-2. *Procedure for processing resource specifications with resource manager functions*

11.3 Standard Geometry

One of the preferences that must be handled by clients is the preferred size and placement of a window or icon. By convention, rather than having the user specify various elements of the size and placement with separate options, clients accept a single *standard geometry string*, which has the following format:

> `<width>x<height>{+-}<xoffset>{+-}<yoffset>`

Items enclosed in <> are integers, and items enclosed in { } are a set from which one item is allowed. The `xoffset` and `yoffset` values are optional. They determine the position of the window or icon—for the top-level window, they are, by convention, interpreted relative to the origin of the root window. The convention is that if the sign of `xoffset` or `yoffset` is positive, they specify that the offset is measured from the top or left edge of the application window to the top or left edge of the screen. If the sign of `xoffset` or `yoffset` is negative, they specify that the offset is measured from the bottom or right edge of the application window to the bottom or right edge of the screen.

After being read in from the command line or from a preference file, this string can be separated into separate x, y, width, and height values with XParseGeometry. See Chapter 12 for an example that uses XParseGeometry.

In addition, there is a function called XGeometry (replaced by XWMGeometry in R4) that can be used to parse a partial geometry specification from the user. XGeometry takes two geometry strings, one specified (presumably) by the user, which might not be complete, and the other, a default geometry string specified by the program, which must be complete. If the user-specified string specifies an element of the geometry, that value is used; otherwise, the corresponding value from program's default geometry string is used. Most current applications use XParseGeometry rather than XGeometry because they hardcode the default geometry values, and therefore, they do not have a second geometry string to pass to XGeometry.

The R3 routine XGeometry and the R4 routine XWMGeometry have very different arguments but the same purpose. One important difference is that XWMGeometry returns a win_gravity value. After calling XWMGeometry, the application should pass this value on to XSetWMProperties, as described in Section 4.3.4. The values returned can be NorthEastGravity, NorthWestGravity, SouthEastGravity or SouthWestGravity.

These functions should not be confused with XGetGeometry, which gets from the server the current geometry string, border width, depth, and root window of the specified window.

11.4 Resource Specification and Matching

A resource specification consists of an optional name of a client, followed by one or more predefined variables that indicate the preference to set, followed by a colon, optional white space, and the actual value of the preference.*

The format of these preference strings is most easily seen by looking at a resource database file, such as the one shown in Example 11-3.

Example 11-3. A simple resource database file

```
*font:                    fixed
.borderWidth:             2

xterm.scrollBar:          on
xterm.title:              xterm
xterm.windowName:         xterm
xterm.boldFont:           8x13
xterm.curses:             off
xterm.internalBorder:     2
xterm.iconStartup:        off
xterm.jumpScroll:         on
xterm.reverseWrap:        true
xterm.saveLines:          700
xterm.visualBell:         off
```

---

*Thanks to Jim Fulton of the X Consortium for providing an explanation of the resource manager on the *comp.windowx* network news group, from which portions of this section are excerpted.

The options which begin with a period apply to all programs unless overruled by a program-specific entry with the same resource name. The last element between a period or asterisk and the colon is the resource name.

This simple example demonstrates the rules as commonly practiced in Xlib applications. However, there are a number of additional rules that come into play in more complex, object-oriented applications, such as those written with the Xt Toolkit. Preferences may apply only to a particular subwindow within an application. For example, the *xmh* mail handler allows the user to set preferences for multiple levels of windows. These levels can be specified explicitly or by using a wildcard syntax, denoted by the asterisk.

As a result, you should think of the syntax for preference specifications, not as:

> *client.keyword: value*

but as:

> *object . . . subobject . . . resourcename: value*

where the hierarchy of objects and subobjects not only usually corresponds to major structures within an application (such as windows, panels, menus, scrollbars, and so on) but also can be a class of such objects.

Individual elements in the hierarchy of objects and subobjects are called *components*. Component names can be either *instance names* or *class names*. By convention, instance names always begin with a lower-case letter, while class names always begin with an upper-case letter. Instances and classes are concepts in object-oriented programming, not normally used in Xlib programming. For a detailed description of instance and classes and how they appear in resource specifications, see Volume Four, *X Toolkit Intrinsics Programming Manual*.

Both instance and class names may include either upper-case or lower-case letters anywhere but in the starting position; in fact, for clarity, a component name is often made up of multiple words concatenated without spaces, with an initial capital serving as the word delimiter. For example, `buttonBox` might be the instance name for a window containing command buttons, while `ButtonBox` would be the corresponding class name.

For example, consider a hypothetical mail-reading program called *xmail*, which is similar to the current *xmh* application.* As shown in Figure 11-3, *xmail* is designed in such a manner that it uses a complex window hierarchy, all the way down to individual command buttons which are small subwindows. If each window is properly assigned a name and class, it becomes easy for the user to specify attributes of any portion of the application.

The top-level window is called `xmail`. It contains a series of vertically-stacked windows (panes), one of which contains all the command buttons controlling the program's functions. This control pane is named `toc` (table of contents). One of the command buttons is used to incorporate (fetch) new mail.

---

*We do not discuss the actual *xmh* application, even though it does use an object-oriented approach, because speaking hypothetically gives us greater freedom to set up illustrative examples.

Figure 11-3. The hypothetical xmail display

This button needs the following resources:

- Label string
- Font
- Foreground color
- Background color
- Foreground color for its highlighted state
- Background color for its highlighted state

A full instance name specifying the background color of the include button might be:

```
xmail.toc.includeButton.backgroundColor
```

Defining class names allows the user to set resource values more freely. The pane containing the buttons could be of class `ButtonBox`, and the buttons themselves are all of class `CommandButton`. Therefore, the background of all the buttons could be identified with:

```
Xmail.ButtonBox.CommandButton.BackgroundColor
```

The user could do something like this:

```
Xmail.ButtonBox.CommandButton.BackgroundColor:  blue
xmail.toc.includeButton.backgroundColor:        red
```

which would make all command buttons blue except the one instance specified (include-Button), which would be red.

It might not be immediately apparent how you could use a class for the name of the application itself. However, consider the emacs family of text editors. Microemacs and GNU emacs could both be considered members of the class Emacs. Or assume that you were using a toolkit to build a group of applications with a similar user interface. It might be desirable to let the user specify attributes for features of all these applications. You might define a general class of vertically paned applications called Vpane.

The distinction between instance names and class names becomes important when you are retrieving an option value from the resource database. Routines such as XrmGet-Resource that retrieve data from the database must specify two separate strings (*retrieval keys*)—one made up completely of instance names, and the other of class names. Both strings must be fully specified.

11.4.1 Tight Bindings and Loose Bindings

The components in a resource specification can be bound together in two ways: by a tight binding (a dot, .) or by a loose binding (an asterisk, *). Thus, xmail.toc.background has three name components tightly bound together, while Vpane*Command.foreground uses both a loose and a tight binding.

Bindings can precede the first component but may not follow the last component. By convention, if no binding is specified before the first component, a tight binding is assumed. For example, xmail.background and .xmail.background both begin with tight bindings before the xmail, while *xmail.background begins with a loose binding.

The difference between tight and loose bindings comes when a function like XrmGet-Resource is comparing two resource specifications. A tight binding means that the components on either side of the binding must be sequential. A loose binding is a sort of wildcard, meaning that there may be unspecified components between the two components that are loosely bound together. For example, xmail.toc.background would match xmail*background and *background, but not xmail.background or background.

Because loose bindings are flexible, they are very useful for defining resource specifications. They allow resource specifications to match many specific applications and will still match if the applications are slightly changed (for example, if an extra level is inserted into the hierarchy.)

A resource specification used to store data into the database can use both loose and tight bindings. This allows the user to specify a data value which can match many different retrieval keys. In contrast, retrieval keys from the database can use only tight bindings. You can only look up one item in the database at a time.

Remember also that a resource specification can mix name and class components, while the retrieval keys are a pair of specifications without values, one consisting purely of name (first character lower-case) components and one consisting purely of class (first character upper-case) components.

11.4.2 The -name Option

If you set up your resource specifications to use the class name for a program instead of an instance name, users can then list instance resources under an arbitrary name that they specify with the *-name* option to a program. For example, if *xterm* were set up this way, with the following resources defined:

```
XTerm*Font:          6x10
smallxterm*Font:     3x5
smallxterm*Geometry: 80x10
bigxterm*Font:       9x15
bigxterm*Geometry:   80x55
```

the user could use the following commands to create *xterm*s of different sizes:

```
xterm &                     (create a normal xterm)
xterm -name smallxterm      (create a small xterm)
xterm -name bigxterm        (create a big xterm)
```

11.4.3 Storage/Access Rules

The algorithm for determining which resource name or names match a given query is the heart of the database. The idea is that resources may be stored with only a partially specified instance and/or class name, while they are accessed with a completely specified instance and class name pair. The lookup algorithm then searches the database for the instance that most closely matches this full instance and class name pair.

The resource manager must solve the problem of how to compare the pair of retrieval keys to a single resource specification. (Actually, it must compare the pair of retrieval keys to many single resource specifications, since the resource manager will compare the retrieval keys against every resource specification in the database, but one at a time.)

The solution of comparing a pair of keys to a single resource specification is simple. The resource manager compares component by component, matching a component from the resource specification against both the corresponding component from the instance retrieval key and the corresponding component from the class retrieval key. If the resource specification component matches either retrieval key component, then that component is considered to match. For example, the resource specification `xmail.toc.Foreground` matches the instance retrieval key `xmail.toc.foreground` and the class retrieval key `Vpane.Box.Foreground`.

Because the resource manager allows loose bindings (wildcards) and mixing names and classes in the resource specification, it is possible for many resource specifications to match a single instance/class retrieval key pair. To solve this problem, the resource manager uses the following precedence rules to determine which is the best match (and only the value from that match will be returned). The precedence rules are, in order of preference:

1. The attribute of the name and class must match. For example, assuming that Xterm allowed multiple levels of resource specification, queries for:

    ```
    xterm.scrollbar.background        (name)
    XTerm.Scrollbar.Background        (class)
    ```

    will not match the following database entry:

    ```
    xterm.scrollbar:  on
    ```

2. Database entries with instance or class prefixed by a dot (.) are more specific than those prefixed by an asterisk (*). For example, the entry `xterm.geometry` is more specific than the entry `xterm*geometry`.

3. Instances are more specific than classes. For example, the entry `*scrollbar.background` is more specific than the entry `*Scrollbar.Background`.

4. An instance or class name that is explicitly stated is more specific than one that is omitted. For example, the entry `Scrollbar*Background` is more specific than the entry `*Background`.

5. Left components are more specific than right components. For example, the entry `xterm*background` is more specific than the entry `scrollbar*background`.

As an example of these rules, assume the following user preference specifications:

```
xmail*background:                      red
*command.font:                         8x13
*command.background:                   blue
*Command.Foreground:                   green
xmail.toc*Command.activeForeground:    black
xmail.toc.border:                      3
```

A query for the name:

```
xmail.toc.messageFunctions.include.activeForeground
```

and class:

```
Vpane.Box.SubBox.Command.Foreground
```

would match `xmail.toc*Command.activeForeground` and return "black." However, it also matches `*Command.Foreground` but with lower preference, so it would not return "green."

The programmer should think carefully when deciding what classes to use. For example, many text applications have some notion of background, foreground, border, pointer, and cursor or marker color. Usually the background is set to one color, and all of the other attributes are set to another, so that they may be seen on a monochrome display. To allow users of color displays to set any or all of them, the colors might be organized into classes as follows:

Table 11-1. Setting Classes

Instance	Class
background	Background
foreground	Foreground
borderColor	Foreground
pointerColor	Foreground
cursorColor	Foreground

Then to configure the application to run in "monochrome" mode but using two colors, the user would only have to use two specifications:

```
obj*Background:  blue
obj*Foreground:  red
```

Then if the user decided to make the cursor yellow but have the pointer and the border remain the same as the foreground, you would only need one new resource specification:

```
obj*cursorColor: yellow
```

All the resource manager rules for matching and precedence are explained in more detail in Volume Four, *X Toolkit Intrinsics Programming Manual*.

11.4.4 Resource Manager Values and Representation Types

The resource manager stores character strings in a structure called an `XrmValue`. Physically, database values consist of a size and an address. The size is specified in machine-dependent units, while the address is a machine-dependent pointer to the character string in uninterpreted machine memory.

The declaration of the `XrmValue` is shown in Example 11-4.

Example 11-4. The XrmValue structure

```
typedef struct {
    unsigned int size;
    caddr_t addr;
} XrmValue, *XrmValuePtr;
```

In addition, a representation type is stored along with each value in the data structure. The corresponding representation type is returned along with the data value when the database is accessed. The type provides a way to distinguish between different representations of the same information. For example, a color may be specified by a color name ("red") or be coded in a hexadecimal string ("#4f6c84"), by a pixel value, or by RGB values. Representation types are user-defined character strings describing the way the data is represented. You specify them when you store data, and you interpret them when you access data. Previous releases of X contained programs to perform automatic type conversion. These converter routines and types were found to be insufficiently general and were removed from Xlib. However, similar conversion functions are now being implemented in the X Toolkit.

You create representation types from simple character strings by using the macro `Xrm-StringToRepresentation`. For example:

```
XrmStringToRepresentation("RGB_value")
```

might be used if the data to be stored was a color represented as an RGB value. Certain functions let you store data without specifying a representation type. These functions always take data in the form of a `char[]` and automatically assign it the representation type `String`. The type `XrmRepresentation` is internally represented as an `XrmQuark`, since it is an ID for a string. (See Section 11.5.2 for details.)

11.5 Other Resource Manager Routines

The resource manager includes a number of other routines that will be of limited use to most application developers. They are discussed briefly here for the sake of completeness.

11.5.1 Putting Resources into the Database

While all most applications will need to do is to merge various sources of user preferences into a database and then read individual values, routines also exist for putting explicit resource values into the database or writing out the database into a file. For example, the *xrdb* program allows a user to write out the current contents of the resource manager database into a file. An application could allow users to modify the application resource specifications file and would then need those routines.

Routines for putting resources include:

`XrmPutResource`	Stores preference data into a resource database.
`XrmPutLineResource`	Stores a single line of preference data into a resource database.
`XrmPutStringResource`	Stores a preference string into a resource database.
`XrmPutFileDatabase`	Writes a resource database into a file.

The resource manager only frees or overwrites entries when new data is stored into a database with `XrmMergeDatabases` or `XrmPutResource` and related routines. A client that does not use these functions should be safe using the addresses to strings returned by routines like `XrmGetResource`.

11.5.2 Quarks

A special data type called a *quark* is used internally by the resource manager to represent strings. They were created to improve the efficiency of the resource manager. The resource manager needs to make many comparisons of strings when it gets data from the database. It must compare, component by component, the name and class specification of the requested resource to each stored key in the database. Quarks are simple identifiers (presently represented as integers) for strings. Thus, instead of comparing strings, the resource manager converts each component of the string into the corresponding quark and compares the quarks instead. This converts lengthy string comparisons into quick numeric comparisons, with the obvious savings in efficiency. The price is the overhead needed to convert back and forth between strings and quarks, but this is a small price for avoiding multiple string comparisons in a large database.

In summary, then, a quark is to a string as an atom is to a property. Quarks, however, are local to the application.

Quarks are implemented using an internal table of strings. The function `XrmString-ToQuark` returns a pointer to the quark for a given string. Clients that do more than just access their resource specifications once might consider calling `XrmStringToQuark` for each string and then using the quark form of the routines that get resources.

The following functions convert between strings and quarks:

- `XrmQuarkToString`
- `XrmStringToBindingQuarkList`
- `XrmStringToQuark`
- `XrmStringToQuarkList`
- `XrmUniqueQuark`

The following routines can be used to work directly on quarks rather than strings when retrieving or storing resources:

- `XrmQGetResource`
- `XrmQGetSearchList`
- `XrmQGetSearchResource`
- `XrmQPutResource`
- `XrmQPutStringResource`

All of the quark routines are unlikely to be used by application developers. However, they will be of use to toolkit developers. See Volume Two, *Xlib Reference Manual*, for more information.

You will need to use a group of special macros with the routines that handle quarks. They are described in Appendix C, *Macros*, of Volume Two, *Xlib Reference Manual*, and listed below. Unfortunately, they do not follow the normal naming convention for macros, since they begin with *Xrm* (no other macros begin with *X*), possibly because the resource manager used to be part of a separate library.

- `XrmClassToString`
- `XrmNameToString`
- `XrmRepresentationToString`
- `XrmStringToClass`
- `XrmStringToName`
- `XrmStringToRepresentation`

12

A Complete Application

While the simple application in Chapter 3 demonstrated the most important X programming techniques, it was far from a complete application. This chapter describes a calculator program that provides for calculations in several bases. This program has a more robust event loop than the simple application in Chapter 3 and demonstrates the use of the resource manager routines for integrating user preferences.

In This Chapter:

12

A Complete Application

Our basic window program in Chapter 3, *Basic Window Program*, did not do all the things an application normally should do. We should have more complete communication with the window manager, parse the command line, and merge these options with the user's defaults to set up user-preferred colors and miscellaneous options. This chapter describes and demonstrates these techniques with a real application, *basecalc*.

The *basecalc* application is a programmer's calculator that allows integer calculations in binary, octal, decimal, and hexadecimal and conversions between these bases. It is not quite as complicated as *xcalc*, the standard calculator for X, but it demonstrates X techniques just as well. *basecalc* also does base conversions, which *xcalc* does not.

Only the sections of the program that illustrate X concepts are shown and described in this chapter. The entire program is shown in Appendix D, *The basecalc Application*.

This program has one characteristic that is not strictly correct in the X environment. It has only one allowable size. If the window manager refuses its request for that size or its main window is reduced in size by the user, it should print a message indicating that it cannot operate in that space. Luckily, the standard window managers *uwm* and *twm* honor the application's size hints and refuse to resize the window. Other window managers might not be so cooperative.

12.1 Description of basecalc

Figure 12-1 shows *basecalc* on the screen. It is a calculator which can perform integer math in decimal, octal, hexadecimal, or binary and can convert values between any of these bases. The calculator may be operated with the pointer by pressing any pointer button on the calculator pads or with the keyboard by typing the same symbols shown on the calculator face.

See the *Preface* for information on how to get the example source code.

The long horizontal window along the top of the calculator is the display, in which the values punched on the calculator and the results are displayed. The digits (0 to 9) and letters (A to F) in the left-hand portion of the calculator keypad are for entering values. The top row of the right-hand portion of the keypad is for base selection. These can be used either to set the

Figure 12-1. The basecalc application on the screen

current base of calculations or to convert a value between bases. Only one of the base indicators is highlighted at a time.

Only valid numbers in the current base are allowed to be entered. Valid pads are black, while invalid ones are light gray. When a pad is triggered by pressing a pointer button, it flashes white, and the operation or value indicated by the pad is executed if the pointer button is released in the same pad. The pad also responds to the pointer entering or leaving the window while a pointer button is pressed.

The calculator also operates from the keyboard. Numbers, letters, and special characters can be typed in (or pasted from another application) to represent all the functions except Clear Entry (CE). The Backspace key also performs this function.

This application runs on any X system, since it uses only the colors black and white. It achieves the appearance of different levels of gray by creating a pattern with differing amounts of black and white. It also provides command line arguments for colors and uses them if the user specifies them and if connected to a color screen.

Here is the list of available functions and how they are used. If you do not plan to be using *basecalc*, skip to Section 12.2, because you will not need to know how to use *basecalc* from the desktop.

All operations work in all bases. You may shift bases at any point in any calculation. The last of any series of consecutive operators pressed will be acted upon.

+,-,*,/	Normal addition, subtraction, multiplication, and division. A number is entered, then one of these operators, then another number, and finally the equal sign, Enter key, or any operator. The result will then be displayed in the window. If the last character entered was an operator, you can continue specifying numbers and operators in alternation.
|, &	AND and OR. Used just like the addition operator. The "|" and "&" symbols on the keyboard trigger this function.
<<, >>	Shift Left and Shift Right. Used just like the addition operator. Enter the number to be shifted, then the ">>" or "<<" pad (or the ">" or "<" keys), and then the number of bits to shift the number, followed by the "=" or Enter key.
^	Exclusive OR. Used just like the addition operator. Sets all bits that are in either number but not both. Available from the caret (^) key.
%	Mod (remainder after division). Used like the addition operator. Available on the percent (%) key.
`	Change sign. This is a unary operator, since it performs its function immediately on the current contents of the display. Its results depend on whether the calculator is in signed or unsigned mode. If in unsigned mode, the result is the unsigned equivalent of a negative number. This function is available from the left single quote key.
~	One's complement. This is a unary operator. It changes all the bits in the value.
CE	Clear Entry. Erases the last value entered. The Backspace key also performs this function.
CD	Clear Digit. Erases the last digit entered.
CA	Clear All. Clears all operator and value registers.
U or S	Unsigned or Signed. Specifies whether all other operations should be performed in signed or unsigned mode.
=	Compute. The Return key also performs this function.

These mathematical operations have nothing to do with X, and how they are implemented is not described here. They are provided so that you can use the program if you have the code and so you can more easily understand the complete code in Appendix D, *The basecalc Application*. In this chapter, we are going to concentrate on the aspects of the program that are standard to X applications. On that note . . .

12.2 Include Files

The include files used in this program are the standard ones, except for the few needed to perform system calls to get the user's home directory, current Rubout key, etc. The <X11/Xresource.h> file is necessary to use the resource manager.

Example 12-1. basecalc — include files

```
#include <X11/Xlib.h>
#include <X11/Xutil.h>
#include <X11/Xresource.h>
#include <X11/cursorfont.h>

#include <stdio.h>

#ifdef SysV
#include <termio.h>
#else
#include <sgtty.h>
#include <sys/ttychars.h>
#endif SysV

#include <ctype.h>
#include <pwd.h>

/* Global declarations file for this application */
#include "basecalc.h"
```

The constant definitions and global variables declared or defined in *./basecalc.h* are shown above the routines in which they are used in the *basecalc* example program. You can take a look at the entire include file in Appendix D.

12.3 The Main of basecalc

The main is a very short and straightforward outline for the major routines to follow.

Example 12-2. basecalc — the main

```
char myDisplayName[256];

/* X11 Integer Programmer's Calculator with base conversions */

main (argc, argv)
int argc;
register char *argv[];
{
    /* So we can use the resource manager data merging functions */
    XrmInitialize();

    /* Parse command line first so we can open display, store any
     * options in a database */
    parseOpenDisp (&argc, argv);

    /* Get server defaults, program defaults, .Xdefaults;
     * merge them and finally the command line */
    mergeDatabases();
```

Example 12-2. basecalc — the main (continued)

```
    /* Extract values from database and convert to form usable
     * by this program */
    extractOpts ();
    /* Load font, make pixmaps, set up arrays of windows */
    initCalc ();

    /* Get keyboard settings for interrupt, delete, etc. */
    initTty ();

    /* Make a standard cursor */
    makeCursor ();

    /* Set standard properties, create and map windows */
    makeWindows (argc, argv);

    /* Get events */
    takeEvents ();

    /* Bow out gracefully */
    XCloseDisplay(display);
    exit (1);
}
```

initTty is not shown in this chapter, but it is included in Appendix D. It simply performs a few system calls to determine which keys are being used for erase, delete, and interrupt.

The following sections describe each routine called in the main. Each section will begin with a brief description of the routine, followed by the declarations from *basecalc.h* that are needed with that routine and then the code.

12.4 Getting User Preferences

This section describes and demonstrates the use of the resource manager in a typical application. For an additional theoretical description of the resource manager, see Chapter 11, *Managing User Preferences*.

12.4.1 User Defaults for basecalc

As described in Chapter 11, the user's default values for options are normally found in the XA_RESOURCE_MANAGER property on the root window. That property is normally set by the user with the *xrdb* program. For compatibility, if there is no XA_RESOURCE_MANAGER property defined (either because *xrdb* was not run or if the property was removed), your program should assume that the defaults can be found in a file called *Xdefaults* in the user's home directory.

Note that XGetDefault, described in Chapter 11, only deals with some of this complexity. It does not read the XA_RESOURCE_MANAGER property, and it does not merge in the command line arguments. That is why, in this example, we have used a different, more thorough technique, using the native resource manager calls.

Here is a sample resource database file with two options for *basecalc*.

Example 12-3. A sample .Xdefaults file

```
basecalc.base:          2
basecalc.unsigned:      False
```

For a complete description of preference matching rules, see Chapter 11. The `basecalc.base` preference sets the base with which the calculator will start and is here specified as binary (base 2). The `basecalc.unsigned` preference specifies whether the calculator should start up in signed mode or unsigned mode.

12.4.2 Parsing the Command Line

`XrmInitialize` must be called before any other resource manager function. (It simply sets up a default `XrmRepresentation` type for strings, but that fact does not affect how the resource manager is used in applications.) After that, the first thing to be done is to parse the command line so that we can read the display argument out of it before opening the display. `parseOpenDisp` does this, loading all the command line options that match resources in the option table into a database for later merging with the user's defaults. Take a look at the code, and then we'll explain it.

Example 12-4. basecalc — the parseOpenDisp routine

```
/* Global variables */
Display *display;
int screen_num;
char myDisplayName[256];

/* Command line options table; we don't do anything with many
 * of these resources, but the program is ready for expansion
 * to allow variable sizes, fonts, etc. */

#define GEOMETRY        "*geometry"
#define ICONGEOMETRY    "*iconGeometry"
#define UNSIGNED        "*unsigned"
#define BASE            "*base"
#define ICONSTARTUP     "*iconStartup"

static int opTableEntries = 25;
static XrmOptionDescRec opTable[] = {
{"-unsigned",       UNSIGNED,       XrmoptionNoArg,     (caddr_t) "off"},
{"-x",              BASE,           XrmoptionNoArg,     (caddr_t) "16"},
{"-hex",            BASE,           XrmoptionNoArg,     (caddr_t) "16"},
{"-dec",            BASE,           XrmoptionNoArg,     (caddr_t) "10"},
{"-oct",            BASE,           XrmoptionNoArg,     (caddr_t) "8"},
{"-binary",         BASE,           XrmoptionNoArg,     (caddr_t) "2"},
{"-geometry",       GEOMETRY,       XrmoptionSepArg,    (caddr_t) NULL},
{"-iconGeometry",   ICON_GEOMETRY,  XrmoptionSepArg,    (caddr_t) NULL},
{"-iconic",         ICONSTARTUP,    XrmoptionNoArg,     (caddr_t) "on"},
{"-background",     "*background",  XrmoptionSepArg,    (caddr_t) NULL},
{"-bg",             "*background",  XrmoptionSepArg,    (caddr_t) NULL},
{"-fg",             "*foreground",  XrmoptionSepArg,    (caddr_t) NULL},
{"-foreground",     "*foreground",  XrmoptionSepArg,    (caddr_t) NULL},
{"-xrm",            NULL,           XrmoptionResArg,    (caddr_t) NULL},
```

Example 12-4. basecalc — the parseOpenDisp routine (continued)

```
{"-display",          ".display",        XrmoptionSepArg,     (caddr_t) NULL},
/* Remainder not currently supported: */
{"-bd",               "*borderColor",    XrmoptionSepArg,     (caddr_t) NULL},
{"-bordercolor",      "*borderColor",    XrmoptionSepArg,     (caddr_t) NULL},
{"-borderwidth",      ".borderWidth",    XrmoptionSepArg,     (caddr_t) NULL
},
{"-bw",               ".borderWidth",    XrmoptionSepArg,     (caddr_t) NULL},
{"-fn",               "*font",           XrmoptionSepArg,     (caddr_t) NULL},
{"-font",             "*font",           XrmoptionSepArg,     (caddr_t) NULL},
{"-name",             ".name",           XrmoptionSepArg,     (caddr_t) NULL},
{"-title",            ".title",          XrmoptionSepArg,     (caddr_t) NULL},
};

static XrmDatabase commandlineDB;

/* Get command line options */
parseOpenDisp (argc, argv)
int *argc;
register char *argv[];
{
    XrmValue value;
    char *str_type[20];

    myDisplayName[0] = '\0';

    XrmParseCommand(&commandlineDB, opTable, opTableEntries, argv[0],
            argc, argv);

    /* Check for any arguments left */
    if (*argc != 1) Usage();

    /* Get display now, because we need it to get other databases */
    if (XrmGetResource(commandlineDB, "basecalc.display",
            "Basecalc.Display", str_type, &value)== True) {
        (void) strncpy(myDisplayName, value.addr, (int) value.size);
    }

    /* Open display */

    if (!(display = XOpenDisplay(myDisplayName))) {
        (void) fprintf(stderr, "%s: Can't open display '%s'\n",
            argv[0], XDisplayName(myDisplayName));
    exit(1);
    }

    screen_num = DefaultScreen(display);
    visual = DefaultVisual(display, screen_num);
    colormap = DefaultColormap(display, screen_num);
}
```

The large options table (opTable) defines all the command line arguments that Xrm-ParseCommand is going to look for. It describes not only what flag to look for but also the style of each option. Some options are a simple flag, others are a flag followed by a value with no space or with a space, and so on. The options table also specifies what to call each option when searching for it in the database.

Example 12-5 shows the structure that defines the options table.

Example 12-5. XrmOptionDescRec, XrmOptionDescList, and XrmOptionKind declarations

```
typedef struct {
    char *option;              /* Option specification string in argv */
    char *resourceName;        /* Binding and resource name (without
                                * application name) */
    XrmOptionKind argKind;     /* Which style of option it is */
    caddr_t value;             /* Value to provide if XrmoptionNoArg */
} XrmOptionDescRec, *XrmOptionDescList;

typedef enum {
    XrmoptionNoArg,            /* Value is specified in
                                * OptionDescRec.value */
    XrmoptionIsArg,            /* Value is the option string itself */
    XrmoptionStickyArg,        /* Value is chars immediately following
                                * option */
    XrmoptionSepArg,           /* Value is next argument in argv */
    XrmoptionResArg,           /* Resource and value in next argument
                                * in argv */
    XrmoptionSkipArg,          /* Ignore this option and next argument
                                * in argv */
    XrmoptionSkipLine          /* Ignore this option and the rest of
                                * argv */
} XrmOptionKind;
```

The styles of command line arguments allowed are as follows:

XrmoptionNoArg   If this flag is present, take the value in the `value` member (the last column) of the options table. For example, the *-u* (unsigned) option for the calculator indicates that the value should be `off` and the calculator should begin in unsigned mode.

XrmoptionIsArg   The flag itself indicates something without any additional information. In the case of the calculator, *-x* or *-h* indicates that it should start up in hexadecimal mode.

XrmoptionStickyArg   The value is the characters immediately following the option with no white space intervening. This is not used in the calculator, but it is like the arguments for *uucico*, where *-sventure* means to call system *venture*.

XrmoptionSepArg   The next item after the white space after this flag is the value of the option. For example, the option *-fg blue* would be of this type and would indicate that blue is the value for the resource specified by *-fg*.

XrmoptionResArg   The resource name and its value are the next argument in `argv` after the white space after this flag. For example, the flag might be *-res* and the resource name/value might be `basecalc*background:white`.

XrmoptionSkipArg   Ignore this option and the next argument in `argv`.

XrmoptionSkipLine   Ignore this option and the rest of `argv`.

As `XrmParseCommand` parses the command line, it removes arguments that it finds in the options table from `argv` and `argc`. Therefore, if `argc` is nonzero after `XrmParse-Command`, at least one of the command line arguments was illegal. The best thing to do is print both the illegal options (by printing `argv`) and the correct option syntax.

If all the options were correctly parsed, then it is time to extract the display name so that we can connect with the display. We need to connect now because we want to get the user's resource database from the server to merge with the command line arguments we already have. If there was no display specified on the command line, we use NULL as usual to connect to the server indicated in the UNIX environment variable DISPLAY. We set the global variable `screen_num` to the default screen number so that we can use it in future macro calls.

It would be possible (and actually preferable) to search the other local databases, namely the *app-defaults/** and *Xdefaults* files, for a display name before connecting to the display. This was not done in *basecalc* because of an oversight.

12.4.3 Getting the Databases

The `mergeDataBases` routine shown in Example 12-6 reads in options from four sources, merges them together in the proper order, and then merges in the database obtained from the command line. As described in Chapter 11, *Managing User Preferences*, the sources and their order of merging are as follows:

- *Classname* file in the *app-defaults* directory.

- *Classname* file in the directory specified by the XUSERFILESEARCHPATH or XAPPLRESDIR environment variables.

- Property set using *xrdb*, accessible through the `XResourceManagerString` macro or, if that is empty, the *Xdefaults* file.

- XENVIRONMENT environment variable or, if not set, *Xdefaults-hostname* file.

- Command line arguments.

Note that even though XUSERFILESEARCHPATH has been added in R4, code to support it can be added in R3, since this will not affect operation under R3.

Let's look at the global declarations and the routine. This routine is quite similar to the routine in the Xt Toolkit that performs the same function (that was its origin).

Example 12-6. basecalc — the GetUsersDataBase routine

```
Display *display;
XrmDatabase rDB;    /* For final merged database */

/* Get program's and user's defaults */
mergeDatabases()
{
    XrmDatabase homeDB, serverDB, applicationDB;

    char filenamebuf[1024];
```

Example 12-6. basecalc — the GetUsersDataBase routine (continued)

```
        char *filename = &filenamebuf[0];
        char *environment;
        char *classname = "Basecalc";
        char name[255];

        (void) strcpy(name, "/usr/lib/X11/app-defaults/");
        (void) strcat(name, classname);
        /* Get application defaults file, if any */
        applicationDB = XrmGetFileDatabase(name);
        (void) XrmMergeDatabases(applicationDB, &rDB);

        /* Merge server defaults, created by xrdb, loaded as a
         * property of the root window when the server initializes
         * and loaded into the display structure on XOpenDisplay;
         * if not defined, use .Xdefaults */
        if (XResourceManagerString(display) != NULL) {
            serverDB = XrmGetStringDatabase(XResourceManagerString
                    (display));
        } else {
            /* Open .Xdefaults file and merge into existing database */
            (void) GetHomeDir(filename);
            (void) strcat(filename, "/.Xdefaults");

            serverDB = XrmGetFileDatabase(filename);
        }
        XrmMergeDatabases(serverDB, &rDB);

        /* Open XENVIRONMENT file or, if not defined, the .Xdefaults,
         * and merge into existing database */
        if ((environment = getenv("XENVIRONMENT")) == NULL) {
            int len;
            environment = GetHomeDir(filename);
            (void) strcat(environment, "/.Xdefaults-");
            len = strlen(environment);
            (void) gethostname(environment+len, 1024-len);
        }
        homeDB = XrmGetFileDatabase(environment);
        XrmMergeDatabases(homeDB, &rDB);

        /* Command line takes precedence over everything */
        XrmMergeDatabases(commandlineDB, &rDB);
}
```

XrmGetFileDatabase reads the application defaults file and loads it into a database, returning a pointer to the database. This database should contain the default values for each configurable variable used in the program. This file should look just like a user preference file, and it should parallel every option in the command line options table. In case this file is unavailable, the application should also have hardcoded defaults for all these values, but it should not have to use them.

Note that Example 12-6 gets the user's database set by *xrdb* from the value returned by the XResourceManagerString function. This function returns a pointer to a string stored in the Display structure. This string is set by XOpenDisplay to the value of the

XA_RESOURCE_MANAGER property on the root window of screen 0.* This string can easily be translated into a database with XrmGetStringDatabase.

12.4.4 Getting Options from the Database

The extractOpts routine performs the final merging of the defaults database with the command line database and then reads options out of the database and sets program variables appropriately. The program does not take advantage of all the options supported in the options table, but it is ready to be expanded to do so.

Example 12-7. basecalc — the extractOpts routine

```
extractOpts()
{
    char *str_type[20];
    char buffer[20];
    long flags;
    XrmValue value;
    int x, y, width, height;
    XColor screen_def;

    /* Get geometry */
    if (XrmGetResource(rDB, "basecalc.geometry",
            "Basecalc.Geometry", str_type, &value)== True) {
        (void) strncpy(Geostr, value.addr, (int) value.size);
    } else {
        Geostr[0] = NULL;
    }

    if (XrmGetResource(rDB, "basecalc.iconGeometry",
            "Basecalc.IconGeometry", str_type, &value)== True) {
        (void) strncpy(iconGeostr, value.addr, (int) value.size);
    } else {
        iconGeostr[0] = NULL;
    }

    if (XrmGetResource(rDB, "basecalc.unsigned", "Basecalc.Unsigned",
            str_type, &value)== True)
        if (strncmp(value.addr, "False", (int) value.size) == 0)
            Unsigned = False;

    if (XrmGetResource(rDB, "basecalc.base", "Basecalc.Base",
            str_type, &value)== True) {
        (void) strncpy(buffer, value.addr, (int) value.size);
        buffer[value.size] = NULL;
        Base = atoi(buffer);
    } else Base = 10;

    if (XrmGetResource(rDB, "basecalc.foreground",
            "Basecalc.Foreground", str_type, &value)== True) {
        (void) strncpy(buffer, value.addr, (int) value.size);
```

---

*Note that because the XA_RESOURCE_MANAGER property is read by XOpenDisplay, it is read only once, during application startup. Therefore, any changes to this property after startup will not be reflected in the application. This property (and all the other resource files) is for initial startup information only.

Example 12-7. basecalc — the extractOpts routine (continued)

```
            if (XParseColor(display, colormap, buffer,
                    &screen_def) == 0)   {
                (void) fprintf(stderr, "basecalc: fg color \
                        specification %s invalid", buffer);
                foreground = BlackPixel(display, screen_num);
            } else {
                /* Accessing visual is cheating, but in the
                 * interests of brevity, we'll do it anyway */
                if ((visual->class == StaticGray) ||
                        (visual->class == GrayScale))
                    foreground = BlackPixel(display, screen_num);
                else if (XAllocColor(display, colormap, &screen_def) ==
                        0) {
                    foreground = BlackPixel(display, screen_num);
                    (void) fprintf(stderr, "basecalc: couldn't allocate \
                            color: %s.\n", buffer);
                }
                else
                    foreground = screen_def.pixel;
            }
        } else {
        foreground = BlackPixel(display, screen_num);
    }

    if (XrmGetResource(rDB, "basecalc.background",
            "Basecalc.Background", str_type, &value)== True) {
        (void) strncpy(buffer, value.addr, (int) value.size);
        if (XParseColor(display, colormap, buffer,
                &screen_def) == 0)   {
            (void) fprintf(stderr, "basecalc: bg color \
                    specification %s invalid", buffer);
            background = WhitePixel(display, screen_num);
        } else {
            if ((visual->class == StaticGray) ||
                    (visual->class == GrayScale))
                background = WhitePixel(display, screen_num);
            else if (XAllocColor(display, colormap, &screen_def) ==
                    0) {
                background = WhitePixel(display, screen_num);
                (void) fprintf(stderr, "basecalc: couldn't allocate \
                        color: %s.\n", buffer);
            }
            else
                background = screen_def.pixel;
        }
    } else {
    background = WhitePixel(display, screen_num);
}

/* One last check to make sure the colors are different! */
if (background == foreground) {
    background = WhitePixel(display, screen_num);
    foreground = BlackPixel(display, screen_num);
}

/* Get window geometry information */
if (Geostr != NULL) {
```

Example 12-7. basecalc — the extractOpts routine (continued)

```
        flags = XParseGeometry(Geostr,
                &x, &y, &width, &height);
        if ((WidthValue|HeightValue) & flags)
            Usage ();
        if (XValue & flags) {
            if (XNegative & flags)
                x = DisplayWidth(display, screen_num) +
                        x - sizehints.width;
            sizehints.flags |= USPosition;
            sizehints.x = x;
        }
        if (YValue & flags) {
            if (YNegative & flags)
                y = DisplayHeight(display, screen_num) +
                        x - sizehints.width;
            sizehints.flags |= USPosition;
            sizehints.y = y;
        }
    }

    /* Get icon geometry information */
    if (iconGeostr != NULL) {
        iconGeostr[0] = '=';
        flags = XParseGeometry(iconGeostr,
                &x, &y, &width, &height);
        if ((WidthValue|HeightValue) & flags)
            Usage ();
        if (XValue & flags) {
            if (XNegative & flags)
                x = DisplayWidth(display, screen_num) +
                        x - iconsizehints.width;
            iconsizehints.flags |= USPosition;
            wmhints.flags |= IconPositionHint;
            wmhints.icon_x = x;
            iconsizehints.x = x;
        }
        if (YValue & flags) {
            if (YNegative & flags)
                y = DisplayHeight(display, screen_num) +
                        x - iconsizehints.width;
            iconsizehints.flags |= USPosition;
            wmhints.flags |= IconPositionHint;
            wmhints.icon_y = y;
            iconsizehints.y = y;
        }
    }
}
```

The variables that are used to access the data returned from the database are `background`, `Base`, `iconGeostr`, `iconOnly`, `foreground`, `Geostr`, and `Unsigned`. The routine then calls `XrmGetResource` for each resource, which places the data which resulted from the combination of the command line and the resource database into user-accessible variables. `Geostr` and `iconGeostr` are used to set up the window manager size hints. Later in the code, the variables `background`, `Base`, `foreground`, `iconOnly`, and `Unsigned` will also be used.

The next step is to get the standard geometry strings from the database, parse them, and use these or the defaults to set the window manager hints to match. This program repeats this process for the main window and for the icon. Strictly speaking, it is not necessary to set window manager hints for the icon, and they are not used for that purpose in this program.

XParseGeometry returns a bitmask which indicates which parts of the geometry string were actually set on the command line or in the resource database. There are symbols to indicate each bit in this mask, and they are:

XValue, YValue   Position of window or icon.

WidthValue, HeightValue   Dimensions of window or icon.

XNegative, YNegative   Indicates whether XValue or YValue is negative.

12.5 Printing a Usage Message

GetOpts calls Usage when the user tries to specify dimensions for the main window or icon, since this program cannot deal with that complexity.

Example 12-8. basecalc — the Usage routine
```
/* Print message to stderr and exit */
Usage ()
{
    fprintf (stderr,
        "%s: [-iconic] [-unsigned] [-hex|x|dec|oct|binary]\
        [-display <display>] [-geometry <geometrystring>]\
        [-iconGeometry <icongeometrystring>\n",
        calcName ? calcName : "basecalc");
    exit (1);
}
```

12.6 Initializing the Calculator

The initCalc routine performs three major functions: it loads the font to be used in all text, creates GCs for foreground and background of the calculator, and then sets the initial pixmaps for all pads. The windows for each pad do not exist yet.

Again, we'll begin with the declarations that are used in the routine.

Example 12-9. basecalc — declarations for initCalc
```
/* Pattern for disabled buttons (Light Gray) */
#define lgray_width 16
#define lgray_height 16
static char lgray_bits[] = {
    0x88, 0x88, 0x22, 0x22, 0x88, 0x88, 0x22, 0x22,
    0x88, 0x88, 0x22, 0x22, 0x88, 0x88, 0x22, 0x22,
    0x88, 0x88, 0x22, 0x22, 0x88, 0x88, 0x22, 0x22,
```

Example 12-9. basecalc — declarations for initCalc (continued)

```
    0x88, 0x88, 0x22, 0x22, 0x88, 0x88, 0x22, 0x22};

/* Background pattern for calculator (Dark Gray) */
#define gray_width 16
#define gray_height 16
static char gray_bits[] = {
    0xaa, 0xaa, 0x55, 0x55, 0xaa, 0xaa, 0x55, 0x55,
    0xaa, 0xaa, 0x55, 0x55, 0xaa, 0xaa, 0x55, 0x55,
    0xaa, 0xaa, 0x55, 0x55, 0xaa, 0xaa, 0x55, 0x55,
    0xaa, 0xaa, 0x55, 0x55, 0xaa, 0xaa, 0x55, 0x55};

#define  WHITE      0
#define  BLACK      1
#define  DARKGRAY   2
#define  LIGHTGRAY  3

int pressedColor =      WHITE;
int unpressedColor =    BLACK;
int disabledColor =     LIGHTGRAY;
int displayColor =      WHITE;

#define NBUTTONS 38

struct windata {
    int  color;    /* Color */
    char *text;    /* Pointer to the text string */
    int  x;        /* x coordinate of text */
    int  y;        /* y coordinate of text */
    int  value;    /* 0 to 16 for number, symbol for operator */
    int  type;     /* Digit, operator, conversion, or special */
} windata[NBUTTONS] = {
    { 1, "                              0 ", 2, 3, 0, WTYP_DISP },

    { 0, "C", 5, 3, 12, WTYP_DIGIT },
    { 0, "D", 5, 3, 13, WTYP_DIGIT },
    { 0, "E", 5, 3, 14, WTYP_DIGIT },
    { 0, "F", 5, 3, 15, WTYP_DIGIT },

    { 0, "8", 5, 3,  8, WTYP_DIGIT },
    { 0, "9", 5, 3,  9, WTYP_DIGIT },
    { 0, "A", 5, 3, 10, WTYP_DIGIT },
    { 0, "B", 5, 3, 11, WTYP_DIGIT },

    { 0, "4", 5, 3, 4, WTYP_DIGIT },
    { 0, "5", 5, 3, 5, WTYP_DIGIT },
    { 0, "6", 5, 3, 6, WTYP_DIGIT },
    { 0, "7", 5, 3, 7, WTYP_DIGIT },

    { 0, "0", 5, 3, 0, WTYP_DIGIT },
    { 0, "1", 5, 3, 1, WTYP_DIGIT },
    { 0, "2", 5, 3, 2, WTYP_DIGIT },
    { 0, "3", 5, 3, 3, WTYP_DIGIT },

    { 0, "CA", 6, 3, OPR_CLRA, WTYP_SPECIAL },
    { 0, "CE", 6, 3, OPR_CLRE, WTYP_SPECIAL },
    { 0, "CD", 6, 3, OPR_CLRD, WTYP_SPECIAL },
    { 0, "=", 17, 2, OPR_ASGN, WTYP_OPERATOR },

    { 0,  "+", 5, 3, OPR_ADD, WTYP_OPERATOR },
    { 0,  "-", 5, 3, OPR_SUB, WTYP_OPERATOR },
```

Example 12-9. basecalc — declarations for initCalc (continued)

```
        { 0,   "*",  5,  4,  OPR_MUL,  WTYP_OPERATOR },
        { 0,   "/",  5,  3,  OPR_DIV,  WTYP_OPERATOR },
        { 0,   "%",  5,  3,  OPR_MOD,  WTYP_OPERATOR },

        { 0,   "|",  5,  3,  OPR_OR,   WTYP_OPERATOR },
        { 0,   "&",  5,  3,  OPR_AND,  WTYP_OPERATOR },
        { 0,   ">>",1,  3,  OPR_SHR,  WTYP_OPERATOR },
        { 0,   "<<",0,  3,  OPR_SHL,  WTYP_OPERATOR },
        { 0,   "^",  5,  3,  OPR_XOR,  WTYP_OPERATOR },

        { 0, "HEX",  2,  3,  16,  WTYP_CONVERSION },
        { 0, "DEC",  2,  3,  10,  WTYP_CONVERSION },
        { 0, "OCT",  2,  3,   8,  WTYP_CONVERSION },
        { 0, "BIN",  2,  3,   2,  WTYP_CONVERSION },

        { 0,  "U",   5,  3,  OPR_UNS, WTYP_SPECIAL },
        { 0,  "\",   5,  3,  OPR_NEG, WTYP_OPERATOR },
        { 0,  "~",   5,  3,  OPR_NOT, WTYP_OPERATOR },
};

/* Font for all numbers and text */
char *myFontName =     "8x13";

/* For keeping track of colors */
GC   fgGC;
GC   bgGC;
```

The data in `lgray` and `gray` are for making pixmaps for tiling in various shades of gray. This program is written to operate correctly on any kind of display. If the display is simple monochrome without grays, you can still get gray shades by creating different pixmaps with slightly different ratios of black and white pixels. The light gray pixmap is used for disabled pads, which are not valid in the current base. The dark gray pixmap is used for the background of the calculator. Simple pixel values of `BlackPixel` and `WhitePixel` are used for valid and selected pads. The symbols BLACK, WHITE, DARKGRAY, and LIGHTGRAY are defined to clarify the code. If foreground and background colors are specified on the command line, they will also be used in the pixmaps, and their colors will be mixed.

The `windata` structure provides information about each subwindow on the calculator: the color, text, position relative to the individual pad subwindows, value (digit or symbol), and type of pad. The first window in the list of data is the display window, where the entered values and results are shown. As you can see, the data for all the windows is initialized, except for the color, which is set in `initCalc`. None of these values change during the operation of the program except the color and the value in the display window.

The `type` member of `windata` indicates which of the four major classes of pads the window fits in. These are WTYP_CONVERSION, WTYP_DIGIT, WTYP_OPERATOR, and WTYP_SPECIAL and represent digits, operators, conversions (bases), and special keys. The special keys are Clear All (CA), Clear Digit (CD), Clear Entry (CE), and Unsigned (U). Each pad within each type is identified with the `value` member of `windata`. For digits, this is the digit itself, and for operators, conversions, and special keys, it is a symbol representing each key.

Last but not least, fgGC and bgGC are two GCs which are used to save the colors between which the pads are changed. The pads have to change back and forth between black and white frequently, and having one GC for each reduces the traffic to the server.

Without further ado, here is the initCalc routine.

Example 12-10. basecalc — the initCalc routine

```
/* Initialize calculator options */
initCalc ()
{
    register int win;
    register int found = -1;
    XGCValues values;
    extern char lgray_bits[];

    if ((theFont = XLoadQueryFont (display, myFontName)) == NULL) {
        (void) fprintf(stderr, "basecalc: can't open font %s\n",
                myFontName);
        exit(-1);
    }

    /* Make the utility pixmaps */
    grayPixmap = makePixmap(gray_bits, gray_width, gray_height);
    lgrayPixmap = makePixmap(lgray_bits, lgray_width, lgray_height);

    /* Make the utility gc's */
    values.font = theFont->fid;
    values.foreground = foreground;
    fgGC = XCreateGC(display, DefaultRootWindow(display),
            GCForeground|GCFont, &values);
    values.foreground = background;
    values.function = GXcopy;
    bgGC = XCreateGC(display, DefaultRootWindow(display),
            GCForeground|GCFont|GCFunction, &values);

    /* Loop through buttons, setting disabled buttons
     * to Color Light Gray; also, find the window which
     * corresponds to the starting display base; also
     * add ascent to y position of text */
    for (win = 1; win < NBUTTONS; win++) {
        if (windata[win].type == WTYP_CONV &&
                windata[win].value == Base) {
            found = win;
        } else
            if (windata[win].type == WTYP_DIG &&
                    windata[win].value >= Base) {
                windata[win].color = disabledColor;
            } else
            if (windata[win].type == WTYP_SPEC &&
                    windata[win].value == OPR_UNS) {
                if (Unsigned)
                    windata[win].text = "U";
                else
                    windata[win].text = "S";
                windata[win].color = pressedColor;
            }
            else
                windata[win].color = unpressedColor;
```

Example 12-10. basecalc — the initCalc routine (continued)

```
            windata[win].y += theFont->max_bounds.ascent;
        }
        windata[0].y += theFont->max_bounds.ascent;
        if (found >= 0) {
            winBase = found;
            windata[found].color = pressedColor;
        } else {
            (void) fprintf(stderr, "basecalc: can't use base %d\n",
                    Base);
        exit(-1);
        }
        windata[0].color = displayColor;
}
```

The first action in this routine is to load the font. The process of loading and using a font should be familiar to you from the discussion and examples in Chapter 6, *Drawing Graphics and Text*.

The routine then calls makePixmap to make pixmaps out of the lgray and gray data in the include file. This routine calls XCreatePixmapFromBitmapData to convert a single-plane pixmap into a pixmap with depth suitable for tiling. Then initCalc creates two GCs, each with a different foreground color. These are used later in drawButton.

Now initCalc begins a loop through all the window data set up in the array of structures called windata. The first operation within the loop is to adjust the position of text in each button according to the font information. Then the pad colors are set according to the Base and Unsigned variables. These variables have default values (10 and U), but they may have been updated according to the command line or the resource database.

Finally, initCalc sets the color of the display window and the current base pad. If the base is not valid, this will not have been caught until now, so the routine prints out a message and exits.

12.7 Making Windows

The makeWindows routine creates a cursor, sets up attributes, and creates the main window, all the pad windows, and the display window. It also creates the icon pixmap from data and then uses it as the background attribute for creating the icon window. The icon will be tiled with this pixmap independent of the icon size. Finally, all the standard properties and window manager hints are set.

There is nothing in makeWindows that you have not seen in previous examples, so we will not show it here. Look at the code in Appendix D, *The basecalc Application*, if you are interested.

12.8 Selecting Events

`selectEvents` selects events for all the windows of the application.

Example 12-11. basecalc — the selectEvents routine

```
selectEvents ()
{
    int win;

    /* Window behind calculator */
    XSelectInput (display, calcWin, KeyPressMask|KeyReleaseMask);

    /* Where results are drawn */
    XSelectInput (display, dispWin, ExposureMask);

    /* Pad windows */
    for (win = 1; win < NBUTTONS; win++)
        XSelectInput (display, Buttons[win].ID,
            ExposureMask|ButtonPressMask|ButtonReleaseMask|
            EnterWindowMask|LeaveWindowMask);
}
```

The entire calculator window requires key events, because we want to be able to operate the calculator from the keyboard as well as with the pointer.

The display window (`dispWin`) requires exposure events, because it must be able to refresh itself for the usual reasons.

All other windows (pads) require exposure events for refresh, button events for selection, and border crossing events so that the button only needs to be released within a pad to activate the pad. This last feature makes it easier to work quickly with the calculator.

12.9 Processing Events

This routine processes events. The top portion of `takeEvents` converts key events to the corresponding button event, and then the bottom sets the colors and flags and draws the button in the new color. Key codes are mapped to ASCII with `XLookupString`, and `keyToWin` is called to get the offset into `windata` that is represented by this key. When key events occur, the appropriate pad is flashed.

Example 12-12. basecalc — the takeEvents routine

```
takeEvents ()
{
    XEvent Event;
    register int win;
    register int Pressed = False;
    register int inWindow = False;
    char buffer[10];
    register char *keyChars = buffer;
    register int keyDown = False;
    int i, nbytes;
```

Example 12-12. basecalc — the takeEvents routine (continued)

```
while (1) {
    /* Get event if key not down */
    if (!keyDown)
        XNextEvent (display, &Event);
    else
        Event.type = KeyRelease;

    /* Map keyboard events to window events */
    if (Event.type == KeyPress || Event.type == KeyRelease) {
        nbytes = XLookupString (&Event, buffer,
            sizeof(buffer), NULL, NULL);
        if (Event.type == KeyPress)
            {
            Event.type = ButtonPress;
            keyDown = True;
            }
        else
            {
            for (i=0; i<60000; i++)
                ; /* Wait */
            Event.type = ButtonRelease;
            }
        if ((Event.xbutton.window =
            keyToWin (keyChars, nbytes)) == None){
            keyDown = False;
            continue;
            }
    }
    for (win=0; win < NBUTTONS; win++)
        if (Buttons[win].ID == Event.xbutton.window)
            break;
    switch (Event.type) {
    case ButtonPress:
        if (windata[win].color == disabledColor)
            break;
        Pressed = win;
        if (!keyDown)
            inWindow = True;
        windata[win].color = pressedColor;
        drawButton (win, 0);
        break;
    case LeaveNotify:
        if (Pressed != win)
            break;
        inWindow = False;
        windata[win].color = unpressedColor;
        drawButton (win, 0);
        break;
    case EnterNotify:
        if (Pressed != win)
            break;
        inWindow = True;
        windata[win].color = pressedColor;
        drawButton (win, 0);
        break;
    case ButtonRelease:
```

Example 12-12. basecalc — the takeEvents routine (continued)

```
                if (windata[win].color == disabledColor ||
                    Pressed != win) {
                     keyDown = False;
                     break;
                }
                Pressed = False;
                windata[win].color = unpressedColor;
                if (keyDown || inWindow)
                    winPressed (win);
                keyDown = False;
                inWindow = False;
                drawButton (win, 0);
                break;
        case Expose:
                drawButton (win, 1);
                break;
        }
        XFlush(display);
    }
}
```

12.10 Drawing a Pad

This routine simply sets colors and draws the text in a pad. Example 12-13 shows the
drawButton routine.

Example 12-13. basecalc — the drawButton routine

```
/* Draw a single pad with its text */
drawButton (win, exposeEvent)
register int win;
{
    register char *string;
    register int x, y;
    struct windata *winp;
    char *Measure;
    XSetWindowAttributes attributes;
    unsigned long valuemask;
    GC gc;

    winp = &windata[win];
    x = winp->x;
    y = winp->y;
    string = winp->text;

    switch (windata[win].color) {
    case WHITE:
        gc = fgGC;
        attributes.background_pixel = background;
        attributes.border_pixel = foreground;
        valuemask = CWBackPixel|CWBorderPixel;
        break;
    case BLACK:
```

Example 12-13. basecalc — the drawButton routine (continued)

```
                    gc = bgGC;
                    attributes.background_pixel = foreground;
                    attributes.border_pixel = background;
                    valuemask = CWBackPixel|CWBorderPixel;
                    break;
            case LIGHTGRAY:
                    gc = bgGC;
                    attributes.background_pixmap = lgrayPixmap;
                    attributes.border_pixel = foreground;
                    valuemask = CWBackPixmap|CWBorderPixel;
                    break;
            }
            if (!exposeEvent){
                XChangeWindowAttributes(display, Buttons[win].self,
                        valuemask, &attributes);
                XClearWindow(display, Buttons[win].self);
            }
            XDrawString (display, Buttons[win].self, gc, x, y, string,
                    strlen (string));
            if (win == 0) {
                switch (Base) {
                    case 10:
                    case 8:
                        Measure = Octmeasure;
                        break;
                    default:
                    case 16:
                    case  2:
                        Measure = Hexmeasure;
                        break;
                }
                XDrawString (display, dispWin, gc, 7, 6, Measure, 31);
            }
    }
```

12.11 Routines Not Shown

The following is a brief description of all the subroutines of *basecalc* that were not shown in this chapter. All of these can be seen in full in Appendix D, *The basecalc Application.*

convButton	Changes the current base and converts a value, if any.
digitButton	Gets a digit and assigns it to Value.
displayVal	Calculates appropriate format string for base.
initTty	Performs system calls to get user's current erase, delete, and interrupt characters.
keyToWin	Translates a keycode as if a pad had been selected.
makePixmap	Makes a pixmap from bitmap data, shown and described in Chapter 6, *Drawing Graphics and Text.*

`operButton`	An operation. Either does it or waits for next value and = .
`printInBase`	Composes the string that should be displayed. Called from `Sprintf`.
`specButton`	Clears a digit, an entry, or all, or toggles unsigned mode.
`Sprintf`	A modified version of `sprintf`, the standard C utility, which does not print in binary. `Sprintf` calls `printInBase`.
`winPressed`	Determines whether pad pressed was a digit, an operator, a conversion, or a special pad.

Complete
Application

13

Other Programming Techniques

As its title implies, this chapter discusses a few orphaned techniques that didn't quite fit in anywhere else. This chapter is important if you want to use one of these techniques, but most readers may just want to skim it.

In This Chapter:

Other
Techniques

13

Other Programming Techniques

This chapter covers a few obscure but occasionally necessary programming techniques. The routines and techniques described here will not be needed in most programs.

The end of the chapter contains information about porting programs from X Version 10 to X Version 11 and from other graphics environments to X Version 11.

13.1 Reading and Writing Properties

Chapter 10, *Interclient Communication*, described many of the usual properties used in communication with the window manager and other clients. Xlib provides convenience routines for reading and writing these properties. But if you establish any other private protocols between two of your applications or between your application and a proprietary window manager, you will need to write your own routines to read and write properties. Example 13-1 is the code for XFetchName that shows how to read a property containing a string.

Example 13-1. Reading a property

```
#include "Xatom.h"

Status XFetchName (dpy, w, name)
    register Display *dpy;
    Window w;
    char **name;
{
    Atom actual_type;
    int actual_format;
    unsigned long nitems;
    unsigned long leftover;
    unsigned char *data = NULL;
    if (XGetWindowProperty(dpy, w, XA_WM_NAME, 0L, (long)BUFSIZ,
            False, XA_STRING, &actual_type, &actual_format,
            &nitems, &leftover, &data) != Success) {
        *name = NULL;
        return (0);
    }
    if ( (actual_type == XA_STRING) &&  (actual_format == 8) ) {
```

Other
Techniques

Example 13-1. Reading a property (continued)

```
    /* The data returned by XGetWindowProperty is guaranteed
     * to contain one extra byte that is null terminated to
     * make retrieving string properties easy */

    *name = (char *)data;
    return(1);
    }
if (data) Xfree ((char *)data);
*name = NULL;
return(0);
}
```

Using XChangeProperty is easier than reading a property with XGetWindow-Property, since there are many fewer arguments. Example 13-2 shows the companion function to XFetchName, XStoreName.

Example 13-2. Writing a property

```
XStoreName (dpy, w, name)
    register Display *dpy;
    Window w;
    char *name;
{
    XChangeProperty(dpy, w, XA_WM_NAME, XA_STRING,
            8, PropModeReplace, (unsigned char *)name,
            name ? strlen(name) : 0);
}
```

13.2 Screen Saver

Screen saver routines are provided to control the blanking of the screen when it has been idle for a time. XSetScreenSaver sets the operation of the screen saver, including:

- How long the display remains idle before it is blanked.

- The time between random pattern motions.

- Whether the application prefers screen blanking or not (regardless of whether the screen is capable of it).

- Whether exposures are generated when the screen is restored.

XActivateScreenSaver and XResetScreenSaver turn the screen saver on and off, respectively, and XForceScreenSaver can turn it on or off according to a flag. XGetScreenSaver returns the current settings of the screen saver.

13.3 Access from Other Hosts and Nodes

X does not provide any protection from unauthorized access to individual windows, pixmaps, or other resources. If a program succeeds in connecting with a server and finds out a resource ID, it can manipulate or even destroy the resource. There are two kinds of security that can prevent connections from being made by clients running on other machines. To provide some minimal level of protection, however, connections are only permitted from machines which are listed on a *host access list*. This is adequate on single-user workstations but obviously breaks down on machines running more than one server. While provisions exist in the server for proper connection authentication, no standard has yet been developed.

The initial access control list is read at startup and reset time. The initial set of hosts allowed to open connections consists of:

- The host the window system is running on.

- On UNIX-based systems, each host listed in the */etc/X?.hosts* file, where *?* indicates the number of the server (the number between : and . in the `display_name` argument to `XOpenDisplay` that would connect to the server). This file should consist of host names separated by newlines. DECnet nodes must terminate in "::" to distinguish them from Internet hosts.

If a host is not in the access control list when the access control mechanism is enabled and the host attempts to establish a connection, the server refuses the connection.

13.3.1 Adding, Removing, or Listing Hosts

You can add, get, or remove hosts with `XAddHost`, `XAddHosts`, `XListHosts`, `XRemoveHost`, and `XRemoveHosts`. All the host access control functions use the `XHostAddress` structure. The members in this structure are:

Example 13-3. The XHostAddress structure

```
typedef struct {
    int family;         /* For example FamilyInternet */
    int length;         /* Length of address, in bytes */
    char *address;      /* Pointer to where to find the bytes */
} XHostAddress;
```

family   Specifies which address family to use (for example, TCP/IP or DECnet). The family symbols `FamilyInternet`, `FamilyDECnet`, and `Family-Chaos` are defined in *<X11/X.h>*.

length   Specifies the length of the address in bytes.

address   Specifies a pointer to the address.

For these functions to execute successfully, the client application must run on the same host as the X server and must have permission in the initial authorization at connection setup before calling these functions.

13.3.2 Enabling and Disabling Access Control

Normally the access control list determines whether a client succeeds in connecting to the server. Sometimes it is more convenient (though less safe) to allow a client or *any* host to have access. In this case, a client running on the same host as the server can call `XDisableAccessControl`. Thereafter, the host access list will no longer be used to filter connection requests. To reset the server to its default condition with access control, use `XEnableAccessControl`. `XSetAccessControl` performs either of these functions according to a flag.

13.4 Getting the Window Hierarchy

`XQueryTree` lets you get the IDs of the windows in any portion of the window hierarchy with a single call. This is the only way to find out the IDs of windows created by other clients. `XQueryTree` gets the root window ID, the parent window ID, and the list of child window IDs given a window. It also returns the number of children.

One possible use of `XQueryTree` is to find out whether your application's top-level window has been reparented by the window manager, and it returns the ID of the new parent.

13.5 Close Down Mode

Normally all resources associated with a client will be destroyed when the connection between the client and the server closes. This can happen without prior warning to either the server or the client when, for example, the network cable is accidentally pulled out of one of the machines or the machine running the server crashes. Therefore, robust applications need a way of recovering from that occurrence. `XSetCloseDownMode` helps implement one method of recovery.

Clients in the default `DestroyAll` close down mode will have all their resources killed when the connection to the server dies. `XSetCloseDownMode` can set two other modes, `RetainPermanent` and `RetainTemporary`, which allow client resources to live on for a time. A client may want its resources to live on to assist in the process of recovering from a broken connection with the server, usually caused by a network failure. When next run after the problem has been corrected, the application could somehow determine which resources were its own and continue operating where it left off. The "somehow" is the crux of the problem. The only way we can think of to allow the client to find out the IDs of its resources after the client is resurrected is for the client to save all the resource IDs in a file (or perhaps in a property, but this would not survive a server crash) immediately after they are created. Then upon startup, it can read this information and see if the specified resources still exist. If they do, it can skip creating them.

A dying connection between the server and client raises other problems, too. Even if a client's resources are put on life support, there is no longer any "brain" behind them. The user's instructions will go unanswered, and there will be no visible warning on the screen that the client is no longer connected. The window manager or some other program, if running on the same machine as the server, could conceivably detect this situation and print a message. However, this kind of functionality in a window manager has not been demonstrated up to now. Otherwise, the user can only be warned that the connection could die and that this would cause the window to freeze (if the client's resources were preserved; the window would disappear if the close down mode had not been set). The user could then restart the client from an *xterm* window to reactivate the window.

XKillClient can kill resources that remain alive after the connection closes. It can kill resources associated with a single client by specifying any resource ID associated with that client, or it can kill all resources of all clients that terminated with mode Retain-Temporary if given the argument AllTemporary. XKillClient might be used by the window manager or conceivably by a separate client to save space in the server by cleaning up resources after clients die that have requested that their resources be kept alive. This should not be done unless the user agrees with it, because it could upset an application's attempt to recover from a broken connection with the server.

13.6 Connection Close Operations

When the connection between the X server and a client is closed, either by a call to XCloseDisplay or by an exiting process, the X server performs these automatic operations:

- Disowns all selections made by the program.

- Releases all passive grabs made by the program.

- Performs an XUngrabPointer and XUngrabKeyboard if the client application had actively grabbed the pointer or the keyboard.

- Performs an XUngrabServer if the client had grabbed the server.

- Marks all resources (including colormap entries) allocated by the client application as permanent or temporary, according to whether the close down mode is Retain-Permanent or RetainTemporary (see Section 13.5).

The X server performs these operations when the close down mode is DestroyAll:

- The *save-set* is a list of other client's windows, referred to as save-set windows (see Section 14.4 for a complete description of save-sets). If any window in the client's save-set is an inferior of a window created by the client, the X server reparents the save-set window to the closest ancestor so that the save-set window is not an inferior of a window created by the client.

- Performs an XMapWindow request on the save-set window if the save-set window is unmapped. The X server does this even if the save-set window was not an inferior of a window created by the client.

- Destroys all windows created by the client, after examining each window in the client's save-set.

- Performs the appropriate free request on all nonwindow resources (Bitmap, Colormap, Cursor, Font, GC, and Pixmap) created by the client.

Additional processing occurs when the *last* connection to the X server closes with close down mode DestroyAll. The X server:

- Resets its state, as if it had just been started. The X server destroys all lingering resources from clients that have terminated in RetainPermanent or RetainTemporary mode.

- Deletes all but the predefined atom IDs.

- Deletes all properties on all root windows.

- Resets all device attributes (key click, bell volume, acceleration) and the access control list.

- Restores the standard root tiles, cursors, default pointing device, and default font path.

- Restores the keyboard focus to PointerRoot.

13.7 Data Management

Xlib provides two ways to help you manage data within an application: the context manager and association tables. The former saves you the trouble of creating arrays and dynamically allocating memory for data to be used only within your application. The latter is a different way of doing the same thing, maintained for backwards compatibility with X10. We will describe only the context manager. If you are interested in investigating association tables, see Appendix B, *X10 Compatibility*.

13.7.1 The Context Manager

Four routines are provided to let you associate data with a window locally in Xlib, rather than in the server as in properties. The context manager routines store and retrieve untyped data according to the display, a window ID, and an assigned context ID. The display argument to the context manager routine (returned from XOpenDisplay) is used as an additional dimension to the array, not as a pointer to the display structure. No requests to the server are made.

First, you call XUniqueContext to obtain an ID for a particular type of information you want to assign to windows. XUniqueContext just provides a unique integer ID every time you call it (you can also make up your own if you wish). This ID indicates to the application what type of information is stored, but none of the calls require you to specify the data type. Then use XSaveContext to store information into the context manager and

`XFindContext` to read it. If you plan to rewrite a particular piece of data corresponding to a window ID and context ID, it is better in terms of time and space to erase the current entry with `XDeleteContext` before calling `XSaveContext` again. `XDelete-Context` does not make the context ID invalid.

If you have many different pieces of data of the same type, such as an array, that must be associated with each window, you have the option of packing it in a single chunk of data and storing it by context or creating a different context ID for each member of the array. The context ID indicates the *meaning* of the data (how you interpret it), not necessarily the C language type.

13.8 The After Function

Every Xlib function that generates a protocol request calls an *after function* just before it returns. This function is normally `NoOp`, but the program may specify the name of any function using `XSetAfterFunction`.

13.9 Coordinate Transformation

`XTranslateCoordinates` translates coordinates relative to one window into the coordinates relative to a second and determines whether the resulting position relative to the second window is in a subwindow of the second window.

Because the window-based coordinate system is so convenient, this function is rarely needed. Since `XTranslateCoordinates` makes a round-trip request, it cannot be used heavily to port to X programs that use global coordinates.

13.10 Porting Programs to X

Any program that runs on an ASCII terminal can be run directly under the terminal emulator *xterm*. The only problem is how to deal with changing the size of the window while the application is running. The application may read the termcap definition to determine the original window size. Look at the X application *resize*, which makes changes to TERMCAP. The *resize* reference page (see Volume Three, *X Window System User's Guide*) suggests a couple of C shell aliases for commands to resize *xterm* windows.

If you have a Berkeley 4.3-compatible tty driver, *xterm* sets the tty driver's row and column attributes when its top-level window is resized. *vi* and *more* and several other programs also look at those attributes when figuring out the terminal size. Also, *xterm* will send a SIGWINCH signal to the controlling process, which, if it is *vi* or *more*, will understand this signal and change its own notion of screen size, repainting the window in the process. This is the best way to deal with window resizing under *xterm*.

Graphics programs face a more difficult porting path. They must be rewritten to use the X library. It is a good idea to use a toolkit rather than trying to write completely in Xlib.

Programs written for single-user systems such as PCs will be a little more difficult, since they must be converted to respond to events instead of asking for one type of input at a time. They must also be modified to work in a multitasking environment.

Byte order is another traditionally thorny issue in porting. Byte order refers to the order in which bytes of data are stored in memory. There are actually four ways for two-byte data to be ordered, since the direction of each byte has two variations and the position of the most significant byte is also variable.

For X pixmaps, byte order is defined by the server and clients with different native byte ordering must swap bytes as necessary. For all other parts of the protocol, the byte order is defined by the client and the server swaps bytes as necessary.

13.10.1 Porting from X10 to X11

X Version 11 is very much different from X Version 10, though it still uses some of the same concepts. It has more than twice as many routines and has several major completely new concepts, such as virtual colormaps, the graphics context, and window manager hints. Porting most X Version 10 programs will essentially require translating all the function calls, adding window manager communication, setting of graphics contexts, and treatment of colors. However, because of the added functionality, there are now better ways to do things in many cases. You should consider carefully whether to do a minimal translation or to do a more extensive rewrite that might achieve better performance.

The MIT distribution includes an X10-to-X11 conversion program (*X10toX11*) that allows X10 clients to run under X11 without even recompiling by translating their X10 requests into X11 requests and tailoring the return values back to X10 format. This program has a performance penalty of 20 percent, according to its authors.

Some of the existing X11 applications are minimal rewrites of X10 programs. Take care before using the existing programs as examples.

Some X10 functions are still supported. They are described in Appendix B, *X10 Compatibility*. The functionality of the X10 XDraw and its variations that fill and tile are supported but are implemented with the X11 drawing routines. Therefore, they are likely to be slow. The association table functions are also available. Both groups of functions can be used by including the file *<X11/X10.h>* at the top of each source file and linking with the *-loldX* library. Reference pages for the X10 compatibility routines are provided in Volume Two, *Xlib Reference Manual*.

13.11 Using Extensions to X

An extension is a set of routines and capabilities that a hardware vendor has provided for use on a particular machine, in addition to the standard X library.

Extensions to X are not second-class citizens, and there should be very little to distinguish the use of an extension from that of the core protocol. The only difference is that the application should check to make sure the extension exists and then query the extension to find out the major opcode, additional event types, and additional error types so that the extension can be integrated properly. If the extensions have been written properly so that they initialize themselves when first called, they should be usable just like other X library functions.

`XListExtensions` returns a list of all extensions supported by the server. Once the name of the desired extension is known, `XQueryExtension` should be called to get specific information about the extension. `XFreeExtensionList` should then be used to free the memory allocated by `XListExtensions`.

14

Window Management

X programs may be expected to cooperate with any one of a number of different window managers. This chapter discusses the design of a simple window manager, not so you will be able to write one but so you will know what to expect from one. As it turns out, some of the techniques used in this program (such as menus) could be adapted for other clients as well. Everyone should at least look through this chapter.

In This Chapter:

14
Window Management

A window manager is a program implemented with Xlib to control the layout of windows on the screen, responding to user requests to move, resize, raise, lower, or iconify windows. The window manager may also enforce a policy for window layout (such as mandating a standard window or icon size and placement) and provide a menu for commonly used shell commands.

This chapter is not primarily for window manager writers, as these are a rare breed. There are several good customizable window managers available, and there is very little reason for users or application writers to want to write their own. Only a few people in the X community are going to be actively involved in writing window managers, and chances are good they will already know all of what is described here. This chapter is presented for two reasons: so that application writers will get a better understanding of how to cooperate with the window manager, and so we can describe and demonstrate the Xlib routines that are provided mainly for the purpose of window management. As it turns out, the examples in this chapter also have elements (such as menus) that are useful in ordinary applications as well.

We'll begin by describing the features and routines in Xlib that are provided mainly to give window managers the authority they need to control window layout and the flexibility to provide a good user interface. These features include the following:

- Substructure redirection, which allows the window manager to intercept requests to change the screen layout. This enables a window manager to enforce a window layout policy.

- Reparenting, which lets the window manager build a frame or other "decoration" around each top-level window. The frame could possibly contain boxes which could be used to move or resize the window.

- The save-set, which ensures that the windows the window manager iconifies or reparents are returned to their original state if the window manager dies unexpectedly.

Then we'll describe what the window manager can do with the properties set by clients, building on the description of interclient communication presented in Chapter 10, *Interclient Communication*.

Finally, we'll describe a simple window manager program. You should find this program helpful not only in demonstrating window management techniques but also for showing Xlib programming in a more complex setting than *basicwin* in Chapter 3, *Basic Window Program*, or *basecalc* in Chapter 12, *A Complete Application*. You should understand both those programs before tackling this one.

14.1 Layout Policy

A window manager may have a policy on how top-level windows will be placed on the screen.

The standard window managers *uwm* and *twm* do not have a window layout policy, but some existing window managers do. For example, the Siemens RTL Tiled window manager mandates that only temporary pop-up windows can overlap. That policy makes exposure a rare occurrence but makes resizing much more common. A second simpler example is the window manager designed by Stellar Computer for its high performance workstations. The Stellar window manager aligns icons along the top edge of the screen, along with the Stellar logo. Since the window manager creates the icons or is passed their IDs through hints, it can distinguish them from other windows on the screen.

Within its window layout policy, the window manager should honor the window size and position hints returned by XGetNormalHints and XGetWMHints as closely as possible (each application sets these hints). Under *uwm* and *twm*, the user selects the size of a newly created window by moving a flashing outline of a window. The size hints provided by the application determine the minimum dimensions, maximum dimensions, and desired increment for the window size, and these are indicated in the motion of the outline. For example, in both *uwm* and *twm*, the minimum size hints take priority over the user's input, so that the user cannot resize the window smaller than the minimum size.

Applications are free to resize or move the children of their top-level windows as necessary. The window manager has no control over these windows.

14.2 Substructure Redirection

The window manager enforces its window layout policy using substructure redirection. When the window manager selects SubstructureRedirectMask on the root window, an attempt by any other client to change the configuration of any child of the root window will fail. Instead an event describing the layout change request will be sent to the window manager. The window manager then reads the event and determines whether to honor the request, modify it, or deny it completely. If it decides to honor the request, it calls the routine that the client called that triggered the event with the same arguments. If it decides to modify the request, it calls the same routine but with modified arguments.

The *structure*, as the term is used here, is the location, size, stacking order, border width, and mapping status of a window. The *substructure* is all these statistics about the children of a particular window. This is the complete set of information about screen layout that the window manager might need in order to implement its policy. *Redirection* means that an event is sent to the client selecting redirection (usually the window manager), and the original structure-changing request is not executed.

The events that are selected by `SubstructureRedirectMask` and the routines that are intercepted are as follows:

- `CirculateRequest` events report when an Xlib function, such as `XCirculate-Subwindows`, `XCirculateSubwindowsDown`, `XCirculateSubwindowsUp`, or `XRestackWindows`, is called to change the stacking order of a group of children.

- `ConfigureRequest` events report when an Xlib function, such as `XConfigure-Window`, `XLowerWindow`, `XMoveResizeWindow`, `XMoveWindow`, `XRaise-Window`, `XResizeWindow`, or `XSetWindowBorderWidth`, is called to resize, move, restack, or change the border width of a window.

- `MapRequest` events report when `XMapWindow` or `XMapSubwindows` is called to map a window.

When `SubstructureRedirectMask` is selected on the root window, the only time that a configuration request on a child of the root window is not intercepted is when the `override_redirect` attribute of that child window has been set to `True`. This is intended for temporary pop-up windows that should not be reparented or affected by the window manager's layout policy.

Only one window manager at a time can select `SubstructureRedirectMask` or `ResizeRedirectMask` on a particular window.

`ResizeRedirectMask` also selects `ConfigureRequest` events when a client has called `XConfigureWindow`, `XMoveResizeWindow`, or `XResizeWindow`. However, if any client has selected `SubstructureRedirectMask` on the parent of the window for which `ResizeRedirectMask` is selected, the `Substructure-RedirectMask` takes precedence.

Substructure redirect allows the window manager to separate the portion of itself that moves and resizes windows from the portion that enforces window policy. While the window reconfiguration section is driven by user events, the policy section can be completely driven from the `*Request` events that signal that the user has proposed a change to the window layout. And since applications will only attempt to resize or move their top-level windows in direct response to a user request, those requests are just as valid as the ones from the window reconfiguration section of the window manager.

14.3 Reparenting

A window manager can decorate windows on the screen with titlebars and place little boxes on the titlebar with which the window can be moved or resized. This is only one possibility, modeled on the user interface on the Macintosh™.

To do this, the window manager creates a child of the root somewhat larger than the top-level window of the application. Then it calls `XReparentWindow`, specifying the top-level window of the application as *win* and the new parent as *parent*. *win* and all its descendants will then be descendants of *parent*.

In the area where the new parent is visible around the top-level window of the application, the window manager can put anything it wants. This could include text, graphics, and small windows which perform certain functions when a button is clicked in them.

The window manager can decorate all top-level windows, but it will normally ignore windows that are mapped with their `override_redirect` attribute set, since no `*Request` events will be generated for them. The window manager may also decorate differently windows that have set the `XA_WM_TRANSIENT_FOR` property and apply its window layout policy to them. The window manager calls `XGetTransientForHint` for each window to get this property.

By the way, it is impossible (except by luck) for the window manager to match the colors of the decoration to the colors of the window it is decorating. A window manager cannot find out what colors a window uses for its border or background because these window attributes cannot be queried.

14.3.1 Shadows

Window shadows can be imperfectly implemented by reparenting top-level windows. The shadow would appear to be the same size as the corresponding window but slightly offset diagonally (see Figure 14-1).

Figure 14-1. Goal of background shadow

What happens if we try to accomplish the following style of background with two windows: one InputOutput window slightly larger in both dimensions than the application's top-level window, and one InputOutput shadow window the same size as the application window, offset into the corner of the InputOnly window?* The larger window would have its background_pixmap attribute set to ParentRelative so that it looked invisible, and the smaller window would have its background set to black or gray to make the shadow. Figure 14-2 shows how the layers are lined up.

Figure 14-2. Window layering for background shadow

When the window with the shadow is moved around the screen when no other applications are on the screen, the shadow looks good. But when the window is moved over other applications, a strange thing happens. The background of the root window shows itself in the "invisible" corner of the shadow, as shown in Figure 14-3.

It turns out that a perfect shadow is not possible without an extension, because the server clips regions of the screen in rectangles, not in the complex shape required by a shadow.† However, if the shadow is only two pixels wide, this approach might look good enough.

---

*See Section 2.4.3 for a description of the characteristics of InputOnly windows.
†As of R4, there is an extension that supports nonrectangular windows.

Corner areas will
not appear
completely invisible.

Figure 14-3. Actual effect of shadow attempt

14.4 Window Save-set

The save-set is a list of windows, usually maintained by the window manager, but including only windows created by other clients. If the window manager dies, all windows listed in the save-set will be reparented back to their closest living ancestor if they were reparented in the first place and mapped if the window manager has unmapped them so that it could map an icon.

The save-set is necessary because the window manager might not exit normally. The user might kill it with Control-C if it is running in the foreground, or more likely, the user might get the process number and kill it. Actually, the actions of the save-set are performed even if the window manager exits normally, so less code is needed since the save-set does the cleaning up.

Window managers almost always place in the save-set all the windows they reparent or iconify, using XAddToSaveSet.

Windows are automatically removed from the save-set when they are destroyed. If this were not the case, the window manager would have to monitor DestroyNotify events and explicitly remove the windows from the save-set.

The routines XRemoveFromSaveSet and XChangeSaveSet are available, but they are not often needed even in window managers. XChangeSaveSet adds or removes a window from the save-set.

14.5 Window Manager – Client Communications

There is no point in reiterating all that was said in Chapter 10, *Interclient Communication*, about the properties that applications set for the window manager. As described there, these properties are hints that the window manager may use or ignore as the programmer sees fit. There is a large amount of flexibility and variety in what window managers can do with the information provided in these hints. Its actions are to some extent constrained by the inter-client communication conventions described in Appendix L, *Interclient Communication Conventions*, of Volume Zero, *X Protocol Reference Manual*, since these conventions are now a standard.

These hints allow the window manager to smooth the user interface so that all the applications running on the system appear integrated. Any good window manager will read most, if not all, of the properties described in this section and try to do with them what is most helpful to applications and users.

14.5.1 Reading the Hints

Hints help the window manager conform to the needs of the application while at the same time letting it control window layout and policy. The window manager gets the hints with the routines shown in Table 14-1.

Table 14-1. Window Manager Hints

Hint	Set (by Application)	Get (by Window Manager)
Window Name (R3)	`XStoreName`	`XFetchName`
Window Name (R4)	`XSetWMName`	`XGetWMName`
Icon Name (R3)	`XSetIconName`	`XGetIconName`
Icon Name (R4)	`XSetWMIconName`	`XGetWMIconName`
Shell Command and Arguments (R3)	`XSetCommand`	use `XGetWindowProperty` to get `XA_WM_COMMAND`
Shell Command and Arguments (R4)	`XSetWMCommand`	`XGetWMCommand`
Icon Pixmap (R3)	`XSetStandardProperties` or `XSetWMHints`	`XGetWMHints`
Icon Pixmap (R4)	`XSetWMProperties` or `XSetWMNormalHints`	`XGetWMNormalHints`
Normal Size Hints (R3)	`XSetNormalHints`	`XGetNormalHints`
Normal Size Hints (R4)	`XSetWMNormalHints`	`XGetWMNormalHints`
WM Hints (R3 & R4)	`XSetWMHints`	`XGetWMHints`
Zoom Hints (R3 only)	`XSetZoomHints`	`XGetZoomHints`

Window Management

Table 14-1. Window Manager Hints (continued)

Hint	Set (by Application)	Get (by Window Manager)
Transient Window	XSetTransientForHint	XGetTransientForHint
Class Hint	XSetClassHint	XGetClassHint
Client Machine (R4 only)	XSetWMClientMachine	XGetWMClientMachine
WM Protocols (R4 only)	XSetWMProtocols	XGetWMProtocols

Getting all of this information within the window manager as described above is simple, with the exception of getting the shell command and arguments. Under R3, the property must be read with XGetWindowProperty, since no convenience function is defined. Under R4, XGetWMCommand is available.

14.5.2 Setting Icon Sizes

The icon size property is the only hint that the window manager should set for applications to read. The window manager may prefer particular sizes of icons to yield a consistent appearance for all icons on the screen. The window manager calls XSetIconSizes (which sets the XA_WM_ICON_SIZE property on the root window), indicating the preferred sizes. The icon size hints include maximum and minimum dimensions and size increments. Once standard window managers evolve that set this property (*uwm* and *twm* do not), applications may have one icon pixmap prepared for each standard window manager.

14.6 Window Management Functions

The functions described in this section are used primarily by the window manager on top-level windows. Applications can also use them on their top-level windows; conventions for doing so are described in Appendix L, *Interclient Communication Conventions*, of Volume Zero, *X Protocol Reference Manual*. Applications can use these routines freely on their subwindows.

XConfigureWindow is the most general routine for changing the configuration of a window, namely its size, position, border width, and stacking position.

The routines to move and resize windows are XMoveWindow, XMoveResizeWindow, and XResizeWindow. The routine to change the border width of a window is XSet-WindowBorderWidth.

Quite a variety of routines are provided to change the stacking order of windows. These operations affect only a single group of siblings. Furthermore, they affect only overlapping siblings. If any of the siblings specified do not overlap, their stacking order is not changed.

`XCirculateSubwindowsDown`

> Moves the lowest mapped sibling to the top of the stacking order.

`XCirculateSubwindowsUp`

> Moves the highest mapped sibling to the bottom of the stacking order.

`XCirculateSubwindows`

> Performs either `XCirculateSubwindowsDown` or `XCirculate-SubwindowsUp` according to a flag.

`XRestackWindows`

> Specifies a list of siblings in the desired stacking order.

`XRaiseWindow`

> Moves a window to the top of the stacking order among its siblings.

`XMapRaised`

> Maps a window, placing it on top of the stacking order of its siblings. For a window mapped for the first time, this is equivalent to `XMapWindow`. But when an already mapped window is unmapped, it retains its stacking order when mapped again with `XMapWindow`.

`XLowerWindow`

> Moves a window to the bottom of the stacking order among its siblings.

`XConfigureWindow`

> Restacks the window according to a `stack_mode` and relative to a particular sibling. This function is also capable of moving, resizing, and changing the border width of a window.

All these functions have the ability to change the screen layout and therefore can be monitored and intercepted by the window manager. They are also commonly used by the window manager itself to allow the user to change the screen layout.

The `stack_mode` of the `XConfigureWindow` routine has five possible values: `Above`, `Below`, `BottomIf`, `TopIf`, and `Opposite`. If the window is simultaneously being moved or resized, this calculation is performed with respect to the window's final size and position, not its initial position. If a sibling and a `stack_mode` are specified, the window is restacked as described in Table 14-2.

Table 14-2. Meaning of Stacking Mode with Sibling Specified

Window Stack Mode	Description
Above	Window is placed just above sibling.
Below	Window is placed just below sibling.
TopIf	If sibling obscures window, then window is placed at the top of the stack.
BottomIf	If window obscures sibling, then window is placed at the bottom of the stack.
Opposite	If any sibling occludes window, then window is placed at the top of the stack, else if window occludes any sibling, then window is placed at the bottom of the stack.

If a `stack_mode` is specified but no sibling is specified, the window is restacked as described in Table 14-3.

Table 14-3. Meaning of Stacking Mode without Sibling

Window Stack Mode	Description
Above	Window is placed at the top of the stack.
Below	Window is placed at the bottom of the stack.
TopIf	If any sibling obscures window, then window is placed at the top of the stack.
BottomIf	If window obscures any sibling, then window is placed at the bottom of the stack.
Opposite	If any sibling occludes window, then window is placed at the top of the stack, else if window occludes any sibling, then window is placed at the bottom of the stack.

Another set of routines that are usually only used by the window manager are the ones that grab and ungrab the server. `XGrabServer` and `XUngrabServer` are used when a program requires total control of the screen, so that output requests from other programs are queued but not displayed. One application of grabbing is to draw temporary moving objects on the screen, such as the outline of a window being moved. This is called *rubber-banding*. The outline (or grid) is drawn with logical function `GXxor`, which, when drawn twice, leaves the screen as it was initially. If the server were not grabbed in between the first drawing and the second of the same line, some other program might update the same part of the display, resulting in glitches after the second drawing. This server grab also speeds up the rubber-banding, because the server stops performing updates to other windows.

14.7 A Basic Window Manager

This section describes the design of a simple window manager called *winman*. This example window manager should be helpful in several ways. It demonstrates many of the Xlib routines that are intended to be used only by window managers. It also shows what a window manager might do with the properties that applications set and how window managers implement icons. This window manager also demonstrates the use of the save-set to make sure that, if it dies, the windows it has iconified will be restored. It does not, however, demonstrate substructure redirection or reparenting. See the code for *uwm* or *twm* for examples of substructure redirection and *twm* for an example of reparenting.

The *winman* program also demonstrates some techniques that may be helpful in ordinary applications, such as how to implement a menu using Xlib. (Most applications will ultimately do this with a toolkit.)

If you have the example programs from O'Reilly and Associates, you can compile and run *winman* to see how it works (how to get this code is described in the *Preface*). Be sure to stop or kill any other window managers running before running *winman*. Both *winman* and the other window manager may get confused because they are not designed to cooperate with each other. The following explanations will be easier to follow if you have used the program.

14.7.1 Operation of the Program

The *winman* program creates a menu composed of horizontal bars and places it in the upper-right corner of the screen, as shown in Figure 14-4.

The menu provides a number of basic functions for manipulating windows on the screen:

Raise   Brings a window to the top of the stack, so that it is fully visible.

Lower   Lowers a window to the bottom so that the area formerly hidden is made visible.

Move   Changes the position of a window on the screen, and raises it.

Resize   Changes the size of a window, and raises it.

CirculateDn   Moves the window on the bottom to the top.

CirculateUp   Moves the window on the top to the bottom.

(De)Iconify   Turns a window into a small marker window or vice versa.

Keybrd Focus   Assigns all keyboard input to the selected window, regardless of the position of the pointer.

New Xterm   Creates a new xterm window, and places it at the upper-left corner of the screen. You can subsequently move or resize the new window with the Move and Resize functions.

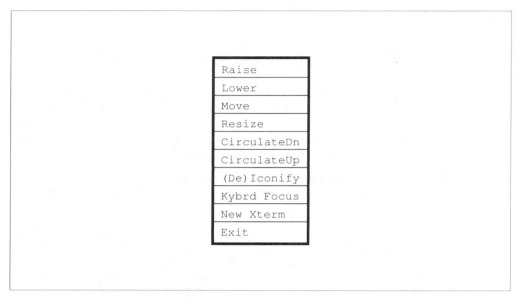

Figure 14-4. The menu created by winman

Exit   It is good practice for all programs to provide a way to quit. (*uwm* requires the user to look up the process number and kill the process.) Since this window manager is primarily for demonstration purposes, this choice is provided to make it easy to kill the program.

All input for the window manager is supplied through the pointer. A cursor (which tracks the pointer) is assigned to the menu to indicate that input in this area selects a menu item. Choices are made from the menu by pressing a pointer button in the appropriate region of the menu. When a menu choice is made, the menu bar and its label change to inverse video. In other words, everything that was black in the bar changes to white and vice versa (*winman* works in black and white on all systems, even those with color). After the choice is made but before the operation is complete, the pointer is grabbed, so that all pointer input is directed to the menu window independent of the position of the pointer. While the pointer is grabbed, *winman*'s cursor changes to a hand and tracks the pointer anywhere on the screen. This reminds you that the window manager is expecting the next pointer input even though the pointer is no longer on the menu. When the chosen operation is complete, the menu is returned to its initial condition, and the pointer grab is released. If this menu was to be used in a normal application, a passive grab would be used instead of the active one used here.

If CirculateDn, CirculateUp, or New Xterm is chosen, selection of a window is not necessary. The circulation operations act on all overlapping windows that are children of the root. The New Xterm choice simply creates a new *xterm* window.

If Raise, Lower, (De)Iconify or Kybrd Focus is chosen, the user must press a pointer button to select a window. (*winman*'s own menu cannot be iconified, because this would make it impossible to recover the window manager menu.) Kybrd Focus sets the keyboard focus window and highlights that window with a white background behind the window.

If Move or Resize is chosen, the user must press a pointer button on the window to be manipulated, drag the pointer with the button held until the outline of the window is in the chosen size or position, and then release the button. (*winman*'s own menu can be moved but not resized.) A moving outline of the window is used to indicate the intended dimensions or position of the window.

14.7.2 Description of the Code of main

Example 14-1 shows the `main` for the *winman* window manager. The `isIcon` routine that is called in `main` is described in Section 14.7.15 below. The `draw_box` routine, also called in `main`, is described in Section 14.7.13. All the rest of *winman*'s code is described in sections following `main`.

Instead of breaking up the code in little pieces as we have done in earlier examples, this time we'll show you `main` together in one place. By this point in the manual, you should know enough to understand most of this code. Any questions you may have should be answered by the description immediately following the code.

Example 14-1. winman — main C program

```
#include <X11/Xlib.h>
#include <X11/Xutil.h>
#include <X11/Xatom.h>
#include <X11/Xos.h>
#include <X11/cursorfont.h>

#include <stdio.h>
#include <signal.h>

#include "bitmaps/focus_frame_bi"      /* Name must be <= 14 chars
                                        * for sys V compatibility */

/* Include file for printing event types */
#include "eventnames.h"

#define MAX_CHOICE 10
#define DRAW 1
#define ERASE 0
#define RAISE 1
#define LOWER 0
#define MOVE 1
#define RESIZE 0
#define NONE 100
#define NOTDEFINED 0
#define BLACK   1
#define WHITE   0

Window focus_window;
Window inverted_pane = NONE;

static char *menu_label[] =
    {
    "Raise",
    "Lower",
    "Move",
    "Resize",
```

Example 14-1. winman — main C program (continued)

```
    "CirculateDn",
    "CirculateUp",
    "(De)Iconify",
    "Kybrd Focus",
    "New Xterm",
    "Exit",
    };

Display *display;
int screen_num;
XFontStruct *font_info;
char icon_name[50];

main()
{
    Window menuwin;
    Window panes[MAX_CHOICE];
    int menu_width, menu_height, x = 0, y = 0, border_width = 4;
    int winindex;
    int cursor_shape;
    Cursor cursor, hand_cursor;
    char *font_name = "9x15";
    int direction, ascent, descent;
    int char_count;
    char *string;
    XCharStruct overall;
    Bool owner_events;
    int pointer_mode;
    int keyboard_mode;
    Window confine_to;
    GC gc, rgc;
    int pane_height;
    Window assoc_win;
    XEvent event;
    unsigned int button;

    if ( (display=XOpenDisplay(NULL)) == NULL ) {
        (void) fprintf( stderr, "winman: cannot connect to \
                X server %s\n", XDisplayName(NULL));
        exit( -1 );
    }

    screen_num = DefaultScreen(display);

    /* Access font */
    font_info = XLoadQueryFont(display,font_name);

    if (font_info == NULL) {
        (void) fprintf( stderr, "winman: Cannot open font %s\n",
                font_name);
        exit( -1 );
    }

    string = menu_label[6];
    char_count = strlen(string);

    /* Determine the extent of each menu pane based on
     * the font size */
```

Example 14-1. winman — main C program (continued)

```
XTextExtents(font_info, string, char_count, &direction, &ascent,
        &descent, &overall);

menu_width = overall.width + 4;
pane_height = overall.ascent + overall.descent + 4;
menu_height = pane_height * MAX_CHOICE;

/* Place the window in upper-right corner*/
x = DisplayWidth(display,screen_num) - menu_width -
        (2*border_width);
y = 0;    /* Appears at top */

/* Create opaque window */
menuwin = XCreateSimpleWindow(display, RootWindow(display,
        screen_num), x, y, menu_width, menu_height,
        border_width, BlackPixel(display,screen_num),
        WhitePixel(display,screen_num));

/* Create the choice windows for the text */
for (winindex = 0; winindex < MAX_CHOICE; winindex++) {
    panes[winindex] = XCreateSimpleWindow(display, menuwin, 0,
            menu_height/MAX_CHOICE*winindex, menu_width,
            pane_height, border_width = 1,
            BlackPixel(display,screen_num),
            WhitePixel(display,screen_num));
    XSelectInput(display, panes[winindex], ButtonPressMask
            | ButtonReleaseMask |  ExposureMask);
}

XSelectInput(display, RootWindow(display, screen_num),
        SubstructureNotifyMask);

/* These do not appear until parent (menuwin) is mapped */
XMapSubwindows(display,menuwin);

/* Create the cursor for the menu */
cursor = XCreateFontCursor(display, XC_left_ptr);
hand_cursor = XCreateFontCursor(display, XC_hand2);

XDefineCursor(display, menuwin, cursor);

focus_window = RootWindow(display, screen_num);

/* Create two graphics contexts for inverting panes (white
 * and black).  We invert the panes by changing the background
 * pixel, clearing the window, and using the GC with the
 * contrasting color to redraw the text.  Another way is using
 * XCopyArea.  The default is to generate GraphicsExpose and
 * NoExpose events to indicate whether the source area was
 * obscured.  Since the logical function is GXinvert, the
 * destination is also the source.  Therefore, if other
 * windows are obscuring parts of the exposed pane, the
 * wrong area will be inverted.  Therefore, we would need
 * to handle GraphicsExpose and NoExpose events.  We'll do
 * it the easier way. */

gc = XCreateGC(display, RootWindow(display, screen_num), 0,
        NULL);
XSetForeground(display, gc, BlackPixel(display, screen_num));
rgc = XCreateGC(display, RootWindow(display, screen_num), 0,
```

Example 14-1. winman — main C program (continued)

```
                    NULL);
        XSetForeground(display, rgc, WhitePixel(display, screen_num));

        /* Map the menu window (and its subwindows) to the screen_num */
        XMapWindow(display, menuwin);

        /* Force child processes to disinherit the TCP file descriptor;
         * this helps the shell command (creating new xterm) forked and
         * executed from the menu to work properly */
        if ((fcntl(ConnectionNumber(display), F_SETFD, 1)) == -1)
            fprintf(stderr, "winman: child cannot disinherit TCP fd");

        /* Loop getting events on the menu window and icons */
        while (1) {
            /* Wait for an event */
            XNextEvent(display, &event);

            /* If expose, draw text in pane if it is pane */
            switch (event.type) {
            case Expose:
                if  (isIcon(event.xexpose.window, event.xexpose.x,
                        event.xexpose.y, &assoc_win, icon_name, False))
                    XDrawString(display, event.xexpose.window, gc, 2,
                            ascent + 2, icon_name, strlen(icon_name));
                else { /* It's a pane, might be inverted */
                    if (inverted_pane == event.xexpose.window)
                        paint_pane(event.xexpose.window, panes, gc, rgc,
                                BLACK);
                    else
                        paint_pane(event.xexpose.window, panes, gc, rgc,
                                WHITE);
                }
                break;
            case ButtonPress:

                paint_pane(event.xbutton.window, panes, gc, rgc, BLACK);

                button = event.xbutton.button;
                inverted_pane = event.xbutton.window;

                /* Get the matching ButtonRelease on same button */
                while (1) {
                    /* Get rid of presses on other buttons */
                    while (XCheckTypedEvent(display, ButtonPress,
                            &event));
                    /* Wait for release; if on correct button, exit */
                    XMaskEvent(display, ButtonReleaseMask, &event);
                    if (event.xbutton.button == button)
                        break;
                }

                /* All events are sent to the grabbing window
                 * regardless of whether this is True or False;
                 * owner_events only affects the distribution
                 * of events when the pointer is within this
                 * application's windows */
                owner_events = True;

                /* We don't want pointer or keyboard events
```

Example 14-1. winman — main C program (continued)

```
            * frozen in the server */
         pointer_mode = GrabModeAsync;
         keyboard_mode = GrabModeAsync;

         /* We don't want to confine the cursor */
         confine_to = None;
         XGrabPointer(display, menuwin, owner_events,
                 ButtonPressMask | ButtonReleaseMask,
                 pointer_mode, keyboard_mode,
                 confine_to, hand_cursor, CurrentTime);

         /* If press and release occurred in same window,
          * do command; if not, do nothing */
         if (inverted_pane == event.xbutton.window) {
             /* Convert window ID to window array index  */
             for (winindex = 0; inverted_pane !=
                     panes[winindex]; winindex++)
                 ;
             switch (winindex) {
             case 0:
                 raise_lower(menuwin, RAISE);
                 break;
             case 1:
                 raise_lower(menuwin, LOWER);
                 break;
             case 2:
                 move_resize(menuwin, hand_cursor, MOVE);
                 break;
             case 3:
                 move_resize(menuwin, hand_cursor, RESIZE);
                 break;
             case 4:
                 circup(menuwin);
                 break;
             case 5:
                 circdn(menuwin);
                 break;
             case 6:
                 iconify(menuwin);
                 break;
             case 7:
                 focus_window = focus(menuwin);
                 break;
             case 8:
                 execute("xterm&");
                 break;

             case 9: /* Exit */
                 XSetInputFocus(display,
                         RootWindow(display,screen_num),
                         RevertToPointerRoot,
                         CurrentTime);
                 /* Turn all icons back into windows */
                 /* Must clear focus highlights */
                 XClearWindow(display, RootWindow(display,
                         screen_num));
                 /* Need to change focus border width back here */
```

Example 14-1. winman — main C program (continued)

```
                    XFlush(display);
                    XCloseDisplay(display);
                    exit(1);
                default:
                    (void) fprintf(stderr,
                            "Something went wrong\n");
                    break;
                } /* End switch */
            } /* End if */

            /* Invert Back Here (logical function is invert) */
            paint_pane(event.xexpose.window, panes, gc, rgc, WHITE);

            inverted_pane = NONE;
            draw_focus_frame();
            XUngrabPointer(display, CurrentTime);
            XFlush(display);
            break;
        case DestroyNotify:
            /* Window we have iconified has died, remove its
             * icon; don't need to remove window from save-set
             * because that is done automatically */
            removeIcon(event.xdestroywindow.window);
            break;
        case CirculateNotify:
        case ConfigureNotify:
        case UnmapNotify:
            /* All these uncover areas of screen_num */
            draw_focus_frame();
            break;
        case CreateNotify:
        case GravityNotify:
        case MapNotify:
        case ReparentNotify:
            /* Don't need these, but get them anyway since
             * we need DestroyNotify and UnmapNotify */
            break;
        case ButtonRelease:
            /* Throw these way, they are spurious here */
            break;
        case MotionNotify:
            /* Throw these way, they are spurious here */
            break;
        default:
            fprintf(stderr, "winman: got unexpected %s event.\n",
                    event_names[event.type]);
        } /* End switch */
    } /* End menu loop (while) */
} /* End main */
```

14.7.3 Window Layering

The first issue that comes up when writing a menu is how to layer the windows that contain each menu item. It would be possible to write a menu that only used one window, placing the text within the window in the right places and highlighting areas when the pointer coordinates in the `ButtonPress` events indicated that an item was chosen. This is a hard way, because it does not take advantage of X's windowing capabilities. It would also be possible to make each menu panel a subwindow of the root window. While this would simplify the event handling and highlighting, we would have to define a cursor for each of the windows. More importantly, the user would have to move all the windows separately if the menu were to be moved, unless we monitored movement of any one of the windows and made the rest follow. There are also other ramifications, including that it would be difficult to identify the menu as a whole to make sure it was not iconified; this would require comparing the IDs in events with the IDs of all the windows. The best solution is a combination of the above approaches.

The menu is created by superimposing ten small `InputOutput` child windows (`defs[ ]`) on one large `InputOutput` parent window (`menuwin`), as shown in Figure 14-5. This has the advantage that there is a single parent window for the window manager, which we can use to locate the panes of the menu and to identify the menu as a whole. You can also assign a cursor to the larger window, and since the smaller windows are its children, the same cursor appears in all of them. This avoids nine cursor assignments.

The nine smaller windows do three other convenient things; their borders make a neat division between areas of the menu, they determine which area of the menu the user chooses, and they define a convenient area to invert from black on white to white on black to indicate which menu choice was made.

14.7.4 Selecting Input

Now that we have decided how to layer the windows to best advantage, it is time to plan what events are going to be needed. The `menuwin` window requires no events, since it is chiefly there to tie together the menu panes. `ButtonPress`, `ButtonRelease`, and `Expose` events are required for the panes, so they can accept a choice and redraw the pane in case anything obscures and then exposes part or all of the menu. `ButtonRelease` events are selected so that we can verify menu choices by making sure the `Button-Release` happens in the same window as the `ButtonPress`. Since the pointer is grabbed during the selection of a window on the screen to be manipulated (a window not associated with the window manager), we do not need to select input on any of these windows. However, we need to know when applications that *winman* has iconified have been killed, so that we can remove the icon. This requires selecting `SubstructureNotify-Mask` on the root window.

Some of the other events selected by `SubstructureNotifyMask` also come in handy for triggering the redrawing of the highlighting background drawn around the focus window by *winman*. This background is drawn on the root window and might have to be redrawn whenever a new area of the root window becomes exposed. It has to be redrawn when

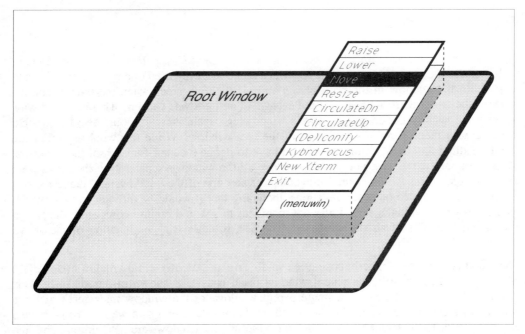

Figure 14-5. Window layering for the menu

CirculateNotify, ConfigureNotify, or UnmapNotify events arrive. This could also have been done by selecting Expose events on the root window, but since we have already selected these other events and they will be sent from the server to Xlib anyway, it improves performance slightly to use them instead of Expose events on the root window.

14.7.5 Handling Input

There are numerous commands available for getting input. The routines used in main are XCheckTypedEvent, XMaskEvent, and XNextEvent.

XCheckTypedEvent   Allows you to choose the types of events to look for, monitors all windows, and does not wait even if no matching event is on the queue.

XMaskEvent   Allows you to choose which event masks of the events to look for, monitoring all windows. It waits until an event arrives.

XNextEvent   Used to get any type of event that occurs in any window. It waits until an event arrives.

These routines were described and most of them demonstrated in Chapter 8, *Events*, and Chapter 9, *The Keyboard and Pointer*. But the way they are used in main might need some explanation. Consider the excerpt from main shown in Example 14-2.

Example 14-2. Using event-getting routines together

```
/* Get the matching ButtonRelease on same button */
while (1) {
    /* Get rid of all presses (on other buttons) */
    while (XCheckTypedEvent(display, ButtonPress,
            &event))
        ;
    /* Wait for release; if on correct button, exit *

    XMaskEvent(display, ButtonReleaseMask, &event);
    if (event.xbutton.button == button) {
        /* Get rid of other releases */
        while (XCheckTypedEvent(display, ButtonRelease,
                &event))
            ;

        break;
    }
}
```

Here we have already read a `ButtonPress` event and are waiting for a `Button-Release` on the same button. This cannot be done with `XMaskEvent` alone, because we might get a `ButtonRelease` on a different button first and there is no way to select or get only the button events on a single button (except by writing a predicate procedure as shown in Example 8-6). Therefore, `XMaskEvent` is called in a loop, and the `button` member in each event must be checked. Furthermore, the `CheckTypedEvent` calls are necessary to make sure that Xlib's queue does not fill up with `ButtonPress` or `ButtonRelease` events that are not wanted, since the code is really waiting for a particular button release. `XCheckTypedEvent` is used again in the routine that actually moves or resizes a window to throw away excess `MotionNotify` events.

The `Expose` event processing in `main` redraws *winman*'s menu only when the `count` field in the `Expose` event is zero, thus responding only to the last `Expose` event in a contiguous series on a single window. Remember that any of the menu panes or any icon can receive `Expose` events. We also minimize redrawing by redrawing only the panes that are exposed.

14.7.6 Inverting an Area

There are at least four possible strategies for inverting a menu pane containing text. They are not all equally good.

One is to use `XCopyArea` to copy the pane to itself using `GXinvert` as the logical function in the GC. This approach is weak because `GXinvert` would not achieve the desired effect on a color system, even though it would work fine on a monochrome system.

The second strategy, adopted in `main`, is to change the background pixel value of the window and change the foreground pixel value in the GC to draw the text in a contrasting color. In *winman*, the colors are black and white, but this approach will work correctly with any two contrasting colors.

The third approach would be to use XDrawImageString to draw the text. XDraw-ImageString draws a complete rectangle, with the text in the foreground pixel value from the GC and the rest of the rectangle in the background pixel value. If this rectangle were the same size as the menu pane, the entire pane could be inverted in color simply by swapping the foreground and background pixel values in the GC. The one weakness of this approach is that the rectangle drawn by XDrawImageString might not leave as much space around the text as you would like. However, this is a very fast approach, useful in menus and for the selection of text, which works in both monochrome and color.

The fourth approach involves a trick using colors allocated by XAllocColorCells. It is possible to allocate colors so that the two contrasting colors in the drawable are swapped by setting to 1 or 0 all the bits in a plane of the drawable. In this technique, the text does not need drawing at all for highlighting, because the plane on which the text is drawn is not modified by the operation to set or clear the bits in the other plane. You would need to allocate four colorcells, two of which contained the foreground RGB values and two the background. This would not work on a monochrome system, since you could not allocate four colorcells. This technique is described in Section 7.4.2.

14.7.7 Cursors

The main creates two cursors: one an arrow for selecting from the menu, and the other a hand for manipulating windows. It uses the call to grab the pointer to change the cursor to the hand. That has the nice side effect that the cursor will automatically change back when the grab is released, so that the cursor window attribute does not need to be changed with XDefineCursor.

14.7.8 Grabbing the Pointer

XGrabPointer is called to allow the user to select a window anywhere on the screen to be manipulated. While the pointer is grabbed, all pointer input is sent to the menu. Note that keyboard input is still sent normally to the application the pointer is in.

The arguments of XGrabPointer can be confusing. The *owner_events* argument affects the distribution of events when the pointer is within this application's windows. Therefore, it does not affect our application, because we are using the grab to get input from outside the menu windows. The *pointer_mode* and *keyboard_mode* arguments also do not apply to the job at hand, so they are set to GrabModeAsync, which does not affect the processing of events. Their other settings cause events to be held in the server until a releasing XAllowEvents call. Finally, the *confine_to* argument also does not fit our job, because we want the pointer to be able to roam around the screen rather than be confined to a window.

That about wraps up the new techniques used in main that have not been used earlier in this manual. Now we'll move on to some of the routines that main calls, beginning with paint_pane.

14.7.9 Painting the Menu

The paint_pane routine displays text in a menu pane. It is called when an exposure event occurs on a pane. When the menu is exposed, all of the exposure events are sent contiguously, refreshing each of the panes that was exposed. When the menu is first mapped, the Expose events trigger the drawing of all the panes for the first time.

Each call of this routine draws the text in one choice window. The first operation compares the window ID from the event with the IDs in the panes array to determine which string from the menu_label array to use.

Window backgrounds are automatically redrawn by the server when exposure occurs. But paint_pane is not always called in response to Expose events; it is also used to invert the pane when a choice is made. Therefore, the request buffer will not necessarily be flushed before the next call to draw the area. Therefore, an XClearWindow call is necessary to redraw the background. (A completely different strategy could have been used. The background could be filled with XFillRectangle instead of using the server.)

Example 14-3. winman — the paint_pane routine

```
static char *menu_label[] = {
    "Raise",
    "Lower",
    "Move",
    "Resize",
    "CirculateDn",
    "CirculateUp",
    "(De)Iconify",
    "Kybrd Focus",
    "New Xterm",
    "Exit",
};

paint_pane(window, panes, ngc, rgc, mode)
Window window;
Window panes[];
GC ngc, rgc;
int mode;
{
    int win;
    int x = 2, y;
    GC gc;

    if (mode == BLACK) {
        XSetWindowBackground(display, window, BlackPixel(display,
                screen_num));
        gc = rgc;
    }
    else {
        XSetWindowBackground(display, window, WhitePixel(display,
                screen_num));
        gc = ngc;
    }
    /* Clearing repaints the background */
    XClearWindow(display, window);
```

Example 14-3.   winman — the paint_pane routine (continued)

```
        /* Find out index of window for label text */
        for (win = 0; window != panes[win]; win++)
            ;

        y = font_info->max_bounds.ascent;

        /* The string length is necessary because strings
         * for XDrawString may not be null terminated */
        XDrawString(display, window, gc, x, y, menu_label[win],
                strlen( menu_label[win]));
}
```

14.7.10   Circulating Windows

The `circup` and `circcdn` routines are simple, because they have no arguments and they require no user input. They simply take all overlapping top-level windows and move the bottom one to the top or the top one to the bottom.

Example 14-4.   winman — the circle up and circle down routines

```
circup(menuwin)
Window menuwin;
{
        XCirculateSubwindowsUp(display, RootWindow(display,screen_num));
        XRaiseWindow(display, menuwin);
}

circcdn(menuwin)
Window menuwin;
{
        XCirculateSubwindowsDown(display, RootWindow(display,screen_num));
        XRaiseWindow(display, menuwin);
}
```

14.7.11   Raising and Lowering Windows

The `raise_lower` routine gets a `ButtonPress` event, finds out which window it occurred in, and raises or lowers the window unless it was the root.

The `XQueryPointer` call is used to get the window ID of the window that the button is pressed in. This call is necessary because the program did not create or select input on the windows that it is going to manipulate.

Example 14-5. winman — the raise and lower routines

```
raise_lower( menuwin, raise_or_lower )
Window menuwin;
Bool raise_or_lower;
{
    XEvent report;
    int root_x,root_y;
    Window child, root;
    int win_x, win_y;
    unsigned int mask;
    unsigned int button;

    /* Wait for ButtonPress, find out which subwindow of root */
    XMaskEvent(display, ButtonPressMask, &report);
    button = report.xbutton.button;
    XQueryPointer(display, RootWindow(display,screen_num), &root,
            &child, &root_x, &root_y, &win_x, &win_y,
            &mask);

    /* If not RootWindow, raise */
    if (child != NULL) {
        if (raise_or_lower == RAISE)
            XRaiseWindow(display, child);
        else
            XLowerWindow(display, child);
        /* Make sure window manager can never be obscured */
        XRaiseWindow(display, menuwin);
    }

    /* Get the matching ButtonRelease on same button */
    while (1) {
        XMaskEvent(display, ButtonReleaseMask, &report);
        if (report.xbutton.button == button) break;
    }
    /* Throw out any remaining events so we start fresh */
    while (XCheckMaskEvent(display, ButtonReleaseMask |
            ButtonPressMask, &report))
        ;

}
```

14.7.12 Moving and Resizing Windows

The move_resize routine is similar to raise_lower but uses the difference in position between a ButtonPress and a ButtonRelease event to determine the change in position or size of the window. It also uses MotionNotify events to draw an outline of the window during the move or resize. During resizing, the upper-left corner of the window stays in place, while the lower-right corner moves the same way the pointer does between the press and the release. The code could be expanded to allow any corner of the window to be resized.

The routine that draws the box for the temporary window outline was described in Chapter 6, *Drawing Graphics and Text*.

If there is an icon associated with the moved window, that icon is not moved. Similarly, if the window moved is an icon, its associated main window is not moved. This is an arbitrary window manager policy decision. Some window managers might legislate a certain relationship between the position of a window and its icon.

Example 14-6. winman — the move and resize routines

```
move_resize(menuwin, hand_cursor, move_or_resize)
Window menuwin;
Cursor hand_cursor;
Bool move_or_resize;
{
        XEvent report;
        XWindowAttributes win_attr;
        int press_x, press_y, release_x, release_y, move_x, move_y;
        static int box_drawn = False;
        int left, right, top, bottom;
        Window root, child;
        Window win_to_configure;
        int win_x, win_y;
        unsigned int mask;
        unsigned int pressed_button;
        XSizeHints size_hints;
        Bool min_size, increment;
        unsigned int width, height;
        int temp_size;
        static GC gc;
        static int first_time = True;
        long user_supplied_mask;

        if (first_time) {
            gc = XCreateGC(display, RootWindow(display,screen_num), 0,
                    NULL);
            XSetSubwindowMode(display, gc, IncludeInferiors);
            XSetForeground(display, gc, BlackPixel(display, screen_num));
            XSetFunction(display, gc, GXxor);
            first_time = False;
            }

        /* Wait for ButtonPress choosing window to configure */
        XMaskEvent(display, ButtonPressMask, &report);
        pressed_button = report.xbutton.button;

        /* Which child of root was press in? */
        XQueryPointer(display, RootWindow(display,screen_num), &root,
                &child, &press_x, &press_y, &win_x,
                &win_y, &mask);
        win_to_configure = child;

        if ((win_to_configure == NULL) ||
                ((win_to_configure == menuwin)
                && (move_or_resize == RESIZE))) {
            /* If in RootWindow or resizing menuwin,
             * get release event and get out */
        while (XCheckMaskEvent(display, ButtonReleaseMask |
            ButtonPressMask, &report))
            ;
            return;
        }
```

Example 14-6. winman — the move and resize routines (continued)

```
        /* Button press was in a valid subwindow of root */

        /* Get original position and size of window */
        XGetWindowAttributes(display, win_to_configure,
                &win_attr);

        /* Get size hints for the window */
#ifdef X11R3
        XGetNormalHints(display, win_to_configure, &size_hints);
#else
        XGetWMNormalHints(display, win_to_configure, &size_hints,
                &user_supplied_mask);
        if (user_supplied_mask & PBaseSize)
           ;/* R4 client */
        else
           ;/* R3 client */
#endif /* X11R3 */
        if (size_hints.flags && PMinSize)
           min_size = True;
        if (size_hints.flags && PResizeInc)
           increment = True;

        /* Now we need pointer motion events */
        XChangeActivePointerGrab(display, PointerMotionHintMask |
                ButtonMotionMask | ButtonReleaseMask |
                OwnerGrabButtonMask, hand_cursor, CurrentTime);

        /* Don't allow other display operations during move
         * because the moving outline drawn with Xor won't
         * work properly otherwise */
        XGrabServer(display);

        /* Move outline of window until button release */
        while  (1) {
            XNextEvent(display, &report);
            switch (report.type) {
               case ButtonRelease:
                  if (report.xbutton.button == pressed_button) {
                      if (box_drawn)
                          /* Undraw box */
                          draw_box(gc, left, top, right, bottom);

                      /* This may seem premature but actually
                       * ButtonRelease indicates that the
                       * rubber-banding is done */
                      XUngrabServer(display);

                      /* Get final window position */
                      XQueryPointer(display, RootWindow(display,
                              screen_num), &root, &child,
                              &release_x, &release_y, &win_x,
                              &win_y, &mask);

                      /* Move or resize window */
                      if (move_or_resize == MOVE)
                          XMoveWindow(display, win_to_configure,
                              win_attr.x + (release_x -
                              press_x), win_attr.y +
                              (release_y - press_y));
```

Example 14-6. winman — the move and resize routines (continued)

```
            else
                XResizeWindow(display, win_to_configure,
                    win_attr.width + (release_x - press_x),
                    win_attr.height + (release_y - press_y));

            XRaiseWindow(display, win_to_configure);
            XFlush(display);
            box_drawn = False;
            while (XCheckMaskEvent(display,
                    ButtonReleaseMask
                    | ButtonPressMask,
                    &report))
                ;
            return;
        }
        break;

    case MotionNotify:
        if (box_drawn == True)
            /* Undraw box */
            draw_box(gc, left, top, right, bottom);

        /* Can get rid of all MotionNotify events in
         * queue, since otherwise the round-trip delays
         * caused by XQueryPointer may cause a backlog
         * of MotionNotify events, which will cause
         * additional wasted XQueryPointer calls */
        while (XCheckTypedEvent(display, MotionNotify,
                &report));

        /* Get current mouse position */
        XQueryPointer(display, RootWindow(display,
                screen_num), &root, &child, &move_x,
                &move_y, &win_x, &win_y, &mask);

        if (move_or_resize == MOVE) {
            left = move_x - press_x + win_attr.x;
            top = move_y - press_y + win_attr.y;
            right = left + win_attr.width;
            bottom = top + win_attr.height;
        }
        else
            {
            if (move_x < win_attr.x)
                move_x = 0;
            if (move_y < win_attr.y )
                move_y = 0;
            left = win_attr.x;
            top = win_attr.y;
            right = left + win_attr.width + move_x
                    - press_x;
            bottom = top + win_attr.height + move_y
                    - press_y;
            /* Must adjust size according to size hints */
            /* Enforce minimum dimensions */
            width = right - left;
```

Example 14-6. winman — the move and resize routines (continued)

```
                        height = bottom - top;

                        /* Make sure dimension are increment of
                         * width_inc and height_inc and at least
                         * min_width and min_height */
                        for (temp_size = size_hints.min_width;
                              temp_size < width;
                              temp_size += size_hints.width_inc)
                            ;

                        for (temp_size = size_hints.min_height;
                              temp_size < height;
                              temp_size += size_hints.height_inc)
                            ;
                        /* Most applications (xterm
                         * included) pad their right
                         * and bottom dimensions by
                         * 2 pixels */
                        bottom = top + temp_size + 2;
                        right = left + temp_size + 2;
                        }

                draw_box(gc, left, top, right, bottom);
                box_drawn = True;
                break;
            default:
                /* StructureNotify events should not appear
                 * here because of the ChangeActivePointerGrab
                 * call, but they do for some reason; anyway,
                 * it doesn't matter */
                /* fprintf(stderr, "unexpected event type %s\n",
                 * report.type); */
                ;
        } /* End switch */
    } /* End outer while */
} /* End move */
```

Figure 14-6 shows an example of the screen during a move operation.

The XChangeActivePointerGrab function is used to narrow the types of events that are received. In other terms, it changes the events that are selected for the window for the duration of the grab. This makes it unnecessary to throw away ButtonPress events that are used early in the program but not needed in this routine.

The server is grabbed in this example to make sure that no other program displays output on the screen while the box is being dragged. This is necessary because the box is drawn and then undrawn with the same command and GC using the GXxor logical function. Graphics drawn twice with Exclusive OR will appear as they started but only if the pixels affected are not changed by any other application in between. If any other client were allowed to draw between the draw and the undraw, the screen might not be returned to normal.

Figure 14-6. Dragging a window outline

Note that the actual color of the rubber-banded line is unpredictable on a color system, because the pixel value is simply the Exclusive OR of what was already there. If a particular color of rubber-banded line is desired, you will have to use the overlay technique described in Section 7.4.2.

14.7.13 The draw_box Routine

The draw_box routine shown in Example 14-7 modifies a GC and draws a box. It raises some interesting issues since it draws on the root window. It is called from the simple window manager program *winman* described in Chapter 14, *Window Management*. Its purpose is to draw an outline of a window during the rubber-banding that shows the user the current size or position of a window being resized or moved. The program also calls this routine to erase the box and to redraw the box to show the current position or size of a window as it is moved.

Example 14-7. The draw_box routine

```
Display *display;
int screen;

draw_box(gc, x, y, width, height)
GC gc;
int x, y,
unsigned int width, height;
{
    /* Set foreground pixel value -- default may be white on white */
```

Example 14-7. The draw_box routine (continued)

```
    XSetForeground(display, gc, BlackPixel(display,screen));

    /* Drawing on root window -- through all windows */
    XSetSubwindowMode(display, gc, IncludeInferiors);

    /* Logical function is XOR, so that double drawing erases box
     * on both color and monochrome screens */
    XSetFunction(display, gc, GXxor);

    XDrawRectangle(display, RootWindow(display,screen), gc, x, y,
            width, height);
}
```

This routine uses a couple of tricks that need explanation. Notice that three elements of the GC are changed and that the drawing request draws on the root window. Since the box may be moved anywhere on the screen during a move operation (by the window manager), the box must be drawn on the root window. We set the foreground color to black so that the box will be visible over the default backgrounds of most windows (white). By default, the subwindow_mode member is set to ClipByChildren, specifying that graphics drawn to a window do not show through child windows. Because we want the entire box to be visible anywhere on the screen, we set the subwindow_mode to IncludeInferiors.

We are using a logical operation of GXxor so that the box can be drawn again to erase itself. This logical operation has the unique feature of returning the pixels to their original state in monochrome or color if the box is drawn twice, as long as none of the pixels were changed between the first and second drawings. To make sure nothing else is drawn in between, the program that calls draw_box grabs the server for the brief period of the window manipulation. Avoid grabbing the server unless absolutely necessary.

14.7.14 (De)Iconifying Windows

The iconify routine must be able to turn a window into an icon or turn an icon back into a window. It is completely up to the window manager to keep track of the association between windows and icons. Therefore, a substantial portion of *winman*'s code is devoted to maintaining a list of the main windows and their associated icon windows. We will look at the code for the routine that main calls, iconify, and then delve into the details of implementing icons.

Example 14-7 shows the iconify routine that is called in response to the user selecting the (De)Iconify item on *winman*'s menu.

Example 14-8. winman — the iconify routine

```
iconify(menuwin)
Window menuwin;
{
    XEvent report;
    extern Window focus_window;
    Window assoc_win;
    int press_x,press_y;
    Window child;
    Window root;
    int win_x, win_y;
    unsigned int mask;
    unsigned int button;

    /* Wait for ButtonPress, any win */
    XMaskEvent(display, ButtonPressMask, &report);
    button = report.xbutton.button;

    /* Find out which subwindow the mouse was in */
    XQueryPointer(display, RootWindow(display,screen_num), &root,
        &child, &press_x, &press_y, &win_x, &win_y, &mask);

    /* Can't iconify rootwindow or menu window */
    if ((child == NULL) || (child == menuwin))
        {
        /* Wait for ButtonRelease before exiting */
        while (1)  {
            XMaskEvent(display, ButtonReleaseMask, &report);
            if (report.xbutton.button == button) break;
            }
        return;
        }

    /* Returned value of isIcon not used here, but
     * it is elsewhere in the code */
    isIcon(child, press_x, press_y, &assoc_win, icon_name, True);
    /* Window selected is unmapped, whether it is icon
     * or main window; the other is then mapped */
    XUnmapWindow(display, child);
    XMapWindow(display, *assoc_win);

    /* Wait for ButtonRelease before exiting */
    /* Get the matching ButtonRelease on same button */
    while (1)  {
        XMaskEvent(display, ButtonReleaseMask, &report);
        if (report.xbutton.button == button) break;
    }
    /* Throw out any remaining events so we start fresh
     * for next op */
    while (XCheckMaskEvent(display, ButtonReleaseMask |
            ButtonPressMask, &report))
        ;
}
```

If the window is not an icon, the window is unmapped and an icon window is created and mapped. If the window is an icon, it is unmapped and the associated main window is remapped. The `iconify` routine guards against iconifying the menu, since there is no way in this program to undo that operation.

The `iconify` routine calls the `isIcon` routine. If the window selected is not an icon, `isIcon` creates an icon window, enters it into a linked list, and returns the icon window's ID. If the window selected is an icon, the associated main window's ID is returned. Either way, the window selected is unmapped and the associated window is mapped.

The routines underlying `isIcon` are a simplified version of the icon-handling code from *uwm*. Notice that these routines are in a separate source file, so they must include the standard include files and declare as `extern` the global variables set in *winman.c*.

Example 14-9. winman — the isIcon routine

```
#include <X11/Xlib.h>
#include <X11/Xatom.h>
#include <X11/Xutil.h>
#include <X11/cursorfont.h>

#include <stdio.h>

extern Display *display;
extern int screen_num;

/* For linked list containing window ID, icon ID, and icon_name;
 * own indicates whether winman created the icon window (True)
 * or was passed it through the WMHints (False) */
typedef struct _windowList {
    struct _windowList *next;
    Window window;
    Window icon;
    Bool own;
    char *icon_name;
} WindowListRec, *WindowList;

WindowList Icons = NULL;

Bool isIcon(win, x, y, assoc, icon_name, makeicon)
Window win;
int x, y;
Window *assoc;
char *icon_name;
Bool makeicon;
{
    WindowList win_list;
    Window makeIcon();

    /* Go through linked list of window-icon structures */
    for (win_list = Icons; win_list; win_list = win_list->next) {
        if (win == win_list->icon) { /* Win is icon */
            *assoc = win_list->window;
            strcpy(icon_name, win_list->icon_name);
            return(True);
        }
        if (win == win_list->window) { /* Win is main window */
            *assoc = win_list->icon;
            strcpy(icon_name, win_list->icon_name);
            return(False);
        }
    }
    /* Window not in list means icon not created yet; create icon
     * and add main window to save-set in case window manager dies */
```

Example 14-9. winman — the isIcon routine (continued)

```
        if (makeicon) {
        *assoc = makeIcon(win, x, y, icon_name);
        XAddToSaveSet(display, win);
    }
    return(False);
}
```

The `isIcon` routine looks through the linked list of structures, of which there is one for each top-level window that has ever been iconified.

- If `win` is found in the structures and it is an icon, `isIcon` returns `True`.

- If `win` is found and it is a main window, `isIcon` returns `False`.

- If `win` is not found at all, `isIcon` calls `makeIcon` to create an icon for the window and then calls `XAddToSaveSet` to add the window to *winman*'s save-set. This code only gets called when an application is being iconified for the first time. Since it is possible that *winman* will get killed before it has a chance to remap the main windows of the applications it has iconified, these windows must be automatically remapped when *winman* dies. That is what the save-set does. (*winman* can be killed by typing Control-C in the window it was invoked from if it has been run in the foreground or with the Exit choice from *winman*'s menu.)

14.7.15 Creating the Icons

The `makeIcon` routine called in `isIcon` is used to read the hints that the application has specified for the icon. As you will recall, the window manager has the option of honoring or ignoring these hints. *winman* honors them to the greatest extent possible. It allows an application to specify an icon pixmap or icon window, an icon name, and the icon's position.

If some or all of these hints are not set, *winman* does the best it can. If no icon window is specified, *winman* creates one. If no icon pixmap is specified, *winman* uses a white background and writes the icon name on it in black.

Example 14-10. winman — the makeIcon routine

```
Window makeIcon(window, x, y, icon_name_return)
Window window;                          /* Associated window */
int x, y;                               /* Current mouse position */
char *icon_name_return;
{
    int icon_x, icon_y;                 /* Icon U. L. X and Y
                                         * coordinates */
    int icon_w, icon_h;                 /* Icon width and height */
    int icon_bdr;                       /* Icon border width */
    int depth;                          /* For XGetGeometry */
    Window root;                        /* For XGetGeometry */
    XSetWindowAttributes icon_attrib;   /* For icon creation */
    unsigned long icon_attrib_mask;
    XWMHints *wmhints;                  /* See if icon position
```

Example 14-10. winman — the makeIcon routine (continued)

```
                                                    * provided */
        XWMHints *XGetWMHints();
        Window FinishIcon();
        char *icon_name;

        /* Process window manager hints.  If icon window hint
         * exists, use it directly.  If icon pixmap hint exists,
         * get its size.  Otherwise, get default size.  If icon
         * position hint exists, use it; otherwise, use the
         * position passed (current mouse position). */
        if (wmhints = XGetWMHints(display, window)) {
            if (wmhints->flags&IconWindowHint)
                /* Icon window was passed; use it as is */
                return(finishIcon(window, wmhints->icon_window,
                    False, icon_name));
            else if (wmhints->flags&IconPixmapHint)
            {
                /* Pixmap was passed.  Determine size of icon
                 * window from pixmap.  Only icon_w and icon_h
                 * are significant. */
                if (!XGetGeometry(display, wmhints->icon_pixmap,
                    &root, &icon_x, &icon_y,
                    &icon_w, &icon_h, &icon_bdr, &depth)) {
                        fprintf(stderr, "winman: client passed invalid \
                            icon pixmap." );
                        return( NULL );
                }
                else {
                    icon_attrib.background_pixmap = wmhints->icon_pixmap;
                    icon_attrib_mask = CWBorderPixel|CWBackPixmap;
                }
            }
            /* Else no window or pixmap passed */
            else {
                icon_name = getDefaultIconSize(window, &icon_w, &icon_h);
                icon_attrib_mask = CWBorderPixel | CWBackPixel;
                icon_attrib.background_pixel = (unsigned long)
                        WhitePixel(display,screen_num);
            }
        }
        /* Else no hints at all exist */
        else {
            icon_name = getDefaultIconSize(window, &icon_w, &icon_h);
            icon_attrib_mask = CWBorderPixel | CWBackPixel;
        }
        /* Pad sizes */
        icon_w += 2;
        icon_h += 2;

        strcpy(icon_name_return, icon_name);

        /* Set the icon border attributes */
        icon_bdr = 2;
        icon_attrib.border_pixel = (unsigned long)
                BlackPixel(display,screen_num);

        /* If icon position hint exists, get it; this also checks
```

Example 14-10. winman — the makeIcon routine (continued)

```
     * to see if wmhints is NULL, which it will be if WMHints
     * were never set at all */
    if (wmhints && (wmhints->flags&IconPositionHint))
    {
         icon_x = wmhints->icon_x;
         icon_y = wmhints->icon_y;
    }
    else
    {
        /* Put it where the mouse was */
        icon_x = x;
        icon_y = y;
    }

    /* Create the icon window */
    return(finishIcon(window, XCreateWindow(display,
            RootWindow(display, screen_num),
            icon_x, icon_y, icon_w, icon_h,
            icon_bdr, 0, CopyFromParent, CopyFromParent,
            icon_attrib_mask, &icon_attrib),
            True, icon_name));
}
```

14.7.16 Getting the Icon Size

We will show you `getDefaultIconSize` (which calls `getIconName`) and then
`finishIcon`, the two routines called from `makeIcon`. `getDefaultIconSize` and
`getIconName` are shown in Example 14-11.

Example 14-11. winman — the getDefaultIconSize and getIconName routines

```
char *
getDefaultIconSize(window, icon_w, icon_h)
Window window;
int *icon_w, *icon_h;
{
    /* Determine the size of the icon window */
    char *icon_name;

    icon_name = getIconName(window);

    *icon_h = font_info->ascent + font_info->descent + 4;
    *icon_w = XTextWidth(font_info, icon_name, strlen(icon_name));

    return(icon_name);
}

char *
getIconName(window)
Window window;
{
    char *name;

    if (XGetIconName( display, window, &name )) return( name );
```

```
     /* Get program name if set */
     if (XFetchName( display, window, &name )) return( name );

     return( "Icon" );
}
```

The routines in Example 14-11 simply get the icon name and determine a size for the icon
from the name, given the font dimensions. If no icon name is available, they use the program
name, and if that is not available, they use the string "Icon." However, this should never happen if the applications are written properly.

14.7.17 Updating the Icon List

Now we'll turn to `finishIcon`, which is called from `makeIcon`. `finishIcon` creates
and defines a cursor for the icon, selects `Expose` events for it, and updates the linked list of
structures to include the new icon and its associated window. (Actually, the cursor should
have been created in another routine, because here it is executed every time a new icon is
created.)

Example 14-12. winman — the finishIcon routine

```
Window finishIcon(window, icon, own, icon_name)
Window window, icon;
Bool own;/* Whether winman created the icon window */
char *icon_name;
{
     WindowList win_list;
     Cursor manCursor;

     /* If icon window didn't get created, return failure */
      if (icon == NULL) return(NULL);

     /* Use the man cursor whenever the mouse is in the
      * icon window */
     manCursor = XCreateFontCursor(display, XC_man);
     XDefineCursor(display, icon, manCursor);

      /* Select events for the icon window */
     XSelectInput(display, icon, ExposureMask);

     /* Set the event window's icon window to be the new
      * icon window */
     win_list = (WindowList) malloc(sizeof(WindowListRec));
     win_list->window = window;
     win_list->icon = icon;
     win_list->own = own;
     win_list->icon_name = icon_name;
     win_list->next = Icons;
     Icons = win_list;

     return(icon);
}
```

One nice user interface possibility is suggested by the code for finishIcon. We could let the user turn an icon back into a main window by pressing some key or button in the icon. To do this, we would select button or key events on the icon and then look for them in one of the event loops in main. If button events were chosen, we would need to identify which window the button event appeared in to distinguish between events from the menu and events in the icon, but this would be easy.

14.7.18 Removing Icons

Finally, we need a way to remove icons for applications that have been iconified but exit while the window manager is running. The main selects StructureNotifyMask to be notified when top-level windows are destroyed and responds by calling removeIcon, which is shown in Example 14-13.

Example 14-13. winman — the removeIcon routine

```
removeIcon(window)
Window window;
{
    WindowList win_list, win_list1;

    for (win_list = Icons; win_list; win_list = win_list->next)
        if (win_list->window == window) {
            if (win_list->own)
                XDestroyWindow(display, win_list->icon);
            break;
        }
    if (win_list) {
        if (win_list==Icons) Icons = Icons->next;
        else
            for (win_list1 = Icons; win_list1->next;
                    win_list1 = win_list1->next)
                if (win_list1->next == win_list) {
                    win_list1->next = win_list->next;
                    break;
                };
    }
}
```

Whether *winman* exits graciously (through the Exit choice on the menu) or by being killed, all the main windows it has iconified have already been placed in the save-set, so that they will automatically be mapped. Therefore, no routine to clear the icons is necessary.

14.7.19 Changing Keyboard Focus

Setting the keyboard focus allows the user to stop worrying about whether the pointer is in the window to be typed into. The underlying function here is XSetInputFocus. It causes keyboard input to go to the selected window regardless of the position of the pointer. When the root window is selected, keyboard events are distributed normally according to the position of the pointer (this is the default situation).

winman highlights the focus window by increasing the width of the border and drawing a white outline around the window. This is necessary because it would not be obvious which application had the focus unless the application itself was programmed to indicate when it has the focus. Of course, applying the keyboard focus to a window that does not use keyboard input, like the main window of *xclock*, would cause your input to be just thrown away and the only indication of what is happening would be the highlighting drawn around the focus window.

The `focus` routine selects a window much like the `raise_lower` function does. If the subwindow returned by `XQueryPointer` is NULL, the pointer must be on the root window, and the focus can be set to the ID of the root window. Otherwise we need to find out if the subwindow is an icon. The focus should be on the real window as opposed to the icon, since the icon is controlled by the window manager and does not accept keyboard input for the application.

To change the border width of the new focus window, we need to get the old width with `XGetWindowAttributes`, and save it so it can be replaced when the focus is changed again.

Example 14-14. winman — the focus routine

```
focus(menuwin)
Window menuwin;
{
    XEvent report;
    int x,y;
    Window child;
    Window root;
    Window assoc_win;
    extern Window focus_window;
    int win_x, win_y;
    unsigned int mask;
    char *icon_name;
    unsigned int button;
    XWindowAttributes win_attr;
    static int old_width;
    static Window old_focus;
    int status;

    /* Wait for ButtonPress, any win */
    XMaskEvent(display, ButtonPressMask, &report);
    button = report.xbutton.button;

    /* Find out which subwindow the mouse was in */

    XQueryPointer(display, RootWindow(display,screen_num), &root,
            &child, &x, &y, &win_x, &win_y, &mask);

    if ((child == NULL) || (isIcon(child, x, y, &assoc_win,
            &icon_name)))
        focus_window = RootWindow(display, screen_num);
    else
        focus_window = child;

    if (focus_window != old_focus)  { /* If focus changed */
        /* If not first time set, set border back */
        if  (old_focus != NULL)
```

Example 14-14. winman — the focus routine (continued)

```
                    XSetWindowBorderWidth(display, old_focus, old_width);

        XSetInputFocus(display, focus_window, RevertToPointerRoot,
                CurrentTime);
        if (focus_window != RootWindow(display, screen_num)) {
                /* Get current border width and add one */
                if (!(status = XGetWindowAttributes(display,
                        focus_window, &win_attr)))
                        fprintf(stderr, "winman: can't get attributes for \
                                focus window\n");
                XSetWindowBorderWidth(display, focus_window,
                        win_attr.border_width + 1);
                /* Keep record so we can change it back */
                old_width = win_attr.border_width;
        }
    }

    /* Get the matching ButtonRelease on same button */
    while (1)  {
        XMaskEvent(display, ButtonReleaseMask, &report);
        if (report.xbutton.button == button) break;
    }

    old_focus = focus_window;
    return(focus_window);
}
```

14.7.20 Drawing the Focus Frame

The focus routine calls draw_focus_frame to further highlight the focus window. There are several ways to do this, ranging from almost trivial to fairly complex. The easiest way is to change the border width and/or color to indicate which window is the focus. Another way is to draw on the root window behind the focus window. This has a slightly different effect in that no highlight would appear on windows where they did not contact the root window. We do both to be absolutely sure the current focus window is well indicated. The window is highlighted by increasing its border width and by tiling a region underneath the current focus window with a pixmap.

A third and more complicated way is to reparent the focus window into a background frame, as described above in Section 14.3. This would work well if the windows already had been reparented to add a titlebar.

The draw_focus_frame routine shown in Example 14-15 also demonstrates the two-step process of creating a useful pixmap from the data in an include file generated by the bitmap program. You must create a bitmap from the data before making a pixmap from the bitmap.

Example 14-15. winman — the draw_focus_frame routine

```
draw_focus_frame()
{
    XWindowAttributes win_attr;
    int frame_width = 4;
    Pixmap focus_tile;
    GC gc;
    int foreground = BlackPixel(display, screen_num);
    int background = WhitePixel(display, screen_num);
    extern Window focus_window;
    Bool first_time = True;

    if (first_time) {
        /* Make Bitmap from bitmap data */
        focus_tile = XCreatePixmapFromBitmapData(display,
                RootWindow(display,screen_num),
                focus_frame_bi_bits, focus_frame_bi_width,
                focus_frame_bi_height, foreground,
                background, DefaultDepth(display, screen_num));

        /* Create graphics context */
        gc = XCreateGC(display, RootWindow(display,screen_num), 0,
                NULL);
        XSetFillStyle(display, gc, FillTiled);
        XSetTile(display, gc, focus_tile);
        first_time = False;
    }

    /* Get rid of old frames */
    XClearWindow(display, RootWindow(display,screen_num));

    /* If focus is RootWindow, no frame drawn */
    if (focus_window == RootWindow(display,screen_num)) return;

    /* Get dimensions and position of focus_window*/
    XGetWindowAttributes(display, focus_window, &win_attr);

    XFillRectangle(display, RootWindow(display,screen_num), gc,
        win_attr.x - frame_width, win_attr.y - frame_width,
        win_attr.width + 2 * (win_attr.border_width + frame_width),
        win_attr.height + 2 * (win_attr.border_width + frame_width));
}
```

14.7.21 Executing a Shell Command

The menu item to create a new *xterm* window uses execute, which is a routine taken
directly from the code for *uwm*. This routine can be used to execute any shell command and,
therefore, may come in handy in virtually any application, not just a window manager.
Example 14-16 shows the execute routine. Obviously, this routine is for UNIX-based
systems. Code for other operating systems can be added between preprocessor directives
(#ifdef, #endif).

Example 14-16. winman — the execute routine

```
#ifdef SYSV
#ifndef hpux
#define vfork() fork()
#endif /* hpux */
#endif /* SYSV */

/* The following procedure is a copy of the implementation of
 * system, modified to reset the handling of SIGINT, SIGQUIT,
 * and SIGHUP before executing */
execute(s)
char *s;
{
    int status, pid, w;
    register int (*istat)(), (*qstat)();

    if ((pid = vfork()) == 0) {
        signal(SIGINT, SIG_DFL);
        signal(SIGQUIT, SIG_DFL);
        signal(SIGHUP, SIG_DFL);
        execl("/bin/sh", "sh", "-c", s, 0);
        _exit(127);
    }
    istat = signal(SIGINT, SIG_IGN);
    qstat = signal(SIGQUIT, SIG_IGN);
    while ((w = wait(&status)) != pid && w != -1)
        ;
    if (w == -1)
        status = -1;
    signal(SIGINT, istat);
    signal(SIGQUIT, qstat);
    return(status);
}
```

There is some code in `main` that helps `execute` do its thing. It makes sure that the new process does not inherit any open files from the parent process, our window manager. Without this call, the child process might affect the operation of the client instead of being completely separate. All routines that execute shell commands should include the code shown in Example 14-17 in the routine that calls `execute`.

Example 14-17. winman — code for assisting execution of shell commands

```
/* Force child processes to disinherit the TCP file .
 * descriptor; this helps the shell command (creating
 * new xterm) forked and executed from the menu to work
 * properly */
if ((fcntl(ConnectionNumber(display), F_SETFD, 1)) == -1)
    fprintf(stderr, "winman: child cannot disinherit TCP fd");
```

Remember that *winman* is only a minimal window manager. It does not perform all the tasks required of window managers as specified by the ICCCM. See Appendix L, *Interclient Communication Conventions*, of Volume Zero, *X Protocol Reference Manual* (as of the second printing), to read about the complete set of requirements for window managers.

A

Specifying Fonts

This appendix describes how to define the names of the default fonts your application will use if the user does not override them.

In This Chapter:

A
Specifying Fonts

This appendix describes how to specify fonts in application code or in resource files. For a detailed description of the conventions for font naming, see Appendix M, *Logical Font Description Conventions*, of Volume Zero, *X Protocol Reference Manual* (as of the second printing).

A.1 Font Specification

Most applications that display text allow the user to specify the font via either the `font` resource or the `-fn` and `-font` command line options.

The X Window System supports many different display fonts with different sizes and type styles. (These are *screen* fonts and are not to be confused with *printer* fonts.)

In Release 3, Adobe Systems, Inc. and Digital Equipment Corporation jointly contributed several families of screen fonts (Courier, Helvetica, New Century Schoolbook, Symbol, and Times) in a variety of sizes, styles, and weights for 75-dots-per-inch (dpi) monitors. Bitstream, Inc. contributed its Charter font family in the same sizes, styles, and weights for both 75- and 100-dpi monitors. In Release 4, Bigelow and Holmes, Inc. and Sun Microsystems, Inc. contributed the Lucida font family and DEC contributed a new terminal emulator font.

In Release 3 and later, fonts are stored in three directories:

Directory	Contents
/usr/lib/X11/fonts/misc	Several fixed-width fonts, the cursor font
/usr/lib/X11/fonts/75dpi	Fixed- and variable-width fonts, 75 dots per inch
/usr/lib/X11/fonts/100dpi	Fixed- and variable-width fonts, 100 dots per inch

These three directories (in this order) comprise X's default font path. The font path can be changed with the `fp` option to the *xset* client, as described in Volume Three, *X Window System User's Guide*. (The font path, together with a great deal of other information about the server defaults, can be listed with *xset query*. All fonts in the font path can be listed with *xlsfonts*, and the characters in a font can be displayed on the screen with *xfd*.

An application can modify the font path using XSetFontPath. However, this should be done carefully to make sure the existing font directories are still searched.

The name of each font file in the font directories has a filename extension of *.snf*, which stands for *server natural format*. Fonts are distributed in *binary distribution format* (*bdf*) and need to be compiled (with a special font compiler) for a given server.

A.1.1 Font Naming Conventions

Font names are not determined by the names of the files in which they are stored. Instead a font's name is determined by the contents of the font property named FONT*. A font can be referred to by this name or by any of the aliases specified in an alias file in the directory containing the font file.

If you run *xlsfonts*, you will get an intimidating list of names similar to the one shown in Figure A-1 which, upon closer examination, contains a great deal of useful information:

Figure A-1. A fully specified font name

This rather verbose line is actually the name of the font stored in the file *courBO10* (in the *75dpi* directory). This font name specifies the foundry (Adobe), font family (Courier), weight (bold) slant (Oblique), set width (normal), size of the font in pixels (10), size of the font in tenths of a point (100, measured in tenths of a point, thus equals 10 points), horizontal resolution (75 dpi), vertical resolution (75 dpi), spacing (m, for monospace), average width in tenths of a pixel (60, measured in tenths of a pixel, thus equals 6 pixels) and character set (iso8859-1).

The meaning of many of these statistics is obvious. Some of the less obvious information is explained below:

foundry   The type foundry (in this case, Adobe) that digitized and supplied the font.

set width   A value describing a font's proportionate width, according to the foundry. Typical set widths include: normal, condensed, narrow, double width. All of the new Release 3 fonts have the set width *normal*.

pixels and points	Type is normally measured in points, a printer's unit equal to 1/72 of an inch. The size of a font in pixels depends on the resolution of the display font in pixels. For example, if the display font has 100-dpi resolution, a 12-point font will have a pixel size of 17, while with 75-dpi resolution, a 12-point font will have a pixel size of 12.
spacing	Either m (monospace, i.e., fixed-width) or p (proportional, i.e., variable-width).

horizontal and vertical resolution

The resolution in dots per inch for which a font is designed. Horizontal and vertical figures are required because a screen may have different capacities for horizontal and vertical resolution.

average width	Mean width of all characters in the font, measured in tenths of a pixel; in this case, 6 pixels.
character set	ISO, the International Standards Organization, has defined character set standards for various languages. The iso8859-1 in Figure A-1 represents the ISO Latin-1 character set, which is used by all of the Release 3 fonts in the *75dpi* and *100dpi* directories. The ISO Latin-1 character set is a superset of the standard ASCII character set, which includes various special characters used in European languages other than English. See Appendix H, *Keysym Reference*, of Volume Two, *Xlib Reference Manual*, for a complete listing and example glyphs of the characters in the ISO Latin-1 character set.

This font naming convention is intended to allow for the unique naming of fonts of any style, resolution, and size. It is powerful but unwieldy.

To display text using the font stored in the file *courBO10*, you could use the resource setting:

```
.yourapp*font:  -adobe-courier-bold-o-normal--10-100-75-75-m-60-iso8859-1
```

Since typing a font name of this length is neither desirable nor practical, the X Window System developers have provided two alternatives: wildcarding and aliasing.

A.1.2 Font Name Wildcarding

Any unnecessary part of a font name can be "wildcarded" by specifying ? for any single character and * for any group of characters.

For example, using a wildcarded font name, the resource specification above could be written:

```
*label:  *courier-bold-o-*-100*
```

(Note that when using wildcards with the −fn command line option, you must take care to quote the font names, since the UNIX shell has special meanings for the wildcard characters * and ?. This can be done by enclosing the entire font name in quotes or by escaping each wildcard character by typing a backslash before it.)

If more than one font in a given directory matches a wildcarded font name, the server chooses the font to use. If fonts from *more than one directory* match the wildcarded name, the server will always choose a font from the directory that is earlier in the font path. Thus, if a wildcarded font name matches a font from both the *75dpi* and the *100dpi* directories and the *75dpi* directory comes first in the font path, the server chooses the font from that directory.

In creating a wildcarded font name, you need to decide which parts of the standard font name must be explicit and which parts can be replaced with wildcards. As the previous example illustrates, you can use a single wildcard character for multiple parts of the font name. For instance, the final asterisk in the example stands for the sequence:

```
-75-75-m-60-iso8859-1
```

in the explicit font name. The idea is to specify enough parts of the font name explicitly so that the server gives you the font you have in mind.

It is helpful to familiarize yourself with the available font families, weights, slants, and point sizes. The following list gives these statistics for the fonts in the directories *75dpi* and *100dpi* in the standard X distribution from MIT.* (The fonts in the *misc* directory are holdovers from Release 2 and have short, manageable names that should not require wildcarding.)

Font families	Charter, Courier, Helvetica, New Century Schoolbook, Symbol, Times
Weights	Medium, bold
Slants	Roman (r), an upright design Italic (i), an italic design, slanted clockwise from vertical Oblique (o), an obliqued upright design, slanted clockwise from vertical
Point sizes	8, 10, 12, 14, 18, 24

If you are unfamiliar with general appearance of a particular font family, try displaying one of the fonts with *xfd*, as described in Volume Three, *X Window System User's Guide*.

As a general rule, we suggest you type the following parts of a font name explicitly:

- Font family
- Weight
- Slant
- Point size

Note that it is better to match the point size field, which is measured in tenths of a point (the 100 in the previous example, equal to 10 points), than the pixel field (the 10). This allows your wildcarded font name to work properly with monitors of different resolutions. For example, say you use the following name to specify a 24-point (size), medium (weight), Italic (slant), Charter (family) font:

```
*charter-medium-i-*-240-*
```

---

*For fonts other than those shipped by MIT, other families, weights, slants, point sizes, etc. may apply.

This will match either of the following two font names (the first for 75-dpi monitors and the second for 100-dpi monitors):

```
-bitstream-charter-medium-i-normal--25-240-75-75-p-136-iso8859-1
-bitstream-charter-medium-i-normal--33-240-100-100-p-136-iso8859-1
```

depending on which directory comes first in your font path. Specifying font size explicitly in pixels (25 for the first or 33 for the second) rather than in points would limit you to matching only one of these fonts.

Given the complexity of font names and the rules of precedence used by the server, you should use wildcards carefully.

A.1.3 Font Name Aliasing

Another way to abbreviate font names is by aliasing—that is, by associating them with alternative names. You can create a file (or files) called *fonts.alias* in any directory in the font search path to set aliases for the fonts in that directory. The X server uses both *fonts.dir* files (see Section A.2.5) and *fonts.alias* files to locate fonts in the font path.

Be aware that when you create or edit a *fonts.alias* file, the server does not *automatically* recognize the aliases in question. You must make the server aware of newly created or edited alias files by resetting the font path with *xset* as described in Section A.2.4.

The *fonts.alias* file has a two-column format similar to the *fonts.dir* file: the first column contains aliases, the second contains the actual font names. If you want to specify an alias that contains spaces, enclose the alias in double quotes. If you want to include double quotes or other special characters as part of an alias, precede each special symbol with a backslash.

When you use an alias to specify a font in a command line, the server searches for the font associated with that alias in every directory in the font path. Therefore, a *fonts.alias* file in one directory can set aliases for fonts in other directories as well. You might choose to create a single aliases file in one directory of the font path to set aliases for the most commonly used fonts in all the directories. Example A-1 shows a sample *fonts.alias* file.

Example A-1. Sample fonts.alias file

```
xterm12   -adobe-courier-medium-r-normal--12-120-75-75-m-70-iso8859-1
xterm14   -adobe-courier-medium-r-normal--14-140-75-75-m-90-iso8859-1
xterm18   -adobe-courier-medium-r-normal--18-180-75-75-m-110-iso8859-1
```

As the names of the aliases suggest, this sample file contains aliases for three fonts (of different point sizes) that are easily readable in *xterm* windows.

You can also use wildcards within the font names in the right-hand column of an alias file. For instance, the alias file above might also be written:

```
    xterm12    *courier-medium-r-*-120*
    xterm14    *courier-medium-r-*-140*
    xterm18    *courier-medium-r-*-180*
```

Once the server is made aware of aliases, you can specify an alias in resource specifications or on the command line:

```
xterm.font: xterm12
```

or:

```
xterm -fn xterm12
```

If you are accustomed to the Release 2 font naming convention (each font name being equivalent to the name of the file in which it is stored, without the *.snf* extension), there is a way to emulate this convention in later releases using alias files. In each directory in the font path, create a *fonts.alias* file containing only the following line:

```
FILE_NAMES_ALIASES
```

Each filename (without the *.snf* extension) will then serve as an alias for the font the file contains. Note that an alias file containing this line applies only to the directory in which it is found. To make every font name equivalent to the name of the file in which it is stored, you need to create a *fonts.alias* file such as this in every font directory.

If you have specified FILE_NAMES_ALIASES in an alias file, you can choose the fonts in that directory by means of their filenames, as we did in the resource example at the end of Chapter 2, *X Concepts*.

A.1.4 Making the Server Aware of Aliases

After you create (or update) an alias file, the server does not automatically recognize the aliases in question. You must make the server aware of newly created or edited alias files by "rehashing" the font path with *xset*. Enter:

```
xset fp rehash
```

on the command line. The *xset* option fp (font path) with the rehash argument causes the server to reread the *fonts.dir* and *fonts.alias* files in the current font path. You need to do this every time you edit an alias file. (You also need to use *xset* if you add or remove fonts. See Volume Three, *X Window System User's Guide*, for details.)

A.1.5 The fonts.dir Files

In addition to font files, each font directory contains a file called *fonts.dir*. The *fonts.dir* files serve, in effect, as databases for the X server. When the X server searches the directories in the default font path, it uses the *fonts.dir* files to locate the font(s) it needs.

Each *fonts.dir* file contains a list of all the font files in the directory with their associated font names in two-column form. (The first column lists the font file and the second column lists the actual font name associated with the file.) The first line in *fonts.dir* lists the number of entries in the file (i.e., the number of fonts in the directory).

Example A-2 shows the *fonts.dir* file from the directory */usr/lib/X11/fonts/100dpi*. As the first line indicates, the directory contains 24 fonts.

Example A-2.   fonts.dir file in /usr/lib/X11/fonts/100dpi

```
24
charBI08.snf    -bitstream-charter-bold-i-normal--11-80-100-100-p-68-iso8859-1
charBI10.snf    -bitstream-charter-bold-i-normal--14-100-100-100-p-86-iso8859-1
charBI12.snf    -bitstream-charter-bold-i-normal--17-120-100-100-p-105-iso8859-1
charBI14.snf    -bitstream-charter-bold-i-normal--19-140-100-100-p-117-iso8859-1
charBI18.snf    -bitstream-charter-bold-i-normal--25-180-100-100-p-154-iso8859-1
charBI24.snf    -bitstream-charter-bold-i-normal--33-240-100-100-p-203-iso8859-1
charB08.snf     -bitstream-charter-bold-r-normal--11-80-100-100-p-69-iso8859-1
charB10.snf     -bitstream-charter-bold-r-normal--14-100-100-100-p-88-iso8859-1
charB12.snf     -bitstream-charter-bold-r-normal--17-120-100-100-p-107-iso8859-1
charB14.snf     -bitstream-charter-bold-r-normal--19-140-100-100-p-119-iso8859-1
charB18.snf     -bitstream-charter-bold-r-normal--25-180-100-100-p-157-iso8859-1
charB24.snf     -bitstream-charter-bold-r-normal--33-240-100-100-p-206-iso8859-1
charI08.snf     -bitstream-charter-medium-i-normal--11-80-100-100-p-60-iso8859-1
charI10.snf     -bitstream-charter-medium-i-normal--14-100-100-100-p-76-iso8859-1
charI12.snf     -bitstream-charter-medium-i-normal--17-120-100-100-p-92-iso8859-1
charI14.snf     -bitstream-charter-medium-i-normal--19-140-100-100-p-103-iso8859-1
charI18.snf     -bitstream-charter-medium-i-normal--25-180-100-100-p-136-iso8859-1
charI24.snf     -bitstream-charter-medium-i-normal--33-240-100-100-p-179-iso8859-1
charR08.snf     -bitstream-charter-medium-r-normal--11-80-100-100-p-61-iso8859-1
charR10.snf     -bitstream-charter-medium-r-normal--14-100-100-100-p-78-iso8859-1
charR12.snf     -bitstream-charter-medium-r-normal--17-120-100-100-p-95-iso8859-1
charR14.snf     -bitstream-charter-medium-r-normal--19-140-100-100-p-106-iso8859-1
charR18.snf     -bitstream-charter-medium-r-normal--25-180-100-100-p-139-iso8859-1
charR24.snf     -bitstream-charter-medium-r-normal--33-240-100-100-p-183-iso8859-1
```

The *fonts.dir* files are created by the *mkfontdir* client when X is installed. *mkfontdir* reads the font files in directories in the font path, extracts the font names, and creates a *fonts.dir* file in each directory. If *fonts.dir* files are present on your system, you probably will not have to deal with them or with *mkfontdir* at all. If the files are not present or if you have to load new fonts or remove existing ones, you will have to create files with *mkfontdir*. See Volume Three, *X Window System User's Guide*, for details.

B

X10 Compatibility

X11 includes a conversion library, so that X10.4 applications can be easily ported to X11, albeit with a loss of performance. In addition, there are a few X10 routines that provide functionality missing in X11, which may still be used. This appendix discusses XDraw and related commands and association table routines for data management.

In This Chapter:

X10 Compatibility

These functions are provided for compatibility with X Version 10. They are considered a part of Xlib even though they exist in a separate library. They can be used by including the file *<X11/X10.h>* and linking with the *-loldX* library.

X Version 11 XDraw now provides all the functionality of the X Version 10 routines XDraw, XDrawDashed, and XDrawPatterned. X Version 11 XDrawFilled now provides the functionality of the old XDrawFilled and XDrawTiled. These routines now use the GC to specify the fill, tile or stipple, line styles, etc.

The association table routines are described next in this appendix. They are also carried over from X10, although their functionality is also provided by the context manager routines described in Chapter 13, *Other Programming Techniques*. However, there are no performance penalties for using association tables if you prefer them.

See Volume Two, *Xlib Reference Manual*, for complete information on using any X10 compatibility function.

B.1 XDraw and XDrawFilled

XDraw and XDrawFilled call other Xlib routines, not the server directly. If you just have straight lines to draw, using XDrawLines or XDrawSegments is much faster. If you want to draw spline curves in a portable fashion, you currently have no choice but to use XDraw until a standard spline extension is adopted.

XDraw draws an arbitrary polygon or curve. The figure drawn is defined by a list of vertices (*vlist*). The points are connected by lines as specified in the flags in the vertex structure. In X Version 11, XDraw provides all the functionality of the X Version 10 routines XDraw, XDrawDashed, and XDrawPatterned. XDrawFilled now provides the functionality of the old XDrawFilled and XDrawTiled. The fill, pattern, line_style, and tile are all controlled by the graphics context. Lines are properly joined according to the GC if they connect and make a closed figure.

The error status returned is the opposite of what it was under X Version 10, conforming to the X Version 11 standard that 0 indicates failure. The `VertexDrawLastPoint` flag and the routines `XAppendVertex` and `XClearVertexFlag` from X Version 10 are not supported.

The *vlist* and *vcount* arguments of `XDraw` and `XDrawFilled` control the line or area that is drawn:

vlist   Specifies a pointer to the list of vertices which indicate what to draw.

vcount   Specifies how many vertices are in *vlist*.

Each `Vertex`, as defined in *<X11/Xlib.h>*, is a structure with the following members:

Example B-1. The Vertex structure for XDraw

```
typedef struct _Vertex {
    short x,y;
    unsigned short flags;
} Vertex;
```

The `x` and `y` members are the coordinates of the vertex. These coordinates are interpreted according to the flags.

The `flags` member, as defined in `Xlib.h`, is a mask made by ORing the symbols listed in Table B-1.

Table B-1. Vertex Flags

Flag	Bit	If Not Set
VertexRelative	0	Absolute
VertexDontDraw	1	Draw
VertexCurved	2	Straight
VertexStartClosed	3	Not closed
VertexEndClosed	4	Not closed

`XDraw` fails (returns 0) only if it runs out of memory or is passed a `Vertex` list which has a vertex with `VertexStartClosed` set not followed by a vertex with `VertexEndClosed` set. The `x` and `y` coordinates in `Vertex` are relative to the upper-left inside corner of the drawable if `VertexRelative` is not specified in `flags` or to the previous vertex if `VertexRelative` is specified. The first vertex must be an absolute vertex.

If `VertexDontDraw` is specified in `flags`, no line or curve is drawn from the previous vertex to this one. This is analogous to picking up the pen and moving it to another place before drawing another line.

If `VertexCurved` is specified in `flags`, a spline algorithm is used to draw a smooth curve from the previous vertex through the current one to the next vertex. Otherwise, a straight line is drawn from the previous vertex to the current one. You should set `VertexCurved` in `flags` only if a previous and next vertex are both defined, either explicitly or through the definition of a closed curve. If `VertexStartClosed` is specified, then this point marks the beginning of a closed curve. This vertex must be followed later in the array by another vertex whose absolute coordinates are identical and which has VertexEnd-Closed specified in its flags.

It is permissible for both the VertexDontDraw and the VertexCurved bits to be 1. This is useful to define the previous point for the smooth curve, without drawing until the current point.

Example B-2 shows a routine that draws a box on the root window for use by the window manager described in Chapter 14, *Window Management*. Of course, you would want to create the GC in the calling routine if draw_box were to be called more than once.

Example B-2. draw_box implemented with X Version 10 XDraw

```
draw_box(display, screen_num, left,top,right,bottom)
Display *display;
int screen_num;
int left,top,right,bottom;
    {
    Vertex corner[5];
    int vertexcount = 5;
    int planes = FIRST_PLANE;
    GC gc;

    /* Create graphics context */
    /* Ignore XGCvalues and use defaults */
    gc = XCreateGC(display, RootWindow(display, screen_num), 0,
            NULL);

    /* Set graphics context to include font */
    XSetFunction(display, gc, GXxor);

    XSetForeground(display, gc, BlackPixel(display,screen_num));

    XSetPlaneMask(display, gc, planes);

    corner[0].x = left;
    corner[0].y = top;
    corner[0].flags = 0;

    corner[1].x = left;
    corner[1].y = bottom;
    corner[1].flags = 0;

    corner[2].x = right;
    corner[2].y = bottom;
    corner[2].flags = 0;

    corner[3].x = right;
    corner[3].y = top;
    corner[3].flags = 0;

    corner[4].x = left;
    corner[4].y = top;
    corner[4].flags = 0;

    XDraw(display, RootWindow(display, screen_num), gc, corner,
            vertexcount);
    XFlush();
    }
```

B.2 Association Tables

Association tables provide a fast lookup table for data that must be searched frequently. They are implemented as a linked list of structures. To use these functions, you must link in *-loldX*, the X10 compatibility library.

Association tables associate arbitrary information with resource IDs. This is similar to the context manager, but the resource IDs used with association tables are existing resources, not created for the purpose of storing data for later retrieval.

An XAssocTable can be used to type X resources. For example, the user may wish to have three or four "types" of windows, each with different properties. This can be accomplished by associating each X window ID with a pointer to a window property data structure defined by the programmer. The generic type for resource IDs is XID.

There are a few guidelines that should be observed when using an XAssocTable:

- All XIDs are relative to the currently active display. Therefore, if you are using multiple displays, you need to be sure the correct display is active before performing an XAssocTable operation. XAssocTable imposes no restrictions on the number of XIDs per table, the number of XIDs per display, or the number of displays per table.

- Because of the hashing scheme used by the association mechanism, the following rules for determining the size of XAssocTables should be followed. Associations will be made and looked up more efficiently if the table size (number of buckets in the hashing system) is a power of two and if there are not more than eight XIDs per bucket.

XCreateAssocTable creates an association table. To create an entry in a specific XAssocTable, use XMakeAssoc. Some size suggestions might be: use 32 buckets per 100 objects; a reasonable maximum number of objects per buckets is 8. XMakeAssoc inserts data into an XAssocTable keyed on an XID. XDeleteAssoc deletes an association in an XAssocTable keyed on its XID. Data is inserted into the table only once. Redundant inserts are meaningless and cause no problems. The queue in each association bucket is sorted from the lowest XID to the highest XID. Redundant deletes (and deletes of nonexistent XIDs) are meaningless and cause no problems. Deleting associations in no way impairs the performance of an XAssocTable.

XLookUpAssoc retrieves the data stored in an XAssocTable by its XID. If an appropriately matching XID can be found in the table, the routine will return the data associated with it. If the XID cannot be found in the table, the routine will return NULL.

XDestroyAssocTable frees the memory associated with a specific XAssocTable. Using an XAssocTable after it has been destroyed is guaranteed to have unpredictable and probably disastrous consequences!

C

Writing Extensions to X

Extensibility is an important part of X. Hooks are provided into Xlib and the protocol so that extensions will have the same performance as the core routines. This appendix provides reference information on how to write extensions and integrate them into Xlib. This appendix is not a tutorial, and you will need to look at existing extensions to figure out how to write one yourself.

In This Chapter:

C
Writing Extensions to X*

Extensions can be added to Xlib only with no protocol addition or to both Xlib and the server with a protocol addition. Several extensions are already available that support nonrectangular windows, 3-D graphics, and alternate input devices and multibuffering. See the code for these for examples of writing extensions.

Because X can only evolve by extension to the core protocol, it is important that extensions not be perceivable as second-class citizens. At some point, some extensions may be adopted as parts of the "X Standard."

Therefore, there should be little to distinguish the use of an extension from that of the core protocol. To avoid having to initialize extensions explicitly in application programs, extensions should perform "lazy evaluations" and automatically initialize themselves when called for the first time.

Extensions written according to these instructions will run at essentially the same performance as the core protocol requests.

It is expected that a given extension to X will consist of multiple requests. Defining ten new features as ten separate extensions is a bad practice. Rather, they should be packaged into a single extension and should use minor opcodes to distinguish the requests.

*This appendix is lightly edited and reformatted from the original MIT material. Before attempting to write extensions, you should be intimately familiar with the *X Window System Protocol, Version 11*, by Robert Scheifler and Ron Newman, and with the server code.

Unfortunately, this appendix does not currently provide sufficient tutorial or contextual information to allow you to build an extension. We intend to provide a more helpful description of how to write extensions in a forthcoming book about the server. In the meantime, several sample extensions are provided with the X core distribution which can be used as examples.

Extensions

C.1 Basic Protocol Support Routines

The basic protocol requests for extensions are XQueryExtension and XList-Extensions. XQueryExtension has the following format:

```
Bool XQueryExtension(display, name, major_opcode,
        first_event, first_error)
    Display *display;
    char *name;
    int *major_opcode;      /* RETURN */
    int *first_event;       /* RETURN */
    int *first_error;       /* RETURN */
```

XQueryExtension determines if the named extension is present. If so, the major opcode for the extension is returned (if it has one). Otherwise, False is returned. Any minor opcode and the request formats are specific to the extension. If the extension involves additional event types, the base support type code is returned. Otherwise, False is returned. The format of the events is specific to the extension. If the extension involves additional error codes, the base error code is returned. Otherwise, False is returned. The format of additional data in the errors is specific to the extension.

The extension name should be in ISO Latin-1 encoding. Upper- and lower-case are distinguished.

XListExtensions returns a list of all extensions supported by the server. It has the following format:

```
char **XListExtensions(display, nextensions)
    Display *display;
    int *nextensions;
```

XFreeExtensionList frees the memory allocated by XListExtensions. It has the following format:

```
XFreeExtensionList(list)
    char **list;
```

C.2 Hooking into Xlib

The functions described in this section allow one to hook into the library. They are not normally used by application programmers but are used by people who need to extend the core X protocol and the X library interface. The functions which generate protocol requests for X are typically called "stubs."

In extensions, stubs first should check to see if they have initialized themselves on a connection. If they have not, they then should call XInitExtension to attempt to initialize themselves on the connection.

If the extension needs to be informed of GC/font allocation or deallocation or if the extension defines new event types, there are several functions that allow an extension to be called when these events occur.

C.2.1 Initializing the Extension

In *<X11/Xlib.h>*, the following structure is defined to return the information from XInit-Extension:

Example C-1. The XExtCodes structure

```
typedef struct _XExtCodes { /* Public to extension, cannot be
                            * changed */
    int extension;          /* Extension number */
    int major_opcode;       /* Major opcode assigned by server */
    int first_event;        /* First event number for the extension */
    int first_error;        /* First error number for the extension */
} XExtCodes;
```

XInitExtension has the following format:

```
XExtCodes *XInitExtension(display, name)
    Display *display;
    char *name;
```

XInitExtension first determines if the extension exists. Then it allocates storage for maintaining the information about the extension on the connection, chains this onto the extension list for the connection, and returns the information the stub implementor will need to access the extension. If the extension does not exist, XInitExtension returns NULL.

In particular, the extension number in the XExtCodes structure is needed in other calls below. This extension number is unique only to a single connection.

Extensions to Xlib that do not require server extensions are permitted. To support this, XAddExtension is provided.

```
XExtCodes *XAddExtension(display)
    Display *display;
```

For local Xlib extensions, XAddExtension allocates the XExtCodes structure, bumps the extension number count, and chains the extension onto the extension list.

C.2.2 Hooks into the Library

The functions described in the following sections allow you to define procedures that are to be called when various circumstances occur. The procedures include creating a new GC for a connection, copying a GC, freeing a GC, creating and freeing fonts, converting events defined by extensions to and from wire format, and error handling.

All of these functions return the previous routine defined for this extension.

C.2.2.1 XESetCloseDisplay

You use this procedure to define a procedure to be called whenever XCloseDisplay is
called. This procedure returns any previously defined procedure, usually NULL. XESet-
CloseDisplay has the following format:

```
int (*XESetCloseDisplay(display, extension, proc))()
     Display *display; /* Display */
     int extension;    /* Extension number */
     int (*proc)();    /* Routine to call when display closed */
```

When XCloseDisplay is called, your routine is called with these arguments:

```
(*proc)(display, codes)
     Display *display;
     XExtCodes *codes;
```

C.2.2.2 XESetCreateGC

You use this procedure to define a procedure to be called whenever a new GC is created.
This procedure returns any previously defined procedure, usually NULL. XESetCreateGC
has the following format:

```
int (*XESetCreateGC(display, extension, proc))()
     Display *display; /* Display */
     int extension;    /* Extension number */
     int (*proc)();    /* Routine to call when GC created */
```

When a GC is created, your routine is called with these arguments:

```
(*proc)(display, gc, codes)
     Display *display;
     GC gc;
     XExtCodes *codes;
```

C.2.2.3 XESetCopyGC

You use this procedure to define a procedure to be called whenever a GC is copied. This
procedure returns any previously defined procedure, usually NULL. XESetCopyGC has the
following format:

```
int (*XESetCopyGC(display, extension, proc))()
     Display *display; /* Display */
     int extension;    /* Extension number */
     int (*proc)();    /* Routine to call when GC copied */
```

When a GC is copied, your routine is called with these arguments:

```
(*proc)(display, gc, codes)
     Display *display;
     GC gc;
     XExtCodes *codes;
```

C.2.2.4 XESetFreeGC

You use this procedure to define a procedure to be called whenever a GC are freed. This procedure returns any previously defined procedure, usually NULL. XESetFreeGC has the following format:

```
int (*XESetFreeGC(display, extension, proc))()
      Display *display; /* Display */
      int extension;    /* Extension number */
      int (*proc)();    /* Routine to call when GC freed */
```

When a GC is freed, your routine is called with these arguments:

```
(*proc)(display, gc, codes)
      Display *display;
      GC gc;
      XExtCodes *codes;
```

C.2.2.5 XESetCreateFont

You use this procedure to define a procedure to be called whenever XLoadQueryFont and XQueryFont are called. This procedure returns any previously defined procedure, usually NULL. XESetCreateFont has the following format:

```
int (*XESetCreateFont(display, extension, proc))()
      Display *display; /* Display */
      int extension;    /* Extension number */
      int (*proc)();    /* Routine to call when font created */
```

When XLoadQueryFont or XQueryFont is called, your routine is called with these arguments:

```
(*proc)(display, fs, codes)
      Display *display;
      XFontStruct *fs;
      XExtCodes *codes;
```

C.2.2.6 XESetFreeFont

You use this procedure to define a procedure to be called whenever XFreeFont is called. This procedure returns any previously defined procedure, usually NULL. XESetFreeFont has the following format:

```
int (*XESetFreeFont(display, extension, proc))()
      Display *display; /* Display */
      int extension;    /* Extension number */
      int (*proc)();    /* Routine to call when font freed */
```

When XFreeFont is called, your routine is called with these arguments:

```
(*proc)(display, fs, codes)
      Display *display;
      XFontStruct *fs;
      XExtCodes *codes;
```

The next two functions allow you to define new events to the library.

C.2.2.7 XESetWireToEvent

There is an implementation limit such that your host event structure size cannot be bigger than the size of the XEvent union of structures. There is also no way to guarantee that more than 24 elements or 96 characters in the structure will be fully portable between machines.

You use XESetWireToEvent to define a procedure to be called when an event needs to be converted from wire format (xEvent) to host format (XEvent). XESetWireToEvent has the following format:

```
int (*XESetWireToEvent(display, event_number, proc))()
    Display *display; /* Display */
    int event_number; /* Event routine to replace */
    Status (*proc)(); /* Routine to call when converting
                       * event */
```

The event number defines which protocol event number to install a conversion routine for. This procedure returns any previously defined procedure.

You can replace a core event conversion routine with one of your own, though this is not encouraged. It would, however, allow you to intercept a core event and modify it before it was queued or otherwise examined.

When Xlib needs to convert an event from wire format to natural host format, your routine is called with these arguments:

```
(*proc)(display, re, event)
    Display *display;
    XEvent *re;
    xEvent *event;
```

Your routine must return status to indicate if the conversion succeeded. The re argument is a pointer to where the host format event should be stored, while the event argument is the 32-byte wire event structure. In the XEvent structure you are creating, you must fill in the five required members of the event structure. You should fill in the type member with the type specified for the xEvent structure. You should copy all other members from the xEvent structure (wire format) to the XEvent structure (host format). Your conversion routine should return True if the event should be queued or False if it should not be queued.

C.2.2.8 XESetEventToWire

You use XESetEventToWire to define a procedure to be called when an event needs to be converted from host format (XEvent) to wire format (xEvent) form. XESetEventToWire has the following format:

```
int (*XESetEventToWire(display, event_number, proc))()
    Display *display; /* Display */
    int event_number; /* Event routine to replace */
    int (*proc)();    /* Routine to call when converting
                       * event */
```

The event number defines which protocol event number to install a conversion routine for. This procedure returns any previously defined procedure. It returns zero if the conversion fails or nonzero otherwise.

You can replace a core event conversion routine with one of your own, though this is not encouraged. It would, however, allow you to intercept a core event and modify it before being sent to another client.

When Xlib needs to convert an event from wire format to natural host format, your routine is called with these arguments:

```
(*proc)(display, re, event)
    Display *display;
    XEvent *re;
    xEvent *event;
```

The `re` argument is a pointer to the host format event, while the `event` argument is a pointer to where the 32-byte wire event structure should be stored. In the `XEvent` structure you are forming, `type` must be the first member and `window` must be the second. You then should fill in `type` with the type from the `xEvent` structure. All other members then should be copied from the wire format to the `XEvent` structure.

C.2.2.9 XESetError

You use this procedure when you want to suppress the calling of the external error handling when an error occurs. This allows status to be returned on a call at the cost of the call being synchronous (though most such routines, like `XAllocColor`, are query operations in any case and are typically programmed to be synchronous). `XESetError` has the following format:

```
int (*XESetError(display, extension, proc))()
    Display *display;  /* Display */
    int extension;     /* Extension number */
    int (*proc)();     /* Routine to call when X error
                        * happens */
```

When Xlib detects a protocol error in `_XReply`, it will call your procedure with these arguments:

```
int (*proc)(display, err, codes, ret_code)
    Display *display;
    xError *err;
    XExtCodes *codes;
    int *ret_code;
```

The `err` argument is a pointer to the 32-byte wire format error. The `codes` argument is a pointer to the extension codes structure. The `ret_code` argument is the return code you may want `_XReply` returned to.

If your routine returns a zero value, the error is not suppressed, and the client's error handler is called. If your routine returns nonzero, the error is suppressed, and `_XReply` returns the value of `ret_code`.

C.2.2.10 XESetErrorString

The Xlib `XGetErrorText` function returns a string to the user for an error. This procedure allows you to define a routine to be called which should return a pointer to the error message. `XESetErrorString` has the following format:

```
char *(*XESetErrorString(display, extension, proc))()
    Display *display;  /* Display */
    int extension;     /* Extension number */
    char *(*proc)();   /* Routine to call to obtain an error
                        * string */
```

The following is an example.

```
char *(*proc)(display, code, codes, buffer, nbytes)
    Display *display;
    int code;
    XExtCodes *codes;
    char *buffer;
    int nbytes;
```

Your procedure is called with the error code detected. You should return a pointer to a null-terminated string containing the error message.

C.2.2.11 XESetFlushGC

The `XESetFlushGC` procedure is identical to `XSetCopyGC`, except that `XESetFlushGC` is called when a GC cache needs to be updated in the server. `XESetFlushGC` has the following format:

```
int (*XESetFlushGC(display, extension, proc))()
    Display *display;  /* Display */
    int extension;     /* Extension number */
    int *(*proc)();    /* Routine to call when GC flushed */
```

C.2.3 Hooks onto Xlib Data Structures

Various Xlib data structures have provisions for extension routines to chain extension-supplied data onto a list. These structures are: `Display`, `GC`, `Screen`, `ScreenFormat`, `Visual`, and `XFontStruct`. Because the list pointer is always the first member in the structure, a single set of routines can be used to manipulate the data on these lists.

The structure in Example C-2 is used in the routines in this section and is defined in *<X11/Xlib.h>*.

Example C-2. The XExtData structure

```
typedef struct _XExtData {
    int number;                /* Number returned by XInitExtension */
    struct _XExtData *next;    /* Next item on list of data for
                                * structure */
    int (*free)();             /* If defined, called to free private */
    char *private;             /* Data private to this extension */
} XExtData;
```

When any of the data structures (Display, GC, Screen, ScreenFormat, Visual, and XFontStruct) are freed, the list is walked, and the *free* routine (if any) is called. If *free* is NULL, then the library will free the data pointed to by *private* and the structure itself.

```
union {
    Display *display;
    GC gc;
    Visual *visual;
    Screen *screen_num;
    ScreenFormat *pixmap_format;
    XFontStruct *font
} XEDataObject;

XExtData **XEHeadOfExtensionList(object)
    XEDataObject object;
```

XEHeadOfExtensionList returns a pointer to the list of extension structures attached to the specified object. In concert with XAddToExtensionList, XEHead-OfExtensionList allows an extension to attach arbitrary data to any of the structures of types contained in XEDataObject.

C.2.3.1 XAddToExtensionList

XAddToExtensionList is used to add extension data onto an Xlib data structure. It has the following format:

```
XAddToExtensionList(structure, ext_data)
    struct _XExtData **structure;  /* Pointer to structure
                                    * to add */
    XExtData *ext_data;            /* Extension data structure
                                    * to add */
```

The *structure* argument is a pointer to one of the data structures listed above (Display, GC, Screen, ScreenFormat, Visual, and XFontStruct).

You must initialize ext_data->number with the extension number before calling this routine.

C.2.3.2 XFindOnExtensionList

XFindOnExtensionList returns the first extension data structure for the extension numbered *number*. It has the following format:

```
XExtData *XFindOnExtensionList(structure, number)
    struct _XExtData **structure;
    int number;   /* Extension number from XInitExtension */
```

It is expected that an extension will add at most one extension data structure to any single data structure's extension data list. There is no way to find additional structures.

C.2.3.3 Allocating a Resource ID

The XAllocID macro, which allocates and returns a resource ID, is defined in *<X11/Xlib.h>*.

```
XAllocID(display)
    Display *display;
```

This macro is a call through the Display structure to the internal resource ID allocator. It returns a resource ID that you can use when creating new resources.

C.3 GC Caching

GCs are cached by the library to allow merging of independent change requests to the same GC into single protocol requests. This is typically called a *write back* cache. Any extension routine whose behavior depends on the contents of a GC must flush the GC cache to make sure the server has up-to-date contents in its GC.

If you extend the GC to add additional resource ID components, you should ensure that the library stub immediately sends the change request. This is because a client can free a resource immediately after using it, so if you only stored the value in the cache without forcing a protocol request, the resource might be destroyed before being set into the GC. You can use the _XFlushGCCache procedure to force the cache to be flushed. The _XFlushGCCache procedure is defined as follows:

```
_XFlushGCCache (display, gc)
    Display *display;
    GC gc;
```

The FlushGC macro checks the dirty bits in the library's GC structure and calls _XFlushGCCache if any members have changed. The FlushGC macro is defined as follows:

```
FlushGC (display, gc)
    Display *display;
    GC gc;
```

C.4 Graphics Batching

If you extend X to add more poly graphics primitives, you may be able to take advantage of facilities in the library that allow back-to-back single calls to be transformed into poly requests. This may dramatically improve performance of programs that are not written using poly requests. In the Display structure is a pointer to an xReq called last_req which is the last request being processed. By checking that the last request type, drawable, GC, and other options are the same as the new one and that there is enough space left in the buffer, you may be able to just extend the previous graphics request by extending the length field of the request and appending the data to the buffer. This can improve naive programs five times or more. For example, here is the source for the XDrawPoint stub.

Example C-3. Example of graphics batching

```
#include "copyright.h"
#include "Xlibint.h"

/* Precompute the maximum size of batching request allowed */

static int size = sizeof(xPolyPointReq) + EPERBATCH * sizeof(xPoint);

XDrawPoint(display, d, gc, x, y)
    register Display *display;
    Drawable d;
    GC gc;
    int x, y;        /* INT16 */
{
    xPoint *point;
    LockDisplay(display);
    FlushGC(display, gc);
    {
    register xPolyPointReq *req = (xPolyPointReq *) display->last_req;
    /* If same as previous request, with same drawable,
     * batch requests */
    if (
            (req->reqType == X_PolyPoint)
        && (req->drawable == d)
        && (req->gc == gc->gid)
        && (req->coordMode == CoordModeOrigin)
        && ((display->bufptr + sizeof (xPoint)) <= display->bufmax)
        && (((char *)display->bufptr - (char *)req) < size) ) {
        point = (xPoint *) display->bufptr;
        req->length += sizeof (xPoint) >> 2;
        display->bufptr += sizeof (xPoint);
        }

    else {
        GetReqExtra(PolyPoint, 4, req);        /* 1 point = 4 bytes */
        req->drawable = d;
        req->gc = gc->gid;
        req->coordMode = CoordModeOrigin;
        point = (xPoint *) (req + 1);
        }
    point->x = x;
    point->y = y;
    }
    UnlockDisplay(display);
    SyncHandle();
}
```

To keep clients from generating very long requests that may monopolize the server, there is a symbol defined in *<X11/Xlibint.h>* called EPERBATCH that limits the number of requests batched. Most of the performance benefit occurs in the first few merged requests. Note that FlushGC is called *before* picking up the value of last_req, since it may modify this field.

C.5 Writing Extension Stubs

All X requests always contain the length of the request, expressed as a 16-bit count of 32-bit entities. This means that a single request can be no more than 256K bytes in length. Some servers may not support single requests of such a length. The value of:

```
XMaxRequestSize(display)
```

returns the maximum length as defined by the server implementation, in units of 4 bytes. For further information, see Volume Zero, *X Protocol Reference Manual*.

C.5.1 Requests, Replies, and Xproto.h

The following discussion may be easier to understand if you look at the *<X11/Xproto.h>* include file. The file contains three sets of definitions that are of interest to the stub implementor: request names, request structures, and reply structures.

You need to generate a file equivalent to *<X11/Xproto.h>* for your extension and need to include it in your stub routine. Each stub routine also must include *<X11/Xlibint.h>*.

The identifiers are deliberately chosen in such a way that, if the request is called X_Do-Something, then its request structure is xDoSomethingReq and its reply is xDo-SomethingReply. The GetReq family of macros, defined in *<X11/Xlibint.h>*, takes advantage of this naming scheme.

For each X request, there is a definition in *<X11/Xproto.h>* that looks similar to this:

```
#define X_DoSomething  42
```

In your extension header file, this is a minor opcode, instead of a major opcode.

C.5.2 Request Format

Every request contains an 8-bit major opcode and a 16-bit length field expressed in units of 4 bytes. Every request consists of 4 bytes of header (containing the major opcode, the length field, and a data byte) followed by zero or more additional bytes of data. The length field defines the total length of the request, including the header. The length field in a request must equal the minimum length required to contain the request. If the specified length is smaller or larger than the required length, the server should generate a BadLength error. Unused bytes in a request are not required to be zero.

Servers have a maximum request size, which varies according to the capabilities of the system. XMaxRequestSize returns the maximum request size (in 4-byte units) supported by the server. Single protocol requests to the server can be no longer than this size. Extensions should be designed in such a way that long protocol requests can be split up into smaller requests. The protocol guarantees the size to be no smaller than 4096 units (16384 bytes). Here is the declaration of XMaxRequestSize:

```
long XMaxRequestSize(display)
    Display *display;
```

Major opcodes 128 through 255 are reserved for extensions. Extensions are intended to contain multiple requests, so extension requests typically have an additional minor opcode encoded in the spare data byte in the request header, but the placement and interpretation of this minor opcode as well as all other fields in extension requests are not defined by the core protocol. Every request is implicitly assigned a sequence number (starting with one) used in replies, errors, and events.

To help but not cure portability problems to certain machines, the B16 and B32 macros have been defined so that they can become bitfield specifications on some machines. For example, on a Cray, these should be used for all 16-bit and 32-bit quantities, as discussed below.

Most protocol requests have a corresponding structure typedef in *<X11/Xproto.h>*, which looks like this:

```
typedef struct _DoSomethingReq {
    CARD8 reqType;      /* X_DoSomething */
    CARD8 someDatum;    /* Used differently in different
                         * requests */
    CARD16 length B16;  /* Total # of bytes in request,
                         * divided by 4 */

    . . .
    /* Request-specific data */
    . . .
} xDoSomethingReq;
```

If a core protocol request has a single 32-bit argument, you need not declare a request structure in your extension header file. Instead such requests use the xResourceReq structure from *<X11/Xproto.h>*. This structure is used for any request whose single argument is of type Atom, Colormap, Cursor, Device, Drawable, Font, GContext, Pixmap, VisualID, or Window.

```
typedef struct _ResourceReq {
    CARD8 reqType;      /* The request type, e.g., X_DoSomething */
    BYTE pad;           /* Not used */
    CARD16 length B16;  /* 2 (= total # of bytes in request,
                         *    divided by 4) */
    CARD32 id B32;      /* Window, Drawable, Font, GContext,
                         * etc. */
} xResourceReq;
```

If convenient, you can do something similar in your extension header file.

In both of these structures, the reqType field identifies the type of the request (for example, X_MapWindow or X_CreatePixmap). The length field tells how long, in units of 4-byte "longwords," the request is. This length includes both the request structure itself and any variable-length data, such as strings or lists, that follow the request structure. Request structures come in different sizes, but all requests are padded to be a multiple of 4 bytes long.

A few protocol requests take no arguments at all. Instead they use the xReq structure from *<X11/Xproto.h>*, which contains only a reqType and a length (and a pad byte).

If the protocol request requires a reply, then *<X11/Xproto.h>* also contains a reply structure `typedef`:

```
typedef struct _DoSomethingReply {
    BYTE type;                      /* Always X_Reply */
    BYTE someDatum;                 /* Used differently in
                                     * different requests */
    CARD16 sequenceNumber B16;      /* # of requests sent so far */
    CARD32 length B32;              /* # of additional bytes,
                                     * divided by 4 */
    ...
    /* Request-specific data */
    ...
} xDoSomethingReply;
```

Most of these reply structures are 32 bytes long. If there are not that many reply values, then they contain a sufficient number of `pad` fields to bring them up to 32 bytes. The length field is the total number of bytes in the request minus 32, divided by 4. This length is nonzero only if:

• The reply structure is followed by variable-length data such as a list or string.

• The reply structure is longer than 32 bytes.

Only `GetKeyboardControl`, `GetWindowAttributes`, `QueryFont`, and `QueryKeymap` have reply structures longer than 32 bytes in the core protocol.

A few protocol requests return replies that contain no data. *<X11/Xproto.h>* does not define reply structures for these. Instead they use the `xGenericReply` structure, which contains only a type, length, and sequence number (and sufficient padding to make it 32 bytes long).

C.5.3 Starting to Write a Stub Routine

An Xlib stub routine should always start like this:

```
#include "Xlibint.h"

XDoSomething (arguments,... )
/* Argument declarations */
{
/* Variable declarations, if any */
... }
```

If the protocol request has a reply, then the variable declarations should include the reply structure for the request. The following is an example.

```
xDoSomethingReply rep;
```

C.5.4 Locking Data Structures

In order to lock the display structure, for systems that want to support multithreaded access to a single display connection, each stub will need to lock its critical section. Generally, this section is the point from just before the appropriate GetReq call documented below until all arguments to the call have been stored into the request. The precise instructions needed for this locking depend upon the machine architecture. Two calls, which are generally implemented as macros, have been provided.

```
LockDisplay(display)
      Display *display;

UnlockDisplay(display)
      Display *display;
```

C.5.5 Sending the Protocol Request and Arguments

After the variable declarations, a stub routine should call one of four macros defined in *<X11/Xlibint.h>*: GetEmptyReq, GetResReq, GetReq, or GetReqExtra. All of these macros take as their first argument the name of the protocol request as declared in *<X11/Xproto.h>*, except with the initial X_ removed. Each one declares a Display structure pointer (called display) and a pointer to a request structure (called req) which is of the appropriate type. The macro then appends the request structure to the request buffer, fills in its type and length field, and sets req to point to it.

If the protocol request has no arguments (for instance, X_GrabServer), then use Get-EmptyReq:

```
GetEmptyReq (DoSomething, req);
```

If the protocol request has a single 32-bit argument (such as Atom, Drawable, Pixmap, Window, and so on), then use GetResReq. The second argument to the macro is the 32-bit object. X_MapWindow is a good example.

```
GetResReq (DoSomething, rid, req);
```

The *rid* argument is the pixmap ID, window ID, or other resource ID.

If the protocol request takes any other argument list, then call GetReq. After the GetReq call, you need to set all the other fields in the request structure, usually from arguments to the stub routine.

```
GetReq (DoSomething, req);
/* Fill in arguments here */
req->arg1 = arg1;
req->arg2 = arg2;
...
```

A few stub routines (such as, XCreateGC and XCreatePixmap) return a resource ID to the caller but pass a resource ID as an argument to the protocol request. Such routines use the macro XAllocID to allocate a resource ID from the range of IDs that were assigned to this client when it opened the connection.

```
rid = req->rid = XAllocID();
...
return (rid);
```

Finally, some stub routines transmit a fixed amount of variable-length data after the request. Typically, these routines (such as XMoveWindow and XSetBackground) are special cases of more general functions like XMoveResizeWindow and XChangeGC. These special case routines use GetReqExtra, which is the same as GetReq, except that it takes an additional argument (the number of extra bytes to allocate in the request buffer after the request structure). This number should always be a multiple of four.

C.5.6 Variable-length Arguments

Some protocol requests take additional variable-length data that follow the xDo-SomethingReq structure. The format of this data varies from request to request. Some requests require a sequence of 8-bit bytes, others a sequence of 16- or 32-bit entities, and still others a sequence of structures.

It is necessary to add the length of any variable-length data to the length field of the request structure. That length field is in units of 32-bit longwords. If the data is a string or other sequence of 8-bit bytes, then you must round the length up and shift it before adding:

```
req->length += (nbytes+3)>>2;
```

To transmit the variable-length data, use the Data macro. If the data fits into the request buffer, then this macro copies it to the buffer. If it does not fit, however, the Data macro calls _XSend, which transmits first the contents of the buffer and then your data. The Data macro takes three arguments: the Display, a pointer to the beginning of the data, and the number of bytes to be sent.

```
Data(display, (char *) data, nbytes);
Data16(display, (short *) data, nbytes);
Data32(display, (long *) data, nbytes);
```

Data, Data16, and Data32 are macros that may use their last argument more than once, so that argument should be a variable rather than an expression such as (nitems * sizeof(item)). You should do that kind of computation in a separate statement before calling them. Use the appropriate macro when sending char, short, or long data.

If the protocol request requires a reply, then call the procedure _XSend instead of the Data macro. _XSend takes the same arguments, but because it sends your data immediately instead of copying it into the request buffer (which would later be flushed anyway by the following call on _XReply), it is faster.

C.5.7 Replies

If the protocol request has a reply, then call _XReply after you have finished dealing with all the fixed and variable-length arguments. _XReply flushes the request buffer and waits for an xReply packet to arrive. If any events arrive in the meantime, _XReply queues them for later use. _XReply has the following format:

```
Status _XReply(display, rep, extra, discard)
    Display *display;
    xReply *rep;
    int extra;    /* Number of 32-bit words expected after
                   * the reply */
    Bool discard; /* Should I discard data following "extra"
                   * words */
```

_XReply waits for a reply packet and copy its contents into the specified rep structure. _XReply handles error and event packets that occur before the reply is received. _XReply takes four arguments:

1. A pointer to a Display structure.

2. A pointer to a reply structure (which must be cast to a pointer to an xReply).

3. The number of additional bytes (beyond sizeof(xReply) = 32 bytes) in the reply structure.

4. A Boolean that tells _XReply to discard any additional bytes beyond those it was told to read.

Because most reply structures are 32 bytes long, the third argument is normally zero. The only core protocol exceptions are the replies to X_GetKeyboardControl, X_Get-WindowAttributes, X_QueryFont, and X_QueryKeymap, which have longer replies.

The last argument should be xFalse if the reply structure is followed by additional variable-length data (such as a list or string). It should be True if there is no variable-length data. This last argument is provided for upward compatibility reasons—to allow a client to communicate properly with a hypothetical later version of the server which sends more data than the client expected. For example, some later version of XGetWindowAttributes might use a larger, but compatible, xGetWindowAttributesReply which contains additional attribute data at the end.

_XReply returns True if it received a reply successfully or False if it received an XError or some other error condition.

For a request with a reply that is not followed by variable-length data, you write something like this:

```
    _XReply (display, (xReply *)&rep, 0, True);
    *ret1 = rep.ret1;
    *ret2 = rep.ret2;
    *ret3 = rep.ret3;
    ...
    UnlockDisplay(display);
    SyncHandle();
    return (rep.ret4);
    }
```

If there is variable-length data after the reply, change the `True` to `False` and use `_XRead` to read the variable-length data.

```
    _XRead(display, data, nbytes)
        Display *display;
        char *data;
        long nbytes;
```

`_XRead` reads the specified number of bytes into data.

```
    _XRead16(display, data, nbytes)
        Display *display;
        short *data;
        long nbytes;
```

`_XRead16` reads the specified number of bytes, unpacking them as 16-bit quantities into the specified array as shorts.

```
    _XRead32(display, data, nbytes)
        Display *display;
        long *data;
        long nbytes;
```

`_XRead32` reads the specified number of bytes, unpacking them as 32-bit quantities into the specified array as longs.

```
    _XRead16Pad(display, data, nbytes)
        Display *display;
        short *data;
        long nbytes;
```

`_XRead16Pad` reads the specified number of bytes, unpacking them as 16-bit quantities into the specified array as shorts. If the number of bytes is not a multiple of four, `_XRead16Pad` reads up to three additional pad bytes.

```
    _XReadPad(display, data, nbytes)
        Display *display;
        char *data;
        long nbytes;
```

`_XReadPad` reads the specified number of bytes into data. If the number of bytes is not a multiple of four, `_XReadPad` reads up to three additional pad bytes.

Each protocol request is a little different. For further information, see the Xlib sources for examples.

C.5.8 Synchronous Calling

To ease debugging, just before returning to the user, each routine should have a call to a routine called `SyncHandle`. This routine generally is implemented as a macro. If synchronous mode is enabled (see the `XSynchronize` reference page in Volume Two, *Xlib Reference Manual*), the request is sent immediately. The library, however, waits until any error the routine could generate at the server has been handled.

C.5.9 Allocating and Deallocating Memory

To support the possible reentrancy of these routines, you must observe several conventions when allocating and deallocating memory. This is most often done when returning data to the user from the window system of a size the caller could not know in advance (for example, a list of fonts or a list of extensions). The standard C library routines on many systems are not protected against signals or other multithreaded use. The following analogies to standard I/O library routines have been defined:

`Xmalloc()`	replaces	`malloc()`
`Xfree()`	replaces	`free()`
`Xcalloc()`	replaces	`calloc()`

These should be used in place of any calls you would make to the normal C library routines.

If you need scratch space inside a critical section (for example, to pack and unpack data to and from wire protocol), the general memory allocators may be too expensive for use (particularly in output routines, which are performance critical). The routine below returns a scratch buffer for your use:

```
char *_XAllocScratch(display, nbytes)
    Display *display;
    unsigned long nbytes;
```

This storage must only be used inside of the critical section of your stub.

C.5.10 Portability Considerations

Many machine architectures, including many of the more recent RISC architectures, will not correctly access data at unaligned locations; their compilers will pad out structures to preserve this characteristic. Many other machines capable of unaligned references pad inside of structures as well to preserve alignment, since accessing aligned data is usually much faster. Since the library and the server use structures to access data at arbitrary points in a byte stream, all data in request and reply packets *must* be naturally aligned. That is, 16-bit data must start on 16-bit boundaries in the request, and 32-bit data must start on 32-bit boundaries. All requests *must* be a multiple of 32 bits in length, to preserve the natural alignment in the data stream. Pad structures out to 32-bit boundaries. Pad information does not have to be zeroed, unless you wish to preserve such fields for future use in your protocol requests. Floating point varies radically between machines and should be avoided completely if at all possible.

This code may run on machines with 16-bit `int`s. So, if any integer argument, variable, or return value either can take only nonnegative values or is declared as a CARD16 in the protocol, be sure to declare it as `unsigned int` and not as `int`. (This, of course, does not apply to Booleans or enumerations.)

Similarly, if any integer argument or return value is declared CARD32 in the protocol, declare it as an `unsigned long` and not as `int` or `long`. This also goes for any internal variables that may take on values larger than the maximum 16-bit unsigned `int`.

The library currently assumes that a `char` is 8 bits, a `short` is 16 bits, an `int` is 16 or 32 bits, and a `long` is 32 bits. The `PackData` macro is a half-hearted attempt to deal with the possibility of 32-bit `short`s. However, much more work is needed to make this really work properly.

C.5.11 Deriving the Correct Extension Opcode

The remaining problem a writer of an extension stub routine faces that the core protocol does not face is to map from the call to the proper major and minor opcodes. While there are a number of strategies, the simplest and fastest is outlined below.

1. Declare an array of pointers, `_NFILE` long, of type `XExtCodes*`. (`_NFILE` is defined in <*stdio.h*> and is the number of file descriptors supported on the system.) Make sure these are all initialized to `NULL`.

2. When your stub is entered, your initialization test is just to use the display pointer passed in to access the file descriptor and an index into the array. If the entry is `NULL`, then this is the first time you are entering the routine for this display. Call your initialization routine, and pass it the display pointer.

3. Enter your initialization routine, call `XInitExtension`, and, if it succeeds, store the pointer returned into this array. Make sure to establish a close display handler to allow you to zero the entry. Do whatever other initialization your extension requires (for example, install event handlers, and so on). Your initialization routine would normally return a pointer to the `XExtCodes` structure for this extension, which is what would normally be found in your array of pointers.

4. After returning from your initialization routine, the stub can now continue normally, because it has its major opcode safely in hand in the `XExtCodes` structure.

D

The basecalc Application

This appendix lists the complete source code for the basecalc application described in Chapter 12. Source code for all examples in this book is available as described in the *Preface*.

D
The basecalc Application

The X Programmer's Calculator (*basecalc*) was described in Chapter 12, *A Complete Application*.

This appendix presents the complete code for *basecalc*, including the following files and routines that were not shown in Chapter 12.

basecalc.h   Include file for this application.

convButton   Changes the current base and converts a value, if any.

digitButton   Gets a digit and assigns it to the variable `Value`.

displayVal   Calculates appropriate format string for base.

initTty   Performs system calls to get user's current erase, delete, and interrupt characters.

keyToWin   Translates a keycode as if a `pad` had been selected.

makePixmap   Makes a pixmap from bitmap data, shown and described in Chapter 6, *Drawing Graphics and Text*.

operButton   An operation, either does it or waits for next value and =.

printInBase   Composes the string that should be displayed. Called from `Sprintf`.

specButton   Clears a digit, an entry, or all, or toggles unsigned mode.

Sprintf   A modified version of the standard C utility `sprintf`, which does not print in binary. `Sprintf` calls `printInBase`.

winPressed   Determines whether `pad` pressed was a digit, an operator, a conversion, or a special `pad`.

Example D-1 shows the *basecalc.h* include file. This include file sets up the structures and global variables used in the calculator application.

Example D-1. The complete basecalc.h file

```
/* Window flags */
#define WTYP_OPER    0x01      /* Operator, +, -, =, etc */
#define WTYP_DIG     0x02      /* Digit 0-9, A-F */
#define WTYP_DISP    0x04      /* Display Window */
#define WTYP_CONV    0x08      /* Converter -- hex, oct, dec, bin */
#define WTYP_SPEC    0x10      /* Special, CE, CA, CD */

/* Operators */
#define OPR_ADD         1
#define OPR_SUB         2
#define OPR_MUL         3
#define OPR_DIV         4
#define OPR_MOD         5
#define OPR_OR          6
#define OPR_AND         7
#define OPR_XOR         8
#define OPR_SHL         9
#define OPR_SHR         10
#define OPR_CLRE        11
#define OPR_CLRD        12
#define OPR_CLRA        13
#define OPR_ASGN        14
#define OPR_NEG         15
#define OPR_NOT         16
#define OPR_UNS         17

/* Colors */
#define   WHITE         0
#define   BLACK         1
#define   DARKGRAY      2
#define   LIGHTGRAY     3

static XrmDatabase commandlineDB, rDB;

int pressedColor =       WHITE;
int unpressedColor =     BLACK;
int disabledColor =      LIGHTGRAY;
int displayColor =       WHITE;

char myDisplayName[256];
char *myFontName = "8x13";

char          *calcName;

Display       *display;
int           screen_num;
Visual        *visual;
Colormap      colormap;
XFontStruct   *theFont;
Cursor        theCursor;
Window        calcWin;
Window        iconWin;
Window        dispWin;
Pixmap        lgrayPixmap;
Pixmap        grayPixmap;
```

```
Pixmap          iconPixmap;

int             foreground;
int             background;

GC              fgGC;
GC              bgGC;

/* Calculator variables */
int       Base = 10;            /* Default base, updated to command line
                                 * or .Xdefaults */
int       Winbase;             /* windata offset for current base, set
                                 * in InitCalc, used in ConvButton */
int       Digit = 0;
long      Value = 0;            /* Current pressed value */
long      Accum = 0;            /* Current results */
Bool      Unsigned = True;      /* Default for U/S key */
int       LastOpt = OPR_ADD;    /* Initial previous operator */
int       CalcReset = 0;
char      Hexmeasure[] = "  .   .   .    .    .   .    .  ";
char      Octmeasure[] = " .  .   .   .   .   .   .   .   .  ";


/* Startup options */
Bool iconOnly = False;

char Geostr[20];
char iconGeostr[20];


/* Command line options table; only resources are entered here...
 * there is a pass over the remaining options after XrmParseCommand
 * is let loose; we don't do anything with many of these resources,
 * but the program is ready for expansion */

#define GEOMETRY           "*geometry"
#define ICONGEOMETRY       "*iconGeometry"
#define UNSIGNED           "*unsigned"
#define BASE               "*base"
#define ICONSTARTUP        "*iconStartup"

static int opTableEntries = 25;
static XrmOptionDescRec opTable[] = {
{"-unsigned",       UNSIGNED,        XrmoptionNoArg,   (caddr_t)   "off"},
{"-x",              BASE,            XrmoptionNoArg,   (caddr_t)   "16"},
{"-hex",            BASE,            XrmoptionNoArg,   (caddr_t)   "16"},
{"-dec",            BASE,            XrmoptionNoArg,   (caddr_t)   "10"},
{"-oct",            BASE,            XrmoptionNoArg,   (caddr_t)   "8"},
{"-binary",         BASE,            XrmoptionNoArg,   (caddr_t)   "2"},
{"-geometry",       GEOMETRY,        XrmoptionSepArg,  (caddr_t)   NULL},
{"-iconGeometry",   ICONGEOMETRY,    XrmoptionSepArg,  (caddr_t)   NULL},
{"-iconic",         ICONSTARTUP,     XrmoptionNoArg,   (caddr_t)   "on"},
{"-background",     "*background",   XrmoptionSepArg,  (caddr_t)   NULL},
{"-bg",             "*background",   XrmoptionSepArg,  (caddr_t)   NULL},
{"-fg",             "*foreground",   XrmoptionSepArg,  (caddr_t)   NULL},
{"-foreground",     "*foreground",   XrmoptionSepArg,  (caddr_t)   NULL},
{"-xrm",            NULL,            XrmoptionResArg,  (caddr_t)   NULL},
{"-display",        ".display",      XrmoptionSepArg,  (caddr_t)   NULL},
/* Remainder not currently supported: */
```

```
{"-bd",              "*borderColor",     XrmoptionSepArg,    (caddr_t)    NULL},
{"-bordercolor",     "*borderColor",     XrmoptionSepArg,    (caddr_t)    NULL},
{"-borderwidth",     ".borderWidth",     XrmoptionSepArg,    (caddr_t)    NULL},
{"-bw",              ".borderWidth",     XrmoptionSepArg,    (caddr_t)    NULL},
{"-fn",              "*font",            XrmoptionSepArg,    (caddr_t)    NULL},
{"-font",            "*font",            XrmoptionSepArg,    (caddr_t)    NULL},
{"-name",            ".name",            XrmoptionSepArg,    (caddr_t)    NULL},
{"-title",           ".title",           XrmoptionSepArg,    (caddr_t)    NULL},
};

/* Keyboard equivalents */
struct KeyCode {
    int   kc_char;
    char  *kc_func;
    int   kc_len;
} KeyCodes[] = {
    { CERASE,  "CD",    2 },
#ifdef SysV
    { 027,     "CE",    2 },
#else
    { CWERASE, "CE",    2 },
#endif SysV
    { CKILL,   "CE",    2 },
    { CINTR,   "CA",    2 },
    { 0,        0,   0 },
};
char QuitChar = CQUIT;

#include "bitmaps/xcalc.icon"
#include "bitmaps/lgray"
#include "bitmaps/gray"

/* Placement variables */
XSizeHints sizehints = {
    PMinSize | PMaxSize | PPosition | PSize | USSize,
    400, 100,          /* x, y */
    300, 139,          /* Width, height */
    300, 139,          /* min_width and min_height */
    300, 139,          /* max_width and max_height */
    0, 0,              /* Width and height increments, not set */
    0, 0, 0, 0,        /* Aspect ratio, not set */
};
XSizeHints iconsizehints = {
    PMinSize | PMaxSize | PPosition | PSize,
    150, 2,
    icon_width, icon_height,
    icon_width, icon_height,
    icon_width, icon_height,
    0, 0,
    0, 0, 0, 0,
};
XWMHints wmhints = {
    InputHint | StateHint | IconWindowHint,
    True,              /* Input model */
    NormalState,       /* Starts up in normal state */
    0,                 /* Icon pixmap -- set later */
    0,                 /* Icon window -- created later */
```

```
    150, 2,            /* Icon position of icon */
    0,                 /* Icon mask pixmap -- not used */
};

/* Configuration of subwindows */
typedef struct _OpaqueFrame {
    Window self;                    /* Window id, filled in later */
    int x, y;                       /* Where to create the window */
    unsigned int width, height;     /* Width and height */
} OpaqueFrame;

#define NBUTTONS 38
OpaqueFrame Buttons[NBUTTONS] = {
    { 0, 3, 5, 292, 18},       /* Display area */

    { 0, 10, 35, 19, 18},      /* c d e f */
    { 0, 37, 35, 19, 18},
    { 0, 63, 35, 19, 18},
    { 0, 91, 35, 19, 18},

    { 0, 10, 60, 19, 18},      /* 8 9 a b */
    { 0, 37, 60, 19, 18},
    { 0, 63, 60, 19, 18},
    { 0, 91, 60, 19, 18},

    { 0, 10, 85, 19, 18},      /* 4 5 6 7 */
    { 0, 37, 85, 19, 18},
    { 0, 63, 85, 19, 18},
    { 0, 91, 85, 19, 18},

    { 0, 10, 110, 19, 18},     /* 0 1 2 3 */
    { 0, 37, 110, 19, 18},
    { 0, 63, 110, 19, 18},
    { 0, 91, 110, 19, 18},

    { 0, 261, 110, 28, 18},    /* ca ce, cd, = */
    { 0, 187, 110, 28, 18},
    { 0, 224, 110, 28, 18},
    { 0, 131, 110, 46, 18},

    { 0, 131, 60, 19, 18},     /* + - * / % */
    { 0, 158, 60, 19, 18},
    { 0, 185, 60, 19, 18},
    { 0, 212, 60, 19, 18},
    { 0, 239, 60, 19, 18},

    { 0, 131, 85, 19, 18},     /* | & << >> ^ */
    { 0, 158, 85, 19, 18},
    { 0, 185, 85, 19, 18},
    { 0, 212, 85, 19, 18},
    { 0, 239, 85, 19, 18},

    { 0, 131, 35, 32, 18},     /* hex oct bin dec */
    { 0, 165, 35, 31, 18},
    { 0, 198, 35, 32, 18},
    { 0, 232, 35, 31, 18},

    { 0, 269, 35, 20, 18},     /* UNS */
    { 0, 269, 60, 20, 18},     /* NEG */
    { 0, 269, 85, 20, 18},     /* NOT */
```

basecalc

```
};

struct windata {
    int   color;      /* Color */
    char *text;       /* Pointer to the text string */
    int   x;          /* x coordinate of text */
    int   y;          /* y coordinate of text */
    int   value;      /* 0-16 for number, symbol for operator */
    int   type;       /* Number, operator, display */
} windata[NBUTTONS] = {
    { 1, "                                0 ", 2, 3, 0, WTYP_DISP },

    { 0, "C", 5, 3, 12, WTYP_DIG },
    { 0, "D", 5, 3, 13, WTYP_DIG },
    { 0, "E", 5, 3, 14, WTYP_DIG },
    { 0, "F", 5, 3, 15, WTYP_DIG },

    { 0, "8", 5, 3,  8, WTYP_DIG },
    { 0, "9", 5, 3,  9, WTYP_DIG },
    { 0, "A", 5, 3, 10, WTYP_DIG },
    { 0, "B", 5, 3, 11, WTYP_DIG },

    { 0, "4", 5, 3, 4, WTYP_DIG },
    { 0, "5", 5, 3, 5, WTYP_DIG },
    { 0, "6", 5, 3, 6, WTYP_DIG },
    { 0, "7", 5, 3, 7, WTYP_DIG },

    { 0, "0", 5, 3, 0, WTYP_DIG },
    { 0, "1", 5, 3, 1, WTYP_DIG },
    { 0, "2", 5, 3, 2, WTYP_DIG },
    { 0, "3", 5, 3, 3, WTYP_DIG },

    { 0, "CA", 6, 3, OPR_CLRA, WTYP_SPEC },
    { 0, "CE", 6, 3, OPR_CLRE, WTYP_SPEC },
    { 0, "CD", 6, 3, OPR_CLRD, WTYP_SPEC },
    { 0, "=", 17, 2, OPR_ASGN, WTYP_OPER },

    { 0,  "+", 5, 3, OPR_ADD, WTYP_OPER },
    { 0,  "-", 5, 3, OPR_SUB, WTYP_OPER },
    { 0,  "*", 5, 4, OPR_MUL, WTYP_OPER },
    { 0,  "/", 5, 3, OPR_DIV, WTYP_OPER },
    { 0,  "%", 5, 3, OPR_MOD, WTYP_OPER },

    { 0,  "|", 5, 3, OPR_OR,  WTYP_OPER },
    { 0,  "&", 5, 3, OPR_AND, WTYP_OPER },
    { 0,  ">>",1, 3, OPR_SHR, WTYP_OPER },
    { 0,  "<<",0, 3, OPR_SHL, WTYP_OPER },
    { 0,  "^", 5, 3, OPR_XOR, WTYP_OPER },

    { 0, "HEX", 2, 3, 16, WTYP_CONV },
    { 0, "DEC", 2, 3, 10, WTYP_CONV },
    { 0, "OCT", 2, 3,  8, WTYP_CONV },
    { 0, "BIN", 2, 3,  2, WTYP_CONV },

    { 0, "U",  5, 3,  OPR_UNS, WTYP_SPEC },
    { 0, "\`", 5, 3,  OPR_NEG, WTYP_OPER },
    { 0, "~",  5, 3,  OPR_NOT, WTYP_OPER },
};
```

Example D-2 is the complete source for the calculator application described in Chapter 12, *A Complete Application*.

Example D-2. Remaining code for basecalc

```
/* X Version 11 Integer Programmer's Calculator, written by
 * Alan Greenspan, modified slightly by Adrian Nye */
#include <X11/Xlib.h>
#include <X11/Xutil.h>
#include <X11/Xresource.h>
#include <X11/cursorfont.h>

#include <stdio.h>

#ifdef SysV
#include <termio.h>
#else
#include <sgtty.h>
#include <sys/ttychars.h>
#endif SysV

#include <ctype.h>
#include <pwd.h>

#include "basecalc.h"

/* Programmer's calculator with number base conversions */
main (argc, argv)
int argc;
register char *argv[];
{
    /* So we can use the resource manager data merging functions */
    XrmInitialize();

    /* Parse command line first so we can open display,
     * store any options in a database  */
    parseOpenDisp (&argc, argv);

    /* Get server defaults, program defaults, .Xdefaults,
     * command line, etc. and merge them */
    mergeDatabases();

    /* Extract values from database for use */
    extractOpts ();

    /* Load font, make pixmaps, set up arrays of windows */
    initCalc ();

    /* Get keyboard settings for interrupt, delete, etc. */
    initTty ();

    /* Make a standard cursor */
    makeCursor ();

    /* Set standard properties, create and map windows */
    makeWindows (argc, argv);

    /* Get events */
    takeEvents ();

    /* Bow out gracefully */
    XCloseDisplay(display);
    exit (1);
```

```
}
static char *getHomeDir( dest )
char *dest;
{
    int uid;
    extern char *getenv();
    extern int getuid();
    extern struct passwd *getpwuid();
    struct passwd *pw;
    register char *ptr;

    if((ptr = getenv("HOME")) != NULL) {
        (void) strcpy(dest, ptr);

    } else {
        if((ptr = getenv("USER")) != NULL) {
            pw = getpwnam(ptr);
        } else {
            uid = getuid();
            pw = getpwuid(uid);
        }
        if (pw) {
            (void) strcpy(dest, pw->pw_dir);
        } else {
            *dest = ' ';
        }
    }
    return dest;
}


/* Get program's and user's defaults */
mergeDatabases()
{
    XrmDatabase homeDB, serverDB, applicationDB;

    char filenamebuf[1024];
    char *filename = &filenamebuf[0];
    char *environment;
    char *classname = "Basecalc";
    char name[255];

    (void) strcpy(name, "/usr/lib/X11/app-defaults/");
    (void) strcat(name, classname);
    /* Get application defaults file, if any */
    applicationDB = XrmGetFileDatabase(name);
    (void) XrmMergeDatabases(applicationDB, &rDB);

    /* MERGE server defaults, these are created by xrdb,
     * loaded as a property of the root window when the server
     * initializes, and loaded into the display structure
     * on XOpenDisplay; if not defined, use .Xdefaults */
    if (XResourceManagerString(display) != NULL) {
        serverDB = XrmGetStringDatabase(XResourceManagerString(display));
    } else {
        /* Open .Xdefaults file and merge into existing data base */
        (void) getHomeDir(filename);
        (void) strcat(filename, "/.Xdefaults");
```

```
            serverDB = XrmGetFileDatabase(filename);
        }
    XrmMergeDatabases(serverDB, &rDB);

    /* Open XENVIRONMENT file or, if not defined, the ~/.Xdefaults,
     * and merge into existing data base */
    if ((environment = getenv("XENVIRONMENT")) == NULL) {
        int len;
        environment = getHomeDir(filename);
        (void) strcat(environment, "/.Xdefaults-");
        len = strlen(environment);
        (void) gethostname(environment+len, 1024-len);
    }
    homeDB = XrmGetFileDatabase(environment);
    XrmMergeDatabases(homeDB, &rDB);

    /* Command line takes precedence over everything */
    XrmMergeDatabases(commandlineDB, &rDB);
}

/* Get command line options */
parseOpenDisp (argc, argv)
int *argc;
register char *argv[];
{

    XrmValue value;
    char *str_type[20];

    myDisplayName[0] = ' ';

    XrmParseCommand(&commandlineDB, opTable, opTableEntries, argv[0],
            argc, argv);

    /* Check for any arguments left */
    if (*argc != 1) Usage();

    /* Get display now, because we need it to get other databases*/
    if (XrmGetResource(commandlineDB, "basecalc.display", "Basecalc.Display",
            str_type, &value)== True) {
        (void) strncpy(myDisplayName, value.addr, (int) value.size);
    }

    /* Open display */
    if (!(display = XOpenDisplay(myDisplayName))) {
        (void) fprintf(stderr, "%s: Can't open display '%s'\n",
            argv[0], XDisplayName(myDisplayName));
        exit(1);
    }

    screen_num = DefaultScreen(display);
    visual = DefaultVisual(display, screen_num);
    colormap = DefaultColormap(display, screen_num);
}

extractOpts()
{
    char *str_type[20];
    char buffer[20];
```

basecalc

```
    long flags;
    XrmValue value;
    int x, y, width, height;
    XColor screen_def;

    /* Get geometry (actually, this is currently ignored) */
    if (XrmGetResource(rDB, "basecalc.geometry", "Basecalc.Geometry",
            str_type, &value)== True) {
        (void) strncpy(Geostr, value.addr, (int) value.size);
    } else {
        Geostr[0] = NULL;
    }

    if (XrmGetResource(rDB, "basecalc.iconGeometry", "Basecalc.IconGeometry",
            str_type, &value)== True) {
        (void) strncpy(iconGeostr, value.addr, (int) value.size);
    } else {
        iconGeostr[0] = NULL;
    }

    if (XrmGetResource(rDB, "basecalc.unsigned", "Basecalc.Unsigned",
            str_type, &value)== True)
        if (strncmp(value.addr, "False", (int) value.size) == 0)
                Unsigned = False;

    if (XrmGetResource(rDB, "basecalc.base", "Basecalc.Base", str_type,
            &value)== True) {
        (void) strncpy(buffer, value.addr, (int) value.size);
        buffer[value.size] = NULL;
        Base = atoi(buffer);
    } else Base = 10;

    if (XrmGetResource(rDB, "basecalc.foreground", "Basecalc.Foreground",
            str_type, &value)== True) {
        (void) strncpy(buffer, value.addr, (int) value.size);
        if (XParseColor(display, colormap, buffer,
            &screen_def) == 0)   {
            (void) fprintf(stderr, "basecalc: fg color specification %s \
                    invalid", buffer);
            foreground = BlackPixel(display, screen_num);
        } else {
            if ((visual->class == StaticGray) || (visual->class ==
                    GrayScale))

                foreground = BlackPixel(display, screen_num);
            else if (XAllocColor(display, colormap, &screen_def) == 0) {
                foreground = BlackPixel(display, screen_num);
                (void) fprintf(stderr, "basecalc: couldn't allocate color: \
                        %s.\n", buffer);
            }
            else
                foreground = screen_def.pixel;
        }
    } else {
        foreground = BlackPixel(display, screen_num);
    }

    if (XrmGetResource(rDB, "basecalc.background", "Basecalc.Background",
```

```
            str_type, &value)== True) {
        (void) strncpy(buffer, value.addr, (int) value.size);
        if (XParseColor(display, colormap, buffer,
            &screen_def) == 0)  {
            (void) fprintf(stderr, "basecalc: bg color specification %s \
                    invalid", buffer);
            background = WhitePixel(display, screen_num);
        } else {
            if ((visual->class == StaticGray) || (visual->class ==
                    GrayScale))
                background = WhitePixel(display, screen_num);
            else if (XAllocColor(display, colormap, &screen_def) == 0) {
                background = WhitePixel(display, screen_num);
                (void) fprintf(stderr, "basecalc: couldn't allocate color: \
                    %s.\n", buffer);
            }
            else
                background = screen_def.pixel;
        }
    } else {
        background = WhitePixel(display, screen_num);
    }

    /* One last check to make sure the colors are different! */
    if (background == foreground) {
        background = WhitePixel(display, screen_num);
        foreground = BlackPixel(display, screen_num);
    }


    /*  Could add a command line option for initial state:
     *  iconOnly[0] = NULL; */

    /* Get window geometry information */
    if (Geostr != NULL) {
        flags = XParseGeometry(Geostr,
            &x, &y, &width, &height);
        if ((WidthValue|HeightValue) & flags)
            Usage ();
        if (XValue & flags) {
            if (XNegative & flags)
                x = DisplayWidth(display, screen_num) +
                    x - sizehints.width;
            sizehints.flags |= USPosition;
            sizehints.x = x;
        }
        if (YValue & flags) {
            if (YNegative & flags)
                y = DisplayHeight(display, screen_num) +
                    x - sizehints.width;
            sizehints.flags |= USPosition;
            sizehints.y = y;
        }
    }

    /* Get icon geometry information */
    if (iconGeostr != NULL) {
        iconGeostr[0] = '=';
```

```
        flags = XParseGeometry(iconGeostr,
            &x, &y, &width, &height);
        if ((WidthValue|HeightValue) & flags)
            Usage ();
        if (XValue & flags) {
            if (XNegative & flags)
                x = DisplayWidth(display, screen_num) +
                    x - iconsizehints.width;
            iconsizehints.flags |= USPosition;
            wmhints.flags |= IconPositionHint;
            wmhints.icon_x = x;
            iconsizehints.x = x;
        }
        if (YValue & flags) {
            if (YNegative & flags)
                y = DisplayHeight(display, screen_num) +
                    x - iconsizehints.width;
            iconsizehints.flags |= USPosition;
            wmhints.flags |= IconPositionHint;
            wmhints.icon_y = y;
            iconsizehints.y = y;
        }
    }
}

/* Print message to stderr and exit */
Usage ()
{
    (void) fprintf (stderr,
        "%s: [-iconic] [-unsigned] [-hex|x|dec|oct|binary] \
        [-display <display>] [-geometry <geometrystring>] \
        [-iconGeometry <icongeometrystring>\n",
        calcName ? calcName : "basecalc");
    exit (1);
}

/* Make a pixmap */
Pixmap
makePixmap(data, width, height)
char *data;
unsigned int width, height;
{
    Pixmap pid;

    pid = XCreatePixmapFromBitmapData(display, DefaultRootWindow(display),
            data, width, height, foreground, background,
            DefaultDepth(display, screen_num));
    return(pid);
}

/* Initialize calculator options */
initCalc ()
{
    register int win;
    register int found = -1;
    XGCValues values;
```

```
    extern char lgray_bits[];

    if ((theFont = XLoadQueryFont (display, myFontName)) == NULL) {
        (void) fprintf(stderr, "basecalc: can't open font %s\n",
                myFontName);
        exit(-1);
    }

    /* Make the utility pixmaps */
    grayPixmap = makePixmap(gray_bits, gray_width, gray_height);
    lgrayPixmap = makePixmap(lgray_bits, lgray_width, lgray_height);

    /* Make the utility gc's */
    values.font = theFont->fid;
    values.foreground = foreground;
    fgGC = XCreateGC(display, DefaultRootWindow(display),
        GCForeground|GCFont, &values);
    values.foreground = background;
    values.function = GXcopy;
    bgGC = XCreateGC(display, DefaultRootWindow(display),
        GCForeground|GCFont|GCFunction, &values);

    /* Loop through buttons, setting disabled buttons to Color
     * Light Gray; also find the window which corresponds to the
     * starting display base; also add ascent to y position of text */
    for (win = 1; win < NBUTTONS; win++) {
        if (windata[win].type == WTYP_CONV &&
            windata[win].value == Base) {
            found = win;
        } else
            if (windata[win].type == WTYP_DIG &&
                windata[win].value >= Base) {
                windata[win].color = disabledColor;
            }
            else
                if (windata[win].type == WTYP_SPEC &&
                    windata[win].value == OPR_UNS) {
                    if (Unsigned)
                        windata[win].text = "U";
                    else
                        windata[win].text = "S";
                    windata[win].color = pressedColor;
                }
                else
                    windata[win].color = unpressedColor;
        windata[win].y += theFont->max_bounds.ascent;
    }
    windata[0].y += theFont->max_bounds.ascent;
    if (found >= 0) {
        Winbase = found;
        windata[found].color = pressedColor;
    } else {
        (void) fprintf(stderr, "basecalc: can't use base %d\n", Base);
        exit(-1);
    }
    windata[0].color = displayColor;
}
```

```
/* Get the user's tty special chars; this is currently 4.2 specific */
initTty ()
{
    register struct KeyCode *KeyCodePtr;
    register int fd;
#ifdef SysV
    struct termio term;
#else
    struct sgttyb tty;
    struct tchars tchars;
    struct ltchars ltchars;
#endif SysV

    if (!isatty(0)) {
        if ((fd = open ("/dev/console", 0)) < 0)
            return;
    } else
        fd = 0;
#ifdef SysV
    (void) ioctl  (fd, TCGETA,   &term);
#else
    (void) ioctl  (fd, TIOCGETP, &tty);
    (void) ioctl  (fd, TIOCGETC, &tchars);
    (void) ioctl  (fd, TIOCGLTC, &ltchars);
#endif SysV
    if (fd)
        (void) close (fd);

    KeyCodePtr = KeyCodes;
#ifdef SysV
    KeyCodePtr++->kc_char = term.c_cc[VERASE];
    KeyCodePtr++;
    KeyCodePtr++->kc_char = term.c_cc[VKILL];
    KeyCodePtr->kc_char = term.c_cc[VINTR];
    QuitChar = term.c_cc[VQUIT];
#else
    KeyCodePtr++->kc_char = tty.sg_erase;
    KeyCodePtr++->kc_char = ltchars.t_werasc;
    KeyCodePtr++->kc_char = tty.sg_kill;
    KeyCodePtr->kc_char = tchars.t_intrc;
    QuitChar = tchars.t_quitc;
#endif SysV
}


/* Make the cursor */
makeCursor ()
{
    theCursor = XCreateFontCursor (display, XC_hand1);
}


/* Set up the selection of events */
selectEvents ()
{
    int win;

    XSelectInput (display, calcWin, KeyPressMask|KeyReleaseMask);
```

```
    XSelectInput (display, dispWin, ExposureMask);
    for (win = 1; win < NBUTTONS; win++)
        XSelectInput (display, Buttons[win].self,
            ExposureMask|
            ButtonPressMask|ButtonReleaseMask|
            EnterWindowMask|LeaveWindowMask);
}

/* Get events and process them */
takeEvents ()
{
    XEvent Event;
    register int win;
    register int Pressed = False;
    register int InWindow = False;
    char buffer[10];
    register char *KeyChars = buffer;
    register int WasKeyDown = False;
    unsigned i, nbytes;

    while (1) {
        if (!WasKeyDown)
            XNextEvent (display, &Event);
        else
            Event.type = KeyRelease;

        /* Map keyboard events to Window events */
        if (Event.type == KeyPress || Event.type == KeyRelease) {
            nbytes = XLookupString (&Event, buffer,
                sizeof(buffer), NULL, NULL);
            if (Event.type == KeyPress) {
                Event.type = ButtonPress;
                WasKeyDown = 1;
            } else {
                for (i=0; i<60000; i++)
                    ;
                Event.type = ButtonRelease;
            }
            if ((Event.xbutton.window =
                keyToWin (KeyChars, nbytes)) == None){
                WasKeyDown = 0;
                continue;
            }
        }
        for (win=0; win < NBUTTONS; win++)
            if (Buttons[win].self == Event.xbutton.window)
                break;
        switch (Event.type) {
        case ButtonPress:
            if (windata[win].color == disabledColor)
                break;
            Pressed = win;
            if (!WasKeyDown)
                InWindow = True;
            windata[win].color = pressedColor;
            drawButton (win, 0);
```

```
                break;
            case LeaveNotify:
                if (Pressed != win)
                    break;
                InWindow = False;
                windata[win].color = unpressedColor;
                drawButton (win, 0);
                break;
            case EnterNotify:
                if (Pressed != win)
                    break;
                InWindow = True;
                windata[win].color = pressedColor;
                drawButton (win, 0);
                break;
            case ButtonRelease:
                if (windata[win].color == disabledColor ||
                    Pressed != win) {
                    WasKeyDown = False;
                    break;
                }
                Pressed = False;
                windata[win].color = unpressedColor;
                if (WasKeyDown || InWindow)
                    winPressed (win);
                WasKeyDown = False;
                InWindow = False;
                drawButton (win, 0);
                break;
            case Expose:
                drawButton (win, 1);
                break;
        }
        XFlush(display);
    }
}

/* Make the calculator windows */
makeWindows (argc, argv)
int argc;
char *argv[];
{
    register int i;
    XSetWindowAttributes attributes;
    char *window_name = "Programmer's Calculator";
    char *icon_name = "basecalc";

    /* Define the border and background for the main window --
     * black border and a patterned background */
    attributes.border_pixel = foreground;
    attributes.background_pixmap = grayPixmap;
    /* Create the main window (calculator frame) as a child of
     * the root window */
    attributes.cursor = theCursor;
    calcWin = XCreateWindow(display, DefaultRootWindow(display),
        sizehints.x, sizehints.y, sizehints.width, sizehints.height,
```

```
            1, DefaultDepth(display, screen_num), InputOutput,
            CopyFromParent, CWBorderPixel|CWBackPixmap|CWCursor,
            &attributes);
#ifdef X11R3
    XSetStandardProperties (display, calcWin, window_name, icon_name,
        NULL, argv, argc, &sizehints);
#endif

    /* Create the icon window and associate it with the calculator */
    iconPixmap = makePixmap(icon_bits, icon_width, icon_height);
    attributes.border_pixel = foreground;
    attributes.background_pixmap = iconPixmap;
    iconWin = XCreateWindow(display, DefaultRootWindow(display),
        iconsizehints.x, iconsizehints.y,
        iconsizehints.width, iconsizehints.height,
        1, DefaultDepth(display, screen_num), InputOutput,
        CopyFromParent, CWBorderPixel|CWBackPixmap,
        &attributes);
    wmhints.icon_window = iconWin;
    wmhints.initial_state = iconOnly ? IconicState : NormalState;
    wmhints.input = True;
    wmhints.flags |= InputHint | StateHint | IconWindowHint;
#ifdef X11R3
    XSetWMHints(display, calcWin, &wmhints);
#else
    {
    XClassHint class_hints;

    /* Format of the window name and icon name arguments
     * has changed in R4 */
    XTextProperty windowName, iconName;

    /* These calls store window_name and icon_name into XTextProperty
     * structures and set their other fields properly */
    if (XStringListToTextProperty(&window_name, 1, &windowName) == 0) {
        (void) fprintf( stderr, "%s: structure allocation for windowName \
                failed.\n", argv[0]);
        exit(-1);
    }

    if (XStringListToTextProperty(&icon_name, 1, &iconName) == 0) {
        (void) fprintf( stderr, "%s: structure allocation for iconName \
                failed.\n", argv[0]);
        exit(-1);
    }

    class_hints.res_name = argv[0];
    class_hints.res_class = "Basicwin";

    XSetWMProperties(display, calcWin, &windowName, &iconName,
            argv, argc, &sizehints, &wmhints,
            &class_hints);
    }
#endif
    /* Create the buttons as subwindows */
    attributes.background_pixmap = lgrayPixmap;
    attributes.border_pixel = foreground;
```

```
    for (i = 0; i < NBUTTONS; i++)
        switch (windata[i].color) {
        case WHITE:
            Buttons[i].self = XCreateSimpleWindow(display, calcWin,
                Buttons[i].x, Buttons[i].y,
                Buttons[i].width, Buttons[i].height,
                1, foreground, background);
            break;
        case BLACK:
            Buttons[i].self = XCreateSimpleWindow(display, calcWin,
                Buttons[i].x, Buttons[i].y,
                Buttons[i].width, Buttons[i].height,
                1, background, foreground);
            break;
        case LIGHTGRAY:
            Buttons[i].self = XCreateWindow(display, calcWin,
                Buttons[i].x, Buttons[i].y,
                Buttons[i].width, Buttons[i].height,
                1, CopyFromParent, InputOutput, CopyFromParent,
                CWBorderPixel|CWBackPixmap, &attributes);
            break;
        }

    /* The display window is distinguished */
    dispWin = Buttons[0].self;

    /* Initialize event catching */
    selectEvents ();

    /* Map the calculator and subwindows */
    XMapSubwindows(display, calcWin);
    XMapWindow(display, calcWin);
}

/* Draw a single button with its text */
drawButton (win, exposeEvent)
register int win;
{
    register char *string;
    register int x, y;
    struct windata *winp;
    char *measure;
    XSetWindowAttributes attributes;
    unsigned long valuemask;
    GC gc;

    winp = &windata[win];
    x = winp->x;
    y = winp->y;
    string = winp->text;

    switch (windata[win].color) {
    case WHITE:
        gc = fgGC;
        attributes.background_pixel = background;
        attributes.border_pixel = foreground;
        valuemask = CWBackPixel|CWBorderPixel;
        break;
```

```
        case BLACK:
            gc = bgGC;
            attributes.background_pixel = foreground;
            attributes.border_pixel = background;
            valuemask = CWBackPixel|CWBorderPixel;
            break;
        case LIGHTGRAY:
            gc = bgGC;
            attributes.background_pixmap = lgrayPixmap;
            attributes.border_pixel = foreground;
            valuemask = CWBackPixmap|CWBorderPixel;
            break;
        }
        if (!exposeEvent){
            XChangeWindowAttributes(display, Buttons[win].self,
                    valuemask, &attributes);
            XClearWindow(display, Buttons[win].self);
        }
        XDrawString (display, Buttons[win].self, gc, x, y, string,
                strlen (string));
        if (win == 0) {
            switch (Base) {
            case 10:
            case 8:
                measure = Octmeasure;
                break;
            default:
            case 16:
            case  2:
                measure = Hexmeasure;
                break;
            }
            XDrawString (display, dispWin, gc, 7, 6, measure, 31);
        }
}


static unsigned int LastDisp = 1;
/* Do the operation corresponding to a key press */
winPressed (win)
{
    register int type;

    type = windata[win].type;
    switch (type) {
    case WTYP_CONV:
        convButton (win);
        displayVal (LastDisp == 1 ? Value : Accum);
        break;
    case WTYP_DIG:
        digitButton (win);
        displayVal (Value);
        LastDisp = 1;
        break;
    case WTYP_OPER:
        if (operButton (win) == 0) {
            displayVal (Accum);
```

```
                LastDisp = 2;
        } else {
            displayVal (Value);
            LastDisp = 1;
        }
        break;
    case WTYP_SPEC:
        specButton (win);
        displayVal (LastDisp == 1 ? Value : Accum);
        LastDisp = 1;
    }
}


/* Handle a conversion button */
convButton (win)
{
    register int i, NewBase, Diff, Digit;
    register int HiBase, LowBase;

    NewBase = windata[win].value;
    windata[Winbase].color = unpressedColor;
    drawButton (Winbase, 0);
    windata[win].color = pressedColor;

    Diff = NewBase - Base;
    if (Diff) {
        if (NewBase > Base) {
            LowBase = Base;
            HiBase = NewBase;
        } else {
            LowBase = NewBase;
            HiBase = Base;
        }
        for (i = 1; i < NBUTTONS; i++) {
            if (windata[i].type == WTYP_DIG) {
                Digit = windata[i].value;
                if (Digit >= LowBase && Digit < HiBase) {
                    if (Diff < 0)
                        windata[i].color = disabledColor;
                    else
                        windata[i].color = unpressedColor;
                    drawButton (i, 0);
                }
            }
        }
    }
    Winbase = win;
    Base = NewBase;
}


/* Handle a digit button */
digitButton (win)
{
    register unsigned long Temp;

    if (CalcReset) {
        CalcReset = 0;
```

```
        Accum = 0;
        Value = 0;
        LastOpt = OPR_ADD;
    }
    Digit = windata[win].value;
    if (Unsigned)
        Temp = (unsigned)Value * (unsigned)Base + Digit;
    else
        Temp = Value * Base + Digit;
    if ((unsigned)Temp/Base != (unsigned)Value) {     /* Overflow? */
        /* Flash the display since the character didn't register */
        windata[0].color =
            (displayColor == WHITE) ? BLACK : WHITE;
        drawButton (0, 0);
        XFlush(display);
        Delay ();
        windata[0].color = displayColor;
        drawButton (0, 0);
        return;
    }
    Value = Temp;
}

/* Handle a special operator */
specButton (win)
{
    register int oper;

    oper = windata[win].value;

    switch (oper) {
    case OPR_CLRD:
        if (LastOpt == OPR_ASGN)
            break;
        Value = (unsigned)Value / Base;
        break;
    case OPR_CLRE:
        Value = 0;
        break;
    case OPR_CLRA:
        Accum = 0;
        Value = 0;
        LastOpt = OPR_ADD;
        break;
    case OPR_UNS:
        Unsigned = !Unsigned;
        windata[win].text = Unsigned ? "U" : "S";
        windata[win].color = pressedColor;
        drawButton (win, 0);
        break;
    }
}

/* Handle an operator */
operButton (win)
{
```

basecalc

```
    register int oper;

    oper = LastOpt;
    LastOpt = windata[win].value;

    CalcReset = 0;
    switch (LastOpt) {
    case OPR_NEG:
        Value = -Value;
        if ((LastOpt = oper) == OPR_ASGN)
            Accum = Value;
        return 1;
    case OPR_NOT:
        Value = ~Value;
        if ((LastOpt = oper) == OPR_ASGN)
            Accum = Value;
        return 1;
    }

    switch (oper) {
    case OPR_ADD:
        if (Unsigned)
            Accum = (unsigned)Accum + (unsigned)Value;
        else
            Accum += Value;
        break;
    case OPR_SUB:
        if (Unsigned)
            Accum = (unsigned)Accum - (unsigned)Value;
        else
            Accum -= Value;
        break;
    case OPR_MUL:
        if (Unsigned)
            Accum = (unsigned)Accum * (unsigned)Value;
        else
            Accum *= Value;
        break;
    case OPR_DIV:
        if (Value == 0)
            break;
        if (Unsigned)
            Accum = (unsigned)Accum / (unsigned)Value;
        else
            Accum /= Value;
        break;
    case OPR_MOD:
        if (Value == 0)
            break;
        if (Unsigned)
            Accum = (unsigned)Accum % (unsigned)Value;
        else
            Accum %= Value;
        break;
    case OPR_OR:
        Accum |= Value;
        break;
```

```
    case OPR_AND:
        Accum &= Value;
        break;
    case OPR_SHR:
        if (Unsigned)
            Accum = (unsigned)Accum >> (unsigned)Value;
        else
            Accum >>= Value;
        break;
    case OPR_SHL:
        if (Unsigned)
            Accum = (unsigned)Accum << (unsigned)Value;
        else
            Accum <<= Value;
        break;
    case OPR_XOR:
        Accum ^= Value;
        break;
    case OPR_ASGN:
        break;
    }
    if (LastOpt == OPR_ASGN) {
        Value = Accum;
        CalcReset = 1;
        return 1;
    }
    Value = 0;
    return 0;
}

/* Display a number in the display window */
displayVal (number)
register long number;
{
    register char *Fmt;
    register char *cp;
    register int i;

    switch (Base) {
    case 16:
        Fmt = "%32x";
        break;
    case 10:
        Fmt = "%32d";
        break;
    case 8:
        Fmt = "%32o";
        break;
    case 2:
        Fmt = "%032b";
        break;
    }
    cp = windata[0].text;
    for (i=32; --i >= 0; )
        *cp++ = ' ';
    *cp = ' ';
```

basecalc

```
    Sprintf (windata[0].text, Fmt, number);
    drawButton (0, 0);
}


/* Translate a key code to a corresponding window */
keyToWin (str, n)
register char *str;
register unsigned n;
{
    register int value = -1;
    register struct KeyCode *KeyCodePtr;
    register char ch;
    register int i;

    if (n > (unsigned) 0) {
        ch = *str;
        if (islower(ch) && isxdigit(ch))
            value = 10 + ch - 'a';
        else
            if (isdigit(ch))
                value = ch - '0';
        if (value >= 0) {
            for (i = 1; i < NBUTTONS; i++)
                if (windata[i].type == WTYP_DIG &&
                    windata[i].value == value)
                    return Buttons[i].self;
        } else {
            /* Do some translations -- these should be driven
             * from the user's terminal erase, kill, etc */
            switch (ch) {
            case 'U':
                if (Unsigned)
                    return -1;
                str = "S";
                n = 1;
                break;
            case 'S':
                if (!Unsigned)
                    return -1;
                str = "U";
                n = 1;
                break;
            case '\r':
            case '\n':
                str = "=";
                n = 1;
                break;
            default:
                if (ch == QuitChar) {
                    XCloseDisplay(display);
                    exit (1);
                }
                KeyCodePtr = KeyCodes;
                while ((n = KeyCodePtr->kc_len) > (unsigned) 0) {
                    if (ch == KeyCodePtr->kc_char) {
                        str = KeyCodePtr->kc_func;
```

```
                            break;
                    }
                    KeyCodePtr++;
                }
                if (n == 0)
                    n = 1;
                break;
            }
            for (i = 1; i < NBUTTONS; i++) {
                if (windata[i].type != WTYP_DIG &&
                    strncmp (windata[i].text, str, (int) n) == 0)
                    return Buttons[i].self;
            }
        }
    }
    return None;
}


/* Specialized version of C Library sprintf
 *
 * %s %c %u %d (==%u) %o %x %b (binary) are recognized
 * %0W... - where 0 means pad with zeros; otherwise, blanks; if W,
 *          the minimum field width is larger than the number */
Sprintf(cp, fmt, x1)
register char *cp;
register char *fmt;
unsigned x1;
{
    register int c, b, sign;
    register unsigned int    *adx;
    register char     *s;
    register unsigned short fw;
    char *printInBase();
    char pad;

    adx = &x1;
loop:
    while ((c = *fmt++) != '%') {
        if (c == ' ') {
            *cp = c;
            return;
        }
        *cp++ = c;
    }
    c = *fmt++;
    if (c == '0') {
        pad = '0';
        c = *fmt++;
    } else
        pad = ' ';

    /* Calculate minimum field width */
    fw = 0;
    while (c >= '0' && c <= '9') {
        fw = fw * 10 + (c - '0');
        c = *fmt++;
```

```
    }
    switch (c) {
    case 's':
        s = (char *)*adx;
        while (c = *s++)
            *cp++ = c;
        break;
    case 'c':
        c = (int)*adx;
        *cp++ = c;
        break;
    default:
        sign = 0;
        switch (c) {
        case 'x':
            b = 16;
            break;
        case 'd':
            if (!Unsigned)
                sign = 1;
        case 'u':
            b = 10;
            break;
        case 'o':
            b = 8;
            break;
        case 'b':
            b = 2;
            break;
        default:
            /* Unknown format */
            b = 0;
            break;
        }
        if (b)
            cp = printInBase (cp, (long)*adx, b, fw, pad, sign);
        break;
    }
    adx++;
    goto loop;
}

/* Print a number n in base b into string cp;
 * minimum field width = fw, pad character = pad */
char *
printInBase (cp, n, b, fw, pad, sign)
register char *cp;
register long n;
register b;
register int fw, pad;
{
    register i, nd, c;
    int     flag;
    int     plmax;
    char d[33];

    c = 1;
```

```
if (sign)
    flag = n < 0;
else
    flag = 0;
if (flag)
    n = (-n);
if (b==2)
    plmax = 32;
else if (b==8)
    plmax = 11;
else if (b==10)
    plmax = 10;
else if (b==16)
    plmax = 8;
if (b==10) {
    if (flag == 0)
        sign = 0;
    flag = 0;
}
for (i=0;i<plmax;i++) {
    if (flag == 0)
        nd = (unsigned)n%b;
    else
        nd = n%b;
    if (flag) {
        nd = (b - 1) - nd + c;
        if (nd >= b) {
            nd -= b;
            c = 1;
        } else
            c = 0;
    }
    d[i] = nd;
    if (flag == 0)
        n = (unsigned)n/b;
    else
        n = n/b;
    if ((n==0) && (flag==0))
        break;
}
if (i==plmax)
    i--;
if (sign) {
    fw--;
    if (pad == '0')
        *cp++ = '-';
}
if (fw > i+1) {
    for (fw -= i+1; fw > 0; fw--)
        *cp++ = pad;
}
if (sign && pad != '0')
    *cp++ = '-';
for (;i>=0;i--)
    *cp++ = "0123456789ABCDEF"[d[i]];
*cp = ' ';
```

Example D-2. Remaining code for basecalc (continued)

```
    return cp;
}

/* Delay a little while */
Delay ()
{
    long tic;

    for (tic = 0; tic < 50000; tic++)
        ;
}
```

E

Event Reference

This appendix provides a detailed description of each event type in a reference page format. The information provided here is essential for a full understanding of the events, how they are selected and propagated, and the intricacies of their operation.

In This Chapter:

E
Event Reference

This appendix describes each event structure in detail and briefly shows how each event type is used. It covers the most common uses of each event type, the information contained in each event structure, how the event is selected, and the side effects of the event, if any. Each event is described on a separate reference page.

E.1 Meaning of Common Structure Elements

Example E-1 shows the XEvent union and a simple event structure that is one member of the union. Several of the members of this structure are present in nearly every event structure. They are described here before we go into the event-specific members (see also Section 8.2.2).

Example E-1. XEvent union and XAnyEvent structure

```
typedef union _XEvent {
    int type;                 /* Must not be changed; first member */
    XAnyEvent xany;
    XButtonEvent xbutton;
    XCirculateEvent xcirculate;
    XCirculateRequestEvent xcirculaterequest;
    XClientMessageEvent xclient;
    XColormapEvent xcolormap;
    XConfigureEvent xconfigure;
    XConfigureRequestEvent xconfigurerequest;
    XCreateWindowEvent xcreatewindow;
    XDestroyWindowEvent xdestroywindow;
    XCrossingEvent xcrossing;
    XExposeEvent xexpose;
    XFocusChangeEvent xfocus;
    XNoExposeEvent xnoexpose;
    XGraphicsExposeEvent xgraphicsexpose;
    XGravityEvent xgravity;
    XKeymapEvent xkeymap;
    XKeyEvent xkey;
    XMapEvent xmap;
    XUnmapEvent xunmap;
    XMappingEvent xmapping;
```

```
    XMapRequestEvent xmaprequest;
    XMotionEvent xmotion;
    XPropertyEvent xproperty;
    XReparentEvent xreparent;
    XResizeRequestEvent xresizerequest;
    XSelectionClearEvent xselectionclear;
    XSelectionEvent xselection;
    XSelectionRequestEvent xselectionrequest;
    XVisibilityEvent xvisibility;
} XEvent;

typedef struct {
    int type;
    unsigned long serial;   /* # of last request processed by server */
    Bool send_event;        /* True if this came from SendEvent
                             * request */
    Display *display;       /* Display the event was read from */
    Window window;          /* window on which event was requested
                             * in event mask */
} XAnyEvent;
```

The first member of the XEvent union is the type of event. When an event is received (with XNextEvent, for example), the application checks the type member in the XEvent union. Then the specific event type is known and the specific event structure (such as xbutton) is used to access information specific to that event type.

Before the branching depending on the event type, only the XEvent union is used. After the branching, only the event structure which contains the specific information for each event type should be used in each branch. For example, if the XEvent union were called report, the report.xexpose structure should be used within the branch for Expose events.

You will notice that each event structure also begins with a type member. This member is rarely used, since it is an identical copy of the type member in the XEvent union.

Most event structures also have a window member. The only ones that do not are selection events (SelectionClear, SelectionNotify, and SelectionRequest) and events selected by the graphics_exposures member of the GC (GraphicsExpose and NoExpose). The window member indicates the event window that selected and received the event. This is the window where the event arrives if it has propagated through the hierarchy as described in Section 8.3.2. One event type may have two different meanings to an application, depending on which window it appears in.

Many of the event structures also have a display and/or root member. The display member identifies the connection to the server that is active. The root member indicates which screen the window that received the event is linked to in the hierarchy. Most programs only use a single screen and therefore do not need to worry about the root member. The display member can be useful, since you can pass the display variable into routines by simply passing a pointer to the event structure, eliminating the need for a separate display argument.

All event structures include a `serial` member that gives the number of the last protocol request processed by the server. This is useful in debugging, since an error can be detected by the server but not reported to the user (or programmer) until the next routine that gets an event. That means several routines may execute successfully after the error occurs. The last request processed will often indicate the request that contained the error.

All event structures also include a `send_event` flag, which, if `True`, indicates that the event was sent by `XSendEvent` (i.e., by another client rather than by the server).

The following pages describe each event type in detail. The events are presented in alphabetical order, each on a separate page. Each page describes the circumstances under which the event is generated, the mask used to select it, the structure itself, its members, and useful programming notes. Note that the description of the structure members does not include those members common to many structures. If you need more information on these members, please refer to this introductory section.

ButtonPress, ButtonRelease

When Generated

There are two types of pointer button events: ButtonPress and ButtonRelease. Both contain the same information.

Select With

May be selected separately, using ButtonPressMask and ButtonReleaseMask.

XEvent Structure Name

```
typedef union _XEvent {
    . . .
    XButtonEvent xbutton;
    . . .
} XEvent;
```

Event Structure

```
typedef struct {
int type;                  /* of event */
unsigned long serial;      /* # of last request processed by server */
Bool send_event;           /* True if this came from a SendEvent request */
Display *display;          /* Display the event was read from */
Window window;             /* event window it is reported relative to */
Window root;               /* root window that the event occurred under */
Window subwindow;          /* child window */
Time time;                 /* when event occurred, in milliseconds */
int x, y;                  /* pointer coordinates relative to receiving
                            * window */
int x_root, y_root;        /* coordinates relative to root */
unsigned int state;        /* mask of all buttons and modifier keys */
unsigned int button;       /* button that triggered event */
Bool same_screen;          /* same screen flag */
} XButtonEvent;
typedef XButtonEvent XButtonPressedEvent;
typedef XButtonEvent XButtonReleasedEvent;
```

Event Structure Members

subwindow   If the source window is the child of the receiving window, then the subwindow member is set to the ID of that child.

time   The server time when the button event occurred, in milliseconds. Time is declared as unsigned long, so it wraps around when it reaches the maximum value of a 32-bit number (every 49.7 days).

x, y   If the receiving window is on the same screen as the root window specified by root, then x and y are the pointer coordinates relative to the receiving window's origin. Otherwise, x and y are zero.

When active button grabs and pointer grabs are in effect (see Section 9.4), the coordinates relative to the receiving window may not be within the window (they may be negative or greater than window height or width).

x_root, y_root   The pointer coordinates relative to the root window which is an ancestor of the event window. If the pointer was on a different screen, these are zero.

state   The state of all the buttons and modifier keys just before the event, represented by a mask of the button and modifier key symbols: Button1Mask, Button2Mask, Button3Mask, Button4Mask, Button5Mask, ControlMask, LockMask, Mod1Mask, Mod2-Mask, Mod3Mask, Mod4Mask, Mod5Mask, and ShiftMask. If a modifier key is pressed and released when no other modifier keys are held, the ButtonPress will have a state member of 0 and the ButtonRelease will have a nonzero state member indicating that itself was held just before the event.

button   A value indicating which button changed state to trigger this event. One of the constants: Button1, Button2, Button3, Button4, or Button5.

same_screen   Indicates whether the pointer is currently on the same screen as this window. This is always True unless the pointer was actively grabbed before the automatic grab could take place.

Notes

Unless an active grab already exists or a passive grab on the button combination that was pressed already exists at a higher level in the hierarchy than where the ButtonPress occurred, an automatic active grab of the pointer takes place when a ButtonPress occurs. Because of the automatic grab, the matching ButtonRelease is sent to the same application that received the ButtonPress event. If OwnerGrabButtonMask has been selected, the ButtonRelease event is delivered to the window which contained the pointer when the button was released, as long as that window belongs to the same client as the window in which the ButtonPress event occurred. If the ButtonRelease occurs outside of the client's windows or OwnerGrabButtonMask was not selected, the ButtonRelease is delivered to the window in which the ButtonPress occurred. The grab is terminated when all buttons are released. During the grab, the cursor associated with the grabbing window will track the pointer anywhere on the screen.

If the application has invoked a passive button grab on an ancestor of the window in which the ButtonPress event occurs, then that grab takes precedence over the automatic grab, and the ButtonRelease will go to that window, or it will be handled normally by that client depending on the owner_events flag in the XGrabButton call.

Event Reference

When Generated

A `CirculateNotify` event reports a call to change the stacking order, and it includes whether the final position is on the top or on the bottom. This event is generated by `XCirculateSubwindows`, `XCirculateSubwindowsDown`, or `XCirculate-SubwindowsUp`. See also the `CirculateRequest` and `ConfigureNotify` reference pages.

Select With

This event is selected with `StructureNotifyMask` in the `XSelectInput` call for the window to be moved or with `SubstructureNotifyMask` for the parent of the window to be moved.

XEvent Structure Name

```
typedef union _XEvent {
    ...
    XCirculateEvent xcirculate;
    ...
} XEvent;
```

Event Structure

```
typedef struct {
    int type;
    unsigned long serial;   /* # of last request processed by server */
    Bool send_event;        /* True if this came from SendEvent request */
    Display *display;       /* Display the event was read from */
    Window event;
    Window window;
    int place;              /* PlaceOnTop, PlaceOnBottom */
} XCirculateEvent;
```

Event Structure Members

event   The window receiving the event. If the event was selected by `Structure-NotifyMask`, event will be the same as window. If the event was selected by `SubstructureNotifyMask`, event will be the parent of window.

window   The window that was restacked.

place   Either `PlaceOnTop` or `PlaceOnBottom`. Indicates whether the window was raised to the top or bottom of the stack.

When Generated

A `CirculateRequest` event reports when `XCirculateSubwindows`, `XCirculate-SubwindowsDown`, `XCirculateSubwindowsUp`, or `XRestackWindows` is called to change the stacking order of a group of children.

This event differs from `CirculateNotify` in that it delivers the parameters of the request before it is carried out. This gives the client that selects this event (usually the window manager) the opportunity to review the request in the light of its window management policy before executing the circulate request itself or to deny the request. (`CirculateNotify` indicates the final outcome of the request.)

Select With

This event is selected for the parent window with `SubstructureRedirectMask`.

XEvent Structure Name

```
typedef union _XEvent {
    ...
    XCirculateRequestEvent xcirculaterequest;
    ...
} XEvent;
```

Event Structure

```
typedef struct {
    int type;
    unsigned long serial; /* # of last request processed by server */
    Bool send_event;      /* True if this came from SendEvent request */
    Display *display;     /* Display the event was read from */
    Window parent;
    Window window;
    int place;            /* PlaceOnTop, PlaceOnBottom */
} XCirculateRequestEvent;
```

Event Structure Members

parent   The parent of the window that was restacked. This is the window that selected the event.

window   The window being restacked.

place   `PlaceOnTop` or `PlaceOnBottom`. Indicates whether the window was to be placed on the top or on the bottom of the stacking order.

ClientMessage

When Generated

A ClientMessage event is sent as a result of a call to XSendEvent by a client to a particular window. Any type of event can be sent with XSendEvent, but it will be distinguished from normal events by the send_event member being set to True. If your program wants to be able to treat events sent with XSendEvent as different from normal events, you can read this member.

Select With

There is no event mask for ClientMessage events, and they are not selected with XSelectInput. Instead XSendEvent directs them to a specific window, which is given as a window ID: the PointerWindow or the InputFocus.

XEvent Structure Name

```
typedef union _XEvent {
    ...
    XClientMessageEvent xclient;
    ...
} XEvent;
```

Event Structure

```
typedef struct {
    int type;
    unsigned long serial;    /* # of last request processed by server */
    Bool send_event;         /* True if this came from SendEvent request */
    Display *display;        /* Display the event was read from */
    Window window;
    Atom message_type;
    int format;
    union {
        char b[20];
        short s[10];
        long l[5];
    } data;
} XClientMessageEvent;
```

Event Structure Members

message_type   An atom that specifies how the data is to be interpreted by the receiving client. The X server places no interpretation on the type or the data, but it must be a list of 8-bit, 16-bit, or 32-bit quantities, so that the X server can correctly swap bytes as necessary. The data always consists of twenty 8-bit values, ten 16-bit values, or five 32-bit values, although each particular message might not make use of all of these values.

format   Specifies the format of the property specified by message_type. This will be on of the values 8, 16, or 32.

ColormapNotify

When Generated

A `ColormapNotify` event reports when the colormap attribute of a window changes or when the colormap specified by the attribute is installed, uninstalled, or freed. This event is generated by `XChangeWindowAttributes`, `XFreeColormap`, `XInstallColormap`, and `XUninstallColormap`.

Select With

This event is selected with `ColormapChangeMask`.

XEvent Structure Name

```
typedef union _XEvent {
    . . .
    XColormapEvent xcolormap;
    . . .
} XEvent;
```

Event Structure

```
typedef struct {
    int type;
    unsigned long serial;   /* # of last request processed by server */
    Bool send_event;        /* True if this came from SendEvent request */
    Display *display;       /* Display the event was read from */
    Window window;
    Colormap colormap;      /* a colormap or None */
    Bool new;
    int state;              /* ColormapInstalled, ColormapUninstalled */
} XColormapEvent;
```

Event Structure Members

window   The window whose associated colormap or attribute changes.

colormap   The colormap associated with the window, either a colormap ID or the constant None. It will be None only if this event was generated due to an `XFree-Colormap` call.

new   `True` when the colormap attribute has been changed, or `False` when the colormap is installed or uninstalled.

state   Either `ColormapInstalled` or `ColormapUninstalled`; it indicates whether the colormap is installed or uninstalled.

When Generated

A `ConfigureNotify` event announces actual changes to a window's configuration (size, position, border, and stacking order). See also the `CirculateRequest` reference page.

Select With

This event is selected for a single window by specifying the window ID of that window with `StructureNotifyMask`. To receive this event for all children of a window, specify the parent window ID with `SubstructureNotifyMask`.

XEvent Structure Name

```
typedef union _XEvent {
    ...
    XConfigureEvent xconfigure;
    ...
} XEvent;
```

Event Structure

```
typedef struct {
    int type;
    unsigned long serial; /* # of last request processed by server */
    Bool send_event;      /* True if this came from SendEvent request */
    Display *display;      /* Display the event was read from */
    Window event;
    Window window;
    int x, y;
    int width, height;
    int border_width;
    Window above;
    Bool override_redirect;
} XConfigureEvent;
```

Event Structure Members

event	The window that selected the event. The `event` and `window` members are identical if the event was selected with `Structure-NotifyMask`.
window	The window whose configuration was changed.
x, y	The final coordinates of the reconfigured window relative to its parent.
width, height	The width and height in pixels of the window after reconfiguration.
border_width	The width in pixels of the border after reconfiguration.
above	If this member is `None`, then the window is on the bottom of the stack with respect to its siblings. Otherwise, the window is immediately on top of the specified sibling window.

override_redirect   The override_redirect attribute of the reconfigured window. If True, it indicates that the client wants this window to be immune to interception by the window manager of configuration requests. Window managers normally should ignore this event if override_redirect is True.

When Generated

A `ConfigureRequest` event reports when another client attempts to change a window's size, position, border, and/or stacking order.

This event differs from `ConfigureNotify` in that it delivers the parameters of the request before it is carried out. This gives the client that selects this event (usually the window manager) the opportunity to revise the requested configuration before executing the `XConfigureWindow` request itself or to deny the request. (`ConfigureNotify` indicates the final outcome of the request.)

Select With

This event is selected for any window in a group of children by specifying the parent window with `SubstructureRedirectMask`.

XEvent Structure Name

```
typedef union _XEvent {
    ...
    XConfigureRequestEvent xconfigurerequest;
    ...
} XEvent;
```

Event Structure

```
typedef struct {
    int type;
    unsigned long serial;  /* # of last request processed by server */
    Bool send_event;       /* True if this came from SendEvent request */
    Display *display;      /* Display the event was read from */
    Window parent;
    Window window;
    int x, y;
    int width, height;
    int border_width;
    Window above;
    int detail;            /* Above, Below, BottomIf, TopIf, Opposite */
    unsigned long value_mask;
} XConfigureRequestEvent;
```

Event Structure Members

parent	The window that selected the event. This is the parent of the window being configured.
window	The window that is being configured.
x, y	The requested position for the upper-left pixel of the window's border relative to the origin of the parent window.
width, height	The requested width and height in pixels for the window.

border_width   The requested border width for the window.

above   None, Above, Below, TopIf, BottomIf, or Opposite. Specifies
                the sibling window on top of which the specified window should be
                placed. If this member has the constant None, then the specified win-
                dow should be placed on the bottom.

Notes

The geometry is derived from the XConfigureWindow request that triggered the event.

Event
Reference

CreateNotify

When Generated

A CreateNotify event reports when a window is created.

Select With

This event is selected on children of a window by specifying the parent window ID with SubstructureNotifyMask. (Note that this event type cannot be selected by StructureNotifyMask).

XEvent Structure Name

```
typedef union _XEvent {
    ...
    XCreateWindowEvent xcreatewindow;
    ...
} XEvent;
```

Event Structure

```
typedef struct {
    int type;
    unsigned long serial;      /* # of last request processed by server */
    Bool send_event;           /* True if this came from SendEvent
                                * request */
    Display *display;          /* Display the event was read from */
    Window parent;             /* parent of the window */
    Window window;             /* window ID of window created */
    int x, y;                  /* window location */
    int width, height;         /* size of window */
    int border_width;          /* border width */
    Bool override_redirect;    /* creation should be overridden */
} XCreateWindowEvent;
```

Event Structure Members

parent   The ID of the created window's parent.

window   The ID of the created window.

x, y   The coordinates of the created window relative to its parent.

width, height   The width and height in pixels of the created window.

border_width   The width in pixels of the border of the created window.

override_redirect   The override_redirect attribute of the created window. If True, it indicates that the client wants this window to be immune to interception by the window manager of configuration requests. Window managers normally should ignore this event if override_redirect is True.

Notes

For descriptions of these members, see the XCreateWindow function and the XSet-
WindowAttributes structure.

When Generated

A DestroyNotify event reports that a window has been destroyed.

Select With

To receive this event type on children of a window, specify the parent window ID and pass SubstructureNotifyMask as part of the event_mask argument to XSelectInput. This event type cannot be selected with StructureNotifyMask.

XEvent Structure Name

```
typedef union _XEvent {
    ...
    XDestroyWindowEvent xdestroywindow;
    ...
} XEvent;
```

Event Structure

```
typedef struct {
    int type;
    unsigned long serial; /* # of last request processed by server */
    Bool send_event;      /* True if this came from SendEvent request */
    Display *display;      /* Display the event was read from */
    Window event;
    Window window;
} XDestroyWindowEvent;
```

Event Structure Members

event   The window that selected the event.

window   The window that was destroyed.

EnterNotify, LeaveNotify

When Generated

EnterNotify and LeaveNotify events occur when the pointer enters or leaves a window.

When the pointer crosses a window border, a LeaveNotify event occurs in the window being left and an EnterNotify event occurs in the window being entered. Whether or not each event is queued for any application depends on whether any application selected the right event on the window in which it occurred.

In addition, EnterNotify and LeaveNotify events are delivered to windows that are *virtually crossed*. These are windows that are between the origin and destination windows in the hierarchy but not necessarily on the screen. Further explanation of virtual crossing is provided two pages following.

Select With

Each of these events can be selected separately with XEnterWindowMask and XLeave-WindowMask.

XEvent Structure Name

```
typedef union _XEvent {
    ...
    XCrossingEvent xcrossing;
    ...
} XEvent;
```

Event Structure

```
typedef struct {
    int type;               /* of event */
    unsigned long serial;   /* # of last request processed by server */
    Bool send_event;        /* True if this came from SendEvent request */
    Display *display;        /* Display the event was read from */
    Window window;          /* event window it is reported relative to */
    Window root;            /* root window that the event occurred on */
    Window subwindow;       /* child window */
    Time time;              /* milliseconds */
    int x, y;               /* pointer x,y coordinates in receiving
                             * window */
    int x_root, y_root;     /* coordinates relative to root */
    int mode;               /* NotifyNormal, NotifyGrab, NotifyUngrab */
    int detail;             /* NotifyAncestor, NotifyInferior,
                             * NotifyNonLinear, NotifyNonLinearVirtual,
                             * NotifyVirtual */
    Bool same_screen;       /* same screen flag */
    Bool focus;             /* boolean focus */
    unsigned int state;     /* key or button mask */
} XCrossingEvent;
typedef XCrossingEvent XEnterWindowEvent;
typedef XCrossingEvent XLeaveWindowEvent;
```

Event Structure Members

The following list describes the members of the XCrossingEvent structure.

subwindow
: In a LeaveNotify event, if the pointer began in a child of the receiving window, then the child member is set to the window ID of the child. Otherwise, it is set to None. For an EnterNotify event, if the pointer ends up in a child of the receiving window, then the child member is set to the window ID of the child. Otherwise, it is set to None.

time
: The server time when the crossing event occurred, in milliseconds. Time is declared as unsigned long, so it wraps around when it reaches the maximum value of a 32-bit number (every 49.7 days).

x, y
: The point of entry or exit of the pointer relative to the event window.

x_root, y_root
: The point of entry or exit of the pointer relative to the root window.

mode
: Normal crossing events or those caused by pointer warps have mode NotifyNormal, events caused by a grab have mode NotifyGrab, and events caused by a released grab have mode NotifyUngrab.

detail
: The value of the detail member depends on the hierarchical relationship between the origin and destination windows and the direction of pointer transfer. Determining which windows receive events and with which detail members is quite complicated. This topic is described in the next section.

same_screen
: Indicates whether the pointer is currently on the same screen as this window. This is always True unless the pointer was actively grabbed before the automatic grab could take place.

focus
: If the receiving window is the focus window or a descendant of the focus window, the focus member is True; otherwise, it is False.

state
: The state of all the buttons and modifier keys just before the event, represented by a mask of the button and modifier key symbols: Button1Mask, Button2Mask, Button3Mask, Button4Mask, Button5Mask, ControlMask, LockMask, Mod1Mask, Mod2-Mask, Mod3Mask, Mod4Mask, Mod5Mask, and ShiftMask.

Virtual Crossing and the detail Member

Virtual crossing occurs when the pointer moves between two windows that do not have a parent-child relationship. Windows between the origin and destination windows in the hierarchy receive EnterNotify and LeaveNotify events. The detail member of each of these events depends on the hierarchical relationship of the origin and destination windows and the direction of pointer transfer.

Virtual crossing is an advanced topic that you should not spend time figuring out unless you have an important reason to use it. We have never seen an application that uses this feature, and we know of no reason for its extreme complexity. With that word of warning, proceed.

Let's say the pointer has moved from one window, the origin, to another, the destination. First, we'll specify what types of events each window gets and then the detail member of each of those events.

The window of origin receives a LeaveNotify event and the destination window receives an EnterNotify event, if they have requested this type of event. If one is an inferior of the other, the detail member of the event received by the inferior is NotifyAncestor and the detail of the event received by the superior is NotifyInferior. If the crossing is between parent and child, these are the only events generated.

However, if the origin and destination windows are not parent and child, other windows are *virtually crossed* and also receive events. If neither window is an ancestor of the other, ancestors of each window, up to but not including the least common ancestor, receive Leave-Notify events, if they are in the same branch of the hierarchy as the origin, and Enter-Notify events, if they are in the same branch as the destination. These events can be used to track the motion of the pointer through the hierarchy.

- In the case of a crossing between a parent and a child of a child, the middle child receives a LeaveNotify with detail NotifyVirtual.

- In the case of a crossing between a child and the parent of its parent, the middle child receives an EnterNotify with detail NotifyVirtual.

- In a crossing between windows whose least common ancestor is two or more windows away, both the origin and destination windows receive events with detail Notify-Nonlinear. The windows between the origin and the destination in the hierarchy, up to but not including their least common ancestor, receive events with detail Notify-NonlinearVirtual. The least common ancestor is the lowest window from which both are descendants.

- If the origin and destination windows are on separate screens, the events and details generated are the same as for two windows not parent and child, except that the root windows of the two screens are considered the least common ancestor. Both root windows also receive events.

Event
Reference

Table E-1 shows the event types generated by a pointer crossing from window *A* to window *B* when window *C* is the least common ancestor of *A* and *B*.

Table E-1. Border Crossing Events and Window Relationship

LeaveNotify	EnterNotify
Origin window (*A*)	Destination window (*B*)
Windows between *A* and *B*, exclusive, if *A* is inferior	Windows between *A* and *B*, exclusive, if *B* is inferior
Windows between *A* and *C*, exclusive	Windows between *B* and *C*, exclusive,
Root window on screen of origin if different from screen of destination	Root window on screen of destination if different from screen of origin

Table E-2 lists the `detail` members in events generated by a pointer crossing from window *A* to window *B*.

Table E-2. Event detail Member and Window Relationship

detail Flag	Window Delivered To
NotifyAncestor	Origin or destination when either is descendant
NotifyInferior	Origin or destination when either is ancestor
NotifyVirtual	Windows between *A* and *B*, exclusive, if either is descendant
NotifyNonlinear	Origin and destination when *A* and *B* are two or more windows distant from least common ancestor *C*
NotifyNonlinearVirtual	Windows between *A* and *C*, exclusive, and between *B* and *C*, exclusive, when *A* and *B* have least common ancestor *C*; also on both root windows if *A* and *B* are on different screens

For example, Figure E-1 shows the events that are generated by a movement from a window (window *A*) to a child (window *B1*) of a sibling (window *B*). This would generate three events: a LeaveNotify with detail NotifyNonlinear for the window *A*, an EnterNotify with detail NotifyNonlinearVirtual for its sibling window *B*, and an EnterNotify with detail NotifyNonlinear for the child (window *B1*).

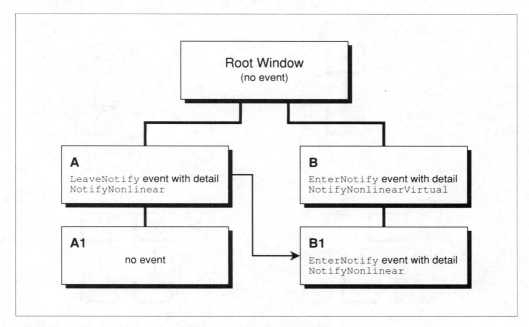

Figure E-1. Events generated by a move between windows

EnterNotify and LeaveNotify events are also generated when the pointer is grabbed, if the pointer was not already inside the grabbing window. In this case, the grabbing window receives an EnterNotify and the window containing the pointer receives a LeaveNotify event, both with mode NotifyUngrab. The pointer position in both events is the position before the grab. The result when the grab is released is exactly the same, except that the two windows receive EnterNotify instead of LeaveNotify and vice versa.

Event Reference

Figure E-2 demonstrates the events and details caused by various pointer transitions, indicated by heavy arrows.

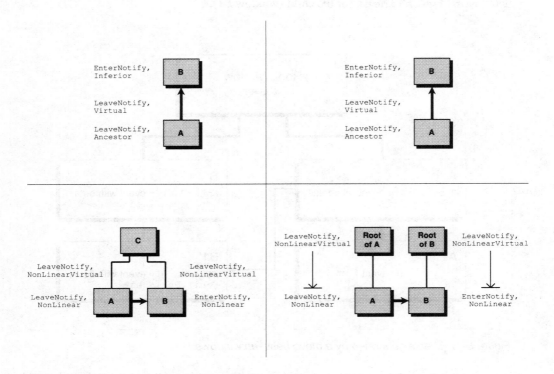

Figure E-2. Border crossing events and detail member for pointer movement from window A to window B, for various window relationships

Expose

When Generated

An Expose event is generated when a window becomes visible or a previously invisible part of a window becomes visible. Only InputOutput windows generate or need to respond to Expose events; InputOnly windows never generate or need to respond to them. The Expose event provides the position and size of the exposed area within the window and a rough count of the number of remaining exposure events for the current window.

Select With

This event is selected with ExposureMask.

XEvent Structure Name

```
typedef union _XEvent {
    ...
    XExposeEvent xexpose;
    ...
} XEvent;
```

Event Structure

```
typedef struct {
    int type;
    unsigned long serial;   /* # of last request processed by server */
    Bool send_event;        /* True if this came from SendEvent request */
    Display *display;       /* Display the event was read from */
    Window window;
    int x, y;
    int width, height;
    int count;              /* If nonzero, at least this many more */
} XExposeEvent;
```

Event Structure Members

x, y   The coordinates of the upper-left corner of the exposed region relative to the origin of the window.

width, height   The width and height in pixels of the exposed region.

count   The approximate number of remaining contiguous Expose events that were generated as a result of a single function call.

Notes

A single action such as a window movement or a function call can generate several exposure events on one window or on several windows. The server guarantees that all exposure events generated from a single action will be sent contiguously, so that they can all be handled before moving on to other event types. This allows an application to keep track of the rectangles specified in contiguous Expose events, set the clip_mask in a GC to the areas specified in the rectangle using `XSetRegion` or `XSetClipRectangles`, and then finally redraw the window clipped with the GC in a single operation after all the `Expose` events have arrived. The last event to arrive is indicated by a `count` of 0. In Release 2, `XUnionRectWith-Region` can be used to add the rectangle in `Expose` events to a region before calling `XSet-Region`.

If your application is able to redraw partial windows, you can also read each exposure event in turn and redraw each area.

FocusIn, FocusOut

When Generated

FocusIn and FocusOut events occur when the keyboard focus window changes as a result of an XSetInputFocus call. They are much like EnterNotify and LeaveNotify events except that they track the focus rather than the pointer.

When a focus change occurs, a FocusOut event is delivered to the old focus window and a FocusIn event to the window which receives the focus. In addition, windows in between these two windows in the window hierarchy are virtually crossed and receive focus change events, as described below. Some or all of the windows between the window containing the pointer at the time of the focus change and the root window also receive focus change events, as described below.

Select With

FocusIn and FocusOut events are selected with FocusChangeMask. They cannot be selected separately.

XEvent Structure Name

```
typedef union _XEvent {
    ...
    XFocusChangeEvent xfocus;
    ...
} XEvent;
```

Event Structure

```
typedef struct {
    int type;               /* FocusIn or FocusOut */
    unsigned long serial;   /* # of last request processed by server */
    Bool send_event;        /* True if this came from SendEvent request */
    Display *display;       /* Display the event was read from */
    Window window;          /* Window of event */
    int mode;               /* NotifyNormal, NotifyGrab, NotifyUngrab */
    int detail;             /* NotifyAncestor, NotifyDetailNone,
                             * NotifyInferior, NotifyNonLinear,
                             * NotifyNonLinearVirtual, NotifyPointer,
                             * NotifyPointerRoot, NotifyVirtual*/
} XFocusChangeEvent;
typedef XFocusChangeEvent XFocusInEvent;
typedef XFocusChangeEvent XFocusOutEvent;
```

Event Structure Members

mode   For events generated when the keyboard is not grabbed, mode is Notify-Normal; when the keyboard is grabbed, mode is NotifyGrab; and when a keyboard is ungrabbed, mode is NotifyUngrab.

detail   The detail member identifies the relationship between the window that receives the event and the origin and destination windows. It will be described in detail after the description of which windows get what types of events.

Notes

The *keyboard focus* is a window that has been designated as the one to receive all keyboard input irrespective of the pointer position. Only the keyboard focus window and its descendants receive keyboard events. By default, the focus window is the root window. Since all windows are descendants of the root, the pointer controls the window that receives input.

Most window managers allow the user to set a focus window to avoid the problem where the pointer sometimes gets bumped into the wrong window and your typing does not go to the intended window. If the pointer is pointing at the root window, all typing is usually lost, since there is no application for this input to propagate to. Some applications may set the keyboard focus so that they can get all keyboard input for a given period of time, but this practice is not encouraged.

Focus events are used when an application wants to act differently when the keyboard focus is set to another window or to itself. FocusChangeMask is used to select FocusIn and FocusOut events.

When a focus change occurs, a FocusOut event is delivered to the old focus window and a FocusIn event is delivered to the window which receives the focus. Windows in between in the hierarchy are virtually crossed and receive one focus change event each depending on the relationship and direction of transfer between the origin and destination windows. Some or all of the windows between the window containing the pointer at the time of the focus change and that window's root window can also receive focus change events. By checking the detail member of FocusIn and FocusOut events, an application can tell which of its windows can receive input.

The detail member gives clues about the relationship of the event receiving window to the origin and destination of the focus. The detail member of FocusIn and FocusOut events is analogous to the detail member of EnterNotify and LeaveNotify events but with even more permutations to make life complicated.

Virtual Focus Crossing and the detail Member

We will now embark on specifying the types of events sent to each window and the detail member in each event, depending on the relative position in the hierarchy of the origin window (old focus), destination window (new focus), and the pointer window (window containing pointer at time of focus change). Don't even try to figure this out unless you have to.

Table E-3 shows the event types generated by a focus transition from window A to window B when window C is the least common ancestor of A and B. This table includes most of the events generated, but not all of them. It is quite possible for a single window to receive more than one focus change event from a single focus change.

Table E-3. FocusIn and FocusOut Events and Window Relationship

FocusOut	FocusIn
Origin window (A)	Destination window (B)
Windows between A and B, exclusive, if A is inferior	Windows between A and B, exclusive, if B is inferior
Windows between A and C, exclusive	Windows between B and C, exclusive
Root window on screen of origin if different from screen of destination	Root window on screen of destination if different from screen of origin
Pointer window up to but not including origin window if pointer window is descendant of origin	Pointer window up to but not including destination window if pointer window is descendant of destination
Pointer window up to and including pointer window's root if transfer was from `PointerRoot`	Pointer window up to and including pointer window's root if transfer was to `PointerRoot`

Table E-4 lists the `detail` members in events generated by a focus transition from window *A* to window *B* when window *C* is the least common ancestor of *A* and *B*, with *P* being the window containing the pointer.

Table E-4. Event detail Member and Window Relationship

`detail` Flag	Window Delivered To
`NotifyAncestor`	Origin or destination when either is descendant
`NotifyInferior`	Origin or destination when either is ancestor
`NotifyVirtual`	Windows between *A* and *B*, exclusive, if either is descendant
`NotifyNonlinear`	Origin and destination when *A* and *B* are two or more windows distant from least common ancestor *C*
`NotifyNonlinearVirtual`	Windows between *A* and *C*, exclusive, and between *B* and *C*, exclusive, when *A* and *B* have least common ancestor *C*; also on both root windows if *A* and *B* are on different screens
`NotifyPointer`	Window *P* and windows up to but not including the origin or destination windows
`NotifyPointerRoot`	Window *P* and all windows up to its root, and all other roots, when focus is set to or from `Pointer-Root`
`NotifyDetailNone`	All roots, when focus is set to or from `None`

Figure E-3 shows all the possible combinations of focus transitions and of origin, destination, and pointer windows and shows the types of events that are generated and their `detail` member. Solid lines indicate branches of the hierarchy. Dotted arrows indicate the direction of transition of the focus. At each end of this arrow are the origin and destination windows, windows *A* to *B*. Arrows ending in a bar indicate that the event type and detail described are delivered to all windows up to the bar.

In any branch, there may be windows that are not shown. Windows in a single branch between two boxes shown will get the event types and details shown beside the branch.

Figure E-3.   FocusIn and FocusOut event schematics

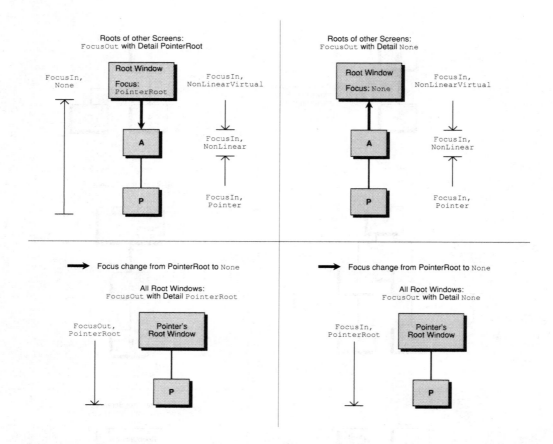

Figure E-3.   FocusIn and FocusOut event schematics (cont.)

FocusIn and FocusOut events are also generated when the keyboard is grabbed, if the focus was not already assigned to the grabbing window. In this case, all windows receive events as if the focus was set from the current focus to the grab window. When the grab is released, the events generated are just as if the focus was set back.

When Generated

GraphicsExpose events indicate that the source area for a XCopyArea or XCopyPlane request was not available because it was outside the source window or obscured by a window. NoExpose events indicate that the source region was completely available.

Select With

These events are not selected with XSelectInput but are sent if the GC in the XCopyArea or XCopyPlane request had its graphics_exposures flag set to True. If graphics_exposures is True in the GC used for the copy, either one NoExpose event or one or more GraphicsExpose events will be generated for every XCopyArea or XCopyPlane call made.

XEvent Structure Name

```
typedef union _XEvent {
    . . .
    XNoExposeEvent xnoexpose;
    XGraphicsExposeEvent xgraphicsexpose;
    . . .
} XEvent;
```

Event Structure

```
typedef struct {
    int type;
    unsigned long serial;  /* # of last request processed by server */
    Bool send_event;       /* True if this came from SendEvent request */
    Display *display;      /* Display the event was read from */
    Drawable drawable;
    int x, y;
    int width, height;
    int count;             /* if nonzero, at least this many more */
    int major_code;        /* core is CopyArea or CopyPlane */
    int minor_code;        /* not defined in the core */
} XGraphicsExposeEvent;

typedef struct {
    int type;
    unsigned long serial;  /* # of last request processed by server */
    Bool send_event;       /* True if this came from SendEvent request */
    Display *display;      /* Display the event was read from */
    Drawable drawable;
    int major_code;        /* core is CopyArea or CopyPlane */
    int minor_code;        /* not defined in the core */
} XNoExposeEvent;
```

Event
Reference

Event Structure Members

`drawable`	A window or an off-screen pixmap. This specifies the destination of the graphics request that generated the event.
`x, y`	The coordinates of the upper-left corner of the exposed region relative to the origin of the window.
`width, height`	The width and height in pixels of the exposed region.
`count`	The approximate number of remaining contiguous `GraphicsExpose` events that were generated as a result of the `XCopyArea` or `XCopy-Plane` call.
`major_code`	The graphics request used. This may be one of the symbols `CopyArea` or `CopyPlane` or a symbol defined by a loaded extension.
`minor_code`	Zero unless the request is part of an extension.

Notes

`Expose` events and `GraphicsExpose` events both indicate the region of a window that was actually exposed (`x`, `y`, `width`, and `height`). Therefore, they can often be handled similarly.

When Generated

A GravityNotify event reports when a window is moved because of a change in the size of its parent. This happens when the win_gravity attribute of the child window is something other than StaticGravity or UnmapGravity.

Select With

This event is selected for a single window by specifying the window ID of that window with StructureNotifyMask. To receive notification of movement due to gravity for a group of siblings, specify the parent window ID with SubstructureNotifyMask.

XEvent Structure Name

```
typedef union _XEvent {
    . . .
    XGravityEvent xgravity;
    . . .
} XEvent;
```

Event Structure

```
typedef struct {
    int type;
    unsigned long serial; /* # of last request processed by server */
    Bool send_event;      /* True if this came from SendEvent request */
    Display *display;      /* Display the event was read from */
    Window event;
    Window window;
    int x, y;
} XGravityEvent;
```

Event Structure Members

event   The window that selected the event.

window   The window that was moved.

x, y   The new coordinates of the window relative to its parent.

KeymapNotify

When Generated

A `KeymapNotify` event reports the state of the keyboard and occurs when the pointer or keyboard focus enters a window. `KeymapNotify` events are reported immediately after `EnterNotify` or `FocusIn` events. This is a way for the application to read the keyboard state as the application is "woken up," since the two triggering events usually indicate that the application is about to receive user input.

Select With

This event is selected with `KeymapStateMask`.

XEvent Structure Name

```
typedef union _XEvent {
    . . .
    XKeymapEvent xkeymap;
    . . .
} XEvent;
```

Event Structure

```
typedef struct {
    int type;
    unsigned long serial; /* # of last request processed by server */
    Bool send_event;      /* True if this came from SendEvent request */
    Display *display;      /* Display the event was read from */
    Window window;
    char key_vector[32];
} XKeymapEvent;
```

Event Structure Members

window   Reports the window which was reported in the `window` member of the preceding `EnterNotify` or `FocusIn` event.

key_vector   A bit vector or mask, each bit representing one physical key, with a total of 256 bits. For a given key, its keycode is its position in the keyboard vector. You can also get this bit vector by calling `XQueryKeymap`.

Notes

The `serial` member of `KeymapNotify` does not contain the serial number of the most recent protocol request processed, because this event always follows immediately after `EnterNotify` or `FocusIn` events in which the `serial` member is valid.

When Generated

KeyPress and KeyRelease events are generated for all keys, even those mapped to modifier keys such as Shift or Control.

Select With

Each type of keyboard event may be selected separately with KeyPressMask and Key-ReleaseMask.

XEvent Structure Name

```
typedef union _XEvent {
    ...
    XKeyEvent xkey;
    ...
} XEvent;
```

Event Structure

```
typedef struct {
    int type;               /* of event */
    unsigned long serial;   /* # of last request processed by server */
    Bool send_event;        /* True if this came from SendEvent request */
    Display *display;       /* Display the event was read from */
    Window window;          /* event window it is reported relative to */
    Window root;            /* root window that the event occurred on */
    Window subwindow;       /* child window */
    Time time;              /* milliseconds */
    int x, y;               /* pointer coordinates relative to receiving
                             * window */
    int x_root, y_root;     /* coordinates relative to root */
    unsigned int state;     /* modifier key and button mask */
    unsigned int keycode;   /* server-dependent code for key */
    Bool same_screen;       /* same screen flag */
} XKeyEvent;
typedef XKeyEvent XKeyPressedEvent;
typedef XKeyEvent XKeyReleasedEvent;
```

Event Structure Members

subwindow   If the source window is the child of the receiving window, then the subwindow member is set to the ID of that child.

time   The server time when the button event occurred, in milliseconds. Time is declared as unsigned long, so it wraps around when it reaches the maximum value of a 32-bit number (every 49.7 days).

x, y   If the receiving window is on the same screen as the root window specified by root, then x and y are the pointer coordinates relative to the receiving window's origin. Otherwise, x and y are zero.

Event Reference

When active button grabs and pointer grabs are in effect (see Section 9.4), the coordinates relative to the receiving window may not be within the window (they may be negative or greater than window height or width).

x_root, y_root   The pointer coordinates relative to the root window which is an ancestor of the event window. If the pointer was on a different screen, these are zero.

state   The state of all the buttons and modifier keys just before the event, represented by a mask of the button and modifier key symbols: Button1Mask, Button2Mask, Button3Mask, Button4Mask, Button5Mask, ControlMask, LockMask, Mod1Mask, Mod2-Mask, Mod3Mask, Mod4Mask, Mod5Mask, and ShiftMask.

keycode   The keycode member contains a server-dependent code for the key that changed state. As such, it should be translated into the portable symbol called a keysym before being used. It can also be converted directly into ASCII with XLookupString. For a description and examples of how to translate keycodes, see Section 9.1.1.

Notes

Remember that not all hardware is capable of generating release events and that only the main keyboard (a-z, A-Z, 0-9), Shift, and Control keys are always found.

Keyboard events are analogous to button events, though, of course, there are many more keys than buttons and the keyboard is not automatically grabbed between press and release.

All the structure members have the same meaning as described for ButtonPress and ButtonRelease events, except that button is replaced by keycode.

When Generated

The X server generates `MapNotify` and `UnmapNotify` events when a window changes state from unmapped to mapped or vice versa.

Select With

To receive these events on a single window, use `StructureNotifyMask` in the call to `XSelectInput` for the window. To receive these events for all children of a particular parent, specify the parent window ID and use `SubstructureNotifyMask`.

XEvent Structure Name

```
typedef union _XEvent {
    . . .
    XMapEvent xmap;
    XUnmapEvent xunmap;
    . . .
} XEvent;
```

Event Structure

```
typedef struct {
    int type;
    unsigned long serial;      /* # of last request processed by server */
    Bool send_event;           /* True if this came from SendEvent request */
    Display *display;          /* Display the event was read from */
    Window event;
    Window window;
    Bool override_redirect;    /* boolean, is override set */
} XMapEvent;

typedef struct {
    int type;
    unsigned long serial;      /* # of last request processed by server */
    Bool send_event;           /* True if this came from SendEvent request */
    Display *display;          /* Display the event was read from */
    Window event;
    Window window;
    Bool from_configure;
} XUnmapEvent;
```

Event Structure Members

event   The window that selected this event.

window   The window that was just mapped or unmapped.

override_redirect (XMapEvent only)
            True or False. The value of the `override_redirect` attribute of the window that was just mapped.

`from_configure` (XUnmapEvent only)

True if the event was generated as a result of a resizing of the window's parent when the window itself had a win_gravity of UnmapGravity. See the description of the win_gravity attribute in Section 4.3.4. False otherwise.

MappingNotify

When Generated

A MappingNotify event is sent when any of the following is changed by another client: the mapping between physical keyboard keys (keycodes) and keysyms, the mapping between modifier keys and logical modifiers, or the mapping between physical and logical pointer buttons. These events are triggered by a call to XSetModifierMapping or XSet-PointerMapping, if the return status is MappingSuccess, or by any call to XChange-KeyboardMapping.

This event type should not be confused with the event that occurs when a window is mapped; that is a MapNotify event. Nor should it be confused with the KeymapNotify event, which reports the state of the keyboard as a mask instead of as a keycode.

Select With

The X server sends MappingNotify events to all clients. It is never selected and cannot be masked with the window attributes.

XEvent Structure Name

```
typedef union _XEvent {
    . . .
    XMappingEvent xmapping;
    . . .
} XEvent;
```

Event Structure

```
typedef struct {
    int type;
    unsigned long serial; /* # of last request processed by server */
    Bool send_event;      /* True if this came from SendEvent request */
    Display *display;      /* Display the event was read from */
    Window window;         /* unused */
    int request;           /* one of MappingMapping, MappingKeyboard,
                            * MappingPointer */
    int first_keycode;     /* first keycode */
    int count;             /* range of change with first_keycode*/
} XMappingEvent;
```

Event Structure Members

request   The kind of mapping change that occurred: MappingModifier for a successful XSetModifierMapping (keyboard Shift, Lock, Control, Meta keys), MappingKeyboard for a successful XChange-KeyboardMapping (other keys), and MappingPointer for a successful XSetPointerMapping (pointer button numbers).

first_keycode If the request member is MappingKeyboard or Mapping-Modifier, then first_keycode indicates the first in a range of key-codes with altered mappings. Otherwise, it is not set.

Event
Reference

count   If the request member is MappingKeyboard or Mapping-Modifier, then count indicates the number of keycodes with altered mappings. Otherwise, it is not set.

Notes

If the request member is MappingKeyboard, clients should call XRefreshKeyboard-Mapping.

The normal response to a request member of MappingPointer or MappingModifier is no action. This is because the clients should use the logical mapping of the buttons and modifiers to allow the user to customize the keyboard if desired. If the application requires a particular mapping regardless of the user's preferences, it should call XGetModifier-Mapping or XGetPointerMapping to find out about the new mapping.

MapRequest

When Generated

A MapRequest event occurs when the functions XMapRaised and XMapWindow are called.

This event differs from MapNotify in that it delivers the parameters of the request before it is carried out. This gives the client that selects this event (usually the window manager) the opportunity to revise the size or position of the window before executing the map request itself or to deny the request. (MapNotify indicates the final outcome of the request.)

Select With

This event is selected by specifying the window ID of the parent of the receiving window with SubstructureRedirectMask. (In addition, the override_redirect member of the XSetWindowAttributes structure for the specified window must be False.)

XEvent Structure Name

```
typedef union _XEvent {
    . . .
    XMapRequestEvent xmaprequest;
    . . .
} XEvent;
```

Event Structure

```
typedef struct {
    int type;
    unsigned long serial; /* # of last request processed by server */
    Bool send_event;      /* True if this came from SendEvent request */
    Display *display;      /* Display the event was read from */
    Window parent;
    Window window;
} XMapRequestEvent;
```

Event Structure Members

parent   The ID of the parent of the window being mapped.

window   The ID of the window being mapped.

MotionNotify

xmotion —

When Generated

A MotionNotify event reports that the user moved the pointer or that a program warped the pointer to a new position within a single window.

Select With

This event is selected with ButtonMotionMask, Button1MotionMask, Button2-MotionMask, Button3MotionMask, Button4MotionMask, Button5MotionMask, PointerMotionHintMask, and PointerMotionMask. These masks determine the specific conditions under which the event is generated.

See Section 8.3.3.3 for a description of selecting button events.

XEvent Structure Name

```
typedef union _XEvent {
    . . .
    XMotionEvent xmotion;
    . . .
} XEvent;
```

Event Structure

```
typedef struct {
    int type;               /* of event */
    unsigned long serial;   /* # of last request processed by server */
    Bool send_event;        /* True if this came from SendEvent request */
    Display *display;       /* Display the event was read from */
    Window window;          /* event window it is reported relative to */
    Window root;            /* root window that the event occurred on */
    Window subwindow;       /* child window */
    Time time;              /* milliseconds */
    int x, y;               /* pointer coordinates relative to receiving
                             * window */
    int x_root, y_root;     /* coordinates relative to root */
    unsigned int state;     /* button and modifier key mask */
    char is_hint;           /* is this a motion hint */
    Bool same_screen;       /* same screen flag */
} XMotionEvent;
typedef XMotionEvent XPointerMovedEvent;
```

Event Structure Members

subwindow   If the source window is the child of the receiving window, then the subwindow member is set to the ID of that child.

time   The server time when the button event occurred, in milliseconds. Time is declared as unsigned long, so it wraps around when it reaches the maximum value of a 32-bit number (every 49.7 days).

x, y   If the receiving window is on the same screen as the root window specified by `root`, then x and y are the pointer coordinates relative to the receiving window's origin. Otherwise, x and y are zero.

When active button grabs and pointer grabs are in effect (see Section 9.4), the coordinates relative to the receiving window may not be within the window (they may be negative or greater than window height or width).

x_root, y_root   The pointer coordinates relative to the root window which is an ancestor of the event window. If the pointer was on a different screen, these are zero.

state   The state of all the buttons and modifier keys just before the event, represented by a mask of the button and modifier key symbols: `Button1Mask`, `Button2Mask`, `Button3Mask`, `Button4Mask`, `Button5Mask`, `ControlMask`, `LockMask`, `Mod1Mask`, `Mod2-Mask`, `Mod3Mask`, `Mod4Mask`, `Mod5Mask`, and `ShiftMask`.

is_hint   Either the constant `NotifyNormal` or `NotifyHint`. `NotifyHint` indicates that the `PointerMotionHintMask` was selected. In this case, just one event is sent when the mouse moves, and the current position can be found by calling `XQueryPointer` or by examining the motion history buffer with `XGetMotionEvents`, if a motion history buffer is available on the server. `NotifyNormal` indicates that the event is real, but it may not be up to date, since there may be many more later motion events on the queue.

same_screen   Indicates whether the pointer is currently on the same screen as this window. This is always `True` unless the pointer was actively grabbed before the automatic grab could take place.

Notes

If the processing you have to do for every motion event is fast, you can probably handle all of them without requiring motion hints. However, if you have extensive processing to do for each one, you might be better off using the hints and calling `XQueryPointer` or using the history buffer if it exists. `XQueryPointer` is a round-trip request, so it can be slow.

`EnterNotify` and `LeaveNotify` events are generated instead of `MotionEvents` if the pointer starts and stops in different windows.

PropertyNotify

When Generated

A `PropertyNotify` event indicates that a property of a window has changed or been deleted. This event can also be used to get the current server time (by appending zero-length data to a property). `PropertyNotify` events are generated by `XChangeProperty`, `XDeleteProperty`, `XGetWindowProperty`, or `XRotateWindowProperties`.

Select With

This event is selected with `PropertyChangeMask`.

XEvent Structure Name

```
typedef union _XEvent {
    . . .
    XPropertyEvent xproperty;
    . . .
} XEvent;
```

Event Structure

```
typedef struct {
    int type;
    unsigned long serial;   /* # of last request processed by server */
    Bool send_event;        /* True if this came from SendEvent request */
    Display *display;       /* Display the event was read from */
    Window window;
    Atom atom;
    Time time;
    int state;              /* property NewValue, property Deleted */
} XPropertyEvent;
```

Event Structure Members

window   The window whose property was changed, not the window that selected the event.

atom   The property that was changed.

state   Either `PropertyNewValue` or `PropertyDelete`. Whether the property was changed to a new value or deleted.

time   The `time` member specifies the server time when the property was changed.

When Generated

A ReparentNotify event reports when a client successfully reparents a window.

Select With

This event is selected with SubstructureNotifyMask by specifying the window ID of the old or the new parent window or with StructureNotifyMask by specifying the window ID.

XEvent Structure Name

```
typedef union _XEvent {
    ...
    XReparentEvent xreparent;
    ...
} XEvent;
```

Event Structure

```
typedef struct {
    int type;
    unsigned long serial; /* # of last request processed by server */
    Bool send_event;      /* True if this came from SendEvent request */
    Display *display;      /* Display the event was read from */
    Window event;
    Window window;
    Window parent;
    int x, y;
    Bool override_redirect;
} XReparentEvent;
```

Event Structure Members

window	The window whose parent window was changed.
parent	The new parent of the window.
x, y	The coordinates of the upper-left pixel of the window's border relative to the new parent window's origin.
override_redirect	The override_redirect attribute of the reparented window. If True, it indicates that the client wants this window to be immune to meddling by the window manager. Window managers normally should not have reparented this window to begin with.

ResizeRequest

When Generated

A `ResizeRequest` event reports another client's attempt to change the size of a window. The X server generates this event type when another client calls `XConfigureWindow`, `XMoveResizeWindow`, or `XResizeWindow`. If this event type is selected, the window is not resized. This gives the client that selects this event (usually the window manager) the opportunity to revise the new size of the window before executing the resize request or to deny the request itself.

Select With

To receive this event type, specify a window ID and pass `ResizeRedirectMask` as part of the `event_mask` argument to `XSelectInput`. Only one client can select this event on a particular window. When selected, this event is triggered instead of resizing the window.

XEvent Structure Name

```
typedef union _XEvent {
    . . .
    XResizeRequestEvent xresizerequest;
    . . .
} XEvent;
```

Event Structure

```
typedef struct {
    int type;
    unsigned long serial;  /* # of last request processed by server */
    Bool send_event;       /* True if this came from SendEvent request */
    Display *display;      /* Display the event was read from */
    Window window;
    int width, height;
} XResizeRequestEvent;
```

Event Structure Members

window   The window whose size another client attempted to change.

width, height   The requested size of the window, not including its border.

SelectionClear

When Generated

A `SelectionClear` event reports to the current owner of a selection that a new owner is being defined.

Select With

This event is not selected. It is sent to the previous selection owner when another client calls `XSetSelectionOwner` for the same selection.

XEvent Structure Name

```
typedef union _XEvent {
    ...
    XSelectionClearEvent xselectionclear;
    ...
} XEvent;
```

Event Structure

```
typedef struct {
    int type;
    unsigned long serial;  /* # of last request processed by server */
    Bool send_event;       /* True if this came from SendEvent request */
    Display *display;      /* Display the event was read from */
    Window window;
    Atom selection;
    Time time;
} XSelectionClearEvent;
```

Event Structure Members

window   The window that is receiving the event and losing the selection.

selection   The selection atom specifying the selection that is changing ownership.

time   The last-change time recorded for the selection.

SelectionNotify

When Generated

A `SelectionNotify` event is sent only by clients, not by the server, by calling `XSend-Event`. The owner of a selection sends this event to a requestor (a client that calls `XConvertSelection` for a given property) when a selection has been converted and stored as a property or when a selection conversion could not be performed (indicated with property `None`).

Select With

There is no event mask for `SelectionNotify` events, and they are not selected with `XSelectInput`. Instead `XSendEvent` directs the event to a specific window, which is given as a window ID: `PointerWindow`, which identifies the window the pointer is in, or `InputFocus`, which identifies the focus window.

XEvent Structure Name

```
typedef union _XEvent {
    ...
    XSelectionEvent xselection;
    ...
} XEvent;
```

Event Structure

```
typedef struct {
    int type;
    unsigned long serial;   /* # of last request processed by server */
    Bool send_event;        /* True if this came from SendEvent request */
    Display *display;       /* Display the event was read from */
    Window requestor;
    Atom selection;
    Atom target;
    Atom property;          /* Atom or None */
    Time time;
} XSelectionEvent;
```

Event Structure Members

The members of this structure have the values specified in the `XConvertSelection` call that triggers the selection owner to send this event, except that the `property` member either will return the atom specifying a property on the requestor window with the data type specified in `target` or will return `None`, which indicates that the data could not be converted into the `target` type.

SelectionRequest

When Generated

A SelectionRequest event is sent to the owner of a selection when another client requests the selection by calling XConvertSelection.

Select With

There is no event mask for SelectionRequest events, and they are not selected with XSelectInput.

XEvent Structure Name

```
typedef union _XEvent {
    ...
    XSelectionRequestEvent xselectionrequest;
    ...
} XEvent;
```

Event Structure

```
typedef struct {
    int type;
    unsigned long serial;  /* # of last request processed by server */
    Bool send_event;       /* True if this came from SendEvent request */
    Display *display;       /* Display the event was read from */
    Window owner;
    Window requestor;
    Atom selection;
    Atom target;
    Atom property;
    Time time;
} XSelectionRequestEvent;
```

Event Structure Members

The members of this structure have the values specified in the XConvertSelection call that triggers this event.

The owner should convert the selection based on the specified target type, if possible. If a property is specified, the owner should store the result as that property on the requestor window and then send a SelectionNotify event to the requestor by calling XSendEvent. If the selection cannot be converted as requested, the owner should send a SelectionNotify event with property set to the constant None.

Event
Reference

VisibilityNotify

When Generated

A `VisibilityNotify` event reports any change in the visibility of the specified window. This event type is never generated on windows whose class is `InputOnly`. All of the window's subwindows are ignored when calculating the visibility of the window.

Select With

This event is selected with `VisibilityChangeMask`.

XEvent Structure Name

```
typedef union _XEvent {
    ...
    XVisibilityEvent xvisibility;
    ...
} XEvent;
```

Event Structure

```
typedef struct {
    int type;
    unsigned long serial;   /* # of last request processed by server */
    Bool send_event;        /* True if this came from SendEvent request */
    Display *display;       /* Display the event was read from */
    Window window;
    int state;              /* VisibilityObscured,
                             * VisibilityPartiallyObscured,
                             * VisibilityUnobscured*/
} XVisibilityEvent;
```

Event Structure Members

state   A symbol indicating the final visibility status of the window: `Visibility-Obscured`, `VisibilityPartiallyObscured`, or `Visibility-Unobscured`.

Notes

Table E-5 lists the transitions that generate `VisibilityNotify` events and the corresponding `state` member of the `XVisibilityEvent` structure.

Table E-5. State Element of the XVisibilityEvent Structure

Visibility Status Before	Visibility Status After	State Member
Partially obscured, fully obscured, or not viewable	Viewable and completely unobscured	`VisibilityUnobscured`
Viewable and completely unobscured, or not viewable	Viewable and partially obscured	`VisibilityPartially-Obscured`
Viewable and completely unobscured, or viewable and partially obscured, or not viewable	Viewable and partially obscured	`VisibilityPartially-Obscured`

Event
Reference

F

The Xmu Library

The Xmu library provides a number of functions that combine Xlib functions in useful ways. This appendix summarizes the available functions. See Appendix J of Volume Two, Xlib Reference Manual, for detailed reference pages for each function.

In This Chapter:

The Xmu Library

The Xmu Library is a collection of miscellaneous (some might say random) utility functions that have been useful in building various applications and Xt Toolkit widgets. Though not defined by any X Consortium standard, this library is written and supported by MIT in the core distribution and therefore should be available on virtually all machines.

The functions in Xmu are briefly described here in several categories: atom manipulation, error handlers, system utilities, window utilities, cursor utilities, graphics functions, selection functions, character set functions, compound text functions, close display functions, event queue functions, and standard colormap functions. For detailed calling sequences for these functions, see Appendix J, *The Xmu Library*, of Volume Two, *Xlib Reference Manual*.

At each release, the number and variety of functions in this library have increased dramatically. It is worthwhile skimming this appendix to see what is available in R4, even if you are familiar with the R3 Xmu library.

Each of the groups of functions listed below has its own header file. Note that the location of the header files of Xmu has changed since R3. In R3, the header files for all X libraries were stored in */usr/include/X11*. The header files for Xmu and Xaw are now located in subdirectories of this directory, named after each library. In other words, the Xmu header files are now located (by default on UNIX-based systems) in */usr/include/X11/Xmu*.

F.1 Atom Functions

These functions allow an application to use various properties that do not have predefined atoms, without having to maintain a global variable to store the atom. Instead Xmu handles calling `XInternAtom` on the first reference and caches the value for all further references. For example, after initializing Xmu's atom-caching facility (with the arcane invocation `XmuInternAtom(display, XmuMakeAtom("NULL"))`), you can get the atom for any property that Xmu knows about, such as CLIPBOARD, simply by using the phrase `XA_CLIPBOARD(display)`.

F.2 Error Handler Functions

`XmuPrintErrorMessage` prints an error message equivalent to Xlib's default error message for protocol errors. It returns a nonzero value if the caller should consider exiting; otherwise, it returns 0. This function can be used when you need to write your own error handler but need to print out an error from within that handler.

`XmuSimpleErrorHandler` is an error handler function you can use in place of the default protocol error handler. It ignores `BadWindow` errors for `XQueryTree` and `XGetWindowAttributes` and ignores `BadDrawable` errors for `XGetGeometry`; it returns 0 in those cases. Otherwise, it prints the default error message and returns a nonzero value if the caller should consider exiting and 0 if the caller should not exit.

F.3 System Utility Functions

`XmuGetHostname` provides an operating-system-independent interface for getting the hostname of the system on which the client is running. This is useful for setting the WM_CLIENT_MACHINE property for the window manager.

F.4 Window Utility Functions

`XmuScreenOfWindow` returns a pointer to the `Screen` structure that describes the screen on which the window was created.

`XmuClientWindow` finds a window at or below the specified window which has a WM_STATE property. If such a window is found, it is returned; otherwise, the argument window is returned. This is used by window managers.

`XmuUpdateMapHints` is a convenience routine for setting (by applications) and reading (by the window manager) the XA_WM_NORMAL_HINTS property. It clears the `PPosition` and `PSize` flags and sets the `USPosition` and `USSize` flags in the hints structure and then stores the hints for the window using `XSetWMNormalHints` and returns `True`. If `NULL` is passed for the hints structure, then the current hints are read back from the window using `XGetWMNormalHints` and are used instead and `True` is returned; otherwise, `False` is returned.

F.5 Cursor Utility Functions

XmuCursorNameToIndex takes the name of a standard cursor and returns its index in the standard cursor font. The cursor names are formed by removing the XC_ prefix from the symbolic constants for cursors listed in Appendix I, *The Cursor Font*, of Volume Two, *Xlib Reference Manual*.

F.6 Graphics Functions

XmuDrawRoundedRectangle draws a rounded rectangle, given x, y, width, height dimensions of the overall rectangle, and ew and eh sizes of a bounding box that the corners are drawn inside of. This function simply calls Xlib's drawing routines.

XmuFillRoundedRectangle simply fills a shape similar to that drawn by XmuDrawRoundedRectangle, in the same way that XFillRectangle fills.

XmuDrawLogo draws the "official" X Window System logo. The bounding box of the logo is given by x, y, width, and height.

XmuCreateStippledPixmap creates a two- by two-pixel pixmap of specified depth on the specified screen, with the top-left and bottom-right pixels drawn in the foreground pixel value and the other two drawn in the background. The pixmap is cached so that multiple requests share the same pixmap. The pixmap should be freed with XmuReleaseStippledPixmap to maintain correct reference counts.

XmuReadBitmapData reads a standard bitmap file description from the specified stream and returns the parsed data in a format suitable for passing to XCreateBitmapFromData

XmuReadBitmapDataFromFile reads a standard bitmap file description from the specified file and returns the parsed data in a format suitable for passing to XCreateBitmapFromData.

XmuLocateBitmapFile reads a file in standard bitmap file format, using XReadBitmapFile, and returns the created bitmap. The filename may be absolute or relative to the global resource named bitmapFilePath with class BitmapFilePath. If the resource is not defined, the default value is the build symbol BITMAPDIR, which is typically */usr/include/X11/bitmaps*.

XmuCreatePixmapFromBitmap creates a pixmap of the specified width, height, and depth on the same screen as the specified drawable and then performs an XCopyPlane from the specified bitmap to the pixmap, using the specified foreground and background pixel values.

F.7 Selection Functions

`XmuConvertStandardSelection` converts the following standard selections: CLASS, CLIENT_WINDOW, DECNET_ADDRESS, HOSTNAME, IP_ADDRESS, NAME, OWNER_OS, TARGETS, TIMESTAMP, and USER. It returns `True` if the conversion was successful, else it returns `False`.

F.8 Character Set Functions

`XmuCopyISOLatin1Lowered` copies a null-terminated string (including the null), changing all Latin-1 upper-case letters to lower-case. `XmuCopyISOLatin1Uppered` copies a null-terminated string (including the null), changing all Latin-1 lower-case letters to upper-case. `XmuCompareISOLatin1` compares two null-terminated Latin-1 strings, ignoring case differences, and returns an integer greater than, equal to, or less than 0, according to whether first is lexicographically greater than, equal to, or less than second. In all three of these routines, the string is assumed to be encoded using ISO 8859-1.

The following functions have the same arguments and function as `XLookupString`, except that they convert to keysyms in different sets.

Function	Converts To
XmuLookupAPL	APL string
XmuLookupArabic	Latin/Arabic (ISO 8859-6) or ASCII control
XmuLookupCyrillic	Latin/Cyrillic (ISO 8859-5) or ASCII control
XmuLookupGreek	Latin/Greek (ISO 8859-7) or ASCII control
XmuLookupHebrew	Latin/Hebrew (ISO 8859-8) or ASCII control string
XmuLookupJISX0201	JIS X0201-1976 encoding, including ASCII control
XmuLookupKana	Latin-1 (ISO 8859-1) and ASCII control in the Graphics Left half (values 0 to 127) and Katakana in the Graphics Right half (values 128 to 255), using the values from JIS X201-1976.
XmuLookupLatin1	Latin-1 (ISO 8859-1) or ASCII control (synonym for XLookupString)
XmuLookupLatin2	Latin-2 (ISO 8859-2) or ASCII control
XmuLookupLatin3	Latin-3 (ISO 8859-3) or ASCII control
XmuLookupLatin4	Latin-4 (ISO 8859-4) or ASCII control

F.9 Compound Text Functions

These functions are for parsing Compound Text strings, decomposing them into individual segments. Four functions are provided for this purpose: `XctCreate`, `XctFree`, `XctNextItem`, `XctReset`. For more information on these functions, see Appendix J, *The Xmu Library*, of Volume Two, *Xlib Reference Manual*.

F.10 CloseDisplay Hook Functions

`XmuAddCloseDisplayHook` adds a function that will be called with the given arguments when `XCloseDisplay` is called. `XmuRemoveCloseDisplayHook` deletes the function that has been added with `XmuAddCloseDisplayHook`. More than one such function can be added.

`XmuLookupCloseDisplayHook` determines if a function is installed.

These functions use the Display Queue Functions internally, which are described next.

F.11 Display Queue Functions

`XmuDQCreate` creates and returns an empty `XmuDisplayQueue` (which is really just a linked list of displays; it is called a queue for historical reasons). The queue is initially empty, but displays can be added using `XmuDQAddDisplay`. Functions can be added for each display, to be called when the display connection is closed. These are called close callbacks. Functions can also be added to be called when the last display connection is closed. These are called free callbacks. The application is responsible for actually freeing the queue, by calling `XmuDQDestroy`.

`XmuDQAddDisplay` does not attempt to prevent duplicate entries in the queue; the caller should use `XmuDQLookupDisplay` to determine if a display has already been added to a queue. The `XmuDQNDisplays` macro returns the number of displays in the specified queue. `XmuDQRemoveDisplay` removes the specified display from the specified queue, without calling its close callbacks. `XmuDQDestroy` releases all memory associated with the specified queue and optionally calls the close callbacks for each display.

F.12 Standard Colormap Functions

XmuAllStandardColormaps creates all of the appropriate standard colormaps for every visual of every screen on a given display. If the property of any standard colormap is already defined, this function will redefine it. This function is intended to be used by window managers or a special client at the start of a session.

XmuVisualStandardColormaps creates all of the appropriate standard colormaps for a given visual on a given screen.

XmuLookupStandardColormap creates a standard colormap if one does not currently exist or replaces the currently existing standard colormap. Given a screen, a visual, and a property, this function will determine the best allocation for the property under the specified visual and whether to create a new colormap or use the default colormap of the screen.

XmuGetColormapAllocation determines the best allocation of reds, greens, and blues in a standard colormap. It is assumed that the visual is appropriate for the colormap property.

XmuStandardColormap creates any one standard colormap, given a visual, a standard colormap atom, and other input, and returns an XStandardColormap structure. Xmu-CreateColormap creates any one colormap, given an XStandardColormap structure.

All colormaps are created with read-only allocations, with the exception of read-only allocations of colors, which fail to return the expected pixel value, and these are individually defined as read/write allocations. This is done so that all the cells defined in the colormap are contiguous, for use in image processing. This typically happens with White and Black in the default map.

Colormaps of static visuals are considered to be successfully created if the map of the static visual matches the definition given in the standard colormap structure.

XmuDeleteStandardColormap removes any standard colormap property, also releasing any resources used by the colormap(s) specified in the property, if possible.

G

Sources of Additional Information

This appendix describes where you can get more information about Xlib and about X in general, including other books on the subject and the various ways to get the source code for X.

In This Chapter:

G
Sources of Additional Information

This appendix lists a few of the official and unofficial sources for information about the X Window System and associated software.

Note that some of this detailed information may become dated rather quickly. The best source of current information is the *comp.windows.x* network news group, described later in this appendix.

G.1 Getting the X Software

At this writing, the current public release level is Release 4. This book documents Release 3 and Release 4. Many people will continue to use R3, since there is a considerable lag time between the date that MIT distributes a new release and the date by which vendors integrate that release into their own products and issue updates. All changes to Xlib in R4 are backwards compatible, although since July 1989, there has been a new X Consortium standard set of interclient communication conventions, first released widely in R4, that require changes from the conventions used in R3.

You can get the X software directly from MIT on three 9-track 1600-BPI magtapes written in UNIX *tar* format or on one 9-track 6250-BPI magtape, along with printed copies of MIT's manuals, by sending a check in U.S. currency for U.S. $400 to:

> MIT Software Distribution Center
> Technology Licensing Office
> MIT E32-300
> 77 Massachusetts Avenue
> Cambridge, MA 02139

Their telephone number is (617) 253-6966, and the "X Ordering Hotline" is (617) 258-8330. If you want the tapes and manuals shipped overseas, the price is $500. The manual set alone is $125, including U.S. shipping, or $175, including overseas shipping.

Other distribution media or formats are not available from the MIT Software Distribution Center but are from other independent vendors such as ICS, mentioned later. The Release tape comes with source code for sample servers for Apollo, DEC, HP, IBM, Sony, Sun, and several other workstations, source code for clients written by MIT, sources for the toolkits

Xt, XView (in R4), Interviews, and Andrew, contributed software written outside MIT, and sources and Postscript files for all MIT's documentation. Note that the servers supplied are sample servers only; commercial vendors typically release optimized (faster) servers for the same machines.

Sites that have access to the Internet can retrieve the distribution from the following machines using anonymous *ftp*. Here are the current sites:

Location	Hostname	Address	Directory
East	*UUNET.uu.net*	192.12.141.129	*X/X.V11R4*
Northeast	*crl.dec.com*	192.58.206.2	*pub/X11/R4*
	expo.lcs.mit.edu	18.30.0.212	*pub/X.V11R4*
Midwest	*giza.cis.ohio-state.edu*	128.146.8.61	*pub/X.V11R4*
	mordred.cs.purdue.edu	128.10.2.2	*pub/X11/R4*
South	*dinorah.wustl.edu*	129.252.118.101	*pub/X.V11R4*
Southeast	*uunet.uu.net*	192.48.96.2	*X/R4*
West	*gatekeeper.dec.com*	128.45.9.52	*pub/X.V11R4*
	nic.mr.net	192.12.250.5	*pub/X.V11R4*

DO NOT do anonymous *ftp* during normal business hours, and please use the machine nearest you.

The distribution is also available by UUCP from UUNET for sites without Internet access. The files are split up to be small enough for UUCP distribution.

G.1.1 Bug Fixes

Critical bug fixes as well as a limited number of important new features are available from the archive server *xstuff@expo.lcs.mit.edu*. Electronic mail sent to this address is forwarded to a program which responds with the requested information. The rest of this section and the two sections that follow it explain how to use *xstuff*.

The *xstuff* server is a mail-response program. This means that you mail it a request and it mails back the response.

The *xstuff* server is a very dumb program. It does not have much error checking. If you do not send it commands that it understands, it will just answer "I don't understand you."

The *xstuff* server reads your entire message before it does anything, so you can have several different commands in a single message. It treats the "Subject:" header line just like any other line of the message. You can use any combination of upper- and lower-case letters in the commands.

The archives are organized into a series of directories and subdirectories. Each directory has an index, and each subdirectory has an index. The top-level index gives you an overview of what is in the subdirectories, and the index for each subdirectory tells you what it contains.

If you are bored with reading documentation and just want to try something, then send the server a message containing the line:

```
send index fixes
```

When you get the index back, it will contain the numbers of all of the fixes and batches of fixes in the archive. Then you can send the server another message asking it to send you the fixes that you want:

```
send fixes 1 5 9 11-20
```

If you are using a mailer that understands "@" notation, send to *xstuff@expo.lcs.mit.edu*. If your mailer deals in "!" notation, try sending to *{someplace}!eddie!expo.lcs.mit.edu!xstuff*. For other mailers, you're on your own.

The server has four commands. Each command must be the first word on a line.

help   The command *help* or *send help* causes the server to send you the help file. No other commands are honored in a message that asks for help (the server figures that you had better read the help message before you do anything else).

index   If your message contains a line whose first word is *index*, then the server will send you the top-level index of the contents of the archive. If there are other words on that line that match the names of subdirectories, then the indexes for those sub-directories are sent instead of the top-level index. For example, you can say:

```
index
```

or:

```
index fixes
```

You can then send back another message to the *xstuff* server, using a *send* command (see below) to ask it to send you the files whose names you learned from that list.

index fixes and *send index fixes* mean the same thing: you can use *send* instead of *index* for getting an index.

If your message has an *index* or a *send index* command, then all other *send* commands will be ignored. This means that you cannot get an index and data in the same request. This is so that index requests can be given high priority.

send   If your message contains a line whose first word is *send*, then the *xstuff* server will send you the item(s) named on the rest of the line. To name an item, you give its directory and its name. For example:

```
send fixes 1-10
```

Once you have named a category, you can put as many names as you like on the rest of the line. They will all be taken from that category. For example:

```
send fixes 1-10 11-20 21-30
```

Each *send* command can reference only one directory. If you would like to get one fix and one of something else, you must use two *send* commands.

You may put as many *send* commands as you like into one message to the server, but the more you ask for, the longer it will take to receive. See Section G.1.3 for an explanation. Actually, it is not strictly true that you can put as many *send* commands as you want into one message. If the server must use UUCP mail to send your files, then it cannot send more than 100K bytes in one message. If you ask for more than it can send, then it will send as much as it can and ignore the rest.

path The *path* command exists to help in case you do not get responses from the server when you mail to it.

Sometimes the server is unable to return mail over the incoming path. There are dozens of reasons why this might happen, and if you are a true wizard, you already know what those reasons are. If you are an apprentice wizard, you might not know all the reasons, but you might know a way to circumvent them.

If you put in a *path* command, then everything that the server mails to you will be mailed to that address rather than to the return address on your mail. The server host *expo.lcs.mit.edu* does not have a direct UUCP connection to anywhere; you must go through *mit-eddie* (the UUCP name of *eddie.mit.edu*) or somewhere else.

G.1.1.1 Notes

The *xstuff* server acknowledges every request by return mail. If you do not get a message back in a day or two, you should assume that something is going wrong and perhaps try a *path* command.

The *xstuff* server does not respond to requests from users named *root*, *system*, *daemon*, or *mailer*. This is to prevent mail loops. If your name is "Bruce Root" or "Jane Daemon" and you can document this, we will happily rewrite the server to remove this restriction. Yes, we know about Norman Mailer and Waverley Root. Norman doesn't use netmail and Waverley is dead.

G.1.1.2 Fairness

The *xstuff* server contains many safeguards to ensure that it is not monopolized by people asking for large amounts of data. The mailer is set up so that it will send no more than a fixed amount of data each day. If the work queue contains more requests than the day's quota, then the unsent files will not be processed until the next day. Whenever the mailer is run to send its day's quota, it sends the shortest requests out first.

If you have a request waiting in the work queue and you send in another request, the new request is added to the old one (thereby increasing its size) rather than being filed anew. This prevents you from being able to send in a large number of small requests as a way of beating the system.

The reason for all of these quotas and limitations is that the delivery resources are finite, and there are many people who would like to make use of the archive.

G.2 Netnews

The Usenet network news is probably the most valuable source of information about X. The current list of public mailing lists that discuss X is as follows:

Mailing List	Description
bug-clx	Bug reports and discussion of the CLX (Common Lisp X) library
x11-3D	People interested in X and three-dimensional graphics
x-ada	X and ada
ximage	People interested in image processing and X
xpert	General discussion of X
xvideo	Discussion of video extensions for X

Requests to join these lists should be sent to *mailing-list-name*-request@expo.lcs.mit.edu, or uunet!expo.lcs.mit.edu!*mailing-list-name*-request (for example, to join the ximage mailing list, send mail to ximage-request@expo.lcs.mit.edu).

The developers of X post notices of fixes to the software to the newsgroup *comp.window.x* (which is the same as *xpert*), and this is where users and developers around the world ask and answer questions.

Information Sources

G.3 Training and Consulting

Numerous independent vendors provide courses on X programming. Several sources that we are aware of include:

- *Integrated Computer Solutions*, 163 Harvard Street, Cambridge, MA 02139; (617) 547-0510. Courses on Xlib, Motif, strategic overviews of X. Also provides consulting services and manages an X user's group.

- *Hands-On Learning*, 27 Cambridge Street, Burlington, MA 01803; (617) 272-0088. Courses on Xlib and Xt.

- X tutorials are now a regular feature of UNIX conventions, such as the UNIX EXPO, Usenix, Uniforum, Xhibition, and the annual X conference at MIT. Also contact hardware vendors for information on courses they offer.

Training companies wishing to be listed here should send us information on the courses they offer.

G.3.1 Telephone Support

X programming is a very new field, and since everyone who knows enough to help you is overworked, you are likely to hear "you're on your own" if you try to call for help. There are currently no support lines, because X was developed by a university, not a system manufacturer or software house. When X becomes widely supported as a commercial product, the situation will change as vendors offer support.

ICS provides telephone support for a fee. See Section G.3 for their telephone number.

G.4 The X Consortium

The X Consortium can be reached at:

> MIT X Consortium
> 545 Technology Square - Room 217
> Cambridge, MA 02139

The Consortium's telephone number is (617) 253-8861; its current members are shown below.

ACER Counterpoint, Inc.	MIPS Computer Systems
Adobe Systems	MITRE Corp.
Advanced Graphics Engineering	Mitsubishi Electric Corporation
Apollo Computer, Inc.	NCR Corporation
Apple Computer, Inc.	NEC Corporation
Ardent Computer	Network Computing Devices, Inc.
AT&T	Nova Graphics International
BULL MTS	NTT Corporation
CalComp	OMRON Tateisi Electronics
Canterbury University, England	Open Software Foundation
Carnegie Mellon University	O'Reilly & Associates, Inc.
CETIA	PCS Computer Systeme GmbH
Codonics, Inc.	Prime Computer, Inc.
Control Data Corporation	Reuters
Cray Research, Inc.	Samsung Software America
Data General	Sequent Computer Systems Inc.
Digital Equipment Corp.	Siemens AG
Eastman Kodak Company	Silicon Graphics Computer Systems
Evans & Sutherland	Societe de Gestion et d'Informatique Publicis
Fujitsu America, Inc.	Software Productivity Consortium
GfxBase	Solbourne Computer Inc.
Hewlett-Packard Company	Sony Corporation
IBM Corporation	Stanford University
INESC*	Stellar Computer Inc.
Integrated Computer Solutions, Inc.	Sun Microsystems, Inc.

---

*Instituto de Engenharia de Sistemas e Computadores, Brazil

Integrated Solutions, Inc.
Interactive Development Environments
Interactive Systems Corp.
Jupiter Systems
Key Systems Engineering Corp.
Landmark Graphics Corp.
Locus Computing Corp.
Matrox International
Megatek Corp.

Tatung Science and Technology
Tektronix, Inc.
Texas Instruments
UNICAD, Inc.
Unisys Corp.
University of Lowell
Visual Technology, Inc.
Wang Laboratories
X/Open Company Ltd.

Most of these companies are preparing products based on X. It should not be long before many different products are available that support X.

G.5 Finding Out for Yourself

X is unusual in that the source code is in the public domain. It should be possible for most X programmers to get a copy of the X source code from the sources listed above. Once you understand how the code is organized, you can look up certain details about how X works as long as you have a good knowledge of C and a little persistence. In "Star Wars," the saying was "Use the Force, Luke." In X, it is "Use the Source, Luke."

Xlib and the server are two distinct chunks of code. Each contains code for sending and receiving information to and from the other over the network using protocol requests, replies, events, and errors. The source tree as supplied on the X distribution tape places the Xlib source in the directory *base/lib/X*, where *base* is the top of the entire source tree. Their server source is placed in *base/server*.

The procedure for finding out something about an Xlib routine is normally to search for the routine in the Xlib code and then figure out what it does. Sometimes the answer can be found there. Many of the routines, however, simply place their arguments in a protocol request and send it to the server. Then you will have to look in the server code for the answer. To find the correct place in the server code, you will need the symbol for the protocol request, which is the first argument in the `GetReq` call.

The server code is much more involved than Xlib itself. The device-dependent portions are in *base/server/ddx*, and the device-independent portions are in *base/server/dix*. The device-independent code should be your first stop, because it is here that protocol requests from Xlib arrive and are dispatched to the appropriate code. Search for the protocol request symbol you found in Xlib. It will appear in several source files. Start with the occurrence in *dispatch.c*, and try to figure out what the code does. This will require following leads to other routines.

If you do not find a routine in *base/server/dix*, then it must be in the device-dependent code. *base/server/ddx* has one directory in it for each brand of hardware to which a sample server has been ported. It also contains the directories */cfb*, */mfb*, */mi*, and */snf*, which contain routines used in writing the sample server device-dependent code. Note that servers may include code ostensibly for other machines. For example, the Sun sample server appears to use code in several of the directories for other servers such as *dec* and *hp*.

Xlib and the X protocol are both defined by specification documents, not by any particular implementation. Never depend on the implementation details of the Xlib or server code. If you do, your code may not run on a machine that has optimized X software. This manual documents only those features of Xlib and X in general that are governed by X Consortium standard specifications. If you follow the guidance you find in this volume and the details in Volume Two, *Xlib Reference Manual*, you will be in good shape.

H

Release Notes

This appendix describes the changes between each release of X Version 11. It begins with the changes in the most recent release and works back to the first release.

In This Chapter:

H
Release Notes

This appendix describes differences between the various releases of the X Window System through Release 4. There were only a few changes in the Xlib interface at each release, and most were backwards compatible. No changes were made in the underlying X protocol.

H.1 Changes from Release 3 to Release 4

We will begin by describing the new functions, and then we will describe the small existing interface changes.

H.1.1 New Routines

Because of the adoption of the ICCCM (*Inter-Client Communication Conventions Manual*) as an X Consortium standard, several Xlib structures had to be changed, and therefore, several of the R3 routines are now superceded by new routines. All R3 routines are still supported, but the superceded routines should not be used in new applications because they do not meet the current conventions. Table H-1 lists the old and new routines.

Table H-1. Superceded R3 Routines and New R4 Routines

Superceded Routine	New Routine	Change
XSetStandardProperties	XSetWMProperties	Added `WM_HINTS` and `WM_CLASS`, format changes
XSetNormalHints	XSetWMNormalHints	New fields in `XSizeHints`
XGetNormalHints	XGetWMNormalHints	New fields in `XSizeHints`
XSetZoomHints	(No replacement)	No longer part of ICCCM
XGetZoomHints	(No replacement)	No longer part of ICCCM
XSetSizeHints	XSetWMSizeHints	New fields in `XSizeHints`
XGetSizeHints	XGetWMSizeHints	New fields in `XSizeHints`
XStoreName	XSetWMName	Property format change
XFetchName	XGetWMName	Property format change
XSetCommand	XSetWMCommand	Property format change

Superceded Routine	New Routine	Change
(No R3 equivalent)	XGetWMCommand	Convenience routine for XGetWindowProperty
XSetIconName	XSetWMIconName	Property format change
XGetIconName	XGetWMIconName	Property format change
XGeometry	XWMGeometry	New fields and arguments
XGetStandardColormap	XGetRGBColormaps	New fields in XStandard-Colormap
XSetStandardColormap	XSetRGBColormaps	New fields in XStandard-Colormap

XSetWMProperties is the new interface for setting all required window manager properties. This function now sets the WM_HINTS and WM_CLASS properties, in addition to the properties set under R3 by XSetStandardProperties. Furthermore, the window name and icon name arguments are now XTextProperty structures that can be filled with the new function XStringListToTextProperty, described below.

All string properties to be set for the window manager have been changed to use XTextProperty structures so that they can use non-Western encodings (which require more than the eight bits of data provided in the R3 STRING property). For this reason, XGetWMCommand replaces XGetCommand, XSetWMCommand replaces XSetCommand, XGetWMIconName replaces XGetIconName, XSetWMIconName replaces XSetIconName, XGetWMName replaces XFetchName, and XSetWMName replaces XStoreName.

XGetWMCommand was added to make it easier for window managers to read the XA_WM_COMMAND property. In R3, XSetCommand was provided but no XGetCommand.

Three new fields have been added to the XSizeHints structure. Two, base_width and base_height, basically supercede the min_width and min_height fields. The x, y, width, and height fields of XSizeHints are no longer used. Instead these values are simply set when creating the top-level window (and the window manager gets these values through substructure redirection in CreateNotify and MapNotify events). The other new field, win_gravity, allows an application to specify that some other portion of the window is to be placed when the window manager allows the user to place windows. The purpose of this, for example, is to allow users that display languages that read from right to left to position the top-right corner of these terminals instead of their top-left corner.

XWMGeometry replaces XGeometry. XWMGeometry calculates geometry values for the top-level window, given a possibly incomplete user-specified geometry string and a complete application default geometry specified using an XSizeHints structure. XWMGeometry also returns a win_gravity value based on which corner of the top-level window the user or application specified, suitable for setting into the XSizeHints structure.

New fields have been added to the `XStandardColormap` structure to return the visual associated with the colormap and also to provide information about who is allowed to delete the colormap. To use the new fields, `XGetStandardColormap` is superceded by `XGet-RGBColormaps` and `XSetStandardColormap` is superceded by `XSet-RGBColormaps`.

The following routines are completely new in R4.

`XSetWMClientMachine` is used by clients to set a new property to be read with `XGet-WMClientMachine` by window or session managers. The property stores the name of the machine on which the client is running, as seen from the server, so that the session manager can stop and restart the client on the right machine. See Chapter 10, *Interclient Communication*.

`XSetWMProtocols` is used by clients to set a new property to be read with `XGet-WMProtocols` by the window manager. This property indicates which of a number of window manager-client protocols the client would like to take part in. Under these protocols, the window manager sends synthetic events to the client to notify the client of certain impending conditions, such as that the client has been granted the keyboard focus or is about to have one of its windows destroyed or that the entire client is about to be killed. See Chapter 10.

`XSetWMColormapWindows` is used by clients to set a new property to be read with `XGetWMColormapWindows` by the window manager. This property tells the window manager that certain subwindows of the client have custom colormaps that will need installing. See Chapter 10.

Five new routines are provided that allocate and zero the fields of structures used in setting the window manager hints: `XAllocClassHint`, `XAllocIconSize`, `XAllocSize-Hints`, `XAllocStandardColormap`, and `XAllocWMHints`. When using these routines, an application declares only a pointer to the structure and then uses one of these routines to allocate the memory. The purpose of doing this is to avoid having compiled-in structure sizes, so that fields can be added to these structures in later releases without causing binary incompatibility. See Chapter 10.

`XGetGCValues` reads most GC component values out of Xlib's local cache. It does not read the dash list or clip mask. See Chapter 5, *The Graphics Context*.

`XIconifyWindow` is to be called by the client to tell the window manager to iconify a window. Similarly, `XWithdrawWindow` tells the window manager to unmap a window without iconifying it. These two routines were added to simplify compliance with the new ICCCM. `XReconfigureWMWindow` is used by clients to reconfigure top-level windows—it works like `XConfigureWindow` except that it handles stacking order changes correctly even if the window or some of its siblings have been reparented. See Chapter 10.

As mentioned above, all of the R3 functions that write or read string properties have been superceded by R4 functions that provide a more flexible property format. All these new functions use the `XTextProperty` structure. Several routines that manipulate these structures are now provided: `XFreeStringList`, `XGetTextProperty`, `XSet-TextProperty`, `XStringListToTextProperty`, and `XTextProperty-ToStringList`. See Chapter 10.

`XListDepths` and `XListPixmapFormats` extract information from the `Display` structure. These are useful when you want to create a window or a pixmap that is not the default depth and not a depth of one plane.

`XrmDestroyDatabase` destroys a resource database, a function that was missing in earlier releases.

The `XScreenNumberOfScreen` function has also been added. It simply returns the screen integer corresponding to the specified pointer to a `Screen` structure. This function is listed with the macros in Appendix C, *Macros*, of Volume Two, *Xlib Reference Manual*.

H.1.2 Existing Interface Changes

The following sections describe the changes in the areas of `XOpenDisplay`, error handlers, nonstandard keysyms and keyboard groups, `XReadBitmapFile`, resource specification syntax, and `XrmParseCommand`.

H.1.2.1 XOpenDisplay

The use of *unix* as a hostname in the DISPLAY environment variable read by `XOpen-Display` is no longer part of the specification (for trademark reasons); use an empty hostname. In other words, setting DISPLAY to ":0.0" will instruct Xlib to make the best local connection to the server running on the same system as this client.

H.1.2.2 Error Handlers

`XSetErrorHandler` and `XIOSetErrorHandler` now return the previous error handler.

```
int (*XSetErrorHandler(handler))()
     int (*handler)(Display *, XErrorEvent *)
int (*XSetIOErrorHandler(handler))()
     int (*handler)(Display *);
```

In `XGetErrorDatabaseText`, for an extension request, the extension name (as given by `XInitExtension`) followed by a period (.) and the minor request protocol number is used for the *message* argument.

H.1.2.3 Nonstandard Keysyms

Keysyms that are not part of the Xlib standard can now be obtained by using `XString-ToKeysym` and `XKeysymToString`. Note that the set of keysyms that are available in this manner and the mechanisms by which Xlib obtains them is implementation-dependent. (In the MIT sample implementation, the resource file */usr/lib/X11/XKeysymDB* is used starting in R4. The keysym name is used as the resource name, and the resource value is the keysym value in upper-case hexadecimal.)

H.1.2.4 XReadBitmapFile

In XReadBitmapFile, the ability to read X10 format is no longer required of an implementation. The ability to read other than the standard format is implementation-dependent.

H.1.2.5 Resource Specification Syntax

As of R4, the BNF notation of a resource specification is now specified:

ResourceLine	=	Comment | ResourceSpec
Comment	=	"!" string | <empty line>
ResourceSpec	=	WhiteSpace ResourceName WhiteSpace ":" WhiteSpace value
ResourceName	=	[Binding] ComponentName {Binding ComponentName}
Binding	=	"." | "*"
WhiteSpace	=	{" " | ""}
ComponentName	=	{"a"–"z" | "A"–"Z" | "0"–"9" | "_" | "-"}
value	=	string
string	=	{<any character not including "\n">}

Note that elements enclosed in curly braces ({...}) indicate zero or more occurrences of the enclosed elements.

To allow values to contain arbitrary octets, the four-character sequence *nnn*, where *n* is a digit in the range of 0 through 7 is recognized and replaced with a single byte that contains this sequence interpreted as an octal number. For example, a value containing a NULL byte can be stored by specifying \\000.

H.1.2.6 XrmParseCommand

In XrmParseCommand, a new value, XrmoptionSkipNArgs, has been added to the XrmOptionKind enum. Note that XrmoptionSkipArg is equivalent to XrmoptionSkipNArgs with the XrmOptionDescRec.value field containing the value one. Note also that the value zero for XrmoptionSkipNArgs indicates that only the option itself is to be skipped.

H.1.2.7 Keyboard Groups

In R4, the concept of keyboard groups has been introduced, and XLookupString implements new semantics to support keyboard groups. Keyboard groups support having two complete sets of keysyms for a keyboard. Which set will be used can be toggled using a particular key. This is implemented by using the first two keysyms in the list for a key as one set and the next two keysyms as the second set.

The standard rules for obtaining a keysym from a KeyPress event make use of only the Group 1 and Group 2 keysyms; no interpretation of other keysyms in the list is given here. Which group to use is determined by modifier state. Switching between groups is controlled by the keysym named MODE SWITCH, by attaching that keysym to some keycode and attaching that keycode to any one of the modifiers Mod1 through Mod5. This modifier is called the "group modifier." For any keycode, Group 1 is used when the group modifier is off and Group 2 is used when the group modifier is on.

Within a group, which keysym to use is also determined by modifier state. The first keysym is used when the Shift and Lock modifiers are off. The second keysym is used when the Shift modifier is on, when the Lock modifier is on and the second keysym is upper-case alphabetic, or when the Lock modifier is on and is interpreted as Shift Lock. Otherwise, when the Lock modifier is on and is interpreted as Caps Lock, the state of the Shift modifier is applied first to select a keysym, but if that keysym is lower-case alphabetic, then the corresponding upper-case keysym is used instead.

If the list of Keysyms (ignoring trailing NoSymbol entries) is a single keysym "K," then the list is treated as if it were the list "K NoSymbol K NoSymbol." If the list (ignoring trailing NoSymbol entries) is a pair of keysyms "$K1$ $K2$," then the list is treated as if it were the list "$K1$ $K2$ $K1$ $K2$." If the list (ignoring trailing NoSymbol entries) is a triple of keysyms "$K1$ $K2$ $K3$," then the list is treated as if it were the list "$K1$ $K2$ $K3$ NoSymbol." When an explicit "void" element is desired in the list, the value VoidSymbol can be used.

The first four elements of the list are split into two groups of keysyms. Group 1 contains the first and second keysyms; Group 2 contains the third and fourth keysyms. Within each group, if the second element of the group is NoSymbol, then the group should be treated as if the second element were the same as the first element, except when the first element is an alphabetic keysym "K" for which both lower-case and upper-case forms are defined. In that case, the group should be treated as if the first element were the lower-case form of "K" and the second element were the upper-case form of "K."

No spatial geometry of the symbols on the key is defined by their order in the keysym list, although a geometry might be defined on a vendor-specific basis. The X server does not use the mapping between keycodes and keysyms. Rather it stores it merely for reading and writing by clients.

The modifier named Lock is intended to be mapped to either a Caps Lock or a Shift Lock key, but which one is left as application-specific and/or user-specific. However, it is suggested that the determination be made according to the associated keysym(s) of the corresponding keycode.

H.2 Changes from Release 2 to Release 3

The following sections describe the changes in the areas of new routines, command line option conventions, fonts, internal changes, server fixes that affect Xlib programming, the Xmu library, and datatype and argument changes.

H.2.1 New Routines

Five new routines were added to Xlib in Release 3. They are all very simple, and in fact, four of them could actually have been simple macros. Here are their definitions:

Example H-1. Code for routines added to Xlib in Release 3

```
long XMaxRequestSize(dpy)
    Display *dpy;
{
    return dpy->max_request_size;
}
char *XResourceManagerString(dpy)
    Display *dpy;
{
    return dpy->xdefaults;
}
unsigned long XDisplayMotionBufferSize(dpy)
    Display *dpy;
{
    return dpy->motion_buffer;
}
XDisplayKeycodes(dpy, min_keycode_return, max_keycode_return)
    Display *dpy;
    int *min_keycode_return, *max_keycode_return;
{
    *min_keycode_return = dpy->min_keycode;
    *max_keycode_return = dpy->max_keycode;
}
VisualID XVisualIDFromVisual(visual)
    Visual *visual;
{
    return visual->visualid;
}
```

`XDisplayMotionBufferSize`, `XMaxRequestSize`, and `XResourceManager-String` are listed in Appendix C, *Macros*, of Volume Two, *Xlib Reference Manual*. `XDisplayKeycodes` and `XVisualIDFromVisual` have their own reference pages in Volume Two.

All of these routines were added to allow applications access to members of structures that are intended to be opaque, namely, `Display` and `Visual`. Applications should reference only the pointers to these structures. When applications are coded without direct reference to members of the opaque structures, this allows the X Consortium or an Xlib implementor on a particular system to change the contents of the `Display` and `Visual` structures, if necessary.

`XMaxRequestSize` tells you the maximum request size on the server in units of four bytes. This would be used when reading and writing properties, since the maximum property data length that can be stored in a single property is one unit (four bytes) less than the value returned by `XMaxRequestSize`.

The `XResourceManagerString` routine accesses the `RESOURCE_MANAGER` property resource database string that is stored in the server with *xrdb* and returned to the client in the `Display` structure by `XOpenDisplay`. This is used by applications that use the resource manager routines to merge appropriate program and user defaults. All serious applications will do this.

`XDisplayMotionBufferSize` tells you whether the server has a motion history buffer, and if it does, how large it is in units of events. Most current servers do not have a motion history buffer, and in that case, this function will return 0.

`XDisplayKeycodes` lets you determine the range of valid keycodes on a particular server. This should not be needed in most applications that use the standard keyboard interface through keysyms. It is only needed if you intend to change the mapping between keycodes and keysyms (server-wide) or perhaps to process key events using keycodes in a non-text application such as for music.

`XVisualIDFromVisual` is provided for completeness. It should not be necessary in most applications and certainly not in those that use `XGetVisualInfo` or `XMatchVisualInfo` to determine color characteristics, since these routines return the `XVisualInfo` structure which contains the `VisualID`.

H.2.2 Command Line Options

The convention until Release 3 was that any command line argument containing : was a display specification and any argument beginning with = was a geometry specification. These no longer hold, and none of the core clients now operate this way. Applications should require an explicit *–display* or *–geometry* option. The = in the geometry specification is now optional.

H.2.3 Fonts

There is no standard that specifies the fonts a server must provide. However, this should not be a portability problem for properly written applications, because fonts should be resources that can be specified by the user or system administrator. You will probably want to "build in" default font names, either in an *app-defaults* file or in your code, but your code ought to be robust enough to fall back on the default font in the GC if all else fails.

We bring this up because the font environment provided in the MIT distribution changed substantially in Release 3. In Release 3, a unified family of fonts were donated by Adobe, Inc. and Bitstream, Inc. These include fonts of various sizes in the Courier, Times Roman, Helvetica, New Century Schoolbook, and Bitstream Charter families in regular weight, bold, and italic and symbol fonts in various sizes from Adobe/DEC are also provided. Furthermore, font aliasing has been added so that font names in code and resource files can be long enough to fully describe a font, but the actual files containing the fonts are still 14 characters or less for compatibility with System V. An organized font naming scheme has also been instituted. For a description of this scheme, see Appendix A, *Specifying Fonts.*

The new font naming scheme is described in even more detail in Appendix M, *Logical Font Description Conventions*, of Volume Zero, *X Protocol Reference Manual* (as of the second printing).

To accommodate the new font naming scheme, wildcards are now permitted as arguments to the Xlib routines XLoadFont, XLoadQueryFont, and XQueryFont. They were already permitted for the routines XListFonts and XListFontsWithInfo.

H.2.4 Internal and Invisible Changes to Xlib

Xlib has been modified internally so that it will compile and run on Cray machines. This does not change the programming interface. Untested support for Mips computers has also been contributed.

Other internal changes include improvements to graphics context cache flushing. The region code was improved, including a fix for overflow on complex regions.

The routines XChangeProperty and XGetWindowProperty now take care of converting arrays of chars, shorts, and longs to and from the formats required by the protocol (8-bit, 16-bit, and 32-bit signed integers, respectively). XGetWindowProperty now always mallocs space for its return data even if the data has zero elements.

XLookupString now has a list of key bindings per display, can cope with modifier mapping changes, handles upper and lower case of all Latin-1 keysyms, does not convert non-Latin-1 keysyms, understands Control 2-8 and /, and uses the preferred protocol definition for CapsLock.

XrmPutFileDatabase will write file with proper special char quoting.

H.2.5 Server Fixes

Some problems that existed in sample server code affected application programming under Release 2. You may wish to inspect programs for workarounds for these problems. We cannot list and explain all the bugs that were found and fixed; see the CHANGES file in the appropriate directory of the X distribution. However, the following changes to the device-independent (dix) portion of the server were among the most likely to affect client programming:

- The AllocColorPlanes request has been fixed to allow allocation of all planes at once.

- Delayed/buffered writes for client events implemented. Delayed writes are simply a performance improvement; the server now queues all events generated by a single request for greater network efficiency. Buffered writes fix a bug that appeared when reading long properties from the server. Client connections would be severed when the client refused or was slow in reading a long message from the server.

- SelectionClear events are now sent to the selection owner (set by XSet-SelectionOwner, not the window creator).

- Font routines and color name lookup routines now fold upper case in names to lower case. Case is no longer significant in the color database, and items in the database differing only in case have been removed.

- Save under support has been added to the device-independent portion of the server. This code supplies save unders to any server which has backing store but not save unders implemented in the device-dependent portion.

- Mixing window gravity and bit gravity has been fixed.

- Many other specious requests also generate Value errors now.

H.2.6 The Xmu Library

A new miscellaneous utilities library has been placed on the X distribution tape. This library is not part of the Xlib standard. It contains routines which only use public interfaces, so that it may be layered on top of any proprietary implementation of Xlib or Xt.

It is intended to support clients in the MIT distribution; vendors may choose not to distribute this library if they wish. Therefore, applications developers who depend on this library should be prepared to treat it as part of their software base when porting.

The following routines apply to Xlib (there are a few not described here that are for use with the X Toolkit):*

- Routines to cache atoms, avoiding multiple server round trips. `XmuMakeAtom` creates and initializes an opaque `AtomRec`. `XmuInternAtom` fetches an atom from cache or server. `XmuInternStrings` fetches multiple atoms as strings. `XmuGetAtomName` returns the name of an atom. `XmuNameOfAtom` returns the name from an `AtomPtr`.

- `XmuCreatePixmapFromBitmap` routine converts a bitmap to a pixmap. The routine uses `XCopyPlane`.

- `XmuConvertStandardSelection` converts a known selection into the appropriate target type.

- `XmuPrintDefaultErrorMessage` prints a nice error that looks like the usual message. Returns 1 if the caller should consider exiting, else 0.

- `XmuDrawRoundedRectangle` draws a rounded rectangle. x, y, w, and h are the dimensions of the rectangle; ew and eh are the sizes of a bounding boxes that each corner is drawn inside of.

- `XmuReadBitmapDataFromFile` reads X10 or X11 format bitmap files and return data.

---

*Note that this is the R3 list of Xmu routines. See Appendix F, *The Xmu Library*, for a list of the R4 routines.

H.2.7 Datatype and Argument Changes

The following changes were made to public datatypes and function arguments in R3.

The `XTimeCoord` structure has its *x* and *y* members changed from type `unsigned short` to `short`.

The `XClientMessageEvent` structure contains a union of three data types. The `l[5]` member has been changed from type `int` to type `long`.

`XAddPixel` has its *value* argument changed from `int` to `long`.

`XCheckMaskEvent` has its *mask* argument changed from `unsigned long` to `long`.

`XCheckWindowEvent` has its *mask* argument changed from `int` to `long`.

The *event_mask* argument of `XMaskEvent`, `XSelectInput`, and `XSendEvent` changed from `unsigned long` to `long`.

The `error_code`, `minor_code`, and `request_code` members of `XErrorEvent` have been changed from type `char` to type `unsigned char`.

H.3 Changes from Release 1 to Release 2

The major change was a completely revised resource manager. The resource manager is now merged into the X library; it was a separate library in Release 1. The routines are now entirely different from the ones in Release 1, although they still serve roughly the same purpose. One added feature is the server resource database set up by the *xrdb* program. This allows the user to specify a single defaults file to be set as a property in the server, so that all applications using the defaults mechanism can use those defaults. This was not done in Release 1, and therefore, the user had to maintain a separate defaults file on each machine on which clients were to run. See Chapter 11, *Managing User Preferences*, for a description of the Release 2 resource manager.

Along with the change in the resource manager routines, the *Xdefaults* file has been superseded by a more general resource database file that can have any name. The user runs *xrdb* with this filename as an argument, and *xrdb* sets a property on the root window containing the database. When applications call `XGetDefault`, this property is the first place where `XGetDefault` searches for the matching value. This change was made so that an *Xdefaults* file would not have to be maintained on every system on which client routines run while displaying on a single server.

The `XUnionRectWithRegion` routine is also new to Release 2. It is provided mainly to simplify the process of coalescing the rectangles returned from a contiguous series of `Expose` events into a single region before setting the clip mask with `XSetRegion`. This is done to optimize the redrawing of windows, as described in Section 3.2.13.1.

The XEventsQueued routine was added to Release 2 to tell how many events are on the queue but in a more flexible way than does XPending. It allows you to choose whether to return immediately if no events are found on Xlib's queue or to flush the connection with the server first. See Section 8.2.6 for a more complete description.

XInsertModifiermapEntry and XDeleteModifiermapEntry were added in Release 2. They make it easier to add or delete a single key to the set of keys mapped to a particular modifier functionality. These routines merely prepare a structure for calling XSetModifierMapping.

Several structures were modified in Release 2. All the event structures had two members added. One is called serial and provides the serial number of the last request successfully processed by the server. This member aids in processing errors and in locating which Xlib call generated the error. The other is called send_event and indicates whether the event was sent from the server or from another client using XSendEvent. In Release 1, the highest bit in the type member was set when the event was sent from another client, but this meant that comparing type against the event type symbols such as Expose would not work for sent events. In Release 2, all events look the same unless the send_event flag is explicitly checked.

Other changes took place in opaque structures (such as Display), but programs should only access these through macros and the other interfaces provided in Xlib so that the changes will not affect properly written programs.

Glossary

X uses many common terms in unique ways. A good example is "children." While most, if not all, of these terms are defined where they are first used in this book, you will undoubtedly find it easier to refresh your memory by looking for them here.

Glossary

This glossary is an expanded version of the glossary in the *Xlib–C Language X Interface*, by Jim Gettys, Ron Newman, and Bob Scheifler.

access control list
> X maintains lists of hosts that are allowed access to each server controlling a display. By default, only the local host may use the display, plus any hosts specified in the *access control list* for that display. This access control list can be changed by clients on the local host. Some server implementations may implement other authorization mechanisms in addition to or instead of this one. The list can currently be found in */etc/X#.hosts*, where # is the number of the display. The access control list is also known as the host access list.

active grab
> Keyboard keys, the keyboard, pointer buttons, the pointer, and the server can be *grabbed* for exclusive use by a client, usually for a short time period. An active grab causes pointer and keyboard events to be sent to the grabbing window regardless of the current position of the pointer. See **passive grab**.

ancestor
> If window *W* is an inferior of window *A*, then *A* is an *ancestor* of *W*. The parent window, the parent's parent window, and so on are all ancestors of the given window. The root window is the ancestor of all windows on a given screen.

association table
> *Association tables* provide a fast lookup table for data that must be searched frequently. Association tables associate arbitrary information with resource IDs. This is similar to the context manager, but the resource IDs used with association tables are existing resources, not created for the purpose of storing data for later retrieval.

atom
> An *atom* is a unique numeric ID corresponding to a string name. Atoms are used to identify properties, types, and selections in order to avoid the overhead of passing arbitrary length property name strings.

background

The `background` member of a GC defines a window's background, which consists of either a solid color or a tile pattern. If a window has a background, it will be repainted automatically by the server whenever there is an `Expose` event on the window. If a window does not have a background, it will be transparent. `background` can be set using the `GCBackground` mask, when the GC is created, or by a call to `XSetBackground`. Default is 1. See also **foreground**.

backing store

When a server maintains the contents of a window, the off-screen saved pixels are known as a *backing store*. This feature is not available on all servers. Use the `DoesBackingStores` macro to determine if this feature is supported.

bit gravity

When a window is resized, the contents of the window are not necessarily discarded. It is possible to request the server (though no guarantees are made) to relocate the previous contents to some region of the resized window. This attraction of window contents for some location of a window is known as *bit gravity*. For example, an application that draws a graph might request that the contents be moved into the lower-left corner, so that the origin of the graph will still appear in the lower-left corner.

bit plane

On a color or gray-scale display, each pixel has more than one bit defined. Data in display memory can be thought of either as pixels (multiple bits per pixel) or as bit planes (one bit plane for each usable bit in the pixel). The *bit plane* is an array of bits the size of the screen.

bitmap

A *bitmap* is a pixmap with a depth of one bit. There is no bitmap type in X11. Instead use a pixmap of depth 1.

border

A window can have a *border* that is zero or more pixels wide. If a window has a border, the border can have a solid color or a tile pattern, and it will be repainted automatically by the server whenever its color or pattern is changed or an `Expose` event occurs on the window.

button grab

Specifies a pointer grab that occurs only when a specified set of keys and/or buttons is held down. This is analogous to a key grab. See **mouse grab**.

byte order

The order in which bytes of data are stored in memory is hardware-dependent. For pixmaps and bitmaps, *byte order* is defined by the server, and clients with different native byte ordering must swap bytes as necessary. For all other parts of the protocol, the byte order is defined by the client, and the server swaps bytes as necessary.

children

The *children* of a window are its first-level subwindows. All of these windows were created with the same window as parent. A client creates its top-level window as a child of the root window.

class

There are two uses of the term *class* in X: window class and visual class. The window class specifies whether a window is InputOnly or InputOutput. See Chapter 2, *X Concepts*, for details. The visual class specifies the color model that is used by a window. See Chapter 7, *Color*, for details.

client

An application program connects to the window system server by an interprocess communication (IPC) path such as a TCP connection or a shared memory buffer. This program is referred to as a *client* of the window system server. More precisely, the client is the IPC path itself; a program with multiple paths open to the server is viewed as multiple clients by the protocol. Server resources survive only as long as the connection remains intact, not as long as a client program remains running. Normally the connection and the program terminate concurrently, but the client's resources may live on if XChangeCloseDownMode has been called.

clip mask

In many graphics routines, a bitmap or list of rectangles can be specified to restrict output to a particular region of the window. The image defined by the bitmap or rectangles is called a *clip mask* or *clipping region*. Output to child windows is automatically clipped to the borders of the parent unless subwindow_mode of the GC is IncludeInferiors. Therefore, the borders of the parent can be thought of as a clip mask or clipping region.

clipping region

See **clip mask**.

colorcell

An entry in a colormap is known as a *colorcell*. An entry contains three values specifying red, green, and blue intensities. These values are always 16-bit unsigned numbers, with zero being minimum intensity. The values are truncated or scaled by the server to match the display hardware. See also **colormap**.

colormap

A *colormap* consists of a set of colorcells. A pixel value indexes into the colormap to produce intensities of red, green, and blue to be displayed. Depending on hardware limitations, one or more colormaps may be installed at one time, such that windows associated with those maps display with true colors. Regardless of the number of installable colormaps, any number of virtual colormaps can be created. When needed, a virtual colormap can be installed and the existing installed colormap might have to be deinstalled. The colormap on most systems is a limited resource that should be conserved by allocating read-only colorcells whenever possible and by selecting RGB values from the predefined color database. Read-only cells may be shared between clients. See also **colorcell**, **DirectColor**, **GrayScale**, **PseudoColor**, **StaticColor**, **StaticGray**, and **TrueColor**.

connection

The IPC path between the server and client is known as a *connection*. A client usually (but not necessarily) has one connection to the server over which requests and events are sent.

containment

A window *contains* the pointer if the window is viewable and the hotspot of the cursor is within a visible region of the window or a visible region of one of its inferiors. The border of the window is included as part of the window for containment. The pointer is in a window if the window contains the pointer but no inferior contains the pointer.

coordinate system

The *coordinate system* has X horizontal and Y vertical pixels, with the origin (0,0) at the upper left. Coordinates are discrete. Each window and pixmap has its own coordinate system. For a window with a border, the origin is inside the border.

cursor

A *cursor* is the visible shape of the pointer on a screen. It consists of a hotspot, a shape bitmap, a mask bitmap, and a pair of pixel values. The cursor defined for a window controls the visible appearance of the pointer when the pointer is in that window.

cut buffer

Cut buffers are a simple but limited method of client communication, sometimes used instead of the selection mechanism. Cut buffers are properties of the root window of screen 0 of a display. They rely on a prior agreement between the two clients regarding the format of the data to be placed in the cut buffers. The data that can be placed in a single cut buffer is limited to the maximum size of a single property. See **selection**.

depth

The *depth* of a window or pixmap is the number of planes that are to be used to represent gray scales or color within a window.

descendants

See **inferiors**.

device

Keyboards, mice, tablets, track-balls, button boxes, etc. are all collectively known as input *devices*.

DirectColor

`DirectColor` is a visual class in which a pixel value is decomposed into three separate subfields for colormap indexing. One subfield indexes an array to produce red intensity values; the second subfield indexes a second array to produce blue intensity values; and the third subfield indexes a third array to produce green intensity values. The RGB (red, green, and blue) values in the colormap entry can be changed dynamically. This visual class is normally found on high performance color workstations. (`XGetVisualInfo`, `XMatchVisualInfo`)

display

A *display* is a set of one or more screens that are driven by a single X server. The Xlib `Display` structure contains all information about the particular display and its screens as well as the state that Xlib needs to communicate with the display over a particular connection.

display function

See **logical function**.

drawable

Both windows and pixmaps may be used as destinations in graphics operations. These are collectively known as *drawables*.

event

Clients are informed of device input or client request side effects asynchronously via *events*. Events are grouped into types; events are never sent to a client by the server unless the client has specifically asked to be informed of that type of event. However, other clients can force events of any type to be sent to any clients. Events are typically reported relative to a window.

event mask

Events are requested relative to a window. The set of event types a client requests relative to a window is described using an *event mask*. See **do_not_propagate_mask** and **event_mask**.

event propagation

Device-related events *propagate* from the source window to ancestor windows until a window that has selected that type of event is reached or until the event is discarded explicitly in a `do_not_propagate_mask` attribute.

event source

The smallest window containing the pointer is the *source* of a device-related event.

event window

An *event window* specifies the ID of the window in which an event appears to have occurred. See **source window**.

exposure

Window *exposure* occurs when a window is first mapped or when another window that obscures it is unmapped, resized, or moved. Servers do not guarantee to preserve the contents of windows when windows are obscured or reconfigured. `Expose` events are sent to clients to inform them when contents of regions of windows have been lost and need to be regenerated.

extension

Named *extensions* to the core protocol can be defined to extend the system. Extension to output requests, resources, and event types are all possible and expected. Extensions can perform at the same level as the core Xlib.

font

The `font` member of a GC specifies which font to use in graphics requests. A font is an array of characters or other bitmap shapes such as cursors. `font` can be set using the `GCFont` mask, when the GC is created, or by a call to `XSetFont`. The default font is installation dependent.

foreground

The `foreground` member of a GC defines the pixel value that will actually be used for drawing pictures or text. `foreground` can be set using the `GCForeground` mask, when the GC is created, or by a call to `XSetForeground`. Default is 0. See also **background**.

frozen events

Clients can *freeze* event processing while they change the screen by grabbing the keyboard or pointer with a certain mode. These events are queued in the server (not in Xlib) until an `XAllowEvents` call with a counteracting mode is given.

GC

The term *GC* is used as a shorthand for graphics context. See **graphics context**.

glyph
> A *glyph* is an image, usually of a character in a font but also possibly a cursor shape or some other shape.

grab
> Keyboard keys, the keyboard, pointer buttons, the pointer, and the server can be *grabbed* for exclusive use by a client, usually for a short time period. In general, these facilities are not intended to be used by normal applications but are intended for various input and window managers to implement various styles of user interfaces. See **active grab** and **passive grab**.

graphics context
> Various information for graphics output is stored in a *graphics context* (GC), such as foreground pixel, background pixel, line width, clipping region, etc. Everything drawn to a window or pixmap is modified by the GC used in the drawing request. GCs are created or altered with XChangeGC, XCopyGC, and XCreateGC.

gravity
> Controls the repositioning of a resized window's contents (bit gravity) or of a resized parent window's subwindows (window gravity). See **bit gravity** and **window gravity**.

GrayScale
> GrayScale is a visual class in which the red, green, and blue values in any given colormap entry are equal, thus producing shades of gray. The gray values can be changed dynamically. GrayScale can be viewed as a degenerate case of PseudoColor. (XGetVisualInfo, XMatchVisualInfo)

hint
> Certain properties, such as the preferred size of a window, are referred to as *hints*, since the window manager makes no guarantee that it will honor them. See **XA_WM_HINTS**, **XA_WM_NORMAL_HINTS**, **XA_WM_SIZE_HINTS**, and **XA_WM_ZOOM_HINTS**.

host access list
> See **access control list**.

hotspot
> A cursor has an associated *hotspot* that defines the point in the cursor which corresponds to the coordinates reported for the pointer.

icon
> An *icon* is a small marker window that indicates that a larger "main" window exists and is available but is not currently mapped on the screen.

identifier

Each resource has an *identifier* or *ID*, a unique value that clients use to name the resource. Any client can use a resource if it knows the resource ID.

inferiors

The *inferiors* of a window are all of the subwindows nested below it: the children, the children's children, etc. The term *descendants* is a synonym.

input focus

See **keyboard focus**.

input manager

Control over keyboard input may be provided by an *input manager* client. This job may also be done by the window manager.

InputOnly window

A window that cannot be used for graphics requests is called an InputOnly window. InputOnly windows are invisible and can be used to control such things as cursors, input event generation, and grabbing. InputOnly windows cannot have InputOutput windows as inferiors.

InputOutput window

The normal kind of window that is used for both input and output is called an InputOutput window. It usually has a background. InputOutput windows can have both InputOutput and InputOnly windows as inferiors.

key grab

Specifies a keyboard *grab* that occurs only when a certain key or key combination is pressed. This is analogous to a button grab. See **keyboard grab**.

keyboard focus

The *keyboard focus* is the window that receives main keyboard input. By default, the focus is the root window, which has the effect of sending input to the window that is being pointed to by the mouse. It is possible to attach the keyboard input to a specific window with XSetInputFocus. Events are then sent to the window independent of the pointer position or, if the *owner_events* argument is True, to the window containing the pointer if it is owned by the same client as the focus window.

keyboard grab

All keyboard input is sent to a specific window (or client, depending on *owner_events*) when the keyboard is *grabbed*. This is analogous to a mouse grab. This is very much like a temporary keyboard focus window.

keyboard vector

A *keyboard vector* represents, in the event structure, the state of the keyboard; the vector consists of 32 bytes of data, with one bit for each keyboard key.

keycode

A *keycode* is a code in the range [8,255], inclusive, that represents a physical or logical key on the keyboard. The mapping between keys and keycodes cannot be changed. A list of keysyms is associated with each keycode.

keysym

A *keysym* is a #defined symbol which is a portable representation of the symbol on the cap of a key. Each key may have several keysyms, corresponding to the key when various modifier keys are pressed. You should interpret key events according to the keysym returned by XLookupString or XLookupKeysym, since this translates server-dependent keycodes into portable keysyms. See **keycode**.

listener

A *listener*-style window manager sets the keyboard focus to a particular window when that window is clicked on with a pointer button. This is the window manager style used with the Apple Macintosh™.

logical function

Logical functions control how the *source* pixel values generated by a graphics request are combined with the *old destination* pixel values already present on the screen or drawable to result in the *final destination* pixel values. A logical function can be changed by a call to XSetFunction. Sometimes called raster operations, raster ops, or display functions.

mapping

A window is said to be *mapped* if a XMapWindow or XMapRaised call has been performed on it. Unmapped windows are never viewable. Mapping makes a window eligible for display. The window will actually be displayed if the following conditions are met: (1) all its ancestors are mapped and (2) it is not obscured by siblings.

mask

A *mask* specifies which values in a specified structure should be read when updating the resource values. One bit in the mask is assigned to every member of its corresponding structure. For example, CWBackgroundPixmap mask is used to indicate that the background_pixmap member of the specified window attributes structure is to be read and the corresponding member in the resource changed. See **structure**.

Glossary

modifier key

A key such as Shift or Control that can modify the meaning of a key event. Shift, Control, Meta, Super, Hyper, Alt, Compose, Apple, Caps Lock, Shift Lock, and similar keys are called *modifier keys*.

monochrome

A *monochrome* screen has only two colors: black and white. Monochrome is a special case of the `StaticGray` visual class, in which there are only two colormap entries.

mouse grab

All mouse input is sent to a specific window (or client, depending on `owner_events`) when the mouse is *grabbed*. This is analogous to a keyboard grab.

obscures

Window *A obscures* window *B* if *A* is higher in the global stacking order and the rectangle defined by the outside edges of *A* intersects the rectangle defined by the outside edges of *B*.

occludes

Window *A occludes* window *B* if both are mapped, if *A* is higher in the global stacking order, and if the rectangle defined by the outside edges of *A* intersects the rectangle defined by the outside edges of *B*. The (fine) distinction between the terms *obscures* and *occludes* is that for *obscures*, the windows have to be mapped, while for *occludes*, they do not. Also note that window borders are included in the calculation. Note that `InputOnly` windows never obscure other windows but can occlude other windows.

owner client

Selections transfer arbitrary information between two clients. An *owner client* owns the data representing the value of a selection, and a requestor client wants it. See **selection**.

padding

Some bytes are inserted in the data stream to maintain alignment of the protocol requests on natural boundaries. This *padding* increases ease of portability to some machine architectures.

parent window

Each new window is created with reference to another previously created window. The new window is referred to as the child, and the reference window as the *parent*. If *C* is a child of *P*, then *P* is the parent of *C*. Only the portion of the child that overlaps the parent is viewable.

passive grab

Keyboard keys, the keyboard, pointer buttons, the pointer, and the server can be grabbed for exclusive use by a client, usually for a short time period. A *passive grab* causes an active grab to begin when a certain key or button combination is pressed. The grab becomes active when the key or button is actually pressed. Before the active grab takes place, nothing has changed. See **active grab**.

pixel value

A *pixel value* is an N-bit value, where N is the number of bit planes used in a particular window or pixmap. For a window, a pixel value indexes a colormap to derive an actual color to be displayed. For a pixmap, a pixel value will be interpreted as a color in the same way when it is copied into a window.

pixmap

A *pixmap* is a three-dimensional array of bits. A pixmap is normally thought of as a two-dimensional array of pixels, where each pixel can be a value from 0 to $(2^N - 1)$, where N is the depth (z-axis) of the pixmap. A pixmap can also be thought of as a stack of N bitmaps.

plane

When a pixmap or a window is thought of as a stack of bitmaps, each bitmap is called a *plane*.

plane_mask

Graphics operations can be restricted to affect only a subset of bit planes in a drawable. The `plane_mask` member of a GC is a bit mask describing which planes are to be modified. Default is all ones. `plane_mask` can be set using the `GCPlaneMask` mask, when the GC is created, or it can be changed by a call to `XSetPlaneMask`.

pointer

The *pointer* is the pointing device currently attached to the cursor and tracked on the screens. This may be a mouse, tablet, track-ball, or joystick, among other things.

pointer grab

A client can actively *grab* control of the pointer, causing button and motion events to be sent to the grabbing client rather than to the client indicated by the pointer.

pointing device

A *pointing device* is typically a mouse or tablet or some other device with effective two-dimensional motion. There is only one visible cursor defined by the core protocol, and it tracks whatever pointing device is currently attached as the pointer.

Glossary

position

A window has a *position*, which locates its upper-left corner relative to its parent's corner.

property

Windows may have associated *properties*, each consisting of a name, a type, a data format, and some data. The protocol places no interpretation on properties; they are intended as a general purpose data storage and intercommunication mechanism for clients. There is, however, a list of predefined properties and property types so that clients might share information such as resize hints, program names, and icon formats with a window manager via properties. In order to avoid passing arbitrary length property name strings, each property name is associated with a corresponding integer value known as an atom. See also **atom**.

property list

The *property list* of a window is the list of properties that have been defined for that window.

PseudoColor

PseudoColor is a visual class in which a pixel value indexes the colormap entry to produce independent red, green, and blue values. That is, the colormap is viewed as an array of triples (RGB values). The RGB values can be changed dynamically. (XGetVisualInfo, XMatchVisualInfo)

quark

A *quark* is an integer ID that identifies a name, class, or type string for the resource manager. Like atoms and resource IDs, quarks eliminate the need to pass strings of arbitrary length over the network. The quark type is XrmQuark, and the types XrmName, XrmClass, and XrmRepresentation are also defined to be XrmQuark.

raise

Changing the stacking order of a window so as to occlude all sibling windows is to *raise* that window.

raster operation

See **logical function**.

real estate

A window management style characterized by the input being sent to whichever window the pointer is in. This is the most common style of input management used in X.

rectangle

A *rectangle* specified by [x,y,w,h] has an (infinitely thin) outline path with corners at [x,y], [x+w,y], [x+w,y+h] and [x,y+h]. When a rectangle is filled, the lower-right edges are not drawn. For example, if w=h=0, nothing would be drawn. For w=h=1, a single pixel would be drawn.

redirect

Window managers (or other clients) may wish to enforce window layout policy in various ways. When a client attempts to change the size or position of a window, the operation may be *redirected* to the window manager, rather than actually being performed. Then the window manager (or other client that redirected the input) is expected to decide whether to allow, modify, or deny the requested operation before making the call itself.

reparenting

The window manager often *reparents* the top-level windows of each application in order to add a titlebar and perhaps resize boxes. In other words, a window with a titlebar is inserted between the root window and each top-level window. See also **save-set**.

reply

Information requested by a client, by routines whose names include the word Query, is sent back to the client with a *reply*. Both events and replies are multiplexed on the same connection. Requests that require replies are known as *round-trip requests*. Most requests do not generate replies. Some requests generate multiple replies. See **round-trip request**.

request

A command to the server is called a *request*. It is a single block of data sent over the connection to the server.

requestor client

Selections transfer arbitrary information between two clients. An owner client owns the data representing the value of a selection, and a *requestor client* wants it. See **selection**.

resource

Windows, pixmaps, cursors, fonts, graphics contexts, and colormaps are known as *resources*. They all have unique identifiers (IDs) associated with them for naming purposes. The lifetime of a resource is bounded by the lifetime of the connection over which the resource was created.

resource manager

Every application should provide command line options that allow users to set colors or patterns for the window border and background; set foreground colors for drawing; start the application at a desired size, position, and configuration; select fonts; and so on. An application must also allow users to specify their own default values (user preferences) for each of these options. There are three and sometimes four sets of options that need to be read and merged: the program's defaults, the user's defaults stored in the root window's XA_RESOURCE_MANAGER property or in the user's *Xdefaults* file, and the command line arguments. The order in which the various options are merged is important. A value for an option in the user's defaults should override the program's default for that option, but a value on the command line would override both the program's and the user's default value. The routines and database structures used for managing user preferences are collectively referred to as the *resource manager*.

RGB values

Red, green, and blue intensity values are used to define a color. These values are always represented as 16-bit unsigned numbers, with 0 the minimum intensity and 65535 the maximum intensity. The X server scales these values to match the display hardware.

root

The *root* of a window, pixmap, or graphics context (GC) is the same as the root of whatever drawable was used when the window, pixmap, or GC was created. These resources can be used only on the screen indicated by this window. See **root window**.

root window

Each screen has a *root window* covering it. It cannot be reconfigured or unmapped but otherwise acts as a full-fledged window. A root window has no parent.

round-trip request

A request to the server that generates a reply is known as a *round-trip request*. Requests that require replies should be avoided when possible since they introduce network delays. See **reply**.

save-set

The *save-set* of a client is a list of other clients' windows which, if they are inferiors of one of the client's windows at connection close, should not be destroyed and which should be reparented and remapped if the client is unmapped. Save-sets are typically used by window managers to avoid lost windows if the manager should terminate abnormally. See **reparenting** for more background information.

scan line

A *scan line* is a list of pixel or bit values viewed as a horizontal row (all values having the same Y coordinate) of an image, with the values ordered by increasing X coordinate values.

scan line order

An image represented in *scan line order* contains scan lines ordered by increasing Y coordinate values.

screen

A server may provide several independent *screens*, which may or may not have physically independent monitors. For instance, it is possible to treat a color monitor as if it were two screens, one color and the other black and white. There is only a single keyboard and pointer shared among the screens. A `Screen` structure contains the information about that screen and is a member of the `Display` structure.

selection

Selections are a means of communication between clients using properties and events. From the user's perspective, a selection is an item of data which can be highlighted in one instance of an application and pasted into another instance of the same or a different application. The client that highlights the data is the owner, and the client into which the data is pasted is the requestor. Properties are used to store the selection data and the type of the data, while events are used to synchronize the transaction and to allow the requestor to indicate the type it prefers for the data and to allow the owner to convert the data to the indicated type if possible. See **cut buffer**.

server

The *server* provides the basic windowing mechanism. It handles IPC connections from clients, demultiplexes graphics requests onto the screens, and multiplexes input back to the appropriate clients. It controls a single keyboard and pointer and one or more screens that make up a single display.

server grab

The server can be *grabbed* by a single client for exclusive use. This prevents processing of any requests from other client connections until the grab is complete. This is typically a transient state to perform such tasks as rubber-banding and pop-up menus or to execute requests indivisibly.

sibling

Children of the same parent window are known as *sibling* windows.

source window

A *source window* specifies the ID of the window in which an event originally happens. See **event window**.

stacking order

Sibling windows may stack on top of each other, obscuring lower windows. This is similar to papers on a desk. The relationship between sibling windows is known as the *stacking order*. The first window in the stacking order is the window on top.

StaticColor

`StaticColor` is a visual class which represents a multiplane color screen with a predefined and read-only hardware colormap. It can be viewed as a degenerate case of `PseudoColor`. (`XGetVisualInfo`, `XMatchVisualInfo`)

StaticGray

`StaticGray` is a visual class which represents a multiplane monochrome screen with a predefined and read-only hardware colormap. It can be viewed as a degenerate case of `GrayScale`, in which the gray values are predefined and read-only. Typically, the values are linearly increasing ramps. (`XGetVisualInfo`, `XMatchVisualInfo`)

Status

Many Xlib functions return a `Status` of zero if it fails and nonzero if it succeeds. If the function does not succeed, its arguments are not changed.

stipple

The `stipple` member of a GC defines a single-plane pixmap that is used to tile a region. Bits set to 1 in the stipple are drawn with the `foreground` pixel value; bits set to 0, with the `background` pixel value. `stipple` can be set using the `GCStipple` mask, when the GC is created, or by a call to `XSetStipple`. Default is the pixmap filled with ones. See **tile**.

structure

Pointers to *structures* are the major way of specifying data to and returning data from Xlib routines. If the routine returns data, the returned value will be a pointer to the data structure, unless the routine returns more then one structure, in which case one or all of the structures will be arguments. When setting the characteristics of an X resource, such as a set of window attributes or a graphics context, both a structure and a mask are specified as arguments. See **mask**.

subwindow_mode

The `subwindow_mode` member of a GC controls whether subwindows obscure their parent. `subwindow_mode` can be set using the `GCSubwindowMode` mask, when the GC is created, or by a call to `XSetSubwindowMode`. Possible values are `ClipByChildren` (the default) or `IncludeInferiors`.

tile

The `tile` member of a GC defines a pixmap used for patterning an area. A tile has the same depth as the drawable it is used to pattern. `tile` can be set using the `GCTile` mask, when the GC is created, or by a call to `XSetTile`. Default is the pixmap is filled with the foreground pixel. See **stipple**.

time

A *time* value in X is expressed in milliseconds, typically since the last server reset. Time values wrap around (after about 49.7 days). One time value, represented by the constant `CurrentTime`, is used by clients to represent the current server time.

top-level window

A child of the root window is referred to as a *top-level window*.

TrueColor

`TrueColor` is a visual class which represents a high performance multiplane display with predefined and read-only RGB values in its hardware colormap. It can be viewed as a degenerate case of `DirectColor`, in which the subfields in the pixel value directly encode the corresponding RGB values. Typically, the values are linearly increasing ramps. (`XGetVisualInfo`, `XMatchVisualInfo`)

type property

A *type property* is used to identify the interpretation of property data. Types are completely uninterpreted by the server; they are solely for the benefit of clients.

viewable

A window is *viewable* if it and all of its ancestors are mapped. This does not imply that any portion of the window is actually visible, since it may be obscured by other windows.

visible

A region of a window is *visible* if someone looking at the screen can actually see it; that is, the window is viewable and the region is not obscured by any other window.

visual

The specifications for color handling for a drawable, including visual class, depth, RGB/pixel, etc., are collectively referred to as a *visual* and are stored in a structure of type `Visual`. The visual accounts for the differences between various types of hardware in determining the way pixel values are translated into visible colors within a window. A screen may support only one of several types of visuals.

Glossary

visual class

This attribute accounts for the differences between various types of display hardware in determining the way in which pixel values are translated into visible colors within a particular window. See **DirectColor, GrayScale, PseudoColor, Static-Color, StaticGray,** and **TrueColor.**

window

An X server controls a bitmapped screen. In order to make it easier to view and control many different tasks at the same time, this screen can be divided up into smaller areas called windows. A window is a rectangular area of any size that works in several ways like a miniature screen. Windows in the screen can be arranged so they all are visible or so they cover each other completely or partially. Each window can be involved in a different activity, and the windows currently in use are placed so they are at least partially visible.

window gravity

When windows are resized, subwindows may be repositioned automatically relative to an edge, a corner, or the center of the window. This attraction of a subwindow to some part of its parent is known as *window gravity*.

window manager

Manipulation of windows on the screen is provided by a *window manager* client. The window manager has authority over the arrangement of windows on the screen and the user interface for selecting which window receives input. See also **redirect.**

XYPixmap

XYPixmap specifies the format for an image. The data for an image is said to be in XYPixmap format if it is organized as a set of bitmaps representing individual bit planes. (XCreateImage, XGetImage, XPutImage)

zoomed window

Some applications not only have a normal size for their top-level window and an icon but also have a *zoomed window* size. This could be used in a painting program (similar to the MacPaint™ fat bits). The zoomed window size preferences can be specified in the window manager hints.

ZPixmap

ZPixmap specifies the format for an image. The data for an image is said to be in ZPixmap format if it is organized as a set of pixel values in scan line order. (XGetImage, XPutImage)

Index

Index

symbols 92
  win_gravity 101
authentication 58, 361
automatic grab
  between button events 294
automatically selected events 259
auto_repeat_mode 297

B

background
  glossary definition 596
  member of GC 125
  specifying 95
background_pixel attribute 97
background_pixmap attribute 96
backing store 103
  definition 30
  glossary definition 596
backing_pixel attribute 103
backing_planes attribute 103
basecalc application 193, 479 -
    506
  basecalc.h include file 480 - 485
  code for calculator application
    485 - 506
  description of 359
  drawButton routine 379 - 380
  example database for 364
  example using 367
  extractOpts routine 369
  getting user defaults 363
  GetUsersDataBase routine 367 -
    368
  how to use 360
  include files 362
  initCalc routine 375 - 376
  main 362
  parseOpenDisp routine 364
  parsing command line 364
  portability of 360
  selectEvents routine 377
  Usage routine 372
basicwin program
  connecting to server 57
  creating icon pixmap 64
  creating windows 62
  include files 55
  main of 55
beep volume 296

bell volume 296
bit gravity
  glossary definition 596
bit plane
  glossary definition 596
bit_gravity attribute 98
  constants 99
bitmap
  client 64
  creating 152
  file format 64, 152 - 153, 565
  glossary definition 596
bits per pixel 30
bitwise OR
  combining mask symbols 242
black background 63
BlackPixel macro 31, 62 - 63, 192
border
  clipping to 27
  glossary definition 596
  specifying color 97
  specifying pattern 97
  width in configuration 24
  width of top-level window 324
border crossing events 291, 525 -
    530
border_pixel attribute 98
border_pixmap attribute 98
buffering 17 - 18
button
  example 421
  grab between 294
  mapping 291, 547
button grab
  glossary definition 596
ButtonMotionMask event mask
    244, 252 - 253
ButtonPress event 246, 294, 512 -
    513
ButtonPressMask event mask 252
ButtonRelease event 246, 294,
    512 - 513
ButtonReleaseMask event mask
    252
byte order 366
  for pixmaps 366
  glossary definition 596

C

caching of GCs in display hardware 119
calculator example 359, 372 - 376
CapButt cap_style 128
CapNotLast cap_style 128
CapProjecting cap_style 128
CapRound cap_style 128
cap_style member of GC 125, 128
changeable colormaps 191
  vs. immutable colormaps 190
character compound 268
character set
  functions in Xmu library 566
characters
  format 156
  metrics 158
child processes 409, 438
child window 27
  drawing through 141
  moving with parent 24
  of root window 26
  stacking relative to parent 28
children
  glossary definition 597
choosing colors 197
circle drawing 138, 148
CirculateNotify event 256, 416,
  514
CirculateRequest event 257 - 258,
  399, 515
circulating windows 28
class
  glossary definition 597
class (resource)
  property 316
class (window) 26
clearing windows 154
click
  key 296
client
  definition 10
  glossary definition 597
  owner 327
  properties 304
  requestor 327
ClientMessage event 245, 259,
  516
client-to-client communication
  327 - 335

client-window manager communication 403 - 404
clip mask
  glossary definition 597
clip mask of GC 119, 124
clip origin of GC 119
  setting 125
CLIPBOARD selection 334
ClipByChildren
  subwindow_mode 141
clipping region
  glossary definition 597
clipping to parent borders 27
close down mode 362
close on fork 409
color
  allocating (description) 182
  allocating read-only 193
  allocating read/write 198 - 208
  choosing 197
  concepts 181
  highlighting 417
  number available vs. possible
    182
  terms 181
  user preference for 197
color mapping on mid-range color
  screen 182
color name database 183 - 185
color names
  ISO Latin encoding 183
color specification
  hexadecimal 185
colorcell 182
  allocating with XAllocColorCells
    202 - 207
  allocating with XAllocColor-
    Planes 207 - 208
  compared to colormaps 191
  definition 30
  glossary definition 597
  read/write 191, 198 - 208
colormap
  and window manager 106, 213
  attribute 106
  changeable vs. immutable 190
  creating 213
  definition 30, 182
  differences of in display hard-
    ware 185 - 191
  functions for manipulating 213
  glossary definition 597
  installing 212

H

hardware *see* display hardware

I

Index

Index

X

Index

Index

About the Author

Adrian Nye is a senior technical writer at O'Reilly and Associates. In addition to the X Window System programming manuals, he has written user's manuals for data acquistion products, and customized UNIX documentation for Sun Microsystems and Prime. Adrian has also worked as a programmer writing educational software in C, and as a mechanical engineer designing offshore oilspill cleanup equipment. He has long-term interests in using his technical writing skills to promote recycling and other environmentally-sound technologies. He graduated from the Massachusetts Institute of Technology in 1984 with a B.S. in Mechanical Engineering.

☐ Please send me the information
I have asked for on the reverse
side of this card.

Name _____

Company _____

Address _____

City _____

State, ZIP _____

(Fill out or tape
business card here)

Nutshell Handbooks

 O'Reilly & Associates, Inc.
632 Petaluma Avenue
Sebastopol CA 95472

☐ Please send me the information
I have asked for on the reverse
side of this card.

Name _____

Company _____

Address _____

City _____

State, ZIP _____

(Fill out or tape
business card here)

Nutshell Handbooks

 O'Reilly & Associates, Inc.
632 Petaluma Avenue
Sebastopol CA 95472

O'Reilly & Associates, Inc.
Creators and Publishers of Nutshell Handbooks

Nutshell Handbooks

Learning the UNIX Operating System
DOS Meets UNIX
Learning the vi Editor
UNIX in a Nutshell, System V
UNIX in a Nutshell, Berkeley

Handbooks on Communications:

*!%@:: A Directory of Electronic
    Mail Addressing and Networks*
Using UUCP and Usenet
Managing UUCP and Usenet

Handbooks on Programming:

Using C on the UNIX System
Checking C Programs with lint
Understanding and Using COFF
Programming with curses
termcap and terminfo
Managing Projects with make

The X Window System series

Vol. 0 *X Protocol Reference Manual*
Vol. 1 *Xlib Programming Manual*
Vol. 2 *Xlib Reference Manual*
Vol. 3 *X Window System User's Guide*
Vol. 4 *X Toolkit Intrinsics
    Programming Manual*
Vol. 5 *X Toolkit Intrinsics Reference
    Manual*
Vol. 7 *XView Programming Manual*

For HyperCard on Macintosh:

UNIX in a Nutshell for HyperCard
(includes 1.8MB of HyperCard
stackware, *User's Guide*, and a copy of
Learning the UNIX Operating System)

Other UNIX books:

UNIX Text Processing

Send me more information on:

☐ Retail sales

☐ Licensing

☐ Review copies for instructors

☐ Magazine press kits for new books

☐ Education policy

☐ Bookstore locations

☐ Overseas distributors

☐ Additional copy of Nutshell News

☐ Upcoming books on the subject:

_____

_____

☐ Writing a Nutshell Handbook

O'Reilly & Associates, Inc.
Creators and Publishers of Nutshell Handbooks

Nutshell Handbooks

Learning the UNIX Operating System
DOS Meets UNIX
Learning the vi Editor
UNIX in a Nutshell, System V
UNIX in a Nutshell, Berkeley

Handbooks on Communications:

*!%@:: A Directory of Electronic
    Mail Addressing and Networks*
Using UUCP and Usenet
Managing UUCP and Usenet

Handbooks on Programming:

Using C on the UNIX System
Checking C Programs with lint
Understanding and Using COFF
Programming with curses
termcap and terminfo
Managing Projects with make

The X Window System series

Vol. 0 *X Protocol Reference Manual*
Vol. 1 *Xlib Programming Manual*
Vol. 2 *Xlib Reference Manual*
Vol. 3 *X Window System User's Guide*
Vol. 4 *X Toolkit Intrinsics
    Programming Manual*
Vol. 5 *X Toolkit Intrinsics Reference
    Manual*
Vol. 7 *XView Programming Manual*

For HyperCard on Macintosh:

UNIX in a Nutshell for HyperCard
(includes 1.8MB of HyperCard
stackware, *User's Guide*, and a copy of
Learning the UNIX Operating System)

Other UNIX books:

UNIX Text Processing

Send me more information on:

☐ Retail sales

☐ Licensing

☐ Review copies for instructors

☐ Magazine press kits for new books

☐ Education policy

☐ Bookstore locations

☐ Overseas distributors

☐ Additional copy of Nutshell News

☐ Upcoming books on the subject:

_____

_____

☐ Writing a Nutshell Handbook